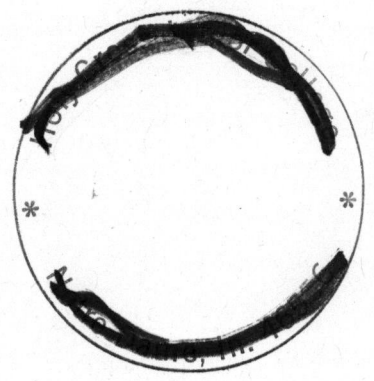

From the Special Introduction by
Harrison Salisbury

". . . the Reports of the National Commission
on the Causes and Prevention of Violence. Hundreds of thousands of words. Staggering man-
hours of investigation. Painstaking analysis.
Learned research. Hypotheses. Statistics. Frequency charts. Historical parallels. Everyone
has been consulted—the illiterate accidental
witness and the psychiatrists, the social theorists, the behavioral scientists, the high priests
of our technological times."

ASSASSINATION AND POLITICAL VIOLENCE

From the Conclusion

"We have shown that the level of assassination
corresponds to the level of political turmoil and
violence in general. In comparison to other nations, the United States experiences a high
level of political violence and assassination
events. The present level of assassination and
political turmoil, however, is no greater than at
times in the past. Violence to achieve political
goals is a thread which runs throughout the
history of the United States."

STATEMENT ON THE STAFF STUDIES

The Commission was directed to "go as far as man's knowledge takes" it in searching for the causes of violence and the means of prevention. These studies are reports to the Commission by independent scholars and lawyers who have served as directors of our staff task forces and study teams; they are not reports by the Commission itself. Publication of any of the reports should not be taken to imply endorsement of their contents by the Commission, or by any member of the Commission's staff, including the Executive Director and other staff officers, not directly responsible for the preparation of the particular report. Both the credit and the responsibility for the reports lie in each case with the directors of the task forces and study teams. The Commission is making the reports available at this time as works of scholarship to be judged on their merits, so that the Commission as well as the public may have the benefit of both reports and informed criticism and comment on their contents.

Dr. Milton S. Eisenhower, *Chairman*

A NEW YORK TIMES BOOK

assassination and political violence

•

A Report to the
National Commission on
the Causes and Prevention of
Violence

•

by
James F. Kirkham
Sheldon G. Levy
William J. Crotty

•

Special Introduction by Harrison E. Salisbury of
The New York Times

PRAEGER PUBLISHERS
NEW YORK • WASHINGTON • LONDON

PRAEGER PUBLISHERS
111 Fourth Avenue, New York, N.Y. 10003, U.S.A.
5, Cromwell Place, London, S.W.7, England

Published in the United States of America in 1970
by Praeger Publishers, Inc.

Library of Congress Catalog Card Number: 74–142215

Produced in cooperation with Bantam Books, Inc.

Printed in the United States of America

CONTENTS

APPENDICES

SPECIAL RESEARCH REPORT

SUPPLEMENTS

TASK FORCE ON ASSASSINATION AND POLITICAL VIOLENCE

Co-Directors

James F. Kirkham
Sheldon G. Levy
William J. Crotty

Staff

Robert C. Herr
Robert C. Nurick
Linda G. Stone

Secretary

Vicky Clinton

Editor

Anthony F. Abell

Commission Staff Officers
Lloyd N. Cutler, *Executive Director*
Thomas D. Barr, *Deputy Director*
James F. Short, Jr., Marvin E. Wolfgang, *Co-Directors of Research*
James S. Campbell, *General Counsel*
William G. McDonald, *Administrative Officer*
Ronald Wolk, *Special Assistant to the Chairman*
Joseph Laitin, *Director of Information*

National Commission on the Causes and Prevention of Violence

Dr. Milton S. Eisenhower, *Chairman*

SPECIAL INTRODUCTION

The bookcase fast is filling up—the one that began with the Report of the Warren Commission and its fat 26 volumes of hearings, documents and exhibits. Beside them stand the dozens of commentaries on the Warren report. Now they are followed by the Reports of the National Commission on the Causes and Prevention of Violence. Hundreds of thousands of words. Staggering man-hours of investigation. Painstaking analysis. Learned research. Hypotheses. Statistics. Frequency charts. Historical parallels. Everyone has been consulted—the illiterate accidental witness and the psychiatrists, the social theorists, the behavioral scientists, the high priests of our technological times.

And still the answer is not yet. Nor an end to the violence and death. The roll grows longer not with each year but with each month. The rattle of gunfire never stills. It may be intermittent, but it soon sounds again.

It began for us with John Fitzgerald Kennedy. And although he was the eighth presidential victim of a violent deadly attack, and the fourth President killed by an assassin, he was for us the first leader gunned down and still the greatest, the shining target of our turbulence, the Sun Emperor of the diverse American land. But Kennedy's death was only the beginning. His assassin (although many still are loath to call him so), Lee Harvey Oswald, died of a bullet within 36 hours of the President. A year later Malcolm X was shot to death in New York City. In 1967 George Lincoln Rockwell fell under gunfire. The next year took the lives of Martin Luther King and Robert Kennedy. And 1969 saw the leaders of the Black Panthers drop, one by one, in murderous progression. New Year's Eve 1970 was ushered in with the brutal murder of Joseph A. Yablonski, leader of the United Mine Workers.

There are those who wince at the juxtaposition of names; the Kennedys, Oswald, Martin Luther King, Malcolm X, George Lincoln Rockwell, the Panthers, a union leader. But the thread of violence ties them together. It is a blood bond and it cannot be severed. In truth these names represent but the peaks of the guns' tattoo, the sick thud of bludgeons, the fatal sadism that soddens the bright beauty of the American dream.

Why? The question haunts us. We cry for an answer. We reject the notion that a single psychotic ne'er-do-well robbed us of John Fitzgerald Kennedy. The crime is too banal, the explanation too shoddy. We admit that Jack Ruby shot Oswald because we saw it on television. But we search for a motivation less trivial. We seduce ourselves with the thought that Malcolm X, Rockwell and the Panthers were violent men. They preached violence, did they not? So there is some element of retribution. Violent men, we tell ourselves, die of violence. But there is less comfort in this rationalization than appears. And we are left with the oedipal tragedies of Robert Kennedy and Martin Luther King and the slaughterhouse brutality of the Yablonski killings.

Small wonder that President after President has named commissions of distinguished citizens to try to find some order in this disorder; to ravel out common clues; to seek answers, explanations and, hopefully, remedies.

Every inquiry quickly discloses the deep strain of violence which has underlain American life from the start—not, perhaps, a deeper violence than has attended the birth of other nations but a strain of remarkable consistency. The American continent was not settled by sedentary men. It was fought for and won. The first settlers made war on the aboriginal inhabitants. They seized the eastern littoral at gunpoint. True, they negotiated treaties, agreements, arrangements. But in the end it was musket fire that took the land and musket fire that held it against the rain of Indian arrows, the chop of the tomahawks. Nor did the settlers fight solely against the red-skinned peoples whose land they were seizing. They fought each other. They sailed the seas with guns at the ready. The oceans were more dangerous than deadly jungles, swarming with "privateers," "bucaneers," pirates, captains with "letters of marque." In other words, armed ocean marauders—out to rob, to kill, to enslave. The only law was the law of gunpowder and cutlass. Nor did the settlers fight only the Indians. They ravaged each other. It was man against man, colony against colony.

The American dream was a bloody dream and the blood did not halt its flow with the long and savage war of independence against the British. "The United States, of course, was born in political violence," this Report points out. For the first 100 years of our national history the frontier, ever opening, ever renewed, was ruled by the gun. War—war against Indians, against Mexicans, between North and South, between sheep- and cattlemen, between grazers and farmers, between those whose economic and social interests collided—was not the exception. It was the rule. Vigilante law—the law of summary justice, enforced by the mob; lynch law—the law of summary terror, enforced by the mob. These were American institutions, as sanctified by practice and custom as the law of the Constitution, the courts and the judges. The authors of this Report note that:

> The prototype of political violence in the United States is the vigilante committee—an extra-legal group that enforces the values of the community by illegal violence. . . .
> . . . The vigilante movement was not unique to the Western plains and mountains; there was as much if not more vigilantism east of the Missouri and Mississippi Rivers. . . . Many vigilante movements led not to order but to increasing disorder and anarchy. . . .
> Today, educated men may view vigilantism with disapproval, but such was not the case in the nineteenth century. In those days, leading citizens were often prominent members of vigilante movements, and proud of it.

To be sure, we do not think of our heritage in this fashion. We think of it in terms of nobility—the Pilgrims and their harsh sufferings on the wild continent; the "treachery" of the redskins in turning on the handfuls of white settlers; the long and arduous efforts by European colonizers to establish a rule of law and justice in the wilderness and to bring the Christian faith to heathen tribes. We romanticize the vigilantes (under the influence of innumerable Western movies glorifying "the law west of Pecos"); we smother the cruelty and atrocities of the Civil War under vistas of moonlight, romance and roses; the horror of Andersonville and Sherman's pillage is flushed down the memory hole. We even tried to sanctify Judge Lynch and the Ku Klux Klan until a more sophisticated generation finally understood what "The Birth of a Nation" was all about. We are horrified today at the Yablonski murders. But death, hatred, violence, the rule of the club and the dynamite stick have been so common in American mining communities that the very counties where the coal deposits lie have been known for years as "bloody" Williamson (in Illinois), "bloody" Harlan (in Kentucky). The fields of Pennsylvania, of Kentucky, of southern Illinois, of Colorado, have often been ravaged for years by open warfare in which hundreds of men and women have lost their lives—events so traditional that the public conscience hardly has felt a twinge.

As for violence against blacks (a subject on which the research of the present volume is weak) it has been so pervasive over such a lengthy period of time that statistics have become meaningless. The story began in Reconstruction days when, for example, in Louisiana 2,000 persons were killed or wounded in the weeks before the 1868 election; in one Florida county the murder toll was 150 within a few months; in Texas a Federal Army commander reported: "Murders of Negroes are so common as to render it impossible to keep accurate accounts of them." So it has gone to the present day. The numbers fluctuate. The violence is constant.

Nor is the story of our violence against each other confined to the blacks. As this study notes:

> Violence has been used by successive generations of native Americans (primarily white Anglo-Saxon Protestants) to oppose a perceived cultural, economic, social, and moral threat posed by successive waves of immigrants from Catholic and non-Teutonic Europe, and to reinforce the moral values of fundamentalist protestantism.

Thus, the notion (which is commonly held in all strata of our society) that the phenomenon of violence and assassination is something new, something "un-American," a peculiar product of the present day, is demonstrably and remarkably mistaken. Violence has marked every step of the creation and building of the American society—violence employed by whites against blacks, by whites against whites, by one segment of the nation against another, by one national or religious strain against another, by one economic group against another. Violence may not be, in the wry expression of Rap Brown, "as American as cherry pie," but it has been synonymous with the American experience from the earliest days.

No underworld has been more prone to the use of the gun and the bomb than the American underworld. Every society about which we know has had its criminal elements. Sometimes, as in eighteenth-century London or thuggee India or the Sicily of the primitive Mafia, the criminal world has been extraordinarily well structured. But never has a nation possessed an underworld which often has become an *overworld* (the domination of New York by the Tweed ring in the 1870's; of Chicago by the Capone mobs, New Jersey by the contemporary Mafia, or a dozen complacent and corrupt metropolises documented by Lincoln Steffens at the turn of the century). In America the underworld adopted not only advanced military technology (Thompson submachine guns, bulletproof steel, incendiary bombs, light artillery, armored cars, etc.), it acquired, modified and employed the mechanisms of modern corporate organization in order efficiently to invest, retain and diversify the enormous profits of criminal operations, often conducted on a global basis (beginning with liquor procurement in Prohibition days and continuing without break to intercontinental manufacture and distribution of narcotics).

It is against this background that contemporary violence must be viewed. And in this context it can come as no surprise that the present period, although clearly violence intensive, is by no means without precedent. Careful sampling of the past demonstrates that there have been four major peaks of violence in 100 years. The first, as might be expected, occurred in the post-Civil War Reconstruction period—probably the most violent period of our national history. A second peak occurred around the turn of the century, another during the Depression days of the 1930's, and the fourth is the present, which had its onset with the opening of the 1960's.

Correlated for population changes, measured in terms of deaths and injuries, the current period has not touched the peaks of the past and, in fact, in ratio to total population, deaths by violence have been lower in the last 30 years than in any comparable period since 1819. In number of persons injured, however, the current period is the most violent.

If, in reality, the present violence has been outdone in the past (and by some indexes is lower than in past periods), why does this seem to us to be a time of such enormous crisis? There are three apparent reasons for this: First of all, newspapers (and radio/TV) with their extensive coverage facilities report more completely on violence than in the past. We are more aware. Second, other peak periods of violence occurred in the distant past—and at times before we were born. We have no precise memory of past violence. We see only what happens today. And in our contemporary experience it is measurably greater than it was a few years ago. Third, it is more dramatic. Endless warfare in "bloody" Harlan County, weekly lynchings in the remote South, the dynamiting of a power flume in the Rockies, a shot fired at an obscure populist leader—none of these events have the impact of the great assassinations, the spectacular outbursts of violence of today. We are living in an Age of Assassination—or so it clearly seems to most Americans. Past comparisons are emotionally invalid. We know that a remarkable number of American Presidents have been assassinated or were targets of fatal attack. But we have lived through an assassination of unbelievable drama followed on national television with the murder of the man under arrest for the killing. Then within a few years the brother of the martyred President died at an assassin's hand. Not even in the trigger-happy, bomb-conditioned capitals of Central America or the Balkans have such fantastic events occurred. We know that this is an era of violence. We have seen with our own eyes the acts of murder and assassination. We read about them in the paper and see them on Walter Cronkite's evening news. Infants too young to know what they are watching have witnessed many of these events on the living room television screen. If a political figure, an agitator, a nonviolent preacher, is shot down anywhere in the United States, we witness the event or something very close to it in our own homes within a matter of hours if not minutes. The news of Lincoln's assassination traveled rapidly. Yet months later there were isolated settlements, solitary homesteads, mountain or wilderness communities which knew neither that he had been shot nor that the war had ended. Today the nation, as never before, is united by electronic bonds of information and intelligence. True, a sparrow may still fall without notice by the nationwide viewing audience. But not a charismatic leader. Or even one of his followers.

This, then, may well explain why the index of violence and assassination seems so remarkably high to all of us. It does not explain why, in absolute terms, it *is* so high.

We turn in all directions seeking light on this problem. We look abroad to the experience of other societies and other nations. The comparisons, for the most part, are odious. The United States has a higher assassination rate—by far—than any other large country. We lead in numbers of assassinations the list of countries of more than 100 million population. And also that of countries over 50 million. Only when we drop down to small nations like Korea, Iran, Cuba, Morocco and Tunisia do we get figures comparable to those of the United States. Countries with dictatorial systems that we consider to possess much more violent societies than our own—Soviet Russia and China, for example—have rates only a fraction of ours. And even unstable new states like India, Indonesia and Pakistan make the U.S.A. look bad.

Historically speaking, violence and assassination have marked almost every society created by man. Man is far from a peaceful animal. The use of violence or terror by the state, be it a medieval kingdom or barony or a contemporary military or political dictatorship, is so customary that it almost goes without note. Regicide was once the commonest way of changing the ruler of the regime. Karl Marx analyzed the state as an apparatus that was employed by a ruling class (be it feudal, bourgeois or monopoly-capitalist) to maintain itself in power. Had he lived to see the so-called "Marxist" society arise in Russia under Lenin's leadership, he would have found one more case history in the employment of terror and force to maintain an elite in power and to suppress political dissent. If the state is taken as a structure organized by human beings who share a common pool of ideas and interests, it obviously will be employed as an instrument by which that society seeks to maintain itself in power. If—as in the case of the Soviet Union—there develop wide gaps between the objectives of those who rule the state and those who are ruled one may anticipate that violence, terror, ruthlessness will tend to increase. This, in fact, was precisely what happened in Russia. In Imperial Russia the power of the state was employed ruthlessly to maintain the clients and elite of the Romanovs in power. The Maximalist oppression of the Romanovs gave rise in the nineteenth century to a fateful escalation of violence, terror and assassination. Russian society split more and more into competitive groups with mutually exclusive objectives—a reformative (but later revolutionary) element seeking to shift the balance of power in the state and a ruling oligarchy (and its supporters) struggling to retain full control. As the state's use of force, the police, arrests, imprisonment, executions and exile increased so did violence on the other side—terroristic acts, assassinations, mass demonstrations, violent challenges to authority—a conflict that waxed and waned for 100 years but finally produced the transfer of power that occurred in 1917.

Some of the aspects of the Russian confrontation, and the birth of a tradition of terror in the Slavic states, both in Russia and in the Balkans, the rise of professional terrorists, particularly in Bulgaria and Serbia, are examined in this volume. The emphasis is largely on the origin and activities of conspiratorial groups seeking to overthrow the existing state system by revolutionary means. While such groups have long existed in the United States (although usually so minute as to bring no real weight on a given socio-political situation), until the most recent times they have not been an appreciable factor in the coefficient of violence and to have not played a measurable or consistent role in Presidential assassinations. The Russian-Slavic experience, however, contains important lessons for the future if persistent and stubborn confrontations continue without effective political accommodations. But, in general the key significance of the East European (or Latin American or Asian) experience is in demonstrating the substantial extent to which America's problems are *sui generis*. We have made them. They grow out of our own traditions, our own deep conflicts, the malfunctioning of our social and Constitutional system, the widening gap between stated ethics and normal conduct, an ingrained American tendency to resort to violence whether in the form of a mob or by employing the pseudo-authority of the police nightstick and a biased court, the persistence into an incredibly complex socio-technological society of habits of conduct that were employed by a primitive society in which violence was perceived as the only reliable means of protection.

The Warren Commission report argues that the assassination of John Fitzgerald Kennedy was an aberrational act, the deed of one alienated, psychotic individual, choosing a victim almost at random among possible targets of importance (the evidence suggested that Oswald had contemplated General Edwin Walker, former Vice President Nixon and possibly even Texas Governor Connolly as alternate targets). To many, this conclusion seemed unsatisfactory and emotionally, if not logically, unfulfilling. In the case of the killing of Robert Kennedy, too, there was evidence that he was but one (the most *available*) of possible victims of an individual whose conduct clearly demonstrated his alienation, his psychopathic view of himself and of the world. The killer of Martin Luther King was obviously a man far out of the mainstream of American life, a man whose prison record, if nothing more, demonstrated his deep aberrational character. Examination of the nature of the actual killers involved in the assassinations of prominent American victims discloses that these are not accidental traits. In *most* cases of assassination the killer is discovered to be not a member of an organized conspiracy, not a member of a group possessing a detailed and principled program of opposition to, let us say, the U.S. system or the American Establishment. He is, instead, a "loner," a man living on the margins of society, paranoid, schizophrenic, possessing a narrow, perverted style of thinking, sometimes perceiving himself as the instrument of a "higher will," more often seeing in his act a rectification of some deep grievance or complaint, usually one of which the man who is slain has had no knowledge, no connection, and one for which he could not by any reasonable logic be regarded as responsible.

The killings—and this goes deep into American history— have been solitary deeds, with a few notable exceptions (the small band of conspirators that centered around John Wilkes Booth and the Puerto Rican Nationalist group that made the attempt on former President Truman's life are examples). The Czars and their leading supporters, the crowned heads of the Balkans and the Austro-Hungarian empire, were almost invariably killed by political conspirators or their agents. This has not been the American pattern. It is this which has caused many Americans to refuse to see a general social or political implication in these supreme examples of American violence. There seems, even with most extensive investi-

gation, to be no direct connection between acts of assassination and generalized manifestations of violence in our society.

It is here that the statistics of political and sociological investigation provide an illuminating framework. While American Presidents, Presidential aspirants and major public and
political figures do not, as a rule, fall as the direct victims of
political assault or political conspiracy, they do die more frequently in periods of social violence. Thus, the two phenomena
seem to spring from one generalized cause. That is, when the
overall level of violence begins to rise in the public at large
there are apt to be prominent victims as well as a multitude
of anonymous ones.

As the authors of the Report conclude:

> We have shown that the level of assassination corre-
> sponds to the level of political turmoil and violence in
> general. In comparison to other nations, the United States
> experiences a high level of political violence and assassi-
> nation events. The present level of assassination and
> political turmoil, however, is no greater than at times
> in the past. Violence to achieve political goals is a thread
> which runs throughout the history of the United States.

The specific source of contemporary violence is clearly
racial. This, also, has been true in one other period of extreme
violence—the postwar Reconstruction era. This does not exclude other accessory sources of violence (for example, the
unusually widespread and pervasive existence of crime and
antisocial patterns, symbolized by the narcotics trade, nation-
wide systems of gambling, etc., and the remarkable turmoil
characteristic of so much of American youth in the past few
years) although other sources are examined only in minor
detail in this study.

But taken in broad terms, the movement to establish
equality of civil, economic, social and political rights for
blacks and whites, getting its inspiration from the U.S.
Supreme Court decisions of the mid-1950's and continuing to
this day, has produced the atmosphere of violence, hatred,
anger, armed combat, open use of guns and clubs, extension
of conflict to every geographical portion of the country and
into every social and economic milieu (especially the large-
scale involvement of the middle class on both sides of the
question). This has created in the country a climate of emo-

tion such as has not been seen in the lives of most Americans and has as a parallel only the turbulence of the Civil War era, before, during and after that conflict. It is a true revolution in the sense that it seeks to shift rights, privileges, property and power from one segment of society to another.

Much of the violence in the United States today, concedes the Report, "lies in the confrontation between blacks and whites."

Yet, even this is not enough to explain the consistently high level of violence in this country.

"... The frontier tradition, with its emphasis on the individual's often violent assertion and protection of his rights," says the Report, "is one explanation. The high level of immigration and the resulting friction between the newer and more established groups is another theme. . ."

The Report notes the racial friction and the use of violence in industrial labor disputes but it adds: "By themselves, these explanations are not sufficient." The Report then goes on to suggest:

> It would appear that supplemental conditions within the American experience help account for the American pattern. For example, there is a predominant emphasis on achieving specified ends or goals, with less consideration given the means for such achievement. . . . American folklore has emphasized direct action and individual initiative. The use of violent acts to achieve personal goals—and, it should be noted here, usually nonpolitical personal ends—if not part of the general cultural mythology, is certainly the image reinforced by the visual and printed media. In many respects, the American cowboy, a powerfully attractive figure in American folk culture, has provided an amalgam of these themes.

To this may be added the American emphasis upon freedom of conscience, freedom of choice, dedication to the individual, his rights, his aims and ambitions, which inevitably conflict with those of other citizens and, as the Report concludes: "Finally, the prevalence of weapons in concert with the emphasis on direct action, the ends to be achieved, the glorification of individual initiative, and ideological commitment. . ."

Anton Chekhov, the great Russian playwright, once said

that if a gun is hanging on the wall when the curtain goes up on a play it must be fired before the curtain falls on the last act. With tens of millions of handguns in the possession of private Americans, as well as police, sheriffs' deputies and a variety of less efficient law enforcement agents, the probability that a portion of these weapons will be used sooner or later against other Americans is great.

Vigilantism—a peculiarly American institution—provides one consistent tendency in American life which ties together, secularizes and justifies the emotional, illogical and often almost suicidal tendency to violence in American life. It has its historical basis and its self-justification (self-preservation is the first law of society). It concedes its own revolutionary nature but equates this with the acts of the American colonists in taking the law into their hands against the British. It is popular—that is, it is ostensibly supported by the majority of the community (quite possibly, as in the case of the blacks, against a real numerical majority). It stands for the *right* against the *wrong*; that is, for the doctrine that its adherents regard as right. And it is evergreen. It springs to life in the most unexpected locales—in recent years the Crown Heights section of Brooklyn, West Hollywood, Florida, and the North Wards of Newark.

"The ideology of vigilantism," the authors of the Report note, "is not dead, but is waiting to be used by the mischievous and the misguided."

What of the future? Obviously, no authors of any report can provide prescriptions for the complex social ills of our time. The Warren Commission was able to make recommendations for the improvement of tactical security of the President—that is, the specific arrangements of the Secret Service to protect him from attack. But it could not guarantee that there would be no future assassinations. As Justice Warren and his colleagues concluded:

> This Commission can recommend no procedures for the future protection of our Presidents which will guarantee security. The demands on the President in the execution of his responsibilities in today's world are so varied and complex and the traditions of the office in a democracy such as ours are so deep-seated as to preclude absolute security.

The Walker Report, examining the violence at the 1968 Chicago Democratic Convention, was compelled to conclude: "Surely this is not the last time that a violent dissenting group will clash head-on with those whose duty it is to enforce the law."

And the authors of the present Report offer a conclusion in the same general vein: "We have not found a specific remedy for assassination and political violence in a democracy apart from the perceived legitimacy of the government and its leaders."

Which is very much like saying: If a democracy works for the very great majority of its citizens we will have no dangerous violence (although presumably still an occasional aberrant act). But if it does not work or is believed not to work or to work unfairly by any substantial group in the population—then violence will be the inevitable handmaiden. For it is in the American tradition to try to right wrongs by aggressive and violent means. If a black man feels he is deprived of his rightful heritage, he will be acting in the great American tradition if he seeks to gain justice by forceful means. If a white feels that his rights are threatened (by blacks, by radical youth, by a religious or ethnic group alien to him) he is acting in the tradition of the country if he uses force and arms to back his beliefs.

Thus, if we are to find a remedy for our Time of Troubles, we will have to seek it in ourselves—in the complex and difficult task of adjusting our wants, our needs, our aspirations, to one another. It is not a task beyond our capabilities. But no one should underestimate its difficulty and danger. Race, politics and traditions can confect a fearsome brew, as anyone may see by a quick look at the festering sores of the world. If America's violence-prone society is to evolve into the just and lawful dream evoked by Washington, Jefferson, Adams and Hamilton, it will take a quality of national dedication and ennobled leadership as great as has been displayed at any time in our nearly 200 years of independent existence. It will not be done quickly nor without a heavy cost of patience, forbearance and understanding.

HARRISON SALISBURY

PREFACE

From the earliest days of organization, the Chairman, Commissioners, and Executive Director of the National Commission on the Causes and Prevention of Violence recognized the importance of research in accomplishing the task of analyzing the many facets of violence in America. As a result of this recognition, the Commission has enjoyed the receptivity, encouragement, and cooperation of a large part of the scientific community in this country. Because of the assistance given in varying degrees by scores of scholars here and abroad, these Task Force reports represent some of the most elaborate work ever done on the major topics they cover.

The Commission was formed on June 10, 1968. By the end of the month, the Executive Director had gathered together a small cadre of capable young lawyers from various Federal agencies and law firms around the country. That group was later augmented by partners borrowed from some of the Nation's major law firms who served without compensation. Such a professional group can be assembled more quickly than university faculty because the latter are not accustomed to quick institutional shifts after making firm commitments of teaching or research at a particular locus. Moreover, the legal profession has long had a major and traditional role in Federal agencies and commissions.

In early July a group of 50 persons from the academic disciplines of sociology, psychology, psychiatry, political science, history, law, and biology were called together on short notice to discuss for 2 days how best the Commission and its staff might proceed to analyze violence. The enthusiastic response of these scientists came at a moment when our Nation was still suffering from the tragedy of Senator Kennedy's assassination.

It was clear from that meeting that the scholars were prepared to join research analysis and action, interpretation, and policy. They were eager to present to the American people the best available data, to bring reason to bear where myth had prevailed. They cautioned against simplistic solutions, but urged application of what is known in the service of sane policies for the benefit of the entire society.

Shortly thereafter the position of Director of Research was created. We assumed the role as a joint undertaking, with common responsibilities. Our function was to enlist social and other scientists to join the staff, to write papers, act as advisers or consultants, and engage in new research. The decentralized structure of the staff, which at its peak numbered 100, required research coordination to reduce duplication and to fill in gaps among the original seven separate Task Forces. In general, the plan was for each Task Force to have a pair of directors: one a social scientist, one a lawyer. In a number of instances, this formal structure bent before the necessities of available personnel but in almost every case the Task Force work program relied on both social scientists and lawyers for its successful completion. In addition to our work with the seven original Task Forces, we provided consultation for the work of the eighth "Investigative" Task Force, formed originally to investigate the disorders at the Democratic and Republican National Conventions and the civil strife in Cleveland during the summer of 1968 and eventually expanded to study campus disorders at several colleges and universities.

Throughout September and October and in December of 1968 the Commission held about 30 days of public hearings related expressly to each of the Task Force areas. About 100 witnesses testified, including many scholars, Government officials, corporate executives as well as militants and activists of various persuasions. In addition to the hearings, the Commission and the staff met privately with scores of persons, including college presidents, religious and youth leaders, and experts in such areas as the media, victim compensation, and firearms. The staff participated actively in structuring and conducting those hearings and conferences and in the questioning of witnesses.

As Research Directors, we participated in structuring the strategy of design for each Task Force, but we listened more than directed. We have known the delicate details of some of the statistical problems and computer runs. We have argued over philosophy and syntax; we have offered bibliographical and other resource materials, we have written portions of reports and copy edited others. In short, we know the enormous energy and devotion, the long hours and accelerated study that members of each Task Force have invested in their labors. In retrospect we are amazed at the high caliber and quantity of the material produced, much of which truly represents the best in research and scholarship. About 150 separate papers and projects were involved in the work culminating in the Task Force reports. We feel less that we have orchestrated than that we have been members of the orchestra, and that together with the entire staff we have helped compose a repertoire of current knowledge about the enormously complex subject of this Commission.

That scholarly research is predominant in the work here presented is evident in the product. But we should like to emphasize that the roles which we occupied were not limited to scholarly inquiry. The Directors of Research were afforded an opportunity to participate in all Commission meetings. We engaged in discussions at the highest levels of decisionmaking, and had great freedom in the selection of scholars, in the control of research budgets, and in the direction and design of research. If this was not unique, it is at least an uncommon degree of prominence accorded research by a national commission.

There were three major levels to our research pursuit: (1) summarizing the state of our present knowledge and clarifying the lacunae where more or new research should be encouraged; (2) accelerating known ongoing research so as to make it available to the Task Forces; (3) undertaking new research projects within the limits of time and funds available. Coming from a university setting where the pace of research is more conducive to reflection and quiet hours analyzing data, we at first thought that completing much meaningful new research within a matter of months was most unlikely. But the need was matched by the talent and enthusiasm of the staff, and the Task Forces very early had begun enough new projects to launch a small university with a score of doctoral theses. It is well to remember also that in each volume here presented, the research reported is on full public display and thereby makes the staff more than usually accountable for their products.

One of the very rewarding aspects of these research under-
takings has been the experience of minds trained in the law
mingling and meshing, sometimes fiercely arguing, with other
minds trained in behavioral science. The organizational structure and the substantive issues of each Task Force required
members from both groups. Intuitive judgment and the logic
of argument and organization blended, not always smoothly,
with the methodology of science and statistical reasoning. Critical and analytical faculties were sharpened as theories confronted facts. The arrogance neither of ignorance nor of
certainty could long endure the doubts and questions of inter-
disciplinary debate. Any sign of approaching the priestly
pontification of scientism was quickly dispelled in the matrix
of mutual criticism. Years required for the normal accumulation of experience were compressed into months of sharing
ideas with others who had equally valid but differing perspec-
tives. Because of this process, these volumes are much richer
than they otherwise might have been.

Partly because of the freedom which the Commission gave
to the Directors of Research and the Directors of each Task
Force, and partly to retain the full integrity of the research
work in publication, these reports of the Task Forces are in
the posture of being submitted to and received by the Commission. These are volumes published under the authority of
the Commission, but they do not necessarily represent the
views or the conclusions of the Commission. The Commission
is presently at work producing its own report, based in part on
the materials presented to it by the Task Forces. Commission
members have, of course, commented on earlier drafts of each
Task Force, and have caused alterations by reason of the
cogency of their remarks and insights. But the final responsibility for what is contained in these volumes rests fully and
properly on the research staffs who labored on them.

In this connection, we should like to acknowledge the special leadership of the Chairman, Dr. Milton S. Eisenhower, in
formulating and supporting the principle of research freedom
and autonomy under which this work has been conducted.

We note, finally, that these volumes are in many respects
incomplete and tentative. The urgency with which papers were
prepared and then integrated into Task Force Reports rendered impossible the successive siftings of data and argument
to which the typical academic article or volume is subjected.

The reports have benefited greatly from the counsel of our colleagues on the Advisory Panel, and from much debate and revision from within the staff. It is our hope, that the total work effort of the Commission staff will be the source and subject of continued research by scholars in the several disciplines, as well as a useful resource for policymakers. We feel certain that public policy and the disciplines will benefit greatly from such further work.

* * *

To the Commission, and especially to its Chairman, for the opportunity they provided for complete research freedom, and to the staff for its prodigious and prolific work, we, who were intermediaries and servants to both, are most grateful.

James F. Short, Jr. Marvin E. Wolfgang
Directors of Research

ACKNOWLEDGMENTS

This Report is necessarily not the work of any one person; it draws together the contributions of many diverse scholars recruited by the Task Force. Accordingly, the Report has breadth of approach and diversity of viewpoint on the many facets of assassination and political violence.

For example, approaches include psychiatric *post facto* examinations of previous assassins; descriptive and historical treatments of assassinations; quantitative comparative analyses of the relationship between acts of political violence and assassinations and the occurrence of assassinations cross-nationally; interpretive discussions of aspects of United States culture which may support violence and, more specifically, violence directed against prominent individuals in the society; and contemporary reports of groups whose rhetoric and previous activities are associated with a variety of kinds of politically violent acts. Each approach contributes a different vantage point from which to examine assassinations and political violence.

The Task Force staff has brought the materials together and has presented them in three major parts: the Report itself, Appendices to the Report, and a Supplement to the Report. The Appendices contain materials that document in greater detail many of the points raised in the Report, including much of the unrefined data employed in the analyses contained within the Report. The Supplement presents more intensive historical and interpretative explorations of political assassinations in other countries and other regions of the world. These studies, along with the quantitative analyses of comparative aspects of violent behavior, assist in placing the experience of the United States in a world context.

In commissioning studies for the Task Force Report, the codirectors attempted to include reports by individuals distinguished in their understanding of the topic in question. The final Report of the Task Force is based on these studies, many of which are incorporated in whole or in part. In a few cases, the editing has been relatively severe. In all cases, at least some minor editorial changes have been made by the staff. In each instance, however, the original author has been identified and the extent of his contribution to the Report described as accurately as possible. In addition, some sections were written entirely by the staff, including much of the introductory and explanatory material. Thus, the result is neither a book of selected readings by different authors nor a presentation which is homogeneous in style and viewpoint. We have instead attempted to combine the different approaches and viewpoints within a systematic structure. This will enable us to treat the resulting product as a whole and draw conclusions based upon all the different approaches to the subject matter.

The codirectors of Task Force I, Assassination and Political Violence, wish to extend their sincere thanks to the Commissioners and the administrative staff of the National Commission on the Causes and Prevention of Violence for their constant help, support, suggestions, and contributions to this report. Essential to all the Task Force Reports, and to this report in particular, was the continuing loyal support of the Executive Director, Lloyd N. Cutler. In addition, we wish to acknowledge a special debt to the Commission's codirectors of research, Dr. James F. Short, Jr., and Dr. Marvin E. Wolfgang, and the Commission's indefatigable administrative officer, Col. William G. McDonald. To single out particular staff members, however, is necessarily unfair. All worked well beyond what could be reasonably expected in helping this and the other Task Forces.

This Report would not exist but for the consultants to the Task Force, and we should like at this point to acknowledge the contributions of each.

Reports submitted by the following were directly drawn upon in one form or another in the text of the Report; as with all consultant papers, some editing was done by the staff.

Consultant	Project Title
Richard Maxwell Brown Department of History College of William and Mary	Violence in American History.

Ivo K. Feierabend
Rosalind Feierabend
Betty A. Nesvold
Franz N. Jaggar
Department of Political Science
San Diego State College
San Diego, Calif.

Political Violence and
Assassination: A Cross-
National Assessment—
1948–1968

Lawrence Z. Freedman, M.D.
Department of Psychiatry
University of Chicago

Assassins of Presidents of the
United States: Their
Motives and Personality
Traits

Clinton E. Grimes
Judith H. Grimes
Department of Political Science
University of Idaho
Moscow, Idaho

Personalism, Partisanship, and
Assassination

Feliks Gross
Department of Sociology
Brooklyn College

Political Violence and Terror in
19th and 20th Century
Russia and Eastern Europe

Carl Leiden
Murray C. Havens
Karl M. Schmitt
James Soukup
Department of Government
University of Texas
Austin, Tex.

Assassinations Worldwide
1918–1969

James McEvoy III
Department of Sociology
University of California, Davis
And
Department of Political Science
University of California,
Berkeley

Components of Political
Violence

Rita J. Simon
Department of Sociology
University of Illinois
Urbana, Ill.

Political Violence Directed at
Public Office Holders: A
Brief Analysis of the
American Scene

Peter B. Young
Summit, N.J.

Whose Law, Whose Order?

Doris Y. Wilkinson
Jerry A. Gaines
Department of Sociology
University of Kentucky
Lexington, Ky.

Sociological Insights into the
Assassin

Jerome Bakst
Anti-Defamation League
New York, N. Y.

Political Extremism and
Violence in the United
States

Reports from the following are reprinted in the Supplement:

Harold Deutsch
Department of History
University of Minnesota
Minneapolis, Minn.

Assassination and Political
Violence in 20th Century
France and Germany

Feliks Gross
Department of Sociology
Brooklyn College
New York, N.Y.

Political Violence and Terror
in Nineteenth and
Twentieth Century Russia
and Eastern Europe

Murray C. Havens
Department of Government
University of Texas
Austin, Tex.

Assassination in Australia

Carl Leiden
Department of Government
University of Texas
Austin, Tex.

Assassination in the Middle
East

Karl M. Schmitt
Department of Government
University of Texas
Austin, Tex.

Assassination in Latin America

James R. Soukup
Department of Government
University of Texas
Austin, Tex.

Assassination in Japan

Denis Szabo
Department of Criminology
University of Montreal

Assassination and Political
Violence in Canada

Inkeri Auttila

Assassination in Finland

Klas Lithner

Assassination in Sweden

Daniel Tretiak
Advanced Studies Group
Westinghouse Electric Corp.
Waltham, Mass.

Political Assassinations in
China, 1600–1968

The following also submitted papers or appeared at hearings before the Commission and provided valuable insights that contributed to the Report:

Dr. David Abrahamsen
Department of Psychiatry
Roosevelt Hospital
New York, N.Y.

Joseph Bensman
Department of Sociology
City College of New York
New York, N.Y.

Social and Instructional Factors Determining the Level of Assassination

Lynne Iglitzin
University of Washington
Seattle, Wash.

Violence and American Democracy

Seymour M. Lipset
Carl Sheingold
Department of Government and Social Relations
Harvard University
Cambridge, Mass.

Values and Political Structure: An Interpretation of the Sources of Extremism and Violence in American Society

Harold L. Nieburg
Department of Political Science
University of Wisconsin
Milwaukee, Wis.

The Political Uses of Assassination

Dr. David A. Rothstein
Michael Reese Hospital
Chicago, Illinois

Richard E. Rubenstein
The Adlai Stevenson Institute
Chicago, Ill.

Assassination and the Breakdown of American Politics

Dore Schary
National Chairman
Anti-Defamation League
B'nai B'rith

Joyce A. Sween
Rae L. Blumberg
Department of Sociology
Northwestern University

Reactions to the Assassination of President John F. Kennedy and Dr. Martin Luther King, Jr.

Henry Alberts Stanford Research Institute	A Study of Game Theory and Probability Models as Employed in the Prediction and Prevention of Assassination
Eduard A. Ziegenhagen Department of Political Science Wayne State University Detroit, Mich.	Systemic Constraints and Political Assassination
Roy Nagle Buffalo, N.Y.	Assassination of President McKinley

The original version of each of the foregoing papers is contained in the files of the Commission, as are the transcripts of the testimony.

One final word of appreciation: with almost no exceptions, the consultants to this Task Force were very generous with their time and professional abilities. Again with almost no exceptions, the amount of work each of the consultants contributed to this Task Force far exceeded the compensation received. In addition, both the Advanced Studies Group of Westinghouse Electric Corporation and the Stanford Research Institute generously donated their services. This Task Force received whole-hearted support from those whose help it sought. Nothing could have been accomplished without that support.

Special thanks is owed Robert C. Herr, who helped direct the work of the Task Force from its inception, and our research assistants, Robert Nurick and Linda Stone, who contributed not only notable ability, but continuing good cheer, notwithstanding the severe pressures of time and performance under which the Task Force operated. Our sincere appreciation is also extended to Victoria Clinton, the secretary of the Task Force, who maintained all its records in addition to assuming the main burden of its clerical work; she cheerfully worked nights and weekends to complete her many tasks.

We appreciate the diligent, painstaking, and patient work of Mr. Anthony F. Abell, who established the overall style for this volume and prepared the manuscript for publication.

The greatest debt of all is owed to Katherine Kirkham, Mary Lois Levy, and Nan Crotty, the wives of the codirectors.

Each of us on very short notice left our wives and small children in other parts of the country to come to Washington, D.C., for the Commission. None of us could or would have imposed that hardship upon our wives without their loyal and enthusiastic support for the work we undertook.

James F. Kirkham*
Sheldon G. Levy†
William J. Crotty‡

James F. Kirkham received an A.B. Degree from Yale in 1954, and an LL.B Degree from the University of California at Berkeley in 1957. He is actively engaged in practice of law in San Francisco where he is a partner with the firm of Pillsbury, Madison & Sutro.

†*Sheldon G. Levy* received an A.B. Degree in Chemistry in 1957, from the College of Wooster, an M.A. Degree in Psychology in 1959, from the University of Michigan, an M.A. Degree in Pure Mathematics in 1962, from the University of Michigan and a Ph.D Degree in Mathematical Psychology in 1963, from the University of Michigan. In addition to various articles, he is the author of *Inferential Statistics in the Behavioral Sciences* (Holt, Rinehart, & Winston, 1968); and, with M. Fried and J. Cole, co-author of *Workbook for Inferential Statistics in the Behavioral Sciences* (Holt, Rinehart, & Winston, 1968).

‡*William J. Crotty* received a B.A. Degree from the University of Massachusetts in 1958, and a Ph.D in Political Science from the University of North Carolina in 1963. In addition to publishing numerous articles and papers in the field of political science, he is the author of the following books: *Political Parties and Political Behavior* (Boston: Allyn and Bacon, 1966), Co-editor with Donald M. Freeman and Douglas S. Gatlin; *Approaches to the Study of Party Organization* (Boston: Allyn and Bacon, 1968), Editor and co-author; *A Methodological Primer for Political Scientists* (Chicago: Rand McNally, 1968), Co-author with Robert Golembiewski and William A. Welsh.

INTRODUCTION

A. Summary

The National Commission on the Causes and Prevention of Violence was established by President Lyndon Johnson immediately after the assassination of Senator Robert Kennedy. Senator Kennedy's assassination occurred within months of that of the Reverend Martin Luther King, Jr., and both followed by less than five years the assassination of President John Kennedy.

The Commission divided its staff into various Task Force groups. This Task Force was to investigate and respond to the questions and issues raised by the phenomenon of assassination and the related phenomenon of political violence. It sought among other things, to shed light on the patterns, if any, that exist in assassination and other acts of political violence; the relationship between assassinations and other forms of political violence; the social and political consequences of assassination; the relative incidence of assassinations and other acts of political violence in the United States vis-a-vis other nations; and the environmental factors that encourage groups or individuals to attack political leaders. This report presents and assesses the evidence available on each of these aspects of political assassinations.[1]

Assassinations have occurred throughout the history of the United States and have been employed on occasion to achieve political and ideological goals, although such use has been limited almost entirely to the Reconstruction period in the South.

The number of assassinations and acts of general political violence in the United States is high, compared with other nations, particularly when with more politically stable and economically developed countries. However, despite the assassinations that have taken place during the 1960's, physical attacks against politically prominent individuals do not appear to be increasing.

The risk of assassination is considerably greater for elective as opposed to appointed public officials in spite of the fact appointed officials may wield greater power. Also, the risk of assassination is directly proportional to the size of constituency of the officeholder. The presidency is the most striking example. In relation to the number of officeholders, the position of President has been the object of by far the greatest proportion of assassination attempts.

Truly "political" assassinations, that is assassinations that are part of a rational scheme to transfer political power from one group to another or to achieve specific policy objectives, are rare in the United States. Assassinations did occur in the Reconstruction period in the South combined with terrorist activities employed in an effort to reimpose white supremacy after the Civil War. But most assassinations in the United States have been the products of individual passion or derangement.

As an example, each of the persons who attempted, either successfully or unsuccessfully, to assassinate Presidents of the United States, with the possible exception of the so-called Puerto Rican nationalists who attacked President Truman, evidenced serious mental illness. None of them were chosen representatives of political movements, although most claimed allegiance to broader political groups and cited political reasons for their act. Each assassin seemed to be acting out some inner pathological need. Despite this, the public, in reaction to the assassinations, has sometimes attempted to tie the assassins to political movements or conspiracies.

The presidential assassins have a number of characteristics in common. Still, we are as yet unable to comprehend the individual and social forces at work sufficiently to be able to identify potential assassins in advance of their attacks. Characteristics common to assassins are shared by a large number of citizens. It is, however, both impossible at this point and probably undesirable in a democratic political system to attempt to identify and isolate potential assassins on any broad scale based on present knowledge.

As a result, prevention of assassinations must remain fundamentally a problem of physical protection. The Secret Service has the principal responsibility for protecting the President and is engaged in a continuing program to evaluate and upgrade its capabilities and to reduce the exposure of the President to risk.

Assuming the assassin to be mentally ill, there remains the question what factors tend to channel such mental illness into an assassination event. Our studies show that assassination correlates highly with general political turmoil. Political turmoil and violence have characterized the United States throughout its history. Levels of political violence appear to crest during periods of accelerated social change. Agrarian reform, abolitionism, the Reconstruction era, the fight to organize labor, and the periodic recrudescence of American nativism in its various forms were each accompanied by high levels of political violence. The 1960's have witnessed a level of violence and political turmoil comparable to other high points of violence in the nation's history.

Also, specific cultural and social factors in the United States may support political violence, including assassinations. Recent years have seen a number of movements that justify violence as a legitimate tactic in seeking political ends. There has been frequent use of rhetoric villifying institutions and individuals. Such rhetoric is frequently a precondition for physical assaults directed against politically prominent individuals. In addition, some segments of the population view our democratic government as ineffectual in meeting the needs of its people.

The likelihood of assassination should decrease as the level of political unrest within the country diminishes.

Neither panic nor complacency is an appropriate response to this Report. We should not surround our elected representatives with guards or otherwise risk isolating political leaders from their contact with the people. Our data suggest that isolated acts of assassination, unconnected with systematic terrorism, rarely bring fundamental change to a nation and have not had such impact in the United States, with the possible exception of the assassination of Abraham Lincoln. On the other hand, our data suggest that isolation of political representatives from the people may have a long-range corrosive effect upon the perceived legitimacy of democratic institutions.

Nor should we seek specific legislation purporting to respond directly to the problem of assassination alone. The most effective defense against assassination in a society that seeks to preserve freedom of the individual is an overwhelming consensus that the government is legitimate and responsive to the people. A government supported by such a consensus will have the political strength and purpose to defend itself firmly and effectively at all levels against those who reject the ideals of democracy.

Thus, we report that the continuing urgent search for strategies to cope with fundamental causes of present disaffection in the United States, such as racial inequality, mounting crime, and the questioned use of military force in our foreign affairs, is of direct relevance to the overall problem of assassination. Such disaffection weakens the consensus upon which the strength of the government is based. We have not found a specific remedy for assassination and political violence in a democracy apart from the perceived legitimacy of the government and its leaders.

B. Organization

The introductory section of this report begins by discussing definitional problems associated with the study of assassination. It presents five categories of assassination, distinguishing between, for example, a palace coup, and the attack of an individual acting out private pathological needs. This part of the report helps to establish a framework in which to evaluate the American experience.

The section also describes preconditions, or factors conducive to assassinations, based on the patterns found in the historical and comparative studies of assassination in a variety of different countries. While, strictly speaking, the precondition to an assassination is a man with a weapon and sufficient motivation to murder a political leader, this section attempts to identify broader, more basic factors that shape an environment conducive to assassination.

The introductory section concludes with an overview of the impact of assassinations upon governmental policies and political institutions, again based upon historical and comparative studies. The conditions necessary for an assassination to provoke fundamental change are reviewed and the likelihood of these occurring at the time of a specific assassination is discussed.[2]

The remainder of the report is divided into four chapters. Chapter 1 describes all attempts on the lives of officeholders in the United States. The perspective is historical and the time period covered is from the inception of the Nation to the present. The offices analyzed are President, US Senator, US Congressman, Governor, State Legislator, Judge, Mayor, and other local offices.

Chapter 2 analyzes in greater detail presidential assassinations, describing the events connected with each assassination and evaluating, to the extent possible, the motives and emotional stability of the assassins. The chapter reports on public reaction to the assassination and the impact that presidential assassinations have had on political institutions and policy. The symbolic attraction of the office of President for assassins is explored, and several general recommendations are put forward to direct attention to the limits of the office, as well as the alternative points of decisionmaking available within the political system. The problems of physical protection of the President are dealt with from the perspective of the Secret Service, the agency charged with this task.

Chapter 3 employs cross-cultural comparative data to compare the American experience with assassinations in other nations. The data show that the United States ranks high in political assassinations. The analysis also describes the relationship between assassination and other forms of political violence. These data, in addition to providing a perspective on assassinations in the United States, contribute a framework and basepoint from which to begin a more intensive exploration of the historical studies of individual nations and regions contained in the supplement to this report.

While Chapter 3 employs quantitative data to discover patterns of political violence among nations, Chapter 4 explores the cultural factors that underlie the high incidence of assassinations and other politically violent acts in the United States. The chapter presents historical overviews of political violence, including both an historical review of the major political movements and groups associated with violence and an analysis of trends in politically violent behavior obtained from a sampling of newspaper accounts over a 150-year period. With this as background, the contemporary levels of violence in the United States are analyzed in several ways. From an original survey of data, the demographic characteristics of those persons in our society who express support for political violence are described. Then, several examples of the rhetoric of violence, drawn from the more extensive materials contained within the appendix to this report, are put forward. Such rhetoric is often a precursor of attacks directed against individuals. The chapter, and the volume, ends with a personalized exploration of two contemporary groups which pose typical problems for those concerned with political violence.

CONCEPTUAL AND STRUCTURAL ANALYSIS OF ASSASSINATION

A. Problems of Definition

Although this is a report about assassination, we do not undertake to define precisely what is meant by an "assassination," nor do we limit consideration in this Report to a particular consistent definition of "assassination." There are at least three separate elements woven into the concept of "assassination" which identify it as a particular kind of murder: (1) a target that is a prominent political figure; (2) a political motive for the killing; (3) the potential political impact of the death or escape from death, as the case may be.

Most murders that would be called "assassinations" contain in greater or lesser degree all three elements, as for example, the killing of a head of state by an agent of a rival political party for the purpose of changing the regime. All three elements, however, do not necessarily coexist. A murder which contains any one of the foregoing three elements should properly be considered in any investigation of the phenomenon of assassination. For example, during the 1920's in Germany, there were a great number of politically motivated killings of persons whose political stature was trivial, but these political killings and assaults had great significance. The terrorism during the Reconstruction era in the South often had nonpolitical figures as its object. In recent years, civil rights workers—not political figures by ordinary definition—have likewise been murdered or assaulted for political motives. Such acts of political terrorism are assassinations in some senses; they should be and are treated as such in this report.

At the other extreme, the head of state or a crucial political figure could be murdered by his estranged wife or simply by a burglar with no political motivation. Nonetheless, the impact upon the political system involved could be profound. Again, in some senses, these would be assassinations and are treated as such in this report.

In assessing the impact of assassination or the level of assassination in a given country, it could be argued that the relevant inquiry becomes, "What factors within a country produce high or low impact upon the removal of a political figure, whether by assassination or not." As Carl Leiden[3] points out, the natural death of a political leader under certain circumstances can have a far more profoundly disruptive political effect than would the assassination of a political leader under other circumstances.

Also, how does one categorize attempts by mentally disturbed persons, such as the typical attacker of a President of the United States? A distinguished psychiatrist and contributer to the Commission, Dr. Lawrence Z. Freedman, has suggested that in some senses, with the possible exception of the attack upon President Truman, there have been no political assassination attempts directed at the President of the United States. The attacks are viewed as products of mental illness with no direct political content. This view is certainly arguable.

Our approach has been to avoid the definitional swamp by simply going around it, using routes dictated by common sense and practicality. In Chapter 1, we have treated all attacks against officeholders in the United States as worthy of our attention, although in most instances the attacks did not have a primary political motivation. In Chapter 2, we treat all attempts upon the lives of Presidents or of presidential candidates as assassinations.

In Chapter 3, our cross-national comparative study of assassination, we draw upon the work of two groups, one headed by Prof. Ivo Feierabend at San Diego State College, and the other headed by Professor Carl Leiden at the University of Texas.

Each group was in a position to make a valuable contribution to the study of assassination despite severe time constraints. Each had already begun gathering relevant data prior to the formation of the Commission. Each group had been working independently. In presenting their materials we adopted the definition of assassination used by each of these groups, although the definitions are not entirely the same. We did so because: (1) no reasonable alternative was feasible or desirable in terms of coordinating and reworking data which had already been gathered by the two groups, and which spoke of different time periods and (2) definitional consistency is irrelevant. Each group made cross-national comparisons only in terms of its own data: that is, all comparisons are based on a consistent definition.

Nor need the definitions used in Chapter 3 be consistent with those used in Chapters 1 and 2. The validity of comparisons of relative incidence of assassination and political violence is unaffected by the fact that the data banks used for comparative purposes may or may not have included all the Presidents of the United States or all the officeholders listed in Chapters 1 and 2 as "assassinations."

In Chapter 4, we have treated low-level political violence as a proper subject for this Report—i.e., violence for political purposes, but not necessarily directed toward political figures. Again, whether the deliberate murder of a Pinkerton guard or a union leader in an earlier time would be considered a "true" assassination is a meaningless question. As we will demonstrate, low-level violence keys into high-level violence. Low-level violence has political implications and impact. Such conduct must be treated in any discussion of political assassination.

B. Categories of Assassination[4]

Acts of assassination can occur in different social and political contexts and may be committed for different reasons. While avoiding the problem of precise definition of assassination as such, it is useful to describe the various categories of assassination and examine the experience of the United States and other regions in the world in light of these categories.

1.   The first category we can identify is assassination by one political elite to replace another without effecting any substantial systemic or ideological change. The purpose of such an assassination is simply to change the identity of the top man and the ruling clique.

This kind of assassination appears in the Middle East. Those accompanying palace revolutions, or coups in Latin America would also come under this heading. Coups in Latin America, however, have not always ended in assassination. The object of the coup has usually relinquished his position and those taking power have been content to let him live.

This type has been successful in countries where the government has little de facto impact upon the vast body of the citizens outside the capital city. As long as governments can come and go with little impact or participation by peon or *fellahin*, as the case may be, palace revolutions appear to be a practical way of gaining power. This type of assassination has not appeared in the United States.

2.   A second category is assassination for the purpose of terrorizing and destroying the legitimacy of the ruling elite in order to effect substantial systemic or ideological change.

Such assassination may be directed against high government officials or against mid-level officials to undermine the effectiveness of the central government at the local or provincial level. When such terror is directed toward a chief of state, the assassin may accomplish part of his goal even though the attempt is unsuccessful. For example, the members of the group which set out to assassinate the Czar in the 1880's realized that they had no realistic chance of short-term success in changing the basic political structure of Czarist Russia. They pointed out, however, that if they forced the Czars to retreat into their palaces or surround themselves with guards, the symbolic separation of the leaders from their people would, in the long run, undermine the legitimacy of the Czarist government.

Our studies show that this kind of assassination is effective in achieving the long-range goals sought, although not so in advancing the short-term goals or careers of the terrorists themselves. Our studies show that, at least in modern history (post-1850), it cannot be said that in the long run any terrorist group was unsuccessful, except in those countries such as Soviet Russia and Nazi Germany where the ruling elite was willing to use massive counter-terror to suppress potentially terroristic groups. Once a terrorist group is well established, the only effective response is either counterterror or agreement to the basic demands of the terrorists—demands which may or may not be compatible with a democratic soeiety. The Nazis, for example, rose to power on a wave of terrorism.

The best defense against terrorism is a government which

has the broad popular support necessary to control terrorist activities through normal channels of law enforcement without resorting to counterterror. Terrorists often correctly perceive that their greatest enemy is the moderate who attempts to remedy whatever perceived injustices form the basis for terrorist strength. It is often these moderates who are the targets of assassination.

For example, Premier Stolypin of Russia, whose energy and force might have made the Duma a practical instrument of constitutional monarchy, fell to an assassin in 1911. Archduke Ferdinand, whose death triggered World War I, advocated federalism and limited autonomy for Serbian nationals within the Austrian Empire. The representatives of Serbian nationalism who killed him apparently feared that this moderate policy might undermine the support upon which they counted.

It should be pointed out that even the strategy of remedying the perceived injustices from which the terrorists gain their strength may not work or may be impractical, because that strategy may be consistent with the basic goals of the central government.

An example is the British presence in both Cyprus and Palestine. It was the British presence itself that was the perceived injustice. In both instances, terrorism was effective in spite of all counter-strategies. As can be seen, terrorism is particularly effective when the government is viewed by a substantial portion of the local population as a foreign conqueror or otherwise illegitimate.

This type of assassination terrorism appeared in the South directly after the Civil War. The imposed ruling class was viewed as illegitimate by a substantial portion of the population. Assassination of Northern Republican officeholders, combined with systematic terrorism practiced on Southerners sympathetic to the then "foreign elite," eventually forced Northern capitulation. The so-called "Southern way of life" was reestablished, and lasted virtually unchallenged until the 1950's.

Even where the government is neither foreign nor otherwise illegitimate, if terrorism has established itself, it may become so institutionalized and professionalized as a way of life that no concession is sufficient. A concession may please one group but offend another. This is apparently what happened in the case of the IMRO, or Black Hand, in the Balkans. Thus, it is important that potential terrorism be recognized and counteracted at an early stage.

3. A third category is assassination by the government in power to suppress political challenge.

This strategy, including mass counterterror, has appeared in Soviet Russia and Nazi Germany. A recent example was the assassination of the leader of the Muslim Brotherhood by the Egyptian Government. Such strategy is not necessarily ideologically based. Machiavelli advised this strategy for the prince who has just come to power—to kill relatives of the previous prince and other potential challengers with promptness in order to make his power secure. Such a strategy is an indication and confession of weakness by the central government. This type of assassination has not occurred in the United States.

4. A fourth category is assassination to propagandize a political or ideological point of view. This is the so-called "propaganda of the deed," popular with anarchists at the turn of the century.

Its purpose is to dramatize and publicize perceived injustice. Some of the assassins of Presidents of the United States may marginally fall within this category, as well as within the fifth category.

The success of such strategies cannot easily be measured, for the assassin does not purport directly to advance his ideology except through publicity. A cause-and-effect relationship cannot be unravelled. For example, the assassination of Archduke Ferdinand may fall in part within this category —to publicize Serbian national aspirations. The effect, we can speculate, was to create upheavals far beyond those anticipated, and still there is no Serbian national state—although Yugoslavia perhaps comes closer than Austria. The speculation remains whether the assassins and the group they represented would prefer Yugoslavia today to the rule of the Austrian Empire prior to World War I.

5. The fifth and last category is assassination unconnected with rational political goals which satisfies only the pathological needs of the mentally disturbed attacker. This represents the typical attacker of Presidents of the United States. Whether such assassinations achieve the goal of the assassin is a matter of psychiatric speculation. To the extent that such assassins seek attention, publicity, and importance, they consistently have achieved their goals in the United States.

C. Preconditions for Assassination[5]

Cross-national comparative studies demonstrate that other forms of political violence correlate highly with and may be preconditions to assassination. That is, political turmoil itself may spawn assassination without regard to distinctions between types of turmoil.

We believe, however, that our studies of assassination in specific regions and countries throughout the world enable us to identify more precisely certain preconditions for assassination.

An analysis of the preconditions of assassination cannot ignore the issue of the kind of government towards which the assassination is directed. The study of assassination and terrorism in the late nineteenth and twentieth centuries demonstrates that the preconditions for assassination under a democracy differ from preconditions under oppressive foreign or autocratic rule, where political expression is not allowed. Where there is oppressive rule, comparative studies suggest three antecedents to assassination: (1) the existence of a political party with an ideology and technique of direct action; (2) perception of oppression; and (3) presence of activists, i.e., persons willing to respond with violence to the conditions of oppression.

In a democracy, however, where physical oppression is absent, its equivalent must be created through (1) a weakening of shared democratic values, or a crisis in which the democratic institutions are incapable of taking effective remedial action; and (2) a pre-assassination process of defamation and vilification of democratic politicians and institutions. The remaining preconditions are also shared with the oppressive rule situation—(3) the existence of a party or groups of persons with an ideology and tactics of direct violence, and (4) the presence of persons with propensities for violence once the antecedents are present.

A number of the preconditions for assassination are latent in the United States. Some groups may perceive the government as oppressive, in which case the model describing oppressive rule is applicable. It is, however, a reverse sentimentalism to distort the overall picture of political conditions in the United States by dwelling on its admitted imperfections. The United States is a remarkably free country. Most of its citizens enjoy perhaps more real freedom, including the freedom from hunger and other material deprivations, than any other nation. Thus, it is the second model, preconditions for assassination in a democracy, which is of particular interest to us.

and the advocacy of violence may have a more profound effect than we have realized. The fact that our most tragic assassinations have been at the hands of persons who were Specifically, the rhetoric of vilification of political leaders mentally deranged, or not part of any political conspiracy, does not weaken the point. As Professor Feliks Gross points out, by way of example:

> Before the assassination of President Gabriel Naru-towicz in 1922 in Poland, in a pre-assassination stage, a vituperous defamation campaign was launched against him by the parties of the right. The assassination was an isolated, political act of killing, not a result of a terroristic tactic. The assassin, Eligious Niewiadomski, believed that he had performed a heroic act and a patriotic duty. There was neither conspiracy nor organized terroristic party. But in the climate of vilification, once the political actor was "morally" branded, eliminated, and destroyed, psychological restraints and controls of a potential assassin were weakened or even removed, and in his view assassination was justified (Supplement, section A).

Professor Gross is not alone with his concern for the impact of such rhetoric. Dan Watts, editor of *The Liberator* magazine, a Negro, and an early advocate of black nationalism, made the same point in an interview with a consultant for this Task Force, that there should be a deescalation of violent talk before it leads to violent action (see Appendix D). On the other hand, a stabilizing strength peculiar to the United States is its unique capacity to absorb and adopt the rhetoric and symbols of radical challenge. To this extent, one can agree with and rejoice in one of the basic theses of Herbert Marcuse that the United States has a tremendous capacity to absorb and thus to emasculate radical challenges. One early exponent of the "hippie" movement complained that the movement was not a success in challenging basic American values because trying to change the United States was like "tilting with a marshmallow; you end up getting smothered."[6] In effect, the movement has been in large part absorbed through diffusion of its symbols into the very establishment which the hippies challenged. This process has a two-fold benefit. In the process of absorbing the destructive radical challenge, the establishment in the United States also experiences renewal and change, not by a destruction of fundamental values, but by an evolutionary awareness and adaptation to the challenging point of view. It is this capacity for absorption and the good-humored refusal of mainstream America to allow itself to be teased into over-reaction by irrelevant symbols—well publicized, short-term exceptions to the contrary notwithstanding—which contributes to America's great capacity for keeping its basic democratic values intact while making the necessary adjustments and responses to continuing change.

D. The Impact of Assassinations on Government Institutions and Policy

It takes a congruence of unusual circumstances for assassinations to achieve fundamental long-run changes within a political system. An assassination of whatever category is not likely in itself to cause any basic alterations in institutional forms or policy.[7] Under a combination of unusual circumstances, however, the removal of a key figure—for example, a Lincoln or Franklin Roosevelt (unsuccessfully attacked just before he took office) in the United States, an Abdullah in Jordan—can have unanticipated and profound implications for the course of the society. The convergence of forces necessary to create high-impact assassinations occurs rather infrequently, however.

Carl Leiden[8] distinguishes between the implications of the assassination act for the survival of the system as against the considerably less consequential difficulties it might create for a particular ruling elite or party. He argues that only in a few very specific cases do assassinations have profound implications for the total political system.

> An assassination can have a high impact when (a) the system is highly centralized, (b) the political support of the victim is highly personal, (c) the "replaceability" of the victim is low, (d) the system is in crisis and/or in a

period of rapid political and social change, and (e) if the death of the victim involves the system in confrontation with other powers. (Supplement, section F)

Applying the foregoing criteria to the United States, we believe that there is little likelihood of an assassination in the United States having a fundamentally destructive impact. Our leaders are either constrained or supported, to the extent that they are either strong or weak, by the institutional framework within which they must operate. Although the federal government has great power, that power is divided among three branches, and the power to control individuals is also shared to a significant degree by the State and local governing bodies. Thus, our government is probably not "highly centralized," that is, our government is not a single hierarchy of power which would be possible for one man to control.

Support of political figures in the United States may result from a charismatic inspiration of personal loyalty among supporters, for example, the two Roosevelts, Bryan, and Lincoln. But such personal support is effectively constrained by our institutions of government. It is impossible for political leaders in the United States to operate outside of institutional forms that set clear restraint on the powers of the office and the eligibility and tenure of its occupants. The political system of the United States also permits many competing centers of power as well as procedures for opposing and replacing those in office.

"Replaceability" of the victim of an assassination is, of course, a concern in the United States, in the sense that no man is a duplicate of another. Each President brings to the office unique qualities which may affect the way he handles a "crisis," "a period of rapid political or social change," or a "confrontation with other powers." Nevertheless, the United States does have an ordered replacement system for its Presidents that has proved successful. The institution of the presidency, with all its powers, limitations, and resources, remains even as one man leaves the office and another succeeds to it. This will continue to be true so long as the United States remains a country governed by law, not by men.

We can take comfort from Professor Leiden's summary statement that "assassination . . . as a *deliberate* instrument of policy is a highly uncertain, risky adventure with little probability that systemic or other far-reaching changes will be brought about."[9]

References

1. The assassins of Dr. King and Robert Kennedy, both of whom were before the courts at the time this Report was being compiled, are not treated here. The public reactions to those assassinations, however, are discussed in Chapter 2.
2. The studies from which these parts of the Report are primarily derived can be found in the Supplement.
3. See Leiden's analysis of assassination in the Middle East in the Supplement F.
4. The following categories are taken directly from a paper submitted by Prof. Feliks Gross, "Political Violence and Terror in Nineteenth and Twentieth Century Russia and Eastern Europe," which appears in section A of the Supplement.
5. This section is drawn primarily from the paper submitted to the Commission by Prof. Feliks Gross.
6. *Yale Alumni Magazine*, November 1967, p. 10.
7. The exception, as pointed out above, is assassination in conjunction with systematic terrorism, which involves the cumulative effect of multiple assassinations.
8. Carl Leiden has co-authored *The Politics of Violence* (Englewood Cliffs, N.J.: Prentice-Hall, 1968) and is preparing with colleagues a book on *The Politics of Assassination.* His reviews of the consequences of assassinations in the Middle East are found in section F of the Supplement.
9. See Supplement F. We are referring to the absence of fundamental impact through assassination upon the political system or upon basic national policies. We do not suggest that there has been no traceable political consequence of assassinations, and in particular we discuss the political consequences traceable to assassinations of Presidents of the United States in Chapter 2.

CHAPTER 1

DEADLY ATTACKS UPON PUBLIC OFFICEHOLDERS IN THE UNITED STATES

A. Introduction[1]

During all stages of our Nation's history, violence has been one response offered to many of the controversial issues confronting our society. The establishment of independence, the relationship of settlers with the American Indian, the slavery and secession questions, and the trade union and civil rights movements are prime examples. Included in this history of violence are deadly attacks on persons holding public office. Chapter 1 is addressed to this particular kind of political violence.

It is important to state clearly at the outset the definition of assassination used in this chapter. We consider "assassinations" all deadly attacks upon public officeholders in the United States by any person for any reason. Included is violence (in the form of direct physical assault, use of firearms, or conspiracies, the aim of which is death or injury) directed at persons both holding or actively aspiring to such office. The offices considered cover a wide range: Presidents, cabinet members, governors, senators, congressmen, mayors, state legislators, judges, tax collectors, state and district attorneys, etc. Not included are politically prominent leaders or workers for social causes or political movements and organizations who did not hold public office, were not actively aspiring to public office, or were not former officeholders.

In specific terms, this section reviews all reported deadly

attacks upon public officeholders or aspirants to public office without regard for motive for the attack—whether "personal" or "political"—from revenue collectors to Presidents. But this section does not consider attacks upon persons such as Martin Luther King, Jr., Medgar Evers, or George Lincoln Rockwell. By including all officeholders who have been the victims of attack, we gain confidence in the validity of our conclusions as to the nature and scope of the problem of deadly political violence in the United States. Virtually none of the deadly attacks against officeholders had a dominant rational political purpose; but most were in some way related to politics. Thus, the soundest approach is to include all such attacks in our investigation; no subjective judgments had to be made about whether the dominant motive for the attack was political, and the entire scope of such violence is before us. In excluding attacks upon all non-officeholders, we again avoid the problem of subjective judgment. Further, we avoid severe historical bias, because the names of the "politically prominent" of a given era tend to fade more rapidly from the pages of history than do the names of officeholders.

Table 1 lists all eighty-one of the recorded assassinations or attempted assassinations in chronological order. Working with this limited but useful definition of assassination, two conclusions can be drawn from the data in Table 1. First, the more powerful and prestigious the office, the greater the likelihood of assassination. Second, there is much greater likelihood that the occupant of or aspirant to an elected public office will be the victim of an assassination than will the occupant of an appointed position, even though the position may be a powerful one, such as Secretary of State, Justice of the Supreme Court, or Attorney General.

The relationships between the importance of the office and the likelihood of assassination are dramatically demonstrated by Table 2. This table compares the proportion of successful or attempted assassinations in four offices which differ significantly in degree of power or prestige.

Despite the crudeness of the estimates upon which the figures in Table 2 are based, the differences among the four categories are still sufficiently large that the relationship between importance or prestige of position and likelihood of assassination is demonstrated. One out of four Presidents has been a target of assassination, compared to approximately one out of every one hundred and sixty-six governors, one out of one hundred and forty-two Senators, and one out of every one thousand congressmen.[2]

We can suggest that the correlation between importance of elected office and likelihood of assassination is affected by the fact that the importance of the office and the size of the constituency are directly related. The President's constituency is much larger than that of any other elected office. Similarly, a senator's or a governor's constituency is greater than that of any congressman. Of the eight senators and eight governors who have been assassination targets, all but one were attacked by members of their own constituency.

The absence of assassination attempts on the vice president may also be consistent with this observation; the office of vice president has no elective independence from the presidency, and, in effect, has no constituency for purposes of this analysis. In any event, the office is sufficiently anomalous that lack of assassination attempts directed at the vice president does not necessarily invalidate the postulated relationship between assassination and size of constituency.

The second point is that persons in elected positions are more likely to be assassinated than are occupants of appointed offices. Of approximately four hundred and fifty cabinet members, and of approximately one hundred and two Supreme Court Justices, only one in each category has been the target of an assassin.

With the exception of attacks upon Republicans in the South during the Reconstruction era, only a very small portion of the deadly attacks against officeholders was rationally calculated to advance political aims of the assassin. With the possible exception of the attack upon President Truman by two self-avowed Puerto Rican nationalists, none of the presidential assassinations or assassination attempts were made under the aegis of any organized political group or to advance any rational strategy for political change. Still, the unbalanced minds of the presidential assassins focused themselves on high political officeholders rather than nonpolitical targets, and the question of why those acts became political still remains.

Similarly, the attacks on other officeholders were related to politics without being "conspiratorial" or "political" in the sense of seeking power. Senator Charles Sumner, the antislavery senator from Massachusetts, was severely beaten on the

Table 1.–Chronological list of political assassinations and assaults.*

Year	Victim	Method of Attack and Result	Location of Attack	Assailant and Professed or Alleged Reason
1835	Andrew Jackson President	Attempted shooting, gun misfired	Washington, D.C.	Richard Lawrence; considered mentally unbalanced; said Jackson was ruining the country.
1856	Charles Sumner Senator, Massachusetts	Assaulted, severely	Washington, D.C.	Congressman Preston Brooks of South Carolina; revenge for antislavery speech made by Sumner.
1857	David C. Broderick Senator, California	Shot in duel, killed	California	David S. Terry; insults over political stand on slavery and legal feud.
1865	Abraham Lincoln President	Shot, killed	Washington, D.C.	John Wilkes Booth; loyalty to the Confederacy; revenge for defeat; slavery issue.
	William H. Seward Secretary of State	Shot, wounded	Washington, D.C.	David Herold, Lewis Paine; part of Lincoln plot.
1867	G. W. Ashburn Delegate to Georgia Constitutional Convention	Shot, killed	Georgia	Unknown; 10 prominent citizens implicated in the murder of the Republican delegate during Reconstruction.
	Almon Case State senator,	Shot, killed	Tennessee	Frank Farris; anti-Union guerrilla leader.
	L. Harris Hiscox delegate to New York Constitutional Convention	Shot, killed	New York	Cole; personal affair over Cole's wife.

*This list represents all acts reported in the New York Times, and other prominent widely circulated newspapers, such as The Washington Post, the Chicago Tribune, the St. Louis Dispatch, etc. Also consulted were basic American histories and interpretative texts of various periods in American history, such as the Reconstruction period, the Depression of the 1930's and the pre-World War I era. It would be foolish to believe that the list prepared for Table 1 accounts for every attempted or successful assassination that has ever occurred in the United States. We are reasonably sure, however, that it accounts for every President, Senator, and Governor; and probably even for every Congressman. But the degree of certainty obviously decreases with the power and publicness of the office involved. Also, under the category "attempted," we do not include "threatening letters" or "crank phone calls"; an overt act must have been committed.

Year	Name / Office	Action	State	Notes
1868	J. W. C. Horne, Judge, Georgia	Shot, killed	Georgia	Unknown Negro; judge shot over incident involving his son and a colored girl.
	H. W. Fowler, Assistant collector of revenues	Shot, killed	Texas	D. B. Bonfoey, collector of Revenues; no motives ascertained.
	John P. Slough, Chief Justice, New Mexico Territory	Shot, killed	New Mexico	Capt. William L. Rynerson; feud and insults over Rynerson's attempt to have Slough recalled.
	V. Chase, Judge, Louisiana	Shot, killed	Louisiana	Band of Rebels; Chase was a Union man.
	Robert Gray, Justice, Louisiana	Shot, killed	Louisiana	Unknown(s).
	Harrington, State legislator; Pennington, State senator, Alabama	Attempted shooting	Alabama	Unknown; ambushed while canvassing county together for Republican Party.
	James Hinds, Representative, Arkansas	Shot, killed	Arkansas	George M. Clark; was Secretary of Democratic Committee; Hinds was campaigning for Republicans, Clark was drunk at the time of shooting.
	B. Saulet, Sheriff, Caddo Parish, Louisiana	Shot, killed	Louisiana	Unknown(s).
	Samuel W. Beall, ex-Lieutenant Governor, Wisconsin	Shot, killed	Montana	George M. Pinney; Beall attacked Pinney over articles Pinney wrote; acquitted as self-defense.
1869	M. McConnel, State senator, Illinois	Shot, killed	Illinois	Unknown; believed to be over property litigation.

Table 1.—Chronological list of political assassinations and assaults. —(Continued)

Year	Victim	Method of Attack and Result	Location of Attack	Assailant and Professed or Alleged Reason
1870	Benjamin Ayers State Legislator, Georgia	Shot, killed	Georgia	Wilson; robbery believed motive
	William S. Lincoln Representative New York	Cane assault	Maryland	Joseph Segar; lost contested seat for Representative from Virginia
	John W. Stevens State senator, North Carolina	Stabbed, hung, killed	North Carolina	Wiley and Mitchelle, apparently acted with consent of Democratic Party of Caswell County; Stevens was a Republican.
	Gaylord Clark District Judge, Texas	Shot, killed	Texas	Frank William; sought judgeship for himself.
	A. P. Crittedon Judge, California	Shot, killed	California	Laura D. Fair, his mistress, when he attempted to break off relationship.
1871	Alden McLaughlin Customs Inspector, Texas	Shot, killed	Texas	Smugglers; in the line of duty.
1873	William Pitt Kellog Governor, Louisiana	Attempted shooting	Louisiana	Charles R. Rainey, Melvin H. Cohen; many disputed his election, open rebellion in parts of Louisiana.
	Samuel Clark Pomeroy ex-Senator, Kansas	Shot, wounded	Washington, D.C.	M. F. Conway; both men had been in Kansas politics at statehood; Conway blamed Pomeroy for his circumstances.
	T. S. Crawford District County Judge Arthur H. Harris District Attorney Monroe, Louisiana	Shot, killed	Louisiana	Assumed to have been ambushed by the Tom Wayne gang, with whom both had previously been involved in a case.

Year	Officeholder	Attack	State	Notes
	Edwin S. McCook, Territorial Secretary of Dakota	Shot, killed	Dakota Territory	P. P. Wintermute; dispute over railroad bonds.
1874	H. P. Farrow, U.S. District Attorney, Georgia	Clubbed, wounded	Georgia	Unknown; had got indictments against five men; papers ranted against him and tried to intimidate jury.
	James O'Brian, ex-State senator, New York	Attempted shooting	New York	Richard Croker, George and Henry Hickey, John Sheridan; Tammany group dispute with O'Brian.
1875	E. G. Johnson, Deputy Collector of Internal Revenue and State legislator, Florida	Shot, killed	Florida	Unknown(s); shot in still house.
	Belden, ex-Parish Judge, Louisiana	Shot, killed	Louisiana	Sherburn; was judge at time; motive unknown.
	Daniel O'Connell, Alderman, New York	Gunthreat	New York	John T. Cox; personal matter over Cox' sister.
	G. A. Roderty, tax collector, Grant Parish, Louisiana	Shot, killed	Louisiana	John B. McCoy, ex-sheriff.
1877	Stephen B. Packard, Governor, Louisiana	Shot, wounded	Louisiana	W. H. Weldon; apparently part of group that challenged legality of election.
1881	James A. Garfield, President	Shot, killed	Maryland	Charles Guiteau; wanted political appointment.
	Smith, State senator, Tennessee	Shot, wounded	Tennessee	John J. Vertress; political feud over way Smith voted, Vertress claimed Smith was bribed.

Table 1.—Chronological list of political assassinations and assaults.—(Continued)

Year	Victim	Method of Attack and Result	Location of Attack	Assailant and Professed or Alleged Reason
1885	John B. Bowman ex-mayor, East St. Louis, Illinois	Shot, killed	Illinois	Unknown; previous attempts made after several men killed in Republican-Democratic clashes at City Hall during his term.
1889	Stephen J. Field Supreme Court Judge	Assaulted	California	David S. Terry; had threatened Field in legal dispute.
	David S. Terry Judge, California	Shot, killed	California	David Nagel, U.S. deputy marshall assigned to guard Field, shot and killed Terry.
	W. L. Pierce Superior Judge, San Diego, California	Shot, wounded	California	W. S. Clendennin; because of unfavorable decision handed down by Pierce.
1890	William P. Taulbee ex-Representative, Kentucky	Shot, killed	Washington	Charles E. Kincaide; feud over articles Kincaide wrote linking Taulbee to scandal; Kincaide acquitted.
1892	R. D. McCotter State senator, North Carolina	Shot, killed	North Carolina	Unknown; assumed to be personal; wife's family did not like his behavior.
1893	Carter H. Harrison mayor, Chicago, Illinois	Shot, killed	Illinois	Patrick E. Prendergast; disappointed officeseeker.
	Henry S. Tyler mayor, Louisville, Kentucky	Threatened with gun	Kentucky	P. J. Schwartz; did not want city limits extended to his property.
1896	Col. Albert Jennings Fountain ex-State legislator, New Mexico Territory	Shot, killed	New Mexico	Unknown; long conflict between cattle association and outlaws backed by opposite political party.

Year	Name	Action	State	Notes
1900	William Goebel, Governor, Kentucky	Shot, killed	Kentucky	Caleb Powers; tried and convicted of conspiracy; disputed election.
1901	William McKinley, President	Shot, killed	New York	Leon F. Czolgosz; anarchist ideology.
1905	Frank Steunenberg, ex-Governor, Idaho	Dynamite, killed	Idaho	Harry Orchard; labor union against which Governor called out troops involved.
1908	John F. Fort, Governor, New Jersey	Attempted bombing	New Jersey	Unknown; suspect either crackpot or parties angered by liquor law enforcement.
1910	William Gaynor, Mayor, New York City	Shot, wounded	New York	John J. Gallagher; fired from city job, angered at Gaynor's trip.
1912	Theodore Roosevelt, President	Shot, wounded	Wisconsin	John Schrank; had vision that McKinley wanted him to avenge his death; Schrank declared insane.
1913	B. P. Windsor, Mayor, Mt. Aubcorn, Illinois	Shot, killed	Illinois	Fay D. State; quarrel over editorial
1917	Henry Cabot Lodge, Senator, Massachusetts	Assaulted	Washington, D.C.	Pacifists: A. Bannwart, Rev. P. H. Drake, Mrs. M. A. Peabody, outbursts because he did not support staying out of war; not serious attempt on life.
1921	Charles Henderson, Senator, Nevada	Shot, wounded	Washington, D.C.	August Grock; personal quarrel over money.
1924	Robert Young Thomas, Jr., Representative, Kentucky	Assaulted	Kentucky	G. Baker; political opponent; Baker angered by Thomas' remarks.
1926	Jeff Stone, mayor, Culp, Illinois	Shot, killed	Illinois	Unknown; suspected political gangster bootlegging tie-in.

Table 1.–Chronological list of political assassinations and assaults.*–(Continued)

Year	Victim	Method of Attack and Result	Location of Attack	Assailant and Professed or Alleged Reason
1933	Franklin Delano Roosevelt President	Attempted shooting	Florida	Guiseppe Zangara; hated rulers and capitalists.
	Anton Cermak mayor, Chicago, Illinois	Shot, killed	Florida	Cermak was hit in hail of bullets aimed at Roosevelt.
1935	Huey P. Long Senator, Louisiana	Shot, killed	Louisiana	Dr. Carl Weiss; apparent concern over Long's power, and having his father-in-law's judgeship taken away.
	Thomas J. Courtney State's attorney, Illinois	Shot, killed	Illinois	Unknown; suspected Capone gang.
1936	J. M. Bolton State legislator, Illinois	Shot, killed	Illinois	Assumed to be gangsters; alliance of crime and politics.
1939	Louis E. Edwards mayor, Long Beach, New York	Shot, killed	New York	Alvin Dooley; angered that Edwards used influence to keep him from being elected to office in police organization.
1945	Warren G. Hooper State senator, Michigan	Shot, killed	Michigan	Conspirators: Harry and Sam Fleisher, Mike Selik, Pete Mahoney; Hooper had been key witness in an investigation.
1947	John William Bricker Senator, Ohio	Shot, wounded	Washington, D.C.	William L. Kaiser; personal grudge over money lost when Bricker was attorney general.
	Hubert H. Humphrey mayor, Minneapolis, Minnesota	Attempted shooting	Minnesota	Unknown; several attempts made conflicts over crime-labor unions.

Year	Name	Attack	State	Notes
1949	Thomas Anglin, State senator, Oklahoma	Shot, wounded	Oklahoma	Jim Scott; personal; Anglin's law firm represented Scott's wife in divorce.
1950	Elihu H. Bailey, mayor, Evarts, Kentucky	Attempted dynamite	Kentucky	Unknown; mayor thought it was bootlegger he was fighting.
	Harry S. Truman, President	Attempted shooting	Washington, D.C.	Oscar Collazo, Griselio Torresola; Puerto Rican Independence
1954	Kenneth Allison Roberts Representative, Alabama Benton Franklin Jensen Representative, Iowa George Hyde Fallon Representative, Maryland Alvin Morell Bentley Representative, Michigan Clifford Davis Representative, Tennessee	Shot, wounded	Washington, D.C.	Puerto Rican extremists: Lolita Lebron, Rafael Cancel Miranda, A. F. Corcera; attack on Congress by independence group.
1958	Paul A. Wallace, State senator, South Carolina	Shot, killed	South Carolina	Henry Rogers; assumed mad, hanged self in mental institution.
1959	J. Lindsay Almond, Jr. Governor, Virginia	Attempted shooting	Virginia	Unknown; suspected segregationist, during school integration period.
1963	John F. Kennedy President	Shot, killed	Texas	Lee Harvey Oswald; motivation unknown.
	John Connally Governor, Texas	Shot, wounded	Texas	Lee Harvey Oswald; accident assuming assassin was aiming at President.
1968	Robert F. Kennedy	Shot, killed	California	Sirhan Sirhan, accused; foreign policy statements vis a vis the Middle East.

Table 2. – *Likelihood of assassination by type of public office*
(1790-1968)

Office	Number of man terms	Estimates of the number holding office	Number of assassinations attempted	Percentage of universality
President	45	35	8[b]	23
Governors[a]	1,710	1,330	8	00.6
Senators[a]	2,271	1,140	8[c]	00.7
Representatives[a]	27,930	8,349	9	00.1

[a]Number of man terms was computed from apportionment census material listed in *Biographical Directory of the American Congress 1774-1961* (Reynolds U.S. Government Printing Office.) The representatives were multiplied by 5 indicating five terms per decade, the Senators by 1.67. The Governors were computed by the number of States in the Union for each census period and then multiplying by 2.5. The figure for estimated Governors actually served was computed by taking 77.8 percent man terms—the same as that for president. The Senators are based on an average of 0.81 per page and Congressmen 5.93 per page for 1,408 pages in the biographical sketch section of the above-cited volume.

[b]Includes Theodore Roosevelt, an ex-President who was also a presidential candidate.

[c]Includes Senator Robert Kennedy who was also presidential candidate.

floor of the Congress by Representative Preston Brooks of South Carolina three days after Sumner had made a strong speech denouncing slavery. Several other public officials were attacked in quarrels over political issues. A number of officeholders were attacked by constituents who harbored a personal grudge over political treatment they thought they had received.

Perhaps as many as eleven public officials were victims of assassination attempts by elements of organized crime. These were mostly lower-level officials who were either involved with the criminals or whose activities represented a threat to organized crime. We may speculate that such attacks were well planned and "political" in the sense of seeking to control legislative or executive conduct vis-a-vis the attackers. These may be the only examples that are comparable to the classic form of "assassination" in other nations, i.e., for direct political payoff.

Of all the assassinations and assassination attempts against officeholders in U.S. history, perhaps only one, excepting those related to organized crime, fits the classic picture of an assassination for a rational political purpose—that of Governor William Goebel of Kentucky in 1900. Goebel narrowly won a hotly contested three-way fight for the governorship between Populist Democrats (Goebel's party), Conservative Democrats, and the incumbent Republicans. Three men associated with the Republican party were convicted of conspiracy to assassinate the Governor.

Other assassinations for rational political purpose might include the caning of Senator Sumner in 1856, the death in a duel of Senator Broderick in 1857 (both based on the passions of the impending Civil War), the assassination of Senator Huey P. Long, and the wounding of the five members of the House of Representatives by the self-appointed advocates of Puerto Rican nationalism.

Perhaps the murder in 1885 of John P. Bowman, former mayor of East St. Louis and a member of the Republican Party, should be added. He was killed by unknown persons, the *New York Times* stating, "The dead man had so many enemies, that police are puzzled where to begin."[3]

Thus it can be seen that a deliberate effort to remove officeholders for rational political purposes is a rarity, even among the eighty-one attacks against officeholders in the United States.

In the next section of this chapter, we use a case method to analyze how the assassinations of different types of officeholders may have varied by the motivation and personal social characteristics of the would-be assassins, and by the context in which the acts have occurred. In the third section, we return to a statistical overview and examine rates of assassination over time and by geographical region. The special issues raised by assassination of a President are treated in detail in Chapter 2 of this report.

B. Case Method Discussion of Assassinations

Presidential Assassinations

In the one hundred and thirty-three years between the attempt made on the life of Andrew Jackson in 1835 and the successful assassination of presidential candidate Robert Kennedy in 1968, seven other Presidents or aspirants to the presidency have been assassination targets. Table 3 lists each of the men involved with a summary description highlighting the main facts surrounding each case.

We can draw several important conclusions about presidential assassinations. Party affiliation, public policies, term of office, and political strength provide few clues about the likelihood of assassination. The men who have been targets differ considerably. For example, Lincoln was the President of a divided nation during a civil war, Garfield was a compromise candidate of a faction-torn party, and McKinley was a popular President of a relatively unified and stable society. All were assassinated.

The list of assassination victims is not limited solely to Presidents who have exhibited strong leadership or enhanced the power of the office. Presidents Lincoln and Kennedy fit this model; Presidents Garfield and McKinley do not. Franklin Roosevelt was shot at before he had a chance to demonstrate his leadership qualities. There are no later reports of attempts on his life. And Woodrow Wilson, who was certainly as strong a President as Truman or Kennedy, was never a target.

Party affiliation does not appear to be relevant except in indicating the hegemony of one party or the other during particular historical periods. The period of Republican dominance from Lincoln to F. D. R. (1860–1932) shows only

Table 3.—Chronological list of political assassinations and assaults of Presidents and presidential candidates

Year	Victim	Political party	Length of administration at time of attack	Location	Method of attack and result	Assailant and professed or alleged reason
1835	Andrew Jackson	Democrat	6 years	Washington, D.C.	pistol, misfired	Richard Lawrence, declared insane; said Jackson was preventing him from obtaining large sums of money.
1865	Abraham Lincoln	Republican	4 years, 1 month	Washington, D.C.	pistol, killed	John W. Booth, loyalty to the Confederacy; revenge for defeat: slavery issue.
1881	James Garfield	Republican	4 months	Washington, D.C.	pistol, killed	Charles Guiteau, disgruntled officeseeker; supporter of opposite faction of Republican Party.
1901	William McKinley	Republican	4 years, 6 months	Buffalo, N.Y.	pistol, killed	Leon F. Czolgosz, anarchist ideology.
1912	Theodore Roosevelt	Progressive (Bull Moose)	Candidate (had served before, 1901-09)	Milwaukee, Wisc.	pistol, wounded	John Schrank, declared insane; had vision that McKinley wanted him to avenge his death.
1933	Franklin D. Roosevelt	Democrat	3 weeks prior to 1st inauguration	Miami, Fla.	pistol, bullets missed the President	Guiseppe Zangara, hated rulers and capitalists.
1950	Harry S. Truman	Democrat	5 years	Washington, D.C.	automatic weapon, prevented from shooting at President	Oscar Collazo and Griselio Torresola; Puerto Rican independence.
1963	John F. Kennedy	Democrat	3 years	Dallas, Tex.	rifle, killed	Lee H. Oswald, motive unknown.
1968	Robert F. Kennedy	Democrat	Candidate	Los Angeles, Calif.	pistol, killed	Sirhan Sirhan, accused.

Republican victims (or, in the case of Theodore Roosevelt, a splinter Republican candidate), while the period of Democratic dominance (1932–68) shows only Democratic victims. This is hardly unexpected, however. Only two Democrats, Grover Cleveland (1884–88, 1892–96) and Woodrow Wilson (1912–20) held office during the first period, and only one Republican, Dwight David Eisenhower, held office (1952–60) during the second. Nor is there any particular era during which assassinations have frequently occurred. From Lincoln to John F. Kennedy, assassination attempts against Presidents or presidential candidates have occurred at fairly regular intervals of one every eleven to twenty-one years. Those of President Jackson (thirty years before Lincoln), and Robert Kennedy (only five years after his brother) deviated from this pattern. Until more time has passed, it is impossible to determine whether the short interval between the Kennedy assassinations has meaning or is simply an anomaly in an otherwise consistent pattern.

The political philosophy of a President or presidential candidate also appears to bear little relevance to an attack. McKinley and Garfield were moderate conservatives, while Kennedy and Truman were liberals; FDR was attacked at a time when his political philosophy was not yet identifiable (indeed, one might have classified him as somewhat conservative on the basis of his balance-the-budget and fiscal-integrity speeches during the presidential campaign of 1932). Of the six attempts in the 20th century, however, it is true that five attempts were made on liberal Presidents or presidential candidates and only one on a conservative President (McKinley). Most Presidents in this century have been of a liberal rather than conservative bent. If Theodore Roosevelt is considered as a liberal, liberals have occupied the White House for forty-three of the last sixty-nine years.

An interesting pattern that does emerge is that the assassination attempts seem to correspond with the general levels of civil strife. The greater such strife, the more likely the President in office will be attacked. In Chapter 4 we set forth a graph of the amount of political violence that occurred in the United States since 1819, based upon a survey of newspaper reports of politically violent incidents since 1819. Every assassination attempt against a President or presidential candidate occurred at or near a peak of civil strife in this country, as shown by the graph.[4]

This pattern is given weight in Chapter 3 of this report, which indicates that the single best predictor of whether a nation will experience assassination attempts is whether that nation experiences high levels of other forms of civil strife. Turmoil in general seems to be a factor which releases, creates, or signals tendencies to assault the President within mentally unbalanced individuals in the population.

Although there may be other factors, the key element in each presidential assassination appears to be the state of mind of the potential assassin. In every case (with the possible exception of the attempt upon Truman) the assailants were alienated figures, and were even confused about the prospects and strategies of the causes they thought they represented.[5] All the assassins but the two who attacked President Truman— Lawrence, Booth, Guiteau, Czolgosz, Zangara, Shrank, and Oswald—showed strong evidence of serious mental disturbance. In addition, each case is conspicuous by the absence of an effective political organization. Even the two presidential assassination attempts which were conspiracies of two or more persons—the attempts against the lives of Lincoln and Truman —were poorly organized, haphazard affairs, and neither would have done much to bring about the triumph of the political causes the assailants favored. Indeed, the assassination of Lincoln was a complete failure in this regard.

We will treat presidential assassination and the special problems raised by such attacks upon the office of President in Chapter 2.

Gubernatorial Assassinations

Only one of the approximately thirteen hundred and thirty men who have held the office of governor from 1790 until the present has been killed. Five others who were targets for political assassination were either wounded or escaped unharmed.[6] In addition, one ex-governor and one ex-lieutenant governor were killed after they had left public office.[7] The first attempt, the killing in self-defense of the ex-lieutenant governor, was in 1868, the last was the wounding of Governor Connally in 1963. Table 4 summarizes the major facts surrounding each case.

The one governor who was assassinated in office was William Goebel. He was declared the victor by his supporters and the state legislature in a disputed election in Kentucky in 1900.

Table 4.—Chronological list of political assassinations and assaults of governors

Year	Victim	Method of attack and result	Location of attack	Assailant and professed or alleged reason
1868	Samuel W. Beall ex-Lieutenant Governor, Wisconsin	Shot, killed	Montana	George M. Pinney; Beall attacked Pinney over articles Pinney wrote; acquitted as self-defense.
1873	William Pitt Kellogg Governor, Louisiana	Attempted shooting	Louisiana	Charles R. Rainey, Melvin H. Cohen; many disputed his election, open rebellion in parts of Louisiana.
1877	Stephen B. Packard Governor, Louisiana	Shot, wounded	Louisiana	W. H. Weldon; apparently part of group that challenged legality of election.
1900	William Goebel Governor, Kentucky	Shot, killed	Kentucky	Caleb Powers; tried and convicted of conspiracy; disputed election.
1905	Frank Steunenberg ex-Governor, Idaho	Dynamite, killed	Idaho	Harry Orchard; labor union against which Governor called out troops.
1908	John F. Fort Governor, New Jersey	Attempted bombing	New Jersey	Unknown; suspect either crackpot or parties angered by liquor-law enforcement.
1959	J. Lindsay Almond, Jr. Governor, Virginia	Attempted shooting	Virginia	Unknown; suspected segregationist, during school integration period.
1963	John Connally Governor, Texas	Shot, wounded	Texas	Lee H. Oswald; Governor was hit while riding with Kennedy when the latter was assassinated.

Goebel had been declared the victor over the Republican incumbent (Taylor) only a few weeks before he was killed. Goebel shared many characteristics with Andrew Johnson—for example, his Populist-like support within the Democratic Party and his antipathy for the old landed aristocracy and "privileged class" that controlled the Democratic Party in Kentucky and throughout much of the South. After Goebel had gained the nomination, the "old school" Democrats left the Party and ran a candidate of their own. Goebel's support came from the small landowners and nonpropertied classes.

Three men were tried and convicted for Goebel's death: Caleb Powers, Henry Youtsey, and James Howard. Powers was secretary of state under the Republican governor. Youtsey was a young lawyer who was employed by the state in the Auditor's Office. He was a strong supporter of the Republican Party. Howard was known as an outlaw with a murder charge hanging over him. During the trial, both testified that they went to Power's office on the morning Goebel was shot, but each claimed that the other did the actual shooting. Powers was charged with conspiracy and convicted along with Youtsey and Howard.

Of the five governors who survived assassination attempts, two, William Kellogg and Stephen Packard, were Republicans who held public office in the South during the Reconstruction period. Both Kellogg and Packard were governors of Louisiana who held office by virtue of the presence of Union troops and Negro police in Louisiana. The Kellogg and Packard cases are part of the one period in American history, the Reconstruction era, during which assassinations were an organized political response to perceived injustice. The Reconstruction period will be discussed in Chapter 4.

The other gubernatorial targets were John Fort of New Jersey (1908), who was the intended recipient of an envelope containing explosives, presumably because of his enforcement of the state liquor laws in the Atlantic City resort area; Lindsay Almond of Virginia (1959), who was the target of an unidentified sniper, presumably because of his recently-adopted "moderate" position on school integration; and John Connally of Texas (1963). It will probably never be known who was Oswald's intended target—Connally, Kennedy, or both. Connally was Secretary of the Navy when Oswald's application to the Navy to have his discharge changed to "honorable" was denied.

The most "sensational" assassination occurred in 1905 when Harry Orchard confessed to the killing of the ex-governor of Idaho, Frank Steunenberg. Steunenberg had been elected as a Populist in 1897, and had the support of the miners. During his term of office, however, a labor dispute arose in which there was a good deal of violence. In response to this violence, Steunenberg called for federal troops to restore law and order. The case attracted notoriety because it involved the leadership of the then powerful IWW, and particularly, the local head of the Western Foundation of Miners, William (Big Bill) Haywood. In his confession, Orchard charged that Haywood had paid him to kill Steunenberg. Orchard also confessed that he was paid to bomb several copper mines, to shoot a detective and a superintendent of a mine, and to assassinate Governor Peabody and several justices of the Idaho Supreme Court. All these successful or attempted acts of violence, Orchard claimed, were at the instigation of Haywood.

The defense, under the direction of Clarence Darrow, charged that Orchard was in the employ of the Mine Owners Association and that he killed Steunenberg only to satisfy a personal grudge. The defense claimed that Orchard had a part interest in a mine which he had been forced to sell below value, and that he blamed Steunenberg for his loss. Haywood was subsequently acquitted and Harry Orchard was sentenced to life imprisonment.

The assassination of William Goebel, and possibly that of Frank Steunenberg, represents violence of direct political motivation not found in presidential assassinations. The Goebel case in particular seems to fit the model of an assassination planned and motivated by representatives of a political movement to enhance the objectives of their cause. In the Steunenberg case, the accusation of involvement of a well-organized political movement was made, but, as pointed out above, the alleged instigator of the plot was acquitted, having defended himself on the ground that the killing was done for personal reasons.

Senatorial Assassinations

Of the approximately eleven hundred men elected to the United States Senate, only two, David C. Broderick in 1859

Table 5.—Chronological list of political assassinations and assaults of Senators

Year	Victim	Method of attack and result	Location of attack	Assailant and professed or alleged reason
1859	Charles Sumner Senator, Massachusetts	Assaulted, severely beaten	Washington, D.C.	Congressman Preston Brooks of South Carolina; revenge for antislavery speech made by Sumner.
1857	David C. Broderick Senator, California	Shot in duel, killed	California	David S. Terry; insults over political stand on slavery and legal feud.
1873	Samuel Clark Pomeroy ex-Senator, Kansas	Shot, wounded	Washington, D.C.	M. F. Conway; both men had been in Kansas politics at statehood; Conway blamed Pomeroy for his circumstances.
1917	Henry Cabot Lodge Senator, Massachusetts	Assaulted	Washington, D.C.	Pacifists: A. Bannwart, Rev. P. H. Drake, Mrs. M. A. Peabody; outbursts because he did not support staying out of war; but not serious attempt on life.
1921	Charles Henderson Senator, Nevada	Shot, wounded	Washington, D.C.	August Grock; personal quarrel over money.
1935	Huey P. Long Senator, Louisiana	Shot killed	Louisiana	Dr. Carl Weiss; apparent concern over Long's power, and having his father-in-law's judgeship taken away.
1947	John William Bricker Senator, Ohio	Shot, wounded	Washington, D.C.	William L. Kaiser; personal grudge over money lost when Bricker was attorney general.

and Huey P. Long in 1935, have been victims of assassination.[8]

Four others, two after their term of office had expired, were targets, but only one of them was seriously hurt.[9] He was Charles Sumner, the strong antislavery senator from Massachusetts, who was attacked on the floor of Congress by Representative Brooks of South Carolina. According to the *New York Times*, Brooks "repeatedly hit Sumner on the head until he collapsed in a pool of blood."[10] Three days before his attack, Sumner had made a strong antislavery speech in which he singled out for special attention South Carolina's senator, Andrew P. Butler, who happened to be Brooks' uncle. According to the *Times*, the attack on Sumner was premeditated. A group of Southerners met the evening before and decided on their course of action. Their intention was to kill the senator from Massachusetts. Why they chose the floor of the Senate (if, in fact, this was their intent), is not explained by the *Times* story.

The other three assassination attempts had little or no rational political content. Senator Bricker (Ohio, 1947) was wounded by one of his constituents who had suffered financial losses fifteen years earlier when Bricker was attorney general of Ohio and who believed Bricker had not done all he should have to help him recover his money. Senator Henderson (Nevada, 1921) was shot and wounded the day after his term of office ended by August Grock, a Reno lawyer who had harbored a grudge against Henderson for twenty-five years because Henderson had refused to act as Grock's attorney in a land suit. Grock had been under treatment for mental "troubles" for several years prior to his attack on Henderson. Ex-Senator Pomeroy (Kansas, 1873) was also wounded by an assailant with a history of mental illness. In this case, Conway (the assailant) had worked together with Pomeroy in state politics and was the first member of Congress from Kansas. But in his later years he apparently became mentally ill, broke his ties with former associates, left his wife, became despondent, and had no means of support. Just a few days prior to his attack on Pomeroy, Conway had tried, unsuccessfully, to borrow money from him.

Of the two successful assassinations, the victim in the first was David C. Broderick, a senator from California, who was shot in a duel in 1859. Broderick was a Democrat who supported the Union. His Republican opponent, in a three-way race (the Democratic Party in California was divided on the slavery issue and each faction put forth a candidate) was State Supreme Court Justice David Terry.[11] Terry accused Broderick of misleading the public concerning his position on the slavery issue, and Broderick in essence called Terry a liar. Terry responded by challenging Broderick to a duel from which Terry emerged the victor. Broderick died of a bullet wound in his left lung. Terry was arrested, tried, and subsequently acquitted.

The victim of the other successful senatorial assassination was the Senator from Louisiana, Huey Pierce Long. Long's assassination, like that of William Goebel, is something of a departure from the American pattern. In reporting Long's death, *Nation* described it as "a deliberate political act, one of the very few in its category in American experience."[12]

Father Coughlin, a friend and political supporter of Long, recognized the difference between Long's assassination and the assassinations of other public officials. He touched on at least one distinctive characteristic by noting that the real target in most of the presidential assassinations was as much the "office" as the particular officeholder. Huey Long was shot not because of the particular office he held, but because his assassin believed that his power had extended far enough to threaten in a very immediate sense the lives of the people he had been elected to represent.

There are other reasons why Long's case is "different." His assassin did not share the social and personal characteristics of many of the presidential assassins, and the public did not respond to him as they had to other political assassins. Carl Weiss, Long's assassin, was a twenty-nine-year-old physician from a wealthy, educated, professional family. His father was also a doctor, and his father-in-law, who was one of the leaders of what remained of the anti-Long forces in Louisiana, was a judge from an old and prominent Southern family. Weiss, who was born in Louisiana, was a successful young man with no history of mental disturbance or imbalance, and with little apparent political interest.

In trying to explain how Carl Weiss came to commit an act that he must have known would (and did) cost him his own life, the press relied mostly on what they assumed to be Weiss' growing concern over Long's well-publicized plan to have legislation introduced which would gerrymander his father-in-law out of public office. Some suggested that Weiss was less disturbed by Long's activities in Louisiana than by the increasing likelihood that Long would make a bid for national power before the 1936 presidential election. Weiss, just a few years before, had witnessed the rise of Hitler and the Nazi movement in Germany. He had been a student in Vienna when Hitler was named Chancellor. To someone with this background, Huey Long in 1935 could have appeared extremely dangerous.

Another unique factor of the Long assassination was the public reaction. While there may always be some who privately applaud the assassination of a public official, the usual response is one of shock, abhorrence, and denunciation. In this case, though, the assassin became a hero. Thousands of people, including prominent business, civic, and social leaders from all over the South, as well as a former Governor of Louisiana (John M. Parker), a Congressman, and the district attorney for Baton Rouge, attended Weiss' funeral.

The public responded to Huey Long's death with as much variety as they had responded to his public policies and political strategies. The fact that he was a controversial figure is still another reason why the Long case does not quite fit into what we have come to consider the American pattern.

Congressional Assassinations

Proportionately, there have been fewer assassinations of congressmen than there have been of governors or senators. Of the approximately eight thousand three hundred and fifty Representatives, only three have been assassinated and seven have been targets of unsuccessful attempts.

Of those seven, five were shot in one episode in 1954. Three members of the Puerto Rican National Party entered the visitors' gallery in the Capitol and by their own admission began shooting in order to bring attention to the American people and the world that Puerto Rico was not free. None of the congressmen was seriously injured.

The two other occasions probably do not merit consideration under assassination attempts. The first occurred in 1836, when Representative William Stanbury drew a gun on Sam Houston after Houston began caning him on Pennsylvania

Table 6.—Chronological list of political assassinations and assaults of congressmen

Year	Victim	Method of attack and result	Location of attack	Assailant and professed or alleged reason
1868	James Hinds Representative, Arkansas	Shot, killed	Arkansas	George M. Clark; was Secretary of Democratic Committee; Hinds was campaigning for Republicans, Clark was drunk at time of shooting.
1870	William Slosson Lincoln Representative, New York	Cane assault	Maryland	Joseph Segar; lost contested seat for Representative from Virginia.
1890	William P. Taulbee ex-Representative, Kentucky	Shot, killed	Washington	Charles E. Kincaide; feud over articles Kincaide wrote linking Taulbee to scandal. Kincaide acquitted.
1924	Robert Young Thomas, Jr. Representative, Kentucky	Assaulted	Kentucky	G. Baker; political opponent; Baker angered by Thomas' remarks.
1954	Kenneth Allison Roberts Representative, Alabama Benton Franklin Jensen Representative, Iowa George Hyde Fallon Representative, Maryland Alvin Morell Bentley Representative, Michigan Clifford Davis Representative, Tennessee	Shot, wounded	Washington, D.C.	Puerto Rican extremists: Lolita Lebron, Rafael Cancel Miranda,' A. F. Corcera; attack on Congress by independence group.

Avenue because Stanbury had accused Houston of misconduct. Neither Houston nor Stanbury was seriously hurt. In 1924, Representative Thomas of Kentucky was attacked by his Republican opponent, George Baker, when Baker became angered at remarks made by Thomas during the congressional campaign.

Three congressmen (two after they had completed their term of office) were fatally wounded by asssasins. Two of them, Representative Hinds from Arkansas, and ex-Congressman W. S. Lincoln from New York, were killed during the Reconstruction period.

Hinds, a former Democrat who had supported Lincoln in 1860, had been a delegate to the Arkansas Constitutional Convention in 1867, and was sent by the Republican ticket to Washington in 1868. His assassin was George Clark, who was secretary of the Democratic committee of Monroe County. Clark was drunk at the time of the shooting and when arrested was in a condition bordering on delirium tremens. W. S. Lincoln, an ex-Congressman from New York, was caned by Joseph Segar, an unsuccessful applicant for a seat in the House as a member-at-large. Segar attacked Lincoln with a cane in a Baltimore train depot the day after a Baltimore paper had carried a story ridiculing his claim to a seat and his general conduct around the House in connection with the matter.

William Taulbee of Kentucky was shot and killed in 1890 by Charles Kincaide, the Washington correspondent for the *Louisville Times*. His is the most recent case of the killing of a representative. Taulbee's case is notable mainly because his assassin gained acquittal on a self-defense charge. Taulbee had apparently been threatening and actually assaulting Kincaide for several months because Kincaide had published a story linking Taulbee with a scandal in the Patent Office. One day, after Taulbee had attacked Kincaide in the main hall of the Capitol, Kincaide shot Taulbee "in self-defense." Sentiment, as reflected in the Washington newspapers and by the names of persons who offered to put up bail for Kincaide, was against the congressman and on the side of the assassin. Kincaide was acquitted.

Mayoral Assassinations

Ten mayors from cities in five states (Illinois, New York, New Jersey, Kentucky, and Minnesota) have been targets of

Table 7.—Chronological list of political assassinations and assaults of mayors

Year	Victim	Method of attack and result	Location of attack	Assailant and professed or alleged reason
1885	John B. Bowman ex-mayor, East St. Louis, Illinois	Shot, killed	Illinois	Unknown; previous attempts made after several men killed in Republican-Democratic clash at City Hall during his term.
1893	Carter H. Harrison mayor, Chicago, Illinois	Shot, killed	Illinois	Patrick E. Prendergast; disappointed officeseeker.
	Henry S. Tyler mayor, Louisville, Kentucky	Threatened with gun	Kentucky	P.J. Schwarz; did not want city limits extended to his property.
1910	William J. Gaynor mayor, New York City	Shot, wounded	New York	John J. Gallagher; fired, from city job, angered at Gaynor's trip.
1913	B.P. Windsor mayor, Mt. Auburn, Illinois	Shot, killed	Illinois	Fay D. Slate; quarrel over editorial.
1926	Jeff Stone mayor, Culp, Illinois	Shot, killed	Illinois	Unknown; suspected political-gangster-bootlegging tie-in.
1933	Anton J. Cermak mayor, Chicago, Illinois	Shot, killed	Florida	Cermak was hit in hail of bullets aimed at Roosevelt.
1939	Louis E. Edwards mayor, Long Beach, New York	Shot, killed	New York	Alvin Dooley; angered that Edwards used influence to keep him from being elected to office in police organization.
1947	Hubert H. Humphrey mayor, Minneapolis, Minnesota	Attempted shooting	Minnesota	Unknown; several attempts made; conflicts over crime-labor unions.
1949	Elihu H. Bailey mayor, Evarts, Kentucky	Attempted dynamite	Kentucky	Unknown; mayor thought it was bootlegger he was fighting.

assassination. Of this number seven were killed and three were unharmed.[13]

Not including Anton Cermak, only two of the ten targets were mayors of large cities: William Gaynor of New York was shot by a watchman who was fired from his job on the New York City docks for incompetence (1910), and Carter Harrison of Chicago was shot and killed by a disgruntled officeseeker (1893).

Three of the other four victims were also mayors of cities in Illinois. In 1885, the former mayor and leader of the Republican Party in East St. Louis, John B. Bowman, was shot and killed by an assassin whom the police were never able to locate. After having been elected to three successive terms of office, Bowman was defeated when he sought a fourth term. He remained an important political figure in the area, and at the time of his death the *New York Times* said: "The dead man had so many enemies, the police are puzzled where to begin."[14]

In 1878, while Bowman was mayor, the local Democrats had tried to capture City Hall by force. Bowman met their advances "with shot and shell, and in the clashes between the two parties, several persons were killed and wounded."[15] Bowman was reelected after the riots. Although the assassin was never found, both the local newspapers and the *Times* were convinced that one of Bowman's numerous political enemies in both parties had hired someone to kill him. In the course of their investigation, the police learned that several earlier attempts were contemplated on Bowman's life. In each instance, the assassin was hired by opposing political factions.

The other two deaths of Illinois mayors were those of B. P. Windsor, the mayor of Mt. Auburn, who was shot by the editor of the local newspaper after a quarrel (1913), and Jeff Stone of Culp, who was killed by gangsters who controlled the bootlegging operations in the area (1926). His assassin was never found.

In 1939, Louis Edward, the mayor of Long Beach, a suburb of New York City, was killed by Alvin Dooley, a police officer. Dooley had been president of the local Policeman's Benevolent Association, and had failed to gain reelection. He claimed that it was the mayor's prestige that prevented his reelection. As mayor, Edward had forced Dooley to pay part of his salary to Dooley's estranged wife.

The assassinations of big city mayors Carter Harrison and William Gaynor contain the same mixture of personal and political elements that were involved in the death of the mayors of the smaller communities. When Harrison's assassin, Eugene Patrick Joseph Prendergast, turned himself in at a local police station, he said: "I am Eugene Patrick Prendergast. I worked hard for Carter Harrison in his campaign. He promised he would make me corporation counsel. He failed to do this and I shot him."[16]

Prendergast also said that he had been justified in killing the mayor because, "he broke his word with me about track elevators." During the campaign, Harrison had said that he favored abolishing railroad crossings at street grades (there had been a number of accidents at the railroad crossings and the plan was to elevate the railroads), but after the election, nothing more was heard about this proposal. Most of the Chicago newspapers used the occasion of the mayor's death to attack Governor Altgeld and Harrison for their policy of laxness toward labor agitators and anarchists. Harrison had been mayor when the Haymarket Riot occurred. According to Louis Adamic, "Harrison went milling in the crowd, and since no trouble was brewing, he instructed the police that no intervention would be necessary and he went home. After he left, the police charged the crowd and the bomb went off." Adamic concludes, "The police were apparently under the orders of one other than the Mayor."[17]

During his time in office, Harrison resisted pressures from propertied groups to suppress the "radical elements" in Chicago. He showed a willingness to permit radicals to carry on activities until they actually violated the laws.[18] Harrison and the newspaper he owned, the *Chicago Times*, praised Governor Altgeld when he pardoned three of the anarchists implicated in the Haymarket Affair. For acts such as these (he also gave members of the Socialist Party jobs in municipal government), Harrison was continuously attacked by wealthy groups in Chicago.

His death took on political significance, for, despite the fact that his assassin had no connection with the socialist-anarchist elements, the newspapers and leaders of the community made the connection. For example, the *Tribune* ran an editorial which said:

Those not in authority, the people at large, well may stop
to consider to what extent the mad act of Prendergast
was due to the mistaken leniency of the State Executive
towards red-handed anarchy, and his dangerous reckless-
ness in the use of the pardoning power and the release of
scores of murderers and other criminals who were convicted and justly punished.[19]

The circumstances of Harrison's death were also compared
with those of President Garfield's (a dozen years earlier), and
the dangers to public figures from disgruntled officeseekers
were widely publicized.

New York Mayor William Gaynor (who died three years
after he was shot) was also the victim of a disappointed
jobseeker. In this case, the assassin had been fired from his job
as a watchman on the New York City docks for incompetence, and had appealed without success to the mayor to reverse the decision of the Civil Service Board. According to the
New York Times, Gallagher claimed in his confession that he
had been haunting the mayor's office for three weeks and kept
repeating, "he took away my bread and meat."[20] Gallagher
shot Gaynor aboard a ship that was to take the Mayor to
Europe. The bullet which lodged itself in Gaynor's larynx was
never removed, and although he lived and was politically active, his health was apparently impaired and his life shortened.

The assassination attempt considerably increased Gaynor's
chances of gaining the Democratic presidential nomination in
1912. Even before the attack, Gaynor had been viewed as a
likely candidate, and his "brush with death" increased those
chances—at least as reported by the New York press.

Two of the three mayors who survived attack by an assassin, Elihu Bailey (Evarts, Ky., 1949) and Hubert H. Humphrey (Minneapolis, 1947), were targets of criminal elements
who were opposed to the clean-up campaigns launched by the
mayors against gambling, bootlegging (Evarts is in a dry
county), and organized crime. Neither Humphrey, who was
shot at three times, nor Bailey, who found twenty-four sticks
of dynamite under his bedroom window, was hurt by the
attempt: their would-be assassins were never found.

In Louisville, Ky., in 1893, P. J. Schwarz, a property owner,
pulled a revolver and told Mayor Henry Tyler that he was
going to kill him because he (Schwarz) thought that the city

limits of Louisville would be extended to include property he owned. The mayor seized Schwarz's weapon and the police carried Schwarz away. The local papers reported that a crank had made an attempt to kill the Mayor.

Thus, of the ten mayors who were victims or intended victims, one had the misfortune of sitting next to a President, three were victims of disgruntled officeseekers, and three were considered threats to the operations of organized crime.

Assassinations of State Legislators

Of the twelve state legislators who were victims or intended victims of assassinations, ten were killed and two were either wounded or escaped unharmed.

During the Reconstruction period, three state representatives were killed and two had attempts made on their lives. The three who were killed were pro-Union men elected to Southern legislatures (Ashburn of Georgia, Stevens of North Carolina, and Case of Tennessee) while the states were still under military control. In none of the cases was the assailant found, although the man who killed Senator Case of Tennessee (Frank Farris), was a well-known member of a guerrilla band, notorious for the atrocities it committed against Union sympathizers during and after the war.

On the morning of Senator Case's murder, Farris rode into Troy (Case's hometown) with a Union man, Morris Kinnan, and while talking with him in a friendly manner in the public square, pulled a gun and shot him. No effort was made to arrest Farris, who then rode off to Case's home, and, after learning from his wife that he had gone into town but was expected back shortly, met him en route and killed him. In reporting the assassination of Senator Case, the *New York Times* wrote:

> That the murder of Senator Case was a well-known and pre-arranged affair is evident from the arrival of the two confederates just in time to give Farris aid if necessary. . . . The outlaws of Ohio County and the adjacent region have been committing outrages with impunity for a long while. The swamps of Reel Foot Lake furnish them a secure hiding place. A young man of this place, while on a recent visit to Jackson, was threatened with a mob for

Table 8. – *Chronological list of political assassinations and assaults of State legislators*

Year	Victim	Method of attack and result	Location of attack	Assailant and professed or alleged reason
1867	G. W. Ashburn delegate to Georgia Constitutional Convention	Shot, killed	Georgia	Unknown; ten prominent citizens implicated in the murder of the Republican delegate during Reconstruction.
	L. Harris Hiscox delegate to New York Constitutional Convention	Shot, killed	New York	Cole; personal affair over Cole's wife.
	Almon Case State senator, Tennessee	Shot, killed	Tennessee	Frank Farris; anti-Union guerrilla leader.
1868	Harrington State legislator; Pennington State senator, Alabama	Attempted shooting	Alabama	Unknown; ambushed while canvassing county together for Republican Party.
1869	M. McConnell State senator, Illinois	Shot, killed	Illinois	Unknown; believed to be over property litigation.
	Benjamin Ayers State legislator, Georgia	Shot, killed	Georgia	Wilson; robbery believed motive.
1870	John W. Stevens State senator, North Carolina	Stabbed, hung, killed	North Carolina	Wiley and Mitchelle; apparently acted with consent of Democratic Party of Caswell County; Stevens was a Republican.
1874	James O'Brian ex-State senator, New York	Attempted shooting	New York	Richard Croker, George and Henry Hickey, John Sheridan; Tammany group dispute witness O'Brian.

Table 8.—(Cont.)

Year	Victim	Method of attack and result	Location of attack	Assailant and professed or alleged reason
1875	E. G. Johnson Deputy Collector of Internal Revenue and State legislator, Florida	Shot, killed	Florida	Unknown(s); shot in still house.
1881	Smith State senator, Tennessee	Shot, wounded	Tennessee	John J. Vertress; political feud over way Smith voted, Vertress claimed Smith was bribed.
1892	R. D. McCotter State senator, North Carolina	Shot, killed	North Carolina	Unknown; assumed to be personal; wife's family did not like his behavior.
1896	Col. Albert Jennings Fountain ex-State legislator, New Mexico Territory	Shot, killed	New Mexico	Unknown; long conflict between cattle association and outlaws backed by opposition political party.
1936	J. M. Bolton State legislator, Illinois	Shot killed	Illinois	Assumed to be gangsters; alliance of crime and politics.
1945	Warren G. Hooper State senator, Michigan	Shot, killed	Michigan	Conspirators: Harry and Sam Fleisher, M. Selik, Pete Mahoney; Hooper had been key witness in an investigation.
1947	Thomas Anglin State senator, Oklahoma	Shot, wounded	Oklahoma	Jim Scott; personal; Anglin's law firm represented Scott's wife in divorce.
1958	Paul A. Wallace State senator, South Carolina	Shot, killed	South Carolina	Henry Rogers; assumed mad, hanged self in mental institution.

speaking favorably of General Sherman. A rebel boasted not long since that there were 1,700 men organized to prevent the enforcement of Brownlow's Law in West Tennessee.[21]

On the day preceding the deaths of Kinnan and Case, a deputy sheriff who was a staunch Union man had been shot and killed by the same group of guerrillas.

A year later in Alabama, the Speaker of the House, Senator Harrington, and another state senator (Pennington) were ambushed while they were canvassing for the Republican Party. They escaped without injury, but the would-be assassin was never found.

Two other assassinations of state legislators occurred in the same decade but were unrelated to the problems posed by Reconstruction policy. L. Harris Hiscox, a delegate to the New York State Constitutional Convention, was shot and killed by General Cole because, according to Cole, Hiscox had tried to seduce his wife while he was away. And in Illinois in 1869, State Senator McConnell was shot in his home by an unknown assailant. According to the Chicago newspapers, the assassination was prompted by McConnell's involvement in litigation concerning valuable property in Chicago.

The next assassination of a state legislator occurred in the South in 1892 when Senator McCotter of Pamlico County, N. C., was ambushed and killed by a group of men. It is assumed that the men belonged to the White Caps (a variation of the Ku Klux Klan), because some time before his death a delegation of White Caps had visited McCotter and warned him to stop seeing "the other woman" and return to his wife. None of the assassins was found.

Three of the remaining four assassinations of state legislators were connected in one way or another with organized crime. Colonel Albert Fountain, a former state legislator of the Territory of New Mexico, was killed (along with his young son) in an ambush. The Territory of New Mexico was the scene of a good deal of open warfare, and the death of Colonel Fountain in 1896 marked the climax of a long-standing feud between him and a Democratic Party judge. The fight was over control of cattle rustling and the prosecution of politically protected rustlers in the Territory. Before Fountain's death, both men (Fountain and Judge Fall) had hired their own gunmen to protect their interests.

In 1936, an Illinois state representative from the West Side of Chicago was shot and killed by what newspapers labelled "men from the rackets." In 1945, State Senator Warren Hooper of Michigan was shot before he could appear as a key witness in an investigation of bribery charges against members of the State legislature. The bribery charges were connected with passage of legislation favorable to parimutuel betting in Michigan.

The most recent assassination of a state legislator occurred in South Carolina in 1958 when County Court Clerk Henry Rogers shot State Senator Paul Wallace while Wallace was listening to election returns indicating that he had gained re-nomination on the Democratic Ticket. Rogers was committed to the State mental hospital, and hanged himself two weeks after he killed Wallace.

The three unsuccessful assassinations of state legislators after the Reconstruction period followed the same pattern as the successful ones: connections with organized crime or purely personal motives. In 1874, former State Senator O'Brian (of New York) swore out a warrant against four criminal gang members for assault and battery. He never pressed charges, presumably because these same men were already under indictment for the murder of a minor state official who had intervened between O'Brian and the assailants to protect O'Brian.

Personal motives were represented in the shooting on the floor of the Senate in Texas of Tom Anglin by a fellow legislator, Jim Scott. Anglin's law firm had represented Scott's wife in a recent divorce proceeding.

State Senator Smith of Tennessee was killed by John Vertress, an attorney who accused Smith of having accepted a bribe. The legislature was considering an investigation into Vertress' charges, and after Vertress shot Smith, the resolution to conduct the investigation was adopted.

The assassinations or attempted assassinations of state legislators share characteristics with the assassinations of both mayors and congressmen. Both state legislators and mayors have been attacked as a result of their ties or conflicts with organized crime, something not found in the murders of higher public officials. Both congressmen and state legislators were assassinated because they were Republicans seeking or holding office in the South during the Reconstruction period.

Judicial Assassinations

The facts that surround the murders of ten state judges provide more evidence about sordid forces that precipitate violence against officeholders than does the information collected about other categories of assassination victims.

Some appear to have little, if any, political content. For example, in 1870, a judge in San Francisco was shot by his mistress after he had broken off their affair in anticipation of his family's return. Another was shot as a result of mistaken identity.[22]

On the other hand, three judges were shot and killed between 1867 and 1875 as a result of intraparty conflict. Chief Justice Slough in the Territory of New Mexico was killed by William Rynerson, a member of the Territorial Senate, after Rynerson demanded that Slough retract insulting remarks made after Rynerson had passed a resolution in the Senate ordering the removal of Slough. Judge Gaylord Clark of the District Court in El Paso, Texas, was killed by Frank William; William had sought the office for himself. Clark was named because party leaders thought his appointment might more adequately serve to unite the radical and conservative wings of the Republican Party. In Louisiana in 1875, a former parish judge was shot by the incumbent.

Three other judges were shot and killed in Louisiana between 1868 and 1873. Judge Crawford of Monroe Parish was killed by an escaped murderer whom Crawford had sentenced to life imprisonment. The same assassin also killed the man who prosecuted him, District Attorney Arthur Harris. Judge Chase of St. Mary's Parish was killed by a band of rebels because of his stand in support of the Union. Judge Robert Gray was shot in his home by "unidentified assailants."

In 1889, Judge Pierce of San Diego, Calif., was shot and seriously wounded by a man whose case he had heard earlier and had decided against.

The last known member of the judiciary who was a victim of assassination was Judge David Terry of the California Supreme Court. This is the same David Terry who, thirty-two years earlier, had killed Senator Broderick in a duel. Judge

Table 9.–Chronological list of political assassinations and assaults of judges

Year	Victim	Method of attack and result	Location of attack	Assailant and professed or alleged reason
1867	John P. Slough Chief Justice, New Mexico Territory	Shot, killed	New Mexico	Captain William L. Rynerson; feud and insults over Rynerson's attempt to have Slough recalled.
1868	J. W. C. Horne Judge, Georgia	Shot, killed	Georgia	Unknown Negro; judge shot over incident involving his son and a colored girl.
	V. Chase Judge, Louisiana	Shot, killed	Louisiana	Band of rebels; Chase was a Union man.
	Robert Gray Justice, Louisiana	Shot, killed	Louisiana	Unknown(s)
1870	A. P. Crittedon Judge, California	Shot, killed	California	Laura D. Fair, his mistress; when he attempted to break off relationship.
	Gaylord Clark District judge, Texas	Shot, killed	Texas	Frank William; had wanted judgeship for himself.
1873	T. S. Crawford Parish Judge Monroe, Louisiana	Shot, killed	Louisiana	Assumed to have been ambushed by the Tom Wayne gang, whose previous trial the judge presided over.
1875	Belden ex-Parish Judge, Louisiana	Shot, killed	Louisiana	Sherburn, was judge at time; motive unknown.
1889	W. L. Pierce Superior Judge, San Diego, California	Shot, wounded	California	W. S. Clendennin; because of decision unfavorable to him handed down by Pierce.
	Stephen J. Field Supreme Court Judge	Assaulted	California	David S. Terry; had threatened Field in legal dispute.
	David S. Terry Judge, California	Shot, killed	California	David Nagel; U.S. deputy marshal assigned to guard Field, shot and killed Terry.

Terry had made verbal threats against Supreme Court Justice Stephen Field. When Justice Field decided to visit his native state of California, the Justice Department sent a U.S. marshal along to protect him (presumably against Terry, who by this time was sixty-six years old).

Both Field and Terry had been powerful political figures in California for years. About ten years earlier, Field sought to be the favorite son candidate for the presidency; Terry, who was one of the delegates, was powerful enough to block his nomination. Terry claimed that Field was a corrupt judge who sold his decisions.[23] The enmity between Field and Terry increased after Field had ruled against Terry's wife when she sued to receive part of Senator Sharon's estate by claiming that she had been Sharon's common-law wife before her marriage to Terry.

When Field's train arrived in Lathrop, Calif., Field and Deputy U.S. Marshal David Nagle went into the dining room at the train station for breakfast. Soon after, Judge Terry and his wife entered the room. Mrs. Terry recognized Justice Field and left.[24] Terry then went over to the table where Field was sitting and slapped him across the face. Nagle arose from his seat and shot Judge Terry through the heart. In the newspaper accounts following Terry's death, Nagle was described in the following manner:

> There is not the slightest doubt that Nagle went, as his associates say, with his finger on the trigger and meant to make short work of Terry, who represented all that was objectionable to him in politics as well as in personal characteristics. Nagle, like many veteran gunfighters, had faith in the old fashioned single action Colt six-shooter.[25]

But the newspapers also claimed that Terry was "prepared to make a deadly assault on Judge Field."[26] Nagle was tried and acquitted, and Field continued to serve as a member of the Supreme Court.

Miscellaneous Assassinations

In this last category we report the assassinations of men who occupied a variety of public offices that are considered generally lower in prestige and power than those in previous sections (see table 10).

Table 10.—Chronological list of political assassinations and assaults of appointed and minor officials

Year	Victim	Method of attack and result	Location of attack	Assailant and professed or alleged reason
1865	William H. Seward Secretary of State	Shot, wounded	Washington, D.C.	David Herold, Lewis Paine; part of Lincoln plot.
1867	H. W. Fowler assistant collector of Revenues.	Shot, killed	Texas	D. B. Bonfoey; collector of Revenues; no motives ascertained.
1868	B. Saulet Sheriff, Caddo Parish, Louisiana.	Shot, killed	Louisiana	Unknown(s).
1871	Alden McLaughlin custom inspector, Texas	Shot, killed	Texas	Smugglers, in the line of duty.
1873	Arthur H. Harris district attorney, Monroe, Louisiana.	Shot, killed	Louisiana	Assumed to have been ambushed by Tom Wayne gang, whom he had previously prosecuted in a case.
	H. P. Farrow. U.S. District Attorney, Georgia.	Clubbed, wounded	Georgia	Unknown; had gotten indictments against 5 men; papers ranted against him and tried to intimidate jury.
	Edwin S. McCook Territorial Secretary of Dakota	Shot, killed	Dakota Territory	P. P. Wintermute; dispute over railroad bonds.
1875	G. A. Roderty tax collector, Grant Parish, Louisiana.	Shot, killed	Louisiana	John B. McCoy, ex-sheriff.
	Daniel O'Connell Alderman, New York	Gun-threat	New York	John T. Cox; personal matter over Cox's sister.
1935	Thomas J. Courtney State's attorney, Illinois	Shot, killed	Illinois	Unknown; suspected Capone gang.

With the exception of the alderman in Brooklyn, whose life was threatened because of an affair with his sister-in-law, and the secretary of the Territory of the Dakotas, who was killed in a dispute about the status of railroad bonds, the other eight targets fall into one of two categories: law enforcement officials and tax collectors.

In the first group, Sheriff Saulet of Caddo Parish, La., was shot in bed by an unidentified assailant in 1868. In 1873, District Attorney Arthur Harris was shot and killed by a man whom he had prosecuted for murder (the case is mentioned in the previous section on judges). Also in 1873, H. P. Farrow, a U.S. district attorney in Georgia, was severely beaten by "unknown assailants" who, it is presumed, were motivated by the fact that Farrow had just obtained an indictment against local white citizens involved in the bloody riots following the election of a Republican governor in Georgia in 1872. In 1935, Thomas Courtney, a state attorney in Illinois, was killed by men believed to have been members of Al Capone's gang. No one was ever brought to trial.

Between 1867 and 1875, four tax collectors were killed in the South. A customs inspector at Corpus Christi was killed by smugglers just before he was scheduled to testify about smuggling activities across the Mexican-Texas border. A deputy collector of Internal Revenue was shot and killed at a still in Florida by unknown assailants; and two others were murdered in Texas and Louisiana by unknown assailants for unexplained reasons.

In this category more than in any other, the number of attempted murders of public officials that our research has been able to uncover is probably less than the number of actual events. But even if the figures reported for this category were to be multiplied tenfold, they would still represent a comparatively small number.

C. Conclusions and Statistical Overview

We return in this last section of Chapter 1 to a statistical overview and note first the distribution of the eighty-one attempted and successful assassinations discovered. Figures 1 and 2 show the number of assassinations over time and by geographic region.

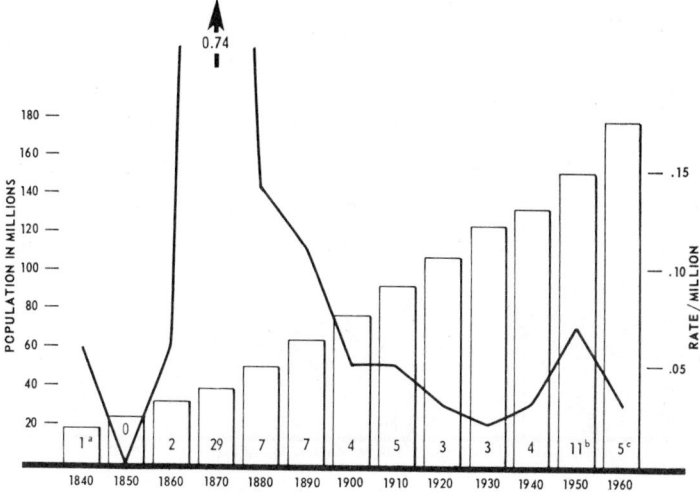

*Figure 1.—Political assassinations and assaults
by decade and population*

---

[a]The number inside the bar graph is the absolute number of assassinations and assaults per ten year period. Assassinations and assaults are
counted for five years on either side of census years; i.e., 1870 includes
from 1865 through 1874.

[b]Includes five congressmen shot by Puerto Rican nationalists in 1954
in a single attack. Otherwise the total would be six, which would indicate no substantial change in the rate of assassination attempts.

[c]Includes Robert F. Kennedy in 1968.

Two facts stand out most sharply. Over two-thirds of the
assassinations occurred in the southern part of the United
States, and over one-third occurred during the Reconstruction
period (that is, in the census period between 1865 and 1874).
Table 11 shows that, of the twenty-nine acts of political violence which occurred during the Reconstruction period, approximately three-quarters took place in the South. A comparison of the number of acts of political violence occurring only
in the South in the twelve census periods shows that one
census period accounted for at least three times as many
attempted or successful assassinations as any other—the Reconstruction period.[27]

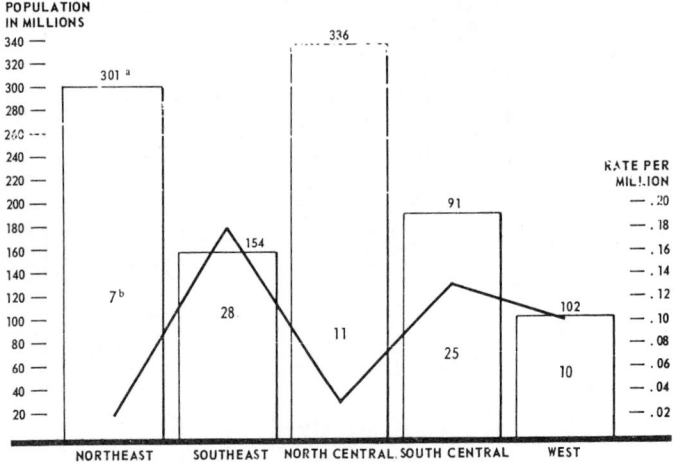

*Figure 2.—Political assassinations and assaults
by geographical region and population*

---

aSummed census totalled for each decade since 1840, see Table 11.
bAbsolute number of assassinations and assaults (81 total)

Northeast	Maine, New Hampshire, Vermont, Massachusetts, Rhode Island, Connecticut, New York, New Jersey, Pennsylvania
Southeast	Delaware, Maryland, D.C., Virginia, West Virginia, North Carolina, South Carolina, Georgia, Florida
North Central	Ohio, Indiana, Illinois, Michigan, Wisconsin, Minnesota, Iowa, Missouri, North Dakota, Nebraska, Kansas
South Central	Kentucky, Tennessee, Alabama, Mississippi, Louisiana, Texas, Oklahoma, Arkansas
Western	Montana, Wyoming, Colorado, New Mexico, Arizona, Utah, Nevada, Idaho, Washington, Oregon, California

The pattern between 1865 and 1875 does not occur anywhere else. In the South, after the Civil War and for as long as federal troops were stationed there, the men who were elected to public office were not considered "legitimate" incumbents of those offices. The level of office was immaterial. Governors, senators, state legislators, etc., were being elected on the Republican Party ticket, primarily, by former slaves and by persons migrating to the South after the war who opposed the traditional Southern white governing classes.

Table 11.—Political assassination and assaults by geographical region and decade

Time period and population	Northeast	Southeast	North Central	South Central	West	Total
1840[a] Assaults and assassinations		1			c	1
Population[b]	6,761	3,925	3,351	3,025		
1850 Assaults and Assassinations						0
Population	8,626	4,679	5,403	4,303	178	
1860 Assaults and Assassinations		1			1	2
Population	10,594	5,364	9,096	5,768	618	
1870 Assaults and assassinations	2	9	2	13	3	29
Population	12,298	5,853	12,981	6,434	990	
1880 Assaults and assassinations	1	2		4		7
Population	14,507	7,597	17,364	8,919	1,767	
1890 Assaults and assassinations		2	2	1	2	7
Population	17,401	8,857	22,362	10.972	3,027	
1900 Assaults and assassinations	1			1	2	4
Population	21,046	10,443	26,333	14,080	4,091	
1910 Assaults and assassinations	2		2		1	5
Population	25,868	12,194	29,888	17,194	7,082	
1920 Assaults and assassinations		2		1		3
Population	29,662	13,990	34,019	19,135	9,213	
1930 Assaults and assassinations		2	1			3
Population	34,427	15,793	38,594	22,064	12,323	
1940 Assaults and assassinations	1		2	1		4
Population	35,976	17,823	40,143	23,842	14,378	

Time period and population	Northeast	Southeast	North Central	South Central	West	Total
1950 Assaults and assassinations		7	2	2	1	11
Population	39,477	21,182	44,460	26,014	20,189	
1960 Assaults and assassinations		2		2	d	5
Population	44,677	25,971	51,619	29,001	28,053	
TOTAL	7	38	11	25	10	81

[a]Assassination and assaults are counted for five years on either side of census dates so that 1870 would include 1865 through 1874.

[b]Population in thousands.

[c]Not part of United States during that census.

[d]Includes Senator Robert F. Kennedy in 1968.

Those who had held public office prior to the Civil War were largely ineligible for such positions because many of them had not yet been "pardoned" for their participation in the War. Also, many Southern white voters were disenfranchised through political manipulation. The governors of Louisiana, such as Kellogg and Packard, held office because of the presence of Northern troops, former slaves who were made policemen, and recently emigrated Northern Republicans.

Thus, many of the men who held public office in the South during this period were not considered to be legitimate incumbents by those they supposedly represented. This is demonstrated by the fact that these men failed to gain reelection when Northern troops were withdrawn and Southern life returned to "normal."

Outside of the Reconstruction period, there seems to be no other distinctive period in American history marked by political violence. The South, both before and after the Civil War, has had more incidents of political violence than any other region, but there is no particular time pattern attached to it.

We turn next to another aspect of the examination of the eighty-one cases. Table 12 summarizes the motives of assassination either given by the assassin or observed by others.

Table 12.—Motives for Assassination

Summary of reasons given or observed for assassination	Frequency
1. In the name of a public issue (i.e., independence for Puerto Rico, slavery, etc.)	20
2. Incumbent perceived as illegitimate	12
3. Involvement with organized crime (as either opponent or collaborator)	11
4. Disgruntled officeseeker	6
5. Accident (i.e., Mayor Cermac, Governor Connally)	3
6. Miscellaneous (including events that occurred prior to incumbent holding office for which he is target; mental derangement of the assassin; matters of "honor")	19
7. No reasons offered or observed	10

All the presidential assassinations fit category one with the possible, but not probable, exception of President Kennedy. Oswald's motives are unknown. None of the gubernatorial, senatorial, or presidential assassinations fit category three, involvement with organized crime.

The pattern suggests that the higher the office, the more impersonal and more political the motive for assassination. The lower the office, the more personal the motive. All the presidential cases, with the exception of the attempt upon President Truman, could also to a greater or lesser degree have been coded under category six—"mental derangement of the assassin." Their somewhat arbitrary inclusion in category one, however, does not distort the point made here. Even if the violence of the assassin was a product of mental derangement, the object of the violence was selected and focused by political issues.

After reviewing, case by case, the acts of political violence in section 2, we find no indicators that isolate *specific* individuals as targets of assassins. Scientists today would be no more likely to predict which Presidents, governors, or senators—let alone holders of lesser offices—might be assassinated than they would in any previous time. Particularly in the case of the higher elected offices, assassination seems to be a function of how a particular officeholder is perceived by an assailant who is by and large outside the main social and political stream of the society, and who is responding to cues that others are not likely to recognize.

References

1. This section is, with minor editing, a paper submitted by Prof. Rita James Simon with the assistance of Sondra Phillips.
2. Whether an incumbent occupies an executive or a legislative office is not significant; note the similarity in the proportion of governors and senators who have been targets.
3. *New York Times,* Nov. 23, 1885, p. 14, col. 2.
4. The only reason Lincoln falls in a trough of the graph rather than at the highest peak is that Civil War military violence was excluded from the newspaper survey to avoid the distortion which that unique event would have introduced.
5. For example, Leon Czolgosz, McKinley's assassin, who purported to be an anarchist, was denounced as a spy in the anarchist newspaper, *Free Society,* a week before he shot the President.
6. One of those included under unsuccessful assassination attempts is John Connally, Governor of Texas, who was wounded while riding in the same car as President Kennedy.
7. An ex-lieutenant governor, Samuel Beall of Wisconsin, was shot and killed in Montana in 1868 by a man named Pinney, an editor of a newspaper in Helena. Beall attacked Pinney because of articles Pinney had written about him, and Pinney shot him. Pinney pleaded self-defense and was acquitted.
8. Because we included Robert Kennedy under the presidential assassinations, we are not counting him in this category.
9. Senator Lodge of Massachusetts was attacked by a group of pacifists for his position on the United States' entry into World War I, but the intent of the protestors was apparently not to kill or even seriously injure the Senator.
10. *New York Times,* May 23, 1856, p. 1.
11. Thirty-two years later the same David Terry was himself killed by a Federal marshal who was assigned to protect Supreme Court Justice Stephen Field from Terry after Terry had made threats against his life.
12. *Nation,* Sept. 18, 1935, p. 309.
13. Included in the number killed is Anton Cermak, mayor of Chicago, who died from an assassin's bullet which almost everyone agrees was intended for President Franklin Roosevelt.
14. *New York Times,* Nov. 23, 1885, p. 15.
15. *Ibid.,* Nov. 21, 1885.
16. *Chicago Sunday Tribune,* Oct. 29, 1893.
17. Louis Adamic, *Dynamite: The Story of Class Violence in America,* (New York: Viking Press, 1934), pp. 72–73.
18. Henry David, *The History of the Hay Market Affair,* (New York: Collier, 1938).

19. *Chicago Tribune,* Nov. 2, 1893, p. 12.
20. *New York Times,* Aug. 10, 1910, p. 1.
21. *New York Times,* Jan. 23, 1874, p. 2, col. 4.
22. The assailant, a Negro in Georgia during the Reconstruction period, was looking for Judge Horne's son because "the son had taken his girl into the field."
23. *Chicago Tribune,* Aug. 17, 1889, p. 1.
24. According to an article in the *New York Times* on Aug. 16, 1889: "The woman [Mrs. Terry] upon encountering him unexpectedly went away, evidently in search of the deadly weapon which she or her husband would have used if Nagle had not anticipated their action."
25. *Chicago Tribune,* Aug. 17, 1889, p. 1, col. 4.
26. *New York Times,* Aug. 16, 1889, pp. 1, 4, col. 3.
27. The unusually large number that appeared in the 1945–54 period includes the one incident in which five Congressmen were shot at in the House of Representatives by Puerto Rican nationalists.

CHAPTER 2

ASSASSINATION ATTEMPTS DIRECTED AT THE OFFICE OF THE PRESIDENT OF THE UNITED STATES

Introduction—Summary

As pointed out in Chapter 1, the presidency has been the object of a disproportionate number of the assassination attempts directed against officeholders in the United States. With the exception of the attempt on the life of President Truman by Puerto Rican nationalists, each presidential assassin has shown signs of serious mental illness; none was the agent of a plot or conspiracy rationally calculated to achieve political goals.

In this chapter, section A consists of short descriptions of each presidential assassination attempt. Section B is a discussion of the psychological characteristics of each of the would-be assassins to determine what patterns emerge. Section C presents a psychiatric perspective upon public reactions to presidential assassinations. Section D describes the reactions of the American public to assassinations, based upon survey data. Section E is an analysis of the political consequences traceable to the assassination of Presidents of the United States. Section F explores possible strategies of prevention: first, strategies to reduce the attractiveness of the office of President to potential assassins, and second, strategies for the physical protection of the President. Section G sets out the conclusions drawn from the previous sections.

A. Presidential Assassination Attempts[1]

Andrew Jackson

The first victim of an assassination attempt was Andrew Jackson. He miraculously escaped death on Jan. 30, 1835, when both pistols of his assailant, Richard Lawrence, misfired.

Lawrence attacked Jackson as he was walking through the rotunda of the Capitol after having attended a funeral service for a congressman. Lawrence, who had stationed himself in the rotunda, fired at Jackson from a range of approximately thirteen feet. The cap went off with a loud report, but the powder did not ignite and the pistol did not fire. Lawrence dropped the first pistol and transferred the other to his right hand. Meanwhile, Jackson rushed at Lawrence with his cane upraised. Lawrence fired the second pistol into Jackson's chest at pointblank range. It also misfired. Subsequent examination of the pistols showed that they were properly loaded. Their misfiring was attributed to humidity and near-miraculous good fortune.

Jackson was no stranger to violence, and his attack in response to the first shot was typical. Jackson had killed a man in a duel in 1806, and had been shot in the shoulder during a brawl in 1813. After he entered the White House, Jackson was hit in the face by a former Navy lieutenant who had been discharged for misappropriating government money. The then elderly Jackson grabbed his cane and chased the man, who ran away. Having been unable to punish him personally, Jackson refused to prosecute his assailant. He said that he always followed his mother's advice never to use the law in response either to assaults or slander; these matters should either be taken care of personally or not at all.

Richard Lawrence was a native Englishman who had moved to Washington with his parents when he was about twelve years old. Little is known of his family life. He was well-behaved as a child and moderate in his habits as an adult. He became a competent house painter and painted landscapes as a hobby. He never married.

At the age of thirty-two, approximately two and one-half years prior to the assassination attempt, a marked change took place in Lawrence's personality. He lost interest in his work and became threatening, violent, and abusive. He began to have delusions. On occasion, he imagined himself to be King Richard III of England. At other times, he claimed to have two great estates in England, or a realm that extended to Rome and Holland. He believed that he had claims for large sums of money against the United States, and began attending sessions of Congress to keep check on the progress of these claims. He came to believe that Jackson, in conspiracy with steamship companies, was preventing him from obtaining this money. In addition, his mind focused upon a hot political issue of the day, Jackson's veto of the bill to recharter the Bank of the United States. Lawrence apparently believed that killing the President would benefit all workingmen by causing the bank to be rechartered.

At the time of his trial, there was a great deal of hostility toward Lawrence among some of Jackson's supporters who suspected that he was part of a Whig conspiracy. Nonetheless, the prosecutor, Francis Scott Key, courageously cooperated with the defense, and helped establish a liberal test for insanity. Lawrence was to be found not guilty by reason of insanity if the deed was the "immediate, unqualified offspring of the disease,"—even if at the time of the attack he comprehended the nature of the act and knew the difference between right and wrong. The jury found Lawrence not guilty by reason of insanity, and he spent the rest of his life in mental institutions.

Abraham Lincoln

On April 14, 1865, John Wilkes Booth entered the Ford Theatre box from which President Lincoln was watching a play. The man assigned to guard Lincoln's box had abandoned his post in favor of a neighboring bar. Booth shot the President in the head with a single-shot derringer. Lincoln immediately lost consciousness, and never recovered.

Lincoln was a tall, physically powerful man who engendered personal feelings of respect and affection. He was killed in the midst of the Nation's celebration that marked the end of the Civil War. The Nation's mood on the day Lincoln was shot is depicted in the tone of an editorial that appeared in the *New York Daily Tribune*:

A new world is born, and the Sun of Peace rises in splendor to send abroad over the land its rays of warmth and light. Never before had a nation so much cause for devout Thanksgiving; never before had a people so much reason for unrestrained congratulations and the very extravagance of joy.[2]

With the exception of the Puerto Rican nationalist attack on President Truman, Lincoln's assassination is the only one that can be considered a genuine conspiracy. It appears, however, that the conspiracy was entirely Booth's creation. The other conspirators were a motley few, and the plot did not have the sanction of Southern leaders.

Booth's father, Junius, was an Englishman. After his marriage, he fell in love with a flower girl and, when he learned she was pregnant, he left England with her and settled in America. John Wilkes was the ninth of ten children born to them. He was illegitimate until his thirteenth birthday, when Junius married his mother after finally obtaining a divorce from his first wife. Booth's father and other brothers were absent for long periods of time on theatrical tours, and he grew up largely under his mother's tutelage. He was unruly and undisciplined.

Booth was said to have been an excellent companion. As he grew older, he was very attracted and attractive to women, and reputedly had many affairs. Although he was apparently engaged at the time of the assassination, his most stable relationship was with a prostitute who, during his absences, lived in her sister's brothel, and presumably practiced her trade while he practiced his.

Booth never completed the equivalent of a high school education. He was apparently unable to apply himself either to formal schooling or later to the formal discipline of acting technique.

Booth decided in his late teens to follow the family career and become an actor. He apparently had a great natural talent, but never developed it properly. Beginning in the shadow of his more famous and accomplished father and older brothers, Booth received mixed or unfavorable reviews until a tour in the South brought him acclaim and an adopted homeland.

Approximately a year and a half before the assassination, Booth's voice began to grow hoarse and weak. Whether this was a result of inadequate voice training or the first symptom of mental illness cannot be known. He began to identify more and more with the Southern cause. He never became a soldier, although he once donned the uniform of a socially prominent

Richmond company to witness the hanging of John Brown. On one occasion he nearly strangled his own brother-in-law for slighting Jefferson Davis. He apparently came to believe that Lincoln had achieved the presidency through fraudulent voting and intended to make himself king.

Booth originally planned to kidnap Lincoln and hold him for ransom in exchange for captured Southern soldiers. The practice of exchanging prisoners had been halted by the North because it worked in favor of the South, with its limited manpower. This plan was not far-fetched under the prevailing conditions, but was frustrated by circumstances. For instance, Booth orginally insisted upon capturing Lincoln in a theater to dramatize the deed. When the war ended, the plot was changed to the assassination of the President, vice president and secretary of state. The man who was to kill the Vice President wavered at the last moment, and did not make an attempt. Secretary of State Seward was viciously attacked, but survived. Only Lincoln was killed.

After shooting the President, Booth leaped to the stage and shouted, *"sic semper tyrannis"*—the motto of the State of Virginia. He broke his leg in the jump to the stage, but escaped for the moment. He wrote that he had acted as an agent of God and that he had only done God's will. Twelve days later he was cornered by Union troops, who surrounded a barn in which he was hiding. He refused to surrender, and the barn was set on fire. He died from a bullet in the head, either by his own hand or by the hand of a Union sergeant who claimed to have shot Booth, also as an agent of God.

The passion engendered by the assassination precluded any semblance of a fair trial for the alleged conspirators. All the conspirators, and probably some who were not conspirators, were tried before a military commission and executed.

James A. Garfield

Charles J. Guiteau shot President James A. Garfield in the back with a pistol on July 2, 1881. They were in a train station where Garfield was leaving for a vacation some four months after having assumed office.

Garfield was a vigorous, forty-eight-year-old soldier, educator, and Congressman, with a full gray beard and the frame of a longshoreman.[3] A dark horse compromise candidate, he had been nominated after a bitter fight between the Stalwart (conservative) and Half-Breed (liberal) wings of the Republican Party. He was nominated on the thirty-sixth ballot, after the two leading contenders, Blaine, the Half-Breed, and Grant, the Stalwart, were unable to obtain a majority of the delegates' votes. Garfield, who leaned to the Half-Breed side, had stayed clear of the feud. To balance the ticket, Chester A. Arthur, a Stalwart, was chosen as his running mate.

Garfield's nomination and subsequent election by a plurality of less than 10,000 votes made clear the necessity to unite the two dissident factions within the party. However, shortly after taking office, segments of the press and his party saw Garfield as favoring the Half-Breeds at the expense of party unity. His nomination of James Blaine, the Half-Breed convention nominee, as secretary of state appeared to support this view.

Guiteau was born in 1841. His mother died when he was seven. His father, Luther W. Guiteau, had a strong interest in the Republican Party and religion, believing with Reverend John H. Noyes, founder of the Oneida community, that the second coming of Christ had already occurred in A.D. 70. He led a useful, respectable, middle-class life for his seventy years.

There was a history of mental illness in the family. One of Guiteau's uncles died insane, the sanity of two of his sisters was questionable, and a niece and nephew, Charles's first cousins, were placed in asylums.

Guiteau, like Oswald, seemed to have spent much of his life seeking some organization or cause to which he could dedicate himself, but each new-found cause seemed to give him neither success nor peace of mind.

Guiteau attempted to enter the University of Michigan, but found he did not have enough credits; he enrolled in high school to meet the requirements. Instead of studying, however, he read the Bible and tracts about the Oneida community which his father sent him. The following summer he joined the Oneida community, an early religious utopian experiment in communism. The community practiced both economic and sexual communism. Copulation was encouraged, but marriage was considered an exploitive ownership relationship.

Guiteau stayed for five years, and then left to found a newspaper to be known as the *New York Theocrat*. He anticipated immediate success and wrote his father, "I claim that I am in the employ of Jesus Christ & Co., the very ablest and strongest firm in the universe."[4] His venture failed, and four months later he was readmitted to the Oneida community. He remained for approximately a year, and then left again. This time he turned against the community, and urged criminal proceedings in an anonymous pamphlet entitled, "An Appeal to All Lovers of Virtue." The pamphlet deplored the sexual license of the Oneida community which he himself had enjoyed.

He studied in a law office, and was licensed to become a lawyer under the lax practices then prevalent. His practice consisted in large part of accepting collection cases on commission, dunning the debtors, and then pocketing the money himself.

He married a sixteen-year-old girl, but the marriage was unsuccessful and they were ultimately divorced on the grounds of Guiteau's adultery. Guiteau began to travel around the country, cheating railroads out of their fares, running out on boarding-house bills, borrowing money whenever he could, and failing to repay. He made a precarious living by publishing religious tracts and lecturing on religious subjects. His ideas were stolen mostly from Reverend Noyes, but according to Guiteau they came directly as an inspiration from God. He also tried, without much success, to sell life insurance.

In 1880, Guiteau focused his wandering attention upon politics. He wrote a speech (apparently never used) for Grant, the Republican candidate of the Stalwart faction, and then changed to Garfield when Garfield received the nomination. When Garfield was elected, Guiteau attributed Garfield's success to his speech and felt himself entitled to the Austrian ambassadorship. He later tempered his ambitions to a consulship in Paris. At first Guiteau's requests were treated courteously although his ambitions had no reasonable basis. Ultimately, he became a pest, and was refused access to the White House.

At this time it occurred to Guiteau that God wanted him to save the country from ruin by eliminating Garfield and restoring the Stalwart faction of the party to power in the person of Chester A. Arthur, the vice president.

Guiteau bought a forty-four caliber pistol with borrowed money. He paid an extra dollar in order to get a fancier handle, because he thought it would look better in a museum. The owner of the gunshop showed Guiteau how to load the revolver and suggested a spot where Guiteau could practice.

Guiteau had several opportunities to kill Garfield. Once, in a train station, he refrained because Mrs. Garfield was with Garfield. On another occasion, it was such a hot, sultry night that Guiteau felt too tired. On the day he finally determined to kill Garfield, Guiteau hired a hack to wait for him and take him immediately to the jail lest angry mobs harm him.

His trial was a circus, and Guiteau reveled in the limelight. He took the position that he had acted as an agent of God and was thus guiltless. He was found guilty and sane, and was hanged in front of a large crowd.

Public opinion ran very high against Guiteau. There were two widely approved attempts to kill him while he was in custody. Plots were imagined as having been spawned by the Stalwarts. Guiteau's sister, in writing of the assassination, conceded that Guiteau had fired at and had wounded the President, but that Garfield had actually been killed by a second assassin hidden in a dark doorway. According to Guiteau's sister, this man was a representative of the Stalwarts, who had treated her noble brother so shamefully and ungratefully.

William McKinley

On Sept. 6, 1901, Leon F. Czolgosz shot William McKinley as the President was about to shake Czolgosz's hand at a reception in the temple of music at the Pan-American Exposition in Buffalo. While Czolgosz was in the reception line he took a pistol out of his pocket and wrapped his hand and the pistol with a handkerchief so that his hand appeared bandaged. The shots were fired at such point-blank range that there were powder burns on McKinley's vest. McKinley died eight days later.

McKinley was an extremely popular President. He was killed less than a year after his reelection to a second term in which he carried every state in the Union outside of the then "solid South" and four silver-mining states. Unlike Garfield, his popular vote was over a million more than his opponent's, and his advantage in electoral votes was almost two to one. During McKinley's first term, the triumph of the United States over the Spanish fleet, the liberation of Cuba, and the acquisition of the Philippines made the United States a world power for the first time.

However one views the foreign policy of the United States

during McKinley's first term, most historians credit him with having brought a new internal unity to the United States.

Czolgosz, the fourth of eight children, was born to Polish immigrant parents four months after they had arrived in the United States. His mother died when he was twelve. He was quiet and shy, with no close friends except Waldek, his older brother.

As a young man, Czolgosz was obsessively neat and possessed an extreme dislike for cruelty, even to the point of refusing to kill insects. He was a steady worker at a Cleveland wire mill from the time he was sixteen until he was twenty-three. During this time, he was a devout Catholic, and on the occasion of a strike at the wire mill, he and his brother prayed fervently, but without favorable result. Thereafter, Czolgosz began to suspect that priests were fooling him, and he ultimately broke with the Church.

At the age of twenty-two, he began to become remote and listless, and at twenty-five he apparently suffered a nervous breakdown. His older brother recalled that he had "gone to pieces." He never returned to a steady job. He retired to the family farm where he read and brooded. He feuded with his stepmother (his father had remarried some years before), and began preparing his own food and eating it in his room—according to Dr. Hastings, "probably because he was under the delusion that his food was being poisoned or at least tampered with."[5]

The assassination of King Humbert I in mid-1900 by an anarchist fascinated Czolgosz. He began reading about anarchism and went to Cleveland to listen to a lecture by Emma Goldman, a leading anarchist, whose speech, incidentally, did not advocate violence. Czolgosz tried to join an anarchist group, but acted so strangely that he was thought to be a police spy. The group published a warning against him just five days before he killed McKinley.[6]

Czolgosz had no remorse for his action. He said that he removed an enemy of the good working people and that one man should not have so much service and another man none.

The country was outraged. Although Czolgosz said he was acting alone, and appeared to have done so, an extensive anarchist plot was believed to have existed. Prominent anarchists were arrested, including Emma Goldman, who was subsequently released. Even Dr. E. C. Spitzka, the most important of the psychiatrists who unsuccessfully testified in 1881 that

Guiteau was insane, hinted at a female conspirator (Emma Goldman) by asserting that Czolgosz's covering his pistol with a handkerchief reflected a feminine touch.

The press wrote many inflammatory editorials attacking anarchist leaders and anarchist ideology. For example, the *New York Herald* wrote:

> There is reason to believe that other anarchists stand ready to complete the work of Czolgosz if the President recovers. This fact will be established if all the ramifications of the conspiracy to kill the President can be brought to light. The authorities are already in possession of evidence pointing in this direction but there is nothing yet to indicate who the men are who will make the next attempt. It is hoped that some of the anarchists now under arrest may reveal the substantial plan.[7]

And *The Washington Post* observed:

> We parade as a matter of patriotic pride those dangerous political dissipations which should be a cause of patriotic sorrow and alarm. We open our arms to the human sewage of Europe; we offer asylum to the outcasts and malefactors of every nation . . .[8]

Local vigilante committees were organized to seek out and attack well-known anarchists and to destroy anarchist communities. Congress, influenced no doubt by Theodore Roosevelt's impassioned plea for legislation,[9] passed a series of laws that added anarchists to the list of excluded immigrants and restricted the activities of those already in this country.

Czolgosz did not testify at his trial, which took place four days after McKinley's funeral. The trial lasted only eight hours and twenty-six minutes, including time for impaneling the jury. The jury brought in the guilty verdict after only thirty-four minutes. No appeal was filed, and Czolgosz was electrocuted. When Czolgosz was being strapped into the electric chair he said, "I killed the President because he was the enemy of the good people—the good working people. I am not sorry for my crime."[10] He was twenty-eight years old.

Theodore Roosevelt

On Oct. 14, 1921, in Milwaukee, John N. Schrank shot Theodore Roosevelt in the chest from a range of about six feet. Roosevelt was emerging from dinner at a hotel and was on his way to give a speech.

Roosevelt, the Rough Rider and hero of San Juan Hill, was vice president when McKinley was assassinated and was elected to another term in his own right. Although he had pledged after the assassination to follow McKinley's policies to the letter, his administration was notable for taking a strong new stand on "trust-busting." He refused the nomination for a second full term, supporting Taft, who was elected. Taft's more conservative policies displeased Roosevelt, and, after four years, he again sought the nomination. When the Republican convention rejected his bid, he accepted the nomination of a third party, the Bull Moose.

Shrank would most likely have killed Roosevelt, had the bullet not spent much of its force passing through Roosevelt's metal glass case and the fifty-page manuscript of a speech he was to give, which was folded double in the breast pocket. According to Donovan, "The bullet had struck him in the right breast an inch below and slightly to the right of the nipple and bored inward and upward about four inches, fracturing the fourth rib."[11] Seeing that he was wounded, Roosevelt coughed into his hand. When he saw no blood, he determined that the bullet had not penetrated his lung and therefore, the wound need not interrupt his speaking schedule. He thereupon intervened with the lynch-minded crowd on Shrank's behalf, went to the lecture hall, and excoriated big business and Republican bossism, with his shirt soaking up blood. Only thereafter did he consent to hospital treatment. "It takes more than that to kill a Bull Moose,"[12] said Roosevelt.

Shrank was born in Bavaria. His father died soon after his birth. His mother remarried and gave Shrank's aunt and uncle the task of rearing the child. The aunt, uncle, and Shrank emigrated to the United States when he was thirteen. Shrank tended bar in his uncle's New York saloon, and at twenty-eight, became the owner. Shrank was orderly and polite, but a loner. He once said, "I never had a friend in my life."[13] He did have a girl friend at one time, but she died along with more than one thousand other persons on the steamship "General Slocum," which burned in the East River.

At the age of thirty, Shrank sold the saloon and thereafter worked only from time to time, otherwise reading, writing, and wandering around New York City. Hastings speculates that perhaps at that time he had become too mentally ill to shoulder the responsibility of keeping the saloon.

As early as 1901, McKinley's ghost appeared to Shrank in a dream and accused Roosevelt of the assassination. Shrank, somewhat atypically, apparently did not identify himself with any particular group or movement. He did develop for himself, however, a political philosophy which he announced in essays. The most important point of his philosophy was that the no-third-term tradition never be violated. On the eleventh anniversary of President McKinley's death, while Roosevelt was campaigning on the Bull Moose platform, the ghost of McKinley again appeared to Shrank, touched him on the shoulder, and told him not to let a murderer become President. This apparently confirmed Shrank's conviction that he must be the agent of God to see that Roosevelt did not live to win what Shrank construed to be a third term—though, of course, it would not be a third *full* term, since Roosevelt had only been elected once in his own right.

Having determined to kill Roosevelt, Shrank set out to stalk him on his campaign tours. In more than two thousand miles and twenty-four days of travel in eight states, Shrank managed to be in the same city at the same time as Roosevelt in only three instances—Chattanooga, Chicago, and Milwaukee. In Chattanooga, Shrank said his nerve momentarily failed him. He refrained from shooting Roosevelt in Chicago for fear of damaging the reputation of that city. He finally acted in Milwaukee.

After Shrank's arrest, the court appointed five psychiatrists to examine him. They unanimously reported that he was insane. There was no further trial, and Shrank spent the rest of his life in Wisconsin mental institutions.

Franklin D. Roosevelt

On Feb. 15, 1933, Guisseppe Zangara attempted to assassinate Franklin D. Roosevelt, then President-elect, while Roosevelt was giving a speech at Bayside Park in Miami, Fla. Zangara, although he arrived an hour and a half before the speech, was too late to get a good seat. When he tried to shoulder his way forward, he was prevented from doing so by a resentful spectator. Just as Roosevelt was leaving, one of the audience left his chair and Zangara, seizing the opportunity, stood on the chair (he was only five feet tall) and fired. The shots missed the President-elect, but fatally wounded Mayor Anton Cermak of Chicago, who was standing near Roosevelt's car. As Secret Service men tried to rush Roosevelt's car from the scene, Roosevelt insisted that the car be stopped to take aboard the wounded Cermak.

Zangara was born in Italy in 1900. When he was two, his mother died and his father remarried before long. When Zangara was six he began school, but after two months his father took him out of school and put him to work. Thereafter, he always resented the fact that he had been unable to go to school, blaming "the capitalists." In addition, he attributed the stomach trouble which plagued him throughout his life to his having had to work at such an early age.

Just after World War I he served for five years in the Italian Army. Sometime during this period he bought a pistol in order to assassinate the King of Italy but was discouraged by the guards and crowd surrounding the king. At the age of twenty-three, shortly after his discharge from the Italian Army, he emigrated to the United States. At first he worked well and without incident as a bricklayer. He prized solitude, had no interest in entertainment, and never went out with girls. He rejected the suggestion of an uncle that he return to Italy to find himself a wife.

He complained constantly of stomach trouble. When he was twenty-five, his appendix was removed, but it turned out to be in fairly good condition. The operation failed to alleviate the stomach condition which Zangara believed was aggravated by cold weather. An autopsy after his execution did not show any abnormality in Zangara's gastrointestinal tract.

Until 1931, Zangara worked without incident, although he frequently expressed resentment over the privileges of the rich and the poor lot of the laborer. Some two years before the assassination attempt, Zangara stopped regular work and did only odd jobs. He traveled to warm regions in hopes of curing his stomach troubles.

In the winter of 1932–33, he was apparently determined to kill President Hoover. However, the cold weather in Washington deterred him. When he learned that President-elect Roosevelt planned to be in Miami, Zangara took this opportunity to assassinate him in a warm climate.

Zangara was found to be sane and electrocuted. He apparently bore no personal ill will toward President Roosevelt, but attempted to kill him simply as the chief of state. He said he would have killed either Hoover or Roosevelt, but once Mr. Hoover had left the office, he would have had no further desire to kill him.

He felt no remorse. He wrote an autobiography when in jail which concludes, "I go contented because I go for my idea. I salute all the poor of the world."

On the day of his execution he sat himself in the electric chair, saying he was not scared of it. He was incensed at the "lousy capitalists" because no one was there to take a picture of him. When strapped in the electric chair, he said, "Go ahead. Push the button."[14]

Harry S. Truman

On Nov. 1, 1950, Oscar Collazo and Griselio Torresola stormed Blair House, intending to kill President Truman. In the melee, twenty-seven shots were fired. Both Torresola and White House policeman Leslie Coffelt were killed. Collazo and two other White House policemen were wounded. President Truman, awakened from his nap, came to the window to see what the noise was about. A guard below shouted for him to get back.

Collazo and Torresola were natives of Puerto Rico and ardent Puerto Rican nationalists. Their attempt on President Truman was not out of personal hatred (Truman in fact had done much to advance self-determination in Puerto Rico), but rather to dramatize the cause of an independent Puerto Rico.

Collazo was thirty-four at the time. He had been born in Puerto Rico, the youngest of fourteen children. His father died when he was six years old, and Collazo went to live with an older brother. Collazo's father had been a small landholder and Collazo always blamed United States imperialism for destroying his father in particular and small Puerto Rican landholders in general. When Collazo was eighteen, he joined the Puerto Rican nationalist party of Albizu Campos. He apparently never ceased to work for the cause of an independent Puerto Rico, and felt that the United States was exploiting his country.

Apart from his ardent support of Puerto Rican nationalism, Collazo could be an example of making the best of life under most difficult circumstances. In his teens, at the very depth of the depression, Collazo came to the United States and worked long, hard hours for little pay. He married and supported his wife, who remained in Puerto Rico. He gave a home to his young daughter. In later years he selflessly helped other Puerto Ricans who had emigrated to New York to make the difficult adjustment.

His last job was that of metal polisher in a firm that made purses. His employer counted him as one of the eight or ten best workers he had. Collazo was elected by his fellow workers to represent them in union negotiations, and was respected by both sides. He divorced his first wife on grounds of unfaithfulness and several years later married a fellow metal polisher who had two daughters by a previous marriage. Collazo was a good family man, and was apparently well-loved by his stepdaughters, who ultimately changed their name to Collazo out of affection for him.

Torresola, except for his ardent Puerto Rican nationalism, was cut from different cloth. Although he was married, he was reputed to be something of a gigolo. He had been fired from his job at a stationery and tobacco shop, and for six months before the assassination attempt had been living on relief in New York.

The attack upon President Truman is unique in that, with the possible exception of the Booth plot, this is the only assassination attempt that meets many of the "formal" requirements of an organized, politically motivated plot. Yet, the attempt does not bear great resemblance to a serious political act.

Perhaps the most unrealistic quality was the man chosen as the assassination target. Shortly after he became President, Truman had sent a special message to Congress recommending that four proposals for changing the status of Puerto Rico, including outright independence, be submitted to the Puerto Ricans for their choice. In 1946, he appointed Jesus T. Pinnero as the first native governor of Puerto Rico, and the following January, under his prodding, Congress granted Puerto Ricans the right to select their own governor and other national officers other than auditor and judges of the Puerto Rican Supreme Court. In 1949, Congress made provision for Puerto Rico to write its own Constitution, to be approved by a referendum among Puerto Ricans. This enabling act was signed by Truman on July 3, 1950. As the first step in the process, a registration of voters was set for November 4 of that same year. Thus, throughout his presidency, Truman showed sympathy for self-determination in Puerto Rico.

From the evidence available, one can only conclude that there was very likely a plot, though a singularly inept one. The evidence lies in other violent acts in support of Puerto Rican independence at about the same time as the assassination attempt, and in documents suggesting a conspiracy. A nationalist coup in Puerto Rico, planned for Nov. 3, 1950, began prematurely in southern Puerto Rico on Oct. 29, 1950, and spread quickly to towns around the island. In San Juan there was intense fighting, and the governor's palace was fired on. Government action quelled the revolt by October 31, the day before the attempt on Truman's life. P. Albizu Campos, president of the nationalist party, was arrested, and his car was found to contain arms.[15]

Other signs of a plot come from documents and statements. At the time he was killed in the shooting outside Blair House, Torresola had in his pocket a letter from Albizu Campos which read as follows:

> My dear Griselio—If for any reason it should be necessary for you to assume the leadership of the movement in the United States, you will do so without hesitation of any kind. We are leaving to your high sense of patriotism and sane judgment everything regarding this matter.
>
> Cordially yours,
> Pedro Albizu Campos.[16]

Collazo claimed after his arrest that it was news of the revolt in Puerto Rico that led to the plan to create a demonstration in Washington, although their first impulse was to go to Puerto Rico to help the rebels. They decided instead to create a violent incident in Washington because it seemed to be a better way of shocking Americans into turning their attention to conditions in Puerto Rico.

Two days later they went to Washington, where they studied a map of the city in a classified directory they found in their hotel room. Then they hired a taxi and had the driver cruise in the vicinity of Blair House (the President's temporary residence during the remodeling of the White House), in order to observe the positions of the guards. Sometime during this two-day period, Torresola gave Collazo a two-hour lesson in the shooting and reloading of his automatic pistol.

Early in the afternoon of November 1, they approached Blair House from opposite directions. Collazo fired first and his gun jammed, a mishap that doomed whatever slight chance for success the plan might have had. The President was never in any danger.

In the subsequent trial, Collazo refused to allow his lawyers to plead insanity. The defense chose to attempt to convince the jury that Collazo had planned only to stage a demonstration in front of Blair House without intending to kill anyone, and that Torresola—who had been killed in the melee—had started the shooting. The jury rejected this assertion and found Collazo guilty of the murder of Coffelt, and the attempted murder of the President and the two White House guards. He was sentenced to death, but President Truman commuted that sentence to life imprisonment. Collazo and Torresola may have been the least mentally disturbed of all the would-be presidential assassins. A psychiatrist who examined Collazo twice concluded that he was not mentally ill. Nonetheless, their plan of action and the relationship of the act to their goals shows little grasp of reality.

There was widespread reaction to their attempt indicating that Puerto Ricans supported neither the would-be assassins nor their political aims. A letter signed by 119,000 Puerto Ricans was delivered to President Truman by the resident Commissioner of Puerto Rico. It declared that, "during 450 years never before have we seen such an arbitrary act of violence as the one carried on recently by a small group of fanatic nationalists."[17] Puerto Rican children raised money for the children of Coffelt, the guard Torresola killed.

American journals, notably the liberal ones which presumably were most sympathetic to the plight of the Puerto Rican people, labeled Collazo and Torresola fanatics and declared that their compatriots were shocked by their action. *The New Republic* argued that the nationalists did not represent the people.[18] *Commonweal* said, "So far as one can tell, going at it without firsthand knowledge, the nationalists' revolt was abortive because it was unsupported."[19]

Nonetheless, in a real sense Collazo and Torresola were patriots. The judge who sentenced Collazo to death said, "The Court has no reason to believe that you are not sincere. The

Court doesn't think you are an inherently evil man. The Court, as an individual, is sorry for you."[20] Collazo was asked if he had anything to say before being sentenced and he replied, "Anything that I had done I did it for the cause of liberty of my country, and I still insist, even to the last, that we have the right to be free."[21]

John F. Kennedy

On Nov. 22, 1963, Lee Harvey Oswald fired three rifle shots in Dallas at a car containing President and Mrs. Kennedy and Governor John Connally of Texas. President Kennedy was killed; Governor Connally was wounded. More is known about this assassination and the assassin than about any other presidential assassination. The details are contained in the Report of the President's Commission on the Assassination of President Kennedy (the Warren Report). There is no reasonable basis for retracing the meticulous steps of the Warren Commission.

Oswald did not have a normal family life. His father died two months before he was born. His mother remarried when Oswald was five, but the marriage only lasted three years. Oswald was a loner; he had few friends. In early adolescence he was diagnosed as an "emotionally quite disturbed youngster" while in public school in New York City.

Oswald apparently tried to submerge his identity in organizations and causes. He joined the Marines at the earliest possible age. He did not succeed; he was resentful of authority, and ultimately obtained an early discharge, ostensibly on hardship grounds to help support his mother. He did return home to his mother upon discharge from the Marines, but then left for Russia. He tried to defect, but the Russians would not accept him as a citizen, although they did allow him to remain as an alien. In Russia Oswald married, but the marriage was not a success; his wife often taunted him for his sexual inadequacies. Oswald did not make a success of his defection to Russia and returned to the United States with his wife.

At first Oswald was steadily employed but was soon unable, for whatever reason, to hold a job. At about this time, he attempted to kill General Edwin A. Walker, firing at and narrowly missing him with a rifle. He apparently attached himself to another cause, this time the revolution in Cuba, but his association with the cause had little basis in reality. He was the sole member of his Fair Play for Cuba Committee, for which he passed out handbills in New Orleans.

Oswald resented the fact that his Marine discharge had been changed from honorable to general in response to his attempted defection. He complained to John Connally, whom Oswald thought was still Secretary of the Navy, although Connally had resigned shortly before.

Oswald, unlike other assassins, denied that he had harmed anyone, although he was seen to have shot Officer Tippit. He is also unique among attackers of a President in using a rifle rather than a pistol.

Oswald was in turn assassinated by Jack Ruby before Oswald's motives and intended target could be determined.

Robert F. Kennedy

On June 4, 1968, Senator Robert F. Kennedy, brother of President Kennedy and candidate for the presidential nomination of the Democratic Party, was assassinated. He was shot in the head with a pistol from pointblank range. A young Jordanian national named Sirhan Bishara Sirhan[22] has been convicted of the crime and his appeal is pending.

B. The Psychology of Presidential Assassins

1. Similarities between Presidential Assassins

All those who have assassinated or attempted to assassinate Presidents of the United States (with the possible exception of the Puerto Rican nationalist attempt upon President Truman) have been mentally disturbed persons who did not kill to advance any rational political plan. One psychiatrist, Dr. Donald W. Hastings, states that all but Collazo and Torresola were insane. Indeed, Dr. Hastings goes so far as to diagnose their mental illness as, "schizophrenia, in most instances a paranoid type."[24]

Such a diagnosis, however, does not tell us why such persons become assassins, or how to identify and distinguish the assassination-prone personality.[25] Furthermore, seven persons—the number of the actual assassins or would-be assassins (excepting Collazo and Torresola)—do not constitute a sufficient sample from which to generalize with any confidence. Yet these men do have a striking number of similarities.

All were male, white, not tall, and slender. Lawrence, Shrank, and Zangara were foreign born. Czolgosz was born a few months after his parents emigrated to the United States, and Booth's parents came to the United States after Booth's mother had become pregnant with their first child, Booth's older brother. Only the parents of Guiteau and Oswald were native born.

On the other hand, neither socioeconomic class nor employment seems to establish a common thread. The families of both Guiteau and Booth can be called middle class, as can Shrank as owner of a bar and tenement property. Booth moved in high social circles in the South. The remainder could be called craftsmen or members of the working class.

All for whom we have information experienced an absence or disruption of the normal family relationship between parent and child.

John Wilkes Booth was an illegitimate child. His father did not marry his mother until John was thirteen. His father and older brothers were away for long periods of time on theatrical tours while he was reared, an unruly child, by his mother.

Guiteau's mother died when he was seven. Czolgosz's mother died when he was twelve. Shrank's father died when Shrank was a child, and his mother remarried, moved to another town, and left Shrank to be reared by an uncle and aunt. Zangara's mother died when he was two, and his father remarried a woman with six daughters. Oswald's father died two months before Oswald was born. His mother remarried when Oswald was about five years old, but the marriage ended in divorce in three years.

The only possible exception, paradoxically, is Lawrence, whose delusions of wealth and high estate fit most perfectly with the popular notion of the madman. As far as can be determined, he alone of all the assassins had the benefit of both parents throughout his childhood.

There is an hypothesis that the absence of a strong father figure may contribute to an assassin's frame of mind. In as many cases as not, the disruption of the family was the early death of the mother, not the absence of the father. However, this does not necessarily defeat the hypothesis. For example,

Guiteau's father, deeply involved in the heterodox religious views of Noyes, may have had little time for his son. Zangara's father took him out of school at the age of six and put him to work. Because of this, Zangara may have felt alienated from his father. What one writer has called "extreme ordinality" may be added to a list of common characteristics[26] Ordinality is the position of a child amongst his siblings by order of birth. Of the eight presidential assassins discussed, including Collazo, two (Shrank and Zangara) were "only" children. Guiteau, Collazo, and Oswald were the youngest in families of three, fourteen, and three children, respectively. Booth was the ninth youngster of ten children. We have no data as to Lawrence's siblings, if any. Only Czolgosz was a middle child, the fourth of eight. Psychiatrists have suggested that ordinality is significant in the development of the personality, and it would seem that ordinal position of the assassins is extreme enough to warrant consideration.

Almost all the assassins were loners who had difficulty making friends of either sex, especially in establishing lasting relationships with women. Booth is an exception, at least in part. He was reputed to be excellent company among men and irresistible to women. He undoubtedly had affairs, and he apparently considered himself engaged to be married at the time of Lincoln's assassination. Nonetheless, the number of affairs he had suggests some inability to establish a mature relationship. When he died, he was found to have the pictures of five different women with him, including one of his fiancee. His most stable relationship was apparently with a prostitute.

Guiteau was somewhat similar to Booth, although he seems to have had no close male friends. For a total of six years he lived in the Oneida community, which practiced sexual communism. Guiteau, by his own admission, had casual liaisons with a number of women there. His subsequent marriage ended in divorce on the grounds of adultery.

Lawrence, Czolgosz, Shrank, Zangara, and Oswald fall most closely into this pattern. All seem to have been quite withdrawn, with very few friends of either sex. Shrank had a girl friend at one point, but she was killed in an accident several years prior to his assassination attempt. We know of no other women in his life. Lawrence never married. Zangara avoided the company of women and never married. Czolgosz wrote that he had no friends except for brother Waldek. Oswald proposed to one girl while in Russia and married another, but was unable to make a success of the marriage.

A striking similarity is the fact that, from one to three years prior to an assassination attempt, each of the assassins apparently became unable to hold a job, although there is no evidence of physical disability in any case.

Lawrence was a competent house painter whose hobby was landscape painting. Two years before his attempt on President Jackson, he quit work and moved in with his sister. Booth did not appear to quit work voluntarily, but approximately a year before the assassination a hoarseness and deterioration of his voice forced him to reduce his acting schedule substantially. Guiteau did not work in the ordinary sense. He lived as a petty swindler, lawyer, pamphleteer, evangelist, and insurance salesman. Nonetheless, there seems to have been a period of deterioration after Guiteau began to focus on politics. At times, just before the assassination, he appeared in public without socks and with his coat collar turned up to hide the fact that he was not wearing a shirt.

Czolgosz left his job at the wire mill where he had been a steady, reliable worker. His brother refers to the fact that he appeared to have a nervous breakdown and to grow listless.

Shrank also quit regular work. When he was twenty-eight, his uncle gave him the family saloon, where he had been tending bar. Two years later Shrank sold the saloon and began drifting, concentrating on reading and writing.

Zangara worked as a bricklayer until about three years before his attempt on Franklin Roosevelt, when he sought to cure his imagined stomach trouble in a warmer climate.

Oswald did not hold a steady job after he returned to the United States from Russia.

Another common characteristic is the tendency to identify with a cause or an ideologically based movement, but being unsuccessful or unable to participate with others in this cause or movement.

Booth identified strongly with the Southern cause. However, he could not or did not participate in the Southern war effort. He put on the Southern uniform to witness the hanging of John Brown. Booth found the experience very moving, and considered John Brown's demeanor and manner of death heroic and admirable. He never wore the uniform again.

Guiteau felt that he was divinely inspired. He tried on two

occasions, once for five years, and once again for a year, to become part of the Oneida religious community. He ultimately identified with the Republican Party and particularly its Stalwart (conservative) wing. In neither case was he successful in becoming part of the organization with which he identified.

Czolgosz was originally a devout Roman Catholic. He became disillusioned with the Church and felt that priests were fakes. He later identified with the anarchist cause, but again he was unsuccessful in relating to or becoming part of the organization.

Shrank and Zangara do not fall into this pattern as neatly as the others. Although Shrank did not appear to identify with any particular group, he did develop a series of essays on political theory with respect to the United States, the most important principle of which was the "no-third-term" concept. Zangara joined the Italian Army at approximately the same age as Oswald joined the Marines. He served for five years, and then emigrated to the United States.

Oswald fits the pattern; he attempted to join the Marines when he was too young, and then enlisted at his earliest opportunity. He was not or could not let himself be accepted in the Marines. In Russia he was again unsuccessful in identifying with and becoming part of the Russian "experiment." Disillusioned, he returned to the United States. His final movement, The Fair Play for Cuba Society of New Orleans, was entirely his creation; he was the only member.

Some of the assassins seem to have been ambivalent with respect to their victim. Guiteau had several opportunities to murder President Garfield, but declined for apparently trivial reasons—the presence of Mrs. Garfield, the oppressive nature of the weather. Shrank followed the Roosevelt campaign, yet in twenty-four days, he managed to cross paths with the presidential candidate on only three occasions.

Ambivalence may also have characterized the other assassins. The misfiring of both of Lawrence's pistols raises the suspicion that Lawrence purposely misloaded them, but experts at the time testified that they were properly loaded.

In every instance the assassin felt no remorse, but felt his act was justified by some transcendent principle of law, divine guidance, or the like. The only possible exception is Oswald, whose assassination by Jack Ruby ended any opportunity to examine his motives directly. The police who held him, however, said that he was a "cool customer." He did not appear to show remorse.

In almost every instance, the assassins seemed to focus on a specific narrow, political issue in addition to harboring a general hostile fixation on the presidency. Lawrence, though basically seeking redress of imagined personal grievance, focused on Jackson's veto of the charter of the United States Bank. The newspapers of the day charged that this act would ruin small business and put people out of jobs. Booth killed to vindicate the position of the South, but also alleged that Lincoln had been elected through vote fraud. Guiteau killed to advance the Stalwart (conservative) wing of the Republican Party. Again the papers had suggested that Garfield, in favoring the Half-Breed (liberal) wing, was destroying the party.

Neither Czolgosz nor Zangara fits this pattern. Although they killed on behalf of the underdog or the working class, apparently they did not focus on one particular narrow issue.

Shrank, on the other hand, followed the typical format. He was generally hostile toward the presidential candidate, and also focused on the narrow issue that Roosevelt was improperly violating the no-third-term precedent. Opposition newspapers had played up the issue by referring to Roosevelt as "the third-termer" rather than by name. The newspapers stopped this practice after Shrank's attack.

Collazo, whose attack on President Truman was based on Puerto Rican nationalism, was examined by a psychiatrist and found to be sane. However, he does fit many of the above criteria: white, small of stature, and showing no remorse. In some regards he does not follow the pattern. His (second) marriage was successful; he was able to hold a job and retain the affection of his family, and became a real part of the movement with which he identified himself.

Although we cannot unravel the significance of the similarities between the assassins, we could make this statement: we could predict after President Kennedy's assassination that the next assassin would probably be short and slight of build, foreign born, and from a broken family—most probably with the father either absent or unresponsive to the child. He would be a loner, unmarried, with no steady female friends, and have a history of good work terminated from one to three years before the assassination attempt by a seeming listlessness and irascibility. He would identify with a political or religious movement, with the assassination triggered by a specific issue which relates to the principles of the cause or movement. Although identifying with the cause, the assassin would not in fact be part of or able to contribute to the movement. Not every presidential assassin has had every one of the foregoing traits, but some combination of the above has characterized them all.

One commentator, Dr. Doris Y. Wilkinson, applies the concept of status incongruence in an attempt to explain presidential assassins.[27] Status incongruence exists where the achievement level of a person is inconsistent with what he expects because of his education or other factors, such as race, sex, ethnicity or nationality, family or social class background, or view of society. The argument can be made that each of the presidential assassins exhibited such an expectation-achievement gap. The question of why the psychic distress derived from status incongruence became politicized in the form of a deadly attack upon a high political officeholder remains unanswered.

One intriguing aspect of the status incongruence approach is that it may provide a partial explanation for two curious facts. First to be noted is the absence of Negroes from our list of presidential assassins—indeed, no Negroes are reported to have attempted to assassinate any high officeholders or persons of political prominence who are white. Second, all the assassins but Guiteau and Oswald either emigrated to America at a young age or were first-generation Americans.

With respect to the Negro phenomenon, it is suggested that, in America, the distinction between black and white has been, until perhaps very recent times, a master-determining status. The black man has a scapegoat. He can blame the system for defining him not in terms of what he does, but what he is. But a white person who fails to achieve his goals, although part of the favored racial class, has no such explanation for his "failure." The hypothesis is too broad, but it is at least a start towards a more specifically explanatory hypothesis.

Applying the expectation-achievement hypothesis to the first-generation phenomenon, the immigrant could explain his absence of status or lack of opportunity in the mother country, but upon immigration to the "land of opportunity" this explanation would seemingly be lost. Still, the immigrant might not have an expectation-achievement gap, because he could perceive his immigrant status as a limiting factor. No such explanation for failure would be available to the first-generation Americans, however. The son of the immigrant—the child who grew up in the "land of opportunity"—might subsequently experience this expectation-achievement gap when conscious of the reality of his failure.

The tragedy of assassination in this nation may be caused in part by the possession of a social ideology or ethic which promises more than is in fact delivered. Again, the hypothesis proves far too much but does provide a starting point for the construction of hypotheses that are more specifically explanatory.

In an attempt to further the limited understanding of what compels people to attack political officeholders, some investigators have examined those imprisoned for threatening a President's life.[28] David Rothstein, for example, has analyzed twenty-seven inmates of the Medical Center for Federal Prisoners in Springfield, Mo., who had indicated an intention to attack the President. The threatmakers bore similiarities to Lee Harvey Oswald. Most came from unhappy homes. They had domineering mothers and weak, ineffectual fathers. Most joined the military service at an early age, yet their experiences proved to be unhappy. Rothstein interprets their actions in threatening the President as the manifestation of a hostility towards their mother redirected against authority symbols— the government and, more specifically, the President.

In another study of forty-eight individuals who attempted to force their way into the White House, Sebastiani and Foy found these individuals to be paranoid, persistent, and self-destructive.[29]

Both studies deal with individuals who threatened the President rather than those who have actually attacked him. The link between such threats and any intention actually to injure a President is not known. It may be that the violent letters to the White House or the attempts to invade its grounds are ends in themselves, designed to attract the type of attention the instigators desire, and not preliminaries to assassinations. No presidential assassin, with the possible exception of Guiteau, has publicized his intentions in advance.

In conclusion, it must be emphasized that we do not know why the characteristics discussed above appear in assassins, nor do we know why in a few instances those characteristics may lead to assassination, while in the overwhelming number of cases there is no such result. Many persons with more disruptive family lives and with the absence of a father figure become mentally healthy, productive citizens or at least do not assume an assassin's role.

2. *A Comparison of the Presidential Assassin and the Normal Citizen*[30]

Dr. Freedman, a psychiatrist and consultant to this Task Force, points out that presidential assassins follow patterns which in other contexts would not only be approved but considered heroic. The typical violent offender strikes out at someone with whom he has at least been acquainted, and often at someone with whom he is intimate. After his attack he is filled with guilt or remorse. But common men—clerks, lawyers, scientists, and the like—can be recruited as soldiers to kill perfect strangers without remorse or regret, in the name of a cause. In this regard, the assassin resembles the patriot, not the typical murderer.

The mentally ill resemble the so-called "well-adjusted" person far more closely than is generally realized. The less severely maladapted who are treated by psychotherapists—and the overwhelming majority of people who get along, more or less successfully, without psychiatric assistance—do so with latent paranoid and grandiose projections, much like the psychotic person. Everyone periodically sees himself as the center of some constellation of human relationships when in fact his role is peripheral or nonexistent. The "normal" person sometimes feels that he is being criticized or snubbed when in actuality he is not. This feeling is very common. The sense of being elevated in the eyes of those around him is comparatively rare. This tendency of the "normal" person to suffer from the disapproval of others is the normal counterpart of the paranoidal projections of the deluded.

In one sense, the assassin grapples with his private misery more concretely, even more practically or realistically, than does the normal person, the neurotic, or the deluded psychotic. However horrible his deed, however pathological his interpretation of events, the assassin is a man who has politicized his private miseries. He has attempted to become part of a social institution which promises him freedom from his overpowering self-loathing. Guiteau and Oswald actually experimented with life in systems that seemed to promise escape from themselves, their fantasies, and their frustrations. Each turned against the community he had attempted to join and then discovered that he carried his private miseries and public disaffections with him wherever he went.

The assassin denies responsibility for his failure. (He does not deny his own failure; he is well aware of that.) He blames his sense of failure on others. However, the assassin does not live in a true community of men. His relationships are not immediate or personal. Unloved, he is unloving. He lacks the quality of empathy. The assassin relates rather to an abstraction such as aggregate man or the political community. The fault as he sees it lies not in himself but in the structure of the community wherein he lives, and it is concentrated in the person who is the leader of that community, the President. The assassin disassociates the presidency from the man who occupies the office, and can kill him because of this lack of human identification which has characterized most of the assassin's relationships.

The assassin combines this capacity to project onto the President the responsibility for his personal misery with an increasing preoccupation with a fanciful, abstract political, or governmental alternative to his unbearable surroundings. If the President is responsible for the failures of his society as well as of himself, then the potential assassin, in the name of all suffering humanity, in the name of an ideology, or as Guiteau claimed, in the name of God, is sometimes impelled even against his own will to carry out his mission. The assassin seeks fame and recognition as the killer of the President and acclamation and martyrdom from the community for having accomplished his "mission." There is, however, no existing community of men for whom this mission is accomplished. It exists only in the fantasy of the assassin. But, in carrying out the assassination, the assassin denies the unreality of his "community," and preserves his delusion.

Dr. Freedman suggests that many persons fall upon a continuum of self-loathing. At one end of the spectrum we find the "normal" people failing in their fondest hopes and ambitions, fighting their sense of worthlessness and failure, but successfully maintaining a balance so they can continue to function in a job, support a family, and make a contribution to society. At the other end of the scale are those whose self-loathing is so great that they must escape to a world of fantasy. This world is so pervasive that they lose touch with reality to such a great extent that they cannot function and must be cared for in mental institutions. At the center is the person perched precariously on the edge of reality. He is incapable of sustained work toward a long-range goal, but is capable of bursts of frenzied activity which are ultimately doomed to failure. Each such failure reinforces the self-loathing and the need, in one tremendous burst of directed planning and energy, to accomplish something of great worth. As Booth remarked, the person who pulled down the Colossus of Rhodes would be famous throughout history. One such act, which can be accomplished in a burst of directed activity and which can assure a person a place in history, however infamous, is the assassination of the President of the United States.

One attempt to explain the politicization of the disordered mind of the assassin[31] is based on the notion that a person requires and creates an "ideal self," i.e., a conception of his own identity, and that he orders his conduct and personality in terms of this conception. When a person's basic identity concept is threatened, he may lash out violently against the threat. Persons usually develop their identity by close contact with fellow human beings during childhood and early adulthood, especially close family members. As they grow to adulthood they continue to define their identity by reacting to persons bearing close relationships to them. Thus, most victims of violent or deadly attack bear a close relationship to the attacker—husband, wife, lover, best friend. These are the persons most in a position to threaten the attacker's basic conception of his identity.

The assassin is unusual in having no such apparent personal relationship to the political figure he attacks. However, assassins of Presidents of the United States have had their normal personal relations disrupted at an early age. Typically, the family was disrupted by the death or absence of one parent. As an only or youngest child, the assassins may have been denied close relationships with siblings. Most of the assassins did not have satisfactory relationships with women. Thus the assassins had insufficient close personal relationships on which to define the basic conception upon which their entire identity depended; they were forced to define and relate their identity not to specific persons but to an abstract such as The State or an ideological movement. Such a person would have a kind of "lover" or "best friend" relationship with The State or ideological movement, and would create his fundamental self-image from this relationship. This sets up the psychological conditions that politicize such a personality to explode in deadly violence against the head of state as the symbol and embodiment of his lover. Under the same conditions, the "normal" person would react violently against an individual—husband, wife, mistress, or best friend, as the case may be.

We realize that we still have not explained why the potential assassin deviates from the large number of persons who share with him the same kind of background but who become well-balanced productive citizens. Nor have we explained why the assassin differs from those who can channel and control their identification with a cause and need for recognition, and whose perception of the goals of their society sufficiently accords with reality that they truly serve their society by selfless acts of heroism.

C. A Psychiatric Perspective Upon Public Reaction To the Murder of a President[32]

There are extraordinary regularities in the sequence of events following the assassination of a President of the United States. Those regularities emanate from the tremendous impact of the death of a President on the American public. The impact is not political as such—as pointed out in section E, no basic policy or structural change in the United States is attributable to a presidential assassination—but a personal, emotional impact.

The first regularity to be noted is that where the assassin has been successful, our system of justice has reacted harshly and primitively. Where the assassin has failed, he has usually been treated with compassion.

The very first assassination attempt, that by Richard Lawrence, could have set a precedent to which the United States could have pointed with great pride. The court, at the courageous instance of the prosecution, adopted a liberal rule for the test of insanity: whether the deed was the "immediate, unqualified offspring of the disease"—even if at the time of the attack, the assassin knew the nature of his act and the difference between right and wrong. The jury found Lawrence not guilty by reason of insanity. Shrank, another unsuccessful assassin, was also recognized as insane, and was hospitalized, not executed.

Successful assassins, however, have all been killed. Oswald was gunned down by Ruby. Booth, historians agree, probably shot himself rather than be arrested, but a Union sergeant, Boston Corbett, claimed to have done the act himself as an agent of God and received wide public approval and acclaim for the alleged killing. Two attempts were made on Guiteau's life prior to his trial and execution, also with widespread though not unanimous approval. The following was written in 1881 of one attempt on his life. It could have been written, with very few changes, in 1963 about Ruby's murder of Oswald.

> I am sorry it should have taken place, for it can only add to the wretchedness of the whole thing. We are disgraced as a nation by such an occurrence. What will foreigners think of us? The assassination of the 2nd of July was a dreadful calamity, but then we can look upon that as the freak of a lunatic or the desperate act of a dangerous and baffled man. But now, when that man is on trial for his life and the judicial hearing is proceeding in a regular way, and with no danger of any but a perfectly just and fair conclusion, to have someone take upon himself the office of executioner is entirely inexcusable. It begins to look as if we were in fact a lawless community . . . This Washington fool steps up and insults every law-abiding citizen of the land by his act.[33]

Czolgosz, Guiteau, and Zangara who, although he missed Franklin Roosevelt, killed Mayor Anton Cermak, appear to have merited treatment as insane persons as much as Lawrence or Shrank. However, all were found sane and executed. The trial of Booth's fellow-conspirators was a disgrace. They were denied their right to a jury and were summarily tried and sentenced to death by a military tribunal. The trial of Guiteau was a circus; although the judge's charge to the jury was fair-minded on the issue of insanity, the jury found him guilty and he was executed in front of a large crowd. The trial of

Czolgosz was a farce that lasted only eight hours and twenty-six minutes. The jury brought in a verdict of guilty after only thirty-four minutes. Thus, one disastrous effect of an assassination may be the failure of our system of justice to respond humanely to the mental illness of the successful assassin.

Perhaps of even greater interest from a psychiatric point of view is the initial and sometimes lasting insistence that the assassin was part of a widespread conspiracy. Lawrence was considered by some to be part of a Whig conspiracy against Jackson. The conspiratorial theories surrounding the assassination of Lincoln still rage, including the view that Cabinet members such as Stanton or even Andrew Johnson headed the plot.

Guiteau's sister has written that, although Guiteau did fire one shot at Garfield, the fatal shot was fired by a member of the Stalwart faction.

Czolgosz was widely assumed to have been an agent of the anarchists. Leading anarchists were arrested, including Emma Goldman. No evidence connecting her with the killing was discovered, and she was subsequently released.

Zangara was seriously mentally disturbed. He freely admitted that his intention was to kill Roosevelt as the head of state. Zangara sprayed five pistol shots in Roosevelt's direction, killing Anton Cermak, Mayor of Chicago. Despite the contrary evidence, the rumor still persists that Zangara was the agent of a gangland conspiracy to kill Chicago's mayor.

The twenty-six volume report of the Warren Commission demonstrates that in all probability no murder in the history of the United States has ever been as thoroughly investigated as that of John F. Kennedy. Evidence was taken from anyone who could possibly have anything to contribute. Probably no trial has exceeded the Warren Commission's efforts to be fair and to conceal nothing that could possibly contribute to public understanding.

Yet the proliferation of conspiracy theories about the assassination of President Kennedy is familiar to all. There is even a book denouncing the books that denounce the Warren Report.[34]

How can we explain the prevalence of theories that presidential assassinations sprang from powerful, widespread conspiracies? These theories are created and maintained tenaciously, despite the absence of evidence and despite empirical demonstration of the irrationality of such theories. Indeed, they are elaborated, like some phobias, by an everwidening network of large and small events that become consciously incorporated into the original theory of conspiracy.

Dr. Freedman attempts neither to disprove the conspiratorial theories nor to strengthen the homicidal-isolate hypothesis. Rather, he asks us to speculate with him about the explanations for the acceptance of conspiratorial theories in the face of seemingly overwhelming evidence which renders them at best inconclusive.

The murder of a President is no ordinary homicide. The impact of the murder of the key figure of the government is so vast, so terrible, so widespread, that it is incomparable to the murder of a private citizen. We are agitated and depressed at even the remote prospect that our elected leader may be killed while in office. In contrast, the death of former Presidents does not concern us nearly as much.

The legal precedents of criminal responsibility and insanity that now apply to all legal acts spring from the early precedents established in these rare cases of assassination. Regicide, as Erskine said in defense of Hadfield, is equated with parricide, the murder of the father. Thus, in our jurisprudal system, culpability and punishability are based on social and personal values which express our horror of killing the father. The violent removal of the father threatens the viability of his offspring. Even the fratricide of Cain in the Old Testament could be compromised by the God-father. Cain, the murderer, was stigmatized but spared. Parricide, however, could never be compromised or ignored. It profaned the killer. It aroused unbearable anxiety and guilt. It demanded retribution by the father's survivors. The anxiety, the guilt, the sense of profanation, and the resultant need to seek absolution and to become eligible once again to be accepted in the sacred brotherhood which shared the common father afflicted the murderer no less poignantly than it did his rudely deprived peers.

Profanation of the father's sexual partner by gaining erotic access to her was only slightly less horrifying an act. The murder of the father and taking his place as the sexual possessor of the mother are the primal crimes of mankind. Nonetheless, Oedipus, the unwitting and unwilling archoffender, was himself a father, and the drama of his redemption and the redemption of his values by and through his children reflects the continuity of the problem.

It is now generally held that the human personality is the product of the enactment in each person's life of this Oedipal drama, no less potent because it is only symbolically and psychically reenacted—indeed, possibly more powerful as a determinant of our adult character than if it were physical fact rather than psychic fantasy. Whether or not these speculations are accepted the empirical evidence demonstrates the awesome significance of parricide to those who are under the paternal influence, bound to each other because of their common bond of ambiguous affection for, awe of, dependence upon, and challenge to the common father figure.

Presidential assassination is, for the overwhelming majority of Americans, the equivalent of parricide. Most Americans felt after the assassination of John F. Kennedy that they had lost a member of their own family, almost always their father. They had responded similarly to the death of President Roosevelt.

Many not only compared their sense of loss to the death of their fathers but expressed a more profound sense of shock, loss, and deprivation than they had felt at the death of their own father. Two-thirds of those interviewed complained not only of depression, but of almost unbearable nervousness and tension. One-half of them could not eat or sleep.

Dr. Freedman suggests that the vast audience which is apparently so willing and anxious to be convinced of a conspiracy exists because the alternative is unbearable. It is unbearable because it makes the entire system of controlled relationships within which they live, and upon which the security and sense of their lives rest, vulnerable to destruction by the vagaries of the totally unpredictable. The most conspicuous and most powerful representative of the principles that shape and guarantee their lives can be destroyed in seconds by the attack by a nonentity. It seems incredible that the man who commands the largest power in the world could be destroyed by a man who commands no one, not even himself. It cannot be that the whole complex and mysterious enterprise of government is unable to protect itself. It must not be that he upon whose decisions so much depends, who determines for millions whether they shall live or die on some battlefield, is incapable of making decisions to prevent the taking of his own life. It cannot be that, in short, the great and all-powerful father from whom all strength and protection comes, is as humble, weak, and vulnerable as one suspects or knows oneself to be.

If we must suffer parricide, if our father is to be taken from us, he must be taken by a most powerful, if malignant, counterforce. We cannot lose him to a casual crank. To do so is to stand shivering and unprotected, not only bereft of our father but exposed within ourselves to our own vulnerability. Far better to be convinced of a manichean diabolism than a trivial mechanical doll as the instrument of our destruction.

Dr. Freedman's analysis, if correct, does not itself disprove the existence of malign far-reaching conspiracies to kill the President. We cannot hope to convince those whose own psychic needs require a belief in such conspiracies. We can, however, comfort the many who accept the overwhelming weight of evidence of the lone, mentally ill assassin, but who still feel disturbed and uneasy about that evidence. This uneasiness is a product of the primal anxieties created by the archetypal crime of parricide—not the inadequacy of the evidence of the lone assassin.

D. A Survey of Public Reaction to Assassinations

This section will deal with the emotional impact of assassination on the American public. The first portion is based upon data collected by a Commission survey[35] concerning six assassinations that have occurred in recent years; President John F. Kennedy, Senator Robert F. Kennedy, Dr. Martin Luther King, Jr., Medgar Evers, Malcolm X, and George Lincoln Rockwell.

In order to make judgments about the impact, different emotions as well as the different targets were examined. The emotions that were examined were presented in the form of scales that had two different poles. In some cases the ends of the scale represented opposite emotions, but this was not the case for every scale. The scales were:

hopeful	1	2	3	4	5	hopeless
not surprised	1	2	3	4	5	shocked
unafraid	1	2	3	4	5	afraid
calm	1	2	3	4	5	angry
sad	1	2	3	4	5	relieved
at a loss	1	2	3	4	5	not affected

The respondent was asked to indicate the number on each scale that best represented his feelings at the time he first heard about the assassination. Table 1 presents the average value that the respondents gave to each variable for each assassination. Each scale had five categories which were scored from one to five. The middle category, which represented a neutral position between the two extremes, received a score of three. Results that fell to the left side of the scale received scores of one or two with the average being less than three for a group of scores. If a group of scores fell primarily to the right side of the scale, the average was above three.

Table 1.—*Average reactions of respondents to each of the assassinations*

SCALE	GEORGE LINCOLN ROCKWELL	SENATOR ROBERT F. KENNEDY	MEDGAR EVERS	MALCOLM X	PRESIDENT JOHN F. KENNEDY	DR. MARTIN LUTHER KING
HOPEFUL–HOPELESS	2.925	4.071	3.412	3.034	4.345	3.637
NOT SURPRISED–SHOCKED	2.401	4.497	3.361	2.607	4.793	3.437
UNAFRAID–AFRAID	2.195	3.398	2.914	2.574	3.752	3.158
CALM–ANGRY	2.226	3.910	3.224	2.642	4.144	3.350
SAD–RELIEVED	3.000	1.316	2.114	2.856	1.216	1.970
AT A LOSS–NOT AFFECTED	3.929	1.837	2.839	3.499	1.471	2.584

```
                                      1.5        2.5        3.5        4.5
                                       |          |          |          |
         SCALE OF POSITIONS  [                                             ]
                                 1.0        2.0        3.0        4.0        5.0
```

Because the assassinations occurred over a five-year period between 1963 and 1968, several refinements must be considered in the interpretations of the data. First, what was the time lapse between the assassination and the survey? The survey, conducted in October of 1968, was closest to the assassinations of Senator Kennedy and Dr. King, and furthest from those of President Kennedy and Medgar Evers. In addition to the time variable, there is also a confounding factor present because while all of those interviewed had heard of the assassinations of President Kennedy, Dr. King, and Senator Kennedy, only seventy-two percent had heard of the Malcolm X assassination, sixty-three percent that of Medgar Evers, and fifty-five percent that of George Lincoln Rockwell. Thus, the table represents the reactions of different sets of respondents, not reactions of the whole survey population.

It can be seen from the table that the reaction of the population to the assassination of President Kennedy was more extreme than the reaction to the other five. This is in spite of the fact that the assassination of President Kennedy, among the major figures, was furthest removed in time from the survey.

The variable that appeared to bring forth the most intense reaction was the scale that went from sad to relieved. It should be recalled that the most extreme "*sad*" response a person could give would be a score of one. The average for respondents on the assassination of President Kennedy was 1.22, for Senator Kennedy it was 1.32; and the next most extreme response was for Dr. King, 1.97. The degree of sadness was significantly greater on the part of the general population to the assassinations of President Kennedy and Senator Kennedy than for any of the others. It is also interesting to note that for none of the assassinations, including that of George Lincoln Rockwell, was the average response on the *relieved* side of the neutral point. In the case of Rockwell, the average was in the middle, between *sad* and *relieved*. The average response to the assassination of Malcolm X, 2.86, was also quite close to this middle category. Of course, the average in itself does not indicate the distribution of responses; although it is on one side of the neutral point, there could be a large number of individuals in the population whose response was on the other side. Figure 1 presents the averages on the *sad-relieved* scale. It can be seen that three pairs emerge. At the extreme *sad* end are President Kennedy and Senator Kennedy. At the neutral point are both Malcolm X and George Lincoln Rockwell. Between those two extreme groups are King and Evers. These three groupings will reappear throughout the analysis.

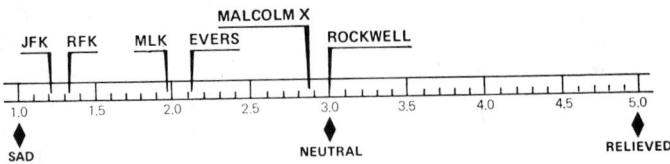

Figure 1.–SAD-RELIEVED SCALE
Intensity of Emotional Reactions to Six Assassinations

The scale that brought the next most intense response was the scale of *not surprised* to *shocked*. Again, there was the greatest surprise at the assassination of President Kennedy, despite the fact that he had been assassinated almost five years before.

It is interesting to note that the degree of shock at the assassinations of Dr. King and Medgar Evers was far less than that for the Kennedys. The degree of shock was about the same for both these individuals, although everyone in the population had heard of the assassination of Martin Luther King, Jr., while less than two-thirds had heard about that of Medgar Evers. Finally, in the case of both Malcolm X and Rockwell, the average response was on the *not surprised* side of the scale. It is possible that, because each of these individuals was a leader of extreme groups within the society, the general impression of the population was that they might meet violent death.

These results are presented in Figure 2. Again the three groups of two appear. In this case, the King-Evers pair is close to the neutral point and is closer to Rockwell-Malcolm X than to the two Kennedys.

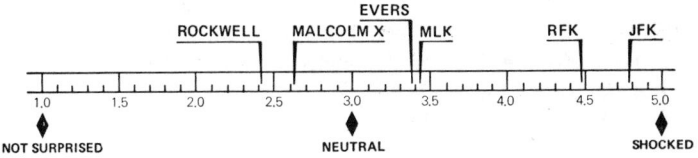

Figure 2.–NOT SURPRISED-SURPRISED SCALE
Intensity of Emotional Reactions to Six Assassinations

The scale that brought forth the third most intense response was *at a loss-not affected*, the last scale on the table. The results here parallel those that have already been presented, although two exceptions should be noted. Although the population in general was more *at a loss* over President Kennedy's assassination than over any of the others, the difference between President Kennedy and Senator Kennedy was greater on this scale than on the previous two. Similarly, it should be noted that again Malcolm X and Rockwell fall on the *not affected* side of the scale. There is, however, a fairly large discrepancy. The population in general was less affected by Rockwell's assassination than by the assassination of Malcolm X. The results are diagramed in Figure 3.

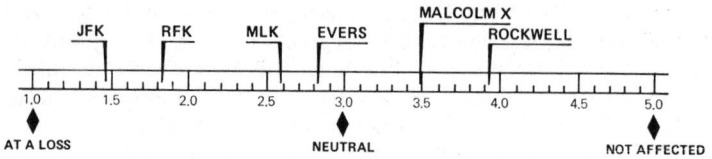

Figure 3.—AT A LOSS-NOT AFFECTED SCALE
Intensity of Emotional Reactions to Six Assassinations

The scale upon which the next most intense responses were given was the *hopeful-hopeless* scale. In this case, the Malcolm X-Rockwell pair falls very close to the neutral point on the scale. Similarly, on the *calm-angry* scale, Malcolm X and Rockwell fall on the opposite side of the scale to that reported for the other assassinations, with Evers and King fairly close to the neutral point. Although comparisons are difficult to make, it appears that aggressive responses on the part of the population to the assassinations of important figures like President Kennedy and Senator Kennedy were less intense than the responses indicating both shock and sadness and a sense of hopelessness or disorientation. These results are presented in Figures 4, 5, and 6.

It must be realized that the above results are based on the average responses of a sample intended to be representative of the entire population of the United States. It is quite possible that not only do the averages for various groups differ from those of the national sample taken together, but that some groups reacted differently to the sequence of assassinations.

1. Emotional Responses of Specific Groups to Assassination

This section will examine the emotions of specific groups. Tables 2 to 7 present the results for each of the scales taken separately.

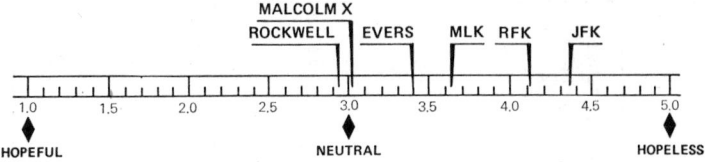

Figure 4.–HOPEFUL-HOPELESS SCALE
Intensity of Emotional Reactions to Six Assassinations

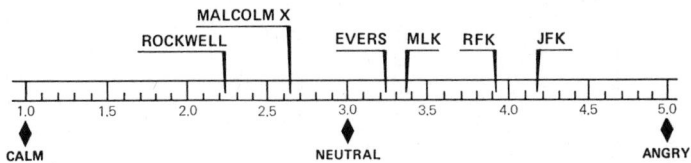

Figure 5.–CALM-ANGRY SCALE
Intensity of Emotional Reactions to Six Assassinations

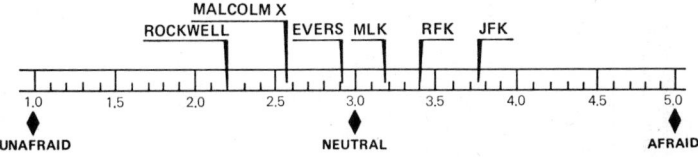

Figure 6.–UNAFRAID-AFRAID SCALE
Intensity of Emotional Reactions to Six Assassinations

Examination of Table 2, which deals with the *hopeful-hopeless* scale, indicates that seventy-eight percent of the population reacted with a feeling of hopelessness to the assassination of President Kennedy. Among Negroes, the percentage was even larger—ninety-one percent, and among suburban residents it was eighty-six percent. In the total population, sixty-eight percent reacted with hopelessness to Senator Kennedy's assassination. But among Negroes this percentage was eighty-three percent, and among the highly politically active it was eighty percent.

For the country as a whole, only forty-six percent reacted to the assassination of Dr. King with hopelessness, but among Negroes the percentage was almost as large as for President Kennedy's—eighty-five percent.

A majority of Negroes also reacted to the assassination of

Table 2.–Analyses of emotional responses to the assassinations hopeful-hopeless scale

ASSASSINATION	HOPEFUL		PERCENT TOTAL SAMPLE	HOPELESS		PERCENT TOTAL SAMPLE
	HIGH GROUPS			HIGH GROUPS		
GEORGE LINCOLN ROCKWELL	30 AND UNDER	24	17	HIGH POL. ACT.	20	12
	NEGRO	23		NEGRO	20	
SENATOR ROBERT F. KENNEDY	RURAL	10	5	NEGRO	83	68
	POL. IMPOTENT	8		HIGH POL. ACT.	80	
	SOUTH	8				
MEDGAR EVERS	WEST	10	6	NEGRO	59	34
	SOME HS	9		HIGH POL. ACT.	49	
MALCOLM X	over 65	21	15	NEGRO	38	17
	8 GRADE OR LESS	20		HIGH POL. ACT.	28	
	WEST	20				
PRESIDENT JOHN F. KENNEDY	RURAL	11	4	NEGRO	91	78
	SOUTH	7		SUBURBAN	86	
DR. MARTIN LUTHER KING	RURAL	16	9	NEGRO	85	46
	(5 GROUPS TIED)	12		HIGH POL. ACT.	61	

Table 3. – Reactions to assassinations
surprised - not surprised scale

ASSASSINATION	NOT SURPRISED		PERCENT TOTAL SAMPLE	SHOCKED		PERCENT TOTAL SAMPLE
	HIGH GROUPS			HIGH GROUPS		
GEORGE LINCOLN ROCKWELL	WEST HIGH POL. ACT	57 57	49	NEGRO INCOME UNDER $5000	21 19	14
SENATOR ROBERT F. KENNEDY	SOUTH POL. IMPORTANT MALE, NON-VET OVER 65	16 13 13 13	8	EAST COLLEGE 51 - 65	91 91 91	86
MEDGAR EVERS	RURAL SOUTH MALE, NON-VET	34 29 29	24	NEGRO 8th GRADE OR LESS	68 59	45
MALCOLM X	RURAL WEST URBAN TOWN EXP WITH VIOLENCE	51 49 49	42	NEGRO HIGH POL. ACT.	48 34	20
PRESIDENT JOHN F. KENNEDY	SOUTH MALE, NON-VET	7 6	3	EAST OVER 65 FEMALES	98 97 97	94
DR. MARTIN LUTHER KING	RURAL SOUTH	47 44	31	NEGRO METRO CITY	84 68	56

Table 4.—Reactions to assassinations
unafraid-afraid scale

ASSASSINATION	UNAFRAID HIGH GROUPS		PERCENT TOTAL SAMPLE	AFRAID HIGH GROUPS		PERCENT TOTAL SAMPLE
GEORGE LINCOLN ROCKWELL	MALE NON-VET	59	48	HIGH POL. ACT.	12	6
	METRO CITY	56		INCOME UNDER 5000	10	
				WEST	10	
SENATOR ROBERT F. KENNEDY	OVER 65	32	20	FEMALES	53	45
	MALE. NON-VET	27		EAST	52	
MEDGAR EVERS	SOME HS	31	25	HIGH POL. ACT.	35	22
	MALE, VET	31		INCOME UNDER 5000	33	
				NEGRO	33	
MALCOLM X	EAST	42	34	NEGRO	21	12
	URBAN TOWN	40		4 GROUPS TIED AT	17	
PRESIDENT JOHN F. KENNEDY	OVER 65	29	17	FEMALES	70	61
	LOW POL. ACT	22		30 AND UNDER	69	
	URBAN TOWN	22		SUBURBAN	69	
DR. MARTIN LUTHER KING	URBAN TOWN	38	27	NEGRO	63	36
	OVER 65	33		METRO CITY	47	
				HIGH POL. ACT.	47	

Table 5.—Reactions to assassinations calm-angry scale

ASSASSINATION	CALM HIGH GROUPS		CALM PERCENT TOTAL SAMPLE	ANGRY HIGH GROUPS		ANGRY PERCENT TOTAL SAMPLE
GEORGE LINCOLN ROCKWELL	MID-WEST	59	49	MID-WEST	18	10
	30 AND UNDER	56		HIGH POL. ACT.	18	
SENATOR ROBERT F. KENNEDY	OVER 65	28	14	EAST	78	58
	8 GRADE OR LESS	24		HIGH POL. ACT.	77	
				EXP. WITH VIOLENCE	77	
MEDGAR EVERS	OVER 65	27	22	HIGH POL. ACT.	58	37
	MALE, VET.	26		NEGRO	56	
	MALE, NON-VET	26				
	WEST	26				
MALCOLM X	URBAN TOWN	44	34	NEGRO	34	17
	OVER 65	40		HIGH POL. ACT.	27	
	ENDORSE STRONG LEADERSHIP ITEM	40				
PRESIDENT JOHN F. KENNEDY	OVER 65	22	13	HIGH POL. ACT.	86	75
	8 GRADE OR LESS	21		EAST	83	
DR. MARTIN LUTHER KING	OVER 65	37	24	NEGRO	78	46
	MALE, NON-VET	32		HIGH POL. ACT.	65	
	8 GRADE OR LESS	32				

Table 6.–Reactions to assassinations
sad-relieved scale

ASSASSINATION	SAD		RELIEVED	
	HIGH GROUPS	PERCENT TOTAL SAMPLE	HIGH GROUPS	PERCENT TOTAL SAMPLE
GEORGE LINCOLN ROCKWELL	HIGH POL. ACT. 30 WEST 29	21	HIGH POL. ACT. 25 TV EFFECT 24	19
SENATOR ROBERT F. KENNEDY	NEGRO 96 FEMALES 95	91	(ALL LOW)	1
MEDGAR EVERS	NEGRO 87 8 GRADE OR LESS 70	56	WEST 11 MALE, VET. 7	4
MALCOLM X	NEGRO 63 METRO CITY 42	26	WEST 22 URBAN TOWN 22	16
PRESIDENT JOHN F. KENNEDY	EAST 97 METRO CITY 97 FINANCIAL SITUATION GETTING WORSE 97	95	(ALL VERY LOW)	1
DR. MARTIN LUTHER KING	NEGRO 95 METRO CITY 76	66	OVER 65 11 (7 GROUPS TIED AT) 10	7

Table 7.—Reactions to assassinations at a loss-not affected scale

ASSASSINATION	AT A LOSS		PERCENT TOTAL SAMPLE	NOT AFFECTED		PERCENT TOTAL SAMPLE
	HIGH GROUPS			HIGH GROUPS		
GEORGE LINCOLN ROCKWELL	INCOME UNDER $5000 NEGRO	15 13	8	RURAL WEST MID-WEST 30 AND UNDER	68 63 63 63	56
SENATOR ROBERT F. KENNEDY	NEGRO METRO CITY	90 82	74	MALE, VET OVER 65	13 12	8
MEDGAR EVERS	NEGRO METRO CITY INCOME UNDER $5000	65 49 36	34	WEST URBAN TOWN	30 30	22
MALCOLM X	NEGRO METRO CITY HIGH POL. ACT.	36 20 20	13	URBAN TOWN RURAL	47 46	38
PRESIDENT JOHN F. KENNEDY	NEGRO METRO CITY	96 91	87	URBAN TOWN LOW POL. ACT.	6 6	4
DR. MARTIN LUTHER KING	NEGRO METRO CITY	93 62	46	SOUTH URBAN TOWN	27 27	21

Medgar Evers with hopelessness—fifty-nine percent—as opposed to thirty-four percent for the whole sample. Similarly, Negroes reacted more strongly to the death of Malcolm X than did the sample as a whole. In fact, the *hopeful* percentage for the sample was almost equal to the *hopeless*—fifteen percent compared to seventeen percent. In the case of George Lincoln Rockwell, a slightly greater percentage was *hopeful* (seventeen percent) than were *hopeless* (twelve percent).

In general, it appears that Negroes have been particularly shaken by the political assassinations that have occurred.

The results, presented in Table 3, are confirmed on the *not surprised-shocked* scale. Again, the pattern repeats itself, although a slightly higher proportion of the citizenry was shocked at each of the assassinations than reacted with the emotion of hopelessness. In the case of George Lincoln Rockwell, more than a majority who heard said that they were not surprised when they heard of the assassination. Even for Malcolm X, the percentage of *not surprised* was forty-two percent, this was twice as large as the percentage that said they were shocked (twenty percent). It is apparent again that Negroes reacted more strongly to the assassinations.

Fear as an emotion did not occur as widely as did either shock or hopelessness. Nevertheless, sixty-one percent of the sample did react this way upon hearing of the assassination of President Kennedy. For Senator Kennedy, the percentage was forty-five percent, but more than half of both females and Easterners reacted with fear to the Senator's assassination. Similarly, although only thirty-six percent of the population reacted with fear to Dr. King's assassination, fully sixty-three percent of the Negroes in the sample indicated that they reacted with this emotion. The picture that is emerging is one of shock and hopelessness over major assassinations in this country and reduced, but still substantial, amounts of fear (see Table 4). Anger was a stronger response than fear in the population. The results for this scale are presented in Table 5. Seventy-five percent of the sample reacted with anger to the assassination of President Kennedy. More than half (fifty-eight percent) also reacted this way to the assassination of Senator Kennedy and almost half (forty-six percent) did so upon hearing of Dr. King's assassination. For particular subgroups in the population, the percentages are even higher. For example, seventy-eight percent of the Negroes reacted with anger to the death of Dr. King and fifty-six percent to that of Medgar Evers. The high politically active also felt a great deal of anger at these assassinations as well as to those of President and Senator Kennedy.

It seems apparent that in such a moment of shock, the nation is in a potentially dangerous mood. In the case of President Kennedy's assassination, a majority were afraid, but an even larger majority were angry, a potentially explosive combination.

The nation reacted with a great deal of sadness to the assassinations (see Table 6)—ninety-five percent to President Kennedy's, ninety-one percent to Senator Kennedy's, sixty-six percent to Dr. King's, and fifty-six percent to Medgar Evers'. Among Negroes, the sadness over the assassination of their leaders was quite great. Ninety-five percent expressed this emotion in the case of Dr. King and eighty-seven percent in the case of Evers. In the case of Malcolm X, the percentage of Negroes who expressed sadness was still a substantial majority —sixty-three percent.

The results of the *at a loss-not affected* scale parallel the percentages for the *calm-angry* scale. They are presented in Table 7. More than ninety percent of the Negro community felt a great loss after each of the "major" assassinations, and a majority expressed this sentiment after the assassination of Medgar Evers. Although the country as a whole was not substantially affected by the Malcolm X assassination, over one-third of the Negro community felt at a loss.

2. Summary

Tables 2 to 7 have presented data for emotional reactions to the six major political assassinations that have occurred in the past six years. In addition, particular groups in the population that were high in the expression of these emotions were presented.

It is apparent that the country was greatly affected by the assassinations. Anger, fear, shock, hopelessness, loss, and sadness were overwhelming reactions to the assassinations of John Kennedy and Robert Kennedy and substantial reactions to Dr. King's. Negroes also expressed these sentiments to a great degree over the assassinations of Medgar Evers and

Malcolm X. Only the assassination of George Lincoln Rockwell evoked relatively little reaction.

3. Polarized Subgroup Analysis

One of the problems in the analysis of attitudes is the
identification of significant subgroups. In this survey, an attempt was made, to select subgroups empirically which would
be fairly homogeneous and maximally different from each
other in their attitudes. The result was a division of the sample
into separate groups defined by more than one attribute at the
same time. Because of the small number of non-whites in a
national sample, it was possible to add only a single characteristic at a time to this grouping. The larger number of cases in
the white part of the sample, allowed several attributes to be
used simultaneously to define the subgroup. The attributes
were selected based on their ability to discriminate among
individuals in their attitudes. Consequently, the use of several
of them simultaneously resulted in even greater discrimination
on the items.

This section will briefly examine some of the subgroups for
their emotional reactions to the various assassinations.

As has been indicated, the most intense reactions were on
the *sad-relieved* scale. This scale will be examined for those
subgroups which differed most in their reactions. Because the
feelings of the population were predominantly at the *sad* end
of the scale for both President Kennedy and Senator Kennedy,
only the most intense response will be considered.

Non-whites and whites were almost identical in their reactions of extreme sadness upon hearing of the death of President Kennedy. For the non-white sample, eighty-seven percent
marked the extreme category, and for whites the figure was
eighty-six percent. There was, however, a substantial amount
of variability among the subgroups. The smallest group to
mark the extreme was the high politically active white Southerners (sixty-seven percent). The highest groups were white
females who had not graduated from high school but who
were high in political activity (100 percent) and the Eastern
whites who had not graduated from high school (99 percent).

In general, the survey indicated that politically active Southern whites are alienated from the federal government to a

much greater extent than would be expected, based on their level of political activity. Among other groups in the population, the high politically active are more supportive of the national government and are usually among the most liberal elements in the population. In the South, however, at least for whites, the issue of segregation appears to be the most politically volatile. This activity has been primarily opposed to federal efforts. Consequently, the interaction of high political activity, being white, and residing in the South, results in a group whose feelings are different on many issues from those of other of the subgroups.

The greatest reaction of sadness to President Kennedy's assassination would be expected to fall among those who felt that he showed great promise and were left without a feeling of direction by his death. This interpretation is somewhat confirmed by an examination of the *at a loss-not affected* scale. The two groups highest in the expression of extreme sadness were also among the highest in expressing the extreme *at a loss* position on that scale. (The highest group on the *at a loss* scale, however, consisted of non-whites who had graduated from high school but had not gone on to college. This result is consistent with the hypothesis that has been presented.) Residence in the West or South was the dominant characteristic among the groups which were low in the extreme *at a loss* reaction. It was in these sections of the country that President Kennedy encountered greatest opposition in his campaign in 1960.

On the *afraid-unafraid* scale, the Eastern non-whites showed the greatest amount of intense fear. This may represent a feeling among this group that they would not make the advances they had hoped they would achieve under the Kennedy administration. Many white residents of the West (white male, white low politically active, and white high politically active Westerners) were among those least likely to give the most intense fear response.

Not only were the Eastern non-whites among the highest in intense fear, they were also among the highest in intense anger over President Kennedy's assassination. On the other hand, Southern white males and Southern whites who had not graduated from high school gave the smallest proportion of intense anger. The spread between the high and low groups was quite large on this scale. Whereas eighty-three percent of the Eastern non-whites fell in the extreme anger category, only thirty-seven percent of the white male Southerners and thirty-eight percent of the Southern whites who had not graduated from high school did.

As expected, similar principles apply in the reactions of the assassination of Senator Kennedy, and such is the case. The extreme sadness category was most likely to be marked by Western non-whites (ninety-six percent) and by male whites living in the East (ninety percent). It was least likely to be marked by politically active white males who had not graduated from high school (fifty percent) and, surprisingly, by white males who had graduated from high school and were medium in political activity (fifty-six percent). One possible explanation for this is the fact that Senator Kennedy was assassinated while his party was divided in a pre-presidential nomination battle, whereas President Kennedy was assassinated after he had assumed leadership of the country. Among the lowest groups were white male Southerners (sixty percent) and white male Westerners (sixty-two percent). The scores of these last two groups were to be expected, based on the results from President Kennedy's assassination.

The greatest proportion of respondents who indicated anger were politically active Eastern whites (sixty-nine percent), Eastern non-whites (sixty-seven percent), and high politically active non-whites. The groups that had the smallest proportion of members who gave a reaction of intense anger consisted of male whites in the South (twenty-five percent) and Southern whites who had not completed high school (twenty-nine percent).

The results for the Martin Luther King, Jr. assassination change drastically because of the great difference in reactions of white and non-white groups. The principles mentioned above also apply here, but the groups to which they apply are markedly different.

Eighty-eight percent of the non-whites, but only forty percent of the whites, marked the most extreme sad position as a response to the King assassination. In general, it appears that the least active and the less educated non-whites responded to the greatest extent (over ninety percent). Among the non-whites, the group having the smallest proportion of extreme sad responses was the highly politically active non-whites (seventy-four percent). This proportion may well have resulted from a greater militancy among the politically active non-whites than they felt was represented in the position of Dr. King. However, it must be noted that the highest white subgroups, the Eastern whites medium in political activity and the highly politically active female whites who had at least graduated from high school, still fell below the lowest non-white subgroup (seventy percent and sixty-nine percent, respectively). For the white subgroup the spread was quite great on this scale, with only twenty-six percent of the male Southerners and twenty-six percent of the low politically active Southerners giving this response.

This pattern was similar on other scales, although the difference between the white and non-white subgroups was even larger in some cases. For example, seventy-five percent of the non-whites and only twenty-two percent of the whites indicated that they felt extremely hopeless upon hearing of the assassination of Dr. King. Similarly, seventy-seven percent of the non-whites and only twenty-three percent of the whites indicated that their feelings were at the extreme *at a loss* position.

Examination of the Evers assassination presents a similar but less intense pattern. It appears that the reactions on most of the scales were more similar for whites and non-whites than on the King assassination. However, Evers may have been seen by non-whites as less directly influential in the possible achievement of important goals. Consequently, there was less hopelessness, anger, fear, etc. expressed by non-whites over his assassination than over that of Dr. King. However, the substantial amount of identification of the non-whites is indicated by the intense sadness response. In this case, sixty-eight percent of the non-whites and only twenty-eight percent of the whites expressed the extreme response.

In the case of Malcolm X, there was even less reaction overall, and there were smaller differences between whites and non-whites. In fact, there was very little difference between the two groups in the amount of fear they expressed upon hearing of the death of Malcolm X. Nevertheless, substantial portions of the non-white community did identify with Malcolm X and did react negatively to his assassination. Again, the greatest difference between the two groups occurred on the *sad-relieved* scale; sixty-three percent of the non-whites and only sixteen percent of the whites expressed sadness over the Malcolm X assassination.

As has been indicated, the Rockwell assassination resulted in the least emotional reaction on the part of the population. Although there was substantial variability among subgroups, the significance of these results is rather difficult to determine. Perhaps the most surprising result is that the group having the largest proportion of members who expressed some degree of sadness were the low politically active non-whites (forty-seven percent). Perhaps this group was reacting more to the concept of assassination than to feelings toward the person himself. Because a smaller proportion of respondents claimed to have heard about the Rockwell assassination, there is also the possibility that memories of this assassination were not as clear as for the others. However, Rockwell was introduced in the interview schedule as the former head of the American Nazi Party. It is also possible, therefore, that the reactions, especially among white subgroups, represent some of the extreme polarization in political viewpoint that exists in the population.[36]

As pointed out above, the reaction of the population to the assassination of President Kennedy was the most extreme among the assassinations examined by the Commission survey, despite the fact that his assassination was furthest removed in time. A number of other studies, closer in time to the death of President Kennedy, have explored the reactions of the public to that assassination.[37] The principal responses of adults to the assassination included sorrow for the President's wife and children (sixty-one percent of those sampled); regret that a young man had been killed at the height of his power (fifty-two percent); shame that such an act could occur in the United States (fifty percent); a sense of loss at the death of one so close and dear (forty-five percent); and anger that anyone would commit such an act (forty-four percent).

A large portion of the national adult population experienced physical and psychological discomfort. Fifty-three percent of the adults interviewed said they had cried; fifty-seven percent said that they were dazed and numb; and forty-eight percent reported that they had trouble getting to sleep. Sixty-eight percent felt very nervous and tense; forty-three percent did not feel like eating; and anywhere from one-fifth to over one-quarter of those interviewed underwent a variety of other nervous reactions—upset stomachs (twenty-two percent), headaches (twenty-five percent), and excessive smoking (twenty-nine percent).

At the time of the interviews, people were confused by the assassin's motives and the rationale for such a crime. About one in three felt that Lee Harvey Oswald, the accused assassin, was mentally ill, although the general reaction seemed to be one of confusion as to the killer's objectives and his reasoning.

About three out of four people (seventy-two percent) were convinced that Oswald was the assassin. However, in response to a question as to whether the murder could be considered the act of one man alone, sixty-two percent of the population believed others were involved in the act. It is difficult to think of an act that violently and horribly removes the chief political officer of the country as the action of an isolated, unstable individual. In their search for a more intelligible explanation, portions of the American public were susceptible to any conspiracy theory that might appear valid.

The tendency to attribute the murder to some broader conspiracy is not a new phenomenon in the aftermath of presidential assassinations. The reaction to the Lincoln assassination, with some justification, centered on talk and investigation of a plot or conspiracy to kill the President. The reactions to the Garfield and McKinley assassinations ran along the same line, leading to accusations against the anarchists in the case of McKinley and the Stalwart Republicans in the case of Garfield. Despite the attribution of the murder to a lone gunman in the assassination of President Kennedy, when respondents were specifically asked, "In your opinion, who or what should really be blamed for the assassination of President Kennedy —aside from the man who actually fired the gun?", only twenty percent could specify any group that they believed ultimately responsible for the death (fifteen percent said the Communists or leftists, five percent said right-wingers or segregationists).

The response of children to the assassination of President Kennedy was at least as intense as that of their parents. The feelings of the children parallel those of their parents (sense of loss, sorrow for the family, anger, and the variety of physical and psychological responses the older people felt). A basic difference in the response patterns, however, was the tendency of children to equate the loss of the President with that of a parent, an especially intensive emotional experience for a child.[38]

One sample of Southern children also showed a sharper

division between the races in speculatively attributing the murder of Martin Luther King, Jr., to an assassin of whom little was publicly known at the time.[39] Black children were three times as likely as whites to believe a white man was responsible (thirty-five to twelve percent) and more likely to attribute the death to "a prejudiced, racist, sick society" (twenty-seven to seventeen percent). White children, on the other hand, were ten times more likely (forty-one to four percent) to argue that, "King himself was to blame." The white children also were considerably less upset by the King assassination, some even justified it.

The responses of the public were also of immediate political concern. In the wake of an assassination, a sense of vindictiveness and anger in the population—quite similar to that resulting from each of the previous presidential murders—was evident in the desire to punish the assassin physically. Little concern was exhibited by respondents for the procedural safeguards implicit in the concept of "due process of law." Only one out of three (thirty-three percent) felt that Oswald should have had a trial, and one in five (twenty percent) was actually pleased when Oswald was shot. The ritualistic trial given Czolgosz and several of the suspected plotters in the Lincoln murder, as well as the speedy executions, indicates that the American public in these circumstances is more concerned with retribution than with any emphasis on traditions and safeguards associated with the concept of the rule of law. "Justice" comes to mean a very immediate and primitive revenge. The handling of accused assassins in 1968 might indicate a change in attitude—a greater willingness to permit the courts to determine guilt or innocence while affording the accused the protections that the system has to offer.

During the period of mourning for President Kennedy, people appeared to be more attracted toward his policy positions and more sympathetic to their enactment. This is one explanation for the number of domestic programs, originally sponsored by Kennedy, which were passed in the year following his death. Democratic Party supporters appeared stronger in their dedication to the party and Republicans were more ambivalent in their attitude toward their party and less likely to employ it as a source of reference in evaluating policy programs.[40] Republicans appeared less willing than Democrats to criticize programs during the early stages of the Johnson administration, and adherents of both parties found themselves more drawn to political figures who supported Kennedy policies and less sympathetic to those who criticized them severely.

The public also tended to idealize the young President in the immediate post-assassination period. Respondents described the deceased President as "intelligent" (eighty percent), "courageous" (sixty-six percent), "hard-working" (fifty-two percent), and "sincere" (forty-eight percent). While only fifty-nine percent indicated that they approved of the way Kennedy was handling the presidency in the last Gallup poll released before his death (Nov. 10, 1963), one-half went so far as to credit him with being "one of the two or three best Presidents the country ever had" in the days immediately following his death.

This phenomenon is not confined to the 1963 presidential assassination. The newspaper and public reactions to the deaths of Garfield and McKinley were reported to be equally profuse. The slain Presidents were eulogized in the most laudatory terms, and were characterized by qualities not necessarily related to their personalities, abilities, or a realistic evaluation of their place in history.

The final stage of the post-assassination period appears to be a unification of people who gain strength from each other and recommit themselves to the goals of the country. The process parallels that of persons who have experienced a natural disaster. They are united by a shared experience that helps to bind them together and provides encouragement for them to continue on. Those who experience grief in a post-assassination period are likely to rededicate themselves to the social values and goals of the total system. In commenting on this process, Christopher Hurn and Mark Messer state that, "One of the consequences of grief . . . may have been to narrow the gap between personal and public concerns, to translate a social event into terms directly relevant to the individual,"[41] and consequently, it might be added, directly relevant to the political system.

E. Political Consequences Traceable to Assassination of Presidents of the United States

The outpouring of grief and shock after the assassination of President John F. Kennedy was typical of the national reaction to each of the previous assassinations of American

Presidents.[42] In this period of national grief, specific legislation associated with the President or the circumstances of his assassination was passed sooner or in a more severe form than would otherwise have been the case. For example, Garfield's assassin, Guiteau, was widely characterized as a "disappointed officeseeker." Legislation to establish a civil service rather than a "spoils" system of appointment had been pending prior to Garfield's assassination, and probably would eventually have been passed. The assassination of Garfield speeded up the process.

McKinley's assassin, Czolgosz, was widely identified with anarchism, considered a "foreign" ideology. Czolgosz's assassination of McKinley probably contributed to the passage, two and one-half years later, of more restrictive immigration laws. This law, however, reflected the general political atmosphere at the time, and did not represent a new or fundamental change.

Only the assassination of Lincoln may have had fundamental long-range political impact. President Andrew Johnson was unable to carry through with Lincoln's permissive and conciliatory attitude towards the Southern States and Lincoln's "soft" position on civil rights for Negroes. It is, of course, impossible for us to know whether the "soft" policy of Lincoln or the "hard" policy of Congress, which embodied itself in the Fourteenth Amendment, would have been the better strategy in the long run for securing equal rights for all, regardless of race.[43] We can, however, infer that Lincoln's popularity, had he lived, would have enabled him to carry out his policy. For better or worse, this difference would have had substantial long-range political impact.

In no case, however, was the legislative and political impact a "logical" response to the assassination. Guiteau's act can not be associated with officeseekers in general, nor Czolgosz's with anarchists, nor Booth's with the Southern aristocracy. None was in any sense a representative of the group with which he was associated. The responses to their acts may, with the hindsight of history, be either approved or disapproved in the individual instance. But none was a response which would have reduced the likelihood of the assassination involved in each case.

In this connection, both John and Robert Kennedy were associated with efforts to pass gun control legislation. Our data indicate that the possible effect of their assassinations with respect to gun control parallels the cases discussed above. It is difficult to determine whether gun control legislation, short of substantial reduction of the rifle population, would reduce the risk of assassination. Gun control legislation may be desirable for other reasons. Surely the judgment of the two martyred brothers in this regard is worthy of careful consideration, and if such legislation is appropriate, it would be an entirely fitting response to their memory to hasten the passage of such legislation.

F. Strategies for the Reduction of Presidential Assassinations

There are two approaches to the reduction of presidential assassinations. One is to improve protection for the man who occupies the office. That protective function is being performed by the Secret Service with the aid and cooperation of other federal and state protective agencies. The continuing efforts of the Secret Service to improve its capability for its protective mission is discussed in "Protection of the President." The other approach, discussed later in this section, is to examine the nature of the office and the campaign for the office to see what changes might reduce the attractiveness of the office to assassins and the exposure of the officeholder to assassination.

1. Protection of the President

Assassination and other acts of political violence are ordinarily symptoms of more fundamental problems. Thus, one response to the problem of assassination must lie in responding to the underlying social, political, cultural, and psychological causes. However, in a nation of hundreds of millions, we cannot deny the possibility of at least a few persons who will become potential assassins, even in the most equitable society. Nor can we avoid the reality that, so long as the United States remains a world power, conditions affecting the development of billions of people in other nations will tend to make the President the object of such murderous displacements. Therefore, the protection of the President from such chance encounters remains an essential requirement.

The report of the Warren Commission set forth a history of presidential protection,[44] including a history of the role of the Secret Service.[45] The Warren Commission also made a number of specific recommendations to the Secret Service,[46] including the formation of a committee specifically to study the function of the Secret Service and to make appropriate recommendations. The Dillon Committee was established and did make the study recommended by the Warren Commission. The studies of the Dillon Committee have not been made public, but they have been received by the President and the Secret Service, and the Secret Service has responded to those recommendations. In addition, the Secret Service has had continuing technological support in refining and upgrading its methods of protection. Mr. Thomas J. Kelley of the Secret Service's protective intelligence division made the following report to the Commission:

> Subsequent to the assassination of President Kennedy, the Department of Defense made its research and development resources available in support of efforts to reduce the vulnerability of important political persons to assassination. The U.S. Secret Service, the Office of Science and Technology, the Office of Director of Defense Research and Engineering, and the Advanced Research Projects Agency participated in a series of studies made by the Rand Corporation, the Research Analysis Corporation, and the Institute for Defense Analysis.
>
> The Rand Corporation took up the broad problem relating to the appearances of the President, and studied the dangers inherent in such appearances. Their studies, completed in July 1964, covered threat detection and evaluation, the planning for public appearances, and the release of public information. They looked into the security coordination between the Secret Service, the White House, Federal agencies, and local and regional police. They studied the use of body armor, the feasibility of detecting weapons such as knives, grenades, or firearms, attacks associated with aircraft, the deterrent image of security measures, screening and surveillance procedures, shielding and evasion techniques, and threat reaction

measures. They submitted a report concerning the French Government's protective systems, the feasibility of a political threat file, and the processing of information.

As the Rand studies approached completion, the Research Analysis Corporation was assigned a field of interest in security threat analysis and research, primarily in travel and public appearance situations. Its reports, received from June 1964 through January 1966, looked into the feasibility of sophisticated weapons and equipment, such as cold liquid weapons and liquid stream projectors, distraction and confusion defense systems, non-lethal weapons, such as the gas-propelled impact projectiles, and the acoustic detection of small-arm fire. It also conducted studies relative to armored automobiles, armored chairs and speaker platforms, helicopters, and blast-containment chambers.

The Institute for Defense Analysis furnished a report in January 1964 relating to threat analysis, the motivation of persons, and the classification of persons and weapons. The Institute's reports suggested that much additional research was needed in the development of transparent armor for automobiles, the development of personal armor, research into the use of men, the use of gaming procedures, and the use of doubles; that general research must be conducted on reaction systems to allow detection of the commencement of an act, such as the detection of bullets when fired. They reflected that research was needed in specific concepts of the use of light to blind an assassin, detection of hidden weapons, and some invisible, relatively silent, method of directing energy to deflect ballistic objects.

In order that the studies might be as objective as possible, the Secret Service's participation during the studies was relatively minor, but at the conclusion, the reports now known as the "STAR Reports" were furnished to and carefully reviewed by the Secret Service. While the people making the studies were aware of the obvious constraints of our society in the protection of a President in a democracy, they did not allow these constraints to affect the avenues in which their research took them. In the evaluation of these reports, the Secret Service, of necessity, took a more pragmatic approach and we found the implementation of some of the recommendations of the study group required conditions which the Secret Service could not control; for instance, the wearing of body armor by Principals and secrecy of movements; and some required ostentatious or oppressive security measures, but the reports were of value in bringing diverse disciplines to bear in the evaluation of the entire range of protective alternatives. They were judged against the realities of the problem and, among other collateral benefits, highlighted the necessity of the participation of other government agencies if maximum protection is to be furnished.

The entire range of protective devices which sprang from the fertile minds of the research group was carefully considered by the Secret Service. While a discussion of those procedures which we have adopted would somewhat reduce their effectiveness, reference to a few of the proposals which were discarded will indicate the breadth of the advisory recommendations. The discarded suggestions ranged from a simple smoke screen device on the Presidential car which would have obscured it in the event of an attack, to sophisticated deflection devices such as one which would cause a stream of air under high pressure to be directed into a pit immediately in front of the President's rostrum, of an intensity which could deflect an object or projectile. Reflecting screens which would cause the Protectee to appear to be standing were suggested, as were blinding lights and highly pitched noises to cause confusion during an attack or to prevent an imminent attack from being successful. A zoom optic surveillance device, with a truck-mounted rotating scanner which would accompany a motorcade and allow improved optical survey of a parade route and the buildings along the route, was one of the suggested devices, as was an electroacoustic detection device which would detect a gun shot when fired and immediately activate a protective shield around the Protectee.

The objections to some of these protective devices are obvious. They could not be utilized when the dangers inherent in them or the impression they would make upon onlookers were considered.

The Secret Service made a decision to place major and

immediate priorities on the development of armored vehicles and related equipment and the adaptation of information handling programs to our needs.

One of the results of the studies of armor was the development by the Secret Service of a series of bullet resistant armored vehicles; each car since 1964 being an improvement on the former; but each retaining the appearance of a conventional vehicle.

There is a continuing dialogue between the Secret Service and the Materials and Mechanics Research Agency to ascertain the feasibility of the development of an armored car capability which would employ bullet resistant material in the manufacture of the car instead of the present method of placing armor material on the standard car. Because the addition of armor adds substantial weight to the vehicle, fabrication of bullet resistant material into automobile bodies would be a breakthrough in the weight problem. The Secret Service is considering a proposal of a research group to inquire if any presently available material will allow such fabrication.

Throughout all the "STAR Reports" there runs the thread of the problem of threat assessment and analysis. The Secret Service has been actively seeking additional studies and assistance in this problem.

Threat assessment is essentially an intelligence activity. As with other efforts to identify hostile opponents and anticipate their intentions, threat assessment requires that we (1) secure what might be called strategic warnings which are the possible sources of attacks against the President; (2) secure tactical warnings of specific attack plans that are about to be or are in the process of being implemented. Our analysis must distinguish between *possible* assassins and potential assassins. The criteria and methods for identifying the former group can probably be improved. More important, however, are our efforts to improve both the criteria for distinguishing potential assassins (a much smaller number of people thought to pose a more serious threat) and the acquisition, evaluation, storage and retrieval, and use of pertinent data on this group.

Subsequent to the assassination of President Kennedy, we began to solicit and receive more information on more people who were thought to represent a danger to the

President. The enormously increased volume could not possibly be handled manually, and we began the development of a data processing system geared to the storage and retrieval of this information. In addition to the acquisition of a computer and the necessary peripheral equipment, the Secret Service expanded its capability in information handling with the addition of a teletype network. We also have a terminal to the National Crime Information Center (NCIC). This link means that if any person whom we are seeking to evaluate is wanted by any police authority in the country participating in the National Crime Information Center, that fact will be immediately reported by our system.

There are still problems in the question of the pertinency of the data, a problem similar to that which this Commission will be considering.

The criteria which we now use has remained substantially from the criteria used in designing the computer system, although our capability to make an effective analysis of the data on hand has been increased. Our computerized data now hopefully make possible a better evaluation and there is a continuing process to refine the criteria to make it more meaningful and at the same time to make handling them practicable and within the capabilities of our resources.

There has been a continuing participation by the Secret Service with agencies and scientific groups dealing with enforcement problems. Specifically, I wish to mention two on-going programs with the Office of Science and Technology. One is a program of consulting with a group of scholars being selected under the aegis of the Office of Science and Technology of the Executive Office of the President for the purpose of evaluating and further developing our criteria. That group is to make recommendations as to the best possible way of making use of the very large amount of information being furnished to us. We are also participating with the Office of Science and Technology in a review of the present state of the art of weapon detection, a matter in which not only we, but the Federal Aviation Agency, has an interest, as well as other groups concerned with the misuse of firearms.

In addition to the armored car program, we are monitoring the advances being made in the fields of body armor, flexible shields, bullet resistant cloth and blankets and armored lecterns.

The Secret Service is a member of the Advisory Committee on the National Crime Information Center; is a member of the Automatic Data Processing Communications Operation Committee in the law enforcement net; participates in the Interdepartmental Automatic Data Processing group sponsored by the Bureau of the Budget; is a member of the Associated Police Communications Officers and participates in the Law Enforcement Teletype System (LETS). The Secret Service is also represented on committees which deal with the gathering of intelligence on a national level, and on a number of classified interdepartmental study groups dealing with advanced protective technology.

The Secret Service is presently making use of the most up-to-date information presently available to the agencies of the Federal Government; it is monitoring pertinent developmental and research programs in the Defense Department, Central Intelligence Agency, and other Government departments and in Private Industry. We have available for use armored vehicles, protective blankets, the latest small arms and hand weapons, both lethal and non-lethal, X-ray equipment for the clearance of packages, baggage, etc., equipment for the containment and defusing of explosives, surveillance equipment, and survival equipment. Our protective communication equipment is provided by the Department of Defense and is the latest and best available. We also make use of protective helicopters for surveillance and to furnish us with the ability to evacuate our Protectees in the event of trouble.

The Secret Service's mission is preventive. Our job is to reduce the possibility of injury to our Protectees through accurate assessment of the level of risk in every environment by the use of intelligence evaluation and, where the incidence of violence or risk becomes too great, to be able to remove our Protectees from the area safely.

To assist us in our responsibility, we have had the ability to call upon other forces in the Government for assistance, and, recently, this ability was made statutory by passage of PL 90–331, on July 6, 1968, giving us,

among other things, the authority to request the other
Federal departments and agencies for assistance in the
performance of all our protective duties under Section
3056, Title 18, United States Code. The Secret Service
feels, therefore, that it has the entire resources of the
Federal Government at its disposal to aid in carrying out
its awesome protective responsibilities and that any equipment necessary can and will be provided.

2. The Symbolic Content of the Office of the President, Other Governmental Institutions, and Assassinations

The relationship between political office and assassination
has been examined in Chapter 1. It appears that offices of high
visibility, substantial power, and symbolic (as well as actual)
importance tend to attract the attention of potential assassins.
The presidency provides the most prominent case in point.
Symbolically, the President is chief of state—the living representative of the continuity in American life, the embodiment
of the political traditions of the nation, and the principal
representative of the country to foreign nations. The President
combines this aspect with the real political and legislative
power reserved in many countries for the national political
leader. The American presidency combines the responsibilities
of the chief of state, a ceremonial position in many nations,
with that of the political leader (Prime Minister in parliamentary systems).

The President is also easily the most highly publicized and
personalized leader in the government. Few aspects of his
private and none of his public life are totally free from public
scrutiny. A quick comparison of the media attention provided
the President with that accorded the Cabinet, legislative leaders, Supreme Court justices, or state officeholders indicates the
inordinate amount of popular attention given to this particular
officeholder. Beyond the actual powers of the office, which are
real enough, the tendency is to direct attention toward this
particular man as the prime mover behind government events.
This, in turn, invites the attention of those who would change
the course of policy by a single violent act or punish the
government for some real or imagined wrong.

The presidency is both the fulcrum of power and the center

of controversy in American politics. The powers attributed to the President's office in the popular mind are probably greater than any position could actually contain. One may speculate that the greater the emphasis on centralizing power upwards within the system, and the greater the emphasis on personalizing it by projecting it to the incumbent of one particular office, the greater the propensity to focus upon the presidency. The phenomenon is not necessarily limited to the attraction of potential assassins. The great attention focused on the presidency is also manifested in the attention given by groups seeking to influence the nomination process.

The Presidency as Symbol[17]

The various institutions of government have different symbolic content in terms of the response they evoke among the governed. The United States, like all political communities, has a special blending of governmental institutions and symbols. Symbolic institutions, such as the presidency, the Congress, and the Supreme Court, were consciously crafted by the writers of the Constitution to draw together a diversity of political communities, each with its own symbolic accouterments. The party system was not consciously fashioned by those drafting the Constitution, but the system is firmly imbedded in law and practice as an institution in the process of government in the United States.

Preeminent among the symbolic institutions of American government is the presidency. Although its historical place in relation to the other two branches of government has fluctuated, today the presidency is a more powerful symbol than either the Supreme Court or the Congress. There are many reasons for this, not the least of which is the presidential form of government itself. Although the writers of the Constitution agreed that the head of state was to be elected by some notables called "electors," the popular election of the President is today considered to be a fact of American political life. He is, therefore, the only nationally elected official, and this fact is much more important than its mere textbook recitation would indicate.

Not only is the President the only nationally elected official, but the executive is the only branch of government headed by a single person. This fact alone makes the office a focus of great interest. The most disinterested citizen can, even with a minimum of effort, symbolize the government in the person of the President. Indeed, studies of the way American children acquire political knowledge indicate that the presidency is one of the first symbols to have meaning for them.

Theodore Roosevelt once said, "A President has a great chance; his position is almost that of a king and a prime minister rolled into one," and Alexander Hamilton remarked, "You nor I, my friend, may not live to see the day, but most assuredly it will come, when every vital interest of the state will be merged in the all-absorbing question of who shall be the next President."[48]

It is notable that the constitutional provisions regarding the presidency are few in number and lack specifics of detail. Fundamentally, the interpretation of the presidency has followed two main lines. One theory holds that, without a specific grant of constitutional or statutory authority, the President should not act. This theory is frequently associated with the view held by President Taft. Another and totally different view holds that the President should act or exercise his authority and influence unless there is a clear prohibition against the exercise of authority or influence either by statute or by the Constitution.

Whether the brevity of the provisions concerning the presidency was intended as a limitation on that office or a conscious invitation to expand the influence of the office is largely an academic question. In the nuclear age, the activist view is not only the fashionable view, but rather the view that seems destined to prevail.

In a provocative article, Gottfried Dietze points out that there is a parallel development between what he calls the aggrandizement of the presidency and the concept of the President as activist. Dietze's argument is that the aggrandizement of the presidency resulted from the fact that the office has become the symbol of democracy.

> Significantly, this aggrandizement, which by the standards of the Founders can only be called revolutionary was most obvious during the most revolutionary periods of American Constitutional development, mainly during the administrations of Jackson, Lincoln, and "progressive" presidents, periods that were characterized by a growth of democracy.[49]

In his argument, Dietze points out that the election of Jackson by almost universal male suffrage increased the power of the presidency. He says, moreover, that Lincoln, the first President to be assassinated, was the heir to this new power.

He further argues that Presidents in the twentieth century added to this power which had its source in the democratization of the office. Dietze writes that in the twentieth century, the President assumed the function of chief legislator as well as Chief Executive. He points out that,

> The increases of assassinations ever since the aggrandizement of the Presidency became obvious makes us wonder. Whereas before the Civil War, none of 15 Presidents was killed, 4 of 20 have been assassinated since then. We bewail the fact that over 11 percent of American Presidents were assassinated. A more proper evaluation of this dilemma would be offered by saying that the percentage of Presidents killed was zero before the aggrandizement of the Presidency had become conspicuous, and rose to as much as 20 percent afterward. Furthermore, it should give us pause that in recent decades, the only objects of assassination were personalities such as Franklin Roosevelt, Truman, and Kennedy, whose strong desires to carry out ambitious social programs made the Presidency appear in its full strength, while Presidents under whom the institution appeared relatively weak such as Harding, Coolidge, Hoover, and Eisenhower, were not objects.[50]

Dietze's article was written before the assassination of Robert Kennedy. But it is reasonably clear that Dietze would regard Robert Kennedy and his view of the presidential office as similar to the activist concept.

The Press and the Presidential Symbol

Dietze's argument is not flawless. It ignores the absence of the attacks upon strong Presidents such as Wilson, and the attacks upon such Presidents as Garfield and McKinley (see section A). His point, however, regarding the historical development of the presidency and the collateral increase in assassination attempts on candidates for and incumbents of the office bears close scrutiny. An important factor paralleling the frequency of assassination attempts against incumbents of the office and candidates for the office has to do with the role of mass communication. In their discussion of the presidency, Polsby and Wildavsky indicate a significant change in the treatment of the presidency by the mass media. They point out that one of the historical factors in the rise of the President as a symbol in American political life is the relationship between the President as the political leader and his political followers as it is filtered through the mass media.[51] They feel that the great mass of citizens is not, in the newspaperman's judgment, so gripped by political issues that their interest can be sustained without the leaven of human interest.

Their point is that the news media in this country are no longer controlled by partisan considerations. There is, in their view, an absence of a rigid partisan tone in the depiction of the everyday activities of the presidency. The emphasis today is on objective news reporting. Therefore, there is a tendency to take the strictly partisan aspect of the presidency out of discussions of that office and to introduce instead what is called the sacerdotal role of the presidency. The President then becomes a kind of guardian of national morale and, as such, the office becomes more of a national symbol. The incumbent of the office is discussed in terms of his private life in such a way which tends to make him "the American." In other words, the President becomes the personification of the American national character. He is no longer the partisan occupant of the institutional office but is rather the symbol of American society.

This also means that for the audience the personality of the news object (in this case the President) takes on a new dimension. It is now possible to know the man in office almost as an intimate, or at least to view him as an intimate.

The consequences of this fact are enormous. The roles of the President as symbol of the government, as personification of the national character, and as leader of the United States in world affairs are now coupled with the role of the President as a figure evoking emotions not unlike those which intimates evoke in one's own circle of familial and social contacts.

The position of the presidency in the roles described above makes him highly vulnerable to those individuals in the society who seek out public objects upon which to displace the hatred born of private motives. This displacement of hatred can be and usually is rationalized in terms of the public interest. Harold Lasswell notes:

> The prominence of hate in politics suggests that we may find that the most important motive is a repressed and powerful hatred of authority, a hatred which has come to partial expression and repression in relation to the father, at least in the function of biological progenitor and sociological father.[52]

Lasswell's early study gives case histories of some who have turned to politics as a means of dealing with their unhappy early lives. The highly potent symbols of government offer ready made objects for displacement.

While the reader may agree that the presidency is the leading symbol against which an assassin might act, other political institutions such as Congress and the Supreme Court, also have symbolic impact. However, these offices differ substantially from that of President.

The Supreme Court

The Supreme Court is a symbol that competes with the presidency. The Court has several important features that have made it the focus of emotional discharge. Antagonism against the Court, often vociferous in character, is not new in American political history. The Court represents an authority symbol almost unsurpassed in elevation. Many of its members tend to be older men, a factor potentially productive of heightened reaction in some personalities. Its decisions count—that is, the Court structures the rules of social reactions in a real way. What it does makes a difference. In these respects, it is similar to the presidency. Moreover, in recent years the Court has become more personalized symbolically as the Warren court —witness the "Impeach Earl Warren" campaigns in response in large measure to a unanimous decision of the Court in favor of school desegregation.

Nonetheless, the emotional discharge evoked by the Court has remained physically harmless. There are two important reasons for this. First, the Court is a multiple body; no single individual dominates. It is difficult to displace one's feelings against a symbol composed of units, though not an impossibility. Second, and parallel with the first feature, is the remoteness of the Court. Unlike occupants of the White House, members of the Court have not been personalized by the mass media. It is difficult to focus on individual members of the Court; with few exceptions they have eschewed publicity.

The tradition of an aesthetic Court is seldom violated by its members. The mass media find it difficult to deal with the Court the same way they deal with the presidency. The Court is a more difficult symbol to convey and to personalize.

A third feature of the Court is its distance from the citizenry. Its members are not elected by the people; there have been no changes in the process of selecting members of the Court, as there have been in selecting the President. The physical contact with the masses that characterizes aspirants for the office of President is almost totally absent for members of the Court. Supreme Court members do not campaign, nor do they go on public fence-mending tours while in office. They are therefore relatively immune to potential violence.

A gradual personalization of the Court in the person of its Chief Justice, however, may be a trend which might expose at least the Chief Justice to a greater danger of assassination. To the extent that the Court becomes "the Warren court" rather than "The Supreme Court," the risk of assassination increases.

Congress

Congress, the branch of government most freighted with symbolic apparatus, should be a serious rival to the presidency in evocative symbolic power. The ritual, rules, and domicile of the Congress combine to reproduce tradition and the majesty of authority and legitimacy. However, several factors render the Congress much less effective as an evocative symbol than the presidency. The Senate has known violence among its own members, and the House was the victim of an attack by Puerto Rican nationalists. Congress is a much more public body than the Supreme Court. Indeed, until the Puerto Rican nationalist attack, little in the way of security was provided for its members during sessions of the Congress. The Congress is, however, a large body of many members. In addition, it is a body whose activities are widely viewed as having results in only a very indirect fashion.

The decisions Congress makes affect people, but it is difficult to trace one of its legislative acts to the final consequence for an individual. That activities of Congress have consequences is not in dispute. However, the fact that the execution of authority is divorced from the legitimating function of Congress makes what the Congress does seem more obscure and ambiguous to the public. Congressmen do not have red telephones to the Kremlin, they do not call out federal marshals, blockade Cuba, or sell fighter aircraft to Israel.

The picture presented by the Congress is made more obscure and ambiguous by the frequent crossing of party lines by members of Congress and by the congressional committee system. A majority party leading the Congress to action against an embattled minority is seldom the picture presented to the public. Dramatic showdown votes on significant matters seldom come to the public because of the nature of congressional rules and practices within the committee system.

Five-hundred and thirty-five individuals are difficult to seize upon collectively as an object against which to vent hatred or any other emotion.

The inability of the press to deal with the Congress as a body is reflected in its presentation of congressional news. The smaller of the two legislative bodies, the Senate, receives much more publicity than the House of Representatives. Individual senators are more newsworthy than their colleagues in the House. This is true not only because the Senate deals with foreign affairs and is the seedbed of future Presidents, but also because the House of Representatives is simply too large to be effectively represented by the press. After all, reporters must deal with symbols that are conveyable—objects that can be grasped by their readers and listeners with a minimum of intellectual effort.

It is difficult to personalize the Congress either by the press or by an individual. Because it is difficult to chart the activity and movement of the Congress as a body, it is even more difficult to trace the action of an individual congressman. The vagueness and ambiguity which surround the function of Congress also surround the function of the congressman; it is probably for this reason that the individual congressman is seldom an object of political violence.

Summary

For reasons we have discussed, no symbol in the United States is more potent than the presidency. Repressed hatred of father, brother, sister, or mother could easily be transferred to this one powerful symbol. What many assassination historians regard as the work of an unbalanced mind may in reality be the work of a mind using the symbolic content of government institutions for its own psychic needs. To say that this is not in part a political act is erroneous; much of what goes on in politics has a similar etiology.

Whether or not the obstacles and impediments which an individual thinks block him in his attainments are social, familial, or political in origin, the highly potent symbol of the presidency could be viewed by the pathological (as well as the neurotic) individual as a source of his inner difficulties. In fact, it is common to see public policies and practices described as alleged sources of personal defeat and unattained achievements. In his preface to Svend Ranulf's *Moral Indignation and Middle Class Psychology*, Lasswell observes:

> The rage which is provoked in erratic acts of deprivation in family, school, and neighborhood is only partly inhibited. There are therefore strong dispositions to escape from internal tensions by "acting out" instead of relying on neurotic symptoms. Among the more extreme types are persons who seek to avenge themselves against fate by committing individual acts of violence. A lone wolf assassin—like Oswald—is more often an indignant, desperate and alienated moralist than a cautious calculator of competing plans of life.[53]

The illustrations can be proliferated. The point is that there are more than a few Americans who, unable to resolve inner psychic disorder, turn to behavior which may have political consequences, and tend to focus upon the most highly potent political symbol in the United States, the office of the presidency.

3. Campaign Style and the Risk of Assassination

Because of the intense symbolically induced focus upon the office of the President, and because the President is widely exposed as a target for the potential assassin during campaign or campaign-related activity, here we examine campaign style and the risk of assassination.

An obvious strategy to reduce the risk of presidential assassination is to limit the access of assassins to their targets by restricting and controlling the public exposure of the President and presidential candidates. Between campaigns, the President may minimize his exposure as a target by carefully choosing speaking opportunities, public appearances, means of travel to engagements, and the extent to which he gives advance notice of his movements. Tight security can result if a President desires.

The presidential campaign, however, presents countervailing considerations.

The ideal from the standpoint of protecting the President from assassination would be to project the candidate to the public through electronic and printed media so that every communication from the candidate could be made from a location which could be made physically secure. The candidate, however, must win votes, and in recent campaigns the candidates have apparently felt the need, in spite of the availability of television and printed media, to expose themselves physically to the voters through speeches, receptions, hand-shaking tours, motorcades, and the like.

We assume that such exposure increases the risk of assassination and examine here possible strategies to reduce that risk and weigh the merits of such strategies.

There are several different questions implicit in any discussion of presidential campaign style which should be kept in mind, quite apart from the risk of assassination: (1) what kind of campaign will produce the greatest number of votes for the candidate? (2) what kind of campaign will best inform the voters of the relevant issues so that they can—if they choose to follow the campaign—make the most intelligent disposition of their vote? (3) what kind of campaign is most apt to inform the candidate how the voters feel on important issues; that is, which can best inform the candidate how to cast *his* vote on the issues confronting the nation, and (4) what kind of campaign would produce amongst the general voters the greatest sense of legitimacy or participation in the political process? The best answer to any one question may not be consistent with the best answer to others.

A fifth issue is often raised in discussion of campaigns and is set forth here in order to be rejected as specious: What kind of campaign would be most dignified? Hoopla and ballyhoo have characterized American presidential campaigns from an early date. The William Henry Harrison campaign of 1840 ("Tippecanoe and Tyler, too") is credited with being the first of the breed. Every campaign since then has drawn, with some variations, on the mass campaign—the buttons and campaign paraphernalia, the large rallies, oversimplified slogans, torchlight parades, and the like.[54] To the extent that this aspect of a campaign is a quadrennial Oktoberfest, it is a harmless folk ritual. To the extent that it evidences and encourages a popular sense of participation in the electoral process, it is desirable. To the extent that the carnival atmosphere overwhelms the serious aspects of the campaign and interferes with communication and discussion of the relative merits of the candidates, it may be viewed as undesirable. Dignity alone in a President has no independent value. By all reports, the man who brought the greatest dignity of manner to the presidency was Warren G. Harding. Lincoln, on the other hand, was widely criticized as lacking dignity.

No matter what we may consider the best campaign style, the overriding consideration will be the first issue: What style of campaign is calculated to get the most votes? We can point out, however, that the effectiveness of whistlestopping and the virtue of the candidate's physical presence in as many different locations as possible may be vastly overrated. The belief in the value of such a campaign style is apparently based upon the 1948 campaign in which Truman, after having campaigned vigorously in whistlestop style, emerged the upset winner against the do-nothing campaign of Dewey. Other factors may well have determined the outcome.[55] Dewey in 1944, Wilkie in 1940, and Landon in 1936 campaigned more than Roosevelt. Smith campaigned more than Hoover in 1928, and Hughes more than Wilson in 1916. Nixon in 1960 logged half again as many miles as Kennedy in what in retrospect is perceived to be an ill-advised attempt to visit every state. Goldwater campaigned more than Johnson in 1964.[56]

We are tempted to conclude that it is the quality more than the quantity of personal exposure which counts. The Kennedy-Nixon television debate in 1960 (it is widely assumed), helped boost the Kennedy candidacy while there was no physical exposure of the candidate whatsoever and a very minimum risk of assassination.

A judgment concerning the kind of campaign that would

most inform the voter of the relevant issues turns on the question of what kinds of issues are relevant to the choice of President, and is a more subtle problem than might appear. Presumably the informed voter in 1916 cast his ballot for Woodrow Wilson as the man who kept America out of the war. That was Wilson's campaign slogan. In 1932, the informed voter cast his ballot for Franklin Roosevelt presumably in part because Roosevelt favored a balanced budget. The informed voter in 1964 learned of Goldwater's position that, if elected, he might commit as many as 250,000 troops to the Vietnam conflict.

The point is that forces beyond the control of the President may force him to take positions opposite to or highly inconsistent with what the informed voter could have learned during the campaign. It may well be that the most relevant issues upon which a voter can inform himself are revealed in the conduct of the candidate under the stress of campaigning. It may be that a candidate's personality and qualities of leadership, as revealed in the hustle and bustle of personal campaign appearances and in his reactions and responses to "irresponsible" attack and the like, are far more relevant than his present position as revealed in a series of formal, highly polished, ghostwritten speeches or position papers on the issues as they then appear. We do not ignore the obvious virtue of reasoned exposition of such issues; we point to other factors of possible crucial importance that would be submerged in a campaign exclusively devoted to a so-called "reasoned analysis" of the issues.

Campaigning is a two-way education. The candidate not only informs the people, but the people inform the candidate. It is said that when then Senator John F. Kennedy was campaigning in the West Virginia primary, he was genuinely shocked and moved by the poverty he saw. The candidate translated this into legislative programs after his return.

Finally, as this Report has demonstrated, it is of critical importance to the problem of reducing the incidence of political violence and assassination that an overwhelming sense of the legitimacy of our governmental institutions be maintained. We believe that people feel more of a sense of personal involvement when the candidate is physically present, though distant, than if he be present, even in a revealing close-up, through the medium of television. For example, though the money goes into the same coffers and for the same purposes, the anticipated physical presence of the President or presidential candidate can sell far more tickets to a party fund-raising dinner and at a far higher price than a warm personal telegram from the President or even his appearance on closed-circuit TV. The sense of personal participation brought by the physical presence of the President is real and must be weighed in considering alternatives to present campaign styles.

In light of the foregoing, we will examine the following areas and make suggestions with respect to: (1) the use of television in lieu of appearances in person; '(2) campaign funding; and (3) the candidate selection process.

We do not suggest that candidates eliminate, or even severely restrict personal appearances. We believe that personal interaction with individual voters, even on a necessarily superficial basis, is a valuable mutual education for both the candidate and the voter.

We have also pointed out, however, that history does not bear out the theory that an attempt to appear in person in front of as many voters in as many regions of the country as possible is effective as a vote-getting strategy. A common-sense and reasonably paced selection of personal appearances is quite likely to be far more effective, not only from the vote-gathering point of view, but also from the point of view of the physical protection of the President.[57] A more limited selection of localities, made in advance, can aid the Secret Service immeasurably.

Television is not a cure-all for the defects of the present campaign system. Recent campaigns have seen efforts to package candidates much like commercial products. The selling aspect of the campaign, commercializing the "image" a contender projects, can overwhelm and supplant more relevant discussions of policy and philosophy. Styling "plugs" like toothpaste commercials for maximum impact may oversimplify and distort the message. The famous "daisy" commercial of the 1964 election campaign is an example.[58]

Television, on the other hand, has great potential for introducing the candidate and his views to the general public in a fully reasoned manner, not in the debased form of an advertisement. One factor which compels campaign managers to select short, high-impact television spots that may be misleading or uninformative is the enormous cost of television time.

The possibility of granting free television time to presidential candidates during the eight weeks preceding the election should be seriously explored. Such free time could be made available only in specified blocks so that the candidates would not be motivated to break up their allotted free time into uninformative advertisements. The candidates would be able to select the format most congenial to a full presentation of themselves and their positions to the public. As pointed out above, such television appearances would entail the least possible risk of assassination.

There are two obvious problems. An enormous cost would be imposed directly on the broadcasting industry, although the public would presumably benefit from the improvement of the quality of the campaign. This time could be treated as the taking of any other property for public use, and the broadcasting companies could be compensated for its fair market value. On the other hand, the public has always asserted—and properly so—a great regulatory interest in the use of television and other broadcasting media. It might not be offensive to fair play to require the three major networks to donate the time in spite of the costs involved. Under the latter alternative, investigation should be made as to whether the most sensible approach would be to require one network to carry a given speech while allowing the others to show commercial programs, thus splitting the burden three ways, or to require all three networks to carry the same speech simultaneously. Simultaneous presentation would eliminate any unfair advantage to the networks not carrying the speech, and would also, in effect, make it more likely that campaign information would get to the public. Previous campaign experience indicates that the public would overwhelmingly prefer to listen to soap operas than to major addresses by a potential Chief Executive. For example, according to the ratings, Goldwater on the evening of October 29, 1964, drew the largest listening audience of the campaign— larger than any audience drawn by Lyndon Johnson. The rival network at the same time was showing "Peyton Place," which drew almost twice as many viewers as the campaign speech.[59]

The other major problem is with minor parties and the "equal time" provision of the law. Many commenters suggest that the political stability of the United States is attributable in large measure to the fact that its political scene is dominated by two major parties, neither one of which has fundamental philosophic or ideological differences. Suggestions that our political institutions be modified to allow for greater participation of minority parties should be given careful and critical attention. Third-party movements have been a relatively common phenomenon in the United States, and such parties should be given a reasonable platform in the marketplace of ideas. One solution would be to limit free time to those parties that qualify to appear on the ballots of a minimum number of states. Another would be to limit free time to the party that obtained at least five percent of the popular vote in the preceding presidential election. A combination of the above two proposals could be used. These suggestions would give reasonable access to minor parties, while eliminating splinter groups with no practical expectation of substantial response at the polls.

The enormous expenditures required to conduct a presidential campaign also place constraints upon campaigns which may lead to a distortion of the campaign process. The possible impact of the high cost of television advertising has already been discussed. The need for money also requires the physical presence of the candidate at many fund-raising occasions, presumably increasing his exposure as a target for assassins, and channeling his energies away from more generally informative campaigning. Serious exploration should be taken regarding the feasibility of public support for presidential campaigns.

The problems, however, are formidable. No matter how much is donated from the public treasury, parties can always use more money and would still be motivated to continue fund-raising activities. Thus, demands would still be made upon the candidate.

A solution might be to make campaign contributions illegal. But, to forbid the public to make political contributions would destroy a tangible and important form of political participation. Further, the practical constraints imposed upon the conduct of the party and its candidate by the necessity to seek funds should not be lightly abandoned, even though the candidate must ultimately be responsible to the public at the polls.

Another difficult problem would be the division of money, not only between the two major parties, but also among third and minor parties in a manner that preserves the stability of our two-party system, yet gives healthy opportunity for challenge and innovation.

Finally, consideration might be given to reevaluating the whole selection process, including the national conventions, employed in determining the contenders for presidential office. We do not recommend eliminating state primaries or party conventions. State primaries and party methods for selecting delegates to national conventions provide a flexibility in the nominating process and a generally stiff test of a politician's acumen. Nonetheless, efforts should be instituted to insure that the party organs selecting delegates for the national conventions are representative of their party's membership and open to influence from the party's base. It would appear reasonable that all states presently offering presidential primaries make these the vehicles for selection of delegates to the national conventions. The voter's decision would be mandatory in convention voting. The Oregon, Wisconsin, and Massachusetts primary laws could serve as models in these regards. Finally, in relation to delegate selection, all delegates to a national convention should be chosen in the year the convention is held. All party elements should be given fair and equal access to influence these selection decisions. This principle, more than the specific proposals, should represent the criteria to be employed in evaluating delegate-choice procedures. Any proposal that would increase the representativeness of the selection process and the accountability of the chosen delegates to party members, broadly defined, should be given consideration. Also the extent to which the national conventions themselves could become orderly vehicles for deciding among potential nominees should be evaluated.[60]

Changes in the present form of presidential campaigns could lessen a presidential candidate's vulnerability to assassination, at the same time increasing the responsiveness of the system's processes to the social demands of its citizens.

G. The Presidency and Assassination: Suggestions and Conclusions

The wide attention the President receives makes him a logical target—if anything about an assassination act can be said to be logical—for those wishing to punish a nation, to strike out at a symbolically powerful figure whom they project as the source of their grievances, to drastically alter governmental policy, or to draw attention to themselves as the author of a memorable event. In addition, the current methods by which presidential candidates seek nomination and election provide many opportunities for assassins. We advance in this section several proposals for reducing the risk of assassination in these circumstances.

To reduce the wide attention given the presidency, greater efforts should be made to develop and publicize the many centers of power within the federal government. The limitations placed on the President and the means of influencing governmental directions by participating in local, county, and State decisionmaking or, on the national level, the alternatives provided by administrative agencies, the courts, and the Congress should be emphasized. This approach portrays a more sophisticated and complex network of governmental institutions, but one more responsive to individual or group needs. It also directs attention away from the presidency as the single, crucial point in political decisionmaking.

To the extent that real social grievances predispose groups and individuals to violence, including assassination, an understanding of the overlapping decision-making centers in government and the agencies directly concerned with a problem could lead to quicker remedial action from the appropriate authorities. Failing this, sanction could be directed specifically against the agency or individual involved—voting against incumbents of particular offices, encouraging legislative overruling of administrative actions, communications directed to superiors, and united, organized resistance to policy decisions. The groups who appreciate the complexities of American government and who can organize to promote their ends will benefit the most from policy decisions. A similar understanding among individuals and groups who believe themselves disadvantaged would serve to channel the struggle for economic and social rewards through the established institutional forms. This would remove the struggle from the violence of the streets or the violent act directed against a symbolic individual or office. This latter approach places conflict within the context of governing institutions and makes it amenable to resolution within the more traditional political structures and values of the nation.

An argument of this nature assumes that the governing institutions of a democracy are open to all groups and are receptive to their problems. To the extent that these assumptions are incorrect, the focus of the country could profitably be directed toward sensitizing democratic political institutions to the interests they are intended to represent. The alternative, the projection of hopes and frustrations onto the presidency, does not describe the realities of the political system or serve the needs of groups who desire to redress what they consider to be inequities.

To reduce the focus on the presidency, to increase the sense of legitimacy of our political agencies and decisionmaking processes by making them more representative, and to reduce exposure of the President by altering presidential campaign practices, this Task Force offers the following recommendations:

1. The Presidency

1. A greater emphasis in press and media treatments on the limitations implicit in the office.

2. Less media exploitation of the personal life of the President and his family.

3. More attention focused on the working nature of the office, i.e., the specific objectives the President is charged to achieve, the resources at his command, and the obstacles in his path. The emphasis should be on the corporate and business aspects of the position rather than on the glamorization and projection of personal attributes.

4. A better understanding of the independence of the bureaucracy, its resistance to change, and its role in framing and executing policy decisions.

5. We do not suggest that the President should isolate himself completely from the people, but he should give consideration, during non-election years, to minimizing exposure of himself as a target by—

(a) Carefully limiting and choosing his public appearances and speaking opportunities.

(b) Using devices such as televised press conferences, televised speeches, and closed circuit television as substitutes for public appearances.

(c) Limiting advance notice of his movements.

2. The Congress

1.   The *role* of the Congress in policymaking needs precise, detailed elaboration. At present, it is poorly understood and its contribution neglected, while examples of its obstructionist influence are well publicized.

2.   The *structure* of the Congress as it relates to policymaking needs clarification and simplification. In particular, the following could be better understood:

> (a) The division of labor and responsibility within the system for framing policy, which would direct attention to the rationale underlying the committee system and the role of institutional officials in promoting legislation.
>
> (b) The structure and influence of the party system in determining committee personnel and promoting legislation, and the congruence of party and institutional factors in promoting legislation.
>
> (c) The complex relationship between the administrative and legislative branches in attempting to achieve policy objectives.

3. The Political Party System

1.   The role of primaries in nominating presidential candidates needs reexamination. In particular, the promise that victories in primary elections insure nominations should be reevaluated. It would appear reasonable that the states holding presidential primaries would require the delegates selected by those procedures to vote for the primary winner. The Oregon, Nebraska, Wisconsin, or Massachusetts primary laws in this regard could serve as standards.

2.   The selection of all delegates to national conventions should be made within one year of those conventions. Party rules should require representation of all party factions in delegate-selection procedures. These selection procedures should be made as accessible to and representative of party members as possible.

3.   The conventions themselves should make certain that representation on committees such as resolutions and membership adequately and fairly encompass all aspects of the party base.

4. Restrictions on voting, such as lengthy residence requirements and inconvenient registration dates, should be minimized.

5. All government—local, state and federal—should assume responsibility for registration. Two possibilities are proposed: (1) the local authorities, through door-to-door canvassing, could enroll voters on permanent registration rolls; or (2) the federal government could issue registration cards, similar to social security cards, qualifying the holder for voting in any locality.

4. Campaign Methods

During election years, presidential candidates should use television, radio, and the printed media extensively, and limit public appearances or speeches. To encourage such limitation, we believe that the Congress should enact laws providing the following:

> (a) Two hours per week (in blocks of at least half-hour segments) of free television time for presidential candidates during the eight weeks prior to the election for candidates of parties which (1) are on the ballot in forty or more states or (2) received five percent or more of the popular vote in the previous presidential election.
>
> (b) Serious consideration to providing campaign funds to minor and major parties on an equitable basis compatible with a free political system.

5. The Federal System Generally

1. Greater emphasis must be placed on the decentralized nature of governing institutions and the many local, state and federal agencies having concurrent jurisdiction in a particular area. The American governing system is pluralistic and provides a number of access points for those wishing to influence policy. An emphasis on their availability would serve to acquaint the citizen with responsive problem-solving agencies of direct consequence to him. Such emphasis would realistically describe the operating political structures within the United States and would serve to deemphasize a perception of the

system as highly centralized and essentially monolithic, with ultimate power residing in the office of the presidency.

2.   An office similar to that of the Scandanavian *ombudsman* should be created at the federal level to represent the complaints of people dealing with federal agencies. This would be beneficial to those with problems and would draw critical attention away from the office of President.

6. Conclusion

Presidential assassinations have not been the product of rational political motive. Although each assassination was felt as a personal loss by the populace, the assassinations have produced no fundamental disruption of our democratic institutions. No substantial changes in the direction of public policy, since the assassination of President Lincoln, are traceable directly to any assassination. Assassination has been a personal, not political tragedy for the nation. This will remain true so long as ours is a government of institutions under law and not of men.

References

1.   These short descriptions were drafted by the staff and based upon data drawn for the most part from Robert Donovan, *The Assassins* (New York: Harper Bros., 1952); Donald W. Hastings, M.D., "The Psychiatry of Presidential Assassination," *The Journal-Lancet,* vol. 85, March, pp. 93–100, April, pp. 157–162, May, pp. 189–192, July, pp. 294–301, 1965; Charles E. Rosenberg, *The Trial of the Assassin Guiteau* (Chicago: University of Chicago Press, 1952); and papers by Task Force consultant, psychiatrist Lawrence Z. Freedman, M.D., and Professor Rita J. Simon.
2.   *New York Daily Tribune,* Apr. 14, 1865, p. 4.
3.   Donovan, *op. cit.,* footnote 1, p. 15.
4.   *Ibid.,* p. 20.
5.   Hastings, *op. cit.,* footnote 1, p. 162.
6.   Donovan, *op. cit.,* footnote 1, p. 97.
7.   *New York Herald,* Sept. 12, 1901, p. 3, col. 2.
8.   *Washington Post,* Sept. 20, 1901, p. 6.
9.   "We should war with relentless efficiency not only against anarchists, but against all active and passive sympathizers

with anarchists—both the advocates of anarchy and the apologists for anarchism were morally accessory to murder before the fact."

10. Donovan, *op. cit.,* footnote 1, p. 107.
11. *Ibid.,* p. 143.
12. *Ibid.,* p. 145.
13. *Ibid.,* p. 131.
14. *Ibid.,* p. 168.
15. *New York Times,* Nov. 5, 1950, p. 2E, sect IV, col. 1.
16. *Ibid.,* Nov. 2, 1950, p. 16, col. 2.
17. *New York Times,* Apr. 7, 1951, p. 32.
18. *New Republic,* vol. 123, Nov. 13, 1950, p. 6.
19. *Commonweal,* vol. 53, Nov. 17, 1950, p. 133.
20. Donovan, *op. cit.,* footnote 1, p. 204.
21. *Ibid.,* p. 204.
22. As this volume goes to press, Sirhan has been convicted by the State of California and sentenced to death. His appeal is underway now.
23. The factual data herein are drawn down from Donovan, *op. cit.,* footnote 1: Hastings, *op. cit.,* footnote 1, and a paper by Task Force consultant, psychiatrist Lawrence Z. Freedman, M.D.
24. Hastings, *op. cit.,* footnote 1, p. 300.
25. Because his trial was pending, we excluded from this and all other sections of this report any consideration of the personality or motivations of Sirhan Bishara Sirhan, the alleged assassin of Senator Robert F. Kennedy.
26. Doris Y. Wilkinson, "The Political Assassin and His Primary Group Relationships," a paper submitted to the Commission.
27. See, "Political Assassination and Status Incongruence: A Sociological Interpretation," a paper submitted to the Commission by Dr. Wilkinson.
28. David A. Rothstein, "Presidential Assassination Syndrome," *Archives of General Psychiatry,* vol. 2, 1964, p. 245, and vol. 15, 1966, p. 260; and Joseph A. Sebastiani and James L. Foy, "Psychotic Visitors to the White House," *American Journal of Psychiatry,* vol. 122, pp. 679–686, March 1965. The discussion in this section draws heavily on the report prepared for the Task Force by Lawrence Z. Freedman, M.D.
29. See Sebastiani and Foy, *op. cit.,* footnote 28.
30. This section consists primarily of portions of a paper submitted to the Commission by Lawrence Z. Freedman.
31. This hypothesis is drawn from "Self-Concepts: The Actual Self and the Ideal Self," by Jerry A. Gaines and Dr. Doris Y. Wilkinson, a paper submitted to the Commission.
32. The materials in this section are taken from the study done by Lawrence Z. Freedman for the Task Force.

33. H. H. Alexander, *The Life of Guiteau and . . . The Trial of Guiteau for Assassinating President Garfield* (Philadelphia: National Publishing Co., 1882); quoted by Hastings, *op. cit.,* footnote 1.

34. Richard Warren Lewis, *The Scavengers and Critics of the Warren Report* (New York: The Delacorte Press, 1967).

35. The survey was designed by staff members of the Commission and consultants and administered by Louis Harris & Associates. The nature of the survey is discussed in more detail in Chapter 4, section C.

36. Sheldon Levy.

37. A number of the most relevant of these research pieces are drawn together in Bradly S. Greenberg and Edwin B. Parker, eds., *The Kennedy Assassination and the American Public* (Stanford, Stanford University Press, 1965), and Martha Wolfenstein and Gilbert Kliman, eds., *Children and the Death of a President* (Garden City, N.Y.: Doubleday, 1965).

38. Wolfenstein and Kliman, *op. cit.,* Footnote 37.

39. Administered by James W. Clark and John W. Soule.

40. David Sears, "Effects of the Assassination of President Kennedy on Political Partisanship," in Greenberg and Parker, *op. cit.,* Footnote 37.

41. Christopher J. Hurn and Mark Messer, "Grief and Rededication," in Greenberg and Parker, *op. cit.,* Footnote 37.

42. This section on the impact of the presidential assassination in the United States is drawn from a paper by Murray Edelman and Rita James Simon, "Presidential Assassinations: Their Meaning and Impact on American Society," *Ethics,* vol. 79, April 1969, pp. 191–221.

43. *Ibid.,* Professors Edelman and Simon argue that the hard position had the effect of restoring the Southern aristocracy to power, cutting out the possibility of an indigenous Southern liberal movement, and ultimately exacerbating racial tensions.

44. Warren Report (app. VII), pp. 504–515.

45. Warren Report, pp. 425–469.

46. *Ibid.,* pp. 454–468.

47. This section is an edited portion of a paper submitted to the Commission by Clinton E. and Judith H. Grimes, entitled, "Personality, Partisanship, and Assassination."

48. *Ibid.*

49. Gottfried Dietze, "Will the Presidency Incite Assassination?" *Ethics,* Oct. 1969, vol. 76, No. 1, p. 19, quoted in Herman Finer, *The Presidency: Crisis and Regeneration* (Chicago: University of Chicago Press, 1960), p. 40.

50. Dietze, *Ibid.,* pp. 22–23.

51. Nelson Polsby and A. Wildavsky, *Presidential Elections* (New York: Charles Scribner's Sons, 1968).

52. Harold Lasswell, *Psychopathology and Politics* (New York: Viking Press, 1968), pp. 75–76.
53. Svend Ranulf, *Moral Indignation and Middle Class Psychology* (New York: Schocken Books, Inc., 1964), p. xiii.
54. Jules Abels, *The Degeneration of our Presidential Election* (New York: Macmillan, 1968).
55. This campaign is interpreted by William J. Crotty, "The Nature and Meaning of Public Opinion" in W. J. Crotty, ed., *Public Opinion and Politics* (New York: Holt, Rinehart & Winston, 1969), pp. 24–30.
56. Abels, *op. cit.,* footnote 54, pp. 34–35.
57. A reasoned argument for such campaigns is made in Stanley Kelly, *Political Campaigning* (Washington, D.C.: The Brookings Institution, 1960). More generally, relevant discussions of campaign practices include Nelson W. Polsby and Aaron B. Wildavsky, *Presidential Elections* (New York: Charles Scribner's Sons, 1964), Gerald Pomper, *Elections in America* (New York: Dodd, Mead & Co., 1968) and Karl A. Lamb and Paul A. Smith, *Campaign Decision-Making: The Presidential Election of 1964* (Belmont, Calif: Wadsworth, 1968).
58. A child is picking a daisy; an atomic explosion obliterates the scene; the viewer is asked to vote for the candidate.
    For examples of the impact of public relations on political campaigning, see Stanley Kelly, *Professional Public Relations and Political Power* (Baltimore: The Johns Hopkins Press, 1956). Herbert M. Baus and William B. Ross, in *Politics Battle Plan* (New York: Macmillan, 1968), supply the perspective on campaigning of a successful California campaign management and public relations team.
59. Abels, *op. cit.,* footnote 54, p. 59.
60. Discussion of convention and nominating procedures is found in Donald B. Johnson, "Delegate Selection for National Conventions," in Cornelius P. Cotter, ed., *Practical Politics in the United States* (Boston: Allyn and Bacon, 1969), pp. 199–238, and Gerald Pomper, *Nominating the President* (Evanston, Ill., Northwestern University Press, 1963).

CHAPTER 3

CROSS-NATIONAL COMPARATIVE STUDY OF ASSASSINATION

Introduction—Summary

In order to determine contemporary factors within our own society that may have contributed to the violence directed towards political figures, we turned to cross-national quantitative studies. Our purpose was twofold: to determine whether the level of assassination is higher for the United States than for other nations, and to determine what political and social factors are most often associated with assassination.

The cross-national comparison showed that the United States was comparatively high in assassinations and that the level of assassination correlates strongly with the level of political violence. Accordingly, in Chapter 4 we examine political violence in the United States.

A. Assassination: A Cross-National Quantitative Perspective

We have two collections of worldwide assassination data. The first is a study of assassination attempts—both successful and unsuccessful—in eighty-eight countries for just over fifty years, from 1918 through October 1968. These data were collected by a team at the University of Texas, headed by Carl Leiden. The second collection of data is of assassination events —including both assassination attempts and assassination plots —in eighty-four countries for a twenty-year period, 1948 through 1967. These data were collected by a team headed by Ivo Feierabend at San Diego State College.[1]

Figure 1 plots the frequency of total assassination events,

including attempts and plots year by year for the twenty-year period (Feierabend). There are four striking peaks of high frequency (1948, 1949, 1963, and 1965), and four lows (1952, 1960, 1961, and the lowest in 1967). Inspection of this graph (that is, trying to draw a straight line that would best fit these scattered points) reveals a slightly negative trend. Hence, one could assert that, on the average, through the twenty years, assassination events are almost constant in their volume of occurrence or, if anything, they may be slightly declining. A comparison of the volume of events for the first half of the time period (1948–57) with that for the second half (1958–67), shows a total of two hundred twenty-two assassinations during the first ten years and one hundred eighty-seven during the second ten years—a decline of sixteen percent. However, from one year to another, the fluctuation is quite considerable.

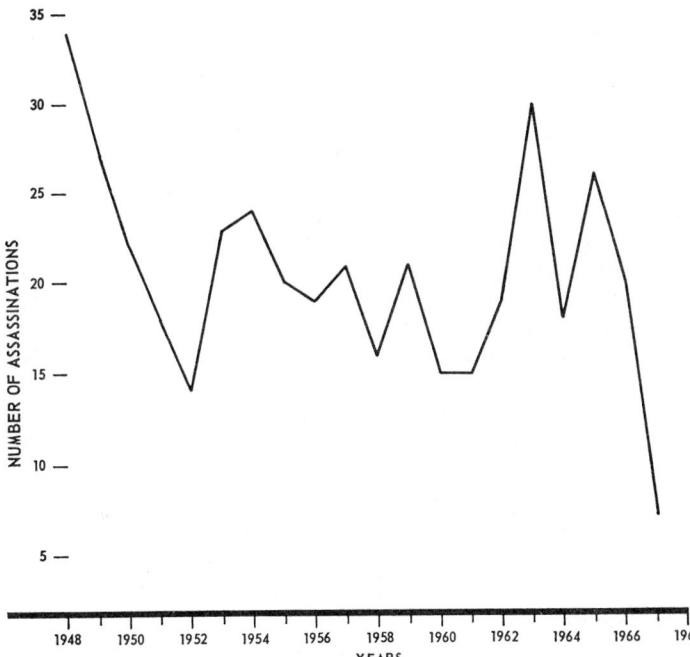

Figure 1.—Global assassination frequency
by year 1948-1968

Figure 2 (the Leiden data) is a similar comparison—frequency of assassination attempts for eighty-eight nations over a fifty-year time period (1918 to October 1968). Figure 3 shows the frequency for the United States over this same period.[2] Figure 2 (the Leiden data) conforms generally with the Feierabend data in showing striking peaks from year to year, but no particular trend in the last fifty years. Indeed, the data show a decline in comparison with population growth, although there are clusterings of years in which there are high incidences of assassination attempts (e.g., 1924-28, 1930-37, 1941-47, 1954-55, and 1957-67). Figure 3 again shows no particular trend.

The number of assassination events in each country also varies widely as shown by the two data collections. Figure 4 shows the number of assassination attempts, both successful and unsuccessful, by country for the last fifty years. These are limited to top ranking officials[3] and ranked from highest to lowest.

Figure 5 lists assassination events by country for the period 1948–67 as collected by the Feierabend group. Again, the countries are ranked from highest to lowest in the number of total assassination events. The data in Figure 5 are broken down between assassination events directed at all persons and those directed at top government officials only. These data include assassination plots as well as actual attempts.[4]

The Leiden data (fig. 4) show the United States as the thirteenth highest of eighty-eight nations over the fifty-year period. The Feierabend data (figure 5) show the United States tied for fifth highest out of eighty-four nations in all assassination events, including plots, in the twenty-year period from 1948–67. If we look at top government officials only, as reported by Feierabend, we find the United States twenty-sixth highest, tied with six other nations. If we ignore assassination plots, we find the United States tied with eleven other countries for twenty-first place.

Although a precise ranking of countries is impossible, we can say with confidence that the United States falls well within the category of those nations that experience a high level of assassination.

It could be argued that population of a country would have a direct bearing on the frequency of assassination. According to this view, it is misleading to compare the absolute frequency of assassination within a large country to that of a

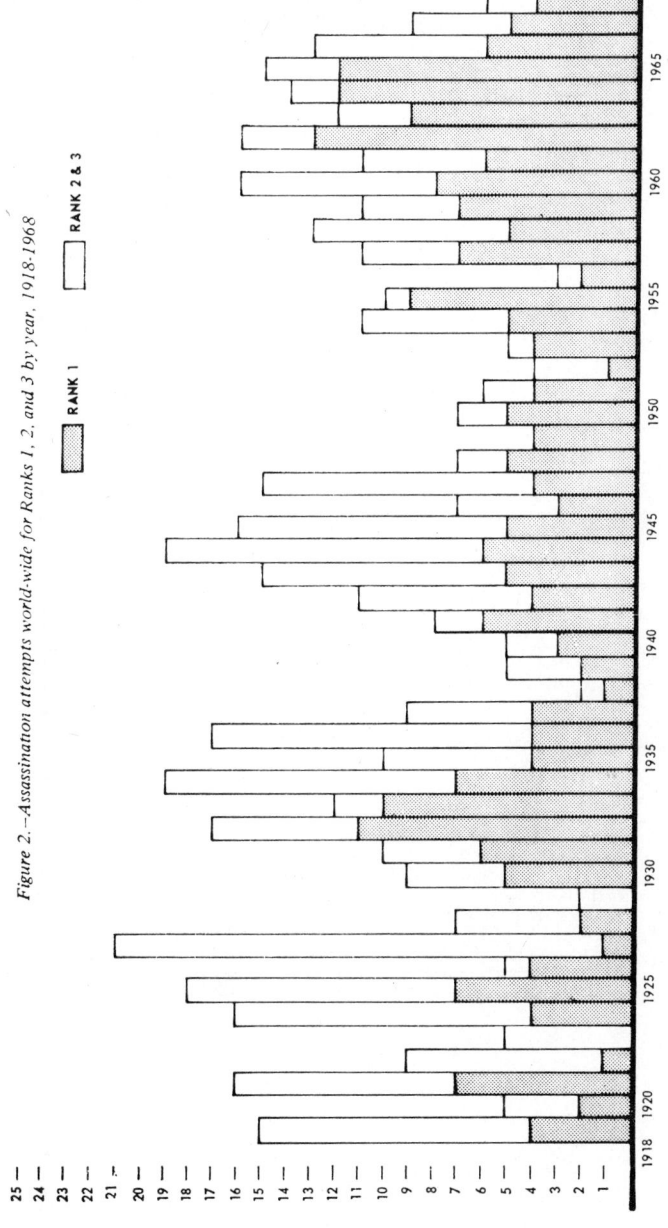

Figure 2.—Assassination attempts world-wide for Ranks 1, 2, and 3 by year, 1918-1968

*Figure 3.—Assassination attempts in the United States for Ranks
1 through 6 by year, 1918-1968*

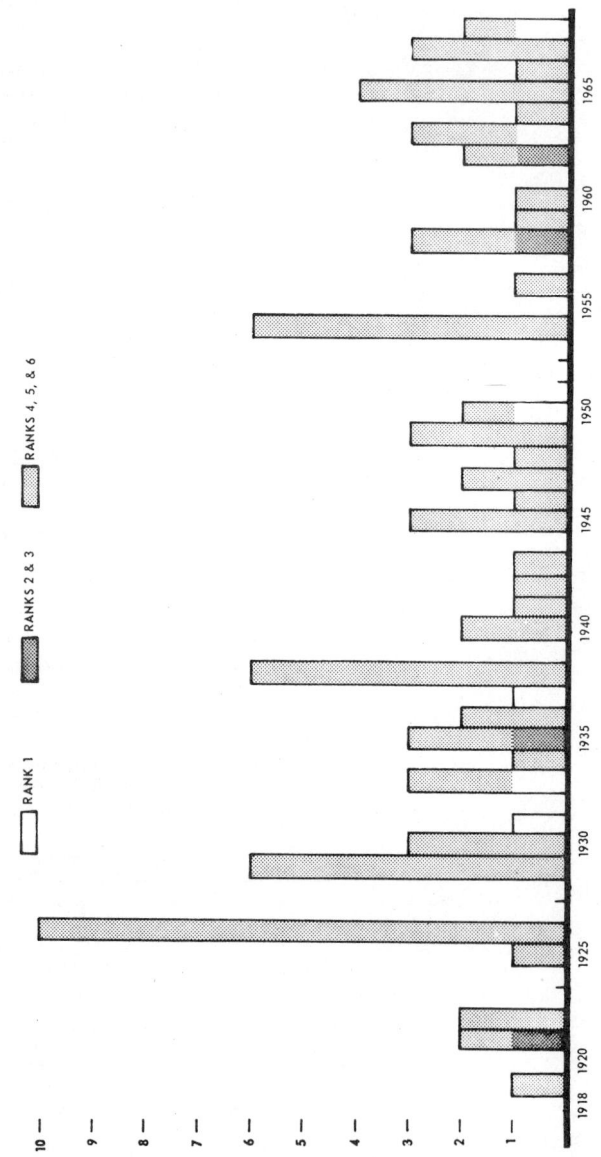

Figure 4.—Assassination attempts by country—(Leiden) 1918-October 1968

Top-ranking officials (Ranks 1, 2, and 3)

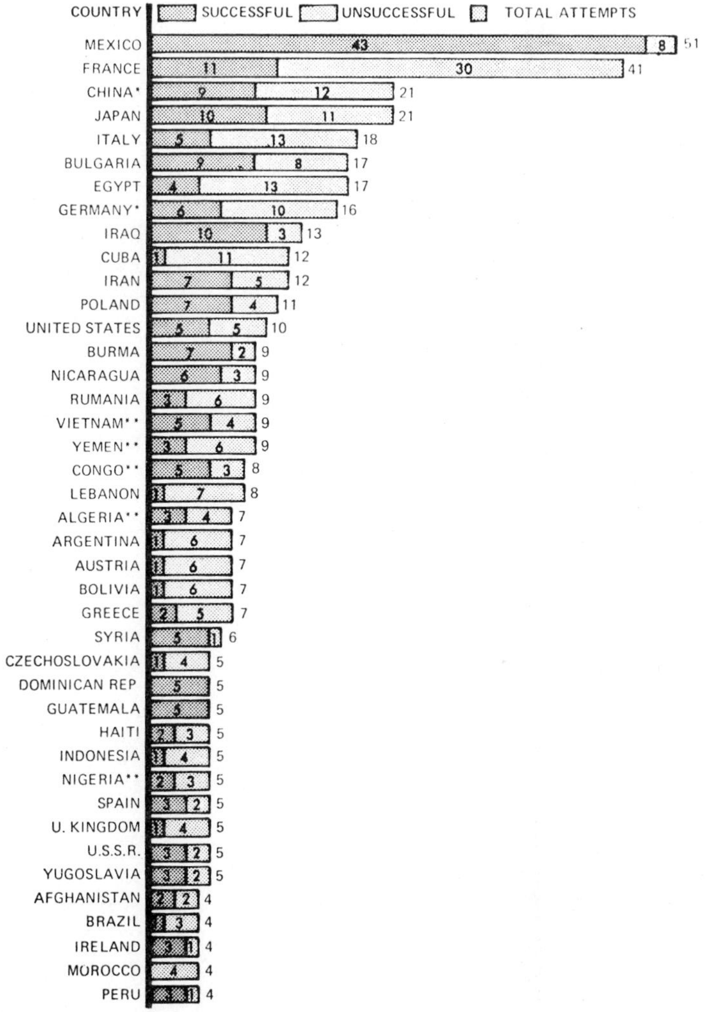

COUNTRY	▨ SUCCESSFUL	☐ UNSUCCESSFUL	☐ TOTAL ATTEMPTS
MEXICO	43	8	51
FRANCE	11	30	41
CHINA*	9	12	21
JAPAN	10	11	21
ITALY	5	13	18
BULGARIA	9	8	17
EGYPT	4	13	17
GERMANY*	6	10	16
IRAQ	10	3	13
CUBA	1	11	12
IRAN	7	5	12
POLAND	7	4	11
UNITED STATES	5	5	10
BURMA	7	2	9
NICARAGUA	6	3	9
RUMANIA	3	6	9
VIETNAM**	5	4	9
YEMEN**	3	6	9
CONGO**	5	3	8
LEBANON	1	7	8
ALGERIA**	3	4	7
ARGENTINA	1	6	7
AUSTRIA	1	6	7
BOLIVIA	1	6	7
GREECE	2	5	7
SYRIA	5	1	6
CZECHOSLOVAKIA	1	4	5
DOMINICAN REP	5		5
GUATEMALA	5		5
HAITI	2	3	5
INDONESIA	1	4	5
NIGERIA**	2	3	5
SPAIN	3	2	5
U. KINGDOM	1	4	5
U.S.S.R.	3	2	5
YUGOSLAVIA	3	2	5
AFGHANISTAN	2	2	4
BRAZIL	1	3	4
IRELAND	3	1	4
MOROCCO	4		4
PERU			4

*Data for all China and all Germany; not divided between Mainland and Taiwan or East and West Germany

**Country not used in Feierabend study

Figure 4 (Continued)

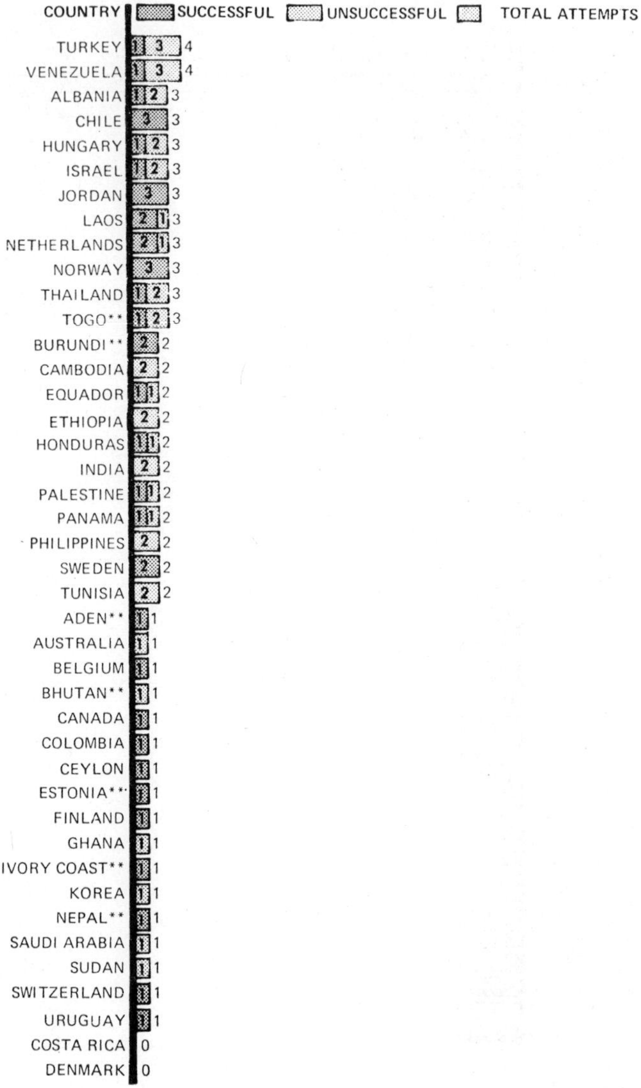

COUNTRY	▓ SUCCESSFUL	▢ UNSUCCESSFUL	▢ TOTAL ATTEMPTS

COUNTRY		TOTAL
TURKEY	1 3	4
VENEZUELA	1 3	4
ALBANIA	1 2	3
CHILE	3	3
HUNGARY	1 2	3
ISRAEL	1 2	3
JORDAN	3	3
LAOS	2 1	3
NETHERLANDS	2 1	3
NORWAY	3	3
THAILAND	1 2	3
TOGO**	1 2	3
BURUNDI**	2	2
CAMBODIA	2	2
EQUADOR	1 1	2
ETHIOPIA	2	2
HONDURAS	1 1	2
INDIA	2	2
PALESTINE	1 1	2
PANAMA	1 1	2
PHILIPPINES	2	2
SWEDEN	2	2
TUNISIA	2	2
ADEN**	1	1
AUSTRALIA	1	1
BELGIUM	1	1
BHUTAN**	1	1
CANADA	1	1
COLOMBIA	1	1
CEYLON	1	1
ESTONIA**	1	1
FINLAND	1	1
GHANA	1	1
IVORY COAST**	1	1
KOREA	1	1
NEPAL**	1	1
SAUDI ARABIA	1	1
SUDAN	1	1
SWITZERLAND	1	1
URUGUAY	1	1
COSTA RICA		0
DENMARK		0

**Country not used in Feierabend study

Figure 4 (Continued)

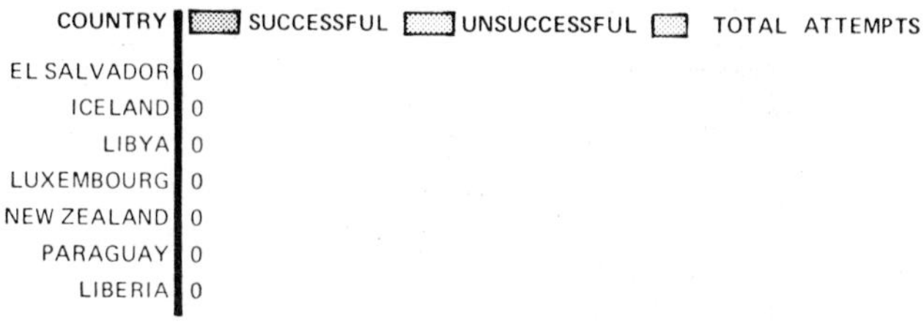

COUNTRY	▓ SUCCESSFUL	▒ UNSUCCESSFUL	⬚ TOTAL ATTEMPTS
EL SALVADOR	0		
ICELAND	0		
LIBYA	0		
LUXEMBOURG	0		
NEW ZEALAND	0		
PARAGUAY	0		
LIBERIA	0		

small one, because the larger population entails the probability of a higher number of assassinations. Therefore, it is unreasonable to class the United States with Cuba, Korea, Iran, Morocco, Tunisia, and the Philippines, since all these countries have fewer than fifty million inhabitants, whereas the United States has over two hundred million.

If this argument is taken at face value, it might lead to a corrective weighting of frequency of assassination by size of population. For example, one might calculate an "assassination per capita" rate by dividing absolute assassination frequency by population. An assassination rate of this type will certainly reorder the positions of countries. All large countries, including the United States, will appear low in this assassination rate, and all small countries will show a high rate, provided they have even one assassination. Thus Cuba, using the Feierabend data with an assassination event frequency of twenty-eight and a population of seven million, shows a rate of four assassination events per million inhabitants. The United States, with sixteen assassination events and a population of almost two hundred million, has a rate of .08 per million inhabitants (or eight per one hundred million), which is only one-fiftieth of Cuba's rate.

However, the assassination rate actually bears very little relationship to population size. There is no evidence that larger countries do, in fact, have more assassinations than smaller ones. One might wish to credit larger countries for their greater forbearance on this type of violence per population unit, or one might instead reject the underlying assumption that a greater population size leads to a higher probability of assassination frequency.

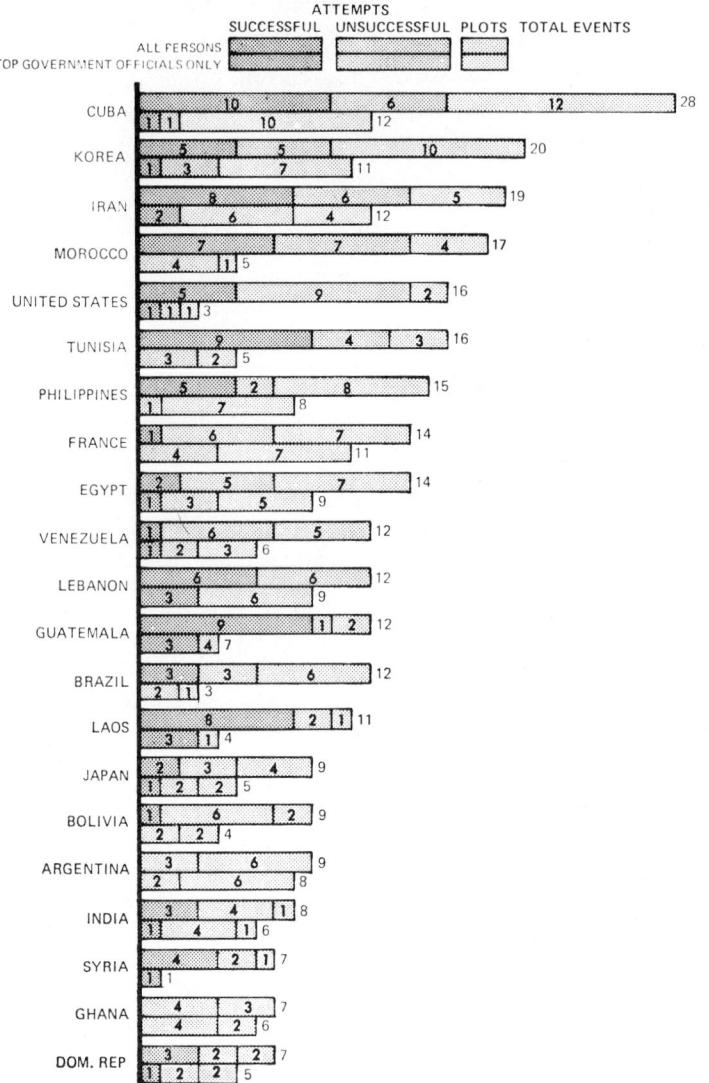

Figure 5.—Assassination events by country (Feierabend)

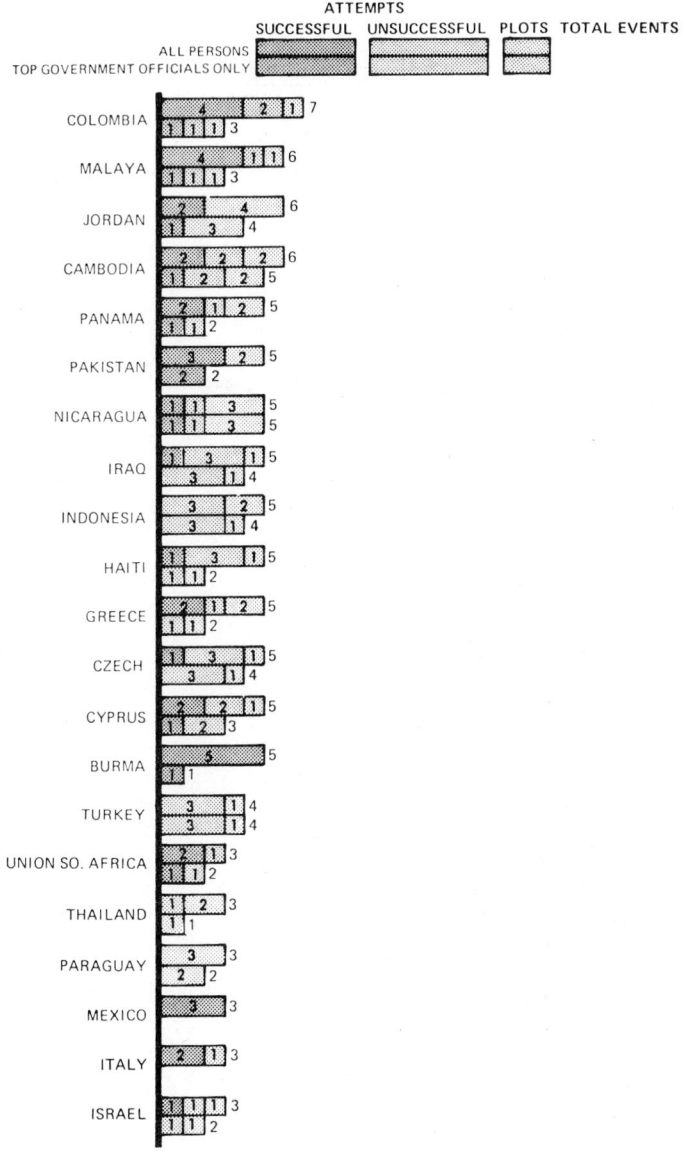

Figure 5.—Assassination Events by Country (Feierabend) continued

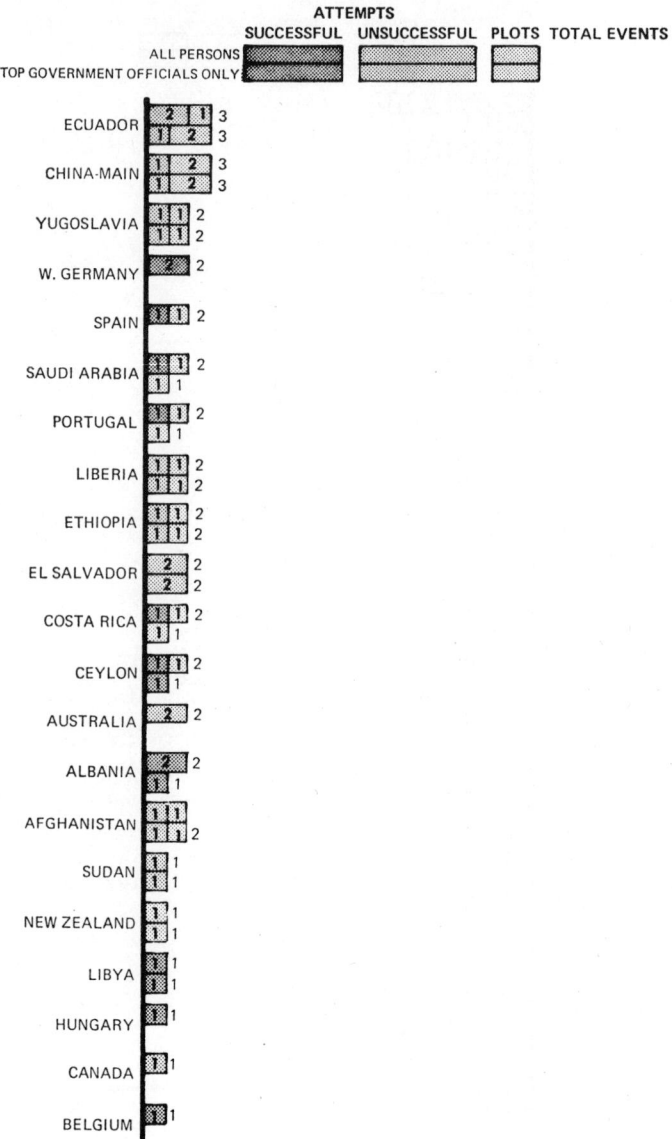

Figure 5.—Assassination Events by Country (Feierabend) continued

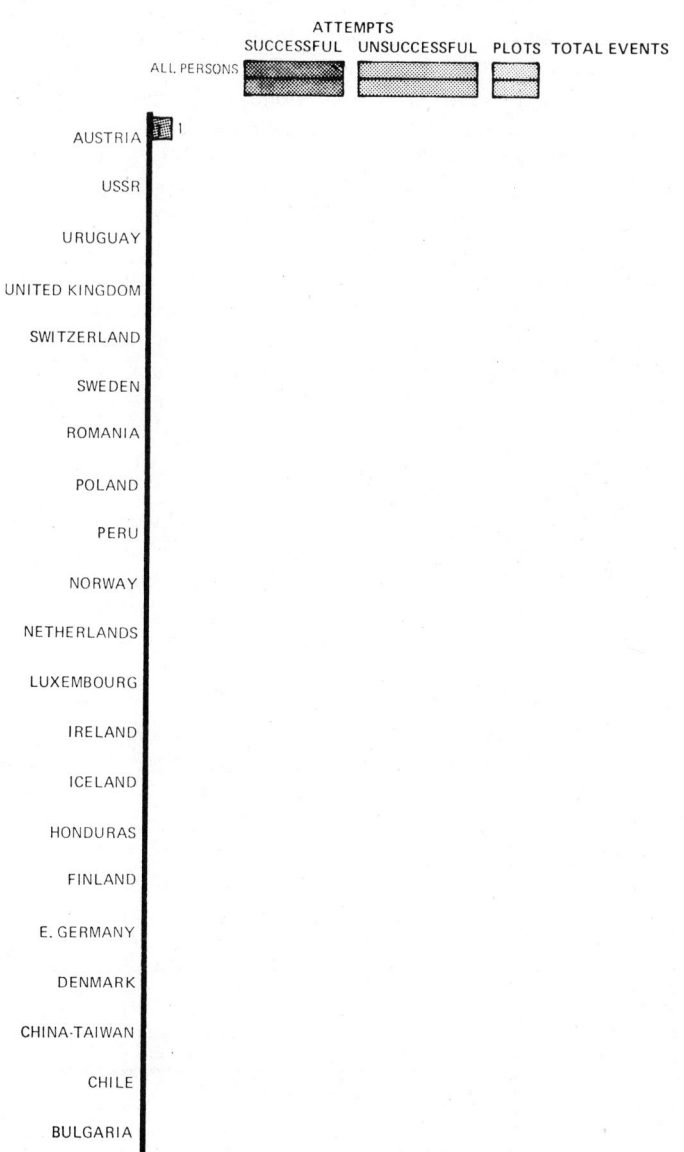

Figure 5.–Assassination events by country (Feierabend) continued

The argument in favor of rejecting population size as a factor may be illustrated by dividing countries into groups according to population. This is done in Tables 1 through 7. Two points are illustrated in these tables. The first is that in each grouping of countries, from smallest to largest in size of population, we find that frequency of assassinations, including plots and attempts, ranges from a very small to a rather high figure. Thus, population itself does not appear to determine the number of assassinations which occur in a nation.[5]

Focusing specifically upon the United States, Table 1 indicates that among the six countries with populations over one hundred million, the United States still ranks first in frequency of assassination events in the last twenty years (Feierabend data) and second over the last fifty years (Leiden data). If the classification is expanded to include countries with populations over fifty million, the United States still ranks first in frequency of assassination events during the last twenty years and fifth out of eleven during the last fifty years. Thus, the conclusion that the United States ranks relatively high in frequency of assassination holds true even with adjustment for population size.

Table 1.—Frequency of assassination in relation to population size of country—over 100 million (1964 population data)

		Feierabend data (1948 - 67) plots and attempts		Leiden data (1918-Oct. 1968) attempts only
Country	Population	All persons	Top Government officials	Top Government officials (Ranks 1-3)
United States	190,700,000	16	3	10
India	467,700,000	8	6	2
Indonesia	101,000,000	5	5	5
Pakistan	100,600,000	5	2	2
China	710,000,000	3	3	21
USSR	227,000,000	0	0	5

Table 2.—Frequency of assassination in relation to
population size of country—over 50 million
(1964 population data)

| Country | Population | Feierabend data (1948 - 67) plots and attempts | | Leiden Data (1918-Oct. 1968) attempts only |
		All persons	Top Government officials	Top Government Officials (Ranks 1-3)
United States	190,700,000	16	3	10
Brazil	78,700,000	12	3	4
Japan	96,200,000	9	5	21
India	467,700,000	8	6	2
Indonesia	101,000,000	5	5	5
Pakistan	100,600,000	5	2	2
China	710,000,000	3	3	21
Italy	50,650,000	3	0	18
West Germany	57,850,000	2	0	16[a]
USSR	227,000,000	0	0	5
U.K.	54,200,000	0	0	5

[a] Includes East and West Germany

Table 3.—Frequency of assassination in relation to
population size of country—20-50 million
(1964 population data)

| Country | Population | Feierabend data (1948-67) plots and attempts | | Leiden data (1918-Oct. 1968) attempts only |
		All persons	Top government officials	Top government officials (ranks 1-3)
Korea	37,500,000	20	11	0
Iran	22,500,000	19	12	12
Philippines	31,200,000	15	8	2
France	48,000,000	14	11	41
Argentina	21,800,000	9	8	7
Burma	23,000,000	5	1	9
Turkey	30,300,000	4	4	4
Mexico	39,000,000	3	0	51
Thailand	29,200,000	3	1	3
Spain	31,200,000	2	0	5
Poland	30,850,000	0	0	11

*Table 4.—Frequency of assassination in relation to
population size of country—10-25 million
(1964 population data)*

Country	Population	Feierabend data (1948-67) plots and attempts		Leiden data (1918-Oct. 1968) attempts only
		All persons	Top government officials	Top government officials (ranks 1-3)
Morocco	12,700,000	17	5	4
Colombia	15,300,000	7	3	1
Burma	23,000,000	5	1	9
Czech.	14,000,000	5	4	5
Yugoslavia	19,200,000	2	2	5
Afghanistan	15,000,000	2	2	4
Australia	11,065,000	2	0	1
Ceylon	10,850,000	2	1	1
Canada	19,100,000	1	0	1
Hungary	10,110,000	1	0	3
Romania	18,875,000	0	0	9
E. Germany	17,100,000	0	0	0[a]
Netherlands	12,050,000	0	0	3
Taiwan	11,900,000	0	0	0
Peru	11,900,000	0	0	4

[a]Leiden data are not divided between East and West Germany and have been recorded under West Germany.

*Table 5.—Frequency of assassination in relation to
population size of country—5-10 million
(1964 population data)*

Country	Population	Feierabend data (1948-67) plots and attempts		Leiden data (1918-Oct. 1968) attempts only
		All persons	Top government officials	Top government officials (ranks 1-3)
Cuba	7,000,000	28	12	12
Venezuela	8,250,000	12	6	4
Syria	5,000,000	7	1	6
Malaya	7,700,000	6	3	0
Cambodia	5,900,000	6	5	2
Greece	8,450,000	5	2	7
Iraq	7,700,000	5	4	13
Saudi Arabia	7,000,000	2	1	1
Belgium	9,300,000	1	0	1
Portugal	9,025,000	2	2	9
Austria	7,175,000	1	0	7
Bulgaria	8,100,000	0	0	17
Chile	8,050,000	0	0	3
Sweden	7,620,000	0	0	2
Switzerland	5,825,000	0	0	1

*Table 6.—Frequency of assassination in relation to
population size of country—2-5 million
(1964 population data)*

Country	Population	Feierabend data (1948-67) plots and attempts		Leiden data (1918-Oct. 1968) attempts only
		All persons	Top government officials	Top government officials (ranks 1-3)
Tunisia	4,400,000	16	5	2
Guatemala	4,150,000	12	4	5
Bolivia	3,650,000	9	4	7
Dom. Rep.	3,400,000	7	5	5
Haiti	4,500,000	5	2	5
Ecuador	4,800,000	3	2	2
Israel	2,435,000	3	2	3
El Salvador	2,725,000	2	2	0
New Zealand	2,575,000	1	1	0
Denmark	4,710,000	0	0	0
Finland	4,565,000	0	0	1
Norway	3,685,000	0	0	3
Ireland	2,825,000	0	0	4
Uruguay	2,450,000	0	0	1
Honduras	2,040,000	0	0	2

*Table 7.—Frequency of assassination in relation to
population size of country—under 2 million
(1964 population data)*

Country	Population	Feierabend data (1948-67) plots and attempts		Leiden data (1918-Oct. 1968) attempts only
		All persons	Top government officials	Top government officials (ranks 1-3)
Lebanon	1,940,000	12	9	8
Laos	1,950,000	10	4	3
Jordan	1,825,000	6	4	3
Nicaragua	1,650,000	5	5	9
Panama	1,185,000	5	2	2
Cyprus	590,000	5	3	0
Paraguay	1,875,000	3	2	0
Albania	1,800,000	2	1	3
Costa Rica	1,350,000	2	1	0
Libya	1,275,000	1	0	0
Luxembourg	325,000	0	0	0
Iceland	190,000	0	0	0

While sheer population size does not tell us what to expect from a country in the way of assassinations, the Feierabend data covering the twenty-year period 1948–67 show that the average rate of assassination events per country varies significantly among different regions of the world. During the twenty-year period, the region with the highest number of assassinations is the Middle East, with an average of 8.23 assassination events per country in this area. Latin America and Asia have approximately the same average assassination scores: 6.2 and 6.0, respectively. All three of these regions are significantly higher in average number of assassinations than are the European countries, for which the average assassination figure is 1.6.

The Leiden data, however, do not yield any significant difference in frequency of assassination by regional groupings. As a matter of fact, Europe has the highest frequency of assassination events during this period, although not by a significant margin. One explanation may be that regional differences that appear in the twenty-year study reflect relatively short-term political and economic factors which vary significantly over the longer fifty-year period. This variation over the fifty-year period would cancel out regional differences over the longer length of time. The impact of various political and economic factors upon assassination and political violence is treated in detail later in this chapter.

B. Political Violence and Assassination[6]

Assassinations, no matter how narrowly or broadly defined, belong among a larger class of politically aggressive and violent behaviors. As such, they undoubtedly must bear some relationship to other acts of internal political turmoil.[7] In an attempt to uncover such a relationship, we used factor analyses of various events of political turmoil.

Factor analysis is a statistical procedure designed to isolate empirical clusterings in the data. In other words, factor analysis determines which events, if any, commonly occur together, and which events occur less frequently together. Events having a strong tendency to occur in conjunction with each other are grouped together and analytically separated from other events. These events are considered as members of a single dimension.

Once an independent dimension has been determined, a search is made for a second dimension, using the identical procedure. This searching for clusterings—or dimensions—continues until no further groups can be found that meet the pre-selected level of statistical explanation. The obvious advantage of this technique is that a large set of complex data can be reduced to a much smaller number of dimensions, each of which can be conceived as a new variable.

Factor analyses were run with respect to two different universes of political turmoil events. One universe was defined very broadly to include not only severe indications of internal political conflict, but also lesser acts of political aggression that might indicate that the political system is laboring under strain. Thirty variables of internal conflict were used for the first universe of political instability events.[8] The second universe of political turmoil was restricted to more violent instances of political aggression.[9]

The factor analysis of the first universe shows that assassination tends to occur most often in conjunction with instances of guerrilla warfare. Assassination also shows a reasonably high association with revolution, but does not correlate significantly with less severe political turmoil. Thus, the evidence is strong that assassinations occur predominantly in nations subject to serious forms of civil disturbance. Nations experiencing predominantly less severe turmoil events show only a modest number of assassination events.

The factor analysis of the second universe, restricted to severe events (strikes, riots, arrests, executions, assassinations, guerrilla warfare, revolt, etc.), verified the first findings. Assassination correlated highly *only* with guerrilla warfare, having no tendency to cluster with other events. In other words, assassination correlates significantly only with certain high levels of internal strife.[10]

These findings were further reinforced and verified by use of a Guttman scalogram. A Guttman scalogram empirically determines, without the use of subjective judgments, whether there is a particular rank order of events such that "lesser" events are normally associated with more "serious" events. In fact, the Guttman scalogram of the violence data was able to create an ordering of events with a very high degree of reliability ($R = 0.97$). That grouping is as follows:

Group 1	Group 2	Group 3	Group 4
Riots, demonstrations, and boycotts	Martial law	Guerilla warfare	Executions
Arrests	Coup d'etat	Assassinations	Civil war
Government action against specific groups	Revolt		
Sabotage			

We found to a high degree of predictability that countries which experienced events listed in group 4 also experienced events in groups 3, 2, and 1. Other countries experienced events in groups 3, 2, and 1, however, without experiencing extreme events listed in group 4. Similarly, the pattern of violence for still other countries was limited to events in groups 2 and 1. Finally, there were countries that experienced events from group 1 only, or others that were beset by no events of this violent nature. These empirical findings show that political violence is an ordered and scalable universe rather than an arbitrary and random occurrence. The data suggest that the occurrence of assassination usually denotes a high degree (point 3), although not necessarily the highest degree (point 4), of internal political turmoil. This is essentially the same pattern of variables isolated by factor analysis. Both techniques suggest that, in the global assessment of assassinations, those countries that experience this political aberration are generally the ones that also experience widespread, highly intense violence.

The foregoing is only one way to look at the underlying structure of internal political turmoil. Another method is to sort political turmoil events in terms of the intensity of aggressive behavior to determine not only the relationship of political turmoil events to each other but also the intensity of quality of the political turmoil. To accomplish this, a seven-point scale was devised, ranging from zero (denoting extreme stability) through six (denoting extreme instability).

Some events indicate far greater aggression than do others. For example, a peaceful demonstration is far less volatile than a civil war. Sorting events in this fashion then becomes an exercise in scaling aggressive behaviors. For this study we defined each point of the scale in terms of specific events representing differing degrees of stability or instability.

An illustration may be given of an item typical of each position on the scale. For example, a general election is an item associated with a zero position. Resignation of a cabinet official falls into the 1 position; peaceful demonstrations into position 2, assassination of a significant political figure (but not a chief of state) into position 3. Mass arrests or assassination of a chief of state occupy position 4, *coups d'etat* position 5, and civil war position 6. The intensity scale was then validated by asking judges to sort the same events along the same continuum. The agreement among judges on the distribution of items was high.

Assassinations were ranked in positions 3 and 4 of the scale, indicative of a considerable degree of internal conflict and crisis, yet not sufficiently intense to be placed among the categories of greatest violence within national political systems.

After the scale was developed, countries were assigned to groups on the basis of the most unstable event they had experienced. Countries that had experienced a civil war were placed in group 6; those which were prey to a *coup d'état* were placed in group 5; countries with mass arrests were assigned to group 4, and so on.

Following the placing of a country in a particular group, the sum total of each country's stability ratings was calculated. To prevent distortion of the data, each country's stability profile was calculated separately for three six-year periods of time (1948–53, 1954–59, 1960–65) and then added together. Thus, many countries that had experienced some highly violent events during the eighteen years have their scores tempered if they were relatively nonviolent in some other six-year period. Some of the Communist-bloc countries fall into this category (Czechoslovakia, Hungary, and Poland). Each experienced a *coup d'état* at the time of the Communist seizure of power in 1948 but, with the exception of Hungary, did not undergo further turmoil of this magnitude in the ensuing years. The stability ratios of each country are set forth in table 8.

Table 8 shows only one country, Indonesia, at the most unstable scale position, 6, indicating that it experienced a civil

Table 8. – Political instability profiles of ninety-four countries, 1948-1965
(stability score shown for each country is grouped score, summed)

1	2	3	4	5	6
NETHERLANDS 04021	U.K. 07112	BELGIUM 10162	FRANCE 13435	ARGENTINA 16445	INDONESIA 18416
LUXEMBG. 03012	GHANA 07106	CHILE 10156	U. OF SO. AFRICA 13422	BOLIVIA 16318	
	AUSTRIA 07057	MEXICO 10111	BRAZIL 13209	CUBA 16283	
	DENMARK 07030	URUGUAY 10100	MOROCCO 13194	IRAQ 16274	
	ICELAND 07026	ISRAEL 10064	PORTUGAL 13190	COLOMBIA 16244	
	W. GERMANY 06087	LIBERIA 10036	TURKEY 13189	BURMA 16213	
	FINLAND 06056	ETHIOPIA 10034	POLAND 13179	VENEZUELA 15429	
	TAIWAN 06039	ITALY 09192	THAILAND 13152	SYRIA 15329	
	AUSTRALIA 06026	LIBYA 09069	JORDAN 13145	KOREA 15291	
	SWEDEN 06020	ROMANIA 09060	CYPRUS 13123	HAITI 15205	
	IRELAND 05031	COSTA RICA 09058	HUNGARY 13113	PERU 15196	
	S. ARABIA 05018	AFGHAN. 09029	PHILIPP. 13105	GREECE 14236	
	N. ZEALAND 05015	CANADA 09029	CZECH. 13100	GUATEM. 14234	
		SWITZER. 08042	CHINA (M) 13086	LEBANON 14212	
		NORWAY 08034	CAMBODIA 13071	EGYPT 14152	
			INDIA 12360	PARAGUAY 14141	
			IRAN 12237	E. GERMANY 14138	
			PAKISTAN 12231	LAOS 14129	
			SUDAN 12189	TUNISIA 14126	
			USSR 12165	HONDURAS 14105	
			ECUADOR 12117	PANAMA 14101	
			NICARAGUA 12096	EL SALVADOR 14079	
			USA 11318		
			SPAIN 11284		
			DOM. REP. 11195		
			CEYLON 11152		
			JAPAN 11123		
			MALAYA 11108		
			YUGOSL. 11077		
			BULGARIA 11071		
			ALBANIA 11067		

war during each of the three six-year periods. No country is at scale position zero, but two (Luxembourg and the Netherlands) are at position 1. The United States is at scale position 4 and at rank order position thirty-eight or thirty-nine, just below the median rank position of forty-two.

As Table 8 shows, when the entire range of political-strife incidents is analyzed, the position of the United States in comparison to other nations is less unfavorable than its assassination profile. Approximately one-half of the nations of the world experienced more civil strife than did the United States in the last twenty years. It is interesting to note, however, that of the European democracies only France had a higher level of civil strife during this period. Thus, the two Western democracies with the highest number of assassination events also show the highest degree of total civil strife.

The system for deriving a national profile of political instability set forth in table 8 gives special weight to the highest strife event that a nation experiences. The first two digits in the scale are determined by the average of the highest strife events occurring in each six-year period. Although giving special weight to the highest strife event yields a valid perspective, it tends to favor nations such as the United States which have experienced many total political-strife events, but not at the most extreme level. Assassination, the highest level of political strife experienced in the United States, is rated 3 or 4 on a six-point scale. To avoid special weighting of the highest strife event, the scores for all instability events for the eighteen-year period were summed. Table 9 shows the scores and ranking of countries. Most of the nations remain in relatively the same rank-order position, yet there are some major shifts. In particular, the United States shows up as one of the most unstable nations in the world.

The last and most important question regarding the violence data is to ascertain the relationship between the assassination profiles and the general violence profiles of the eighty-four countries for the twenty-year period. One such relationship is presented in table 10, which splits the countries into groups experiencing high frequencies of assassination events (three or more) and those experiencing low frequencies (two or less), and ranks them on the six scale positions of political instability as set out in table 8. Table 10 shows a definite relationship between political instability and assassination. Countries with high frequencies of assassination fall predominantly at positions 4 and 5 on the instability scale. None falls at scale position 1 and only one country is at scale position 2. Countries low in assassination frequency are primarily from scale positions 2, 3, and to some extent, 4. None is from position 6, and only four are from scale position 5.

From the information in table 10, we may say that general political violence appears to be among the more efficient predictors of assassination. That is, if we were to single out one characteristic of a national system without knowing the country's profile, general political violence would give the best clue as to whether the political system is assassination-prone. To illustrate the point from table 10, if we were to predict high and low frequency of assassinations occurring in the eighty-four countries, we could be right in sixty-six cases, and proba-

Table 9.—Political instability profiles for eighty-four countries (summed, 1948-65)

Country	Score	Country	Score	Country	Score
Luxembourg	12	West Germany	87	Turkey	189
New Zealand	15	Nicaragua	96	Portugal	190
Saudi Arabia	18	Czechoslovakia	100	Italy	191
Sweden	20	Uruguay	100	Morocco	194
Netherlands	21	Panama	101	Dominican Republic	195
Iceland	26	Honduras	105	Peru	196
Australia	26	Philippines	105	Haiti	205
Afghanistan	29	Ghana	106	Brazil	208
Denmark	30	Malaya	108	Lebanon	212
Ireland	31	Mexico	111	Burma	213
Ethiopia	34	Hungary	113	Pakistan	231
Norway	34	United Kingdom	116	Guatemala	234
Liberia	36	Ecuador	117	Greece	236
China (Taiwan)	39	Cyprus	123	Iran	237
Switzerland	42	Japan	123	Colombia	244
Finland	56	Tunisia	126	Iraq	274
Austria	57	Laos	129	Cuba	281
Costa Rica	58	East Germany	138	Spain	284
Romania	60	Paraguay	141	Korea	291
Israel	64	Jordan	145	United States	319
Albania	67	Ceylon	152	Bolivia	323
Libya	69	Thailand	152	Syria	329
Bulgaria	71	Egypt	153	India	360
Cambodia	71	Chile	156	Indonesia	416
Yugoslavia	77	Belgium	162	Union So. Africa	427
El Salvador	79	USSR	165	Venezuela	429
Canada	83	Poland	179	France	435
China (Mainland)	86	Sudan	189	Argentina	445

Table 10.—Relationship between assassinations and political instability for a 20 year period, 1948-1967

	STABILITY			INSTABILITY		
	1	**2**	**3**	**4**	**5**	**6**
ASSASSINATION HIGH (THREE AND ABOVE)	(none)	GHANA 7	ITALY 3, ISRAEL 3, MEXICO 3	MALAYA 6, JAPAN 9, DOM. REP 7, UNITED STATES 16, NICARAGUA 5, ECUADOR 3, PAKISTAN 5, IRAN 19, INDIA 8, CAMBODIA 6, CHINA–MAIN 3, CZECH 5, PHILIPPINES 15, CYPRUS 5, JORDAN 6, THAILAND 3, TURKEY 4, MOROCCO 17, BRAZIL 12, UNION SO. AFRICA 3, FRANCE 14	PANAMA 5, TUNISIA 16, LAOS 10, PARAGUAY 3, EGYPT 14, LEBANON 12, GUATEMALA 12, GREECE 5, KOREA 20, HAITI 5, SYRIA 7, VENEZUELA 12, BURMA 5, COLOMBIA 7, IRAQ 5, CUBA 28, BOLIVIA 9, ARGENTINA 9	INDONESIA 5
(count)	0	1	3	21	—	1
ASSASSINATION LOW (TWO AND BELOW)	IRELAND 0, LUXEMBOURG 0, NETHERLANDS 0	NEW ZEALAND 1, SAUDI ARABIA 2, SWEDEN 0, AUSTRALIA 2, CHINA–TAIWAN 0, FINLAND 0, WEST GERMANY 2, ICELAND 0, DENMARK 0, AUSTRIA 1, UNITED KINGDOM 0	NORWAY 0, SWITZERLAND 0, CANADA 1, AFGHANISTAN 2, COSTA RICA 2, ROMANIA 0, USSR 0, LIBYA 1, ETHIOPIA 2, LIBERIA 2, URUGUAY 0, CHILE 0, BELGIUM 1	ALBANIA 2, BULGARIA 0, YUGOSLAVIA 1, CEYLON 2, SPAIN 2, SUDAN 1, HUNGARY 2, POLAND 0, PORTUGAL 2	EL SALVADOR 2, HONDURAS 0, EAST GERMANY 0, PERU 0	(none)
(count)	3	11	12	10	4	0

bly wrong in eighteen cases; significantly, this relationship would hold true for the United States. This is an educated guess rather than a reliance on chance alone.

Thus, if we can isolate some factors that lead to political violence in general, we can also help explain and ultimately reduce incidents of assassination.

C. Violence, Assassination, and Political Variables

The findings of the cross-national study suggest that political violence is not a random occurrence. Violence appears to be related to a number of conditions in the environment of political systems. If this is the case, the occurrence of assassination may also be pinpointed within broader patterns of cross-national behavior and national characteristics. We have selected seven such factors for analysis:

1. Development or modernity level.
2. Systemic frustration, or systemic satisfaction levels.
3. Rate of socioeconomic change.
4. Permissiveness—coerciveness of political regime.
5. External aggression level.
6. Level of minority tension.
7. Homicide and suicide rates.

Each will be discussed separately. At the end of this section, the degree of relationship between each of these factors and the frequency of assassination and political violence is indicated in a summary table (table 31) which shows the correlation coefficients among these variables.

1. Level of Development and Political Violence

We developed an index of level of development or modernity based on eight indicators: GNP per capita, literacy level, radios and newspapers per one thousand population, rate of urbanization, caloric intake per person per day, number of persons per physician, and percentage of population having telephones.[11] Standard scores for each country on each of these indicators were averaged to yield an overall estimate of level of attainment. The resulting distribution of countries was divided into three groups.

The twenty-four countries scoring highest were designated

Modern. The twenty-three countries falling at the lowest end of the continuum were called Traditional, although perhaps Low Development would be a better designation. The thirty-seven countries falling between the Modern and Traditional groups were termed Transitional. We then determined the relationship, if any, between modernity level and the level of political violence in general and assassination in particular. Table 11 shows the relationship between modernity level and political violence in general.

There is a definite tendency for the Modern countries to be politically stable. On the other hand, a preponderance of Transitional countries give evidence of instability. Among the Traditional countries, the tendency toward stability is about equal to the tendency toward instability.

A somewhat similar pattern occurs between level of development and frequency of assassination (see table 12). Only five of twenty-four Modern countries, or twenty-one percent, experience a high frequency of assassination. This relationship is reversed for both Transitional and Traditional countries, however. Well over half the countries at both of these lower levels of development have had more than three assassinations in the past twenty years.

Thus it appears that there is a definite relationship between level of development and incidence of political violence, including assassination. Developed countries tend to experience lower levels of political unrest and assassination than do less developed countries. There are exceptions to this rule at all three levels of development. Among Modern countries, the United States and France are notable exceptions. Among nations at the two lower levels of development, about one-third are exceptions. It also must be noted that no difference between the incidence of political violence in Traditional and Transitional countries is apparent in table 12, and only a small difference in table 11. Both groups show a tendency toward political instability and assassination.

We may also examine assassination frequency in relation to a more detailed breakdown of level of development. The results are indicated in table 13. The five different levels of development labelled in this table are taken from the *World Handbook of Political and Social Indicators.*[12] The division into five groups is based on only one indicator: GNP in 1957 U.S. dollars.

Table 13 shows a tendency for countries at the lowest level

Table 11—Stability-instability by level of modernity

	I. Traditional	II. Transitional	III. Modern	
Unstable (126-445)	Bolivia Burma Haiti India Indonesia Iran Iraq Jordan Laos Morocco Pakistan Sudan 12	Brazil Ceylon Chile Colombia Cuba Dom. Rep. Egypt Greece Guatemala Italy Korea Lebanon Paraguay Peru Poland Portugal Spain Syria Thailand Tunisia Turkey Union South Africa Venezuela 23	Argentina Belgium East Germany France United States USSR 6	41
Stable (012-125)	Afghanistan Cambodia China-Taiwan China-Main Ethiopia Ghana Malaya Liberia Libya Philippines Saudi Arabia 11	Albania Bulgaria Costa Rica Cyprus Ecuador El Salvador Honduras Hungary Japan Mexico Nicaragua Panama Romania Yugoslavia 14	Australia Austria Canada Czechoslovakia Denmark Finland Iceland Ireland Israel Luxembourg Netherlands New Zealand Norway Sweden Switzerland United Kingdom Uruguay West Germany 18	43
	23	37	24	84

Chi-square value=13.71
p < 0.01

Table 12. – Frequency of assassination by level of modernity

	I. Traditional	II. Transitional	III. Modern	
High frequency of assassinations (3 or more)	Bolivia (9) Burma (5) Cambodia (6) China–Main (3) Ghana (7) Haiti (5) India (8) Indonesia (5) Iran (19) Iraq (5) Jordan (6) Laos (10) Malaya (6) Morocco (17) Pakistan(5) Philippines (15)	Brazil (12) Colombia (7) Cuba (28) Cyprus (5) Dom. Rep. (7) Ecuador (3) Egypt (14) Greece (5) Guatemala (12) Italy (3) Korea (20) Japan (9) Lebanon (12) Mexico (3) Nicaragua (5) Panama (5) Paraguay (3) Syria (7) Thailand (3) Tunisia (16) Turkey (4) Union So. Africa (3) Venezuela (12)	Argentina (9) Czechoslovakia (5) France (14) Israel (3) United States (16) United Kingdom (6) Uruguay (0) USSR (0) W. Germany (2)	44
	16	23	5	
Low frequency of assassinations (2 or less)	Afghanistan (2) China–Taiwan (0) Ethiopia (2) Liberia (2) Libya (1) Saudi Arabia (2) Sudan (1)	Albania (2) Bulgaria (0) Ceylon (2) Chile (0) Costa Rica (2) El Salvador (2) Honduras (0) Hungary (1) Peru (0) Poland (0) Portugal (2) Romania (0) Spain (2) Yugoslavia (2)	Australia (2) Austria (1) Belgium (1) Canada (1) Denmark (0) E. Germany (0) Finland (0) Iceland (0) Ireland (0) Luxembourg (0) Netherlands (0) New Zealand (1) Norway (0) Sweden (0) Switzerland (0)	40
	7	14	19	
	27	33	24	84

Chi-Sq. value = 7.76
p 0.05

of development to experience a low assassination level, while the so-called Traditional group of countries show the highest incidence. Unfortunately, the total number of Traditional Primitive Societies is very small. Two-thirds of them, however, experience few assassinations. The trend is in the opposite direction at the next two levels of development. Among Traditional civilizations, the ratio of countries with a high frequency of assassinations to those with a low incidence is seven to one. In Transitional societies, the same ratio is slightly in excess of two to one. At the fourth level of development, however, among Industrial Revolution Societies, countries are equally divided between those that are high and those that are low in assassination frequency. Finally, at the highest level of development, among High Mass-Consumption Societies, the trend is markedly in the direction of a low frequency of assassinations. Only two countries are exceptions to the trend, the United States and France.

2. Systemic Frustration—Satisfaction and Political Violence

Another condition selected as potentially related to the level of political unrest is the degree of systemic frustration experienced within a society.[13] The notion of systemic frustration is closely related to level of socioeconomic development. It refers to the gap or ratio between social wants and social satisfactions within a society, and is postulated to be curvilinearly related to the modernity level. Traditional and Modern societies should both be relatively satisfied, while Transitional societies should be relatively unsatisfied, because they have been awakened to a desire for a new way of life but are only beginning to achieve it.

To measure the level of systemic frustration, we devised a Frustration index by forming a ratio from the eight indicators used in the Modernity index. Literacy and urbanization comprised the numerator of the ratio, indicating level of want formation within the society. This choice was based on notions of social mobilization, in which literacy and city life are two media through which persons in developing societies may gain knowledge of new patterns. The remaining six indicators, GNP per capita, caloric intake, radios, newspapers, physicians, and telephones, were regarded as measures of want satisfaction, forming the denominator of the ratio.

Table 13.—Frequency of assassination by level of development

	I. Traditional primitive societies	II. Traditional civilizations	III. Transitional societies	IV. Industrial revolution societies	V. High mass-consumption societies	
High frequency of assassinations (3 or more)	Burma (5) Laos (10)	Bolivia (9) Cambodia (6) China–Main (3) Haiti (5) Pakistan (8) Thailand (3)	Dom. Rep. (7) Ecuador (3) Egypt (14) Ghana (7) Guatemala (12) Indonesia (5) Iran (19) Iraq (5) Jordan (6) Korea (20) Morocco (17) Nicaragua (5) Paraguay (3) Philippines (15) Syria (7) Tunisia (16) Turkey (4)	Argentina (9) Brazil (13) Colombia (7) Czechoslovakia (5) Cyprus (3) Greece (5) Italy (3) Israel (3) Japan (9) Lebanon (12) Malaya (6) Mexico (3) Panama (5) Union So. Africa (14) Venezuela (12)	France (14) United States (16)	
	2	7	17	15	2	43
Low frequency of assassinations (2 or less)	Afghanistan (2) Ethiopia (2) Libya (1) Sudan (1)	Liberia (2)	Albania (2) Ceylon (2) China–Taiwan (0) El Salvador (2) Honduras (0) Peru (0) Portugal (2) Saudi Arabia (2)	Austria (1) Bulgaria (0) Chile (0) Costa Rica (2) East Germany (0) Finland (1) Hungary (0) Iceland (0) Ireland (0) Poland (0) Romania (0) Spain (2) Uruguay (0) USSR (0) Yugoslavia (2)	Australia (2) Belgium (1) Canada (1) Denmark (0) Luxembourg (0) Netherlands (0) New Zealand (1) Norway (0) Sweden (0) Switzerland (0) United Kingdom (0) West Germany (2)	
	4	1	8	15	12	40
	6	8	25	30	14	83

Chi-square value = 16.57
$p < 0.001$

Table 14. – *Stability-instability by systemic satisfaction*

	Low satisfaction	High satisfaction		
Unstable (126-445)	Bolivia Brazil Ceylon Chile Colombia Cuba Dominican Republic Egypt Greece Guatemala Haiti India Iraq Italy Korea	Paraguay Peru Spain Syria Thailand Turkey Venezuela	Argentina Belgium France Indonesia Iran Lebanon Morocco Pakistan Portugal Tunisia Union of South Africa United States	
		22	12	34
Stable (012-125)	Bulgaria Cyprus Ecuador El Salvador Japan Panama Philippines Mexico Nicaragua Yugoslavia		Australia Austria Canada Costa Rica Czechoslovakia Denmark Finland Iceland Ireland Israel Netherlands	New Zealand Norway Sweden Switzerland United Kingdom Uruguay West Germany
		10	18	28
		32	30	62

Chi-square value=4.07
$p < 0.05$

Table 14 gives the relationship between systemic satisfaction level and level of political unrest, while table 15 relates systemic satisfaction to assassination frequency.[14]

The relationships shown in these tables indicate that satisfied countries are less prone to political instability and assassination than are frustrated societies. Two-thirds of the countries that are low in systemic satisfaction are politically unstable; sixty percent of countries high in systemic satisfaction are politically stable. We find a similar relationship indicated in table 15 between systemic satisfaction and frequency of assassination. Seventy-eight percent of the countries low in systemic satisfaction have had two or fewer assassinations.

We may say, then, that the level of systemic satisfaction within a society shows a relationship to the degree of political instability experienced by that society, as well as to the incidence of assassination.

3. Rate of Socioeconomic Change and Political Violence

A third measure related to the level of political unrest and assassination frequency is the rate of socioeconomic change experienced within a society. We hypothesized that a high rate of socioeconomic change would entail a high level of political violence. Conversely, less rapid change will mean a more stable society.

In order to measure the rate of socioeconomic change, data on nine economic indicators were collected for a twenty-eight-year period, 1935–62. The indicators were: literacy level, primary and postprimary education levels, infant mortality rate, caloric intake, radios, urbanization level, national income, and cost of living. The rate of change was calculated in percentage terms, thus showing the countries with a high base level (modern industrialized states by and large) as having a low rate of change, and countries with a low base level (underdeveloped societies) as having a higher annual percentage rate of change.[15]

The relationship between rate of change and political instability is shown in table 16. Again we find a similar pattern. Approximately seventy percent of the countries which experienced a high percentage rate of change are politically unstable.

Table 15.—Frequency of assassination by systemic satisfaction

	Low satisfaction	High satisfaction		
High frequency of assassinations (3 or more)	Bolivia (9) Brazil (12) Colombia (7) Cuba (28) Cyprus (5) Dom. Rep. (7) Ecuador (3) Egypt (14) Greece (5) Guatemala (12) Haiti (5) India (8) Iraq (5) Italy (3) Japan (9) Korea (20) Mexico (3) Nicaragua (5) Panama (5) Paraguay (3) Philippines (15) Syria (7) Thailand (3) Turkey (4) Venezuela (12) 25	Argentina (9) Czechoslovakia (5) France (14) Indonesia (5) Iran (19) Israel (3) Lebanon (12) Morocco (17) Pakistan (5) Tunisia (16) Union South Africa (3) United States (16) 12		37
Low frequency of assassinations (2 or less)	Bulgaria (0) Ceylon (2) Chile (0) El Salvador (2) Peru (0) Spain (2) Yugoslavia (2) 7	Australia (2) Austria (1) Belgium (1) Canada (1) Costa Rica (0) Denmark (0) Finland (0) Iceland (0) Ireland (0) Netherlands (0)	New Zealand (1) Norway (0) Portugal (2) Sweden (0) Switzerland (0) United Kingdom (0) Uruguay (0) West Germany (2) 18	25
	32	30		62

Chi-square value = 7.83
$p < 0.01$

Table 16.—Stability-instability by rate of socio-economic change

	Low rate of change	High rate of change	
Unstable (126-445)	Argentina Belgium Chile Cuba France Greece Guatemala Italy Pakistan Paraguay Spain Union of South Africa United States	Bolivia Brazil Burma Ceylon Colombia Dominican Republic Egypt Haiti India Indonesia Iraq Korea Morocco	Poland Peru Portugal Syria Thailand Tunisia Turkey USSR Venezuela
	13	22	35
Stable (012-125)	Australia Austria Bulgaria Canada China—Taiwan Denmark Ecuador Finland Hungary Iceland Ireland Israel Luxembourg Mexico Netherlands New Zealand Norway Philippines Sweden Switzerland United Kingdom Uruguay West Germany	Cambodia Costa Rica El Salvador Ghana Honduras Japan Panama Yugoslavia Malaya	
	23	9	32
	36	31	67

Chi-square value = 5.68
$p < 0.05$

And sixty-three percent of the countries with a low rate of change are politically stable.

We find evidence of an almost identical relationship between rate of socioeconomic change and frequency of assassination. As shown in table 17, approximately seventy percent of the countries with a high rate of socioeconomic change had three or more assassinations, while sixty-one percent of the countries with a low rate of change exhibit a low frequency of assassination.

4. Coerciveness of Political Regimes and Political Violence

To measure the elusive and complicated notion of permissiveness—coerciveness of political systems, the following general questions were formulated and then applied as a yardstick against which to rate the various nations:

(1) To what degree are civil rights present and protected?

(2) To what extent is political opposition tolerated and effective?

(3) How democratic is the polity?

These broad questions were then refined in terms of some fifty specific rating criteria. A six-point scale was devised to assess each of the eighty-four countries for the time period 1948–60. Point 1 on the scale was defined as highly permissive, point 6 as highly coercive.[16]

This is undoubtedly a rough procedure to estimate a complex variable, yet the profiles find considerable support in works of other authors interested in analyzing similar aspects of political regimes.[17]

The relationships between coerciveness of regime, political instability, and frequency of assassination are presented in tables 18 and 19. These figures are subdivided to indicate the six different levels of permissiveness–coerciveness. Both tables show very much the same pattern.

Coerciveness levels 1 and 2 (permissive states), as well as 6 (highly coercive states), are conspicuously populated by countries experiencing low levels of political unrest and a low frequency of assassination. In both tables there are twenty-six countries in this category as compared to seven countries that indicate the opposite combination. On the other hand, coer-

Table 17. – Frequency of assassination by rate of socio-economic change

	Low rate of change	High rate of change	
High frequency of assassinations (3 or more)	Argentina (9) Cuba (28) Ecuador (2) France (14) Greece (5) Guatemala (12) Israel (3) Italy (3) Mexico (3) Pakistan (5) Paraguay (3) Philippines (15) Union South Africa (3) United States (16)	Bolivia (9) Panama (5) Brazil (12) Syria (7) Burma (5) Thailand (3) Cambodia (6) Tunisia (16) Colombia (7) Turkey (4) Dominican Republic (7)Venezuela (12) Egypt (14) Ghana (7) Haiti (5) India (8) Indonesia (5) Iraq (5) Japan (9) South Korea (20) Malaya (6) Morocco (17)	36
	14	22	
Low frequency of assassinations (2 or less)	Australia (2) Norway (0) Austria (1) Spain (2) Belgium (0) Sweden (0) Bulgaria (0) Switzerland (0) Canada (1) United Kingdom (0) China–Taiwan (0) Uruguay (0) Chile (0) West Germany (2) Denmark (0) Finland (0) Hungary (1) Iceland (0) Ireland (0) Luxembourg (0) Netherlands (0) New Zealand (1)	Ceylon (2) Costa Rica (2) El Salvador (2) Honduras (0) Peru (0) Poland (0) Portugal (0) USSR (0) Yugoslavia (2)	31
	22	9	
Chi-square value = 5.96 $p < 0.05$	36	31	67

Table 18.–Stability-instability by level of coerciveness (scaled)

	Permissive					Coercive	
	1	2	3	4	5	6	
Unstable (126-445)	United States	Belgium Italy	Brazil Burma Ceylon Chile France Greece India Pakistan Turkey	Bolivia Colombia Guatemala Indonesia Iran Iraq Jordan Laos Lebanon Peru Syria Sudan Thailand Tunisia	Argentina Cuba Egypt Haiti Korea Morocco Paraguay Portugal Spain Union South Africa Venezuela	Dom. Republic East Germany Poland USSR	
	1	2	9	14	11	4	41
Stable (012-125)	Australia Canada Denmark Netherlands Norway Sweden Switzerland United Kingdom	Costa Rica Finland Iceland Ireland Israel Luxembourg Mexico New Zealand Uruguay West Germany	Austria Cambodia Japan Malaya Panama Philippines	Cyprus Ecuador El Salvador Ghana Honduras Liberia Libya	Afghanistan Ethiopia Nicaragua Saudi Arabia	Albania Bulgaria China–Mainland China–Taiwan Czechoslovakia Hungary Romania Yugoslavia	
	8	10	6	7	4	8	43
Chi-square value = 18.69 p < 0.01	9	12	15	21	15	12	84

Table 19—Frequency of assassination by level of coerciveness (scaled)

	Permissive 1	2	3	4	5	Coercive 6	
High frequency of assassinations (3 or more)	United States (16)	Israel (3) Italy (3) Mexico (3)	Brazil (12) Burma (5) Cambodia (6) France (14) Greece (5) India (8) Japan (9) Malaya (6) Pakistan (5) Panama (5) Philippines (15) Turkey (4)	Bolivia (9) Colombia (7) Cyprus (5) Ecuador (3) Ghana (7) Guatemala (12) Indonesia (5) Iran (19) Iraq (5) Jordan (6) Laos (10) Lebanon (12) Syria (7) Thailand (3) Tunisia (16)	Argentina (9) Cuba (28) Egypt (14) Haiti (5) Korea (20) Morocco (17) Nicaragua (5) Paraguay (3) Union So. Africa (3) Venezuela (12)	China–Main (3) Czechoslovakia (5) Dom. Re. (7)	44
	1	3	12	15	10	3	
Low frequency of assassinations (2 or less)	Australia (2) Canada (1) Denmark (0) Netherlands (0) Norway (0) Sweden (0) Switzerland (0) United Kingdom (0)	Belgium (1) Costa Rica (2) Finland (0) Iceland (0) Ireland (0) Luxembourg (0) New Zealand (1) Uruguay (0) West Germany (2)	Austria (1) Ceylon (2) Chile (0)	El Salvador (2) Honduras (0) Liberia (2) Libya (1) Peru (0) Sudan (1)	Afghanistan (2) Ethiopia (2) Portugal (2) Saudi Arabia (2) Spain (2)	Albania (2) Bulgaria (0) China–Taiwan (0) E. Germany (0) Hungary (1) Poland (0) Romania (0) USSR (0) Yugoslavia (2)	40
	8	9	3	6	5	9	
	9	12	15	21	15	12	84

Chi-square value=22.24
p<0.001

civeness levels 3, 4, and 5 include a greater percentage of unstable countries and countries experiencing a high frequency of assassination. Thirty-four countries at these mid-levels of coerciveness are unstable, as compared to seventeen that are stable; thirty-seven countries experience a high frequency of assassination and only fourteen a low frequency.

These tables show that assassinations and political violence are more likely to occur at mid-levels of coerciveness (3, 4, 5) than with highly permissive (1, 2) or highly coercive (6) regimes.

Only extremely coercive systems (totalitarian states) are able to deter assassins and expressions of political violence. Permissiveness appears to be associated with the lowest amount of violence; moderate coerciveness of political regimes appears to be associated in the highest amount of violence. Again, the United States appears as a notable exception.

5. External Aggression, Minority Tension, Homicide, and Suicide

We also investigated the relationship between political violence and assassination and four kinds of violent aggressive behavior—external aggression, minority tension, homicide, and suicide. The data on homicide and suicide rates are derived from United Nations statistical compilations. In order to assess the level of minority tension, a special data collection was compiled from *Deadline Data*, including thirty countries for the time period 1955–65.[18] The data on external conflict are drawn from the work of Rummel and Tanter and cover the time period 1955–60.[19]

These external aggression and minority-tension events were scaled in very much the same fashion as the political instability data. The scaled values were then used to profile the nations of the sample. Some sixty different types of events were distinguished in the minority-tension data collection. These included the thirty events discussed above (see footnote 8), used to denote political instability as well as events having specific reference to minority-majority actions, such as granting of autonomy, banning of institution, police, or military escort. The external hostility events included protests, accusations, threats, anti-foreign demonstrations, expulsion of diplomatic officials, mobilizations, negative sanctions, troop movements, severing of diplomatic relations, and military actions.

The relationship between these variables and political instability and assassination is presented in tables 20 through 32. Nations involved in external conflict tend to be more politically unstable and to experience high assassination frequency than do nations with less hostile relations (see tables 20 and 21).

The relationship between the minority-tension level and both general political instability and assassination frequency is shown in tables 22–24. Only thirty-one countries are included in these tables; these are the countries that have minority groups of sufficient strength to experience either actual or potential conflict of this type. Tables 22 and 23 indicate the relationship when the countries are divided into only two categories, while table 24 divides minority conflict into the six categories of the minority-hostility scale. According to table 22, countries high on minority hostility also tend to be high on political instability. In table 23, we find that countries high on minority hostility are high on assassinations, but the complementary trend of low minority hostility/low frequency of assassinations is not in evidence. This is shown in table 24 where one-third of the countries (10/29) in scale position 5 on minority hostility are also high in frequency of assassination. The patterning indicates that among countries with sizeable minority groups, two-thirds experience high instability. Also, two-thirds experience a high frequency of assassination.

The relationship of homicide and suicide[20] to political instability and to assassination is given in tables 24–30. Tables 25 and 26 compare homicide rates to stability profiles and frequency of assassination, respectively. Tables 27 and 28 do the same for suicide. The relationships for homicide and suicide yield reverse pictures. Homicide rates are positively related to both level of political instability and assassination frequency. On the other hand, seventy-eight percent of the countries high on suicide have experienced a low frequency of assassination, while sixty-one percent of countries low in suicides have had a high frequency of assassination.

Tables 29 and 30 combine homicide/suicide rates and compare them to both political instability and to frequency of assassination. Comparing the two center columns of table 30, we see a very marked tendency for inverse patterns of homicide/suicide to relate to incidence of assassination. Among countries demonstrating the syndrome of high homicide-low suicide, eighty percent have a high incidence of assassination.

Table 20.–Stability-instability by level of international aggressiveness

	Low external aggression		High external aggression		
Unstable (126-445)	Belgium Bolivia Brazil Ceylon Colombia Dom. Republic Greece	Italy Peru Poland Portugal Spain Thailand	Argentina Burma Chile Cuba East Germany Egypt France Guatemala Haiti India Indonesia Iran	Iraq Jordan South Korea Lebanon Pakistan Paraguay Turkey Union South Africa USSR United States of America Venezuela	
		13		23	36
Stable (012-125)	Afghanistan Bulgaria Canada Czechoslovakia Denmark Ecuador El Salvador Ethiopia Finland Ireland Japan Liberia	Netherlands New Zealand Norway Panama Philippines Romania Saudi Arabia Sweden Switzerland Uruguay	Albania Australia Cambodia China–Mainland China–Taiwan Costa Rica Honduras Hungary Israel Mexico Nicaragua	United Kingdom West Germany Yugoslavia	
		22		14	36
		35		37	72

Chi-square value = 6.69
p < 0.01

Table 21.—Frequency of assassination by level of international aggressiveness

	Low external aggression	High external aggression		
High frequency of assassinations (3 or more)	Brazil (12) Bolivia (9) Colombia (7) Czechoslovakia (5) Dominican Rep. (7) Ecuador (3) Greece (5) Italy (3) Japan (9) Panama (5) Philippines (15) Thailand (3)	Argentina (9) Burma (5) Cambodia (6) China–Main (3) Cuba (28) Egypt (14) France (14) Guatemala (12) Haiti (5) India (8) Indonesia (5) Iran (19) Iraq (5)	Israel (3) Jordan (6) Lebanon (12) Mexico (3) Nicaragua (5) Pakistan (5) Paraguay (3) South Korea (20) Turkey (4) Union South Africa (3) United States (16) Venezuela (12)	37
	12	25	35	
Low frequency of assassinations (2 or less)	Afghanistan (2) Belgium (1) Bulgaria (0) Canada (1) Ceylon (2) Denmark (0) El Salvador (2) Ethiopia (2) Finland (0) Ireland (0) Liberia (2) Netherlands (0)	New Zealand (1) Norway (0) Peru (0) Poland (0) Portugal (2) Rumania (0) Saudi Arabia (2) Spain (2) Sweden (0) Switzerland (0) Uruguay (0)	Albania (2) Australia (2) Chile (0) Costa Rica (2) East Germany (0) Honduras (0) Hungary (1) China–Taiwan (0) United Kingdom (0) USSR (0) West Germany (2) Yugoslavia (2)	35
	23	12		
Chi-square value = 3.56 $p < 0.10$	35	37	72	

Table 22 – Stability-instability by level of minority hostility

	Low Minority Hostility			High Minority Hostility			
Unstable (126-445)	Egypt Haiti	Syria Thailand	6	Ceylon India Indonesia Iran	Peru Tunisia Turkey United States	13	19
Stable (012-125)	Bulgaria Canada Czechoslovakia Mexico Netherlands	New Zealand Philippines Switzerland United Kingdom Yugoslavia	10	Cyprus Israel		2	12
			16			15	31

Chi-square value = 5.95
$p < 0.05$

Table 23. – Frequency of assassination by level of minority hostility

	Low minority hostility	High minority hostility		
High Frequency of assassinations (3 or more)	Czechoslovakia (5) Haiti (5) Mexico (3) Philippines (1) Thailand (3)	Cyprus (5) Egypt (14) India (8) Indonesia (5) Iran (19 Iraq (5) Israel (3) Lebanon (12)	Morocco (17) Pakistan (5) Syria (7) Tunisia (16) Turkey (4) USA (16) Union South Africa (3)	
	5		15	20
Low Frequency of assassinations (2 or less)	Bulgaria (0) Chile (0) Netherlands (0) United Kingdom (0) New Zealand (0) Yugoslavia (2)	Belgium (1) Canada (1) Ceylon (2) Switzerland (0) Peru (0)		
	6		5	11
	11		20	31

Chi-square value = 1.57

$p < 0.25$

Table 24.—Frequency of assassination by level of minority hostility (scaled)

	Low minority hostility					High minority hostility	
	1	2	3	4	5	6	
High frequency of assassinations (3 or more)	Mexico (3)		Czechoslovakia (5) Haiti (5) Philippines (15) Thailand (3)	Egypt (14) Lebanon (12) Syria (7)	India (8) Indonesia (5) Iran (19) Israel (3) Morocco (17) Pakistan (5) Tunisia (16) Turkey (4) United States (16) Union South Africa (3)	Cyprus (5) Iraq (5)	
	1	0	4	3	10	2	20
Low frequency of assassinations (2 or less)	New Zealand (1)	Netherlands(0)	Bulgaria (0) Chile (0) United Kingdom (0) Yugoslavia (2)	Canada (1) Switzerland (0)	Belgium (1) Ceylon (2) Peru (0)		
	1	1	4	2	3	0	11
Chi-square value = 4.76 p < 0.50	2	1	8	5	13	2	31

Table 25.—Stability-Instability by Homicide Rate

	Low homicide	High homicide	
Unstable (126-445)	Belgium France Greece Italy Poland Portugal Spain	Brazil Burma Ceylon Chile Colombia Dom. Republic Egypt Guatemala India Jordan Peru USA	
	7	12	
Stable (012-125)	Austria Canada China—Taiwan Czechoslovakia Denmark Iceland Ireland Luxembourg Netherlands New Zealand Norway Sweden Switzerland United Kingdom West Germany	Australia Bulgaria Costa Rica Ecuador Finland Hungary Japan Mexico Nicaragua Panama Philippines Uruguay	
	15	12	24
	22		

Chi-square value= 1.34 $p < 0.25$

Table 26.—Frequency of assassination by homicide rate

	Low homicide	High homicide	Total
High frequency of assassinations (3 or more)	Czechoslovakia (5) France Greece (5) Italy (3) 4	Brazil (12) Burma (5) Colombia (7) Dom. Rep. (7) Ecuador (3) Egypt (14) Guatemala (12) India (8) Japan (9) Jordan (6) Mexico (3) Nicaragua (5) Panama (5) Philippines (15) United States (16) 15	19
Low frequency of assassinations (2 or less)	Austria (1) Belgium (1) Canada (1) China—Taiwan (0) Denmark (0) Iceland (0) Ireland (0) Luxembourg (0) Netherlands (0) New Zealand (1) Norway (0) Poland (0) Portugal (2) Spain (2) Sweden (0) Switzerland (0) United Kingdom (0) West Germany (2) 18	Australia (2) Bulgaria (0) Ceylon (2) Chile (0) Costa Rica (2) Finland (0) Hungary (1) Peru (0) Uruguay (0) 9	27
	22	24	46

Chi-square value = 7.56
$p < 0.01$

Table 27.—Stability-instability by suicide rate

	Low suicide	High suicide	
Unstable (126-445)	Burma Chile Colombia Dom. Republic Egypt Greece Guatemala India Italy Jordan Peru Spain	Belgium Brazil Ceylon France Poland Portugal USA	
	12	7	19
Stable (012-125)	Canada Costa Rica Ecuador Ireland Mexico Netherlands New Zealand Nicaragua Norway Panama Philippines	Australia Austria Bulgaria China—Taiwan Czechoslovakia Denmark Finland Hungary Iceland Japan Luxembourg Sweden Switzerland United Kingdom Uruguay West Germany	
	11	16	27
	23	23	46

Chi-square value = 1.43
$p < 0.25$

Table 28.—Frequency of assassination by suicide rate

	Low suicide	High suicide	
High frequency of assassinations (3 or more)	Burma (5) Colombia (7) Dom. Rep. (7) Ecuador (3) Egypt (14) Greece (5) Guatemala (12) India (8) Italy (3) Jordan (6) Mexico (3) Nicaragua (5) Panama (5) Philippines (15) 14	Brazil (12) Czechoslovakia (5) France (14) Japan (9) United States (16) 5	19
Low frequency of assassinations (2 or less)	Canada (1) Chile (0) Costa Rica (2) Ireland (0) Netherlands (0) New Zealand (1) Norway (0) Peru (0) Spain (2) 9	Australia (2) Austria (1) Belgium (1) Bulgaria (0) Ceylon (2) China—Taiwan (0) Denmark (0) Finland (0) Hungary (1) Iceland (0) Luxembourg (0) Poland (0) Portugal (2) Sweden (0) Switzerland (0) United Kingdom (0) Uruguay (0) West Germany (2) 18	27
	23	23	46

Chi-square value = 5.86
$p < 0.05$

Table 29.—Stability-instability by combined suicide and homicide rates

	Low suicide Low homicide	High suicide Low homicide	Low suicide High homicide	High suicide High homicide	
Unstable (126-445)	Greece Italy Spain	Belgium France Poland Dominican Republic Egypt Guatemala India Jordan Peru	Burma Chile Colombia	Brazil Ceylon USA	
	3	4	9	3	19
Stable (012-125)	Canada Ireland Netherlands New Zealand Norway	Austria China—Taiwan Czechoslovakia Denmark Iceland Luxembourg Sweden Switzerland United Kingdom West Germany	Costa Rica Ecuador Mexico Nicaragua Panama Philippines	Australia Bulgaria Finland Hungary Japan Uruguay	
	5	10	6	6	27
	8	14	15	9	46

Chi-square value = 33.84
P < 0.001

Table 30. – Frequency of assassination by combined suicide and homicide rates

	Low suicide Low homicide	High suicide Low homicide	Low suicide High homicide	High suicide High homicide	
High frequency of assassinations (3 or more)	Greece (5) Italy (3)	Czechoslovakia (5) France (14)	Burma (5) Columbia (7) Dom. Republic (7) Ecuador (3) Egypt (14) Guatemala (12) India (8) Jordan (6) Mexico (3) Nicaragua (5) Panama (5) Philippines (15)	Brazil (12) Japan (9) USA (16)	
	2	2	12	3	19
Low frequency of assassinations (2 or less)	Canada (1) Ireland (0) Netherlands (0) New Zealand (1) Norway (0) Spain (2)	Austria (1) Belgium (1) China–Taiwan (0) Denmark (0) Iceland (0) Luxembourg (0) Poland (0) Portugal (2) Sweden (0) Switzerland (0) United Kingdom (0) West Germany (2)	Chile (0) Costa Rica (2) Peru (0)	Australia (2) Bulgaria (0) Ceylon (2) Finland (0) Hungary (1) Uruguay (0)	
	6	12	3	6	27
	8	14	15	9	46

Chi-square value = 14.59
$p < 0.01$

Table 31.—*Correlation coefficients of ecological indicators, political instability, and frequency of assassinations*[a]

	Assassinations		Instability (summed scores) (1948-65)
	New York Times		
	Raw	Transformed	
Level of modernity (84) [b]	-.229	-.402	-.382
Level of systemic satisfaction (62)	-.261	-.431	-.569
Rate of socioeconomic change (67)	.269	.415	.517
Level of coerciveness (84)	.153	.198	.311
Level of international aggressiveness (72)	.318	.319	.409
Level of minority hostility (31)	.300	.346	.440
Homicide rate (46)	.278	.377	.427
Suicide rate (46)	.265	-.319	-.378
Instability (summed scores)	.528	.628	

[a] A correlation coefficient is a measure of the degree to which two variables are related. The mathematical value which this coefficient may take ranges from -1.00 to +1.00. A coefficient of 1.00 (whether plus or minus) indicates perfect interrelationship among two variables, so that a unit change in one produces a unit change in the other. A zero correlation indicates no relationship whatsoever. The closer the coefficient to 1.00 the closer the relationship between the two variables.

[b] Number in parenthesis indicates the number of countries examined for each category.

Table 32. – Relationship between level of development, coerciveness of regime, rate of socioeconomic change and assassination frequency, political instability, external aggression

	Modernity-low coerciveness-mid 3-4-5 change-high	Modernity-low coe-low-high 1-2-6 change-high	Modernity-high coerciveness-mid 3-4-5 change-high	Modernity-low coe-low-high 1-2-6 change-low	Modernity-high coerciveness-mid 3-4-5 change-low	Modernity-low coerciveness-mid 3-4-5 change-low	Modernity-high coe-low-high 1-2-6 change-high	Modernity-high coe-low-high 1-2-6 change-low	Totals
Low assas. stable low external aggression	El Salvador							Bulgaria Canada Denmark Finland Ireland Netherlands New Zealand Norway Sweden Switzerland Uruguay	12
Low assas. stable high external aggression	Honduras				China-Taiwan		Costa Rica	Australia United Kingdom West Germany	6
High assas. stable low external aggression		Ecuador Philippines		Japan Panama				Italy	5
Low assas. unstable low external aggression	Ceylon Peru Portugal					Spain		Belgium	5
Low assas. unstable high external aggression						Chile	USSR		2
High assas. stable high external aggression					Mexico			Israel	2
High assas. unstable low external aggression	Colombia Bolivia Brazil Thailand		Dominican Republic			Greece			6
High assas. unstable high external aggression	Iraq Korea Turkey Venezuela Burma Cambodia Haiti India Indonesia	Egypt Guatemala Pakistan Paraguay				Argentina Cuba France Union of South Africa		USA	16
Totals	18	6	1	2	2	7	2	18	50

Among countries showing the reverse pattern, eighty-six percent have a low incidence of assassination. The pattern for countries either high or low on both homicide and suicide is not clear cut. All show a greater tendency toward a low frequency of assassination. The United States is an exception however, because it is high on homicide, high on suicide, and high on assassination.

All the relationships discussed above are summarized in table 31, which shows the relationship of each factor to both political violence and frequency of assassination. The last column of the table shows the degree of relationship between the two forms of violence: assassination and general political instability. The first impression gained from the table is that some of the variables show more interrelationship than do others.

The factor that shows the strongest relationship to assassination frequency is the general level of political violence within the society, indicating that, when assassinations are frequent, other forms of political violence also tend to be present. The two conditions that appear to have the closest relationship to both assassination and political instability are systemic satisfaction level and rate of socioeconomic change. These relationships show that societies experiencing systemic frustration and a high rate of socioeconomic change are prone to political violence in general and assassination in particular. Level of coerciveness of political regime shows the weakest relationship to both forms of violence. This reflects the fact that coerciveness is curvilinearly related to violence and assassination, as pointed out above. The correlation values taken as a group range from 0.2 to 0.6, with the majority at approximately 0.4, indicating a moderate degree of relationship. Thus each has a certain potential for explaining the occurrence of political violence and assassination.

D. Conclusions

What can be said regarding the cross-national pattern of violence and assassination? Do our findings help to explain the incidence of assassination in the United States?

(1) Perhaps the broadest generalization we may offer is that violence, viewed cross-nationally, is not a random occurrence. Political, social, and ecological factors are associated

with it, sufficiently so that a knowledge of these associated factors can improve our prediction of political violence beyond the chance level. On the other hand, the relationships are not sufficiently persuasive to claim that we have provided a complete explanation. Insufficient information and imperfect data manipulation and measurement cause unknown errors. The occurrence of other variables which we did not take into account would also undoubtedly improve predictability.

(2) The second broad generalization is that assassinations show a similar pattern to internal political violence and instability. Whatever is related to violent and aggressive behavior within countries is also related to the occurrence of assassinations.

More specifically:

(a) A high rate of assassination is directly related to systemic frustration, external aggression, minority tensions, and homicide rates, as well as to political instability and violence. In other words, the higher the levels of systemic frustration, external aggression, minority tension, homicide rates, and general political violence within a society, the higher the assassination rates.

(b) A high rate of assassination is inversely related to measures of modernity and suicide. Thus the higher the level of modernity and the higher the level of suicides within a society, the less likelihood there is of assassination.

(c) Frequency of assassination is curvilinearly related to coerciveness of political regime. Permissive, democratic societies and highly coercive regimes are less prone to assassination than are countries at midlevels of coerciveness.

It is important to stress the fact that these relationships also hold true for aggregate measures of internal political aggression and violence.

In the previous discussion, the global pattern of violence was examined in reference to each selected variable. It is of equal interest to look at combined patterns. In table 32, six variables are examined simultaneously. The rows of the table combine three forms of political aggression: assassination frequency, political instability, and international (or external) aggression. Each variable is separated, yielding eight possible combinations. The rows are ordered from the most peaceful combination (low frequency of assassination, political stability, and low level of external aggression) to the most aggressive combination (high frequency of assassination, political instability, and high level of external aggression). The columns combine three of the most significant ecological variables: modernity level, rate of socioeconomic change, and level of permissiveness–coerciveness of regime. Again the variables are separated yielding eight combinations. The columns are ordered from highest potential violence (low level of modernity, midlevels of coerciveness, and high rate of socioeconomic change) to lowest potential violence (high level of modernity, permissiveness levels 1, 2, or 6, and low rate of socioeconomic change).

There is a very pronounced patterning here that identifies syndromes of political aggression and non-aggression in the contemporary world. Eleven countries appear in the upper right-hand corner of the table. These are modern states which have permissive regimes, experience a low rate of socioeconomic change, and are low on the three measures of political aggression. They have experienced few assassinations, and enjoy low levels of internal and external aggression. Nine of these eleven nations may be identified as Western-style democracies. One country, Uruguay, is in Latin America, and the other, Bulgaria, is from the Communist bloc. The latter is not permissive but rather comes from the other extreme of the permissiveness—coerciveness dimension (scale value 6). There are three additional Western democracies that fit the non-aggressive syndrome despite the fact that they are high in external aggression.

At the other end of the table, in the lower left-hand corner, the opposite syndrome is in evidence. Nine countries are high on three forms of aggression (assassination, general political unrest, and external aggression) and also high on three types of systemic frustration. These are low in modernity, at midlevels of political coerciveness, and experience high rates of socioeconomic change. These countries are drawn from three areas of the world: Asia, Latin America, and the Middle East. Four other countries have the same high levels of systemic frustration and exhibit a high frequency of assassination and a high level of general political unrest, but are low in external aggression. Three of these nations are from Latin America; one is from Asia. Four additional countries are high on all three forms of political aggression, while high on two of three types of systemic frustration. These countries are also from Asia, Latin America, and the Middle East.

We thus have fourteen countries that come close to fitting a non-aggressive syndrome and seventeen that approximate an aggressive syndrome. There are fifty-six countries in the table; hence, fifty-five percent of the sample may be accounted for in terms of these two syndromes. Furthermore, forty-one cells are empty, indicating that two-thirds of the potentially possible combinations of variables do not exist. If chance alone were operating and there were no relationship among these six variables, these cells would not remain empty.

There are also exceptions to the pattern sprinkled throughout the table. The largest group of deviants are the four countries that are high on all three forms of political aggression, yet satisfied on two of three indicators. The most completely deviant countries in the table are El Salvador and the United States. The former is non-aggressive despite experiencing all the preconditions supposedly conducive to political violence. The United States is high on three forms of violence, despite internal conditions which should predispose political tranquility. Furthermore, in view of the high frequency of assassinations in the United States, it cannot be claimed that we are a case of only borderline deviancy. The United States ranks fifth of the eighty-four countries surveyed in terms of the total number of assassination events experienced, although this high rank is somewhat reduced in the other subcategories of assassination. Among the group of Western democracies, the United States has experienced sixteen assassinations, while ten other countries never had an assassination. It is in this respect that the deviant nature of the United States is most dramatically illustrated.

There is a strong suggestion that, in the global pattern, assassinations tend to occur with other events of a rather high intensity of violence, and, specifically, that they occur in conjunction with guerrilla warfare. In the United States, however, the events of the highest intensity of violence, apart from assassinations, are riots and demonstrations. Not only is the United States a deviant case in terms of excessive frequency of assassinations, but the pattern of violence is also atypical in comparison to that of other nations.

Because the United States is clearly a deviant in these respects, it may be difficult to arrive at an adequate explanation in terms of the variables we have chosen for this cross-national analysis. There must be other circumstances that we have omitted which are responsible for this country's political behavior. These circumstances may be presumed to be largely absent from the comparable group of nations, that is, the modern, Western democracies which, on the whole, experience a low assassination rate. None of the correlation coefficients between our selected set of ecological variables and the occurrence of instability and assassinations is so high as to provide a set of clear-cut determinants.

Although additional variables may be responsible, there are still findings in the previous section that may at least suggest dimensions to be explored further in seeking explanations for this country's assassination rate. It will be remembered that the assassination rate is a concomitant of the level of general political aggression. In the case of the United States, assassinations occurred predominantly during the 1960's. This was also a period of heightened political violence. In the 1956–60 period, for example, the United States experienced no events that registered higher than position 3 on the six-point instability scale, but from 1961 to 1965, twelve percent of this country's events were at scale position 4.

Another possible explanation is the association between assassination and external violence. In this respect also, the United States is no deviant. In very specific terms, considering American foreign policy and the internal responses to it, the Vietnam war undoubtedly is a strong factor in creating politically anomic behavior. A somewhat comparable case can be seen in France's controversial involvement in Algeria. Nine of France's fourteen assassination events, or sixty-four percent, took place during the years 1957–62 (thirty percent of the total time period).

There is one circumstance in the United States, as well as in many other nations, that must be judged a powerful explanatory factor in increasing political violence. This is the level of tension among ethnic, racial, linguistic, religious, and other groups within society. Among the sixteen assassinations which have occurred in the United States during the last twenty years, seven can be attributed to this problem. Furthermore, of the twelve assassinations occurring in the 1960's, six stem from the minority problem.

The presence of minority groups is one of the variables in the present study that is not sufficiently refined to yield a more accurate picture and perhaps a more persuasive pattern of association. Too much is left unexplained about the nature of the minority, the goals, the type of country, and the response of the majority that develops minority-majority tensions. Even in this early stage of cross-national investigation, it belongs among the predictors of internal violence and assassination. The United States fits the expected patterns as present in tables 24–26, which show that minority hostility relates to political violence and assassination.

The correlation of minority-group tensions with political violence and assassination does not mean that minority groups necessarily are the agents of violence or assassination. Indeed, Negroes, the minority group with whom most of the tension is associated, seem to be the victims rather than the assassins.

The existence of minority-group tensions seems to be a symptom of other underlying social factors which lead to political violence but which may not be apparent in a statistical overview. For example, on a statistical average, the United States is a modern nation experiencing a relatively low rate of socioeconomic change and a low level of governmental coerciveness. However, we can speculate that certain significant groups within the United States, such as Negroes, experience midlevel coerciveness, a high rate of socioeconomic change, and a low rate of modernity as compared with their perception of other groups in the society.

We can perhaps think of the current "black revolution" as a previously isolated but now politically significant and participant stratum of the population reaching toward modern, satisfied, stable, permissive, democratic, Western society at an increasingly accelerated rate of speed. This social substratum could be conceived as similar to the transitional nations in the global pattern. It is equally subject to rising expectations and the feeling of systemic frustration. In this sense, then, the American Negro community could be conceived as largely transitional, frustrated, and at present subject to a rapid rate of social change.

Even the aggregate permissiveness of the dominant political regime may be considered at midlevels of coerciveness in its relationship to this social segment. Furthermore, the emergence of transitional societies in its midst also forces rapid social change on the rest of society. Thus the United States should perhaps be considered a "high change" society at present. In conjunction with some other selected characteristics, this fits rather well the picture of the violent or assassination syndrome.

Although this assessment of the domestic scene in the United States might seem persuasive, it is but a speculative generalization in the perspective of the broader global picture. In relying largely on aggregate data, the present analysis does not reach the subtleties inherent in specific case studies.

The present effort can only hope to reveal the more obvious patterns, and note the more striking deviations. Furthermore, macroscopic cross-national analysis is at a stage of development where one must be sufficiently humble to state that patterns are seen only through a haze of imperfect information, imprecisions of data manipulation, and measurement error.

In sum, the pattern we have determined by cross-national investigation indicates that the characteristics of an assassination-prone society are very similar to those of a society beset by a high level of political unrest. This is to be expected, because assassinations are one facet of a politically unstable behavior pattern. The traits which have been isolated in this analysis to describe the aggressive nation are: a low level of modernity, high systemic frustration, a high rate of socioeconomic change, a high level of need for achievement, midlevels of coerciveness of political regime, a high level of external aggression, a high level of minority hostility, a high level of homicide, and a low level of suicide. This is a general pattern from which individual nations may deviate to greater or lesser degree. The United States shows a high frequency of assassination without exhibiting the low level of development traits characteristic of other assassination-prone societies. On the other hand, it does show a high level of external aggression, a high level of minority hostility, and a high incidence of homicide. Furthermore, it shows an increasing tendency toward political unrest. All these traits are aggressive behaviors. Also, as discussed above, the typical criteria found cross-nationally that lead to political violence may exist for certain important groups within the total U.S. society.

Appendix A to this report sets forth each assassination event collected by the Leiden and Feierabend groups.

References

1. The members of the Leiden team include Carl Leiden, Murray Havens, Karl Schmitt, and James Soukup. The members

of the Feierabend team consist of Ivo Feierabend, Rosalind
Feierabend, Betty A. Nesvold, and Franz N. Jaggar, with
assistance from Rosemary J. Roth, K. Linden Smithson,
Robert Kaufman, and Antonia E. Williams. A list of assassination events collected by both Feierabend and Leiden is set
forth in Appendix A to this report. The two sets of data do
not always correspond. Differences of definition, differences
of judgment in applying definitions, and different sources of
data lead to varying counts of assassination events. Thus, no
significance can be drawn, for example, from the specific
ranking of a country in assassination events from either set
of data or a peaking of assassination events *in any one year.*
The two sets of data discussed herein do correspond generally. In the analyses that follow, we have not relied upon a
specific rank ordering of countries. We have done no more
than divide countries broadly into high and low assassination
event countries. The data allow us to make such broad distinctions with confidence. However, an examination was made
of those countries which appear on both the Leiden and
Feierabend lists. The countries were ranked in terms of the
total number of attempts in each list. Computation of the
Spearman rank order correlation resulted in a high degree of
agreement ($r_s = +0.80$) between the two investigators.

2. The Leiden data rank assassination attempts by the prominence of the target in six categories: rank 1, heads of state,
heads of government, or dictators, e.g., Presidents, Kings,
Premiers, or former holders of these positions; rank 2, cabinet ministers, ambassadors, vice presidents, leading judges,
bureaucrats, and legislators; rank 3, high military officers;
rank 4, provincial governors, second-level officeholders and
chargés d'affairs; rank 5, politically prominent private citizens;
and rank 6, third-level officeholders and lower ranking
officials. Figure 2 plots frequency of attacks against ranks 1,
2, and 3 only because it was felt that reporting error worldwide would make use of data with respect to the lower ranks
too unreliable. All ranks are plotted for the United States in
Figure 3.

3. The Leiden group defines such officials as: (1) heads of state;
(2) cabinet ministers, ambassadors, vice presidents, leading
judges, leading bureaucrats, and leading legislators; (3) high
ranking military officers. Not included, for example, are governors of States of the United States and members of Congress unless they have particular political prominence.

4. The complete definition of assassination event as used by the
Feierabend group is set forth in Appendix A.

5. Further corroboration of this lack of relationship may be
shown mathematically from the data. The Feierabend group

took assassination data from both the *New York Times Index* and *Deadline Data* and compared those with population size both directly and using a log transformation $(X+1)$ to compensate for the highly skewed nature of the assassination data. A correlation of 1.0 or -1.0 is perfect; a correlation of zero would mean a complete absence of any correlation. The correlation obtained between assassination events and population size both logged and unlogged ranged from a high of .093 to a low of .035—*i.e.*, virtually no correlation whatsoever.

6. The remainder of this chapter is an edited version of the paper, "Political Violence and Assassination: A Cross-National Analysis," prepared by Ivo K. Feierabend, Rosalind L. Feierabend, Betty A. Nesvold, and Franz Jaggar. The data on ecological variables and political violence were collected as a portion of the research project, "Systemic Conditions of Political Aggression," supported by the National Science Foundation. Grants Nos. GS–1417 and GS–1781.

7. As for the assassination events, political turmoil data were collected for the same eighty-four nations for the period 1948–65 from *Deadline Data on World Affairs* and the *Yearbooks* of the *Encyclopaedia Britannica*. Altogether some 8,000 events are contained in this data collection.

8. Elections, vacation of office, significant change of laws, acquisition of office, crisis within a non-governmental organization, organization of opposition party, repressive action against specific groups, microstrikes, general strikes, macrostrikes, microdemonstrations, macrodemonstrations, microriots, macroriots, severe macroriots, arrests of few insignificant persons, assassination, martial law, execution of significant persons, execution of insignificant persons, terrorism and sabotage, guerrilla warfare, civil war, *coups d'état*, revolts, and exile.

9. Riots and demonstrations, boycotts, arrests, repressive action against specific groups, sabotage, martial law, *coup d'etat*, revolt, guerrilla warfare, assassination, execution, and civil war.

10. The finding that assassination tends to occur in conjunction with guerrilla warfare has support in the results obtained by other researchers. It should be pointed out, however, that in one research investigation, assassination occurred on a common dimension with riots, strikes, and demonstrations, a pattern that is typical of the United States. See Rummel and Tanter referenced in full at footnote 19.

11. These indicators, which are based primarily on UN statistics for 1948–55, are further discussed in: Ivo K. and Rosalind L. Feierabend, "Aggressive Behaviors Within Polities, 1948–

1962: A Cross-National Study," *Journal of Conflict Resolution,* Sept. 1966, pp. 249–271; Betty A. Nesvold, "Turmoil to Civil War: A Cross-National Survey," Ph.D. thesis, (University of Minnesota, 1968); and Betty A. Nesvold, "Modernity, Social Frustration, and Stability of Political Systems: A Cross-National Study," M.A. thesis, San Diego State College, 1964.

12. Bruce M. Russett, Hayward R. Alker, Jr., Karl W. Deutsch, and Harold D. Lasswell, *World Handbook of Political and Social Indicators,* (New Haven: Yale University Press, 1964), pp. 294–298.

13. See Feierabend and Feierabend, "Aggressive Behaviors Within Polities," *op. cit.,* footnote 11.

14. The cutting points on the variables in these two tables, as well as in all the contingency tables in this report, were set at the median values on each dimension, thus equalizing the number of cases in the marginals. If we were to manipulate this cutting point, we would increase the chi-square value. If this were done, to discover the threshold values of the predictor indicator, for example, the size of the chi-square value and the correlation coefficients might seem less discrepant. (See, for example, the statistically nonsignificant chi-square value and the significant correlation in the case of the relationships between political violence and homicides and suicides, tables 16–19.)

15. For a more thorough discussion, see Feierabend and Feierabend, "Aggressive Behaviors Within Polities"; research paper written at San Diego State College, 1965, and Wallace W. Conroe, "A Cross-National Analysis of the Impact of Modernization Upon Political Stability," M.A. thesis, San Diego State College, 1965.

16. For greater detail, see Ivo K. Feierabend and Rosalind L. Feierabend, "The Relationship Between Frustration, Coerciveness, International Tension and Political Instability: A Cross-National Study," paper presented at the Annual Meeting of the American Psychological Association, New York City, Sept. 1966; and Jennifer G. Walton, "Correlates of Coerciveness and Permissiveness of National Political Systems: A Cross-National Study," M.A. thesis, San Diego State College, 1965.

17. The coerciveness profiles show a correlation of $r = 0.67$ to the Political Development index developed by Phillips Cutright. ("National Political Development: Measurement and Analysis," *American Sociological Review,* April, 1963, pp. 253–264). This index uses as its criteria the extent of opposition in national legislatures and the mode of acquisition and tenure of office by chief executives. The types of political

systems classified by Coleman in Gabriel A. Almond and James S. Coleman, *The Politics of Developing Areas* (Princeton: Princeton University Press, 1960) also show similarity to our coerciveness index, as do the nation typologies emerging in 'Arthur S. Banks and Phillip M. Gregg, "Grouping Political Systems: Q-Factor Analysis of a Cross-Polity Survey," *The American Behavioral Scientist,* Nov. 1965, pp. 3–6. For more detail, see Walton, *op. cit.* footnote 16, and Norman M. Howard, "Modernity, Rate of Change and Coerciveness of Political Systems: A Cross-National Study," M.A. thesis, San Diego State College, 1966.

18. The minority data were collected by the authors as a portion of the Systemic Conditions of Political Aggression project; see footnote 6, *supra.*

19. This data collection comes from Rudolph J. Rummel, "Dimensions of Conflict Behavior Within and Between Nations," *General Systems Yearbook,* vol. 8, pp. 1–50, 1963, and Raymond Tanter, "Dimensions of Conflict Behavior Within and Between Nations, 1958–60," *Journal of Conflict Resolution,* March, 1966, pp. 41–64. For the scaling of the data and other information, see Feierabend and Feierabend, *op. cit.,* footnote 16; Frank W. Scanland III, "International Conflict and Internal Frustration: A Cross-Policy Study," M.A. thesis, San Diego State College, 1968; and John Stuart Chambers, Jr., "Hostility and Amity in International Relations: A Transactional Study," M.A. thesis, San Diego State College, 1966. Also, Ivo K. Feierabend and Rosalind L. Feierabend, "Level of Development and Inter-Nation Behavior," in Richard Butwell, Ed., *Foreign Policy and the Developing Nations* (forthcoming University of Kentucky Press, 1969), pp. 135–188.

20. For a discussion of these variables, see Robert W. Winslow, "Social Integration, Suicide, and Homicide: A Cross-National Study," a paper delivered at the Annual Meeting of the Pacific Sociological Association, San Francisco, March 1968.

CHAPTER 4

POLITICAL VIOLENCE IN THE UNITED STATES

Introduction—Summary

Assassination may be viewed as an extreme case along the continuum of political violence. Less extreme forms of political violence are far more common, in the United States as elsewhere, and the cross-national quantitative studies of Chapter 3 demonstrate that the incidence of assassination in a country and the level of political violence are closely related. It is appropriate therefore, in reporting on the phenomenon of assassination in the United States, to examine the present data on the broader spectrum of political violence in the United States.

In this chapter, section A gives an historical overview of violence in the United States. The analysis demonstrates that violence to achieve political goals has been endemic to the United States since its inception.

Section B presents original data with respect to the intensity of political violence today as compared to violence in the United States since 1819. The major conclusion is that the United States, at several prior stages in its history, has experienced political violence of a comparable intensity to the present day. But the data also show that the 1960's rank among the most intensely violent periods in our history, and that periods of comparable violence have not occurred since the late 1920's or the turn of the century.

Section C is an analysis of data collected by a national survey designed by the Commission staff. That analysis attempts to identify the demographic characteristics of those who give verbal support for political violence. Those data suggest, as do the cross-national data presented in Chapter 3, that the confrontation between black aspirations and whites directly threatened by those aspirations is the most significant source of willingness to use violence in general for political goals.

Section D presents an original collection of the contemporary rhetoric of vilification of political figures and the rhetoric of the advocacy of violence. The studies (particularly those of assassination in other regions) indicate that a high intensity of such rhetoric of vilification and violence is frequently a pre-conditioning to incidents of assassination. Finally, in section E, again using original data collected for the Commission, two specific contemporary groups within the United States associated with violent acts and violent rhetoric are examined: the North Carolina Ku Klux Klan and the North Ward Citizens Council of Newark, N.J.

Our data suggest that violence is a concomitant of substantial social change, and appears among those groups most directly affected, either favorably or unfavorably, by such change. We suggest the obvious: political violence can be reduced by mitigating the dislocations, hardships, and threats that arise from rapid social change. Above all, the major burden of problems associated with change should not either by inadvertence or design fall upon specific subgroups of the population.

A. Historical Overview of Political Violence in the United States

The United States, of course, was born in political violence. The British soldiers killed by the shots heard round the world were real people—young men serving their country. The following is a highly condensed historical overview of political violence in the United States beginning with vigilantism.[1] This subject is treated extensively in the report to the Commission by the History Task Force.

1. Vigilantism

The prototype of political violence in the United States is the vigilante committee—an extra-legal group that enforces the values of the community by illegal violence. Vigilantism is a phenomenon apparently unique to the United States.

The first large-scale vigilante movement occurred in the South Carolina back country in the late 1760's. A tradition of vigilantism took root in response to a typical American problem: the absence of effective law and order in the frontier region. It was a problem that occurred again and again beyond the Appalachian Mountains, and stimulated the formation of countless frontier vigilante movements.

The first phase of American vigilantism, mainly before the Civil War, dealt largely with the threat of frontier horsethieves and counterfeiters. Virtually every state or territory west of the Appalachians had one or more well-organized, relentless vigilante movement. The vigilante movement was not unique to the Western plains and mountains; there was as much if not more vigilantism east of the Missouri and Mississippi Rivers. The main thrust of vigilantism was to reestablish in each newly settled frontier area the values of property and law and order.[2]

Vigilante movements were usually under the control of the frontier elite and represented their social values and preferences. This was true of the first vigilante band in South Carolina (1767–69) known as "Regulators"—the original but now obsolete term for vigilantes.[3] It was also true of the greatest of all American vigilante movements, the San Francisco vigilante committee of 1856, which was dominated lock, stock, and barrel by the leading merchants of the city who wanted to stamp out alleged crime and political corruption.

Although the typical vigilante movement was dominated by social conservatives who desired to establish order and stability in newly settled areas, there were a disconcerting number of departures from the norm. Many vigilante movements led not to order but to increasing disorder and anarchy. Frequently, the strife between vigilantes and their opponents (aggravated by individual, family, and political hatreds) became so bitter that the governor had to call out the militia to restore order. When the Bald Knobbers of the Missouri Ozarks rose in 1887 to curb the evils of theft, liquor, gambling, and prostitution in Christian County, intervention by outside authorities was finally needed to suppress the movement.[4]

Today, educated men may view vigilantism with disapproval, but such was not the case in the nineteenth century. In those days, leading citizens were often prominent members of vigilante movements, and proud of it. Included in a "Who's Who of American Vigilantism" would be United States senators and congressmen, governors, judges, wealthy capitalists, generals, lawyers, and even clergymen. Presidents of the United States have not been immune to the vigilante infection. During his presidency, Andrew Jackson once approved the vigilante methods of Iowa pioneers pending the clarification of their territorial status.[5] As a young cattlerancher in North Dakota, Theodore Roosevelt was refused admittance to a vigilante band that was being formed to deal with rustlers and horsethieves.[6]

The post-Civil War era also saw the climax of a movement with strong affinities to vigilantism: the anti-horsethief association movement, which grew predominantly in the rural Midwest and Southwest after the Civil War, although its roots were to be found in the Northwest as early as the 1790's. The anti-horsethief society pattern involved state charter of local associations that were often vested with constabulary power. By 1900, the anti-horsethief association movement numbered hundreds of thousands of members in a belt stretching from the Great Lakes to the Rio Grande. Forming a flexible and inexpensive (the members shared costs whenever they arose) supplement to immobile, expensive, and inefficient local law enforcement, the association afforded the farmer insurance against the threat of horse and other types of theft. The movement died only with the rapid development of the automobile about the time of World War I.[7]

2. Abolitionism and Anti-Abolitionism

The abolitionist movement spawned more righteousness, blood, and misery on both sides than any other movement in the history of the United States. Abolitionists used violence to oppose slavery—for example, John Brown's raid on Harper's Ferry in 1859—and anti-abolitionists resorted to violence to support slavery. "Bleeding Kansas," a horrible precursor to the Civil War itself, was a violent struggle between pro- and anti-slavery forces in the Kansas Territory. The ultimate solution of the slavery question, of course, was the most violent struggle ever to engage our society: the Civil War.[8] The bloody legacy of the war and its ineffectual solution to the relationships of white and black America continue to this day.[9]

3. Reimposing White Supremacy in the South after the Civil War (the First Ku Klux Klan)

The white elite of the old Confederacy used violence—from beating and flogging to burning at the stake—to regain political supremacy in the South and prevent the social, economic, and political advancement of the Negro. The first Ku Klux Klan, which lasted from 1865 to 1876, was a principal means of administering this violence in the South. It eventually attracted thousands of embittered and fearful men and declared as its fundamental objective, " 'The *MAINTENANCE OF THE SUPREMACY OF THE WHITE RACE*' in this Republic by terror and intimidation."[10]

The inevitable end was extreme violence. From 1867 until 1871, the Klan helped overthrow the Reconstruction governments of North Carolina, Tennessee, and Georgia, and was responsible (according to the findings of a Congressional investigation in 1871) for hangings, shootings, whippings, and mutilations numbering in the thousands. In Louisiana, at least two thousand were killed or wounded in the few weeks preceding the presidential election of 1868. Seventy-five killings were reported in Georgia, and one hundred and nine in Alabama. In a single county in northern Florida, more than one hundred and fifty men were murdered within a few months. The commanding general of federal troops in Texas reported: "Murders of Negroes are so common as to render it impossible to keep accurate accounts of them."[11]

4. Defense of American Nativism and Moralism— Native American Party—Know-Nothings— White Caps—Second Ku Klux Klan

Violence has been used by successive generations of native Americans (primarily white Anglo-Saxon Protestants) to oppose a perceived cultural, economic, social, and moral threat posed by successive waves of immigrants from Catholic and non-Teutonic Europe, and to reinforce the moral values of fundamentalist protestantism.

The first victims of bigotry and most of the violence were Roman Catholics and foreigners—most specifically the Irish immigrants who had begun settling in the Eastern cities and manufacturing areas during the 1830's and 1840's. An anti-Catholic, anti-immigrant political organization, the Native American Party, took root in these areas and rose to power as Irish immigration increased. The new party's literature and street oratory were designed to instill fear and excite passions. One document, signed by nine hundred party members and sent to Congress, expressed fears concerning "the rapid and extraordinary increase of the foreign population," which would "ere long expose the institutions of the country to serious danger."[12] In 1843, the Native American Party elected a mayor of New York and sent several members to Congress.[13]

The party also held a number of street meetings and parades in the heart of a predominantly Irish Philadelphia neighborhood in 1844, to which native Americans were asked to come "prepared for defense."[14] Months of street rioting ensued; several persons were killed and many injured. Two Catholic churches, two parochial schools, and at least a dozen homes owned by Catholics were burned to the ground. The militia was called, but units of the U.S. Cavalry and Marines had to be summoned before the riots were quelled.[15]

One of the anti-Catholic books of the period, *Foreign Conspiracies Against the Liberties of the United States*, by Samuel F. B. Morse, had called for the establishment of an "Anti-Popery Union."[16] When the "Know-Nothings" (officially, the Grand Council of the United States of North America) appeared in the 1850's, Morse heartily endorsed them.[17]

The new organization, which derived its name from instructions to its members to say "I know nothing," when questioned about it, was formed to keep Catholics and foreigners out of political office—in the organization's own words, "Thwarting the machinations and subverting the deadly plans of the Jesuit and Papist."[18]

Violence broke out in Boston in May 1854, when Know-Nothings, inflamed by street preachers, attacked a Catholic church, smashing windows and tearing down its cross, and then went on to destroy the homes of Irish Catholics in the neighborhood.[19] During this and the following year, there were many instances of mob violence and destruction of property directed at the Irish and Catholic churches.

In the national election of 1854, the Know-Nothings, organized politically as the American Party, elected governors in nine states and sent one hundred and four of its members to the House of Representatives (then a body of two hundred and thirty-four). In 1856 former President Millard Fillmore, the Know-Nothing presidential candidate, polled almost one million votes, about one in every five votes cast.[20]

The Know-Nothing movement declined after the 1856 election and disappeared during the Civil War. During the 1880's and 1890's, however, the American Protective Association (APA) appeared with the Know-Nothing spirit and much of the organization's literature to continue the anti-Catholic rhetoric of provocation.[21]

The White Cap movement, dedicated to the defense of "traditional moral values," arose in southern Indiana in the 1880's, and soon spread to all sections of the country. The movement generally used flogging as a mode of punishment. White Capping varied greatly throughout the country. In Mississippi, South Carolina, and north Texas, the White Caps were anti-Negro; in south Texas they were anti-Mexican; and in northern New Mexico the White Caps were composed of poor Mexican herders and ranchers who battled land-enclosing rich Mexicans and Americans.[22]

In general, White Capping was a spontaneous movement for the moral regulation of the poor whites and ne'er-do-wells of rural America. Drunken, shiftless, wife-beating whites and loose women were typical targets of White Cap violence. Vigilantism dating back to the South Carolina Regulators of 1767–69 had often been concerned with the moral regulation of incorrigible whites, and White Capping can be considered in part a throwback to the early era of frontier vigilantism. At the same time, White Capping seems to have been an important link between the first and second Ku Klux Klans. White Cap methods of punishment and costume seem to have been influenced by the first Klan, while their attacks on immoral and shiftless whites foreshadowed the main thrust of the second Klan of the 1920's.

White Capping began in the 1880's, about a decade after the first Klan, and by the turn of the century had become a generic term for local American violence. At the time of World War I, the movement was fading from view, and shortly thereafter the second Ku Klux Klan rose to take its place.[23]

The second Ku Klux Klan burned, beat, flogged, and lynched to preserve native Protestant superiority over Catholic, Jew, and immigrant, to preserve fundamentalist Protestant moral (primarily sexual) values, and to suppress the aspirations of Negro Americans in the South, Mexican Americans in the Southwest, and orientals in California.[24] The second Klan was founded in Georgia, in 1915, but achieved substantial political power in the North and West as well as in the South. Klansmen established a virtual dictatorship over political life in Indiana, and were politically powerful in Colorado, Oregon, New Jersey, Texas, Oklahoma, Maine, Louisiana, and even some sections of New York. By 1925, the year after it had become a national issue at a presidential convention, the Klan could boast a membership of between four and five million Americans, more than ten times that of the first hooded empire.

Violence remained the heart of its program. The *New York World* compiled statistics on Klan violence for the period between October 1920 and October 1921, while the movement was still growing. The results were:

> Four killings, one mutilation, one branding with acid, 42 floggings, 27 tar-and-feather parties, five kidnappings, 43 persons warned to leave town or otherwise threatened, 14 communities threatened by warning posters, and 16 parades by masked men with warning placards.[25]

During a congressional investigation in 1921, Representative Leonidas C. Dyer of Missouri provided a summary of the second Klan's operations:

> During the past year a constant succession of violent and criminal assaults on individuals, consisting of abductions, flogging, brandings, irreparable mutilations, applications of tar and feathers to men and women, and in several instances, murders, have been reported from various parts of the country . . . . Terrorization, active or passive, of the colored people in American communities, has been one of the Klan's principal objects.[26]

In later years, the anti-Semitism and race theories of the movement led the second Klan, in 1940, to join with the pro-Nazi German-American Bund in a large New Jersey rally where a forty-foot cross was burned and Nazi marching songs were sung.[27]

5. Agrarian Reform

From its very beginning, the United States has experienced violence from a series of movements in behalf of the suffering farmer or yeoman. Often these movements—generally considered to be liberal in their political character—have been formed for the purposes of redressing the economic grievances of the farmer; at times they have been land-reform movements. The dissident farmer movements have been deemed among the most heroic of all American movements of political insurgence; they have been the special favorites of historians who, with admiration and sympathy, have chronicled their ups and downs. There have been a host of these agrarian uprisings in both the colonial and national periods of our history. The initial agrarian uprising was that behind Nathaniel Bacon in late seventeenth century Virginia,[28] followed by the New Jersey land rioters of the eighteenth century.[29] The 1760's saw the Paxton Boys[30] movement of Pennsylvania and the New York anti-rent movement (which stretched on into the nineteenth century).[31] After the Revolutionary War were Shays' Rebellion in Massachusetts (1786–87),[32] the Whiskey Rebellion in western Pennsylvania (1794),[33] and Fries' Rebellion in eastern Pennsylvania (1799). Further west—in the Mississippi Valley before the Civil War—the Claims Clubs defended the land occupancy of squatters.[34]

After the Civil War, a plethora of economic problems gave rise to the Grangers, the Greenbackers, the Farmers' Alliance (which originally began in central Texas as a quasi-vigilante movement), and the Populist Party. About the same time there appeared a land reform movement in California which fought the monopoly landholdings of the Southern Pacific Railroad.[35] In New Mexico there appeared the aforementioned White Cap movement of poor Mexicans against the land-enclosing tactics of well-to-do Mexicans and Americans. Western Kentucky and the Ohio-Mississippi Valley area were the scene of a tobacco farmers' cooperative movement in the early 1900's which sought to end the control by the American Tobacco Company and foreign companies over the tobacco marketing system.[36]

Farmers became increasingly attracted to the Socialist Party, and the non-industrial state of Oklahoma soon led the nation in Socialist Party members. During World War I, a pacifist, anti-draft movement of Sharecroppers and small farmers in Oklahoma resulted in the "Green Corn Rebellion."[37] In 1915, the radical Nonpartisan League rose in North Dakota, enacting many reforms in that state and inspiring similar progressive farm movements in other states of the Northwest. The Farm Bloc emerged in Congress in the 1920's to promote legislation for easing the agricultural depression. When conditions worsened in the 1930's, the Farmers' Holiday Association was formed in the Midwest to lead farmer strikes and boycotts against the economic system.[38] In our own 1960's, the National Farmers' Organization has adopted similar tactics.

The insurgent-farmer movements have thus formed one of the longest and most enduring chronicles in the history of American reform, but have been troubled again and again by violence. Nathaniel Bacon's movement became a full-fledged rebellion which resulted in the burning of Jamestown. The New Jersey land rioters used violence to press their claims against the Jersey land companies. The New York anti-rent movement frequently used force against dominant landlords. The North Carolina Regulators rioted against the courthouse rings that burdened them with heavy taxes and fees.

The Paxton Boys of Pennsylvania followed their Indian massacre with a march on Philadelphia. The followers of Daniel Shays in Massachusetts disrupted court sessions to delay land foreclosures. Pennsylvania farmers rebelled against taxes on liquor and land in the Whiskey and Fries uprisings. The Western Claim Clubs (which, paradoxically, were sometimes dominated by land speculators pursuing their own interests) used intimidation to protect "squatters' rights."

The land reform movement in California gave birth to a "Night Rider" league in Tulare County, 1878–80, to resist railroad land agents. The tobacco farmer cooperative movement in Kentucky did not succeed in breaking monopoly domination of the marketing system until its Night Rider organization raided several western Kentucky towns, destroyed tobacco warehouses, and abused non-cooperating farmers. The New Mexican White Caps employed a reign of terror to fight the land-enclosure movement. The "Green Corn" rebels of Oklahoma contemplated a peaceful march on Washington, but armed themselves and committed a few acts of violence before the movement was halted. The Farmers' Holiday Association dumped milk cans, blocked roads, and manhandled opponents. Farmer grievances have been serious. Farmers repeatedly used a higher law—the need to right insufferable wrongs, the very justification of the American Revolution—to justify the use of violence in uprising after uprising.

6. Labor Violence

Historians have portrayed the labor movement in American history with the same sort of admiration as the agrarian uprisings. Most would agree that, by raising the health and living standard of the workingman, the American labor movement has been a significant factor in advancing the social well-being of the nation. But the labor movement has the same history of achieving glorious ends by inglorious means—violence—that characterized the agrarian movement.

A rudimentary labor movement existed in the port cities of the colonial period. While there was no organization of laborers as such, sailors, longshoremen, and other workers of the maritime industry occasionally rioted—stirred up, perhaps, by sporadic economic stringency.

The advent of the Industrial Revolution in the nineteenth century saw the birth of the labor movement. The tremendous growth of American industry after the Civil War was a prime factor. Various labor organizations mushroomed: The Knights of Labor, American Railway Union, American Federation of Labor, Western Federation of Miners (WFM), and the Industrial Workers of the World (IWW). All made the strike a major weapon, and in case after case violence accompanied the strike.[39]

The blame lay not on the side of labor alone. The unyielding attitude of the owners in regard to wages, hours, working conditions, and the desire to unionize led to the calling of these strikes. Violent attempts to suppress unions and break up strikes frequently contributed to the violence. However, laborers were often more than ready to resort to violence, as many of the great upheavals after the Civil War indicate.[40]

The great railroad strike of 1877 triggered massive riots that reached the level of insurrection in Pittsburgh. At the same time, the decade-long troubles with the Molly Maguires in the coal fields of eastern Pennsylvania came to a head. The Molly Maguires was a secret organization of Irish miners who fought their employers with assassination and mayhem.[41]

Events such as the Haymarket Riot in Chicago (1886),[42] the Homestead strike (1892)[43] the Idaho silver mining troubles in Coeur d'Alene (1892 ff.), and the 1910 dynamiting of the *Los Angeles Times* building[44] (by the McNamara brothers of the supposedly conservative American Federation of Labor) led Louis Adamic to label this period as "the era of dynamite" in American labor relations.[45] The last great era of violence in the history of American labor came in the 1930's with the sitdown strike movement which accompanied the successful drive to unionize the automobile and other great mass-production industries.

7. Political Violence in Contemporary America

a. The Third Ku Klux Klan

The Klan rose again after World War II, this time in the form of numerous autonomous groups and confederations of "klaverns" throughout the South. Although most of its violence was directed against Negroes or civil rights workers, Jews and Catholics also were targets.[46] The loosely organized Klans are the most widespread and pervasive terrorist organizations presently on the American scene. The North Carolina Klan is documented and discussed in detail below and in Appendix D.

b. Black Extremist Groups

In the black community, murder and intimidation appear to be the principal weapons of the extremist fringe of militant groups. The Black Panther Party, first organized in Oakland, Calif., in 1966, now has units in many major metropolitan black ghettos. They have been involved in "shoot outs" with police,[47] and one Black Panther leader, Huey Newton, has been convicted of voluntary manslaughter in the killing of an Oakland policeman.[48]

Another extremist group is the Revolutionary Action Movement (RAM), which is dedicated to black revolution and takes its ideological cues from Robert F. Williams, a radical Negro recently returned from residence in Communist China.

Two alleged members of the Revolutionary Action Movement, Herman B. Ferguson, former New York City elementary school assistant principal and Freedom and Peace Party candidate for U.S. Senator, and Arthur Harris, a young black militant, were sentenced on Oct. 3, 1968, to three and one-half to seven years in prison for conspiring to murder moderate civil rights leaders Roy Wilkins, executive director of the NAACP, and Whitney Young, Jr., former national director of the Urban League. Ferguson and Harris were said to have denounced Wilkins and Young as "puppets" who had "sold out" the Negro people.[49]

During the trial, the name of the late Senator Robert F. Kennedy was introduced as having been on a list of persons "who should be assassinated." According to Edward Lee Howlette, an undercover agent who was the prosecution's key witness, Ferguson said that Kennedy's name was one of five on a list given him by Philadelphian Maxwell Stanford, who has been described by the FBI as the national leader of RAM.[50]

Apart from such relatively small and recently organized groups, however, there are few organized groups in the black community that use violence to achieve political aims. Spontaneous Negro riots may erupt as a form of political protest, but the black equivalent of the Ku Klux Klan has not yet appeared.

The black community has been as fertile in recent years in creating and using a rhetoric of violence as has white America. This may precondition the more extensive use of organized political violence by certain members of the black community.

c. The Extreme Right and the New Left

Organized violence to achieve political goals is also used by the extreme Right and elements of the New Left. The two groups are very similar in style and tactics.

It has been pointed out that the tactics of the New Left are virtually identical with those used at an early stage by the Nazis—a party traditionally grouped on the far Right.[51] To the extent that the New Left has an ideology, it candidly rejects, as did the Nazis, the rights embodied in the first ten amendments to the Constitution (such as freedom of expression), and an active advocacy of points of view that deviate from the values perceived by the adherents of the New Left.

The extreme Right often purports to act in defense of the first ten amendment rights, which advocating conduct which is directly contrary. Both the extreme Right and the New Left approve of violence as a tactic; indeed, some segments of the New Left express the view that violence for its own sake is a liberating, manhood-redeeming goal. The New Left rejects the notion of majority rule, for the majority is not necessarily correct in its view and policies, and the extreme Right rejects the implications of majority rule even when ostensibly acting in "defense" of the United States.

The position of the extreme Right becomes crystal clear when the necessity for defense is examined from their perspective. For example, the Minutemen, an extreme rightist group, has persistently protested that guns and guerrilla training are meant only for that moment when America is actually invaded by the "enemy." The October 1968 issue of *The Patriot* ("official" newspaper of the Minutemen's Michigan Patriotic Party), states:

> MAKE NO MISTAKE ABOUT IT ... THE UNITED STATES HAS BEEN INVADED AND THE ENEMY NOW OCCUPIES THE KEY POSITIONS OF CONTROL: Education, Psychiatry, entertainment, communications, religion, government, the labor unions, and the news media. It is through these critical areas that the enemy has been able to influence and control the thought processes of the American people to a point of robotistic existence.[52]

The Minutemen's rationale for bringing the force of arms to bear on political affairs was expressed in 1961 by Lt. Gen. Pedro A. del Valle, USMC (Ret.), president of the Defenders of the American Constitution, Inc., of Armond Beach, Fla. General de Valle issued a "revised version" of the Declaration of Independence which began:

> When a free and sovereign people find their elected servants in government, and their appointed advisors, following a course of action contrary to their oath of office, destructive of the Constitution they have sworn to uphold, and leading relentlessly to the loss of their freedom and their sovereignty, they must perforce take the most effective action to restore sane constitutional government, or perish as a free and sovereign people.[53]

Attacks upon the legitimacy of democratic government and the loyalty of key government officials often characterize a preassassination stage in a country's history.[54] The extreme Right and some elements of the New Left merit concern because they help to create an environment of violence in which the assassination of political figures by mentally unstable persons becomes more likely.

B. Historical Comparison of the Intensity of Political Violence In the United States[55]

The previous section demonstrates that political violence has characterized the United States since its birth. To obtain a less subjective measure of such violence, the Task Force made a sampling of newspapers to compare the rate of incidents of political violence over the last one hundred and fifty years.[56] The incidents that were recorded ranged from riots and group assaults on individuals to individual assaults on local, state, or federal officeholders. We defined "political reasons" to include socioeconomic, ethnic, or religious reasons of community-wide implications. The aim was to determine, among other things, whether the United States was, in fact, becoming a more violent nation.[57]

The results of this sampling are shown in Figures 1 and 2. Figure 1 groups incidents of violence by five-year periods, and Figure 2 by ten-year periods; the results for both groupings are consistent. In both figures three curves are presented. The solid line represents the actual number of events recorded.[58] The other two curves represent the ratio of the number of events to the population of the country during the period involved, and the ratio of the number of events to the number of pages contained in the newspaper issues examined. The absolute number of incidents shows a significant rising trend since 1819, with dips during the decade prior to the turn of the century, the two decades on either side of and including World War I, and the decade including World War II. The figures show peaks of violence during the post-Reconstruction period and the turn of the century, a sharp rise during the depression, and a very striking increase during the 1960's, which show by far the largest absolute number of politically violent events.

Using the absolute number of events, however, distorts the picture, for the one hundred and fifty years covered by the study were a time of rapidly rising population and rapidly increasing coverage and dissemination of information. Therefore, two additional curves are shown—one which adjusts the absolute number of incidents for population, and one which adjusts the absolute number of violent incidents for number of pages in the newspapers. Both adjustments must, of course, be considered as highly approximate. For example, simply adjusting for gross population takes no direct account of increased urbanization. Adjusting for newspaper pages makes no direct adjustment for the number of column inches devoted to news as opposed to advertisements, the increasing speed with which news could be disseminated with the invention of the telegraph, radio, etc., and, most important, it takes no account of variations, if any, of incidents deemed newsworthy. Crude as those adjustments are, together they give a more complete picture of the comparative intensity of political violence across the United States since 1819. Within the limitations of the sampling and adjustment technique, the results present an accurate picture.

The three curves indicate in general that the United States has in the past experienced high levels of violence comparable in intensity to the present day. The country does not appear to be passing through a period of unique internal political violence. The curves, consistent with generally accepted historical analysis, suggest that past violence has been associated with specific issues, such as agrarian reform, abolitionism, reconstruction, and labor violence. The turmoil of the 1960's shows up, however, as a peak at least comparable to the high points of violence in the nation's past. Relative to the impact of this violence upon the public, the intensity of violence in the 1960's has probably not been duplicated since the turn of the century, or at least since the late 1920's. Thus, most persons today have not experienced a comparably violent period of American history. The curves indicate that the level of political violence peaked in the post-Reconstruction era and began a downward trend; in the 1960's there has been a sharp rise to a level approximating the post-Reconstruction era.

Figures 1 and 2 show the number of violent events without considering the intensity of that violence. To attain an approximate measure of the comparative intensity of violence, the frequency of personal injuries and the frequency of deaths were separately examined. This division is of particular signif-

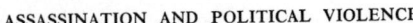

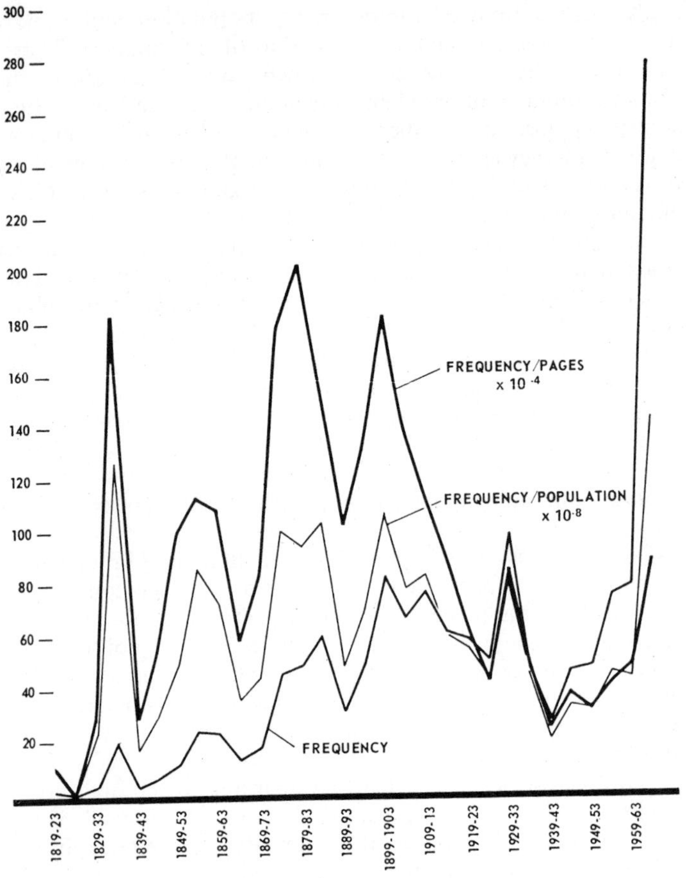

Figure 1.—Rate of incidents of political violence, 5 year intervals

icance in view of the fact that, included in the definition of "violent" events were those which resulted not only in personal injury but also in injury to property and disruption of normal activity. Death and injury are considered separately. The death and injury frequencies are broken down into injury and death to the targets on the one hand and to the attackers on the other. They are further separated into incidents involving injury or death to a single individual, group incidents

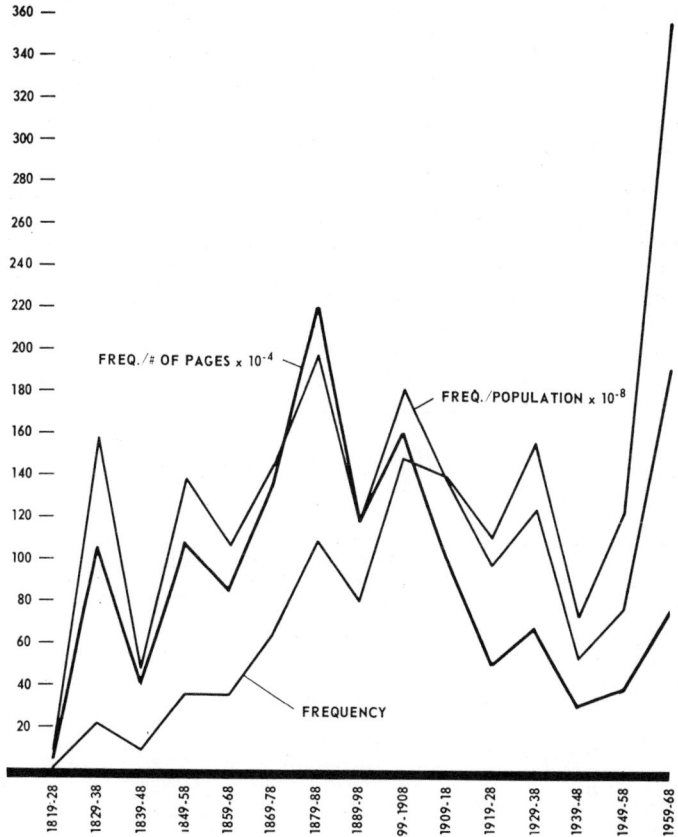

Figure 2. – Rate of incidents of political violence, 10 year intervals

where injuries occurred to fifty or fewer individuals, and group incidents where injuries occurred to more than fifty persons.

It is important for sampling stability to separate the incidents of more than fifty injuries. The number of events in which a large number of deaths or injuries occurred is still quite small, but one or two large events in a given period greatly alter the results for that period. Because no more than one newspaper issue per week was selected, it is possible that other large events occurred but were not included. The stability of the results is greatly decreased by the addition of the large events. In order to give greater stability to the sample, the results were grouped into thirty-year periods.

The frequency of deaths is presented in Table 1, from which several conclusions can be drawn. The first is that for none of the three categories has the last thirty years been the most violent in the United States, even in terms of absolute number of incidents. In fact, even without adjustments for population and the amount of reporting, the number of deaths is far below those of other periods. In absolute number of deaths, the peak occurs in the interval from 1879 to 1908. This judgment is consistent with historical analyses that have examined the post-Reconstruction period and the early labor violence. The Civil War era, 1849–78, also appears to have

Table 1.—Frequency of deaths.

For targets

Interval	Individuals	Groups 50 or fewer	Row total	Groups over 50	Grand total
1819-1848	5	17	22	0	22
1849-1878	17	31	48	300	348
1879-1908	63.4	148	211.4	75	286.4
1909-1938	37.4	107.8	145.2	0	145.2
1939-1968	39.6	22	61.6	0	61.6

For attackers

Interval	Individuals	Groups 50 or fewer	Row total	Groups over 50	Grand total
1819-1848	0	5	5	0	5
1849-1878	0	24	24	0	24
1879-1908	2	76.8	78.8	75	153.8
1909-1938	4.4	30.8	35.2	0	35.2
1939-1968	4.4	24.2	28.6	0	28.6

Total deaths,
targets and attackers

Interval	Individuals	Groups 50 or fewer	Row total	Groups over 50	Grand total
1819-1848	5	22	27	0	27
1849-1878	17	55	72	300	372
1879-1908	65.4	224.8	290.2	150	440.2
1909-1938	41.8	138.6	180.4	0	180.4
1939-1968	44	46.2	90.2	0	90.2

been violent, even though war deaths were excluded from the study.

If adjustment is made for population or newspaper size, the result is even more striking. *The ratio of deaths to total population and to newspaper size is lower during the last thirty years than for any thirty-year period since 1819. This holds true for all three categories.*[59]

Table 2 presents these data with respect to the absolute number of injuries. Injuries are consistent with deaths, if injury only to targets is considered. Peaks occur where expected in the next two most recent thirty-year periods, which include post-Reconstruction early labor movement violence, and depression violence.

Table 2.—Frequency of injuries

To targets

Interval	Individuals	Groups 50 or fewer	Row total	Groups over 50	Grand total
1819-1848	2	22	24	300	324
1849-1878	12	31	43	375	418
1879-1908	33.4	273.6	307	75	382
1909-1938	28.6	297	325.6	3135	3460.6
1939-1968	13.2	227	240.2	0	240.2

To attackers

Interval	Individuals	Groups 50 or fewer	Row total	Groups over 50	Grand total
1819-1848	0	18	18	0	19
1849-1878	1	28	29	0	29
1879-1908	5	61.6	62.1	75	141.6
1909-1938	4.4	156.6	161	4180	4341
1939-1968	6.6	598.4	605	5665	6270

Total injuries,
targets and attackers

Interval	Individuals	Groups 50 or fewer	Row total	Groups over 50	Grand total
1819-1848	2	40	42	300	342
1849-1878	13	59	72	375	457
1879-1908	38.4	335.2	373.6	150	523.6
1909-1938	33	453.6	486.6	7315	7801.6
1939-1968	19.8	825.4	845.2	5665	6510.2

The most recent period appears far more violent with respect to injuries than to deaths. When injury to attackers as well as targets is included, however, the picture shifts with the two most recent periods by far the most violent.

The anomaly is emphasized when adjustments are again made for population and newspaper size. Figure 3 presents the same four curves for injuries. When incidents involving injuries to fifty or more are excluded, the curves show a small increasing trend, with a previous high point during the 1879 to

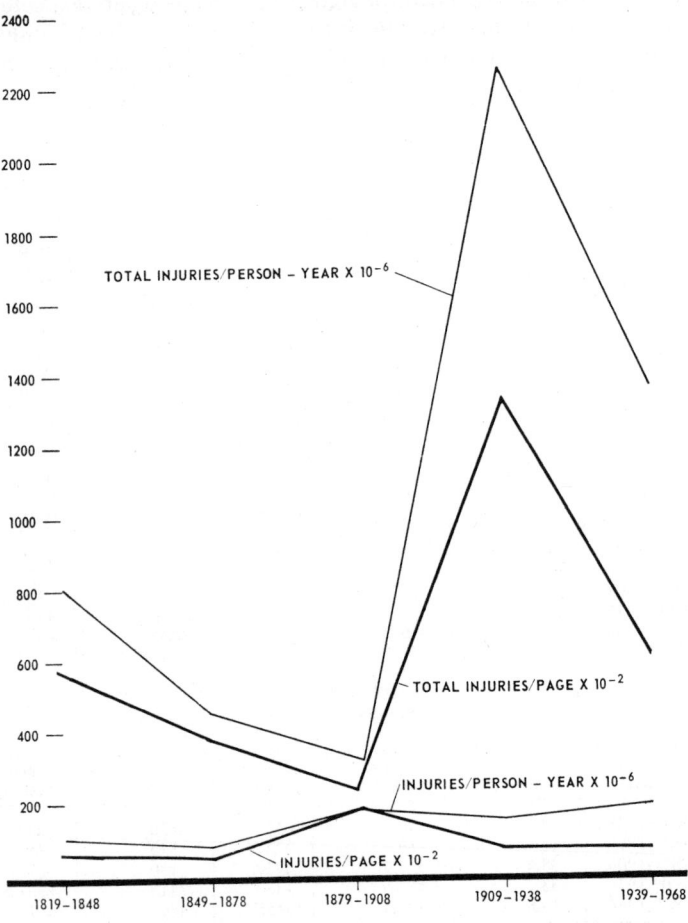

Figure 3.—Injuries through time adjusted for population and newspaper size

1908 period. When total injuries are considered, 1879 to 1908 becomes the low point, and the last two thirty-year periods show up as the most violent of all by a substantial margin.

No one hypothesis seems to account satisfactorily for this. Injuries could have increased because crowds have become larger. Of course, the increase in crowd size would not detract from genuine changes in the levels of violence. It may be that the improvement in medical facilities has reduced what otherwise might have been fatalities. It may be that newspaper reporters have been more sensitive to political violence in recent decades. A combination of factors is most likely involved.

One factor that is clearly of significance is the increased newspaper coverage of incidents of political violence. Because a sampling technique was used, an incident reported in only one issue was much less likely to be noted than one covered in several issues. The effect would be to skew the data toward greater violence in recent years.

We cite the following two examples from an earlier era, reprinted in its entirety:

> Washington *Daily National Intelligentsia,* March 30, 1834, p. 3, col. 2: "The Hon. Ben T. Major, State Senator in Missouri, was stabbed a short time since at Warsaw, in that state, by a Mr. Cherry, and died of the wound. Cause, a political quarrel."

> New York *Times,* June 28, 1854, page 1, col. 6:
> RIOT AT RIPLEY, OHIO—Cincinnati, Monday, June 26. A riot occurred at Ripley, Ohio, on Saturday night, caused by the inmates of a coffeehouse throwing rotten eggs into temperance meeting. The temperance men rifled the coffeehouse, and then visited all the liquor shops in town, and those that did not agree to give up their businesses were assaulted. No lives were lost. The weather is oppressively hot and business is very dull.

In addition, death is a more extreme consequence of political violence than injury, and may well be a more stable measure of the intensity of the violence. The data do not distinguish serious injury from slight injury. It is likely that increased interest in political violence may have resulted in reporting as "injuries," events which would not previously have been so reported. As pointed out above, it is the reported number of injuries to attacking groups that appears inconsistent with the other data.

Last, data is presented on the reasons or motivation for the violence. Table 3 presents the results for broad categories of motivation, and Table 4 sets forth a selection of the particular subcategories that contributed the most to the trend within those broad categories.

Table 3. – Frequencies of reasons for politically violent events over time.

Interval	Personal motivation	Action against authority	Foreign affairs protest	To change official leadership	Reaction of official groups	Protests based on group antagonisms	Total
1819-1849	6	0	0	0	0	16	22
1849-1878	27	11	0	0	2	60	100
1879-1908	89.7	18.4	0	3.2	12.4	178	301.7
1909-1938	50.6	77	6.6	6.6	33	191.4	365.2
1939-1968	61.6	123.2	39.6	2.2	4.4	235.4	466.4
Total	234.9	229.6	46.2	12	51.8	680.8	1255.3

The information collected is consistent with other historical analysis. Several trends appear in the data. In Table 3, personal motivation is shown to rise as a reason for attack during the 1800's but after the turn of the century, it falls quite rapidly. In contrast, action against authority shows a sharp rise within the last two thirty-year periods. Foreign affairs protests are heavily concentrated in the most recent thirty-year period. It thus would appear that personal motivations for politically violent events have in general been replaced by more deep-seated controversies over the role of government.

Table 3 indicates that there have been very few attempts to change official leadership through politically violent events. Although Table 3 shows that there has been a steady increase in protests based on group antagonisms, the sharp rises occurred prior to the turn of the century. There is an exceptionally high point, relative to population, in the post-Reconstruction era.

An important finding is that there has been a sharp decrease in political violence based on the reactions of official groups. The period in which this type of reaction was greatest was in the World War I depression era; in fact, that period accounts for almost two-thirds of the recorded incidents.

Table 4.—Frequencies of specific reasons for politically violent events over time

Code numbers[a]	Personal motivation				Action against authority				Foreign affairs protest		To change official leadership	Protests based on group antagonisms						Reaction of official groups
	1	2	3	4	5	6	15	16	23	25	31	40	41	42	43	44	45	50
1819–1848		2	3.0	0	0	0	0	0	0	0	0	2.0	1.0	9.0	1.0	1.0	0	0
1849–1878	4.0	11.0	27.0	0	7.0	1.0	2.0	1.0	0	0	0	3.0	14.0	23.0	11.0	3.0	2.0	0
1879–1908	3.2	41.0	42.4	3.2	2.0	2.0	7.0	4.2	0	0	3.2	3.0	69.4	68.8	20.0	9.6	1.0	2.0
1909–1938	8.8	17.4	19.8	4.4	8.3	8.8	15.4	17.6	0	6.6	6.6	4.4	103.4	37.6	26.4	2.2	6.6	17.6
1939–1968	13.2	6.6	6.6	35.2	13.2	57.2	15.4	13.2	28.6	9.0	2.2	8.8	55.0	116.6	15.4	13.2	11.0	2.2

[a]Code Numbers

1. Economic gain
2. Personal revenge
3. Political disagreement
4. To gain political advantage
5. To obtain a political goal
6. Response to social conditions
15. Protest police action
16. Protest action of local officials
23. Protest current involvement in war
25. To protest government action in foreign affairs
31. To effect change in political personnel
40. Religious antagonism
41. Labor antagonism
42. Racial antagonism
43. Political antagonism
44. Differences in social viewpoints
45. Internal group antagonisms
50. To maintain official authority by police

The general impression is that protests currently are more impersonal; that is, they involve protests against actions of authorities, group antagonisms, or, in the latest period, foreign affairs protests. Attempts to change official leadership have always been low in frequency. Official reactions as a basis for political violence occurred with frequency only in the 1879 to 1938 period. Personal motivation, although fairly high, has been decreasing since the post-Reconstruction era.

Table 4 shows some interesting changes within the broad categories. For example, although there has been a decline in the general category of personal motivation, there are counter-trends with subcategories. Personal revenge and political disagreements were the major reasons in the post-Reconstruction era, while most of the incidents in the latest thirty-year period have been to gain political advantage.

In the "action against authority" category, changes result from the striking increase in the number of events in response to social conditions. The foreign affairs increase arises from contemporary protests over involvement in wars, specifically the Vietnam war.

Examination of group antagonism shows relatively few politically violent events due to religious antagonism. Similarly, relatively few incidents have been reported that deal with differences in social viewpoints or internal group antagonism. Further, although there have been more events based on political antagonism in recent periods, this is not a major category, and the number has decreased in the last thirty years.

Almost all the events based on group antagonism have occurred either because of labor or race. As expected, the level for labor increases sharply in the post-Reconstruction era, reaches a peak during the World War I-Depression era, and then drops sharply in the most recent period. Relative to population, in fact, the number of politically violent events based on labor antagonism is less during this most recent period than for any but the pre-Civil War period. On the other hand, racial violence has been highest during the latest period, although relative to population it was highest in the post-Reconstruction era.

General Summary of the Newspaper Study

As has been noted, the data from the newspaper study must be treated with caution. They are based upon a sampling drawn from only one newspaper for each given period of time.

Some crude adjustments were made for population and newspaper space. The study has been an attempt to supplement intuitive historical judgments about levels of political violence over a period of one hundred fifty years. The basic conclusions of this study are:

1. The absolute number of politically violent events has increased greatly in recent years. However, adjustments for both newspaper size and population indicate that this period of history is no more politically violent than previous high points of political violence in our history.

2. With respect to the intensity of such events, the number of deaths as a result of political violence is far less in the most recent period than it has been in others.

3. The total number of injuries for both attackers and targets is quite high during the last thirty-year period. However, the number is below that of the World War I-Depression period (1909–38). Data based on death provide a different picture from that based on injury, but the best judgment must still be that the present period is no more violent than some previous ones, and may be significantly less in violence resulting in death.

4. The motivation for political violence shows important changes. Group antagonisms and action against authority have been an increasing basis for politically violent events. Labor and racial antagonisms have dominated the picture. The post-Reconstruction era and the present period have witnessed the largest amounts of racial strife; the period between these two (World War I-Depression) saw the height of labor violence.

5. Some motivations for political violence have been almost entirely absent in the history of the United States. Political violence to change official leadership and religious antagonism have been rare. Except for the period in which the greatest amount of labor violence occurred (1909–38), violence by official authority to maintain control has also been quite low.

C. Profile of Support Within the United States for Political Violence

This section seeks to identify the characteristics of persons within the United States who support political violence, based upon an analysis of a national cross-section sample survey designed by the Commission and administered by Louis Harris and Associates.[60] We seek to isolate both social-structural and personality factors which are causally related to support of political violence, and in turn to isolate for analysis groups of persons who are disproportionately supportive of violent political acts.[61] The survey was conducted in the latter part of October 1968, with a total sample of 1176 adults. Initial comparisons of the survey data with census data indicate that the sample conforms closely with the expected distributions of basic demographic characteristics of the population. The only exception is a slight overrepresentation of Negro respondents.[62]

Table 5 – Factors*

Factor I	Anomic authoritarianism
Item No.	Item
16	A few strong leaders
13	People better off in old days
01	Justice rough and ready
14	Friendship lacking in world today
09	Everything changes so quickly these days
15	What young people need most is strong discipline

Factor II	Political vengeance
Item No.	Item
25	Sometimes I have felt the best thing might be the death of political leaders
22	Government is enemy, not friend of people like me
07	Some politicians have deserved death threats

Factor III	Acceptance of political violence
Item No.	Item
10	If people go into politics they more or less have to expect that they might get killed
18	Politicians who change too fast have to expect death threats
21	A lot more people in government and politics will probably be assassinated in the next few years

Factor IV	Police violence
Item No.	Item
24	Police wrong to beat up unarmed protestors
06	Police frequently use more force than necessary
20	Anyone who insults a cop has no complaint
19	Sex criminals should be whipped

Factor V	Military violence
Item No.	Item
12	In dealing with other countries we are frequently justified in using military force
03	Government too ready to use military force
17	Unfortunate many civilians are killed but can't be avoided in a war

*See complete list of items on pp. 240–41.

A copy of the entire interview schedule is to be found in the Appendix to this report. It contains much of the standard demographic and political information in addition to items designed (1) to yield attitudinal responses which might indicate support for or approval of violence to achieve political goals in general, and (2) to determine by direct questions one's willingness to support the use of violence in political situations perceived as unjust.[63]

We wish to caution against the tendency to leap from analyses of attitudes to expectations of behavior. It is important to remember that the results of this survey are based on a sample of the population who were interviewed in their own homes. In addition to the possible biases that may exist in the interview situation, there is the problem of deciding, on the basis of publicly expressed attitudes, the behavior in which individuals are likely to engage. The relationship is difficult to determine. Nevertheless, attitudes that are expressed in private to interviewers have been found to relate to the behavior of individuals, and the material is, therefore, important for developing tentative hypotheses about the basis of political violence in the general population.

One finding of interest is that the attitudinal factors which appear to predict the use of political violence in general do not predict one way or the other stated approval of violence in situations of perceived governmental injustice. The two approaches apparently reveal different dimensions of support for political violence. We will discuss each dimension in order.

1. Analysis of Groups Whose Attitudinal Responses Indicate Support for Political Violence

In order to discover basic underlying dimensions of attitudes, a factor analysis* was completed by Louis Harris and Associates.[65] Five factors emerged from the twenty-five original items. Those factors are set forth in Table 5, and the loading factors are shown in Table 6.

---

*This analysis is based upon responses to a series of twenty-five attitude-scale types of items administered to each respondent. Those items are listed below. Included in those items are short forms of the California F-Scale and the Anomy Scale developed by McClosky and Scharr. Other items, designed by James McEvoy III and William A. Gamson, sought attitudes on police violence, military violence, personal violence, politically related violence (both legitimate and illegitimate) and paramilitary groups.

Table 6 – Factor loadings

Factor I	Factor II	Factor III	Factor IV	Factor V
.6910	.7370	.7938	.7867	.7051
.6593	.6837	.7346	.6190	.6857
.6507	.6054	.6576	.6127	.5591
.5902			.3558	
.5160				
.4674				

Factor I emerged from the items (with one exception) drawn from previously developed scales, the F-Scale and the Anomy Scale. This factor was named "Anomic Authoritarianism." Factor II, which we have called "Political Vengeance," was drawn from three items which seem very directly to indicate approval of politically directed violence and the perception that the government was a hostile force and threatening to the respondent.

Factor III, "Acceptance of Political Violence" is based upon three items which appear to denote a less hostile set of attitudes about political violence. Passive acceptance of vio-

---

List of Items

1. Justice may have been a little rough and ready in the days of the Old West, but things worked better than they do today with all the legal red tape.
2. When a boy is growing up, it is more important for him to have a few fist fights.
3. Our government is too ready to use military force in dealing with other countries.
4. One of the best reasons for people to have guns is to make sure that the government doesn't get too much power.
5. The people running the government in Washington would do a good job if everybody left them alone instead of trying to influence them all the time.
6. The police frequently use more force than they need to when carrying out their duties.
7. Some politicians who have had their lives threatened probably deserve it.
8. Human nature being what it is, there must always be war and conflict.
9. Everything changes so quickly these days that I often have trouble deciding which are the right rules to follow.
10. If people go into politics, they more or less have to accept the fact that they might get killed.
11. Groups have the right to train their members in marksmanship and underground warfare tactics in order to help put down any conspiracies that might occur in the country.

lence rather than the active participation and support indicated in Factor II seem to be the attitudes shown here.

Factor IV, "Police Violence," is based on items which seem to measure support or disapproval of police violence. Factor V, "Military Violence," is based upon items with similar intent dealing with military force. Table 7 presents the correlations of the items in the factors.

2. Political Vengeance

For this analysis, we selected Factor II, "Political Vengeance," as the dependent variable (or variable to be "explained"). The three items in Factor II seem to offer a direct opportunity to support or reject violence as a political strategy and also to combine acceptance or rejection of political violence with a measure of the degree to which a respondent distrusted the federal government. Each of the items in this factor which concerns political violence is acceptably related to the "Government is the enemy" item, the correlations being

---

12. In dealing with other countries in the world, we are frequently justified in using military force.
13. People were better off in the old days when everyone knew just how he was expected to act.
14. What is lacking in the world today is the old kind of friendship that lasted for a lifetime.
15. What young people need most of all is strong discipline by their parents.
16. A few strong leaders could make this country better than all the laws and talk.
17. It is unfortunate that many civilians are killed by bombing in a war, but this cannot be avoided.
18. Politicians who try to change things too fast have to expect that their lives may be threatened.
19. Sex criminals deserve more than prison, they should be publicly whipped or worse.
20. Any man who insults a policeman has no complaint if he gets roughed up in return.
21. A lot more people in Government and politics will probably be assassinated in the next few years.
22. The Government in Washington is the enemy, not the friend, of people like me.
23. Some people don't understand anything but force.
24. The police are wrong to beat up unarmed protesters, even when these people are rude and call them names.
25. Sometimes I have felt that the best thing for our country might be the death of some of our political leaders.

.196 and .267, respectively. The other correlations of the items within each of the five factors are set forth in Table 7.

Table 7–Factor Intercorrelations, (unweighted) Pearson R
I. Anomic authoritarianism

	16	13	01	14	09	15
16		.267	.240	.227	.243	.248
13		-	.300	.379	.308	.251
01			-	.267	.245	.259
14				-	.254	.387
09					-	.183

II. Political vengeance			III. Acceptance of political violence			
	25	22	07	10	18	21
25	-	.267	.251	10	-	.441	.303
22		-	.196	18		-	.310
07			-	21			-

IV. Police Violence				V. Military violence		
	24	06	20	19	12	03	17
24	-	.250	-.130	-.078	12	-	.012	.310
06		-	- 130	-.026	03		-	.019
20			-	.283	17			-
19								

In the next section we will attempt to validate the selection of Factor II, "Political Vengeance," as the key factor for analysis. Following that discussion, we will proceed to an analysis of the politically vengeant person.

3. Political Vengeance and Other Types of Violence: An Attempt at Validation of the Measure

In order to validate the measure of Political Vengeance, we correlated it with a number of different measures drawn from the survey data. In addition to the four factors identified above, the following measures were used:

Assassination Relief. Among other data sought in the survey was the degree of emotional distress, neutrality, or satisfaction experienced by the respondents after the assassinations of President Kennedy, Malcolm X, George Lincoln Rockwell, Medgar Evers, Martin Luther King, Jr., and Senator Robert Kennedy. We asked respondents to indicate to what degree they felt "Hopeless," "Shocked," "Afraid," "Angry," "Relieved," and "Not Affected" at the time of each assassination. The resulting Assassination Relief Index isolated those who were the least "hopeless" and the most "relieved" with respect to each assassination and then each respondent's score was combined in a summary over all the assassinations. The relationship of this measure of approval of real political violence (assassinations) and Political Vengeance was fairly high—a correlation of .226.

Revolutionary Violence. This index isolated those who said they would approve illegal sit-ins or the use of violence to counter perceived governmental injustices in four situations: (1) where Congress has imposed an unfair tax; (2) where Congress had forbidden free-speech criticism of the government; (3) where the government is arresting Negroes although there had been no trouble; and (4) where the government is arresting and shooting innocent people to maintain power (see Appendix, questions 18–21).

Personal Violence. This index isolated persons who said they had slapped, kicked, punched, or beaten another person in anger as an adult. There was no relationship between this measure of violence and Political Vengeance.

Firearm Ownership. This index isolated the group of people who owned firearms. This factor did not correlate with any of the measures of political violence, but it was not controlled to isolate those who owned pistols from rifle and shotgun owners.

The correlations of the foregoing indexes and factors are set out in Table 8a.[66]

As shown in Table 8a, the Political Vengeance factor is related to several other factors which by their correlation partially validate that factor as a measure of support for political violence. For example, the correlations between the Police Violence factor and the Political Vengeance factor is +.221 and the correlation between the Assassination Relief scale is +.226. These are rather significant correlations in view of the number of respondents in the survey.

There is a somewhat more modest association between the Vengeance and Military Violence factors ($r=.149$), but it is in the expected direction, indicating that Political Vengeance and approval of the use of military force are associated far beyond the chance level.

The strongest correlation is the positive relationship between Political Vengeance and Acceptance of Political Violence ($r=.300$). This suggests that Political Vengeance is accompa-

Table 8a.—Inter-factor Correlations

	ASSASSINATION RELIEF	REVOLUTIONARY VIOLENCE	PERSONAL VIOLENCE	ANOMIC AUTHORITARIANISM FACTOR I	POLITICAL VENGEANCE FACTOR II	ACCEPTANCE OF POLITICAL VIOLENCE FACTOR III	POLICE VIOLENCE FACTOR IV	MILITARY VIOLENCE FACTOR V
ASSASSINATION RELIEF	—							
REVOLUTIONARY VIOLENCE	.007	—						
PERSONAL VIOLENCE	-.006	.162	—					
ANOMIC AUTHORITARIANISM	.153	-.248	-.058	—				
POLITICAL VENGEANCE	.226	.068	.014	.246	—			
ACCEPTANCE OF POLITICAL VIOLENCE	.164	.008	.018	.356	.300	—		
POLICE VIOLENCE	.051	.024	-.007	.310	.221	.295	—	
MILITARY VIOLENCE	-.034	-.029	-.007	.335	.149	.304	.204	—
FIREARMS OWNERSHIP (UNCONTROLLED FOR PISTOLS)	.041	.060	.080	.012	.020	.002	-.071	.042

nied by a willingness to tolerate or accept as inevitable the occurrence of political violence.

A further examination of the Political Vengeance factor showed that the addition of the Acceptance of Political Violence factor did not substantially improve the predictive power of the Political Vengeance factor when it was tested against other violence-related variables such as the personal violence scale, authoritarianism, military violence and the like. A chart was constructed using the Political Vengeance and Acceptance of Political Violence factors. The scales were trichotomized into low, medium, and high, and a nine-cell typology resulted. The first cell contained persons very low on both Political Vengeance and Acceptance of Political Violence, and the ninth cell contained persons who were very high on both these measures. An examination of this chart indicated that, while Acceptance of Political Violence did not decrease or increase agreement with violence-related items against which they were run, cells in which persons were high on the Political Vengeance factor were equally good predictors of these measures as were cells in which the high vengeance and high acceptance respondents were located. In other words, the addition of the acceptance factor made no difference in the level of support or opposition to other measures of violence.

Thus, both a complex attitudinal measure of support for violence and a measure of relative approval of real political murders (the assassination relief scale) are positively associated with our measure of Political Vengeance, leading us to conclude that it is an acceptable attitudinal measure of support for political violence.

4. Analysis of the Social Structural Characteristics of the "Politically Vengeant"

Accepting the Political Vengeance factor as a valid indicator of support for political violence, we now move to the question of what accentuates the presence of this behavior in the American population.[67] For example, what are the demographic and social status correlations of high vengeance? What influence does the political system have on vengeance, and how often is strong policy opposition accompanied by a willingness to support political violence? We may also be able to give some very limited tests to several theoretical ideas which might be useful in predicting what groups in society might be prone to support political violence. Among these are the theory of relative deprivation, the class conflict model, and the influence of racial conflict on political vengeance.

For the purposes of this analysis, the scores individual respondents received on the Political Vengeance factor (hereafter called "Vengeance") were combined into four groups. These groups were formed by collapsing the total distribution of the factor so that each group (with the exception of group 3) contained the number of respondents falling in two groups of scores on the original scale. In the case of the high group, identified as group 3, there were so few cases at the very extreme end of the distribution that this group was constructed to include all cases beyond a score of 9 on the Vengeance factor. An examination of Figure 5, will make this process clear. Thus, the original scores, ranging from 3 to 15 on the Vengeance factor, have been collapsed into four groups, as follows:

Group 0 = score of 3 or 4 on the Vengeance Factor
Group 1 = score of 5 or 6 on the Vengeance Factor
Group 2 = score of 7 or 8 on the Vengeance Factor
Group 3 = score of 9 through 15 on the Vengeance Factor.

According to Figure 5, there are one hundred and five cases that fall one standard deviation to the right of the mean of the scores (scores 9 and 10) or about nine percent of the sample: an additional 36 cases (about three percent of the sample) fall two standard deviations to the right of the mean.

Thus more than twelve percent of the adult population in the country can be thought of as having relatively high levels of political vengeance. We do not, of course, know if this is a proportion of the population that is greater or smaller than at

Figure 5.—Frequency distribution of scores of respondents on factor II, political vengeance

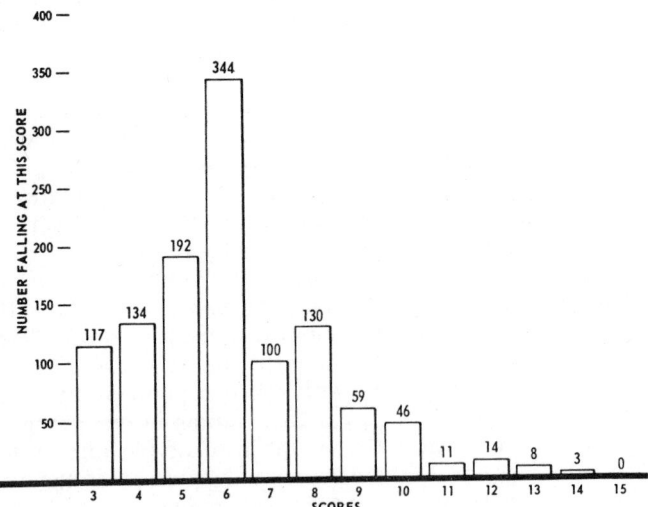

some other time in our history. It is safe to conclude, however, that political vengeance, and, by inference, support for political violence, is not a trivial or diminutive problem. One of every ten Americans supports statements that are, when viewed from the perspective of the responses of the remaining ninety percent of the population, rather highly supportive of political murder. Further, this support is accompanied by extreme distrust of the government. Translated into the terms of the resident civilian adult population, more than twelve million people in the United States share the views of the respondents at the higher end of the Vengeance scale.

5. Demographic Correlates of Political Vengeance

Race. Race was an important predictor of political vengeance. Figure 6 shows the distribution of two racial groups on the Vengeance scale from 0 through 3. About the same proportion of whites and blacks fall at the lowest end of the Vengeance scale, but as we approach the higher end, the proportion of Negroes increases; at the highest point on the scale there are, proportionally speaking, twice as many Negroes as whites. Such an extreme difference requires further explanation, and considerable attention will be devoted to the factor of race in the sections devoted to this question.

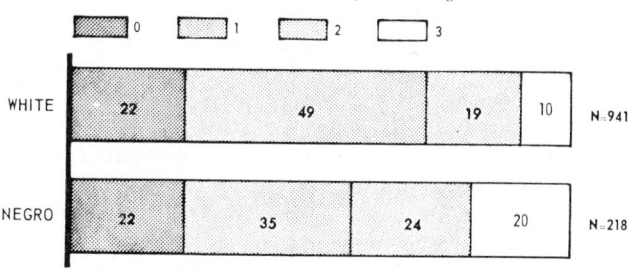

Figure 6.—Racial factor in political vengeance

Regional difference. Figure 7 shows the distribution of regional groups by political vengeance. Although this table includes all respondents (i.e., both black and white), it is nevertheless interesting to note that the South contributes twice as

Figure 7. - Regional factor in political vengeance

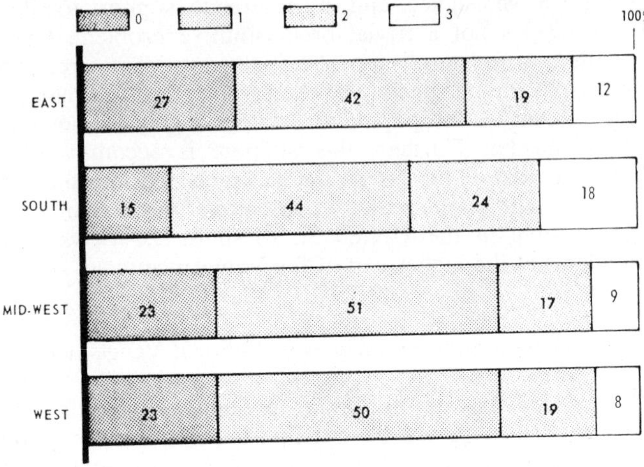

many highly vengeant persons as the Midwest, more than twice as many as the West, and a third more than the East.

Many commentators have observed that the South is the locale of a violent culture. Martin Luther King, Jr., John Kennedy, Medgar Evers, and George Lincoln Rockwell were all assassinated in the South, the scene for years of lynchings, bombings, and other kinds of terror used to suppress the black and sometimes the white population. It is clear from the figure that this culture of violence is not a "one percenter" phenomenon. Almost twenty percent of the Southerners score at the high end of the Vengeance scale, and, unlike other regions, only fifteen percent of the Southern respondents manifest a relatively low level of vengeance.

It might be argued that these differences in part result from the fact that the South has a greater proportion of lower income persons with lower levels of formal education; it will certainly be necessary to control for income level and educational level in further examinations of this finding. However, with the data available, it is possible to control for race. This also has the effect of introducing a limited control for education and income, for blacks are, especially in the South, least likely to have high or middle incomes or relatively high levels of formal education. Figure 8 shows the distribution of Ven-

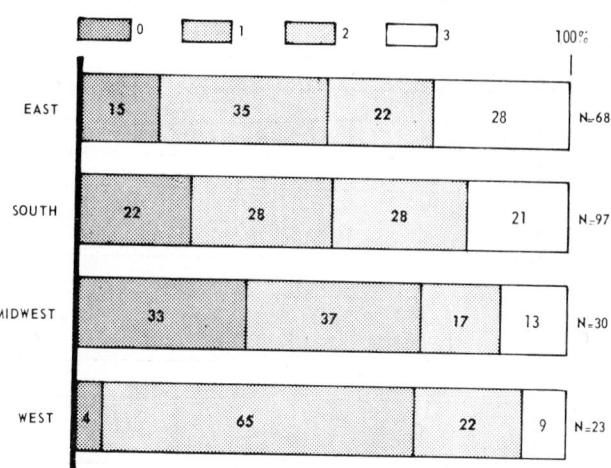

Figure 8. — Distribution of vengeance by region for blacks

geance by region for blacks, and Figure 9 shows the same data for whites. These figures show that the pattern of Southern violence is especially prevalent among whites. Southern whites are twice as likely to be highly vengeant as Eastern or Western whites, and almost twice as likely as Midwestern whites. The pattern changes, however, for blacks. The Eastern blacks are by far the most vengeant segment of the population, with twenty-eight percent falling at the high end of the Vengeance Scale. Southern blacks are next, followed by Midwestern and Western respondents.

Negroes in the Eastern States are largely located in the great urban ghettos of New York, New Jersey, Boston, Philadelphia, and Washington, D.C. Other sources of data indicate that these ghettos are the scene of much militant political activity and it is to be expected that this activity, along with the deplorable conditions of life in these areas, would yield great distrust of and hostility toward the government. Riots in these and other cities constitute further evidence that urban blacks have been disproportionately hostile to the government. Regrettably, we do not know from these data whether the relative hostility of the black population in these areas has increased or declined. However, it is certain that a disproportionately large

Figure 9.—Distribution of vengeance by region for whites

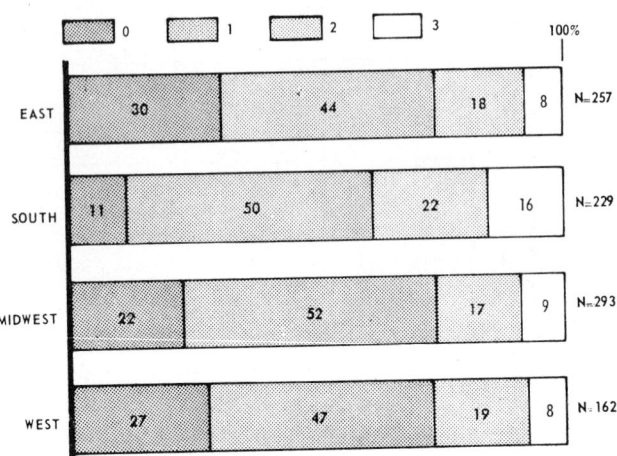

number of blacks, especially Eastern urban blacks, express profound hostility toward the government; more than a quarter of this population expresses rather general support for the statements that make up the Vengeance scale.

Income and Education. As we have noted before, income and education are both variables that have a strong effect on the level of support or opposition that a respondent shows on the Vengeance scale. In general, the effect can be seen as a strong inverse relationship between increasing levels of income and education and support for political vengeance. Figures 10 and 11 present the distribution of education and income on the Vengeance scale. These figures clearly show that, as income and education increase, the proportion of respondents in the high vengeance cells of the figure declines rapidly. For example, at the lowest levels of education—persons having an eighth grade education or less—roughly twenty-two percent —are found in the high vengeance group. This proportion falls to about seven percent among those who attended college and declines to zero among those with a college degree. There is a slight increase in vengeance among persons in the sample with postgraduate degrees, but the number of cases is so small that this cannot be viewed as significant.

The same general pattern can be seen in the figure reporting

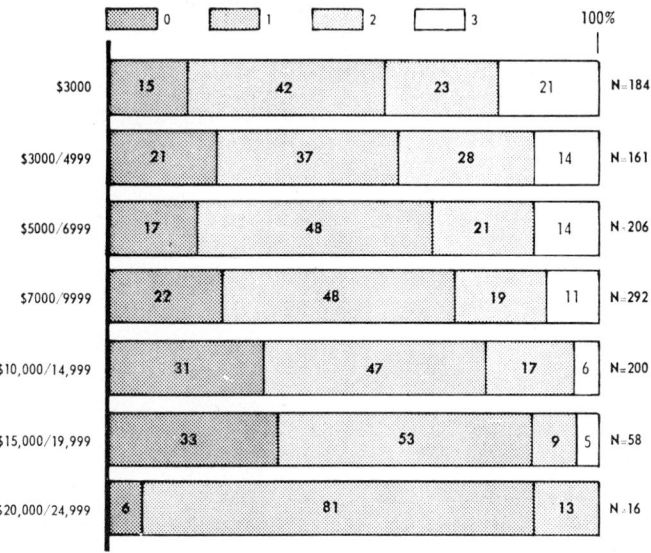

Figure 10. – Vengeance and combined family income

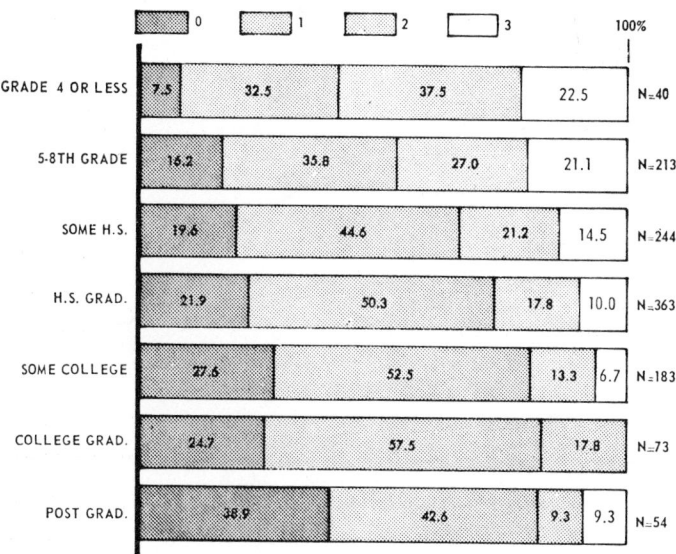

Figure 11. – Vengeance and education level

combined family income. At the lowest levels of income, between fourteen and twenty-one percent of the respondents fall at the high end of the Vengeance scale; at the higher levels, between zero and six percent are at the same level on the Vengeance scale.

It remains to be seen whether or not increased levels of income have the effect of diminishing vengeance among both racial groups. Figure 12 considers only persons at the two

Figure 12.–Proportion of income groups at high and low ends of the vengeance scale

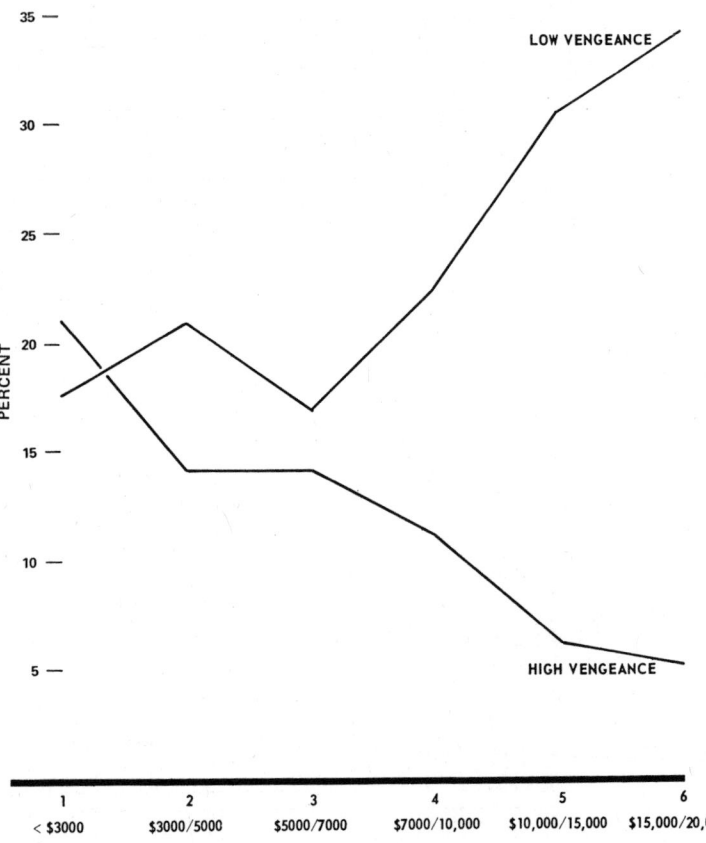

extreme ends of the Vengeance scale. The line labelled "Low Vengeance" is made up of persons with a score of zero on the scale and those labelled "High Vengeance" are persons with a score of three. Figures 13 and 14 present the same data for whites and blacks. In these two figures, however, the income groups have been compressed from eight categories to five in order to increase the number of respondents in each income group at the extreme end of the Vengeance scale.

As Figure 12 indicates, there is a strong and almost linear decline in the proportion of persons at the high and low ends of the Vengeance scale as income increases and decreases. Essentially, this figure is simply a repetition of the data found in Figure 10 except for its exclusion of the middle range of scores on the Vengeance scale. Figure 13 presents the same data for whites, and it is quite clear that a similar pattern prevails among this group; as income increases, vengeance declines, as income decreases, vengeance increases. Figure 14,

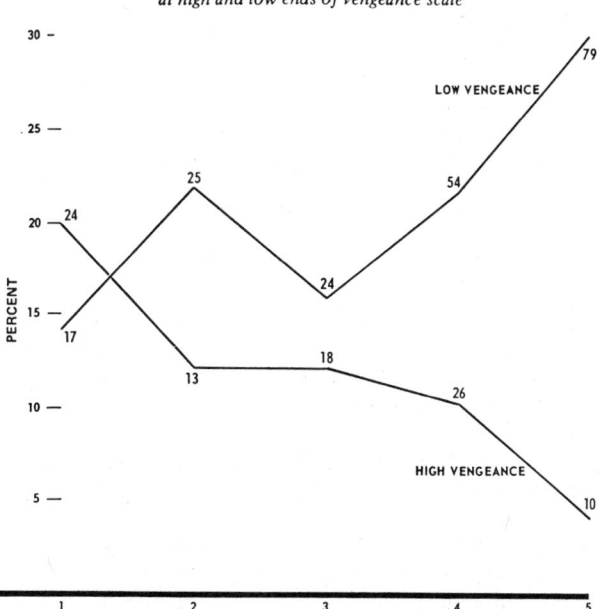

Figure 13.—Proportion of income groups among whites at high and low ends of vengeance scale

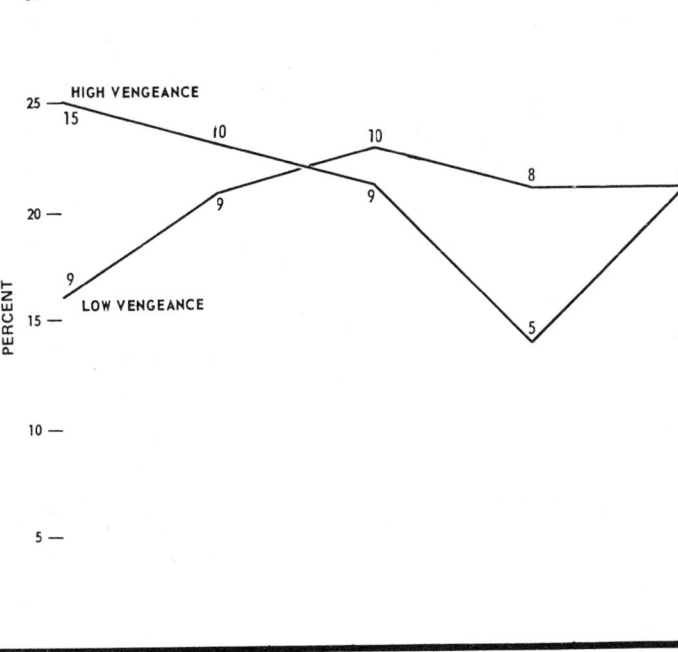

*Figure 14.—Proportion of income groups among blacks
at high and low ends of vengeance scale*

on the other hand, presents quite a different picture. Although the number of cases in this figure is rather small, it is still clear that increasing income levels among blacks does not have the same effect as it does for whites. Why is this the case?

Under a classical formulation of the class-conflict argument, we would expect that as we examine more and more deprived segments of the population there should be greater and greater levels of hostility to governmental structures—except at the very lowest level, where we should find little or no revolutionary sentiment. The curve for whites in Figure 13 gives some support to this argument, despite the fact that the relationship at the lowest level is not the expected direction. Although this is an extremely crude formulation of the class-conflict hypothesis and an equally crude measure (i.e., simply family income), the argument in general is supported within the white population.

The picture for blacks, however, suggests two alternative formulations. On the one hand, the blacks may form the segment of the population that, in the contemporary United States, is the functional equivalent of the classical lumpenproletariat; perhaps they should not therefore be expected to show great differences in their hostility toward the government despite increasing income level. This argument is rather insubstantial, for, as we have seen, blacks are much more likely than whites to be high on political vengeance and cannot, therefore, be treated as a prerevolutionary segment in the classical Marxian sense. Therefore, it seems most reasonable to conclude at this stage of the analysis that factors more important than simple class position are operating to produce the generalized support for vengeance found among the blacks. A number of possible factors might be: racial discrimination, relative deprivation irrespective of income level, the presence and increasing appeal of separatist and black-militant ideologies, and the allocation of federal monies for military expenditures at the expense of programs designed to improve the lives and expectations of the black population of the country. It may be that simply increasing income levels among Negroes will not necessarily increase their confidence in the government and the social system.

Unless the factors that have produced such high levels of distrust among the black population are attacked at the same time that their relative poverty is reduced, programs simply designed to increase income may not have the intended effect, i.e., the successful integration of the black population into the value and class system of the United States.

Figures 15 and 16 report educational levels of blacks and whites. The general pattern here is the same found in the data on income, except that increasing levels of education appear to have a stronger effect on vengeance among whites than does income. The data from the high and low groups on the Vengeance scale are repeated in Figure 17, where the pattern is quite clear. Figure 18 is based on Figures 15 and 16, where vengeance is examined by the educational level of white and black respondents. Inspection of these figures indicates that low-vengeance blacks and whites have about the same proportion of respondents at each level of education, with vengeance varying inversely with increasing education. In the case of the high-vengeance blacks and whites, the two curves diverge

Figure 15.—Education and vengeance for blacks

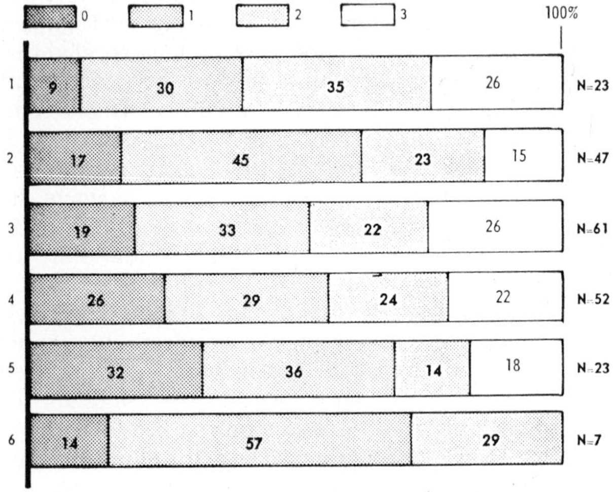

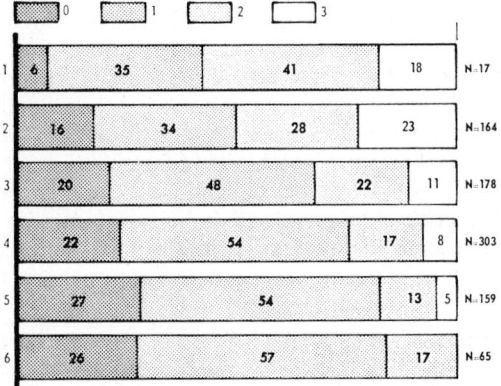

Figure 16.—Education and vengeance for whites

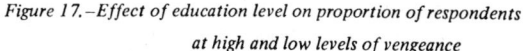

Figure 17.–Effect of education level on proportion of respondents
at high and low levels of vengeance

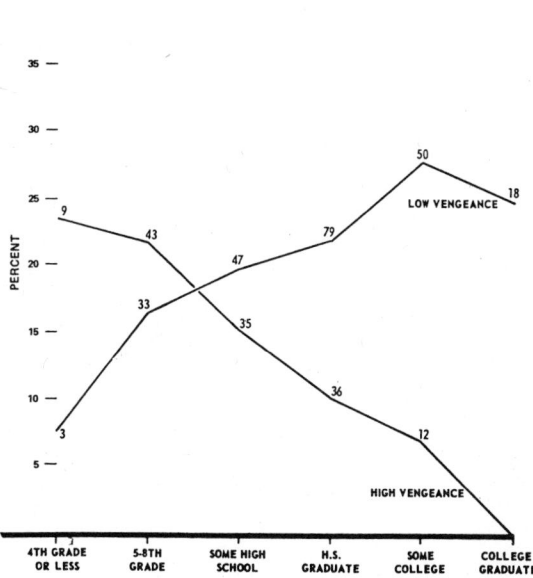

rather sharply. As educational attainment increases among
whites, the proportion of high-vengeance respondents falls off
rapidly. This is not the case with blacks, among whom a large
proportion of highly vengeant respondents are found at all but
the highest educational levels. Again, however, the number of
cases used to establish these curves is very small and should be
taken as a suggestion rather than a substantial finding. Nevertheless, the overall effect of education on diminishing support
for the Vengeance scale is far greater for whites than it is for
blacks.

6. Vengeance and the Political System: Party Identification
and Policy Orientation

We have already seen (Table 8a) that high assassination
relief scores are related to political vengeance and that politi-

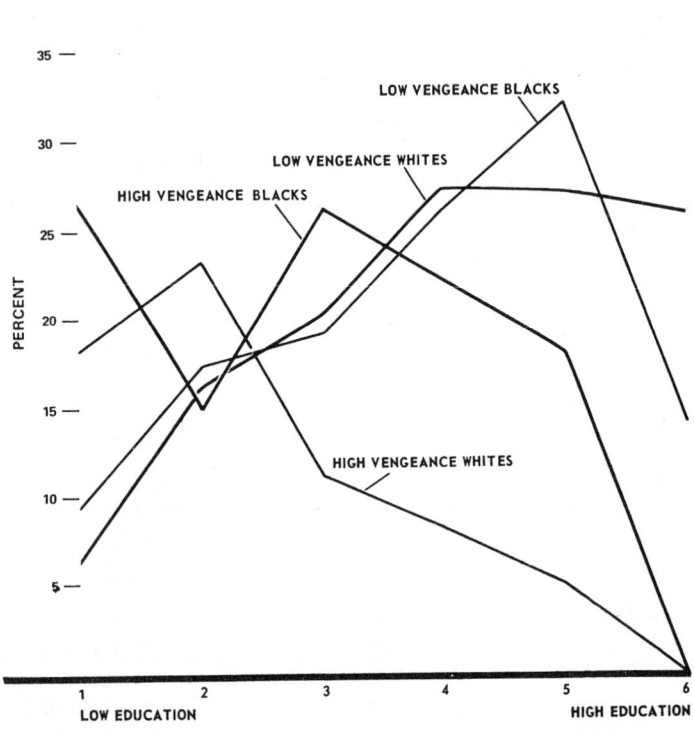

Figure 18.—Proportion of high and low vengeance groups
by race at various levels of education

cal vengeance is closely tied to the concept of political trust.
We therefore ought not to expect that our highly vengeant
respondents have "normal" attitudes about the American political system. Nevertheless, it is worth while to give further
consideration to the question of the political attachments of
highly vengeant respondents. Let us look first at the national
election of 1968.

Interest in the election is shown in Figure 19 for the persons
reporting that they were "very interested" in the election and
those "not much interested" in it. Presumably, disinterest in
national elections is in part an indicator of alienation from the
political system, and we should expect to find greater propor-

tions of the low-interest respondents at the higher ends of the Vengeance scale. In fact, we do. Again, however, when race is controlled, blacks are found to contribute higher proportions of persons who are both disinterested in the election and highly vengeant. Indeed, thirty percent of the blacks in the "not much interested" group were at the high end of the Vengeance scale, compared with fourteen percent for whites. This underlines our previous analyses: blacks are disproportionately alienated from the political system and express this alienation in the form of disinterest in one major intersection of public opinion and political policy.

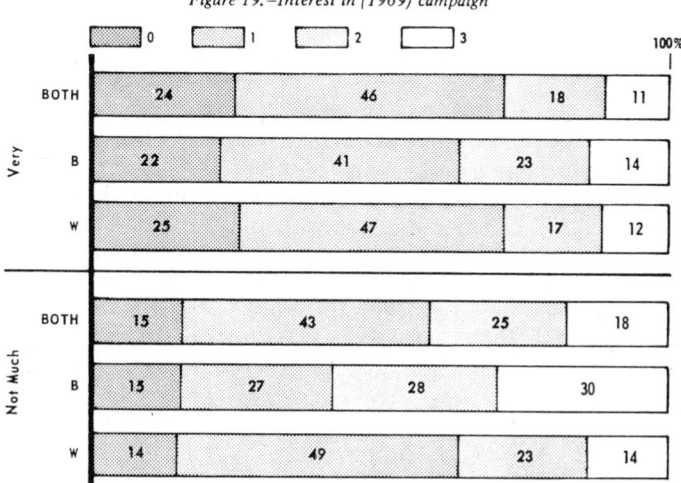

Figure 19. – Interest in (1969) campaign

a. America's Presidential Elections

A rather different pattern emerges when we look at the presidential preference of our respondents in the national election of 1968. Figure 20 reports these distributions for the entire sample.

Although there were no substantial differences between Nixon and Humphrey supporters in the proportion of these groups located at the high end of the Vengeance scale, persons who supported George Wallace contributed, proportionately,

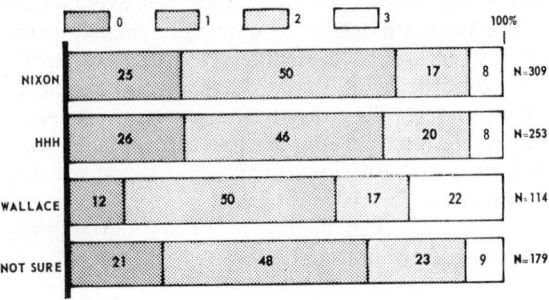

Figure 20.—Presidential choice (all respondents)

almost three times as many highly vengeant respondents as either the pro-Nixon or pro-Humphrey groups.

As we might expect, Wallace supporters were ninety-nine percent white. Wallace's campaign was partially based on appeals to racism, and was also replete with violent or emotionally charged references to many of America's political leaders —threatening to throw some of them in the Potomac, calling others traitors and communist sympathizers. This tactic evidently appealed strongly to about a fourth of his supporters. Among the set of highly vengeant white respondents with a presidential preference, just under half of them—forty-five and two-tenths percent—were found in the ranks of the Wallace supporters.

Wallace was successful in mobilizing by far the greatest share of politically vengeant white persons in the national election of 1968. He did so on the basis of appeals similar to those which have mobilized the opposition of the blacks to our political system. The implications of this finding are ominous indeed. Political vengeance is highest in two groups in the society who have little attachment to its political system and who have increasingly become the political, and in some cases revolutionary, targets of militant demagogues who openly espouse violence as a means of social change.

Figure 21 reports the partisan identification of the respondents in the sample. The question asked, "Regardless of how you may vote, do you usually consider yourself a Democrat, a Republican, an Independent or what?" There is little difference between the two major parties in their level of vengeance, with Republicans having a lower proportion at the high end of the

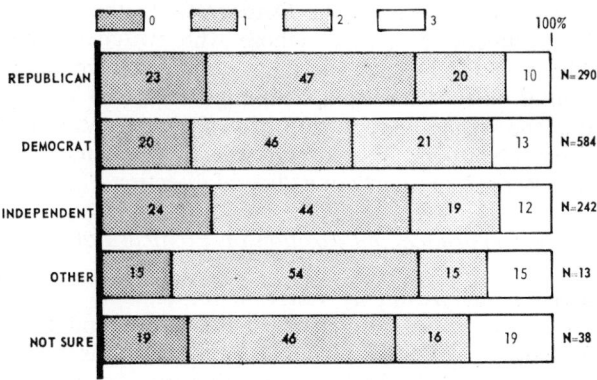

Figure 21.—Party identification

vengeance scale—conceivably a product of their generally higher levels of education and income. "Other" (specific party) and "Not sure" reflect a disproportionate number of the politically vengeant but the low number of such respondents makes any detailed discussion impossible. In particular, the impact of Wallace's American Independent Party cannot be assessed although such respondents should technically have listed themselves in the "Other" category; many may have called themselves "Independent" (American Independent Party) or Democratic. We can speculate that some persons attracted by Wallace but with a traditional party loyalty would appear in the "Not sure" category.

A final measure of political attachment and party switching produced a finding that is consistent with our expectations about political vengeance. Figure 22 reports the percentage of

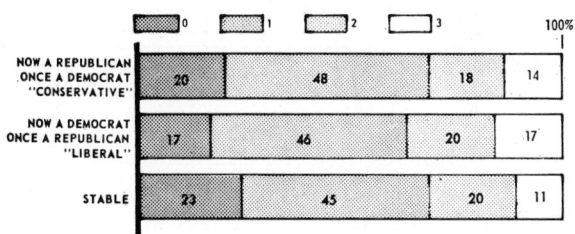

Figure 22.—Party switching

persons reporting party switches in a "conservative direction" (those who switched from the Democratic to the Republican Party), a "liberal direction" (those who switched from the Republican to the Democratic Party), and those remaining in their initial party. Consistent with Figure 21, the group contributing the smallest proportion of vengeant respondents was the stable identifiers. The largest was those switching away from the Republican Party in a "liberal direction."

b. Vengeance and Position on Political Issues

When we analyze highly vengeant respondents in terms of their positions on selected political issues, we find that they tend to cluster at the two extremes. In other words, persons at the extremes are much higher in the proportion of respondents at the high end of the Vengeance scale. Figure 23 reports the distribution of opinion on the issues of preferred policy in Vietnam. While reading this table, it must be remembered that this question was asked before the bombing halt was ordered by former President Lyndon Johnson early in November 1968. As this figure shows, the proportion of highly vengeant respondents decreases as one moves toward the middle of the figure. The central column, containing persons favoring a continuation of the then current U.S. policy, contributes the smallest proportion of highly vengeant respondents. This same pattern

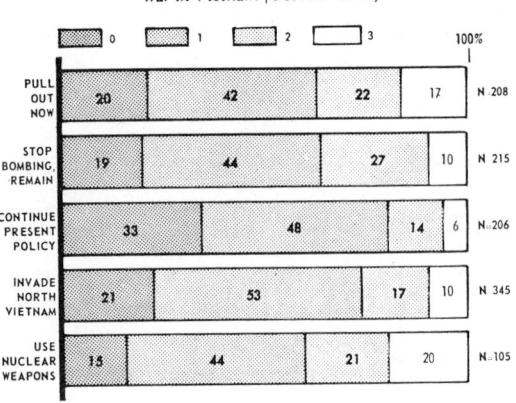

Figure 23.—Policy favored as a solution to war in Vietnam (October 1968)

appears in Figure 24, which reports respondents' views on the speed of integration. Those stating that integration was proceeding too slowly and those saying it was proceeding too rapidly are more than twice as likely to have highly vengeant respondents in their ranks as the group who state that integration is going at "about the right" speed.

Figure 24.—Political vengeance and speed of integration—both races

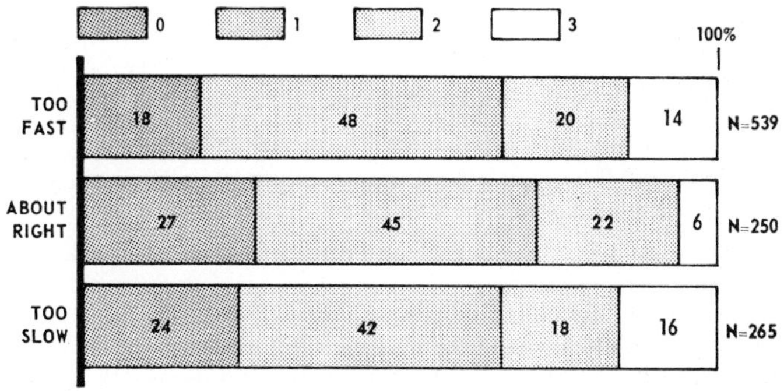

	0	1	2	3	100%
TOO FAST	18	48	20	14	N=539
ABOUT RIGHT	27	45	22	6	N=250
TOO SLOW	24	42	18	16	N=265

Another measure of policy relating to civil rights (Figure 25) shows that persons favoring segregation are far more likely to be highly vengeant than those favoring integration or "something in between."

Figure 25.—Political vengeance and segregation—both races

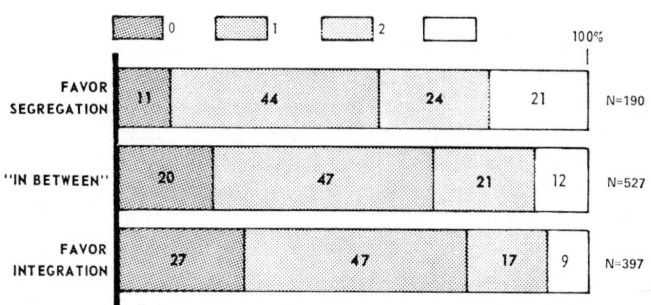

	0	1	2		100%
FAVOR SEGREGATION	11	44	24	21	N=190
"IN BETWEEN"	20	47	21	12	N=527
FAVOR INTEGRATION	27	47	17	9	N=397

c. Conclusions to Political Vengeance Analysis

We have seen that region has had a substantial effect on the production of vengeance, with urban blacks and Southern whites being the most vengeant. Race is a high predictor of vengeance, as are low levels of education and income. The psychological variable, Anomic Authoritarianism, and the acceptance of political violence variable are closely associated with vengeance. Vengeance itself is very closely tied to low levels of political trust and adherence to the extreme positions upon the various political issues discussed above (Figures 23, 24, and 25).

7. Analysis of Persons Who Indicate Support For The Use of Illegal Tactics or Violence in Response to Perceived Governmental Injustice

As noted in the introduction to this section, one extremely interesting relationship which appears from the data is the very weak (r=.068) correlation of the Political Vengeance measure to the measure of willingness to support "revolutionary violence." For the convenience of comprehension, the correlation matrix set forth in Table 8a is repeated here as Table 8b. The revolutionary violence measure was constructed from questions posing hypothetical situations in which the government is portrayed as having enacted increasingly repressive and dictatorial policies which would be expected to produce hostile responses from the population.

For example, the first hypothetical situation involved the imposition of a highly unjust tax by Congress, and the last involved the arrest and execution of innocent people by the government to keep itself in power. A series of responses were also proposed, including expressing an opinion about the matter, organizing a group concerned about it, illegally sitting in, and finally an armed revolt against the government. The Revolutionary Violence index was produced by considering only the two most extreme responses: participate in an illegal sit-in, and armed assault.

Because the Revolutionary Violence items attempt to measure opposition, though illegal or violent, to unjust and repressive governmental action, and because the vengeance measure

Table 8b.—Inter-factor correlations

	ASSASSINATION RELIEF	REVOLUTIONARY VIOLENCE	PERSONAL VIOLENCE	ANOMIC AUTHORITARIANISM FACTOR I	POLITICAL VENGEANCE FACTOR II	ACCEPTANCE OF POLITICAL VIOLENCE FACTOR III	POLICE VIOLENCE FACTOR IV	MILITARY VIOLENCE FACTOR V
ASSASSINATION RELIEF	—							
REVOLUTIONARY VIOLENCE	.007	—						
PERSONAL VIOLENCE	-.006	.162	—					
ANOMIC AUTHORITARIANISM	.153	-.248	-.058	—				
POLITICAL VENGEANCE	.226	.068	.014	.246	—			
ACCEPTANCE OF POLITICAL VIOLENCE	.164	.008	.018	.356	.300	—		
POLICE VIOLENCE	.051	.024	-.007	.310	.221	.295	—	
MILITARY VIOLENCE	-.034	-.029	-.007	.335	149	.304	.204	—
FIREARMS OWNERSHIP (UNCONTROLLED FOR PISTOLS)	.041	.060	.080	.012	.020	.002	-.071	.042

is based on items that seem to measure indiscriminate support for political violence, we need not be surprised at the absence of a relationship between these two variables. To the extent that the questions about governmental injustice reveal "civil libertarianism," we might expect the correlation with Political Vengeance to be negative. To the extent that the violence or illegality of the response eliminate those committed to the democratic form of government, we might expect the correlation with Political Vengeance to be positive. Pehaps the best conclusion at this stage of the analysis is that these are really two distinct types of violence and that the two sets of responses merit further study.

The fact that "Political Vengeance" and "Revolutionary Violence" did not tap the same groups is demonstrated by their different relationships to other violence factors investigated, as shown in Table 8b. Anomic Authoritarianism is a salient example.

The Anomy scale was initially devised to measure a person's relationship to the social structure—in particular to isolate those persons who were socially alienated and detached from contemporary values. The authoritarianism scale was an attempt to isolate persons who, among other things, placed a great emphasis on toughness, were non-introspective, presumably tolerant of authoritarian governments because of their general submission to authority figures, and were ethnocentric. The Anomic Authoritarianism factor is strongly associated with many of the other variables in the matrix, such as Police Violence (r=.310), Acceptance of Violence (r=.356), Military Violence (r=.335) and, of course, with Political Vengeance (r=.246). The social-psychological constructs which underlie the scales of authoritarianism and anomy are precisely those which we would expect to contribute a disproportionate number of persons to society who are potentially violent or who support violence in political and other forms. There is, however, a strong *negative* correlation between the anomic authoritarianism factor and the revolutionary violence scale (r= —.228). Thus, the persons who were high on items which purport to measure detachment from the social system and submissiveness to authority were very low on a measure of their willingness openly to oppose authority even when unjust, yet high in their support of violence in political contexts in general.

There are other striking differences. Acceptance of violence correlates very highly with Political Vengeance (r=.300), but not at all with Revolutionary Violence (r=.008). Perhaps more significantly, the Assassination Relief measure also correlates highly with Political Vengeance (r=.226), but not at all with Revolutionary Violence (r=.007). In addition, Acceptance of Police Violence correlates with Political Vengence (r=.221), but again not at all with Revolutionary Violence (r=.024).

Another difference, although not so strong and perhaps in an unexpected direction, is the moderate correlation between Revolutionary Violence and the experience and use of Personal Violence (r=.162), and the absence of any such correlation with Political Vengeance (r=.014).

Thus, the persons who say they would respond with illegal or violent acts to governmental injustice—the "revolutionarily violent"—are quite unlikely to be anomic or authoritarian, and are likely to have had experience in personal violence (fist fights and the like). Apart from this, none of the other violence factors we have investigated serves to isolate revolutionarily violent persons from the rest of society.[68]

Thus we turn to an item-by-item analysis of the responses to each of the questions from which the revolutionary violence scale was derived in an attempt to shed some light on the revolutionarily violent and to analyze the significance of different responses to different items in the revolutionary violence measure.

Item-by-item analysis of responses to
perceived governmental injustice.

The Hypothetical Situations

The following situations were presented to the respondents:
1. Imagine that Congress has passed a law that makes you pay just as many dollars in taxes as people who make a lot more money than you do.
2. Imagine that Congress has just passed a law prohibiting anyone from saying anything against the government.
3. Imagine that the government has just arrested and imprisoned many of the Negroes in your community even though there had been no trouble.
4. Imagine that, in order to keep control of the country, the government starts arresting and shooting large numbers of innocent people including members of your family.

Approval—Disapproval

Respondents were first asked if they strongly approved, approved, disapproved, or strongly disapproved of each situation that was described. The results are presented in Table 9.

Table 9.—Degree of Approval-Disapproval For
Each of the Four Hypothetical Situations[a]

	Taxes	Free speech	Negro arrest	Shooting innocent people
Strongly approve	2	2	1	1
Approve	1	2	0	0
Disapprove	21⎫	27⎫	31⎫	10⎫
Strongly disapprove	74⎭95	68⎭95	65⎭96	87⎭97
Not sure	2	3	4	1

[a]Columns do not always equal one hundred due to rounding of figures.

Actions That Individuals Would Take

For each of the situations, respondents were asked to indicate which of the following responses they felt it would be all right to take:

1. Express an opinion to friends on what is happening.
2. Sign a petition about what is happening.
3. Organize a group who is interested in what is happening.
4. If nothing else worked, participate in an illegal sit-in to express one's feelings about what is happening.
5. If nothing else worked, participate in a physical assault or armed action because of feeling about what is happening.

In addition to being asked what actions the respondent felt it would be all right to take, he was also asked, if he responded yes, whether he himself would be likely to engage in it. The results are presented in Table 10.

Table 11 describes the extent to which the respondents would themselves take any given action. There are two numbers presented for each action. The first is the percentage of respondents who agreed that a particular action was all right and who then said they were likely to engage in it themselves. The second figure applies this percentage to the total number

*Table 10.—Percentages endorsing each
response by issue*

Action	Issue			
	Taxes	Free speech	Negro arrest	Shooting innocent people
Express opinion	74	73	76	67
Sign petition	73	73	69	65
Organize a group	61	64	61	67
Illegal sit-in	11	17	18	37
Physical assault	3	9	9	48

Table 11.—Percentage taking personal action

	Taxes	Free speech	Negro arrest	Shooting innocent people
Express opinion	93/69	94/69	94/71	97/65
Sign petition	88/64	89/65	88/61	94/61
Organize a group	54/33	65/42	64/39	83/56
Illegal sit-in	53/ 6	66/11	69/12	83/31
Physical assault	43/ 1	71/ 6	59/ 5	86/41

of respondents approving the action. In other words, seventy-four percent of the total respondents said it was all right to express an opinion with respect to the "taxes" item (Table 10). Of those seventy-four percent, ninety-three percent said they themselves would take that action (Table 11, first number). Ninety-three percent of seventy-four percent is sixty-nine percent (Table 11, second number), or the total of all respondents who responded both "all right" and "likely to take the action themselves."

It would appear that the four items are in ascending degree of injustice, from unfair taxes to shooting innocent people. The results of overall disapproval, thus, are somewhat unexpected. (The total level of disapproval for each item was virtually unanimous and not significantly different, though it did tend to scale slightly upward, as expected.) When strong disapproval alone is considered, we find that while shooting innocent people scores highest, the next highest response is to unfair taxes, with arrest of Negroes receiving the least amount of strong disapproval. The expected pattern of responses, however, returns if we consider only the most serious action responses—illegal sit-in and physical assault. The percentage of respondents who stated both approval of those actions and willingness to engage in those actions was lowest with respect to unfair taxes, tied as to prohibiting free speech and arresting Negroes, and was highest by a wide margin as to shooting innocent people.

The Political Activist

The foregoing responses were analyzed in terms of a number of factors. We selected for more detailed discussion one of these variables, which we called "Political Activity." It was selected because it appeared to produce the most consistently significant explanation for "revolutionary violence," i.e., high levels of stated approval of the most severe forms of response to governmental injustice and a high level of willingness to engage in such activities. This variable was constructed by asking all respondents to indicate which actions they personally had taken to express their views about political or social issues. Their replies follow:

	Percent who have taken action
Discuss with friends	97
Write a letter to a newspaper or to an elected official.	32
Contribute money to an organization concerned about the issue.	32
Sign a petition.	53
Express your opinion in person to a Government official.	27
Organize a group.	8
Participate in a legally permitted demonstration.	8
Participate in an illegal but nonviolent demonstration.	3
Participate in a riot (Less than ½ of 1 percent)	

The first action, discussion with friends, is so universal that it does not sufficiently discriminate between groups. The last two actions were engaged in so infrequently that they provided too few cases for analysis. Accordingly, our political activity factor was confined to consideration of the six other actions on the list.

All respondents were classified into three groups according to the number of different activities they had participated in: low (No or one activity), moderate (two, three, or four activities), and high (five or more activities). As expected, when actually applied to the survey data, the Political Activity index appears to be the variable which is most consistently explanatory of the more severe responses in each of the four hypothetical situations of governmental injustice.

For example, the political activity factor as applied to the unfair tax and the infringement of free speech items is shown in Tables 12 and 13:

At the least severe level (expressing an opinion or signing a petition), there appear to be no significant group differences, but starting at the next level (organizing a group), the Political Activity index becomes highly discriminatory. For example, with regard to infringement of free speech, three times as many of the highly politically active would participate in illegal sit-ins, if nothing else worked, than would those of low political activity (eleven percent vs. thirty-four percent). The

Table 12.—All right response by political activity—free speech infringement

Response	Political activity		
	Low	Mod-erate	High
Express an opinion to friends.	74	72	73
Sign a petition.	67	76	75
Organize a group.	54	66	82
If nothing else worked, participate in an illegal sit-in to express one's feelings.	11	16	34
If nothing else worked, participate in a physical assault or armed action.	4	8	21

Table 13.—*All right response by political activity—unfair tax laws*

Response	Political activity		
	Low	Mod- erate	High
Express an opinion to friends.	76	73	74
Sign a petition.	66	76	78
Organize a group.	51	62	81
If nothing else worked, participate in an illegal sit-in to express one's feelings.	9	9	22
If nothing else worked, participate in a physical assault or armed action.	3	2	6

ratio increases to five times (four percent vs. twenty-one percent) with respect to physical assault or armed action.

A high score on the Political Activity index was also a high predictor of severe action responses in the "shooting of innocent people" item[69] (Table 14).

Table 14.—*All right response—shooting innocent people*

Response	Moderate	High political activity
Participants in illegal sit-in	37	56
Physical assault or armed action	48	71

The Political Activity factor is related to a stated willingness to take the approved action. For example, in the "shooting innocent people" item, the percentage of those stating approval who also said they would take the action themselves is as follows:

	Activity		
	Low	Mod- erate	High
Participate in illegal sit-in	73	85	91
Physical assault or armed action	74	89	91

We cannot assume that high Political Activity factor entirely explains high Revolutionary Violence. As demonstrated above, however, the politically active do account to a highly significant degree for Revolutionary Violence, and their demographic profile differs greatly from the "politically vengeant" discussed in the first part of this section.

The demographic profile of the political activist is shown in Table 15, which sets forth the Political Activity index for each variable considered. In brief, Table 15 shows that the most politically active are younger, have higher incomes, feel confident of their financial future, are males, are well educated, and are salaried or self-employed rather than hourly workers. A heavier than average proportion is Jewish, a smaller proportion Protestant. A high proportion was reared in a large city, and a disproportionately high number now lives in the suburbs. They are strongly represented in the West and heavily underrepresented in the South. Race alone does not predict political activity; the proportion of Negroes among the active group is as large as among the inactive group.

Given such a disparity in demographic profile between the political activist and the politically vengeant, the absence of a negative correlation between Revolutionary Violence and Political Vengeance suggests that there are significant elements other than political activism that enter into Revolutionary Violence.

Another way to focus upon the distinction between Political Vengeance and Revolutionary Violence, is through analysis of another item, the so-called Senator item.

Response to "Legitimate" Political Conduct Perceived as Highly Harmful to the Community—The "Senator" Item

The respondents to the survey were told:

> Your senator has blocked legislation which you believe is essential to protect the rights of every citizen. The senator has come to your town and is making a speech in a public auditorium to gain support for his point of view.

A senator is duly elected official who has the right in a democracy to block legislation even when some persons may strongly disagree with such action. Furthermore, he is engaged in the classic kind of conduct contemplated by democratic procedures—making a speech in an effort to gain support. On the other hand, the legislation he is blocking is "essential to

Table 15.—Political activity (percent)

Age	Low	Moderate	High
18–20	2	4	3
21–30	19	23	25
31–40	16	21	27
41–50	17	18	17
51–60	18	16	17
61–65	6	3	2
Over 65	22	15	9
Race			
White	78	86	81
Negro	20	12	18
Other	2	2	1
Income			
Under $3,000	21	22	4
$3,000–$4,999	20	11	6
$5,000–$6,999	18	19	17
$7,000–$9,999	25	25	20
$10,000–$14,999	13	22	32
$15,000–$19,999	2	8	12
$20,000–$24,999	1	2	4
$25,000 and over	*	2	5
Financial status in last few years			
Getting better	37	49	56
Getting worse	17	15	11
Stayed the same	45	35	32
Not sure	1	1	1
Financial status in next few years			
Get better	40	51	57
Get worse	10	10	6
Stay the way it is	39	33	34
Not sure	11	6	3
Sex			
Male	47	49	70
Female	53	51	30

Table 15.—(continued)

Education	Low	Moderate	High
4th grade or less	6	1	1
5th to 8th grade	27	14	3
Some high school	28	17	13
High school graduate	28	36	22
Some college	8	19	29
College graduate	2	8	15
Postgraduate	1	5	17
Employment status			
Hourly wage	39	30	24
Salaried	23	37	45
Self-employed	11	13	18
Retired	19	13	9
Student	—	1	2
Military service	*	1	1
Housewife	3	2	—
Unemployed	2	1	—
Other	3	2	1
Religion			
Protestant	69	64	56
Catholic	26	28	25
Jewish	1	2	6
Other	3	4	8
Not classified	1	2	5
Church attendance			
Regularly	38	44	45
Often	13	14	12
Seldom	41	35	33
Never	8	7	10
Where brought up			
Farm	39	28	18
Town	27	28	29
Small city	13	16	13
Large city	21	28	40
Military service			
Veteran	39	56	46
Active	1	1	1
Reserve	1	2	4
Never been in service	59	41	49

Table 15.—(continued)

Region	Low	Moderate	High
East	26	28	33
Midwest	28	30	24
South	36	24	14
West	10	18	29
Size of community			
Metro city	31	27	32
Suburban	18	29	36
Urban town	21	21	20
Rural	30	23	12

protect the rights of every citizen." The responses to the dilemma might shed light upon the nature of the revolutionarily violent and the politically vengeant.

Respondents were asked to indicate which of a selected list of activities they would condone, and which they themselves would be likely to participate in. The results of the entire line of questioning are detailed in Table 16.

Table 16.—Percentage condoning and participating in activities

Response	Condone	Likely to participate
Carry signs expressing disapproval of the position of the Senator	92	59
Boo during pauses in the Senator's speech where the Senator was expecting applause	36	66
Participate with others in systematically booing and stamping feet so that the Senator was unable to continue his speech and be heard	17	60
Throw rotten tomatoes or other objects which could not harm the Senator but which would demonstrate disapproval	5	55
Throw empty bottles or other objects which could not do serious or permanent harm to the Senator but which would demonstrate the extent of disapproval	2	20
Use a gun or other weapon to inflict serious enough harm to the Senator so that he would have to turn over his position to another person	1	14

Significantly, the data showed that the politically active, although more prone to approve booing, were no more likely than the average to condone more extreme forms of dissent. This tends to suggest that the politically active do not consider "revolutionary" violence an appropriate response to highly disfavored political conduct which is within the bounds of the democratic process.

Likewise, blacks do not differ from whites in refusing to condone the most extreme response of using a gun or other weapon (two percent), as would be expected under the Political Activist model, but not expected under the Political Vengeance model. Blacks do, however, tend more to condone booing (fifty-five percent), booing and stamping in rhythm (thirty-seven percent), and throwing rotten tomatoes (sixteen percent) and bottles (seven percent).

In addition to asking what the respondents would condone or do themselves, the survey asked what their friends would condone and what activities their friends would be likely to engage in. The results are set forth in Table 17.

Table 17.—Percentages of those condoning and likely to participate (responses for self and for friends)

	Self		Friends	
Response	Condone	Likely	Condone	Likely
Carry a sign	92	59	90	70
Boo	36	66	49	81
Participate in booing and stamping of feet	17	60	30	78
Throw tomatoes	5	55	13	63
Throw empty bottles	2	20	7	48
Use a gun	1	14	3	52

Only in the case of the first response is there a greater percentage of stated endorsement for the individual than for his friends. Beginning with the second most serious response, the percentage for friends is greater than for the individual himself. This relationship continues through all of the remaining responses. The politically active, however, responded above the average level for all acts except for inflicting serious physical harm.

	Total (percent)	High political activity (percent)
Carry signs	90	93
Boo	49	68
Systematically boo and stamp feet	30	41
Throw rotten tomatoes	13	20
Throw empty bottles	7	11
Use a gun or other weapon	3	3

The picture with respect to Negroes also changes with the "friends" response. For all the more serious responses a much greater proportion of non-whites than whites indicated that their friends would condone such an action. In the case of booing, fifty-nine percent of the non-whites indicated that their friends would support this action, while only forty-six percent of the white respondents do. In the next case, the percentages are forty-six to twenty-six percent, and so on. In fact, fully one out of every five non-whites said that they thought their friends would condone throwing bottles at the Senator, whereas only one out of twenty-five whites gave this response for their friends.

Response	Percent, Friends overall rates	Percent, Friends White	Percent, Friends Nonwhite
Carry signs	90	90 (n=657)	91 (n=158)
Boo	49	46 (n=332)	59 (n=102)
Systematically boo and stamp feet	30	26 (n=187)	47 (n=81)
Throw tomatoes	13	9 (n=69)	28 (n=49)
Throw empty bottles	7	4 (n=31)	20 (n=34)
Use a gun or other weapon	3	2 (n=11)	7 (n=12)

Conclusion

The foregoing section is only a brief analysis of the data collected by the commission survey. We can, however, make the following tentative conclusions: Our finding with respect to political vengeance supports the basic assertions of the National Advisory Commission on Civil Disorders (the Kerner Commission) which summarizes its studies of recent disorders as follows: "Our nation is moving toward two societies, one black, one white—separate and unequal."[70] Blacks in the United States, particularly those in urban ghettos, are manifesting their distrust of America's political institutions and political system in ways that are strongly supportive of political violence. Whites, particularly those directly threatened by the prospect of black equality, are also responding with violent opposition to this same political system. The net result is the formation of large groups in our society who are violently antagonistic toward each other and, at the same time, hostile to the political order as we know it. This division in the society may be characterized as the formation of two warring camps of white racists and black militants. These two groups are so intensely hostile to the political system that they are willing to use violence against their political enemies and against the government in their quest for realization of their values and goals.

Our findings with respect to revolutionary violence indicate that those who state a willingness to respond with violence to perceived governmental injustice differ from the politically vengeant. To a significant extent, the latter group is composed of political activists; young, highly educated, urban, and with a relatively high income. This is the very group from which our democratic system should expect to derive its greatest support. This group tends to respond with violence to perceived governmental injustice, although our data suggests that they will tolerate, without violent response, political actions of which they highly disapprove if these actions still fall within the bounds of democratic procedure.

We believe that the findings in this section strongly support the basic finding of this report: i.e., the remedy for political violence in general, and assassination in particular, lies in meeting the root causes of social unrest and perceived injustice. We have found no shortcut to political tranquility.

D. The Rhetoric of Vilification and Violence in Contemporary America

Although assassination for political purposes has been virtually nonexistent in the United States, political groups within our society, especially those of an extremist nature, have used violence as a means to achieve their ends. In the 1960's, violence by extremist groups, such as the Ku Klux Klan, the Black Panthers, and the Minutemen, has been a tactical device intended to achieve specified goals. Violent behavior also draws public attention to the organizations and their causes.

These groups use a rhetoric of vilification and violence. Groups advocating violent behavior justify its use and acceptance to achieve objectives of the organization. For the individual disposed to engage in violent acts, advocacy of violence by the group provides him with a rationale for his behavior and even the promise of increased acceptance within the group.

Some of this rhetoric goes beyond the advocacy of violence in general and the moral justification for individual acts of violence. Such rhetoric often pinpoints and vilifies a specific target—Martin Luther King, Jr., Robert Kennedy, the incumbent President, members of the police force (indiscriminately chosen), and the like. Some literature even goes on to indicate the weapon best suited for the task, appraising and evaluating the alternatives conveniently available or providing information as to where they may be obtained.

A group that uses the rhetoric of vilification and violence as an acceptable political stratagem, then, can supply an individual with a motive, a climate receptive to the act, the potential admiration of his peers, the target, a justification for the behavior, and information on the capability and availability of weapons. When these factors are combined with any psychological aberrations or personality disorders an individual might have, a tragedy may result.

Systematic vilification of political leaders has been identified as one of the preconditions for assassination in a democracy.[71] Posters are among the means used for political influence. In most, political figures are identified as criminals and in some cases home and office addresses are given as well as the usual route of travel between the two. The sources of these verbal and pictorial attacks are both left and right wing.

An extensive collection of the rhetoric of vilification and violence employed by contemporary groups appears in Appendix B.[72] The material illustrates the climate of violence encouraged by these groups, their directives for group members to arm and kill other human beings, their advice on weaponry, and specific examples of group-connected violent acts.

The evidence set forth in Appendix B indicates that exhortations to violence are connected with violent acts. We do not suggest that because this relationship exists the present scope of the protection of speech under the First Amendment to the U.S. Constitution should be narrowed. We do report that our studies indicate violent and inflammatory rhetoric and deliberate vilification of officeholders have a seriously corrosive effect upon democratic institutions and may be a substantial preconditioning factor for extreme political violence, including assassination. There appears to be no need for responsible journalists to depict the President of the United States as a deliberate murderer of children or a vice president as a sewer rat. Sewer rats should be killed. Do we mean to suggest that? Should we suggest that?

We repeat: we do not suggest any limitation of the right of free speech. Too much is to be lost by any such limitation. We do suggest that much more is to be gained from a responsible use of free speech than may have been previously realized. All of us should consider what we really mean before we attribute epithets such as traitor, murderer, fascist, and communist to those with whom we disagree.

E. Two Contemporary Violent or Potentially Violent White Vigilante-Type Groups

Our data, in particular section C of this chapter, have shown that a special potential for political violence exists in black ghettos and in those segments of the white population directly threatened by black aspirations. The black urban ghetto has been analyzed, among other places, in the report of the National Commission on Civil Disorders (the Kerner Commission). In analyzing the problems which lead to the violent and potentially violent confrontations between black and white, the white side of the equation is too often simply dismissed as "racism." Racism, however, is a symptom of underlying social conditions. These conditions must be identified if the violence associated with white racism is to be reduced.

We selected for study two current American vigilante-type movements, neither a stranger to violence, and both responding to a perception of a black threat; (1) The North Carolina Ku Klux Klan—a product of the rural poor whites in the

South, called by Peter Young, consultant to this Task Force, the White Ghetto; and (2) The North Ward Citizens' Council of Newark, an example of a so-called backlash group.

This section is drawn from the work of Peter Young, consultant to this Task Force. He collected important original material of great value which included tape recordings of a Ku Klux Klan rally, interviews with Exalted Cyclops Billy Glowers and Grand Dragon J. Robert Jones, a Klan-sponsored radio program, semi-underground "segregationist" records distributed through the Klan, and an interview with Reverend Will Campbell, a churchman long concerned with ministering to the poor rural white ghetto from which the Klan draws its strength. In addition, Mr. Young tape-recorded a campaign speech and an interview with Tony Imperiale, leader of the North Ward Citizens' Council in Newark, N.J., a so-called vigilante group representative of the white northern urban backlash. He also interviewed Dan Watts, editor of the black nationalist magazine, *The Liberator,* and Paul Krassner, editor of *The Realist* and founder of the Youth International Party (Yippies). These tapes are summarized in Appendix D.

He describes the development of this interest as follows:

The first Klan rally I attended was held on the outskirts of Hillsboro, N.C., about ten miles from the wellspring of Southern liberalism at Chapel Hill where I had been a graduate student in the late 1950's. I was at the rally as a newsman, representing WRAL–TV of Raleigh.

It was a small rally—only about 1,500 of the faithful in their dirt-stained dungarees and their sweat-stained gingham dresses. And as those raucous cries of *nigger, nigger* split the Southern night, I was shaken—perhaps *stricken* is more accurate—by the realization that the drive for minimal justice in behalf of black people had come to this: the ordinary white people of the South, God's people, were on the edge of a collective nervous breakdown composed in roughly equal parts of ignorance, rage and paranoia. . . .

I felt as though I had blundered into the scene of an awful disaster—with the dead, dying, maimed and crippled all around me. If you have read *Catch-22* by Joseph Heller, you will recall the scene in which the protagonist,

Yossarian, goes into the back of the plane to give first aid to Snowden. Yossarian thinks that he is dealing with a relatively minor wound, until he unzips Snowden's flak suit and the youngster's insides come tumbling out all in a heap on the floor of the aircraft.

After some months of debating with myself I committed my life into the hands of precisely those wounded men, women and children I saw in that first Klan cow pasture.

So I do not pretend to be a neutral, unbiased observer.

The section on the North Carolina Ku Klux Klan that follows uses Mr. Young's words, selected and organized from the prolific material provided to this Task Force.

1. North Carolina Ku Klux Klan (White Ghetto)[73]

The forgotten man in America's continuing racial crisis is the low-income white. He it is who has carved out, against considerable odds, a struggling, marginal existence symbolized by the little house, the car, the television set, and the tax bill that comes due each year.

Life has not been easy for this man; he is unimpressed by the argument that the average Negro has suffered even more. It is the low-income white whose precarious life style is directly and immediately threatened by the improvement in status of the Negro and his reaching out (with governmental backing) for better horizons which include a job, a decent home, and education for his children.

The reaction of the low-income white to the rise of the Negro was easily predictable. The white reacted with an explosive mixture of fear and hate. Since nobody else seemed to care about his situation, he became a sitting duck (in North Carolina) for recruitment by the Ku Klux Klan.

The stork did not bring 20,000 Kluxers to North Carolina. They were made here, in this America, our North Carolina, just as surely as the textiles, tobacco and furniture are also products of "Variety Vacationland." These Kluxers, organized into more than 200 chartered Klan units, came out of the white ghetto as the indigenous leaders of a gravely wounded people.

Southern leaders have tended to minimize the importance of this phenomenon. In North Carolina in 1965, Governor Dan K. Moore said there were only "618 hard-core Klansmen" in the Tar Heel State. The Governor defined a hard-core Klansman as one who would drive hundreds of miles each week to attend Klan rallies and transact Klan business, all without pay, as a sort of labor of love. Dragon J. R. [Bob] Jones quite correctly replied that if the Governor's own definition were accepted, then there were more "hard-core" Klansmen in the State than hard-core Democrats or Republicans.

A similar game is being played on the national level. The gaping wounds of American black people can no longer be denied, but it is still possible for a little while longer yet to maintain the fiction that this is an isolated case and that the ordinary white American is doing very well indeed in this paradise of free enterprise and democracy. But truth will out—in fact, it already has. (The white ghetto exists just as surely as the black.)

My dictionary defines a ghetto as "any section of a city in which many members of some national or racial group live, or to which they are restricted." This definition does not have to be stretched very far in order for us to talk about the white ghetto of the Carolina Klan.[74]

The average Tar Heel Kluxer (as I have known him) was born into grinding poverty, poorly educated in substandard schools, economically exploited and officially harassed.

Most white Americans (and many black people) have some difficulty in believing that in this year 1968, in this prosperous America, that *white* citizens exist by the millions in an environment which is so lacking in elemental respects as to be fertile breeding ground for hatred which is finally expressed in a murderous racism.

Permit me, then, to quote at some length from the report of *another* Presidential Commission, the National Advisory Commission on Rural Poverty (Chairman Edward Breathitt), which issued its report in September, 1967. The quoted excerpts are from the Rural Poverty Commission's summary of its report:

"Rural poverty is so widespread, and so acute, as to be a national disgrace, and its consequences have swept into our cities, violently. . . . They (the programs) were developed without anticipating the vast changes in technology, and the consequences of this technology to rural people . . . Most rural programs still do not take the speed and consequences of technological change into account[75] . . . In contrast to the urban poor, the rural poor, notably the white, are not well organized, and have few spokesmen for bringing the nation's attention to their problems[76] . . . The more vocal and better organized urban poor gain most of the benefits of current antipoverty programs[77] . . . the Nation's major social welfare and labor legislation largely bypassed rural Americans . . . we have been oblivious of the rural poor . . . Rural poverty in the United States has no geographic boundaries. It is acute in the South, but it is present and serious in the East, the West and the North. Rural poverty is not limited to Negroes . . . whites outnumber nonwhites among the rural poor by a wide margin . . . Hunger, even among children, does exist among the rural poor . . . The rural poor have gone, and now go, to poor schools . . . Unemployment and underemployment are major problems in rural America . . . Most of the rural South is one vast poverty area . . . The community in rural poverty areas has all but disappeared as an effective institution."[78]

Those who profess surprise that an organization such as "The Klan" should emerge from the environment described above are naive. What do they expect?

As far as a descriptive picture of "the white ghetto" is concerned, there is nothing I can add to what is already so abundantly in the record from this previous Commission. But I can add several observations:

1. The appointment of each new Commission (including the Commission on Violence) is greeted by most citizens with a withering blast of cynicism. We have had a plethora of Commissions, federal and state, telling us rather precisely what is wrong and what needs to be done. Yet nothing is done; the recommendations are not followed. The problems continue. It is not so much that the recommendations are ignored: they are usually good for a "special" from Walter Cronkite. Rather, The System

seems *unable* to do what its own best experts proclaim is essential. It is not entirely facetious to suggest that we might need still another Presidential Commission to examine the question of why previous Commissions have proven so ineffective!

2. We hear a great deal of easy talk these days (often from men whose colonial ancestors whirl in their graves) to the effect that "there is never any excuse or justification for violence, no matter how bad conditions may be." It would be more correct, and not at all hypocritical, to say that people's violence is often misdirected in terms of target and frequently counter-productive in terms of result. The fact is that the grievances so well summarized by the Rural Poverty Commission far exceed those grievances which caused our forefathers to separate (*violently*) from a distant and rather benign king. The same, of course, can also be said, and must be said, for our black and white brothers trapped in the misery of deteriorating cities. It was the Kerner Commission, which dissected *that* environment.

3. I am not in the business of comparing misery, of saying that Group A in the southern country side is more miserable (or less) than Group B in the northern metropolis.[79] I am simply saying that for *both* Group A and Group B—and perhaps Groups C through G as well —the level of unrelieved misery has long since passed the tolerance threshold, and we are therefore—surprise! surprise!—confronted by an explosive level of alienation that is marked by frequent incidents of violence.

4. For the low-income Southern white—whose grievances are numerous, legitimate and painfully real—it comes therefore as an unbearable shock to hear repeated expressions of governmental concern for the problems of *black* people. Never mind that these expressions are almost invariably hypocritical, designed simply for vote-getting purposes. The point is that the low-income Southern white—that bigot, that redneck, that racist, that hate-monger—doesn't even get the hypocritical expressions of concern from the government which is also *his*. It is exactly at this point that the average white ghetto citizen displaces his hatred from government officials (where it belongs) to his black neighbors, who also are victims of

the very same shell game. This shell game is *profitable* for some; the driving of a deep wedge between ordinary white and black citizens is precisely what perpetuates the power of a tiny minority, the country club elite. Quite often, the Klansman, as indigenous leader in the white ghetto, has a better understanding of this than do his followers. Example: the young preacher at the Klan rally at Four Oaks, N.C., shouted to the multitudes—"When they say HEW, they mean *nigger* health, they mean *nigger* education, they mean *nigger* welfare! You and I are just going to have to suffer it out by ourselves, the best way we can, like we always done."[80] But is this Klan preacher, at rock bottom, furious with "niggers" or "they"? To ask such a question is to answer it. And it is similarly no accident that the *overt* expressions of hostility in the Wallace campaign are always directed at "pseudo-intellectuals, pointy-headed guideline writers,"etc.

(The white ghetto citizen has committed violent and atrocious acts—against both Negroes and whites—those whites such as civil rights workers which he sees as challenging his world. Their rhetoric is deadly sick with hatred for Negroes. See Appendix D, for many examples, as well as Appendix B.)

But at some level of his being, the white ghetto citizen knows he is living a lie. Dimly, he recalls his many human contacts with black people all along the twisted trail of his life. He *is* on fire with hatred, as the result of a difficult life in an impoverished environment; this diffused hatred is suddenly focused on "the nigger," as if the latter were a lightning rod for all the ailments of the world. Yet in the very act of picking up his gun and acting out his hatred, the white ghetto citizen protests that it is not "niggers" whom he *really* hates. And to a considerable extent, he is right. What we call "racism" is more the expression than the cause of the highly contagious, collective frustration which afflicts the white ghetto these days in epidemic proportions.

You see, there is a magnificent Gravy Train which continues even now to roll across the American landscape. But unfortunately, it does not make all the required stops.[81]

White and Black Ghettos

Similarities and Differences

Similarities

1. No liquid capital for investment.

2. Low level of skills—people becoming "obsolete."

3. Feelings of powerlessness, rage, alienation, etc.

4. Fierce compensatory pride.

5. Heavily armed and arming.

6. Violence as a life style—has been expressed internally, but now is beginning to be externalized.

7. Infrastructure of indigenous, secret organizations operating outside the legal, constitutional framework.

8. Significant political activity outside two-party system.

Differences

1. White ghetto: No intellectual leadership or indigenous professional services.

   Black ghetto: Increasingly adequate intellectual leadership—black cultural explosion.

2. White ghetto: Family structure still intact, but under increasing strain.

   Black ghetto: Family structure splintered—no father figure, matriarchy.

3. White ghetto: Vices largely private and unorganized, with possible exception of "moonshine" liquor.

   Black ghetto: Racket-ridden community—heroin, prostitution, numbers, etc.

4. White ghetto: Few, if any, *constructive* governmental programs—much abuse, threats, etc.

Black ghetto: Many poorly conceived, mismanaged governmental and private programs—innumerable expressions of concern. Hopes aroused, then dashed.

5. White ghetto: Constant harassment from most *state and federal* law enforcement agencies but not ordinarily local police.

Black ghetto: Constant harassment from *local* police.

6. White ghetto: Advanced paranoid delusions that United States is about to be taken (or already has been taken) by Communist-Jewish-black conspiracy.

Black ghetto: Mild paranoid delusions among militants that official policy of *overt* genocide is just over the horizon.

2. North Ward Citizens' Council
(Urban Backlash)

The North Ward Citizens' Council in Newark, N.J., has been labeled a white vigilante group and has been identified with the so-called "white backlash." With the help of Peter Young, we taped a campaign speech and an interview with Mr. Anthony Imperiale, head of the North Ward Citizens' Committee, who was running for city councilman-at-large. His campaign speeches were demonstrably successful; he won his seat by a greater majority than any other candidate. Thus, the campaign speech and the interview, both of which are summarized in the appendix, merit the reader's special attention.

From the speech and interview we can conclude that the persons to whom Mr. Imperiale apparently appeals are not sick persons. They are, however, learning to resent what appears to them to be the position of favoritism taken by the government toward the urban Negro. They are beginning, like the Klansmen, to see the government as hostile rather than responsive to the needs of their community. They are quick to spot and resent the hypocrisy of the white legislator who requires the integration of the public school to which they must send their children because they cannot afford the private school to which the legislator sends his children.

Klan resurgence in North Carolina and white backlash vigilantism in Northern cities is a warning signal that the American racial crisis is not going to be solved at the expense of the low-income white. We have already heard from the Negro precincts that the crisis cannot be solved at their expense. This crisis can only be solved, not at someone else's expense, but at ours.

F. Summary: Cultural Origins and Impact of Violence

As the previous portions of this report have pointed out, much of the violence in the United States today is based on the confrontation between black and white. We attempt, however, to go beyond the specific violence-producing circumstances of today to identify, if possible, the cultural basis for the recurrent resort to violence to redress perceived grievances throughout United States history.

Such violence in the United States, though directed toward broadly political issues, has not been directly associated with formal political parties. Indeed, the two-party system of the United States has been a remarkably stable mechanism. For one hundred eighty years, with the exception of the Reconstruction period, political power at local, state, and federal levels has shifted nonviolently from party to party.

Nor have third-party movements been violent, even though our system is designed to make them unsuccessful.[82] The ballot, not the bullet, was the method used by the Populists of the 1890's, the different progressive parties of 1912, 1924, and 1948, the various socialist parties, and the plethora of other minor political parties that have arisen, including the Communist Party.

Organized political violence *has* characterized single-issue movements, almost all of which were ultimately successful in their broad goals. The values which this violence imposed on the social structure have often been adopted, and the violence condoned, by significant groups within the United States. Examples include the Abolitionist movement, the labor movement, agrarian movements of various kinds, the white supremacy movement in the South, and the temperance movement. The last two examples are not exceptions to the generality that the values supported by violence were ultimately adopted by the majority involved. The first Ku Klux Klan was successful in reimposing white supremacy which lasted nearly a century, until its serious challenge in the present decade. The temperance movement was successful in imposing prohibition. The experiment in prohibition was ultimately rejected, as we trust the experiment in white supremacy will ultimately be rejected, but the values espoused by movements characterized by violence were at least temporarily adopted by the dominant society.

Many theories have been advanced to explain the apparent high level of violence found within the United States, of which assassination is but one manifestation. The frontier tradition, with its emphasis on the individual's often violent assertion and protection of his rights, is one explanation. The high level of immigration and the resulting friction between the newer and more established groups is another theme found in the analysis of violence within American society. Slavery, the Civil War, and the Reconstruction period eroded faith in legal processes as the chief means of resolving social conflict. Violence by groups seeking to direct attention to their plight and to force the political system to respond to their needs is another frequent theme. Violence is identified with the recognition of trade unions, the periodic revivals of the Klan, and the recent riots in urban areas.

By themselves, these explanations are not sufficient. Australia, for example, has a similar frontier tradition and has had immigration of different ethnic groups, although not on the scale of this country. Yet, assassination is virtually nonexistent in Australia; there have been only two unsuccessful attempts and one known assassination in the history of the country.

It would appear that supplemental conditions within the American experience help account for the American pattern. For example, there is a predominant emphasis on achieving specified ends or goals, with less consideration given the means for such achievement. In times of upheaval, little attention has been given to the procedural and institutional facilities designed to achieve change within the society. American folklore has also emphasized direct action and individual initiative. The use of violent acts to achieve personal goals—and, it should be noted here, usually nonpolitical personal ends—if not part of the general cultural mythology, is certainly the image reinforced by the visual and printed media. In many respects, the American cowboy, a powerfully attractive figure in American folk culture, has proved an amalgam of these themes. It is noteworthy that the heroes have been individuals who acted on their own to achieve their ends—Billy the Kid, Jesse James, and the classic portrayal of the Western sheriff.

Equally compelling within the American experience has been the emphasis placed on freedom of conscience. Many of the founding fathers sought to escape religious persecution. This search for freedom of conscience has continued to serve as a reason for migration to this country. The dedication to individual conscience, a product of the earlier Calvinist tradition, and the willingness to suffer ostracism and employ unconventional, even potentially violent, means to realize goals unpopular to a majority of citizens are recurrent and accepted strains in American social history.

Finally, the prevalence of weapons in concert with the emphasis on direct action, the ends to be achieved, the glorification of individual initiative, and ideological commitment are supplementary explanations of the currents of violence throughout American history.

Perhaps the best insight into the subtle and perplexing relationship between political violence and American values and culture can be gained through an examination of vigilantism.[83] Vigilantism became such a pervasive feature of American life that it developed its own self-justifying ideology. There were four main elements in the philosophy of vigilantism:

(1) *Self-preservation.* It is the first law of society and the basis upon which its structure is built. To the vigilante, the threat of crime and disorder justified taking the law into one's own hands as an act of self-preservation.

(2) *The right of revolution.* Vigilante leaders recognized that taking the law into their own hands was, in effect, a revolutionary act against the authority of the state. They made this a virtue, claimed revolution as a right, and cited for their precedent the American Revolution of 1776.

(3) *Popular sovereignty.* To Americans of the nineteenth century, popular sovereignty meant that the rule of the people was superior to all else. The people, joined together for self-

preservation in a vigilante movement, saw their organization as transcending the regular system of law and order, should the latter prove incapable of protecting life and property.

(4) *The doctrine of vigilance.* This doctrine swept America in the first half of the nineteenth century. For some reason it was the passion of Americans to be *vigilant* in all things and against all manner of threats and dangers. Vigilance committees and associations were formed in all areas of the nation, a great many of them having nothing whatever to do with the classic problems of crime and disorder. The widespread doctrine of vigilance was a powerful underpinning for classic vigilantism.

Vigilantism was often effective in the short run. Corruption was rooted out, outlaws were expelled, and "law and order" were reimposed. Those were only accomplished, however, at long-term cost, as the tradition of lawless vigilantism has grafted itself on this nation's value structure.

Along with vigilante ideology grew that of anti-vigilantism. From the very beginning, there was always a cogent and vigorous philosophy that held that due process of law was among the most precious values of the Anglo-American legal heritage; that true law and order meant observing the letter of the law as well as the spirit; and finally, that the only way to get real law and order was to make the regular system work. The philosophers of anti-vigilantism were on strong ground in holding that, far from enhancing respect for law and order, vigilantism bred an insidious disrespect for law and order and planted in men the arbitrary tendency to judge for themselves when they should be orderly and lawful.

The vigilante tradition lives on. It has become a permanent part of American heritage. The memory of vigilantism is kept green by movies and television, by our novels and stories. The ideology of vigilantism is not dead, but is waiting to be used by the mischievous and the misguided. Since 1964, a number of quasi-vigilante movements have arisen: the neighborhood patrol movement of Crown Heights in Brooklyn (1964), the People's Civic Association of the East New York, Brownsville, and Flatbush areas of Brooklyn (1967), the North Ward Citizens' Council of Newark (1967–68), and the self-styled "vigilantes" of West Hollywood, Fla. (1968). Similar in character has been the Negro movement of Deacons for Defense and Justice in Bogalusa, La. (1965) and other Southern localities.

None of these movements has, to our knowledge, taken the law into its own hands, but officials are rightly concerned that this will be the next step. The police and other concerned officials look upon these organizations as vigilantes, and refer to them as such. New Left, old Right, and even the traditional center appear to be seriously considering extralegal violence as an appropriate tactic. As we hope to have demonstrated, such violence is not peripheral to a study of assassination, but strongly and directly relates, along with the rhetoric of vilification and violence, to it.

By far the strongest tradition in American history is the anti-vigilante adherence to due process of law, but vigilantism is also a strong and recurrent part of the cultural heritage of the United States.

The tension between these two competing principles may explain how a nation which is impatient with rules resorts often to direct action. Far more violent than comparable countries, it has nonetheless persevered, with remarkable stability as a free nation under law through periods of social change and unrest.

Conclusion

We have shown that the level of assassination corresponds to the level of political turmoil and violence in general. In comparison to other nations, the United States experiences a high level of political violence and assassination events. The present level of assassination and political turmoil, however, is no greater than at times in the past. Violence to achieve political goals is a thread which runs throughout the history of the United States.

Our data indicate that the greatest source of violence today lies in the confrontation between blacks and whites. Other specific issues have spawned similar levels of violence in the past: agrarian reform, abolitionism, labor violence, etc. In each instance, single-issue "radical" movements, not formal political parties, were the immediate source of violence. The two parties formed a basis of stability while society eventually ameliorated the conditions which gave birth to violence.

To point out that the violence of today has parallels in our past history does not lessen the need for urgency and creative intelligence in attacking immediate causes of violence. We repeat the conclusion as set forth in the beginning of this report:

The continuing urgent search for strategies to cope with the fundamental causes of present disaffection in the United States, such as racial inequality, mounting crime, and the questioned use of military force in our foreign affairs, is of direct and not peripheral relevance to the problem of assassination. Such disaffection weakens the consensus upon which the strength of the government is based. We have not found a specific remedy for assassination and political violence in a democracy apart from the perceived legitimacy of the government and its leaders.

References

1. Much of this section is drawn directly from Richard Maxwell Brown, "Violence in American History," a paper written for the Commission (hereinafter cited as "Commission Paper") and from a paper submitted by the Anti-Defamation League. References 2–50 are those in the two papers.
2. Brown, Commission Paper.
3. Richard Maxwell Brown, *The South Carolina Regulators,* (Cambridge: Harvard University Press, 1963).
4. Lucille Morris, *Bald Knobbers* (Caldwell, Idaho: Caxton Printers, Ltd., 1939).
5. Eliphalet Price, "The Trial and Execution of Patrick O'Conner at the Dubuque Mines in the Summer of 1834," *Palimpset,* I (1920), pp. 86–97.
6. Ray H. Hattison, "Roosevelt and the Stockmen's Association," *North Dakota History,* XVII, 2 (1950), p. 85.
7. Brown, Commission Paper.
8. Allan Nevins, *The Emergence of Lincoln:* vol. II, *Prologue to Civil War* (New York: Charles Scribner's Sons, 1950), 1859–61.
9. Brown, Commission Paper.
10. "The Ku Klux Klan—1965," Anti-Defamation League of B'nai B'rith *Facts,* May 1965, p. 324.
11. Gustavus Myers, *History of Bigotry in the United States* (New York: Random House, 1943), p. 216.
12. *Ibid.,* p. 111.
13. Arnold Forster, "Violence on the Fanatical Left and Right," *Annals,* vol. 364, March 1966, p. 143.
14. Myers, *op. cit.,* footnote 11, p. 120.

15. Forster, *op. cit.*, footnote 13, p. 143.
16. Myers, *op. cit.*, footnote 11, p. 106.
17. *Ibid.*, p. 129.
18. *Ibid.*, p. 132.
19. *Ibid.*, p. 139.
20. Forster, *op. cit.*, footnote 13, p. 143.
21. Myers, *op. cit.*, footnote 11, p. 163.
22. Brown, Commission Paper.
23. *Ibid.*
24. David M. Chalmers, *Hooded Americanism* (Garden City, N.Y.: Doubleday, 1965), p. 2.
25. Samuel Tenenbaum, *Why Men Hate* (New York: Beechurst Press. 1947), p. 236.
26. Myers, *op. cit.*, footnote 11, p. 223.
27. *op. cit.*, footnote 10, p. 325.
28. William E. Washburn, *The Governor and the Rebel* (Chapel Hill: University of North Carolina Press, 1957).
29. Gary S. Horowitz, "New Jersey Land Riots 1745–1755" (unpublished Ph.D. dissertation, Ohio State University, 1966).
30. Brooke Hindle, "The March of the Paxton Boys," *William and Mary Quarterly,* III (Oct. 1946), pp. 461–486.
31. Irving Mark, *Agrarian Conflicts in Colonial New York, 1711–1775* (Port Washington, N.Y.: I. J. Friedman, 1965); David M. Ellis, *Landlords and Farmers in the Hudson-Mohawk Region,* 1790–1850 (Ithaca, N.Y., Cornell University Press, 1946).
32. Marian L. Starkey, *A Little Rebellion* (New York: Alfred A. Knopf, 1955).
33. Leland D. Baldwin, *Whiskey Rebels: The Story of a Frontier Uprising* (Pittsburgh: University of Pittsburgh Press, 1939).
34. Brown, Commission Paper.
35. James L. Brown, *The Mussel Slough Tragedy, 1880* (no publisher, 1958).
36. James O. Nall, *The Tobacco Nightriders of Kentucky and Tennessee* (Louisville, Kentucky: Standard Press, 1939).
37. John Womack, Jr., "Oklahoma's Green Corn Rebellion; The Importance of Fools" (unpublished, A. B. thesis, Harvard College, 1959).
38. John L. Shover, *Cornbelt Rebellion: The Farmers' Holiday Association* (Urbana, Ill.: University of Illinois Press, 1965).
39. Louis Adamic, *Dynamite: The Story of Class Violence in America* (New York: Viking Press, 1934).
40. Samuel Yellen, *American Labor Struggles* (New York: S. A. Russell, 1936).
41. Wayne G. Broehl, Jr., *The Molly Maguires* (Cambridge: Harvard University Press, 1964).

42. Henry David, *The History of the Haymarket Affair* (New York: Farrar Rinehart, Inc., 1936).

43. Leon Wolff, *Lockout, The Story of the Homestead Strike of 1892* (New York: Harper & Row, 1965).

44. Brown, Commission Paper.

45. Adamic, *op. cit.,* footnote 39.

46. Chalmers, *op. cit.,* footnote 24, pp. 324–327.

47. *Los Angeles Times,* Aug. 8, 1968, p. 3.

48. *New York Times,* Sept. 9, 1968, p. 1.

49. *Ibid.,* Oct. 4, 1968, p. 20.

50. *Ibid.,* June 6, 1968, p. 18.

51. By Professor Feliks Gross, Brooklyn College, City University of New York.

52. Quoted in Commission Paper by the ADL, p. 113.

53. Task Force, Dec. 1961, p. 2. Quoted in Commission Paper by the ADL, p. 107.

54. See Feliks Gross, "Political Violence and Terror in Nineteenth and Twentieth Century Russia and Eastern Europe," Supplement.

55. The following section is based upon original research conceived and executed by various members of Task Force I.

56. The Washington *Daily National Intelligencer* was used from 1819–51; the *New York Times* was used from 1951–68. Before 1900, one issue per week was examined, selected by choosing at random a date in the month and then picking all issues in that month that fell on exactly the same day of the week as the date that was selected; for the next month, a new date within the month was selected as the starting point. Beginning with 1900, two issues per month were examined, the first issue by picking a random date in the first week of the month and then selecting the issue that fell exactly two weeks later. All charts used herein adjust for the difference in sampling after 1900 by multiplying the number of post-1900 incidents by 2.2. In total, approximately 6,000 newspaper issues were sampled. Each issue was examined completely and all politically violent events recorded. The definition of "political violence" that we used was quite broad: included were any violent events involving a politically prominent person or public officeholder and any violent event that arose from political party, racial, social, economic, or religious group hostilities. An event was considered violent if injury to person or property occurred, or if disruption of normal activity occurred. These events were numerically coded into categories that had been previously developed, and then analyzed statistically.

57. The Civil War makes that the most politically violent period in our history. Because of the uniqueness of that event, we

have not coded the military violence of that war and omit completely any discussion of military violence during the Civil War.

58. Adjusted for change in sampling technique beginning in 1900.

59. For the adjustment for newspapers, the denominator consists of the number of pages that were examined during the thirty-year interval. For the adjustment for population, the denominator is based on the number of people in the country for each year during the thirty-year period. These population figures were then summed for each of the thirty-year periods.

60. The design of the survey was a joint effort including Dr. Sandra Ball of the Commission staff, Dr. Sheldon Levy, and Dr. James McEvoy, consultant to the Commission, and others.

61. The first portion of this section is an edited version of a paper submitted to the Commission by Dr. James McEvoy III of the University of California. The tables and other data are those of Dr. McEvoy.

62. Dr. McEvoy in his paper uses unweighted data. The analysis run for the Commission by Louis Harris and Associates uses data that has been weighted to compensate for the over-representation of Negroes in the sample. Thus, the data used by the Commission, furnished by Louis Harris and Associates, and the data discussed in the portion of this section based upon the work of Dr. McEvoy, differ slightly from each other.

63. It is important to note that an analysis of these data cannot isolate persons who are themselves violent, but instead isolate only persons who give disproportionate support to verbal statements of approval of violence. We than have assumed that such persons contribute significantly to the maintenance of a culture of violence in the United States which in turn, we assume, affects the incidence of politically violent events.

64. No reference.

65. Louis Harris and Associates derived the factors by varimax rotation using weighted data.

66. Scales, or more properly, indices were created for each of these factors. Respondent's score on any given index was based on the sum of the selected item scores for the set of items in the index. Any missing data from the items in each factor deleted the respondent from further computation of a summary score for that factor.

67. One caveat which must apply to all analyses herein is that the data are not controlled for acquiescence response set, i.e., the extent to which the persons interviewed responded in the manner they thought the interviewer expected rather than how they actually felt about the items. The degree to which

this phenomenon influenced the outcome of the distributions on the Political Vengeance and other factors discussed above is not known. Because of the strong inverse relationship between Political Vengeance and level of formal education (discussed below) there is reason to believe that acquiescence response set—rather than true agreement with the content of the items in the Political Vengeance factor—may have influenced this distribution to some extent.

68. End of the portion of this section based on the paper submitted by Dr. McEvoy. The remainder of this section was written by the staff, based on the article by Louis Harris and Associates on the survey it conducted for the Commission.

69. As expected, in the Negro-arrest item, race is the most strongly significant variable, with more Negroes than whites willing to engage in more severe activity.

70. *Report of the National Advisory Commission on Civil Disorders* (New York: Bantam Books, 1968), p. 1.

71. By Feliks Gross, whose analysis of assassination appears in the Supplement.

72. That Appendix is taken from the report by the Anti-Defamation League.

73. Some portions of the following are taken from an article by Peter Young, published in the Duke *Chronicle,* Feb. 8 and Feb. 11, 1966.

74. It should be carefully noted that the white ghetto psychosis—composed in roughly equal parts of ignorance, rage, and paranoia—is spreading not only into the North, but more importantly into significant sections of the middle class.

75. The First Inaugural Address of President Woodrow Wilson, delivered March 4, 1913, comments succinctly on this point: "There can be no equality of opportunity, the first essential of justice in the body politic, if men and women and children be not shielded in their lives, their very vitality, from the consequences of great industrial and social processes which they cannot alter, control or singly cope with. Society must see to it that it does not itself crush or weaken or damage its own constituent parts."

76. Curiously, I could not find in the otherwise admirable Rural Poverty Commission Report so much as a mention of the Ku Klux Klan. This is just another example of the old mechanism of denial. If we do not utter the dirty words, "Ku Klux Klan," perhaps we'll wake up to find that it never happened. The Rural Poverty Commission would have done better to say that Southern white rural poor are remarkably well organized, but not along lines approved by the larger society.

77. And the urban poor, for the most part, regard these poverty

programs as a cruel hoax, in black ghetto terminology, "a hustle." I think they're right.

78. Again, the otherwise admirable Rural Poverty Commission misses the critical point. The idea of community did indeed disappear in the white rural South, only to be resurrected by the people themselves flocking into the dusty cow pastures. This is one of the most important and attractive aspects of "The Klan."

79. Though I am not in that business, I recognize that some folks are. And for them I have prepared a chart showing similarities and differences between white and black ghettoes, which appears at the end of this report.

80. At United Klans of America rally, Four Oaks, N.C., Sept. 28, 1968, taped with the full knowledge, consent, and cooperation of North Carolina Klan leaders. A copy of this tape has been filed with the Commission.

81. More on alienation in mainstream America is contained in other reports of the Commission staff and in Appendix C of this report.

82. In our single-member district plurality electoral system, the man who has the most votes wins all and the runners up get no share of the political power. This as a practical matter impells any group seeking power to become part of one of the major parties with a chance to carry an entire electoral district.

83. The discussion of vigilantism is drawn directly from Brown's Commission Paper.

APPENDIX A

DATA ON ASSASSINATION EVENTS

This appendix sets forth each assassination event collected by the Leiden group and by the Feierabend group.

I. The following is a list of each incident of attempted assassination both successful and unsuccessful, collected by the Leiden group for the period 1918 to October, 1968, arranged chronologically. [This list was collected primarily from newspaper files and other available sources within a very short time by different investigators.]

The key to the rank code is as follows:
1. Head of state, head of government, or dictator; former head of state or head of state-elect, e.g., presidents, kings, premiers.
2. Cabinet ministers; ambassadors; vice presidents; leading judges, bureaucrats, legislators (but not necessarily former holders of those offices).
3. High ranking military officers.
4. Provincial governors; in general second level officeholders; chargé d'affaires.
5. Private persons but prominent politically.
6. Third level officeholders, lower ranking officers.

The key to the result code is as follows:
1. Unsuccessful—target not killed.
2. Successful—target killed.

1. Data Collected by Leiden Group

Name	Country	Date	Rank	Result
William Frederick	Holland	11/12/18	5	1
Henry	Germany	11/25/18	5	1
Paes, Sidonia	Portugal	12/ 7/18	1	1
Kuratchenko	Russia	12/11/18	6	2
Paes, Sidonia	Portugal	12/16/18	1	2
Zapata, Emiliano	Mexico	/19	3	2
Luxemburg, Rosa	Germany	1/ /19	5	2
Liebknecht, Karl	Germany	1/18/19	5	2
Russky	Russia	1/27/19	3	2
Wong, T.H.	U.S., D.C.	2/ 1/19	4	2
Paul Alexandrovitch	Russia	2/ 3/19	5	2
Eisner, Kurt	Germany	2/29/19	1	1
Clemenceau, Georges	France	2/29/19	1	1
Baronorsky, Lugan	Russia	3/14/19	5	2

Trotsky, Leon	Russia	3/15/19	2	1
Blanquet, A.	Mexico	4/19/19	3	2
Radko, Dimitrieff	Russia	5/ /19	3	2
Paderewski, M.	Poland	5/15/19	1	1
Habibullah Khan	Afghan	5/17/19	1	2
Tidioa	Russia	7/28/19	5	1
Tinoco, Joaquin	Costa Rica	8/15/19	1	1
Said, Mohammed	Egypt	9/ 2/19	1	1
Ponti	Italy	9/ 2/19	2	1
Baron Saito	Korea	9/ 4/19	4	1
Lettow-Vorbeck	Germany	9/ 9/19	3	1
Kolchak	Russia	9/23/19	3	1
Haase, Hugo	Germany	10/ 8/19	2	2
Hati, Ahmed	Russia	10/27/19	6	2
Ferry	Hungary	11/ /19	3	2
Borky	Hungary	11/ /19	6	2
Hollan, Alexander	Hungary	11/ /19	5	2
Menkina	Hungary	11/ /19	6	2
Lord French	Ireland	11/ 5/19	3	1
Cohen	Egypt	11/22/19	6	2
Guajardo, Jesus	Mexico	/20	3	2
Sullivan, A.M.	Ireland	1/11/20	5	1
Redmond	Ireland	1/22/20	6	2
MacCurtain, T.	Ireland	3/20/20	6	2
Bell	Ireland	3/27/20	6	2
Romanovsky	Turkey	4/ 7/20	3	2
Wilkinson, T.G.	Ireland	5/14/20	5	2
Carranza, V.	Mexico	5/21/20	1	2
Tewfik Nessim Pasha	India	6/13/20	6	2
Wilson, L.	Ireland	6/16/20	6	2
Smyth	Ireland	7/19/20	6	2
Brooke, F.	Ireland	7/31/20	4	2
Droubi Pasha	Syria	8/23/20	1	2
Abderhaman	Syria	8/23/20	2	2
Willoughby	India	8/28/20	6	2
Johnstone	Ireland	8/31/20	6	2
Saito	Japan	9/ 6/20	4	2
MacCurtain, Mrs. T.	Ireland	9/26/20	5	1
Dejelal Munif Bey	Hungary	12/24/20	5	2
Tronkiewitz, M.	Russia	/21	6	2
Fatzeas, Stefan	Greece	1/ 8/21	6	2
Singh, Shir	Germany	1/22/21	5	2
Holmes	Ireland	1/30/21	6	2
Captain King	Ireland	2/ 2/21	6	1
Dixon, R.	Ireland	2/ 3/21	6	2
Craven, F.W.	Ireland	2/ 4/21	6	2
Cumming	Ireland	3/ 6/21	3	2
Clancy	Ireland	3/ 8/21	6	2
O'Callaghan	Ireland	3/ 8/21	5	2
Dato, Eduardo	Spain	3/ 9/21	1	2
Gaxiola, Angel	Mexico	3/10/21	6	2
Talaat Pasha	Germany	3/16/21	2	2
Quinones, F.	Cuba	4/ 3/21	4	2
Vicars, Sir A.	Ireland	4/14/21	6	2
MacKinnon	Ireland	4/16/21	6	2
Ferris	Ireland	5/ 8/21	6	1
Gonzales, M.	Mexico	5/ 8/21	6	1
Moguel, J.	Mexico	5/ 8/21	6	2
Blake	Ireland	5/17/21	6	2
Viscaino, Fernando	Mexico	6/ /21	3	2

Peacock	Ireland	6/ 2/21	6	2
Gareis	Germany	6/12/21	6	2
Challoner	Ireland	6/21/21	6	1
Lambert	Ireland	6/21/21	6	2
Pilsudski, General J.	Poland	7/14/21	1	1
Draskovics, M.	Yugoslavia	7/22/21	2	2
Erzberger, Matthias	Germany	8/ /21	5	2
Robles, J.A.	Mexico	8/10/21	3	2
Ball, L.H.	U.S., D.C.	8/19/21	2	1
Rakovsky, Count J. Andressy	Hungary	9/26/21	1	1
Pilsudski, General J.	Poland	9/27/21	1	1
Dos Santos, Machado	Portugal	10/21/21	1	2
Granjo, Antonio	Portugal	10/21/21	1	2
Silva, Carlos	Portugal	10/21/21	2	2
Mara, Carlos	Portugal	10/21/21	3	2
Dimitroff, Alexander	Bulgaria	10/23/21	2	2
Takashi Hara	Japan	11/ 5/21	1	2
Helst, O.	U.S., Ill.	11/20/21	6	1
Jones, Dr. Zmable	Argentina	11/21/21	4	2
Meade, P.	Ireland	12/13/21	5	1
Carrasco, Juan	Mexico	/22	3	2
Murguia, Francisco	Mexico	/22	3	2
Villa, Pancho	Mexico	/22	5	1
Pruneda, Antonio	Mexico	2/ /22	3	2
Ruiz, Antonio	Mexico	2/ /22	3	2
Ritavuari	Finland	2/15/22	2	2
Perez Lazono, Julian	Spain	3/17/22	5	2
Tsang Hou	France	3/22/22	5	1
Tcheng Loe-	France	3/22/22	5	1
Harrison	Ireland	3/28/22	6	1
Milukoff, Paul N.	Germany	3/29/22	5	1
Cardinal Pompilj	Italy	4/ 8/22	5	1
Conner, P.	U.S., N.Y.	4/14/22	5	2
Scheidemann, Philipp	Germany	6/ /22	5	1
Flanagan, W.	Ireland	6/ 5/22	6	2
Aragone, Juan F.	Spain	6/19/22	5	1
London	U.S., Okla.	6/21/22	6	1
Wilson, Sir Henry	England	6/23/22	3	2
Rathenau, Walter	Germany	6/24/22	2	2
Blanco, Lucio	Mexico	7/ /22	3	2
Martinex, Candido	Mexico	7/ /22	6	2
Denize	Haiti	7/30/22	6	2
Cremonesi	Italy	8/14/22	5	2
Baron Udekem D'Acoz	Belgium	8/14/22	5	2
Narutowicz, Gabriel	Poland	12/16/22	1	2
Stambuliski, Alexander	Bulgaria	1/23	1	2
Alvarado, Salvador	Mexico	/23	3	2
Buelna, Rafael	Mexico	/23	3	2
Estrada, Enrique	Mexico	/23	3	2
Vigil Garcia, Manuel	Mexico	/23	4	1
Villa, Pancho	Mexico	/23	5	1
Fenni, Mohammed	Switzerland	1/11/23	5	1
Plateau, Marius	France	1/23/23	5	2
Ali Chukri Bey	Turkey	4/ 1/23	5	2
Card. Soldevilla y Romero	Spain	6/ 5/23	5	2
Swan	Palestine	6/19/23	6	2
Villa, Pancho	Mexico	7/20/23	5	2
Dashkaloff, M.	Czechoslovakia	8/27/23	5	2
Conati	Albania	8/29/23	6	2
Scorti	Albania	8/29/23	6	2

DeLeon, R.	Mexico	10/ 4/23	6	1
Rodriguez, A.	Mexico	11/ 4/23	3	2
Vorovsky, Vaslaw	Switzerland	11/ 4/23	5	2
Colonel Krastitch	Bulgaria	11/ 4/23	4	1
Sgarapuievitch	Bulgaria	11/26/23	6	2
Amendola, G.	Italy	12/23/23	2	1
Alecsa	Lithuania	12/30/23	5	2
Zaghloul Pasha	Egypt	/24	1	1
Gomez, Jose F.	Mexico	/24	6	2
Imbrie, Robert	Iran	/24	6	2
Trevino, Ramon	Mexico	/24	5	2
Duparinof, L.	Bulgaria	1/ 6/24	5	2
Heintz	Germany	1/10/24	4	2
Daudet, Philippe	France	1/18/24	5	2
Field Jurado, Francisco	Mexico	1/23/24	2	2
Guminger, E.	Germany	1/31/24	6	2
Buonservici, N.	France	2/21/24	5	1
Dieguez, Manuel	Mexico	4/ /24	3	2
Garcia, Alredo R.	Mexico	4/ /24	3	2
Ocampo, Cristoforo	Mexico	4/ /24	3	2
Vigil Garcia, Manuel	Mexico	4/ /24	4	2
Delong, G.B.	Albania	4/ 7/24	5	2
Coleman, R.L.	Albania	4/ 7/24	5	2
Maycotte, Fortunato	Mexico	5/14/24	3	2
Cicaria, R.P.	Spain	5/30/24	6	2
Baron Saito	Korea	5/30/24	4	1
Matteoti, Giacomo	Italy	6/ /24	2	2
Seipel, Ignatz	Austria	6/ 2/24	1	1
Petkoff, M.	Bulgaria	6/16/24	2	2
DeHaan, Israel	Palestine	7/ 2/24	5	2
Zaghloul Pasha	Egypt	7/13/24	1	1
Fukuda	Japan	9/ 3/24	3	1
Casalini, A.	Italy	9/13/24	4	2
Alexandroff, T.	Bulgaria	9/16/24	5	2
Kovatcheff	Bulgaria	9/16/24	6	2
Menocal, M.G.	Cuba	10/ 6/24	1	1
Morones	Mexico	11/13/24	4	1
Guerrero	Mexico	11/13/24	4	1
Stack, Sir Lee	Egypt	11/19/24	3	2
Greene, Alejandro	Mexico	12/ /24	3	2
Greene, Carlos	Mexico	12/ /24	3	2
Segouia, Fernando	Mexico	12/ /24	3	2
Selas, M.	Cuba	1/ 4/25	6	2
Kato	Japan	1/11/25	1	1
El Maraghi, Mustapha	Egypt	1/29/25	5	1
Mileff, N.	Bulgaria	2/14/25	2	2
Strachinicoff, T.	Bulgaria	2/19/25	4	2
Beginski	Poland	3/31/25	5	2
Wierzorkiewicz	Poland	3/31/25	5	2
Acosta	Mexico	4/ 2/25	3	2
Boris	Bulgaria	4/15/25	1	1
Gheorgieff	Bulgaria	4/15/25	3	2
Iltcheff, M.	Bulgaria	4/15/25	6	2
Tsankoff, Alex.	Bulgaria	4/17/25	1	1
Klaoff	Bulgaria	4/17/25	2	1
General Davidof	Bulgaria	4/18/25	3	2
Colonchef	Bulgaria	4/18/25	4	2
Kissof	Bulgaria	4/18/25	4	2
Neresof	Bulgaria	4/18/25	5	2
Ratchef	Bulgaria	4/18/25	4	2

Menkoff	Bulgaria	4/21/25	6	2
Yankoff, R.	Bulgaria	4/22/25	6	2
Muravieff	Bulgaria	4/23/25	5	2
Tchountoulof	Bulgaria	4/24/25	5	2
Ivanoff, V.	Bulgaria	4/27/25	5	2
Boumethoka, A.	Bulgaria	4/29/25	5	2
Grantcharoff	Bulgaria	4/30/25	5	2
Boris	Bulgaria	5/ 2/25	1	1
Kossowsky	Bulgaria	5/ 8/25	4	2
Petrini	Bulgaria	5/ 8/25	4	2
Panizza, Todor	Austria	5/10/25	5	2
Amaral, F.	Portugal	5/17/25	6	1
Kirk, Buck	U.S., W.Va.	5/20/25	6	2
Fukuda, M.	Japan	5/25/25	3	1
Tehouparinoff	Bulgaria	5/31/25	6	2
Helling, Herman	Germany	6/ /25	5	2
Mikhailoff, P.	Bulgaria	6/16/25	5	2
Abramson	Palestine	6/17/25	6	1
Amendola, Giovanni	Italy	7/ /25	2	2
Hsu Sung-Chi	China	7/ 9/25	2	1
Wu Hon Min	China	7/ 9/25	4	1
Bretherton, H.G.	Mexico	7/19/25	6	1
Kasselo, A.	Poland	7/31/25	6	2
Maurer, Robert	Mexico	8/ 3/25	5	2
Richard, M.	Martinique	8/23/25	4	1
Perez, M.	Mexico	9/ 5/25	4	2
Burilo	Bulgaria	9/ 8/25	5	2
Karkalasheff	Bulgaria	9/ 8/25	5	2
Mussolini, Benito	Italy	9/11/25	1	1
Cruz, C.	Mexico	9/11/25	6	2
Carol	Rumania	9/13/25	1	1
Lupporini, Cavaliere	Italy	10/ 4/25	5	2
Benciolini, G.	Italy	10/ 6/25	5	2
Barde, H.	Switzerland	10/18/25	5	1
Tsankoff, Danoso	Bulgaria	10/30/25	5	2
Mussolini, Benito	Italy	11/ 4/25	1	1
Hong Chow-Ling	China	12/ 9/25	3	1
Dammers, Heinrich	Germany	12/12/25	5	2
Kuo Sing-Ling	China	12/26/25	3	2
Hsu Shu-Cheng	China	12/31/25	3	2
Panitza, Todor	Bulgaria	/26	5	2
Sloat, E.C. Jr.	U.S., N.J.	1/15/26	6	1
Flores, Angel	Mexico	4/ 4/26	3	2
Mussolini, Benito	Italy	4/ 8/26	1	1
Esparragoza, Father Gregorio	Mexico	4/21/26	5	2
McSwiggin, William H.	U.S., Ill.	4/25/26	6	2
Kato	Korea	4/26/26	6	1
Takayama	Korea	4/26/26	6	2
Peltasohn	Germany	5/21/26	6	1
Petlura, Simon	Poland	5/25/26	1	2
Knight, C.	Mexico	6/ 5/26	6	2
Beschapely, Gregoire	France	6/11/26	5	2
Oskilko, Radziwill	Poland	6/22/26	5	2
Luter, A.A.	U.S., Tex.	6/23/26	5	1
Vincent, Mordel	Mexico	7/ 7/26	5	1
Zimmerman, Felton	Cuba	7/ 7/26	5	2
Yerman, J.	U.S., Ill.	7/11/26	6	2
Mellett, Don R.	U.S., Ohio	7/17/26	5	2
Donaldson, Bert	U.S., Ga.	8/ 1/26	6	2
DeLloyd, Salustio	Mexico	8/ 5/26	6	2

Dunfee, S.	U.S., Ohio	8/ 6/26	6	2
Almeida, Jose	Mexico	8/ 9/26	5	2
Violante, Raymundo	Mexico	8/ 9/26	5	2
Pineda, J.	Mexico	8/26/26	4	2
Graff	Germany	9/12/26	6	2
Princess Louise (Sweden)	Japan	9/18/26	5	1
Mussolini, B.	Italy	10/13/26	1	1
Coutinho de Azevedo	Mozambique	11/ 4/26	4	1
Stone, J.	U.S., Ill.	11/ 8/26	6	2
Mejia, Marcelos	Mexico	11/18/26	4	1
Dale, G.D.	U.S., Ind.	11/26/26	5	1
Marina, Fernando	Argentina	12/ 2/26	6	2
Cantoni, Aldo	Argentina	12/ 2/26	4	1
Atanasoff, Philip A.	Bulgaria	12/12/26	5	1
Ivanoff, Slawe	Bulgaria	12/12/26	6	1
Adams, J.	U.S., Ill.	12/13/26	6	2
Diaz	Nicaragua	12/24/26	1	1
Swami Shradanand	India	12/24/26	5	2
Salazar, Alberto	Mexico	/27	3	2
Cisneros, Antonio	Mexico	1/24/27	4	2
Smetana	Lithuania	1/30/27	5	2
Hernandez, T.	Mexico	2/10/27	6	2
Nelson, G.	Mexico	2/20/27	3	2
Ikonomoff, M.	Bulgaria	3/ 7/27	4	2
Kantor, Ernst	Germany	4/11/27	5	1
Cinarski	Poland	4/15/27	6	2
Uribe, Father David	Mexico	4/16/27	5	2
Voikoff, Peter	Poland	4/20/27	2	2
Archbishop Chryostomos	Greece	5/22/27	5	1
Turoff	Russia	6/13/27	6	2
O'Higgins, K.C.	Ireland	7/11/27	2	2
Har, L.M.	Canada	8/10/27	3	2
Park, W.	Canada	8/10/27	5	2
Steger, E.	Germany	9/ 5/27	6	1
Nardini, Count Carlo	France	9/13/27	6	2
Artura Lasso de la Vega	Mexico	10/ /27	3	2
Olivera, Norberto C.	Mexico	10/ /27	3	2
Rodriguez, Alredo	Mexico	10/ /27	3	2
Ariza, Carlos B.	Mexico	10/ 3/27	3	2
Peralta, Miguel A.	Mexico	10/ 3/27	3	2
Vidal, Carlos A.	Mexico	10/ 3/27	3	2
Peralta, Daniel	Mexico	10/ 3/27	3	2
Serrano, Francisco	Mexico	10/ 3/27	3	2
Pena, Augusto	Mexico	10/ 3/27	5	2
Martinez de Escobar, Rafael	Mexico	10/ 3/27	5	2
Monteverde, Enrique	Mexico	10/ 3/27	5	2
Capetillo, Alonso	Mexico	10/ 3/27	5	2
Mendez, Ernesto V.	Mexico	10/ 3/27	6	2
Almada, Octavio R.	Mexico	10/ 3/27	6	2
Villa Arce, Jose	Mexico	10/ 3/27	5	2
Gonzalez, Otilio	Mexico	10/ 3/27	5	2
Jauregui, Antonio	Mexico	10/ 3/27	5	2
Hermosillo, Luis	Mexico	10/ 5/27	3	2
Kovachevitch	Yugoslavia	10/ 6/27	3	2
Moran, Jose C.	Mexico	10/ 6/27	3	2
Tsena Bey	Czechoslovakia	10/15/27	2	2
Aguilar, Oscar	Mexico	11/ /27	3	2
Gavriloff, Mirailo	Yugoslavia	11/ 2/27	5	2
Gavriloff, Risto	Yugoslavia	11/ 2/27	5	2
Gomez, Arnulfo	Mexico	11/ 5/27	3	2

Obregon, Alvaro	Mexico	11/13/27	1	1
Raditch, Stefan	Yugoslavia	/28	2	2
Mena, Luis	Nicaragua	5/20/28	3	2
Basaritchik, G.	Yugoslavia	6/21/28	4	2
Raditch, P.	Yugoslavia	6/21/28	4	2
Jacobobovitch, Ivan	Rumania	7/ 3/28	5	2
Protogueroff, Alex	Bulgaria	7/ 9/28	3	2
Morones, Luis	Mexico	7/15/28	2	1
Calles, P.E.	Mexico	7/17/28	1	1
Obregon, Alvaro	Mexico	7/17/28	1	2
Ristovitch, V.	Yugoslavia	8/ 6/28	5	2
Patrezi, Luigi	Canada	8/30/28	5	2
Nanders, G.	Yugoslavia	11/20/28	5	2
Constantinovitch	Bulgaria	11/26/28	6	2
Bebi, A.	Czechoslovakia	12/ 1/28	5	2
Clavery	Algeria	12/12/28	3	2
Debenne	Algeria	12/12/28	6	2
Pasquet	Algeria	12/12/28	6	2
Mella, Julio Antonio	Cuba	/29	5	2
Chu Yun-Fung	China	3/10/29	3	2
Schlegel, T.	Yugoslavia	3/23/29	5	2
Aderholt, O.F.	U.S., N.C.	6/ 8/29	6	2
Holt, P.	U.S., Mont.	8/22/29	6	2
Holmes, J.A.	U.S., Tex.	9/14/29	6	2
Wiggins, Mrs. E.M.	U.S., N.C.	9/15/29	5	2
Krokowski, T.	U.S., Pa.	10/ 7/29	6	2
Galmot, Jean	French Guiana	10/12/29	5	2
Zertuche, Antonio R.	Mexico	11/ 2/29	3	1
Bentwick	Palestine	11/24/29	4	1
Ashby, P.H.	U.S., Ky.	11/25/29	6	2
Filho, Sousa	Brazil	12/ /29	4	2
Wessel, Horst	Germany	1/14/30	5	2
Viana, F. Melo	Brazil	2/ /30	2	1
Ibarra, Leon	Mexico	2/ /30	3	2
Ortiz-Rubio, P.	Mexico	2/ 5/30	1	1
Barlow, Christopher	Nigeria	2/ 9/30	6	2
Po Ching-King	China	2/18/30	5	2
Wang Po-Ling	China	2/18/30	5	2
Florian, A.	Czechoslovakia	2/19/30	6	2
Kramer, Emil	Germany	2/19/30	5	2
Lewis	India	2/24/30	6	2
Poundeff, V.	Bulgaria	3/ 5/30	5	2
Unya	Estonia	4/ 5/30	3	2
Ghulum Agha	India	4/22/30	6	1
Leguia	Peru	4/26/30	1	1
Dr. Rintelen	Austria	5/18/30	4	1
Lord Strickland	Malta	5/24/30	4	1
Von Baligand, Dr. Henry A.	Portugal	6/ 8/30	2	2
Chiesti, Giuseppe	Albania	6/29/30	6	2
Pessoa, Joao	Brazil	7/ /30	4	2
Angelescu, M.	Rumania	7/22/30	4	1
Dennis, E.J.	U.S., S.C.	7/25/30	6	1
Rusteika	Lithuania	8/19/30	6	1
Sidky, Ismail Pasha	Egypt	8/26/30	1	1
Tegart, Charles	India	8/26/30	6	1
Hobson, Eric	India	8/30/30	6	1
Lowman, Francis	India	8/30/30	6	2
Dabski, M.	Poland	9/ 1/30	5	1
Khaneband, Hassanand	India	9/ 8/30	6	2
Freeman, R.L.	U.S., Ga.	9/ 9/30	6	2

Holtz, Max	Germany	9/ 9/30	5	1
Compmany	Spain	9/24/30	6	2
Jenkins, J.B.	U.S., Ga.	10/ 2/30	6	2
Simpson, Lenox	China	10/ 2/30	6	1
Aziz, Khan Buhadan	India	10/ 4/30	6	1
Sottosanti	Italy	10/ 5/30	5	2
Suassuna	Brazil	10/11/30	4	2
Pilsudski, General J.	Poland	10/14/30	1	1
Hamaguchi, Yuko	Japan	11/14/30	1	2
Kirkhan, Said	Russia	11/21/30	4	2
Ludendorff	Germany	11/29/30	5	1
Mukerji	India	12/ /30	6	2
Simpson	India	12/ 8/30	6	2
Graf, Herbert	Germany	1/ 1/31	5	2
Schneider, Willi	Germany	1/ 1/31	5	2
Ali, S.	India	1/14/31	6	1
Curtis	India	1/14/31	6	1
Moriotcheto, Traiiko	Bulgaria	1/14/31	5	2
Mussolini, B.	Italy	2/ /31	1	1
Beritch, A.	Yugoslavia	2/ 5/31	6	2
Ghurkoff	Bulgaria	2/ 9/31	5	2
Barnes, Captain	India	2/18/31	6	2
Guzzi, Ercole	France	2/19/31	6	1
Zog	Austria	2/21/31	1	1
Topola, Major	Austria	2/21/31	6	2
Machado, Gerardo	U.S., N.Y.	2/25/31	1	1
Lal, Munshi	India	3/ 2/31	6	2
Lassally	Germany	3/13/31	5	1
Pertchetch	Austria	3/16/31	5	1
Aniekieff	Japan	3/17/31	6	1
Henning, E.	Germany	3/17/31	6	2
Stern, T.H.	Iraq	4/ 1/31	6	2
Heaney, Captain G.F.	Burma	4/11/31	6	2
Peddie, James	India	4/11/31	6	2
Austin, W.H.	India	5/ 9/31	6	2
Chanan Singh	India	5/14/31	5	2
Husain, Jawad	India	6/ 9/31	5	2
Ruseff, N.	Bulgaria	7/19/31	5	2
Soong, T.V.	China	7/23/31	2	1
Hotson, Sir J.E.B.	India	7/23/31	4	1
Garlick, R.R.	India	7/28/31	6	2
Chiang Kai-Shek	China	7/30/31	1	1
Tejada	Mexico	8/ 8/31	4	1
Soong, T.V.	China	8/23/31	2	1
Holowkos, T.	Poland	8/30/31	2	2
Ismet Inonu	Greece	10/ 2/31	1	1
Stepanoff	Bulgaria	10/27/31	2	1
Hsuan Tung	China	11/ 9/31	1	1
Barakat, S.	Syria	/32	1	1
Sanchez Cerro, L.M.	Peru	/32	1	1
Soong, T.V.	China	1/ 3/32	2	1
Hirohito	Japan	1/ 8/32	1	1
Gentile, G.	France	1/ 9/32	6	1
Winkler, F.	Austria	1/16/32	2	1
Carmona, E. Fragosa	Portugal	1/17/32	1	1
Jackson, Ir S.	India	2/ 7/32	4	1
Inouye, J.	Japan	2/ 9/32	4	2
Dan, Baron T.	Japan	3/ 5/32	5	2
Czechowski, E.	Poland	3/23/32	2	2
Soong, T.V.	China	3/25/32	2	1

Luther, Hans	Germany	4/ 9/32	1	1
Casares Quiroga, S.	Spain	4/20/32	2	1
Sidky, Pasha	Egypt	5/ 6/32	1	1
Doumer, Paul	France	5/ 7/32	1	2
Inukai	Japan	5/16/32	1	2
Michailoff, Prof. D.	Bulgaria	5/17/32	5	1
Mussolini, B.	Italy	6 6/32	1	1
Chiang Kai-Shek	China	6/10/32	1	1
Machado, Gerardo	Cuba	6/11/32	1	1
Popovitch, V.	Yugoslavia	6/23/32	5	2
Wu Kwang-Tsung	China	9/22/32	3	2
Watson, Sir A.	India	9/29/32	5	1
Bethlen, Count	Hungary	10/20/32	5	2
Fostoa, G. de	Span. Guinea	11/16/32	4	2
Roosevelt, F.D.	U.S., Fla.	3/ 6/33	1	1
Cermak, Anton	U.S., Fla.	3/ 6/33	4	2
Chen Chi-Tang	China	3/10/33	5	1
Sanchez Cerro, L.M.	Peru	4/30/33	1	2
Yuh Sueh-Chung	China	5/ 6/33	4	1
Chang Ching-Yao	China	5/ 8/33	3	2
Napetoff, P.	Bulgaria	5/13/33	5	2
Sidky, Pasha	Egypt	5/17/33	1	1
Venizelos, E.	Greece	6/ 7/33	1	1
Mohammad Aziz Khan	Germany	6/ 7/33	2	2
Steidle, R.	Austria	6/12/33	5	1
Burge, B.E.J.	India	9/ 3/33	6	2
Grau San Martin, Ramon	Cuba	10/ 4/33	1	1
Dollfus, Engelbert	Austria	10/ 4/33	1	1
Carol	Rumania	10/12/33	1	1
Benavides, C.P.	Peru	10/23/33	1	1
Nadir Shah	Afghanistan	11/ 8/33	1	2
Primo de Rivera, J.A.	Spain	11/13/33	5	1
Wakatzuki, Baron	Japan	11/21/33	5	1
Tourian, L.E.	U.S., N.Y.	12/25/33	5	2
Duca, Ion G.	Rumania	12/30/33	1	2
Taymurtash, Abdul Husayn	Iran	/34	4	2
Khosrow, Arab Kai	Iran	/34	4	2
Chang, Pai-Yuan	China	1/11/34	3	2
Sandino, A.C.	Nicaragua	2/23/34	1	2
Estrada, F.	Nicaragua	2/23/34	3	2
Umanzor, J.P.	Nicaragua	2/23/34	3	2
de la Torriente, C.	Cuba	3/ 8/34	2	1
Primo de Rivera, J.A.	Spain	4/11/34	5	1
Koerbel, Edward	Austria	4/12/34	6	2
Fey, Major Emil	Austria	4/15/34	2	1
Huang Shao-Wen	China	4/18/34	6	2
Anderson, Sir J.	India	5/ 9/34	4	1
Von Papen, F.	Germany	6/ /34	1	1
Von Schleicher, K.	Germany	6/ /34	1	2
Roehm, Ernst	Germany	6/ /34	5	2
Hwang Fu	China	6/ 3/34	4	1
Berenguer, Fernando	Spain	6/ 7/34	3	2
Berenguer, Damaso	Spain	6/ 7/34	3	1
Primo de Rivera, J.A.	Spain	6/10/34	5	1
Mendieta, Carlos	Cuba	6/16/34	1	1
Pieracki, Colonel B.	Poland	6/16/34	2	2
Von Bredow, Kurt	Germany	6/30/34	3	2
Heines, Lt. Edmund	Germany	6/30/34	5	2
Von Kahr, Gustav	Germany	6/30/34	5	2
Klausener, Erich	Germany	6/30/34	5	2

Stempfle, Bernhard	Germany	6/30/34	5	2
Strasser, Gregor	Germany	6/30/34	5	2
Dollfus, Engelbert	Austria	7/25/34	1	2
Wadij, J.	Poland	7/26/34	5	2
Alexander	France	10/ 9/34	1	2
Barthou, Jean Louis	France	10/ 9/34	2	2
Pommer, Archbishop J.	Latvia	10/13/34	5	2
Moreland, J.C.	U.S., Ill.	11/ 4/34	6	1
Chiang Kai-Shek	China	11/ 9/34	1	1
Kolodyer, M.	Yugoslavia	11/28/34	5	1
Kiroff, S.M.	Russia	12/ 1/34	5	2
Kondylis, George	Greece	12/25/34	2	1
Miro Quesada, Jose A.	Peru	/35	5	2
Kasravi, Ahmad	Iran	/35	5	2
Mirza, Firuz	Iran	/35	4	2
Rojas	Spain	/35	6	1
Wilhelm II	Netherlands	1/28/35	1	1
Songram, Luang Bipul	Thailand	2/24/35	2	1
Shoriki, M.	Japan	2/24/35	5	2
Abdul Aziz	Saudi Arabia	3/16/35	1	1
Courtney, T.J.	U.S., Ill.	3/25/35	6	1
Yeftich.	Yugoslavia	4/ 6/35	1	1
Terra	Uruguay	6/ 3/35	1	1
Nagata, Tetsuzan	Japan	8/12/35	3	2
Ghilardi, L. de	Albania	8/16/35	3	2
Middleton, E.C.	U.S., Ky.	9/ 5/35	6	2
Long, Huey P.	U.S., La.	9/ 8/35	2	2
Sun Chuan-Fang	China	11/14/35	3	2
Tang Yu-Jen	China	12/26/35	4	2
Harrison, John	Ireland	12/27/35	6	1
Assad, Sardar	Iran	/36	2	2
Hazhir, Abdul Husayn	Iran	/36	2	2
Gomez, Eustaquio	Venezuela	/36	5	2
De Serval, Luis	Spain	/36	5	2
Niemerower, J.I.	Rumania	1/12/36	5	1
Ganeff, M.	Bulgaria	1/18/36	5	2
Deskoff	Spain	1/21/36	6	2
Ni	Mongolia	1/21/36	5	2
Gustluff, Sigmund	Switzerland	2/ 4/36	5	2
Chien Wha	China	2/ 7/36	5	2
Donkin, R.	Zanzibar	2/11/36	6	1
Eberwein, C.	U.S., N.J.	2/11/36	6	2
Humphrey, Ian	Zanzibar	2/11/36	6	2
Jones, J.P.	Zanzibar	2/11/36	6	1
Skinner, Leslie	Zanzibar	2/11/36	6	1
Blum	France	2/13/36	2	1
Aluwihara, W.H.	Ceylon	2/24/36	6	1
Riggs, E.F.	U.S., P.R.	2/24/36	6	2
Okada, Admiral	Japan	2/26/36	1	2
Saito, Viscount	Japan	2/26/36	1	2
Suzuki, Admiral	Japan	2/26/36	2	1
Takakashi	Japan	2/26/36	2	1
Watanake, General	Japan	2/26/36	3	2
Makino, Count	Japan	2/26/36	4	1
Stoyadinovitch	Yugoslavia	3/ 7/36	1	1
Asua, L.J.	Spain	3/13/36	4	1
Martinez, Dr. Alfredo	Spain	3/23/36	4	2
Somerville, H.B.	Ireland	3/25/36	3	2
Torres de Sanchez, Count L.	Spain	4/ 5/36	5	1
Ortega Gasset, Eduardo	Spain	4/ 7/36	6	1

Rojas	Spain	4/ 7/36	6	1
Pedregal, M..	Spain	4/15/36	6	1
Madia, Josep	Spain	4/28/36	5	2
Madia, Miguel	Spain	4/28/36	5	2
Gonzales, Major	Cuba	5/11/36	3	1
Pedraza, J.	Cuba	5/30/36	6	1
Li Shengta	China	6/ 1/36	3	2
Schlick, Moritz	Austria	6/22/36	5	2
Urdaneta, I.	Panama	6/23/36	2	1
Sotelo, Calvo	Spain	7/13/36	2	2
Edward VIII	England	7/17/36	1	1
Garcia Lorca	Spain	8/18/36	5	2
Al-Askari, Sayyid Jaefar	Iraq	10/ /36	2	2
Falconde, M.	France	10/12/36	5	1
Yang Yung-Tai	China	10/26/36	6	2
Martin, V.	Brazil	12/24/36	4	2
Villaboas, J.	Brazil	12/24/36	4	2
Grove, M.	Chile	12/29/36	2	1
Ed-Dawlah, Solat	Iran	/37	5	2
Calles, P.E.	U.S., Calif.	1/ 2/37	1	1
Salah, Suleiman Bey	Palestine	1/23/37	5	2
Shukry, Hassan Bey	Palestine	1/23/37	6	1
Wang I-Chch	China	2/ 4/37	3	2
Graziani, Gen. Rudolfo	Ethiopia	2/21/37	2	1
Leolta, Gen. Aurelio	Ethiopia	2/21/37	3	1
Kyrillos, Abuna	Ethiopia	2/21/37	5	1
Garcia, R.	Mexico	3/14/37	6	2
Liu To-Chuan	China	4/30/37	3	1
Ascasso, Francisco	Spain	5/ 7/37	5	2
Sesa, A.	Spain	5/ 7/37	4	2
Salazar, A.	Portugal	7/ 7/37	1	1
Koc, Colonel Adam	Poland	7/17/37	5	1
Sidki, Bakr	Iraq	8/12/37	1	2
Ali Jawad, Muhammad	Iraq	8/12/37	6	2
McEwan, P.R.	Palestine	9/27/37	6	2
Andrews, L.Y.	Palestine	9/27/37	6	2
Marriner, J.T.	Lebanon	10/13/37	6	2
Nahas Pasha	Egypt	11/28/37	1	1
Chinna, Swami	India	2/28/38	5	2
Clark, J.R.	U.S., Ky.	4/12/38	6	2
Dykes, James	U.S., Ky.	4/12/38	6	1
Bargas, Getulio	Brazil	5/11/38	1	1
Epps, F.O.	U.S., Ga.	7/10/38	6	2
Combs, Lee	U.S., Ky.	8/ 5/38	6	2
Combs, Lewis	U.S., Ky.	8/ 5/38	5	1
Deaton, Walter	U.S., Ky.	8/ 5/38	6	1
Peeff, Jordan	Bulgaria	10/10/38	3	2
Rath, Ernst Von	France	11/ 7/38	6	2
Trivulzio, Prince Luigi	Italy	11/ 9/38	5	2
Cedillo, Saturnillo	Mexico	/39	3	2
Sanderson, G.D.	Palestine	1/ 1/39	6	2
Tegart, Sir C.	Palestine	1/ 1/39	6	1
Blum	Palestine	1/ 4/39	5	2
Bernstein	Palestine	1/ 4/39	5	2
Keith-Roach	Palestine	1/ 6/39	6	1
Shahbandar, Dr.	Lebanon	1/17/39	2	1
Acosta, Pedro	Cuba	1/24/39	6	2
Cristescu	Rumania	1/27/39	5	2
Bingham, Hugh	Palestine	2/ 3/39	6	1
Chow Chi-Tang	China	2/ 7/39	6	2

Koo Pingtsun	China	2/ 7/39	6	2
Stambouli, Hadi	Palestine	2/10/39	6	1
Calinescu, M.	Rumania	2/13/39	2	1
Gazzera, Dr. Franco	Ethiopia	2/13/39	6	2
Chen Loh	China	2/21/39	4	2
Li, M.	China	2/22/39	5	2
Kruschev, N.	Poland	2/28/39	5	1
Tao Shan-Chen	China	3/ 1/39	6	1
Nashashibi, Adnan	Palestine	3/ 6/39	5	2
Sternberg, Dr.	Palestine	3/ 7/39	6	1
Monck-Mason, G.E,A,C,	Iraq	4/ 5/39	6	2
Calinescu, Armand	Rumania	9/21/39	1	2
Hitler, Adolph	Germany	11/ 8/39	1	1
Balmaseda, Miguel	Cuba	12/10/39	5	2
Almazan, Juan	Mexico	/40	1	1
Haydar, Rustum	Iraq	1/18/40	2	2
Velazquez Rivera, Gen. R.	Dom. Rep.	1/29/40	3	2
Arani, Dr. Taqi	Iran	2/ /40	5	2
Bakior, Ivan	Yugoslavia	2/ 8/40	5	2
Sumuano, E.	Mexico	2/ 9/40	6	2
Ferrara, Dr. Oreste	Cuba	3/10/40	4	2
Lamington, Lord	England	3/10/40	5	1
Dane, Sir L.	England	3/13/40	5	1
O'Dwyer, Sir Michael	England	3/13/40	5	2
Santo Mauro, Duke of	France	4/ 5/40	5	2
Rataj, Maciej	Poland	5/ /40	5	2
Leimer, E.	Czechoslovakia	5/ 6/40	5	2
Rodriguez, Felix	Mexico	7/ 7/40	5	2
Ma You-Feng	China	8/10/40	5	2
Daussa, Dr. R.V.	Cuba	8/16/40	5	2
Chang Han-Yen	China	8/20/40	5	2
Trotsky, L.	Mexico	8/21/40	5	2
Bombelec, Count	Yugoslavia	9/18/40	5	1
Garcia Mendez, A.M.	U.S., P.R.	9/30/40	6	1
Fu Siau-En	China	10/11/40	4	2
Carias, Andino	Honduras	10/24/40	1	1
Garcia de Caturla, Alejandro	Cuba	11/13/40	6	2
Perry, R.F.	U.S., Ala.	11/23/40	6	2
Iorga, Nicolas	Rumania	11/29/40	1	2
Fernandez Fiallo, Dr. R.	Cuba	11/29/40	5	2
Frugoni, E.	Uruguay	12/31/40	4	1
Boris	Bulgaria	/41	1	1
Boris	Bulgaria	/41	1	1
Boris	Bulgaria	/41	1	1
Victor Emmanuel	Albania	/41	1	1
Mandique, M.	Cuba	1/14/41	5	2
Doering	Rumania	1/21/41	6	2
Keswick, W.J.	China	1/24/41	6	1
Erroll, Earl of	Kenya	1/24/41	5	2
Sanchez Errazuriz, E.	Chile	1/28/41	5	2
Menendez, Bernardo	Cuba	2/ 1/41	6	2
Baldes Lamas, J.	Cuba	2/ 1/41	6	2
Cortina, J.M.	Cuba	4/ 1/41	2	1
Ayala, J.	Cuba	4/26/41	5	2
Zaydin Almendares, R.	Cuba	4/30/41	4	1
Pinto, F.	Chile	5/17/41	5	2
Fernando Pinto, Sepulveda	Chile	5/18/41	5	2
Faget, M.	Cuba	6/ 3/41	6	1
Kusocinski, J.	Poland	6/18/41	5	2
Hiranuma	Japan	8/14/41	2	2

Laval, Pierre	France	8/28/41	1	1
Deat, Marcel	France	8/28/41	5	1
Durvez, P.	France	8/28/41	6	1
Gitton, M.	France	9/ 6/41	5	2
Frank, K.H.	Czechoslovakia	10/ 7/41	4	1
Holtz, K.F.	France	10/21/41	6	2
Alessandri, Arturo	Chile	12/ 6/41	1	1
Okanda, S.	U.S., Calif.	12/21/41	5	2
Paringaux, Y.	France	1/ 6/42	2	2
Von Papen, Franz	Turkey	2/25/42	2	1
Zarate-Albarran, Gov. A.	Mexico	3/ 7/42	4	2
Deat, Marcel	France	3/28/42	5	1
Ebeid Pasha	Egypt	4/14/42	2	1
Heydrich, Reinhard	Czechoslovakia	5/28/42	4	2
Enriquez, General A.	Ecuador	5/31/42	1	2
Clement, A.	France	6/ 3/42	5	2
Louer, J.	France	6/11/42	5	2
Demaret, Jean	Belgium	7/ 9/42	6	2
Frank, Waldo	Argentina	8/ 3/42	5	1
Gachelin, H.	France	8/ 8/42	5	2
Griffiths, Dr.	Iran	8/10/42	5	2
Tojo	Japan	8/13/42	1	1
Chahab	Iran	8/24/42	3	2
Drosch, Dr.	Yugoslavia	8/28/42	6	2
Mulletti, General	Albania	8/31/42	3	1
Tojo	Japan	9/ 9/42	1	1
O'Brien, D.	Ireland	9/10/42	6	2
Lebrasse	France	9/12/42	6	2
Rondoz, Marcel	Belgium	9/26/42	5	2
Antonescu, M.	Rumania	10/ 1/42	2	1
Van Nieuwenhuyse	Belgium	10/ 2/42	5	2
Box, John M.	U.S., Miss.	10/19/42	6	2
Teughels, J.	Belgium	11/21/42	6	2
Antonescu, M.	Rumania	12/ 6/42	1	1
Darlan, Jean	Algeria	12/24/42	3	2
Verdier, Jean	France	/43	6	1
Tresca, Carlo	U.S., N.Y.	1/11/43	5	2
Beraud, Henri	France	1/12/43	5	1
Haas, Wilhelm	Belgium	1/22/43	4	2
Camacho, Manuel A.	Mexico	2/ 4/43	1	1
Seyffardt, Gen. Heordrik A.	Netherlands	2/ 5/43	3	2
Fernandez Pelaez, J.	Cuba	2/ 6/43	5	2
Seyffardt, H.A.	Netherlands	2/ 9/43	3	2
Ruiz Guinazu	Argentina	2/11/43	2	1
Ravenzwaai, C. Van	Netherlands	2/12/43	4	2
Reydon, Dr. H.	Netherlands	2/12/43	6	2
Loukoff	Bulgaria	2/14/43	3	2
Desslain, M.	Belgium	2/18/43	6	2
Van Stenlandt, Albrecht	Belgium	2/21/43	6	2
Glad, Dr. Wolfgang	Belgium	2/26/43	3	2
Akkers, Jan	Belgium	3/ 9/43	5	2
Savo, G.	Albania	3/21/43	6	2
Brynder, J.E.	Belgium	4/ 9/43	5	2
Curvers, Julien	Belgium	4/ 9/43	5	2
Harnack, Von	Germany	4/11/43	5	2
Janeff, Sotir	Bulgaria	4/15/43	4	2
Colin, Paul	Belgium	4/16/43	5	2
Yamamoto, Isoroku	Japan	4/17/43	3	2
Hoffman, K.	Poland	4/20/43	6	2
Chevalier, Maurice	Belgium	4/21/43	5	1

Corteville, Cyrille	Belgium	4/21/43	6	2
Gassowski, Paul	France	4/25/43	6	2
Fischer, L.	Poland	4/29/43	4	1
Laval, P.	France	5/ 1/43	1	1
Cathala, Pierre	France	5/ 1/43	2	1
Dietz, Hugo	Poland	5/ 2/43	6	2
Kurtz, B.	Poland	5/ 2/43	6	2
Nitsche, Georg	Norway	5/ 6/43	6	2
Olitsch, Kurt	Norway	5/ 6/43	6	2
Krueger, Gen. W.	Poland	5/10/43	4	2
Rebus, O.	Poland	5/15/43	6	2
Baksh, K.B.A.	India	5/15/43	5	2
Dirr, Raymond	France	5/18/43	6	2
Guerin, Michel	France	5/18/43	5	2
Leng Yun	China	5/30/43	6	2
Haudevin, Pierre	France	5/31/43	6	1
Bouisson, Jean	France	5/31/43	6	2
Klevkoff, Sapria	Bulgaria	6/ 1/43	6	2
Abdul Ilah	Iraq	6/ 5/43	1	1
Posthuma, Dr. F.E.	Netherlands	6/ 8/43	4	2
Joltekenoff, Vassal	Bulgaria	6/ 9/43	6	2
Ehrenlichter, L.	Russia	6/26/43	6	2
Schmidt, F.	France	6/28/43	5	2
Tissot, Paul	France	6/30/43	6	2
Labreau, Maurice	Belgium	7/ 4/43	5	2
Arrarista, Carolino	Mexico	7/17/43	5	2
Aletrino, L.	Rumania	7/22/43	5	2
Chierci	Italy	8/ 1/43	6	2
Boris	Bulgaria	8/24/43	1	2
DelaPlace, Jose	France	8/26/43	5	2
Cinquin, Francois	France	8/26/43	5	2
Varoteaux, Marcel	France	9/21/43	5	2
Ritter, Julius	France	9/29/43	6	2
Jolicoeur, Dr.	France	10/ 1/43	5	2
Darbelle, Lucie	France	10/10/43	5	2
Lespinasse, Paul	France	10/12/43	6	1
De Brinon	France	10/20/43	2	1
De Jong, Adrianus M.	Netherlands	10/20/43	5	2
Barthelet, Jean	France	10/27/43	6	2
Legnani	Italy	10/28/43	3	2
Escofier, Eugene	France	11/ 8/43	5	2
Edde, Emile	Lebanon	11/14/43	1	1
Philippon, J.	France	11/16/43	3	2
Bonamy, Andre	France	11/18/43	4	2
Verdier, Jean	France	12/ 7/43	6	2
Marion, J.	France	1/ 3/44	3	2
Toomver	Estonia	1/ 4/44	6	2
Hobel, Hans	Italy	1/ 5/44	4	2
Munk, K.	Denmark	1/ 6/44	5	2
Kaerra, Leo	Denmark	1/14/44	5	1
Serlin, J.	France	1/15/44	5	2
Mittica	Italy	1/15/44	6	2
Kalyvas	Greece	1/29/44	2	2
Harvy, J.	France	2/13/44	6	2
Tan Shu-Kuei	China	2/14/44	6	2
Ludberg, H.	Poland	2/18/44	6	2
Loaiza, Colonel Rodolfo	Mexico	2/22/44	4	2
Tommasini, D.	France	2/29/44	5	2
Thompson, S.	Denmark	3/26/44	5	2
Marion, P.	France	4/ 4/44	2	2

Herrerias, I.	Mexico	4/ 4/44	5	2
Chen Yao-Tsu	China	4/ 7/44	4	2
Ibsen, Jense Albert	Denmark	4/ 9/44	5	2
Camacho, Manuel A.	Mexico	4/10/44	1	1
Mussolini, B.	Italy	4/25/44	1	1
Ingarano, Colonel	Italy	4/30/44	6	1
Grunwald, O.	Poland	5/ 1/44	6	2
Sergius, Metropolitan of Vilna	Poland	5/ 1/44	5	2
Humbert	Italy	6/10/44	2	1
Herland, E.	Norway	6/14/44	3	2
Parodi	Italy	6/21/44	3	2
Koch, Lt.	Italy	6/22/44	6	2
Norse, T.	Norway	6/27/44	6	2
Henriot, Philippe	France	6/28/44	2	2
Rolls, S.	Norway	7/ 6/44	6	2
Mandel, Georges	France	7/ 7/44	5	2
DeGrelle, Edward	Belgium	7/ 8/44	5	2
Arze, Jose A.	Bolivia	7/10/44	5	1
Bartelemy, Georges	France	7/10/44	5	2
Hitler, Adolf	Germany	7/20/44	1	1
Von Stuelpnagel	France	7/25/44	3	2
Mussolini, B.	Italy	8/ 7/44	1	1
McMichael, Sir Harold	Palestine	8/13/44	4	1
Sandhoe, P.	Denmark	3/13/44	6	2
DeGaulle, Charles	France	8/28/44	1	1
Carretta, D.	Italy	9/19/44	5	2
Lalis, Etienne	France	9/21/44	5	2
Picout, Andre	France	9/21/44	5	2
Pavolini	Italy	9/26/44	5	1
Cordova, Alejandro	Guatemala	10/ 3/44	5	2
Noguera Gomez	Nicaragua	10/10/44	5	2
Lakatos	Hungary	10/12/44	1	1
Wikin, T.J.	Palestine	10/12/44	6	2
MacMichael, Sir Harold	Palestine	10/12/44	4	1
Gilbert, H.	Denmark	10/15/44	5	1
Corado	Guatemala	10/23/44	3	2
Calvo, L	Bolivia	11/ /44	4	2
Capriles, F.	Boliva	11/ /44	4	2
Boncour, Jean Paul	France	11/ 1/44	4	1
Moyne, Lord	Egypt	11/ 6/44	2	2
Keitel	Germany	11/18/44	3	1
Marion	France	11/18/44	3	2
LeLong	France	11/18/44	6	2
Stahr, J.E.	Denmark	11/19/44	6	2
Voigt, R.	Norway	12/10/44	6	2
Fitzpatrick, W.J.	U.S., N.Y.	1/ 6/45	6	2
Hooper, W.G.	U.S., Mich.	1/12/45	6	2
Ribbentrop, Joachim Von	Germany	1/15/45	2	1
Pospichal, E.J.	U.S., N.Y.	1/29/45	5	2
Castro, Rosendo G.	Mexico	1/30/45	4	2
Hitler, Adolf	Germany	2/ /45	1	1
Freisler	Germany	2/ /45	6	2
Loret, Giulio	Italy	2/ /45	5	2
Fujui, Y.	Macao	2/ 4/45	6	2
Martinsen, General Carl	Norway	2/ 8/45	3	2
Fitzhum, Josef	Austria	2/17/45	6	2
Maher Pasha, Ahmed	Egypt	2/24/45	1	2
Radescu, Nicolai	Rumania	2/25/45	1	1
Sarraut, Maurice	France	3/ /45	5	2
Alvarez	Cuba	3/12/45	2	1

Sforza, Count Carlos	Italy	3/12/45	5	1
Berlinguer, M.	Italy	3/14/45	6	1
Llanillo, Dr. Eugenio	Cuba	3/16/45	5	2
Oppenhof, Franz	Germany	3/25/45	6	2
Schirach, Baldur Von	Germany	3/25/45	5	1
Salotti	Italy	4/13/45	5	1
Dietrich, Sepp	Austria	4/19/45	2	1
Enriquez, E.	Cuba	4/25/45	4	2
Benes, E.	Czechoslovakia	5/ /45	1	1
Moravec, E.	Czechoslovakia	6/ /45	5	2
Sokol, S.	Poland	6/18/45	5	2
Hill, General M.	Chile	7/31/45	3	1
Passalides, M. Jean	Greece	8/ /45	5	1
Nejedly, Z.	Czechoslovakia	8/30/45	2	1
Gottwald, K.	Czechoslovakia	8/30/45	2	1
Basch, Victor	France	9/27/45	5	2
Anba, Theophilus	Egypt	10/ 2/45	5	2
De Gasperi	Italy	10/ 3/45	2	1
Lassen, R.	Denmark	10/18/45	6	2
Mallaby	Indonesia	10/31/45	3	2
Horikiri	Japan	11/ 9/45	2	1
Arntzen	Norway	11/28/45	2	2
Brito, Colonel A.	Cuba	11/29/45	5	2
Ostrom, E.N.	Indonesia	12/ /45	5	2
Nahas Pasha, M.	Egypt	12/ 7/45	1	1
Nan Ung	Korea	12/22/45	5	1
Chudzik	Poland	/46	6	1
Osman Pasha	Egypt	1/ 6/46	5	2
Cofran, E.	Germany	1/13/46	6	2
Moulheim, Tarrad	Syria	1/13/46	4	2
Joglar, R.D.	Cuba	1/20/46	5	2
Chang Hsi-Fu	Manchuria	2/28/46	4	2
Sung Chu-Hsiang	Manchuria	3/ 9/46	5	2
Baig, M.M.	India	4/10/46	5	2
Song Chin-Woo	Korea	4/11/46	5	2
Imperial, R.	Philippine Is.	4/24/46	4	2
Aumeran	Algeria	5/ /46	3	1
Mahidol, Ananda	Thailand	6/11/46	1	2
Atherton, T.	Yugoslavia	6/12/46	6	2
Tandogan, Nevzat	Turkey	7/10/46	4	2
Roxas, Dr. P.M.	Philippine Is.	7/16/46	6	2
Villaroel, Gualberto	Bolivia	7/21/46	1	2
Khan, Sir S.A.	India	8/26/46	4	2
Monje Gutierrez, T.	Bolivia	9/ /46	1	1
Hartshorne, E.Y.	Germany	9/ 1/46	6	2
Martinez Fernandez, L.J.	Cuba	9/ 8/46	5	1
Rajagopalachari	India	9/18/46	2	1
Scioborek, B.	Poland	9/24/46	5	2
Donald, T.S.	India	9/28/46	6	2
Rodrigues Araya, A.	Argentina	10/ 4/46	5	1
Chang Taik Sang	Korea	10/22/46	6	1
Charles, Sir Noel	Italy	10/31/46	2	1
Scottoriggio, J.	U.S., N.Y.	11/12/46	5	2
Buitenzorg	Indonesia	11/19/46	6	2
Husseini, Fawzi	Palestine	11/24/46	5	2
Gonzalez Piloto, D.	Cuba	11/27/46	6	2
Ricci	Sweden	12/ /46	2	2
Zeinati, Emir Mohammed	Palestine	12/27/46	5	2
Levin, I.	Palestine	12/27/46	5	2
Glountchitch	Italy	2/ 1/47	6	2

Sachs, Camille	Germany	2/ 1/47	6	1
DeWinton, R.W.M.	Italy	2/11/47	3	2
Swerozewski, General Karl	Poland	3/ /47	5	2
McNear, George P	U.S., Ill.	3/10/47	5	2
Zeugous, John	Greece	3/21/47	5	2
Contopoulos, Christos	Greece	4/ /47	5	2
Davey, Peter	Aden	4/15/47	6	2
Fawsitt, Dermott	Ireland	4/26/47	6	1
Lonquest, A.E.	Palestine	4/28/47	6	2
Anglin, Tom	U.S., Okla.	5/ /47	6	1
Bevin, Ernest	England	5/ 5/47	2	1
Eden, Anthony	England	5/ 5/47	2	1
Santin, Antonio	Italy	6/ /47	5	1
San U Aung	Burma	7/19/47	1	2
Thakin Mya	Burma	7/19/47	2	2
Mahn Ba Khaing	Burma	7/19/47	2	2
Abdul Bazak	Burma	7/19/47	2	2
U Ba Win	Burma	7/19/47	2	2
U Ba Choe	Burma	7/19/47	2	2
Sao Sam Heun	Burma	7/19/47	2	2
Tut, U Tin	Burma	8/ /47	2	1
Zeglicky, Tadeusz	Poland	8/11/47	4	2
Tonski, Stanislaw	Poland	8/11/47	5	2
Ukmar	Trieste	8/27/47	5	1
Khristian, Abbe	Trieste	8/27/47	5	2
Buselitch, Abbe	Trieste	8/27/47	5	2
Taha, Sami	Palestine	9/ /47	5	2
Masaryk, Jan	Czechoslovakia	9/12/47	2	1
Paul	Greece	9/23/47	1	1
Ramadier, Paul	France	10/ 7/47	1	1
Truong Dinh Tri	Indochina	10/10/47	5	2
Nu Thakin	Burma	11/ /47	1	1
Chang Duk Soo	Korea	12/ /47	5	2
Nizam of Hyderabad	India	12/ 5/47	4	1
Masud, Muhammad	Iran	/48	5	2
Wasson, Thomas C.	Palestine	/48	6	2
Gandhi, M.K.	India	1/20/48	5	1
Gandhi, M.K.	India	1/30/48	5	2
Coirier	Italy	1/31/48	6	1
DeFreminville	Italy	1/31/48	6	1
Yahya, ibn Mohammed	Yemen	2/17/48	1	2
Gaitan, Jorge E.	Colombia	4/ 9/48	1	2
Reuther, Walter	U.S., Mich.	4/20/48	5	1
Nahas Pasha, Mustafa	Egypt	4/25/48	1	1
Ladas, Christos	Greece	5/ 1/48	2	2
Tut, U Tin	Burma	9/ /48	5	2
Arevalo Y Veitia, Juan	Cuba	9/ 1/48	5	2
Bernadotte, Count Folke	Israel	9/17/48	2	2
Serot, Colonel Andre	Israel	9/17/48	6	2
Nukrashy Pasha, Mahmoud	Egypt	12/28/48	1	2
Pahlavi, Mohammad Reza, Shah	Iran	/49	1	1
Kostelnik, Dr. Ivov O.G.	Russia	1/ 9/49	5	2
Lucie-Smith, Sir John	Sierra Leone	1/ 9/49	4	1
Raulin-Laboureur, Ede	France	1/21/49	4	2
Al-Banna, Hasan	Egypt	2/ /49	5	2
Maule, A.C.	Poland	2/17/49	6	2
Bailey, E.H.	U.S., Ky.	4/26/49	6	1
Quezon, Mrs. Manuel	Philippine Is.	4/29/49	5	2
Reuther, Victor	U.S., Mich.	6/ 7/49	5	1
Torlonia, Alessandro	Italy	6/20/49	5	2
Saada, Antun	Lebanon	7/ /49	5	2

Arana, Francisco Javier	Guatemala	7/19/49	1	2
Al-Barazi, Muhsin	Syria	8/14/49	1	2
Zaim, Husni	Syria	8/14/49	1	2
Stewart, Duncan George	Malaysia	12/ /49	4	2
Christenson, F.J.	U.S., Ill.	12/12/49	5	2
Hazhir, Abdul-Husayn	Iran	/50	1	2
Castaneda	Philippine Is.	1/18/50	3	1
Gallostra, Jose	Mexico	3/ /50	6	2
Do Van Nang	Vietnam	3/ 4/50	5	2
Alwani, Sheikh Adil	Syria	3/ 7/50	6	2
El Solh, Riad El	Lebanon	3/10/50	1	1
Armstrong, V.S.	U.S., Pa.	3/12/50	6	2
Weston, J.	South Africa	7/26/50	3	2
Nasir, Muhammad	Syria	7/31/50	6	2
Graile, C.	Cuba	9/ 4/50	4	2
Al-Hinnawi, Colonel Sami	Lebanon	10/31/50	1	2
Truman, Harry S.	U.S., D.C.	11/ 1/50	1	1
Delgado Chalbaud, Carlos	Venezuela	11/13/50	1	2
Razmara, Ali	Iran	3/ 8/51	1	2
Zangareh, Abdul Hamid	Iran	3/20/51	2	1
Haas	Vietnam	5/15/51	4	2
Rincon, J.	Colombia	6/15/51	5	2
Henriquez	Cuba	6/29/51	4	1
Al-Sulh, Riad	Jordan	7/16/51	1	2
Abdullah	Jordan	7/20/51	1	2
Chanson	Vietnam	7/31/51	3	2
Thai Lap-Thanh	Vietnam	7/31/51	4	2
Mazuera, H.J.	Colombia	9/23/51	5	2
Liaquat, Ali Khan	Pakistan	10/16/51	1	2
Escalante	Cuba	10/17/51	4	1
Ousman, C.	Saudi Arabia	10/19/51	6	2
Raymond	Cambodia	10/31/51	4	2
Waruhiu	Kenya	/52	6	2
Ben Hamouda, Si Sliman	Tunisia	2/15/52	5	2
Fatemi, Hussein	Iran	2/16/52	2	2
Farouk	Egypt	3/ /52	1	1
Rosselin, Bernard	France	3/ /52	6	2
Zevaco	Tunisia	4/ 2/52	6	1
Palmer, Colonel	Jordan	4/10/52	6	2
Harjono, Colonel	Netherlands	5/21/52	6	1
Pinkas, Zvi	Israel	6/21/52	2	1
Didier, Paul	France	7/16/52	6	1
Chenik	Tunisia	7/21/52	4	1
Chedly Hayder	Tunisia	7/28/52	6	1
Drummond, Sir Jack	Switzerland	8/ 5/52	4	2
Carrion, Alejandro	Ecuador	10/ /52	5	1
Hached, Ferhat	Tunisia	12/ 5/52	5	2
Somoza, Anastasio	Nicaragua	/53	1	1
Beria, Lavrenti	Russia	/53	2	2
Peron, J.	Argentina	4/15/53	1	1
Brassat	France	4/21/53	6	2
Rais, Dr. Ben	Tunisia	5/ 1/53	4	1
Kastalli, Chedly	Tunisia	5/ 2/53	6	2
Azzedine Bey	Tunisia	7/ 2/53	5	2
Peck, Mrs. Bernard	Spain	8/ /53	5	2
Muhammad, Sidi	Morocco	9/11/53	1	1
Chakir, Hedi	Tunisia	9/13/53	5	2
Sierra, G.R.G.	Cuba	10/25/53	5	2
Belasco Ibarra, Jose M.	Ecuador	11/ /53	1	1
Adenauer, K.	Germany	/54	1	1

Galoui, Si Hadi Thami	Morocco	2/19/54	4	1
Roberts, Kenneth	U.S., D.C.	3/ 1/54	4	1
Jensen, Ben F.	U.S., D.C.	3/ 1/54	4	1
Bentley, Alvin M.	U.S., D.C.	3/ 1/54	4	1
Davis, Clifford	U.S., D.C.	3/ 1/54	4	1
Fulton, George H.	U.S., D.C.	3/ 1/54	4	1
Muhammad	Morocco	3/ 5/54	1	1
Montalvo, J.	Guatemala	3/16/54	4	1
Faisal II	Pakistan	3/24/54	1	1
Patterson, A.L.	U.S., Ala.	6/19/54	6	2
Hauteville, General	Morocco	6/20/54	3	1
Eyraud, Dr.	Morocco	6/30/54	5	2
Lacerda, Carlos	Brazil	8/ 5/54	5	1
Vaz, Ruben Florentino	Brazil	8/ 5/54	6	2
Kow Worawong	Laos	9/20/54	2	2
Azhari, Ismail	Sudan	10/27/54	1	1
Nasser, Gamal Abdel	Egypt	10/27/54	1	1
Remon, Jose Antonio	Panama	1/ 2/55	1	2
Ben Shain, Abdallah	Morocco	1/ 4/55	6	2
Cutino, Arthur	Morocco	1/ 8/55	5	1
Hoffman, J.	Germany	2/ 5/55	4	1
Shalky, Ibrahim Al-	Libya	2/ 8/55	6	2
Tran Van Lam	Vietnam	3/ /55	4	1
Moulay Idriss	Morocco	3/ 2/55	5	2
Nehru, J.	India	3/12/55	1	1
Quiroz, F.L.	Bolivia	3/13/55	6	2
Armitage, Sir Robert	Cyprus	4/ 2/55	4	1
Boniface	Morocco	4/10/55	5	2
Paz Estenssoro, Victor	Bolivia	4/19/55	1	1
Al-Malki, Lt. Col. Adnan	Syria	4/22/55	1	2
Dupuy	Algeria	5/ /55	6	2
Adenauer, K.	Germany	5/14/55	1	1
Armitage, Sir Robert	Cyprus	5/24/55	4	1
Ellis, Eric	Bermuda	5/24/55	6	1
Guidon	Morocco	6/ /55	6	2
Naceur, Ridoub Amar Ben	Algeria	6/ /55	6	2
Ben Azouz, Mekki	Tunisia	6/ 3/55	5	1
Lemaigre-Dubreuil, Jacques	Morocco	6/14/55	5	2
Peron, Juan	Argentina	6/16/55	1	1
Russo, Tomas	Argentina	6/16/55	3	2
Desanti, Mark	Morocco	6/17/55	5	1
Allal, Said	Morocco	6/20/55	6	1
Lebean	Morocco	6/20/55	6	1
Tubman, W.S.	Liberia	6/25/55	1	1
Naciri, Mohamed	Morocco	6/27/55	4	1
Cernak, Matus	W.Germany	7/ 5/55	5	2
Talow, Michael	Morocco	9/16/55	6	2
Courvoisier, Raymond	Lebanon	10/24/55	4	1
Gallo, Joseph	Algeria	11/ 3/55	6	1
Nkrumah, K.	Gold Coast	11/12/55	1	1
Ala, Hussein	Iran	11/17/55	1	1
Berdadi	Morocco	11/20/55	5	2
Djurhuus, K.	Denmark	11/21/55	4	1
Harding, Sir John	Cyprus	11/26/55	4	1
Boutaleb	Morocco	11/30/55	5	2
Diouri, Mustapha	Morocco	11/30/55	5	1
Laraki	Morocco	11/30/55	5	2
Mouakit, Mohammed	Morocco	11/30/55	5	1
Galindez, Jesus de	Dom. Rep.	/56	5	2
Mao Tse-Tung	China	2/28/56	1	1

Riesel, V.	U.S., N.Y.	4/ 6/56	5	1
Harding, Sir John	Britain	6/ 4/56	4	1
Batista, F.	Cuba	6/26/56	1	1
Shaw Bernard V.	Cyprus	6/26/56	6	1
Hernandez, J.T.	Mexico	9/ 6/56	5	2
Somoza, Anastasio	Nicaragua	9/21/56	1	2
Chang, John M.	S. Korea	9/28/56	2	1
Salas Canizares, R.	Cuba	10/ /56	2	2
Blanco Rio, Antonio	Cuba	10/ /56	4	2
de la Maza, Octavio	Dom. Rep.	/57	5	2
Piedra, Orlando	Cuba	1/13/57	6	1
Jahid, Ghassan	Lebanon	2/19/57	6	2
Ngo Dinh Diem	Vietnam	2/23/57	1	1
Batista, Fulgencio	Cuba	3/13/57	1	1
Azikiwe, N.	Nigeria	4/17/57	1	1
Salah, Kamal Eddine	Somalia	4/17/57	6	2
Voroshilov, K.	Indonesia	5/25/57	2	1
Chekhol, Ali	France	5/27/57	5	2
Koussa, Addi	Algeria	6/ 5/57	5	2
Massu, J.	Algeria	6/24/57	3	1
Rojas, Isaac	Argentina	6/24/57	3	1
Zahir Shah, Mohammed	Afghanistan	7/12/57	1	1
Daud Khan, Sardar	Afghanistan	7/12/57	1	1
Castillo Armas, Carlos	Guatemala	7/26/57	1	2
Si Henni Jah Ahmed	Algeria	8/ 8/57	5	2
Borgeaud, Henri	France	11/ 1/57	4	1
Barakrok, Abdelkader	France	11/28/57	2	1
Sukarno, A.	Indonesia	12/ 1/57	1	1
Arboleda de Uribe	Colombia	2/ /58	5	1
Paramo Arias	Colombia	2/ /58	5	1
Sardi Garces	Colombia	2/ /58	5	1
Soustelle, Jacques	France	2/ 8/58	2	1
Arbelaez-Cifuentes, Fabio	Colombia	3/12/58	5	2
Figuerola, Jose	Argentina	3/14/58	5	1
Sevillano, Emilio	Argentina	3/14/58	5	1
Chapel, Jean	Algeria	3/26/58	4	1
Pharaon, Henri	Lebanon	3/27/58	5	1
Harahap, Burhanuddin	Indonesia	4/ 7/58	5	2
Mohr, Dr. Ernst Guenther	Germany	4/10/58	4	1
Devieux, Samuel	U.S., D.C.	4/14/58	2	2
El-Solh, Sami	Lebanon	4/20/58	1	1
Dejoie, Louis	Haiti	5/ 4/58	2	2
Duncan, Victor	Haiti	5/ 4/58	5	2
Sabalat, Ernst	Haiti	5/ 4/58	5	2
Drew, Gerald A.	Haiti	5/ 7/58	2	1
Mitry, Nasib El-	Lebanon	5/ 8/58	5	2
Khan Sahib, Dr.	Pakistan	5/ 9/58	5	2
Haas, Arthur D.	Haiti	5/11/58	5	1
Rey, Santiago	Cuba	6/13/58	5	2
Balboalopez, Angelico	Cuba	6/18/58	5	1
Marquez Monreal, Jose de Jesus	Mexico	6/22/58	5	2
Shuttlesworth, F.L.	U.S., Ala.	6/29/58	5	1
Rivero Aguero, Nicolas	Cuba	7/ 1/58	5	1
Abboud Abdul Arzzak	Lebanon	7/11/58	5	1
Abdul Ilah	Iraq	7/14/58	1	2
Faisal II	Iraq	7/14/58	1	2
El-Khalry, Khulousy	Iraq	7/14/58	2	2
Ibrahim Hashim	Iraq	7/14/58	2	2
Toukan, Suleiman	Iraq	7/14/58	2	2
Nuri Al-Said	Iraq	7/16/58	1	2

El-Solh, Sami	Lebanon	7/29/58	1	1
Salah Samarai	Lebanon	8/30/58	6	2
Soustelle, Jacques	France	9/15/58	2	1
Wentworth, John Page	Cyprus	9/18/58	6	1
King, Martin Luther, Jr.	U.S., N.Y.	9/20/58	5	1
Chmine, Mohammed	France	9/21/58	6	2
Vega, Anibal	Cuba	9/29/58	4	2
El-Sohl Wadih	Lebanon	10/13/58	6	1
Ameziane, Ait Ahcene	Germany	11/ 5/58	5	2
Ah Ann	Malaya	11/ 6/58	5	2
Chai Swee Sang	Malaya	11/ 6/58	5	2
Thuveney, Auguste	Morocco	11/23/58	5	2
Kassem, Abdul Karim	Iraq	/59	1	1
Guerrero Rosario, Teofilo	Dom. Rep.	2/ /59	5	2
Altamirano Herrera, Rafael	Mexico	3/ 7/59	4	2
Aris, El	Lebanon	3/16/59	5	1
Almond, James	U.S., Va.	4/12/59	4	1
Inonu, Ismet	Turkey	5/ 3/59	1	1
Rodriguez Echazabal	Haiti	5/ 3/59	2	1
Karami	Lebanon	5/19/59	2	1
Rodriguez Echazabal	Haiti	6/ 7/59	2	1
Somoza Debayle, Luis A.	Nicaragua	6/ 8/59	1	1
Shakerch, G.D.	Iraq	6/22/59	5	2
Buis, Dale R.	Vietnam	7/10/59	6	2
Moghabghab, N.	Lebanon	7/29/59	4	2
Suramarit, Norodom	Cambodia	9/ 1/59	1	1
Busso	Argentina	9/18/59	5	1
Bandaranaike, Solomon W.R.	Ceylon	9/25/59	1	2
Kassem, Abdul Karim	Iraq	10/ 8/59	1	1
Plaza	Argentina	10/24/59	5	1
Naim, Sardar Mohammed	Afghanistan	11/24/59	2	1
Rodriguez Reyes, M.	Mexico	12/ 4/59	2	1
Ibrahim, Bin	Oman	12/13/59	2	1
Hakim, A.	Lebanon	12/19/59	5	1
Botet	Argentina	12/20/59	5	2
Ben Messaoud, Ali	Algeria	/60	3	2
Pardo Llada, Jose	Cuba	1/ 9/60	5	1
Kemajou, Daniel	Cameroon	1/13/60	5	1
Lemos, Laercio	Brazil	2/ 6/60	5	2
Sihanouk, Norodom	Cambodia	2/18/60	1	1
Rousseau, Dr. Roger	Haiti	3/ 2/60	5	2
Sukarno, A.	Indonesia	3/ 9/60	1	1
Cabrera, Rene	Argentina	3/12/60	6	1
Lagalaye, Juan	Argentina	3/27/60	3	1
Frondizi, Arturo	Argentina	3/28/60	1	1
Henrik Verwoerd	South Africa	4/ /60	1	1
Sevilla Sacasa, Dr. Oscar	Nicaragua	4/ 1/60	5	1
Calderon Forero, Jairo Alberto	Dom. Rep.	4/14/60	5	2
Chabert, Paul-Emile	Laos	4/21/60	6	2
Abdesselam, Robert	France	5/ 4/60	4	1
Ben Mahmoud	Algeria	5/19/60	5	2
Kawakami, Jotaro	Japan	6/17/60	5	2
Betancourt, Romulo	Venezuela	6/24/60	1	1
Henriques, Josue Lopez	Venezuela	6/24/60	2	1
Armas Perez, Ramon	Venezuela	6/24/60	6	2
Sequero, Francisco R.	Dom. Rep.	6/24/60	5	1
Lumumba, Patrice	Congo	7/ 8/60	1	1
Kishi, Nobusake	Japan	7/14/60	1	1
Asafu-Adjaye, Sir Edward D.	England	7/23/60	2	1
Higgins, Mark H.	Congo	7/25/60	5	2

Altamirano, Alberto J.	Mexico	7/28/60	5	2
Pathammavong, Sounthone	Laos	8/ 9/60	3	2
Majali, Hazza	Jordan	8/29/60	1	2
Assem Taijo	Jordan	8/29/60	6	2
Ishasat, Mamdoh	Jordan	8/29/60	6	2
Zuha Iddin Hammoud	Jordan	8/29/60	4	2
Lumumba, Patrice	Congo	9/15/60	1	1
Zevaco, Raoul	Algeria	9/29/60	5	2
Asanuma, Inejiro	Japan	10/12/60	2	2
Moumie, Dr. Felix	Switzerland	10/16/60	2	2
Kalowa, Boniface	Congo	10/26/60	6	2
Heard, Roby H.	U.S., Calif.	11/12/60	5	2
Hodgson, Edward	Congo	11/23/60	5	2
Knauf, Elton G.	Congo	11/23/60	5	2
Mirabel de Tavarez, Dr. Minerva	Dom. Rep.	11/29/60	5	2
Mirabel de Gozman, Maria Teresa	Dom. Rep.	11/29/60	5	2
Mirabel de Gonzales, Patricia	Dom. Rep.	11/29/60	5	2
Newaye,Germane	Ethiopia	12/24/60	4	2
Strom, Carl W.	Bolivia	12/25/60	2	1
Ben Youssef, Salah	Germany	/61	5	2
Lumumba, Patrice	Congo	1/17/61	1	2
Mpolo, Maurice	Congo	1/17/61	2	2
Okito, Joseph	Congo	1/17/61	2	2
Bourguiba, Habib	Tunisia	1/26/61	1	1
Finant, Joseph	Congo	2/ /61	6	2
Songolo, Alphonse	Congo	2/ /61	5	2
Yahya, Ahmed Ibn	Yemen	3/ /61	1	1
Trujillo Molina, Rafael	Dom. Rep.	5/30/61	1	2
de la Maza, Ernesto	Dom. Rep.	5/31/61	5	2
Roman Fernandez, Jose R.	Dom. Rep.	6/ /61	2	2
Diaz, Juan Tomas	Dom. Rep.	6/ /61	3	2
Imbert Barrera, Segundo	Dom. Rep.	6/ /61	3	2
Baez Diaz, Miguel A.	Dom. Rep.	6/ /61	5	2
Diaz	Dom. Rep.	6/ /61	5	2
Garcia Guerrero, Amado	Dom. Rep.	6/ /61	6	2
Haviera, Juan	Dom. Rep.	6/ /61	5	2
de la Maza	Dom. Rep.	6/ /61	5	2
de la Maza, Antonio	Dom. Rep.	6/ /61	6	2
Roman Fernandez	Dom. Rep.	6/ /61	5	2
DeGaulle, C.	France	9/ 9/61	1	1
Rivagasore, Louis	Burundi	10/ /61	1	2
Caceres, Luis M.	Dom. Rep.	11/18/61	5	2
Diaz, Modesto	Dom. Rep.	11/18/61	5	2
Estrella Sadhala, Salvador	Dom. Rep.	11/18/61	5	2
Livio Cedeno, Pedro	Dom. Rep.	11/18/61	5	2
Pastoriza, Roberto	Dom. Rep.	11/18/61	5	2
Tejeda Pimentel, Huascon	Dom. Rep.	11/18/61	5	2
Olympio, S.	Togo	1/22/62	1	1
Mahendra, King	Nepal	1/24/62	1	1
Gizenga, Antoine	Congo	1/28/62	2	1
Stogner, H.D.	Congo	2/15/62	6	2
Ngo Dinh Diem	S. Vietnam	2/27/62	1	1
Salan, R.	France	5/ /62	3	1
Sukarno, A.	Indonesia	5/14/62	1	1
DeGaulle, Charles	France	5/22/62	1	1
DeGaulle, Charles	France	5/31/62	1	1
DeGaulle, Charles	France	6/15/62	1	1
Tovey, N.	Bahamas	6/16/62	6	2
DeGaulle, Charles	France	8/23/62	1	1
DeGaulle, Charles	France	9/13/62	1	1
Al-Badr, Muhammad	Yemen	9/28/62	1	1

Nkrumah, Kwame	Ghana	9/29/62	1	1
DeGaulle, Charles	France	10/22/62	1	1
Joachim, Paul	U.S., Ill.	10/23/62	3	2
Hoffa, James	U.S., Tenn.	12/ 6/62	5	1
Bourgiuba, Habib	Tunisia	12/27/62	1	1
Chausevanh	Laos	/63	6	2
Ketsana	Laos	/63	6	2
Konthi	Laos	/63	6	2
Olympio, Sylvanus	Togo	1/13/63	1	2
DeGaulle, Charles	France	1/29/63	1	1
Kassem, Abdul Karim	Iraq	2/ 9/63	1	2
DeGaulle, Charles	France	3/ 1/63	1	1
Lafond, Henri	France	3/ 6/63	5	2
Houphouet-Boigny, Felix	Ivory Coast	4/11/63	1	1
Khemisti, Mohammed	Algeria	4/11/63	2	2
Djafawi, Abdul Aziz Ben Saud	France	4/17/63	5	2
Kouyoumjian, Shavarsh	Syria	4/17/63	5	1
Nolting, Frederick	S. Vietnam	5/28/63	2	1
Evers, Medgar	U.S., Miss.	6/12/63	5	2
Betancourt, Romulo	Venezuela	6/13/63	1	1
Savang Vathana	Laos	10/31/63	1	1
Ngo Dinh Diem	S. Vietnam	11/ 2/63	1	2
Ngo Dinh Nhu	S. Vietnam	11/ 2/63	2	2
Kennedy, John F.	U.S., Tex.	11/22/63	1	2
Connally, John B.	U.S., Tex.	11/22/63	4	1
Oswald, Lee Harvey	U.S., Tex.	11/23/63	5	2
Leuang	Laos	12/ 6/63	6	2
Henderson, George	Aden	12/10/63	4	2
Barrientos Ortuno, Lt. Gen.	Bolivia	/64	1	1
Barrientos Ortuno, Lt. Gen.	Bolivia	/64	1	1
DeGaulle, Charles	France	1/18/64	1	1
Blitzstein, Marc	Martinique	1/24/64	5	2
Hassan II	Morocco	2/ 4/64	1	1
Ketsana Vongsonavanh	Laos	2/12/64	6	2
DeGaulle, Charles	France	2/13/64	1	1
Inonu, Ismet	Turkey	2/22/64	1	1
Prasuth	Laos	3/18/64	6	2
DeGaulle, Charles	France	3/19/64	1	1
Reischauer, Edwin	Japan	3/24/64	2	1
DeGaulle, Charles	France	3/25/64	1	1
DeGaulle, Charles	France	4/ 1/64	1	1
Dorji, Jigme P.	Bhutan	4/ 5/64	1	2
Welcome, Verda	U.S., Md.	4/11/64	6	1
Arias, Roberto	Panama	5/21/64	5	1
Calvo, Escolastico	Panama	5/21/64	5	1
Ben Bella, A.	Algeria	6/ 1/64	1	1
Agede, Abate	Sweden	6/ 5/64	2	2
Sanyal, H.N.	India	9/ /64	4	2
Al-Shishakli, Gen. Adib	Brazil	9/27/64	1	2
Wiesenthal, Simon	Austria	12/20/64	5	1
Pahlavi, Mohd. Reza Shah	Iran	/65	1	1
Ngendandumwe, Pierre	Burundi	1/15/65	1	2
Mansour, Hassan Ali	Iran	1/21/65	1	2
Kairon, Pratap Singh	India	2/ 6/65	6	2
Matsokota, Lazare	Congo	2/15/65	2	2
Pouabou, Joseph	Congo	2/15/65	2	2
Massouemi, Anselme	Congo	2/15/65	4	2
Malcolm X	U.S., N.Y.	2/22/65	5	2
Reeb, Rev. James J.	U.S., Ala.	3/ 9/65	5	2
Barriento Ortuno, Lt. Gen. Rene	Bolivia	3/21/65	1	1

Liuzzo, Viola	U.S., Ala.	3/25/65	5	2
DeGaulle, Charles	France	3/28/65	1	1
Al-Zubairy, Mohd.	Yemen	4/ 1/65	4	2
Diori, Hamani	Nigeria	4/14/65	1	1
Arreaga, Col. Ernesto M.	Guatemala	5/21/65	4	2
DeGaulle, Charles	France	5/24/65	1	1
DeGaulle, Charles	France	7/17/65	1	1
Taylor, Maxwell D.	Vietnam	7/20/65	2	1
Castro, Fidel	Cuba	7/27/65	1	1
Aragones, Emilio	Cuba	7/27/65	5	1
Daniels, Jonathan M.	U.S., Ala.	8/ /65	5	2
Al-Sallal, Abdullah	Yemen	8/ 7/65	1	1
Charles, Sir Arthur	Aden	9/13/65	4	2
Macapagal, Diosdado	Philippine Is.	10/29/65	1	1
Mendez Montenegro, Mario	Guatemala	10/31/65	1	2
Ali Benahmed	Aden	11/ 4/65	5	2
Balewa, Sir Abubakar	Nigeria	1/15/66	1	2
Okotie-Eboh, Festus	Nigeria	1/15/66	2	2
Akintola, Sumuel L.	Nigeria	1/15/66	4	2
Bello, Sir Ahmadu	Nigeria	1/15/66	4	2
El-Airiny, Abdullah	Yemen	4/13/66	2	2
Iriani, Abdul	Yemen	4/14/66	2	2
Rahoumi, Ahmed	Yemen	4/14/66	2	1
Hernandez Martinez, Maximliano	Honduras	5/18/66	3	2
Calwell, Arthur	Australia	6/ /66	2	1
Meredith, James	U.S., Miss.	6/ 6/66	5	1
Kittakachorn, Thanom	Thailand	7/ /66	1	1
Nasser, G.A.	Egypt	7/ /66	1	1
Ironsi Aguiyi, J.T.V.	Nigeria	7/30/66	1	2
Costa E Silva, Arthur	Brazil	8/ /66	1	1
Bassendawah, Ahmed	Aden	8/ /66	4	2
Verwoerd, Hendrik F.	S. Africa	9/ 6/66	1	2
Van Der Poel, J.	England	9/13/66	6	2
Van, Tran Van	S. Vietnam	12/ 7/66	2	2
Aptheker, Dr. Herbert	U.S., N.Y.	/67	5	1
Khider, Mohammed	Spain	1/ 3/67	5	2
Diop, Demba	Senegal	2/ 3/67	2	2
Hassan, Sayed Mohammed	Aden	2/26/67	4	2
Mackawee, Abdul Q.	Aden	2/2-/67	5	1
Nagi, Mohammed	Aden	3/ 5/67	6	2
Girgerah, Abdurrahman	Aden	3/20/67	2	2
Senghor, Leopold S.	Senegal	3/22/67	1	1
Senghor, Leopold	Senegal	3/23/67	1	1
Shamshair, Haider	Aden	4/ 4/67	6	2
Qassem, Abdurrahim	Aden	4/19/67	5	2
Amoodi, Sheik Salem Al-	Aden	4/19/67	5	2
Eyadema, Etienne	Togo	4/24/67	1	1
Yafai, Haidera Saleh Mohammed	Aden	5/ 8/67	5	2
Gonzalez, Rodolfo	Venezuela	5/28/67	4	2
Bohlen, Charles E.	France	6/ 9/67	2	1
Wilkins, Roy	U.S., N.Y.	6/22/67	5	1
Duvalier, Francois	Haiti	6/25/67	1	1
Fedama, Sheik Ali Salih	Aden	7/ 3/67	5	2
Bun, Lam	Hong Kong	8/ /67	5	2
Rockwell, George Lincoln	U.S., Va.	8/26/67	5	2
Eshkol, Levi	Israel	9/28/67	1	1
Guevara, Che	Bolivia	11/ /67	5	2
Bui Quang San	S. Vietnam	12/14/67	2	2
Munro, Ernest A.	Guatemala	1/ /68	6	2
Webber, John D., Jr.	Guatemala	1/ /68	6	2

King, Martin Luther, Jr.	U.S., Tenn.	4/ 6/68	5	2
Boumedienne, H.	Algeria	4/25/68	1	1
Chiari, Modesto	Panama	5/25/68	5	2
Chamoun, Camille	Lebanon	5/31/68	1	1
Kennedy, Robert F.	U.S., Calif.	6/ 5/68	2	2
Al-Iryani, Abdul Rahman	Yemen	7/ 7/68	1	1
Kachailov, Yevgeny N.	Russia	7/26/68	4	2
Manzanas, Militon	Spain	8/ 2/68	6	2
Papadopoulis, George	Greece	8/13/68	1	1
Mein, John Gordon	Guatemala	8/28/68	2	2
El-Farrah, Shawki	Gaza	9/16/68	6	2
Chandler, Charles R.	Brazil	10/12/68	6	2
Roman, Jose	Philippine Is.	10/21/68	6	2

2. Data Collected by Feierabend Group

The following is the definition of assassination used by the Feierabend group and a print out of assassination attempts and plots data, collected by the Feierabend group for the period 1948 through 1967. Included as well is the complete code index. The data are arranged by country alphabetically.

Definition of Assassination Event

An assassination event was defined as an act that consists of a plotted, attempted or actual murder of a prominent political figure (elite) by an individual (assassin) who performs this act in other than a governmental role. This definition draws a distinction between political execution and assassination. An execution may be regarded as a political killing, but it is initiated by the organs of the state, while an assassination can always be characterized as an illegal act. A prominent figure must be the target of the killing, since the killing of lesser members of the political community is included within a wider category of internal political turmoil, namely, terrorism. Finally, we used a minimal definition to distinguish assassination from homicide. The target of the aggressive act must be a political figure rather than a private person. The killing of a prime minister by a member of an insurrectionist or underground group clearly qualifies as an assassination. So does an act by a deranged individual who tries to kill, not just any individual, but the individual in his political role—as President, for example.

There are three additional aspects of our definition. (1) We included assassinations carried out by agents of foreign governments and assassinations perpetrated against a political figure while he was visiting on foreign soil. (2) There is implicit the notion of premeditation in our definition, thus ruling out accidental and "crime of passion" types of killings. (3) We counted assassination plots and alleged plots within our data, although they are distinguished from assassination attempts. It is impossible to determine, in the case of alleged plots, whether the plot in fact existed and was discovered by the regime, or whether it served as an excuse for a wave of political arrests.

Within the notion of prominent public figure, we counted all top governmental officeholders, heads of state and government, presidential candidates, cabinet members, legislators, and judges. We also included military figures, chiefs of staff, generals, and occasionally colonels if they seemed to play an important role in the political arena. Some important local officials, such as mayors of cities or chiefs of police, qualified in our definition of political prominence. Beyond governmental officeholders, we included leaders öf political parties, large trade unions, social and religious movements, leaders of minority groups and other prominent members of important, visible social institutions. Undoubtedly, the definition of political prominence is difficult and, at times, drawing a meaningful line between prominence and non-prominence was tortuous.

ASSASSINATION CODE INDEX
and
EXPLANATORY NOTES

1. DATA BANK ID.
Col. 1-2

2. COUNTRY
Col. 3-5

001 - Afghanistan	029 - Finland	057 - New Zealand
002 - Albania	030 - France	058 - Nicaragua
003 - Argentina	031 - Ghana	059 - Norway
004 - Australia	032 - Greece	060 - Pakistan
005 - Austria	033 - Guatemala	061 - Panama
006 - Belgium	034 - Haiti	062 - Paraguay
007 - Bolivia	035 - Honduras	063 - Peru
008 - Brazil	036 - Hungary	064 - Philippines
009 - Bulgaria	037 - Iceland	065 - Poland
010 - Burma	038 - India	066 - Portugal
011 - Cambodia	039 - Indonesia	067 - Romania
012 - Canada	040 - Iran	068 - Saudi Arabia
013 - Ceylon	041 - Iraq	069 - Spain
014 - Chile	042 - Ireland	070 - Sudan
015 - China (Taiwan)	043 - Israel	071 - Sweden
016 - China (Mainland)	044 - Italy	072 - Switzerland
017 - Colombia	045 - Japan	073 - Syria
018 - Costa Rica	046 - Jordan	074 - Thailand
019 - Cuba	047 - Korea	075 - Tunisia
020 - Cyprus	048 - Laos	076 - Turkey
021 - Czechoslovakia	049 - Lebanon	077 - Union of South Africa
022 - Denmark	050 - Liberia	078 - United Kingdom
023 - Dominican Republic	051 - Libya	079 - United States
024 - East Germany	052 - Luxembourg	080 - Uruguay
025 - Ecuador	053 - Malaya	081 - U.S.S.R.
026 - Egypt	054 - Mexico	082 - Venezuela
027 - El Salvador	055 - Morocco	083 - West Germany
028 - Ethiopia	056 - Netherlands	084 - Yugoslavia

West Germany = Federal Republic of Germany
United Kingdom = Sum of data for England, Wales, Northern Ireland, Scotland
Egypt = United Arab Republic

3. DATE
Col. 6-7 (month)
Col. 8-9 (day)
Col. 10-11 (year)

4. OUTCOME
Col. 12
1-successful
2-unsuccessful

5. ACTION
Col. 13
1-attempt
2-plot

6. MINORITY HOSTILITY
Col. 14

1-Yes
2-No

7. NATURE OF TENSION (reason for event)
Col. 15

1-political
2-religious
3-economic
4-ethnic
5-educational

8. TYPE OF GROUP
Col. 16-17 initiator
Col. 18-19 target

01-unspecified
02-clandestine (group, movement, paramil.)
03-social or political movement/leader
04-extremist political group
05-extremist political group-Communist
06-refugee/leader

10-economic
11-big business/managers/professional
12-small business/shopkeepers
13-agriculture
14-worker/laborer
15-trade union group/leader

20-Chief of State or military junta
21-former Chief of State
22-member of cabinet
23-presidential candidate
24-other national govt. official
25-political party/leader
26-judicial (national)
27-legislative (national)
28-military
29-police
30-Monarch
31-hereditary heir
32-tribal chief or official
33-colonial official
34-foreign government official
35-state governor
36-state legislator
37-state judiciary
38-other state official
39-major

40-educational, unspecified
41-educational, students
42-educational, professor/teacher
43-educational, leader/administrator
44-press/owners/correspondents
45-radio/television

50-religious leader

60-medical/doctors/physicians

80-International Organization

9. NATURE OF GROUP
Col. 20-22 initiator
Col. 23-25 target
*** code only if minority involved***

999 - no data
001 - all minorities
002 - majority of minorities
003 - Arab
004 - Assamese
005 - Baluchi
006 - Bantu
007 - Bengali
008 - Berber
009 -
010 - Buddist
011 - Catholic
012 - Chinese
013 - Christian
014 - Christian, Battak
015 - Christian, Copt
016 - Colored
017 - Croats
018 - French
019 - Gujarti
020 - Hindu
021 - Hindu, Balinese
022 - Indian (India)
023 - Indian (Western Hemisphere)
024 - Indian, Mulatto
025 - Indian, Negro
026 - Italian
027 - Jewish
028 - Jakartan
029 - Kannada
030 - Kurd
031 - Macedonian
032 - Madurese
033 - Magyar
034 - Malay
035 - Malayalam
036 - Maori
037 - Marathi
038 - Menangkaban
040 - Mestizo-Indian
041 - Moor (Ceylon)
042 - Moslem
043 - Moslem, Bosnian
044 - Moslem, Malay
045 - Mulatto
046 - Negro
047 - Negro-Mestizo
048 - Negro-Mulatto
049 - Oriya
050 - Protestant
051 - Punjabi
052 - Scotch
053 - Sikh
054 - Slovak
055 - Slovene
056 - Sudanese

057 - Sundhi
058 - Swedish
059 - Tamil
060 - Tamil, Ceylon
061 - Torajada
062 - Turkish
063 - Walloon
064 - Welsh
065 - Moslem, Druse
066 - Moslem, Sunni
067 - Moslem, Maronite
068 - Puerto Rican
069 - Buganese
070 - Flemish
071 - Sinhalese
072 - Episcopal
073 - Jurassian
074 - Dukobors, Orthodox
075 - Dukobors, Extremist
076 - Spanish
077 - German
078 - Telegu
079 - Nagas (India)
080 - Moslem, Shia
081 - Mexican-Americans
082 - Nungs (S. Vietnam)
083 - Papuans
084 - Karens (Burma)
085 - Oriental
086 - Cao Dai, Hoa Hao, etc.
087 - Sumatrins (Indonesia)
088 - Rumanians
089 - English
090 - Bahais (Iran)
091 - Huks (Philippines)
092 - Greeks (Cyprus)
093 - Kachens (Burma)
094 - Bedouins (Syria)
095 - Biharis (India)
096 - Greek Orthodox
097 - Georgian (USSR)
098 - Sorbs (E. Germany)

110 - Moslem Brotherhood
111 - Dutch

200 - majority
201 - Majority group
          sympathetic to
          minority
202 - Majority group
          unsympathetic to
          minority group

300 - Government, federal
          national

301 - Government, state
           provincial
302 - Government, local
           municipal

303 - Government, foreign
304 - United Nations
305 - Colonial government

10. NUMBER KILLED
Col. 26
      1 through 9

11. NUMBER WOUNDED
Col. 27
      1 through 9

12. TARGET NAME AND DESCRIPTION
Col. 31-54

13. ASSASSIN NAME AND DESCRIPTION
Col. 55-69

14. REFERENCE
      Col. 70-71 (month)
      Col. 72-73 (day)
      Col. 74-75 (year)
      Col. 77-78 (page number)
      Col. 80   (column number)

NOTE: If an EB appears in columns 78-80, then the reference is the Encyclopedia Brittanica Yearbook.

NOTE: If a DD appears in columns 79-80, then the reference is the Deadline Data service.

In all other cases the reference is the *New York Times*.

EXPLANATORY NOTES:

ASSASSINATION CODE INDEX

Field 3.   DATE
a)   In cases where the assassination date is not known the DATE field is filled with zeroes indicating missing data. Thus, if the code 040059 appeared in the DATE field, the assassination would have taken place in April on an unknown day in 1959.

b)   Since the data were collected from the *New York Times Index* in the majority of cases, the date of the assassination event is given as the date of the *New York Times* issue in which the article appeared, unless specific reference was given to the actual date in the index. The time lag between the assassination event and the date the story was reported in the *New York Times* is typically one to three days.

Field 4.   OUTCOME
             An assassination is coded as successful only if the
             primary target of the assassination is killed.

Field 5.   ACTION
   a)   An assassination is operationally defined as the suc-
             cessful or unsuccessful premeditated murder of a
             politically significant person. The assassin must ac-
             tively try to murder the target or be apprehended in
             the attempt.

   b)   An assassination plot is by definition unsuccessful
             since it never reaches the stage of attempted murder.
             Typically, the government will report that a plot to
             assassinate the Chief of State has been broken up and
             the ringleaders arrested.

Field 6.   MINORITY HOSTILITY
             Minority hostility is coded "yes" whenever the target
             and the assassin are of different minority groups or
             one is of a majority and the other of a minority
             group. The groups involved are further described by
             the coding in Field 9 NATURE OF GROUP. Field 9
             is always coded if Field 6 is coded "yes."

Field 7.   NATURE OF TENSION
             This coding tries to discriminate among the reasons
             or motivations for the assassination event. If the
             reason cannot be determined then a "1" (political) is
             coded.

2. Data Collected by Feierabend Group

ASSASSINATION EVENTS-BY COUNTRY

PRINTOUT

Code	Flag	Name	Note	Date
0010711572210130	00	ZAHIR SHAH, KING		071257,18.1
0011124592210122	01	NAIM, MIN	ANTI-COMMUNIST	112459,30.6
0021024491210427	10	BISBASH, DEPUTY		102449,09.7
0020405501212222	10	SHEHU DEP PREMIER	SHEHU A, UND SEC	040550,02.2
0030925482213420	00	PERON, PRES		092548,25.1
0030225502210125	01	MINSK H, RADICAL PTY		022850,21.1
0030329512210120	00	PERON, PRES	REYES C	032951,11.3
0030427522210120	00	PERON, PRES	USA, CHARGED	042752,22.1
0030000532210120	00	PERON, PRES		EE
0030505532210122	00	REMORIN, MIN	OLIVER RC, NTLST	050553,05.3
0030816552210320	00	PERON, PRES		081655,01.5
0030624572210122	00	ROJAS, VICE-PRES		062455,30.7
0030813642210121	00	FRONDIZI A, EX-PRES		DD
0040313602210128	00	CABRERA, MAJ	HOME BOMBED	031360,04.6
0040622662210125	01	CALDWELL, OPP LAB PTY LDR	KOCAN PR	062266,05.2
0050506521210129	10	LAPUSNYIK, SEC POL CHF		060562,01.2
0060819501210105	10	LAHAUT L, COMM PTY CHRMN	GUNMEN	081950,01.6
0070419552210120	00	PAZ ESTENSSORO, PRES		041955,13.2
0070503561210139	10	ROCA H, GUAYARAMERIA	POLIT OPP	050456,06.8
0070125582210120	00	SUAZO SILES, PRES		012558,05.6
0071226602210134	00	STROM, AMB. (US)	HOME BOMBED	122660,02.4
0070226642210128	00	ORTUNO B, GEN	SHOT	022664,02.5
0070816642210124	00	BARRIENTOS, VP	CAR BOMBED	081664,64.4
0070906642210124	00	BARRIENTOS, VP	HOUSE BOMBED	092264,06.1
0070323652210123	00	BARRIENTOS, GEN		032365,10.4
0070523652210123	00	BARRIENTOS, GEN		052365,04.1
0080417482210522	00	PEREIRA DE COSTA, MIN		041748,05.5
0080910501210136	10	ARTTIAGA G, STATE LEGIS		091050,04.1
0080654421210144	01	LACERDA, ANTI-VARGUS ED		080654,04.3

Code	ID Number	Name / Target	Description	Date
00	008062756222210120	KUBITSCHEK, PRES	ANARCHISTS, COMM	062756,10.1
10	008021457112210127	MARQUES DE SILVA J	GOV FALCO AVDES	021457,11.4
08	008101663222210135	LACERDA, GOV	GOULART AVDES	101563,15.1
08	008112864222210125	LACERDA		091164.28.6
08	008030765222210124	GOVT LDRS		030765,03.1
08	008030965222210128	ALVES BASTOS, GEN	BRIZOLA, EX-GOV	030965.23.4
08	008030866222212935	MENEGHETTI, GOV	COMMUNISTS	030866,19.8
10	008072566212210523	COSTA DE SILVA, GEN		072666,14.6
10	008111666112210136	ROCHA J, OPP PTY		111666,12.2
10	010041148112210531	TAW, PRINCE		041148,22.1
10	010041248112210524	SAN U AUNG AND GOVT LDRS		041248.03.1
10	010008304811210527	THEIN SAW BA, EX-LEG	BOMB	103148,75.4
10	010009184811210522	TUT U TIN, EX-FOR MIN	BOMB IN CAR	091948,42.1
90	010009024911110224084200	HLA SAO TIN, SAWBWA	KARENS	090349,02.5
10	010101145011210125	IOE KOEUX, DEMO PTY LDR	SERVANT	011650,06.4
10	010111000511110133	DE RAYMOND J, FR COMMISS		EB
08	010110901592210130	SURAMARIT, KING	BOMB	090159,57.1
08	010110901592210130	NORODOM SURAMARIT, KING		090159,57.1
08	010102146022210120	SIHANOUK, PREM	CIA, CHARGED	021460,12.2
08	010102096722210130	SIHANOUK N, PRINCE		021967,25.5
08	010205196622210127	MEM PARLIAMENT		051966,06.5
08	010131202582210124	GOONETILEKE, GOV GEN	CHARTIER PJ	120258,10.5
10	010309265911215020	BANDARANIKE, PM	BUDDHIST MONK	092659,01.2
01	010160818512212820	MAO TSE TUNG	BARRET, EXMIL AT	081851,02.5
08	010160112582210122	CHOU EN LAI, PREMIER		013158.02.7
08	010160307582210520	CHAING KAI SHEK, PRES	NIEH SHIH-MEN	030758,05.3
10	010170409481210125	GAITAN J, LIB PTY LDR		EB
10	010170410481212524	GRITAN JE, SENATOR		041048,01.8
10	010170525482212525	RESTREPO BOTERO	GUNMAN	052548,12.6
10	010170622481212525	HENAO BLANCO B, LIB LDR		062248,19.4
04	004170110562110121	LLERAS CAMARGE, EX-PRES		011056,05.5
10	010170314581210123	ARBELAEZ CIFUENTES		030458,08.5
08	010170427652210120	VALENCIA, PRES		042765,22.5
10	010180302481210101	VALERDE, PTY SUPP		030248,15.3
08	008180514562210120	FIGUERES S, PRES	BAKER AP, HOND	051456,03.4

ID	Code	Name	Note	Ref
0190717481121010129	10	HERNANDEZ VEGA		071748,05.6
0190901481121010115	10	AREVALO Y VEITIA, LAB LDR		EB
0190107492221013420	00	SOCARRAS P, PRES	DOM REP CHARGED	010749,10.3
0190405491121010141	10	FUENTES J, STUDENT LDR		040549,14.6
0190419492121010103	01	SALAZAR LF, REV LDR		042049,03.2
0190902491121010125	10	SALAZAR G, SOCIALIST LDR		090249,07.5
0190749492121010427	00	MASFERRER, REP		091749,02.6
0190927501121010122	10	PANIAGUA RT, TRES UND SEC		092750,27.2
0190213521121010122	10	PINO A, EX-MIN OF INT		021352,35.8
0190214521121010124	10	COSINO DEL PINO, XSEC INT		021452,04.4
0191112521121010144	10	GONZALES-REBULL, PUB		111252,02.2
0190127552221014120	00	BATISTA, PRES ELECT	STUDENTS	012755,05.6
0191007562221010220	00	BATISTA, PRES	SOCARRAS, EXPRES	100756,06.5
0191029561121010128	10	BLANCO RICO, CHF MIL INT		102956,06.3
0191115572121010129	00	PIEDRA, POLICE AIDE		011557,12.4
0190615572221010124	00	REY, MIN OF INT		061557,03.5
0190930581121010103	10	VEGA A		093058,08.6
0190203592221010120	00	CASTRO	NYE, US LINKED	020359,15.1
0190203592221012820	00	CASTRO	COBRAS	020359,15.1
0190327592221010120	00	CASTRO		032759,07.6
0190329592221010120	00	CASTRO	DE LA FE	032959,32.6
0190607592121010124	00	ECHAZABAL, AMB	KNIFE	060759,01.4
0191022592121010120	00	CASTRO F, PREMIER	USA, CHARGED	102359,01.2
0190715602121010129	10	NOGUERIA, M, MAJ		071560,02.1
0190726612221010128	00	CASTRO RAUL	ARTIME, CIA LNK	080961,01.5
0190306662221010120	00	CASTRO F, PREMIER	USA, CHARGED	030666,25.1
0190807672221010120	00	CASTRO F	CIA CHARGED	080767,13.1
0191014672221010120	00	CASTRO F	USA, CHARGED	101467,01.6
02003225621140233092305	00	HARDING	SOPHOCLEOS N	032256,01.2
0200617561121010234	10	BOTELER, US VICE CONSUL		061756,17.1
02011075611140233092305	00	WILLIAMSON, AST DIST COMR		110756,36.8
0200813612221013434	00	NASSER	ISR. AGENTS-CYP	081661,04.6
0200204642121010122	00	KYPRIANOU, MIN		020464,05.4
0210229482121010522	01	ORTINA, JUSTICE MIN		022948,01.1
0211210482121212820	00	GOTTWALD, PRES		121048,20.3

021030650112101125	10	TAUSINGER, SLOVAK COM LDR		030650,04.5
021020952222210120	08	GOTTWALD, PRES	RSIANSKY, GHUSAK	020952,04.6
021012254212101120	01	ZAPOTOCKY		012254,07.4
023042751122101120	00	TRUJILLO, PRES		042751,17.1
023100452112101104	10	REQUENA, REGIME FOE		100452,03.8
023012960222101120	00	TRUJILLO, PRES		012960,01.5
023060161112122820	10	TRUJILLO, PRES	DIAZ JT, GEN	060161,01.8
023070465212101123	00	BALAGUER	SHOTS INTO HOME	070465,12.3
023101765112105525	10	CABRAL ORTIZ AS		101765,26.6
023122065212101120	08	CAAMANO		122065,01.6
025110449212101120	00	PLAZA LASSO	OPP BOMB PLOT	110449,08.4
025101253222101420	00	VELASCO	MONTUFAR, COL	101253,05.8
025092454212127827	01	CANARTE BARBERO, DEPUTY		092454,06.4
026042648212101121	01	NAHAS PASHA, EX-PREMIER		042648,01.7
026112648212101120	00	NOKRASHY PASHA, PREMIER		122948,01.4
026122948112042011020	10	NOKRASHY PASHA, PREMIER		122948,01.4
026021349112010420110200	10	BANA H EL, CHF MOSLEM BRO	HASSAN, MOS BRO	021349,01.6
02605114921120427110200	00	GOUDA, DEP CHMBS PRES		050649,11.2
02608245122120430110200	00	FAROUK, KING		082451,08.2
02610275421110420110200	00	NASSER ABDUL, PREMIER	MOSLEM BRO	102754,09.1
02610315422110425211200	00	REV COMMAND COUNCIL	MOSLEM BRO	103154,05.1
026112661222213420	00	NASSER	LATIF, MOSLEM BRO	112761,08.4
026012862222213420	00	NASSER	LATIF, MOSLEM BRO	012962,04.5
026032363212101142	00	KLEINWAECHTER, SCIENTIST	MATTEI, 3 FR REP	032363,01.4
02609276522120220110200	00	NASSER	BELLIVIER, FR	092765,02.1
02610056522120224110200	00	GOVT OFFICIALS	ISRAELI AGENTS	100565,04.3
02603006622210420110200	00	NASSER	MOSLEM BRO	071966,08.5
02709145721210620	00	LEMUS, PRES	MOSLEM BRO	EB
027120563212101122	00	FINANCE MIN	RAMADAN S	120563,02.4
028072751221221230	00	HAILE SELASSIE, EMP	REFUGEE	072751,08.4
02807136221210122	00	ABEYE ABEBE, MIN INT		DD
030012149212101124	01	RALIN-LABOUREUR, DEPUTY	MIN OF STATE	012149,14.3
03005265711110203003003	00	CHEKKAL ALI, PRO FRENCH	MACHINE GUNNED	052757,01.8
030103157211210227	00	BORGEAUD H, ALGERIAN SEN	SAKOK M BEN	110157,05.4
030112757221210222	00	BARAKROK A, ALG SEC STATE	N AFR TERRORIST	112857,06.5

030091061121210220	00	DEGAULLE C, PRES	OAS	091961,01.5
030110461222104020	00	DEGAULLE C, PRES	RT WING OPP	110461,02.8
030052262222102200	00	DEGAULLE, PRES	OAS	052262,09.3
030061962222210120	00	DEGAULLE, PRES	GUERTITOT	061962,08.3
030082362212102200	01	DEGAULLE, PRES	OAS	082362,01.7
030112862222212820	00	DEGAULLE, PRES	GRAS, EX-LT	112862,02.5
030030163222210120	00	POMPIDOU, PREMIER	TERRORISTS	030163,01.4
030082964212101200	00	DEGAULLE, PRES		082964,18.2
030052665222110200	00	DEGAULLE, PRES		052665,03.1
030022566222210122	00	MATANZIMA, CHF MIN		022566,03.7
031111255221210120	00	NKRUMAH K, PM	BOMB HOME	111255,03.8
031111158222101204	00	NKRUMAH K, INT MIN		111159,08.3
031052459222101200	00	NKRUMAH, PRIM MIN		052459,31.1
031053061222101200	00	MAGA		053061,05.1
031080262221212420	00	NKRUMAH	ADJEI, MIN	080262,03.6
031010364221210120	00	NKRUMAH, PRES		010364,01.8
031030364212129200	00	NKRUMAH, PRES	AMETEWEE, EX-POL	030364,11.1
032050248112105240	10	LADES, MIN	COMM YOUTH	050248,01.2
032012549221210522	00	KANALLOPOULOS, MIN	COMMUNISTS	012549,16.4
032031249222210528	00	VAN FLEET, LT GEN	COMMUNISTS	031249,04.7
032052463112101270	11	LAMBRAKIS, DEP	MOTORCYCLIST	052463,03.6
032071364222210420	00	PREMIER	RIGHT WING PLT	DD
033071949112101280	10	ARANA, COL, C/S		071949,01.2
033011254221210127	01	ARRIOLA, CONGRESS PRES		01254.04.7
033072057112105200	10	CASTILLO ARMAS, PRES	SANCHEZ RV, COMMO	072857,01.8
033012357222210224	00	OLIVA, NAT SEC CHIEF	OPP LDRS	102257,01.6
033012562222212520	10	YDIGORAS, PRES	REVOL PTY	DD
033012562112101290	10	GONZALES R, CHF SECRT POL		DD
033012662112105290	10	ONELLE, POLICE CHF		012662,05.4
033052265112105220	10	ARRIAGO, VICE MIN	COMM TERR	052265,08.4
033110165112101230	10	MENDEZ MONTENEGRO, REV PTY		110165,16.4
033050566112101240	10	MORALES B, PRESS SEC		-050566,39.8
033081666112102030	10	ORELLANO PORTILLO, ANTICM	TERRORISTS	082166,10.1
033050467112101020	10	ALDANA RM, EX-GUER LDR		050467,13.1
034070748112101240	10	GOVT PRINT OFF DIR		070748,04.7

034091858221210120	00	DUVALIER, PRES	EDELSON AM	091858,11.6
034052092121210134	00	ESCHAZABAL, CUBAN AMB		050359,20.5
034060759212101 34	00	ESCHAZABAL, CUBAN AMB		060759,28.6
034063067121210120	10	DUVALIER, PRES		063067,18.1
036110556112102 25	00	GERO, EX HEAD COMM PTY	REBELS	110556,25.1
038012148212101 03	10	GANDHI		012148,04.3
038013148112101 03	00	GANDHI	GODSE, MOS. FAN.	013148,01.6
038072049212101 20	00	NEHRU, PM	BOMB PATH PLANE	072049,13.5
038080350222104 20	00	NEHRU, PM	HINDU EXTR PLOT	080350,10.6
038050553212101 20	00	NEHRU	BOMB RR TRACK	050553,06.4
038031355212101 20	00	NEHRU, PM	KOCHALE B, KNIFE	031355,01.7
038082261111104350792 00	00	AO I, CHRM OF NAGA STATE	NAGA TERRORIST	082561,09.1
038020765112101 22	10	KAIRON, EX-CHF MIN		020765,09.2
039120157222101 20	00	SUKARNO, PRES		120157,01.3
039030960212128 20	00	SUKARNO, PRES	MAUKAUR, LT	030960,03.6
039010862211102201 11200	00	SUKARNO	DUTCH PROF	010862,04.4
039051462212102 20	00	SUKARNO	DARUL ISLAM	051462,01.6
039052965222101 20	00	SUKARNO, PRES	USA, UK, CHARGED	052965,04.1
040021448112101 44	10	MASOOD M, NEWSPAPER ED		021448,05.3
040020549212104 30	01	PAHLEVI MR, SHAH		020549,01.6
040110549112101 21	10	HAJIR, EX-PREMIER	IMMANI H	110549,02.5
040052850112101 44	10	DEHGHAN, EDITOR		052850,20.6
040030851112102 44	10	RAZMARA, PREMIER	RASTEGAR AM	030851,01.6
040032651222104 28	10	HEJAZI, TEHERAN MIL GOV	FADAYAM ISLAM	032751,01.2
040032651112102 44	10	ZANGANEH, EX-EDUC MIN	GHOMI, FADAYAM I	032631,08.6
040032851222104 30	00	SHAH	FADAYAM ISLAM	032851,06.5
040021552212101 22	01	FATEMI H	MOSLEM FANATIC	021552,01.5
040021652212101 22	01	FATEMI, DEP PREMIER	FADAYAM ISLAM	021652,01.5
040030253221202 20	00	MOSSADEGH		030253,01.8
040040753221202 120	00	MOSSADEGH	ROYAL FAMILY	040753,01.7
040042753112101 29	10	AFSHARTOUS, POLICE CHF	STRANGLED	042753,01.5
040031454212101 22	01	FATEM H, FOREIGN MIN		031454,01.2
040091154222105 30	00	SHAH AND GOV OFFICIALS		091154,01.3
040111755212102 20	01	ALA, PREMIER	COMM ORG	111855,01.3
040111462112312 24	10	CHF LAND REFORM	MOSLEM FANATIC	DD

ID	Code	Name	Detail	Reference
0400122655112101022	10	MANSOUR, PREMIER	BOKHARAII M	012265,06.3
0400412652121110030	00	SHAH	SUB-MACHINE GUN	041265,10.5
0410324542121010130	00	FEISAL, KING		032454,03.6
0411008592121010120	01	KASSIM		100859,01.2
0411014592221010120	00	KASSIM		101659,01.1
0411025592121010120	00	KASSIM		102559,05.4
0410100661111022803020	0200	MUSTAFA B, COL	KURDS	020466,11.7
0430718481121010180	10	BERNADOTTE, UN MEDIATOR		091848,02.6
0430724552121010222	10	ROKACH I, MIN		072455,31.5
0431030572221010120	08	BEN GURION, PREMIER	DUEK M	103057,01.7
0440715482121014105	05	TOGLIATTI, DEPUTY, COMM	PALLANTE, STDT	071548,01.2
0440620491121010131	01	TORLONIA, PRINCE		062049,08.5
0440328551121010538	10	CHRISTIAN DEM LOCAL LDR		032855,04.2
0450721482221010105	22	TOKUDA, PTY GEN SEC		072148,13.1
0450706491121010122	00	SHIMOYAMA, TRANSPORT MIN		070649,16.3
0450714602121010420	00	KISHI, PREM	ARAMAKI, T	071460,02.1
0450126011214003	01	ASANUMA, SOCIALIST LDR	YAMAGUCHI, O STU	101260,01.5
0450820612221010134	10	MIKOYAS, USSR	PLOT IN JAPAN	082061,13.1
0451219612221010420	00	IKEDA, PREMIER	ULTRA RIGHTIST	121261,17.1
0450716632221010422	00	KONO, MIN	ULTRA-RIGHTIST	071663,04.4
0451105632121010410	00	IKEDA, PREMIER	RIGHTIST	110563,15.4
0450324642121024024	00	REISCHAUER, AMB	STUDENT	032464,04.4
0460721511112100431	10	ABDULLAH, KING	MASHU, MOSLEM	072151,01.6
0460713582221010130	00	HUSSEIN, KING		071358,23.3
0460329602221010124	00	MAJALI, PREM	UAR, CHARGED	032960,30.5
0460830601121010124	10	MAJALI, PREM	TIME BOMB	083060,01.6
0460315632221010130	10	HUSSEIN, KING		030563,03.6
0460501642221010130	00	HUSSEIN, KING		050164,05.5
0470125482121010129	00	CHANG, POLICE CHIEF	ANZTAHIR	012548,40.7
0470619481121010128	10	BAK, COL	SHOT IN SLEEP	061948,06.5
0470203492221010280	10	UN COMMITTEE MEMBERS		021249,01.5
0470804491121212821	10	KIM KOO, EX-PROV LDR	AN DU HI, LT	080449,10.2
0470813491121010529	10	KIM HO SIK, POLICE CAPT	LEE YUNG WOON	081349,02.7
0470605502221010120	10	RHEE, PRES	CHO MAI	060550,08.6
0471226502121010222	00	TEX BAN CHANG, VICE MIN		122650,02.6

ID	Code	Name	Note	Date
04706145222210524	00	GOVT LDRS	COMMUNISTS	061452,02.6
04706255221210120	00	RHEE, PRES	TAI RS, ULT-NAT	062552,01.8
04711209532210520	00	GOVT LDRS	COMMUNISTS	120953,04.7
04701195521212834	00	TAYLOR M, US ARMY C/S	KIM KAI OK, MAJ	011955,03.7
04703245522210520	00	RHEE S, PRES	COMMUNISTS	032455,10.4
04710085522212520	10	RHEE S, PRES	HO KJ, IND PTY	100855,07.1
04701305611212828	11	KIM CHANG YONG, ARMY INT	HUH TAI YUNG	013056,03.4
04709285621210122	00	CHANG, VICE PRES	KIM-SANG BOON	092856,06.5
04703096011210125	00	PTY LEADERS		DD
04701146222210120	00	PARK CHUNG KEE, PRES		011362,02.2
04710296322210120	00	PARK, PRES		102963,12.5
04709196422210120	00	PARK, PRES		091964,03.4
04708146522210524	10	GOVT OFFICIALS	NORTH KOREANS	081465,03.4
04809205411210522	10	KOUVORAVONG	COMM TERRORISTS	092054,01.4
04802126311210128	11	VONGSAVONG K, EX-C/S		DD
04803156311210124	10	KHAMPHUEY THAO, INSP EDUC		DD
04804026311210122	10	QUINIM PHOLSENA, MIN		040263,01.8
04804076311210122	10	TIM BURIPHAT, MIN		040763,01.7
04804136311210129	00	VISAPHANTHONG KHANTI, COL		041363,04.6
04804206321210122	10	PHOUMI VOGNVICHIT, MIN	PLANE SHOT	042063,02.4
04812066311210128	10	LEUANG, COL INTEL CHIEF		120663,07.3
04803176411210128	01	PRASEUTH, INT OFFICER		032064,06.5
04803136621210131	00	NITH NIKHAM, PRINCE		031366,32.7
04903155021210120	10	SOLH R ES-, PREMIER	SYRIAN ARMY	031550,04.5
04910315011210134	10	HINNAWI, GEN	BARAZI A	103150,14.4
04907175111210322	00	SOLH R ES-, EX-PREMIER	SYR NAT SOC PTY	071751,12.2
04907185321210123	00	ABBOUD, PRES CAND	POL OPPONENT	072453,05.3
04907245311210123	00	ABBOUD, PRES CAND		072453,05.3
04911235621210120	00	EL YAFI, PREMIER		112356,21.2
04907305821210120	00	SOLH R ES-, PREMIER		073058,01.7
04908105811210125	10	HAMMOUD A, PTY LDR		DD
04905195921210120	10	KARAMI, PREMIER		051959,05.1
04907275911210122	00	MOGHABHAB N, EX-MIN		DD
04903076121210120	10	SALAAM	5 PERSONS	070161,04.3
04905176611210144	10	MROWA K		051766,06.5

ID	Code	Name	Note	Ref
0500062455211212520	00	TUBMAN, PRES	OPPOSITION PTY	062455,01.2
0500206632322210120	00	TUBMAN, PRES	SINUSSI, QNREL	020663,03.1
0511006541121312122	10	SHALHI, PALACE AFF MIN		100654,05.2
0530113501121010133	10	STEWART, BRITISH GOV		011350,05.6
0530428502121210233	00	GIMSON F, GOV		EB
0531007511121210524	10	GURNEY H, HIGH COMR		100751,01.6
0530502531121210505	10	COMM GUER LDR	BODYGUARD	050253,06.5
0530915531121210505	10	COMM GUER LDR	COMMUNIST	091553,04.3
0531010572222210120	00	RAHMAN, PRIME MIN		101057,04.5
0540218481121210124	10	ANGULO M. SENATOR		021848,10.6
0540622581121210503	10	MONREAL J MARGUEZ		062258,26.2
0540307591121010127	10	ALTAMIRANO H, SEN	MARTINEZ E	030759,08.1
0550061248211103350 42027	10	HAJOUI MOHAMMED, PASHA	MOSLEM FANATIC	061248,13.1
0550912532121210130	01	SULTAN		091253,01.6
0550226542121210130	00	CALIPH OF CASABLANCA		022654,03.1
0550306542121010130	01	SULTAN OF MOROCCO		030654,01.4
0550317541121210124	10	HAROUCINS SB, MORD OFF		031754,06.2
0550526542121010121	00	GUILLAUMS		052654,01.3
0550621541121210133	01	D-HAUTEVILLE, MAJ GEN		062154,04.4
0550630541121010144	10	EYRAUD, PUBLISHER		EB
0550830542121010127	10	ISTIQUAL MEMBER		083054,05.2
0551017541121010112	01	SLIIAI, SHEIKH		101754,12.2
0550302551121210725	10	MOULAY IDRISS, DEMFREEMEN		030255,05.5
0550612551114281100 3018	10	LEMAIGRE-DUBREVIL		061355,02.3
0551030551121210103	10	RAISSI BOUCHAID		103055,16.1
0550418562211013401 8303	00	MENDES-FRANCE	2FR IN MOROCCO	041856,10.6
0550509561121210125	10	LARAQUI, DEM IND PTY SEC		051056,04.5
0550228602221210131	00	HASSAN, PRINCE		022860,20.3
0571232352222210122	00	HOLLAND, PM		122352,04.8
0580422512221210120	00	SOMOZA, PRES-ELECT	LOPEZ PEREZ R	042251,17.1
0580406541121210120	00	SOMOZA, PRESIDENT	GOMEZ R	040654,17.1
0580923561121210120	00	SOMOZA, PRES	PRO-CUBANS	092356,01.8
0580423582221210120	00	SOMOZA, PRES	RED SHIRTS	042358,15.4
0580925642221210120	00	SCHICK, PRES		092564,16.4
0600315492221210282	00	KHAN AQ, NW PRVNCE PREM		031549,12.3

Code	Flag	Subject	Reference	ID
06010175111210420	10	LIAQUAT ALI KAHN, PM	AKTAR S, MOSLEM	101751,01.2
06005095811212720	10	ALI SHAHED	LEGISLATORS	EB
06007105822210124	08	GOVT MINS		071058,06.3
06013065112210144	10	ZAQURESHI, JOURNALIST		013065,05.5
06107214822210120	08	JIMENEZ, PRES		072148,02.3
06103025122210129	08	REMON, POLICE CHIEF	NICARAGUANS	030251,09.1
06101025511210120	10	REMON, PRES	MIRO R, GUIZADO	010355,01.8
06105216421212444	01	CALVO E, ED LA HORA	BOYD A	DD
06106016611214141	10	NAVAS J, STDT LDR	GRANADOS M	071566,02.5
06203294922212522	10	RIVERA SCHREIBER, SECGEN	COX CM, APRISTA	032949,03.8
06211055622210124	08	GOV AIDES, COLORADO PTY		110556,11.3
06210026422212820	08	STROESSNER. PRES		100264,12.2
06401174822210120	08	QUIRINO, PRES	MILITARY	011749,08.7
06404294911140203091200	20	QUEZON, WIFE OF 1ST PRES	HUKS	042949,01.5
06407124921210123	08	LAUREL JP, PRES CAND		071249,10.6
06403045022140224091200	08	GOVT OFFICIALS	HUKS	030450,05.5
06411025011110227091200	10	FELICIANO J, CONG	HUKS	110250,02.5
06407295122220222091200	00	QUIRINO, PRES	HUKS	072951,03.6
06401025321211435	01	PROVINCIAL GOV	WORKER	010253,18.6
06409085722210123	00	MANAHAN, PRES CAND		090857,33.1
06410135722210120	00	GARCIA, PRES		101357,03.3
06406226022110220091200	08	GARCIA, PRES	HUKS	062260,05.5
06411206122210120	08	MACAPAGAL		112061,17.4
06407316211110139091200	10	MAGALLOWS		073162,11.5
06404256322210320	08	MACAPAGAL, PRES		042563,14.3
06405226611210144	10	GARCIA A, PUB		052266,79.8
06407186611110239091200	10	MAYOR	HUKS	071866,11.5
06606255022210120	00	SALAZAR, PREMIER		062550,29.1
06604286511210128	10	DELGADO, GEN		042865,06.1
06805045722210130	00	SAUD. KING	EGYPT LINKED	050457,01.7
06809276511122804200110	10	BEN MUSSAED KHALID	MILITARY	092765,02.1
06902215011212824	10	GALLOSTRA J, MIN	FLEITAS GS	022150,15.3
06905256222210106	08	PERON, EX-PRES OF ARG		052562,07.1
07010275421210120	08	AZHARI, PREMIER		102754,24.8
07310135021210128	00	SHISHAKLI, AST CHF STAFF	SHARABATE, EXMIN	101350,05.3

ID	Code	Description	Group	Ref
0730201521121010121	10	EL KODSI, EX PRES	SOCIALISTS	021052,06.8
0730419551112527	10	SHISHEKLY G,	SOC NATL PTY	041955,10.4
0730423551112528	10	MAKLI COL A, DEP C/S		042355,04.3
0730825552110128	01	SALEH H, MIL PROSECUTOR		082555,09.5
0730222562212528	00	3 HIGH MIL OFFICERS	SOC NAT PTY MEM	022256,30.6
0730227571110103	10	JEDID, COL, PTY LDR		022757,08.4
0740521482121010144	01	THONGWANITCH S, NEWSMAN		052148,13.8
0740311572210124	00	GOVT LDRS		031457,09.1
0740821662210120	00	THANOM KITTIKACHORN, PRM	SOROT HEMAWONG	082166,15.4
0750615522210131	00	BEY OF TUNIS	POISON PLOT	061552,18.1
0750316531210432	10	MAHDIA CHIEF	NATIONALISTS	031653,03.1
0750503531210428	10	KASTAUI, TUNIS CC VP	NATIONALISTS	050353,01.5
0750602532110122	00	RAIS, MIN		060253,03.6
0750602532110122	00	RAIS B, MIN OF COMMERCE	GUNMAN	060253,03.6
0750702531110131	00	AZZEDINE BEY, PRINCE		070253,01.4
0750718531210132	10	PRO-FRENCH CHIEF		071853,05.3
0750909531110132	10	PRO-FRENCH SHEIK		090953,13.3
0750913532110129	10	TOUMI, GEN, PRO-FR INSP		091353,10.1
0750914531210125	01	NATIONALIST LDR		091453,12.3
0750531542110120	10	M-ZALI, PREMIER		053054,10.1
0750803541110129	00	PR INSPECTOR OF SOUSSE		080454,03.1
0750523551110225	10	DESTOUR PTY LDR		052455,07.1
0750327561110227	10	BOUZAINE H, DEPUTY	TERRORIST	032756,17.1
0750301582210120	00	BOURGUIBA, PRES	BEN YOUSSEH S	030158,04.1
0751227622212820	00	BOURGUIBA	MEHREZI	122762,02.3
0761117492212520	00	INONU, PRES	NATION PTY MEM	111749,01.2
0761007572121012122	00	CABINET MINS		100757,02.5
0760129612121120	00	OPPOSITION LDR	MENDERES, EXPREM	012961,24.3
0760222642121010120	00	INONU, PREMIER	SUNA M	022264,01.8
0770410602121011320	01	VERWOERD, PRIME MIN	PRATT WHT FRMR	041060,01.6
0770207631210132	10	GOOBOZA, CHF TEMBU TRIBE	POQO MEMBERS	DD
0770906661110120	10	VERWOERD, PRIME MIN	TSAFENDAS, WHITE	090766,01.8
0790420482130115	01	REUTHER W, LAB LDR		EB
07911015021140420068200	00	TRUMAN H, PRES	PR NATIONALISTS	110250,01.7
07903015421110427068200	05	REPRESENTATIVES	PR NATLS	EB

Code		Subject	Name	Reference
07904125921210135	01	ALMOND, GOV OF VIRG.		041259,70.5
07904026122210120	08	KENNEDY JF, PRES		040261,48.5
07912026222210115	08	HOFFA JR, TEAMSTER UNION	SWANSON W	120662,47.3
07904126321210124	08	WALKER		041263,12.2
07905126321150103200046	08	KING AD, REVEREND		DD
07906136311140103200046	10	EVERS MEDGAR, CIV RTS LDR		061363,01.8
07911236311210120	10	KENNEDY J, CONNALLY J		112363,01.7
07911246311210101	10	OSWALD LH,	OSWALD LEE H	DD,
07902156522140103200046	08	KING MARTIN L, CIV RTS LDR	RUBY J	022465,28.1
07902226511210103	10	MALCOLM X, BLK MUSLIMS		022265,01.2
07903216521150103200046	08	KING AD, REVEREND	HAGAN T	DD
07907206521211124	08	TAYLOR MAXWELL, AMB		DD
07908266711210125	10	ROCKWELL L, AM NAZI PTY		072065,01.7
08211145011212820	10	DELGADO CHALBAUD, PRES	SNIPER	082667,01.2
08204215122210021	08	BETANCOURT, EX-PRES	URBINA, GEN	111450,01.6
08203285222210124	08	ADENAUER	MIL JUNTA	042151,09.7
08212185722210124	08	ALLEGED PLOTS	BOMB IN MAIL	032852,04.5
08206256021210120	10	BETANCOURT, PRES		121857,20.4
08202086321210525	08	LEONI R, DEM ACTION PTY		062560,01.6
08202136321210528	08	GONZALEZ J, COL		DD
08206136321210528	08	BETANCOURT, PRES		DD
08211276322210123	08	PRES CANDIDATES	BOMBS IN MAIL	061363,01.1
08212026321210128	08	MARACAY, US MIL	HOUSE BOMBED	112763,03.6
08204276522210120	08	LEONI, PRES		110263,10.7
08212136621210228	08	MOREAN SOTO, ARMY C/S		042765,22.5
08308156111210106	10	SALAH BEN YOUSSEF	3 FOREIGNERS	121466,17.1
08404055922210320017200	08	TITO	CROATS	081561,10.3
08404376721210120	08	TITO, PRES	CRABOVAC M	040559,06.2
				032767,06.4

APPENDIX B

THE RHETORIC OF VILIFICATION AND VIOLENCE*

1. White Racist Groups

Item: Quotations from *White Power,* by George Lincoln Rockwell, p. 291: (referring to "Black Plague"—Negro people)—"It is going to take bloody violence and killing to solve this problem . . .

"To stop a plague of bed bugs takes *killing,* not words.

"To stop a plague of traitors, agitators and black half-animals is going to take *killing,* not words."

Item: From George Lincoln Rockwell's *White Power.*

p. 406: "How long before our masses of great Americans get mad enough to say, as we must, 'To hell with all the pretense and fancy talk! It's time to name the damnable Jewish, Zionist, "nigger" and Communist enemy, fight him, and kill those who are trying to commit treason, enslave us, or kill us! It's time to fight!' "

Item: The "Defensive Legion of Registered Americans," a front group for the National Knights of the Ku Klux Klan, headed by Atlanta attorney James R. Venable, used the mails in 1964 to distribute a document warning that, "blood will surely flow in the streets," and adding, "Let it flow! Let us arm our homes to make sure that Negro-Jew blood flows—not ours." The document recommended 12-gauge shotguns, high-powered rifles and telescopic sights "for distance shooting," and hollow-nosed bullets that "go clear through your game, whether two-legged or four."

Item: National Klan Wizard Venable has advised on how to retain segregated schools: "Let's close them up. Let's burn them if it comes to that."

* This material was collected for the Commission by the Anti-Defamation League of B'nai B'rith.

Item: A directive from the White Knights of the Ku Klux Klan, of Mississippi, an independent Klan that has been especially violence-prone—even by KKK standards—declared that an atheist or traitor in the community could be destroyed by social or economic pressure in most cases, but advised:

"If they continue to resist, they must be physically destroyed before they can damage our Christian civilization further to destroy us."

Item: Police in Atlanta, Ga., reported in 1958 finding the minutes of an NSRP (National States Rights Party) meeting which had begun with this prayer:

"Our heavenly father, we beseech thee to know that we will fight this battle to our last ounce of energy and to the enemy's last drop of blood. Amen."

Item: A publication of the NSRP, Maryland chapter, *Race and Nation*, declared:

"American youth is waking. It mouths the approved, worn-out 'conservative' slogans, but it is not conservative. It is Nationalist. Ideology is crumbling before ethnology. The Destiny of America points to another civil war within twenty years. An issue of such magnitude can only be settled by blood, for this is always the price of freedom."

Item: A letter from one Chet Schwarzkopf, of Atascadero, Calif., published in the *Imperial Nighthawk,* organ of James Venable's National Knights of the Ku Klux Klan, read as follows:

"Encouraged by 'liberals'—plus Washington's weakling stand—America's black primates have waxed ever-more vicious and kill-hungry.

"Anthropoids of their ilk will fear and obey one thing only —force, in the form of Hot Lead.

"Mow them down without mercy—carpet the streets with their dead—and the remainder will become 'good niggers.' "

Item: Robert Shelton, Imperial Wizard of the United Klans, published the following advice in his publication, *Fiery Cross* (applying an ambiguous usage to the word "kill"):

"When WILL our white men and women WAKE UP? The only scourge in America today is the leper Jew. Kill him, and we have no more trouble about Communism, Negroes, money, taxes, economy, or political crooks in office or getting along with the rest of the world. Kill him economically, politically, and socially. Do THIS, and the white race of all the earth will owe Americans an undying debt of gratitude."

Item: On July 16, 1965, Connie Lynch was the main speaker at an NSRP rally in Anniston, Ala. He said to the audience:

"If it takes killing to get the Negroes out of the white man's streets and to protect our constitutional rights, I say, yes, kill them."

Item: Connie Lynch, a National States Rights Party organizer and an itinerant preacher with a long background of anti-Semitism, was the chief speaker at a Ku Klux Klan rally outside St. Augustine, Fla., on Sept. 18, 1963, where he declared that, "the Klan is on the move again, and it is not going to let niggers and Jews take over the country." He then commented on the Birmingham, Ala., church bombing that took the lives of four Negro children:

"Little niggers ain't little children. Children are human . . . so, if there's four less niggers tonight, then I say good for whoever planted the bomb. We're all better off."

Lynch then stated what he thought should be the fate of a Negro dentist who lived in the city:

"You've got a burr-headed bastard of a dentist in St. Augustine that ought not to live . . . He ought to wake up tomorrow with a bullet between his eyes . . . If you were half the men you claim to be, you'd kill him before sunup."

Before the rally ended, the dentist, who had been present in the area, was beaten along with three other Negroes, and eventually spent 14 days in a hospital recovering from his injuries.

Item: "DEATH TO JEW TRAITORS AND RACE-MIXERS!"—*Rockwell Report*, November 15, 1962.

"Let me show you how we can SMASH NIGGER POWER! Niggers operate as a national gang: we need a national WHITE 'GANG'! . . .

"We need a savage, mean and vicious NATIONAL GANG of WHITE MEN, operating on a political basis, just like a swarm of deadly PIRANHAS!"

— *White Power*, Sept. 1, 1967
(written by Rockwell before his death)

"WHITES Must Keep GUNS! Gun Control Must Fail!"
— *Ibid.*

2. Right Wing Extremists

Item: In July, 1966, Robert DePugh, leader of the Minutemen, founded a "political" party, the Patriotic Party, as a Minutemen front, and set forth a program more in keeping with his established ideas than with political action in the traditional sense:

(1) Political action *alone* will not suffice.

(2) A new political party cannot win *by conventional means*.

(3) A new party *can* win if it serves its proper function as the political arm of a complete patriotic resistance movement.

In 1961, DePugh issued a booklet, *Principles of Guerrilla Warfare*, containing 50 "principles" ranging from methods of ambush and sniping to those of bombing and sabotage—many borrowed from the techniques of Mao.

Item: From *The Minutemen*, by J. Harry Jones, Jr. (Doubleday & Co., 1968), p. 92 (quoting a Minutemen publication):

Traitors beware! Even now the cross hairs are on the back of your necks. . . .

On February 27, 1963, the existence of the House Committee on Un-American Activities was . . . challenged in the House of Representatives . . . Twenty Congressmen voted against it. . . .

Here then, are the Judases who seem willing not only to sell out their country for thirty pieces of silver but to go on record and brag about it.

IN MEMORIAM

James Roosevelt (Calif.), George Brown, Jr. (Calif.), W. E. Edwards (Calif.), Edward Roybal (Calif.), William Fitts Ryan (N.Y.), Abraham Multer (N.Y.), Leonard Farbstein (N.Y.), Benjamin Rosenthal (N.Y.), Mrs. Edith Green (Ore.), Robert Duncan (Ore.), Robert W. Kastenmeier (Wisc.), Barratt O'Hara (Ill.), Thomas L. Ashely (O.) Charles Diggs (Mich.), John Dingell (Mich.), Lucien Nedzi (Mich.), Neil Staebler (Mich.), Donald Fraser (Minn.), Henry Gonzalez (Tex.), Thomas Gill (Hawaii).

Item: The Minutemen rhetoric is presented without the warning that fantasy may be involved. For example, in 1963, the Minutemen publication, *On Target,* listed the names of 20 Congressmen who had voted against the House Committee on Un-American Activities, and prefaced the list with the following warning to the Congressmen:

> ... patriots are not going to let you take their freedom away from them. They have learned the silent knife, the strangler's cord, the target rifle that hits sparrows at 200 yards. Only their leaders restrain them. Traitors beware! Even now the cross-hairs are on the back of your necks.

3. Black Extremist Groups

Item: From *The Black Panther,* May 4, 1968, from Credo for Rioters and Looters, p. 24:

> America, you will be cleansed by fire, by blood, by death. We who perform your ablution must step up our burning—bigger and better fires, one flame for all America, an all-American flame; we must step up our looting —loot, until we storm your last hoarding place, till we trample your last stolen jewel into your ashes beneath our naked black feet; we must step up our sniping—until the last pig is dead, shot to death with his own gun and the bullets in his guts that he had meant for the people. . . . We know that there are those amongst your people who are innocent, those who were brainwashed and manipulated out of their own humanity, out of their minds, out of their lives. We know who these are. These will help us burn you. These will help us loot. These will help us kill you. . . .

Item: The Communications Secretary of the Black Panthers, Kathleen Cleaver, is the wife of the Party's Minister of Information, Eldridge Cleaver, a candidate for President of the United States in 1968 of the Peace and Freedom Party. In an article that appeared in the February 10, 1968, issue of *People's World,* a Communist-oriented West Coast paper, Mrs. Cleaver summed up the outlook of the Black Panther Party with respect to the question of violence:

"The question of violence is not a question among the

oppressed; the only questions are tactical and practical; how to exercise what kind of violence with what kind of preparation and for what ends. . . .

"The Black Panther Party for Self-Defense—specifically in the Bay Area on the question of police violence—adopted a program of self-defense; the ideological and programmatic extensions of that program are the dialectics of a national liberation struggle. Violence formed the Afro-American nation de facto during the period of slavery; violence will establish the Afro-American nation politically during the period of national liberation struggles the world over. . . ."

4. The New Left

Item: By John Veneziale, Sept. 25, 1967, Skid Row Chapter, SDS (Students for a Democratic Society):

". . . I don't think the working class people of this country will ever take the student seriously until students become people again, and come off the campus, and be willing to kill and die for their (i.e., the people's) freedom."

Item: On Aug. 27, 1967, Lincoln Lynch, then CORE associate director, told 300 persons at a black mobilization rally in Chicago sponsored by the Student Non-Violent Coordinating Committee (SNCC): "If America doesn't come around, we're gonna burn it down. If there isn't a place in America for the Negro, then there won't be any America."

Item: Writing on the use of black power in a 1967 issue of Harlem CORE's publication *Rights & Reviews*, school teacher Ralph Edwards concluded:

> Any true proponent of Black Power should be *committed* to a special kind of violence—defensive violence. Yes, defensive violence, as opposed to the aggressive violence heaped upon us. . . . Defensive violence is the violence that opposes violence; it is an antiviolent violence, if you will. The idea, in any case, is far less self-annihilating than this nonsense about militant nonviolence whose most intelligible manifestation has been the blood of little black children.

Item: Malcolm X, who had called the assassination of President Kennedy a case of "chickens coming home to roost," was himself assassinated—by followers of the black Muslim sect from which he had defected. A few months later, a Harlem man named Clarence Smith (also known as "Allah" and 13X), who was believed to be a chief successor to Malcolm, threatened:

"We're going to kill the cops and all the white people—women and children, too. We're going to start a blood bath now, and if we don't get our share of poverty funds, blood will flow."

Item: H. Rap Brown advised Negroes in Washington, D.C., on July 27, 1967, to "get you some guns" and, if the Nation's Capital did not satisfy their demands, "burn this town down." Among other statements by Brown were the following:

Black people have been looting. I say there should be more shooting than looting, so if you loot, loot a gun store.

You've got to decide for yourself if you kill your enemy, because that is an individual decision. But the white man is your enemy. You got to destroy your enemy.

If you give me a gun and tell me to shoot my enemy, I might shoot Lady Bird.

Brown also assailed President Johnson as a "wild, mad dog, an outlaw from Texas."

Item: In a talk at San Francisco State College on Oct. 9, 1968, Black Panther Eldridge Cleaver shouted:

"If Huey isn't freed, we're going to free him, and we're going to do it with guns."

5. Schooling in Weaponry

Item: A Georgia UKA klavern, posing as a civic club, sponsored a series of demonstrations in the use of explosives, firearms, and guerrilla warfare after the klavern had proposed that the only way to stop integration was through "acts of violence such as arson and bombings."

Item: Like other extremist organizations of the right wing, the NSRP has opposed gun control legislation and has urged the stocking of weapons by its supporters. In a newsletter in February 1968, one of its leaders, Stoner, wrote:

If the politicians in office were honest and not controlled by the Jews, they would be calling upon all White Christians to arm themselves and stock up on ammunition instead of trying to disarm law abiding citizens . . .

Since racial civil war is already raging in America in its early stages, we Whites would be fools to ignore it. This civil war is not along geographical lines; it is not North versus South. It is a civil war with loyal White Christian Americans on one side and the Jews, communists and blacks on the other side. The object of the Jews and Negroes is to enslave or exterminate every White person in America. If we allowed that to happen, America would no longer be a White nation. . . .

Item: From *The Thunderbolt*:

". . . the NSRP (National States Rights Party) believes that every White patriot should own and possess sufficient arms and extra large quantities of ammunition. . . . We are exercising our Constitutional right to possess firearms and ammunition and say, 'Let the Jews be damned.' "

Item: Robert Scoggins, the UKA Grand Dragon for South Carolina, on gun registration:

"If you register your gun with anybody, you're a nut. When the conspiracy comes for your firearm, give it to 'em like this grand dragon is going to—right between the eyes."

Item: An appeal that ran in George Rockwell's *White Power* (the issue of Sept. 1, 1967, which appeared a few days after Rockwell himself had become an assassination victim of neo-Nazi violence) follows:

MORE GUNS! . . .

If you can spare any kind of weapons, ship them by express to 'Mike Brown' (Nazi activist and leader in the confrontation with Black Panthers) at Box 986, San Leandro, Calif.

The appeal resulted when Brown felt his arsenal for the previous confrontation was inadequate. He had then by his own account: "Three .303 bolt action enfields, one 7-mm bolt action mauser, one 12-ga. pump shotgun, two 38 revolvers, and a 9-mm luger. . . ."

Item: In 1968, the National Socialist White People's Party, of Arlington, Va. (George Lincoln Rockwell's party, now run by his heirs), announced a new subsidiary, NS Arms, to handle mail-order gun sales. Among the weapons made available through NS Arms were:

> Riot Gun . . . 12-ga., 5-shot, rapid-fire, pump action. The perfect weapon for self-defense and crowd control. . . .
> FN Model 1949 Semi-Automatic Rifle . . . This is the perfect rapid-fire sniper rifle. . . .
> Madsden Bolt-Action Rifle . . . With armor-piercing ammunition, this weapon will penetrate an engine block. . . .
> Astra .25-Caliber Semi-Automatic Pistol . . . The perfect weapon for concealing in a small area . . .
> Chemical Mace. First time offered to the public. . . . MK IV, large canister; will control a whole crowd; contains approx. 80 bursts, $10.95; with holster, $13.95. . . .

The NS bulletin offering the above for sale set forth the following rationale:

"The federal government has and will do everything in its power to see that Whites are disarmed. National Socialists must arm themselves and as many other White men who can be found to fight in the coming war—while there is still time."

The message ended:

"HEIL HITLER!"

Item: A magazine, *Black Politics*, is published in Berkeley and declares in its "Statement of Purpose" that it supports "the liberation of the oppressed masses of the world . . .

"We are part of the Black liberation movement and believe that freedom, justice, and equality must be attained by those means that the oppressed think necessary."

In its summer, 1968, issue, *Black Politics* editorialized:

"We favor gun control laws that will provide every black adult, free of charge, a rifle and handgun from the federal government until the danger of attack by racists of any kind is over."

The editorial was immediately followed by an article by George Prosser entitled, "Teach Yourself to Shoot," advocating the purchase of arms and a membership in the National Rifle Association. The article concluded with these words:

"You will acquire a deep understanding of that ancient Christian moral principle, as applied to aimed fire, *'It is better to give than to receive.'* "

Item: The May 18, 1968, issue of *The Black Panther* quoted Chairman Bobby Seale as declaring, in answer to a question about firearms at a meeting held a few days earlier:

"Every black man should have a shotgun, a 357 magnum or a .38 in his pad to defend it. . . . every woman should understand that weapon. . . ."

Item: The Minutemen's clandestine bulletins and publications, circulated to the membership, are quite specific about firearms. The following appeared in a January, 1966, bulletin:

"Don't overlook the potential of .22 long rifles, pistols or rifles, as guerrilla warfare or resistance weapons. These advantages include ready availability, light weight, fast accurate second and third shots, due to absence of recoil, light weight and readily available ammunition, good accuracy, simplicity of care, and comparatively small report when fired. The .22 can be silenced completely with materials that are always available. Although the .22 lacks killing power, this can readily be increased by filling hollow point bullets with poison."

Item: The Minutemen publication, *On Target* (issue of December 1966), was equally specific when it urged its members to arm themselves without delay. It offered five specific pieces of advice:

1. Buy a gun that is new or nearly new. . . .
2. Expect to pay a good price for a good gun. . . .
3. Avoid civilian-made copies of military-made firearms. This especially applies to copies of the .30 carbine. . . .
4. Try to buy your gun in such a way that it cannot be traced to you. If you live in a state or city that requires a permit to buy a gun, go to some other state that does not have such a requirement. Most dealers will ask your name but few will ask for identification.
5. Don't wait—buy your gun now. . . .

Item: The Black Panthers publish a bi-weekly tabloid, *The Black Panther*, which is filled with pictures and drawings of rifles and submachineguns. The Nov. 23, 1967, issue carried a page bearing the slogan "Guns Baby Guns." So did the May 4, 1968 issue.

Black Panthers have been ordered to arm themselves and defend their homes by force of arms, on pain of expulsion from the Party. A so-called "Executive Mandate No. 3" published in the March 16, 1968, issue and signed by Huey Newton, read in part as follows:

> It is . . . mandated as a general order to all members of the Black Panther Party for Self-Defense that all members must acquire the technical equipment to defend their homes and their dependents and shall do so. Any member of the Party having such technical equipment who fails to defend his threshold shall be expelled from the Party for life.

Item: In his Nov., 1965, *Bulletin*, under the heading, "Manufacture of Explosives," Robert DePugh of the Minutemen provided his members with the formula and directions for making nitroglycerine, and full details of the precise processes used in making "simple" plastic bombs, detonators, fuses, Molotov cocktails, and incendiary devices—complete with directions on "how to use."

Item: More on guns from the Minutemen *Bulletin* of January, 1966.

> Suppose the reader has no gun at all and is planning to buy one gun only . . . What shall it be? Though it will surprise many people, my recommendation is a .22 caliber semi-automatic pistol . . .
>
> It's true that the .22 lacks the "shock" effect of a more powerful cartridge, but this is largely compensated for by the ease of putting a well-placed shot into heart or brain. When needed for a second well-aimed shot can be fired quicker from a .22 than from a more powerful weapon. . . .

(Note: A .22 caliber pistol fired the shots that killed Senator Robert F. Kennedy.)

> As a deadly weapon, their effect can be greatly increased by using hollow-point bullets filled with poison. If needed, the hole in the point can be opened up further with a small drill. Sodium or potassium cyanide are two fast acting and easily obtainable poisons. Pharmacists or medical doctors will have ready access to succinyl choline or tubocurarine which are excellent when used in powdered form. If nothing better is available ordinary household lye (thirty cents for a pound can at your local grocery store) will do nicely.

For a small hideaway gun, the .25 Browning automatic is unsurpassed. A man wearing slacks and sports shirt can easily carry one of these in his side pants pocket without its ever being noticed. Quality of material and workmanship on all Browning firearms is excellent.

If my one-and-only gun were to be a rifle, once again it would be a .22. First choice would be the Browning semi-automatic which retails at $69.50. This particular rifle can be quickly divided into two parts by just pushing a button and giving the barrel a half twist. The two pieces could then be carried easily in a small suitcase.

The gun can be reassembled just as quickly and is very accurate . . .

6. The Relationship Between the Rhetoric of Violence and Violent Action

The groups which foster a rhetoric of violence produce or attract members who are willing to resort to violent action. The contemporary groups which produce the most vehement rhetoric of violence—the Ku Klux Klan, the Black Panthers and other Negro extremist groups, and the Minutemen—have produced members who use violence to attain their goals. A more expert documentation of the relationship between rhetoric and violent action follows.

Item: The relationship between the prior rhetoric of violence and actual incidents of violence was dramatically demonstrated in Meridian, Miss., on June 30, 1968, with the death of Mrs. Kathy Ainsworth, 26, a popular and attractive fifth-grade teacher from Jackson. Described as being "adored by her students and their parents," Mrs. Ainsworth was, nonetheless, a Ku Klux Klan terrorist by night. She was shot to death by police officers in Meridian when she and a 21-year-old Klansman were surprised while allegedly trying to dynamite the home of a Jewish businessman. (Her companion, Thomas Albert Tarrants III, emptied a submachine gun firing at police, and critically injured one officer and a bystander before he himself was wounded.)

In Mrs. Ainsworth's possession at the time of her death were a loaded pistol, Klan membership cards, a card from

Gerald Smith's anti-Jewish Christian Nationalist Crusade, and a pamphlet from the anti-Semitic Christian Education Association, of Union, N.J., which declared that "at least 90 per cent of all Jews are Communists," and urged all "red-blooded Americans" to "rise up and rid the country of your enemy."

Still other publications were found in her desk at the Ainsworth's Jackson home. These included *We Will Survive*, a manual, often used by the paramilitary Minutemen, which features anti-Semitic and anti-Negro hate messages along with instructions on the use of firearms and the making of bombs; copies of KKK reports; and hate publications warning of a "Communist-Jewish conspiracy," such as *The Thunderbolt*, the organ of the violent National States Rights Party.

The anti-Communist paranoia and exhortation to violence of the Minutemen has been set forth above. One example of their violent acts:

On Aug. 24, 1968, a group of Minutemen allegedly tried to burn down a pacifist camp near Voluntown, Conn. The armed invaders fought a close range gun battle with police, and four of them were wounded.

The anti-police rhetoric of the Black Panthers was recounted previously.

On August 5, 1968, in Los Angeles, two policemen were hospitalized with multiple wounds suffered in a shootout in which three Black Panther members were killed. According to police, the two officers halted a car containing four Negroes whom they said had acted suspiciously. Police said they were preparing to search the men when one drew a weapon and fired at them. According to a Black Panther official, police halted the car, jumped out and started shooting, and one of the Panthers attempted to defend himself with a gun. (*Los Angeles Times*, Aug. 8, 1968).

Item: The Black Panthers first made major news on May 2, 1967, when some 40 members of the organization invaded the legislative chambers of the California state capitol building at Sacramento, carrying loaded rifles, shotguns, and pistols. The alleged purpose of the invasion was to discourage the Legislature from adopting more stringent gun control legislation. Six of the Panthers, including Chairman Bobby Seale, were sent to jail with sentences of three months. (The *New York Times*, Aug. 11, 1967).

In April, 1968, while awaiting trial on the charges, Seale was arrested and found guilty of carrying a gun near a jail—a felony. Seale was given three years' probation on the charge and ordered not to carry a gun, not to associate with anyone who does, not to associate with persons having known criminal records, and to get a job. (*San Francisco Chronicle*, May 24, 1968).

Item: Huey Newton of the Black Panthers was convicted in September 1968, of voluntary manslaughter in the killing of an Oakland policeman. His trial lasted eight weeks and was made into a *cause celebre* by the Panthers and groups sympathetic to them, who raised the slogan "Free Huey!"

Item: Also in April, 1968, Black Panther Information Minister Eldridge Cleaver and five other Panthers were involved in a gun battle with police and were charged with attempted murder and attempted assault. Cleaver was wounded and another Panther killed. The accused Panthers pleaded not guilty. (*New York Times*, Sept. 18, 1968).

APPENDIX C

ALIENATION TODAY CONVEYED THROUGH THE WORDS OF PETER YOUNG

"Something is happening
But you don't know what it is,
Do you Mister Jones"

Bob Dylan

What's happening is that whole chunks of the American citizenry are modifying their traditional allegiance to the central government in favor of more personalized commitments *much* closer to home. This is what some people mean when they talk about "the sickness" abroad in the land. And because I am a part of this phenomenon, I naturally choose to regard it as a sign of *health*. We have *been* sick; but now we are raised from the dead (as it were), all of us in motion towards an existential freedom that operates outside the traditional legal framework with its apparatus of FBI agents and courts.

This country is not innocent, nor are those who own it and run it. Neither wealth nor power have been distributed equitably. The most solemn promises have not been kept, and the land is now littered with human wreckage. Yes, there is violence and hatred abroad in the land. And there is more to come. Naturally. Did you really expect anything else?

Group behavior which is "extremist" finds its lowest common denominator in the reality of *powerlessness*. This goes for the white ghetto, the black ghetto and the rebellious young —to name just three of the groups which are now in motion towards a new distribution of the wealth and the power. The young theoreticians of the Students for a Democratic Society, led by Tom Hayden, were quite correct in 1962 when they drafted a manifesto at Port Huron, Michigan, which called for "participatory democracy." Denied channels of expression within the formal society, various groups first retreated to form a veritable community-within-the-community, then came charging back in to open up new channels with a variety of crude, ugly, vulgar, often illegal techniques.

They (we) are modifying our traditional allegiance not out of perverse wickedness or because of the influence of "outside agitators," but rather because The American System *you* help to manage is no longer meeting our most elementary needs.

What North Carolina Governor Terry Sanford used to call "The Mainstream of America" is polluted, both literally and symbolically: the polluted air is thick enough to chew; the polluted rivers and streams are almost thick enough to plow. The streets are not safe. Racketeers have more "clout" at City Hall (and Washington) than the average citizen. The tax laws are rigged in favor of the super-rich. The courts and prisons are rigged against the white and black poor. The vast blessings of American productivity have not been distributed equitably. And a stupid, vicious, immoral and unconstitutional war drags on endlessly in the swamps of Southeast Asia.

All of these obvious grievances (and many others) help set in motion a revolutionary *process*. The wonder is not that there is so much violence in this America; *the wonder is that there is so little.*

Will tomorrow's America be totalitarian? Or will it be what we have never known and always sought—a pluralist democracy operating through decentralized units of political and economic power?

While you can not stop the revolutionary process, I think it safe to say that you are in a position to influence greatly the final outcome. *All* groups are in motion, and all roads are open. This is at one and the same time both our nightmare *and* our hope.

Naturally, there are those who can not live with the risk and the suspense of this extraordinary America. Panic rises in the breast of the elitist, when he contemplates *all* the vulgar people "doing their own thing." Witness this recent statement from Mr. Walter Lippmann:

"Necessity may dictate the repression of uncontrollable violence."

What necessity? *Whose* necessity? And the answer is, Mr. Lippmann's necessity. (And *yours?*)

Does Mr. Lippmann mean sending the National Guard back into the Central Ward of Newark, so that automatic weapons can once again rake the high-rise projects and thereby kill innocent old black women and their grandchildren in their own little living rooms?

Does Mr. Lippmann look forward to still another skull-busting session between the Chicago police and some of our more exotic and profane young people?

Or does Mr. Lippmann perhaps anticipate a mass roundup of the men, women and children of the white ghetto and their subsequent detention (without benefit of due process) in the very same camps that were used for that very same obscene purpose with more than 100,000 *citizens* of Japanese ancestry during World War II? [I have made it] my solemn duty to discuss that neglected chapter from the history books with "the boys" of the Carolina Klan. I thought then—and I think *now*—that those boys should have a good idea of what *you* are capable of doing in moments of panic.

To summarize the point:

I think it *most* important that the Commission understand full well that *nobody* I know is going to play the role of Docile Jew while somebody else plays the role of Manicured Nazi. That's why the guns are out there; that's why *both* white and black ghetto folks are planning to ignore and/or defy stringent gun control legislation.

When my vital interests are threatened, I am *not* going to consult my well-worn copy of the U.S. Constitution or even the latest decision by Justice Fortas. As a Muslim leader said [of the Constitution] in one of our conversations: "Later for *that* garbage, Baby." I resort to a different piece of paper when challenged, namely, The Declaration of Independence, with its emphasis on the inalienable right of the ugly, vulgar, but sovereign people to rise up in their wrath and alter or abolish the out-of-touch structure which still rules over their lives—long after the mechanics of contractual consent have atrophied and withered away. I will consult with my various friends. And *we* will decide what action is necessary and appropriate to defend the interests at stake. You can no longer define our reality. We'll do that now for ourselves, thank you.

*   *   *

"Look out!
The Saints are coming through!
And it's all over now,
Baby Blue."

Bob Dylan

APPENDIX D

THE CONTEMPORARY KU KLUX KLAN *

1. The Traditional Perspective

Though the Klan had been quiet during World War II, there were cells in every major Southern community from Virginia to Texas before V-J Day. The Klan groups were reported to be more irresponsible—because less centralized—than at any other time in history. The lack of central control persisted, and the story of the KKK from the immediate post-war years until the early 1960's is one of splintering and dissension, with one group or another in momentary ascendancy and no clear national leadership.

Cross burnings, a traditional Klan weapon of intimidation often used to spread the fear of violence among Negroes, integrationists or dissenters, became widespread early in 1945 —three "fiery crosses" were lighted in Knoxville, Tenn., on March 18; five near Birmingham, Ala., on March 28; two in August near Flemington, N.J., visible nearly 60 miles away; five in October in Miami, Fla., outside the homes of eleven Negro families.

The largest of the Klan groups—The Association of Georgia Klans, Inc., headed by Dr. Samuel Green, one of the last leaders of the pre-war "second Klan"—dominated the scene until 1949. In April of that year, Green's Klan was declared a subversive organization by the U.S. Attorney General. In August, Green died, and the Klans became a plethora of fragmented and competing factions.

Fearful of a changing climate of public opinion in the

---

*This report was prepared for the commission by the Anti-Defamation League of B'nai B'rith from its own sources.

South, Green sought to disassociate his Klan from violence. In the last weeks of his life, Green was incensed by a rise in Klan violence. He revoked the charter of the Chattanooga, Tenn., klavern because of its alleged involvement in terrorist raids and floggings, and of the Trenton, Ga., klavern because it had been linked to an incident in which seven Negroes were flogged.

In Alabama, a band of masked Klansmen raided a Negro Girl Scout camp, near Bessemer on June 12, 1948. They closed down the camp and ordered two white instructors to "get out of town" within 24 hours. During the following months, communities in the Birmingham area saw a wave of kidnappings, floggings, and cross burnings. On June 12, 1949, hooded Klansmen dragged a white woman from her home in Birmingham and threatened to burn her at the stake as they burned a cross on her lawn. On June 20, hooded night riders beat a Birmingham housewife because they disapproved of her suitor. The suitor and three other men, one a cripple, were kidnapped and flogged the same night.

In July 1949, Klansmen in central Florida became involved in a wave of anti-Negro terrorism following the rape of a white woman. Negro homes in the Groveland area were burned and pillaged over a period of three days until the National Guard was called in.

During the remainder of the year, cross burnings and other acts of KKK intimidation were reported throughout the South, on the West Coast, in Chicago, Washington, D.C., and Long Island, N.Y.

Two years of Klan terror in North and South Carolina began during the summer of 1950, attributed to members of the Association of Carolina Klans, headed by Thomas L. Hamilton, an ally of Florida's Grand Dragon Bill Hendrix. On August 26, in Horry County, S.C., a large group of robed and armed Klansmen raided a Negro night club and abducted its owner after a melee in which hundreds of gunshots were fired. Along with a dozen of his associates, Grand Dragon Hamilton himself was arrested and charged with conspiring to commit mob violence. (A grand jury failed to indict them.)

In March 1951, also in Horry County, a mob of 25 robed and masked men abducted and whipped a disabled World War II veteran and his crippled uncle. A series of floggings also marked this period.

Violence and the words that provoke violence continued their relationship as marks of Thomas Hamilton's Carolina Klans. Balked by an anti-mask law in South Carolina, Hamilton crossed the State line to organize a klavern in Columbus County, N.C. where hoods could still be worn.

The move was followed by a series of brutal nighttime kidnappings and floggings which terrorized the citizens of Columbus County for more than a year. Appointing themselves guardians of morality, the nightraiders beat and flogged Negroes who stepped out of their racial "place" and also white persons for such offenses as drunkenness or failure to attend church regularly. Several Negro women had their heads shaved in the form of a cross for allegedly having consorted with white men.

As violence continued, Hamilton, early in 1952, disbanded the Columbus County klavern for procedural irregularities. A few weeks later, on February 16, a score of FBI agents, assisted by local police, arrested 11 former members of Hamilton's klavern, charging them with violations of the Federal Kidnapping Law (two of the flogging victims had been carried across the state line). Ten of the 11 were eventually convicted.

Later in 1952, North Carolina authorities arrested additional Klansmen involved in other incidents of violence—including Hamilton himself. He pleaded guilty to having conspired to flog three Negroes and was sentenced to four years at hard labor. The arrests and convictions temporarily destroyed the Carolina Klans.

Segregation found political (more influential, less violent) supporters during the next three years, and it was not until 1956 when the efforts of those groups failed to stem the trend toward integration in the South that the Ku Klux Klans revived, with cross burnings and roadside rallies again increasing. In San Antonio, Tex., a cross was burned at a busy intersection—its purpose, according to a new Klan leader, to "let the niggers, Jews, and Catholics know we're back in operation."

In Alabama, Asa E. Carter, a well-known racist, formed a new KKK organization composed of "squads and platoons with areas of responsibility" to serve as a type of patrol against integration.

In September 1957, six Alabama Klansmen decided to abduct a Negro and throw a scare into him as a protest against

Negro efforts to desegregate schools in Birmingham. They found a poor handyman named Judge Aaron, dragged him to a small house with a dirt floor, and there castrated him, afterward pouring hot turpentine onto his wounds. (The man survived his ordeal, and four of the Klansmen received 20-year terms.) The sordid incident highlighted a long series of outrages against Negroes by Alabama Klansmen during the summer and fall of 1957.

In South Carolina that summer, three members of Greenville County's KKK unit, including the county leader, were charged with beating a 58-year-old Negro man with blackjacks and sticks because he had been mixing with white people —taking care of seven white children while their mother was in a hospital. The four Klansmen were convicted.

In February 1958, police in Charlotte, N. C., thwarted the bombing of the Woodland School, a Negro elementary school, when they caught two Klansmen at the school carrying sticks of dynamite with detonator caps and a fuse. The two, plus a third (also a Klansman) were convicted and imprisoned.

The 1960's—Klan Membership and Violence on the Rise

The year 1960 was marked by a sharp increase in Klan activities and by the consolidation of previously splintered groups in seven states. The new confederation, the National Knights of the KKK, showed its strength in a coordinated series of cross burnings on Saturday, March 26. Newspapers in the South reported sightings of more than 1,000 fiery crosses on that day throughout Alabama, Florida, Georgia, South Carolina, and several other states.

There is evidence that Klansmen from Florida and southern Georgia were mobilized for, and took part in, the race riots that lasted for almost a week in Jacksonville, Fla., beginning on "Axe-Handle Saturday"—Aug. 27, 1960. Tactics to counteract the sit-in movement, of which Jacksonville was then a target, were discussed at a meeting of the Jacksonville klavern of the Florida Knights of the KKK four days earlier. A call was sent out to other Klan units urging them to converge on Jacksonville on Saturday and to bring Klan sympathizers with them. (They were urged to leave all KKK identification at home.) Scores of Klansmen and other whites appeared in downtown Jacksonville on Saturday morning. Stores selling axe-handles and baseball bats did a rushing business—one store alone reporting the sale of 50 axe handles. Violence broke out by noon. Sporadic disorders and racial violence continued for several days.

The Ku Klux Klans in America had begun a significant resurgence by the time of Axe Handle Saturday—and, to a great extent, had achieved a unity it had not seen since before World War II. The chief Klan organization of the resurgence was the United Klans of America, headed by Imperial Wizard Robert M. Shelton in Tuscaloosa, Ala. with units in 18 States. An investigation of KKK groups by the House Committee on Un-American Activities in 1965–66 revealed that most Klan members in the United States belonged to UKA–affiliated "klaverns" and "realms."

The first half of the 1960's was a time of intensive civil rights activity in the Southern States—rallies, sit-ins, and huge marches—and consequently the time for extremist segregationists to fight harder for their own political goals. In its rhetoric, the Ku Klux Klan had made it clear that such goals would be achieved through violence if necessary. Not surprisingly, the record of the period is a record of violence against Negroes and others interested in the cause of civil rights.

The most memorable cases:

(1) The slaying, near Philadelphia, Miss., on June 21, 1964, of civil rights workers James Chaney (Negro), Andrew Goodman (white), and Michael Schwerner (white). Twenty-one men, six of them said by the FBI to be members of Mississippi's White Knights of the KKK, were arrested. Eighteen were eventually tried on federal charges of conspiracy to commit murder. The government marshaled overwhelming evidence that the roadside triple murder had been the direct result of a Klan extermination plot. Seven of the 18 were convicted by an all-white jury. Among those convicted were Sam Holloway Bowers, Jr., Imperial Wizard (President) of the White Knights of the Ku Klux Klan, and Cecil Ray Price, the chief deputy sheriff of Neshoba County.

(2) The murder of Lemuel Penn, a Negro educator

who was gunned down from a passing automobile while driving home to Washington from Fort Benning, Ga., on July 11, 1964. Four Klansmen were arrested and charged with murder. Two of them were tried and acquitted. In 1966, however, the same two, charged with joining in a Klan conspiracy to kill Negroes, in violation of the victims' civil rights, were convicted in a federal court.

(3) The murder of Viola Gregg Liuzzo, a white civil rights worker, on a lonely highway in Lowndes County, Ala., on March 25, 1965, immediately after the completion of the Selma-to-Montgomery Freedom March. Three Klansmen were indicted by a federal grand jury for rights violations. In November 1965, the three were convicted on the federal charges and were sentenced to 10 years in prison. In April 1967, the U.S. Circuit Court of Appeals upheld the convictions.

(4) The Jan. 10, 1966, firebomb murder of Vernon F. Dahmer, a Negro civil rights leader. On March 16, 1968, an all-white Mississippi jury found Cecil V. Sessum, a reputed Klansman, guilty of the crime. An FBI agent testified that the White Knights of the KKK had met prior to Dahmer's death and plotted to get rid of him because he was "getting too many niggers to vote," and that three Klansmen had acknowledged attending the secret meeting. It was alleged also that a "practice run" of the bombing had been ordered by Wizard Bowers himself before the actual crime.

The Klan violence of the 1960's has been directed primarily against the advocates of civil rights for Negroes; as civil rights activity slackened after 1965, instances of violence somewhat decreased in number. They did not end. The Klan slaying of Vernon Dahmer came in 1966. Later in the year the Grand Dragon of a midwestern state was one of three Klansmen arrested after the bombing of an office of the National Association for the Advancement of Colored People. In 1967 and 1968, at least 20 acts of violence have been attributed to the Mississippi White Knights alone. There is evidence of the Ku Klux Klan's acceptance of terrorism as a political weapon. A partial chronology of violence in the South by Klan members of Klan type elements follows:

1962

Sept. 1	Louisiana	Crosses were burned by the Klan in front of the state capitol in Baton Rouge; three Negro schools in Hodge and near Bosco; at a Negro minister's home in Bastrop; and in eleven other north Louisiana towns.
Sept. 3	Albany Ga.	A cross was burned at a Klan meeting.
Sept. 5	Dallas Ga.	A group of masked riders attempted to force their way into the home of a Negro, but were forced to flee when they were fired on.
Oct. 4	Greenville Miss.	A cross was burned near the home of Hodding Carter, editor-publisher of the Delta *Democrat-Times*.
Oct. 13	Birmingham Ala.	A man was beaten at a Klan rally after he declared: "Mob violence is no answer to anything."
Dec. 14	Birmingham Ala.	The New Bethel Baptist Church, a Negro church, was damaged by a bomb.

1963

Feb. 4	Mobile Ala.	A cross was burned in front of the home of a Negro minister, who had urged desegregation of a high school.
Feb. 7	Bossier City La.	Four men were arrested following the painting of some 30 KKK signs on sidewalks, stores, buildings, traffic signs and driveways.

March 24	Birmingham Ala.	A bomb exploded at the home of a Negro, injuring two of the five occupants.
May 11	Birmingham Ala.	Blasts ripped the home of Rev. A. D. King and the A. G. Gaston Motel.
May 12	Anniston Ala.	Shots were fired at the homes of two Negroes. On May 20, a one-time Klan leader, Kenneth Adams, was arrested and on May 25 was convicted for these assaults. He was sentenced to 180 days in jail and fined $100 on each of the shooting counts. Freed on bond pending an appeal. (Adams was also accused of firing a shot into a Negro church on May 12. On April 8, 1964, a jury found him innocent.)
May 17	Alexandria La.	A cross was burned in front of the home of relatives of a Negro youth who was in jail, charged with rape of a white woman.
June 8	Tuscaloosa Ala.	A cross was burned at a Klan meeting.
June 18	Gillett Ark.	A dynamite blast blew out the front door of a Negro church.
June 26	Gulfport Miss.	An explosion damaged the offices of a Negro doctor, who was president of the local NAACP chapter.
June 30	Jackson Miss.	An explosion collapsed a two-family frame house; four Negro men escaped injury.
July 14	Atlanta Ga.	A cross was burned at a Klan meeting.

July 27	Anderson S. C.	Klan meeting featured a cross burning.
August 15	Birmingham Ala.	Tear gas bombs were detonated at a department store which had recently been desegregated.
August 21	Birmingham Ala.	The home of Negro attorney Arthur D. Shores was bombed.
August 26	Columbia S. C.	A packet of dynamite blew a crater near the home of a Negro girl scheduled to enter the University of South Carolina.
August 26	Buras La.	An explosion wrecked a classroom and started a fire in an integrated Catholic school.
Sept. 1	Winnsboro La.	Crosses were burned in front of several schools, one night after a Klan rally.
Sept. 4	Birmingham Ala.	The home of Arthur D. Shores was blasted again.
Sept. 7	Ocala Fla.	A 35-foot cross was burned at a Klan rally.
Sept. 8	Birmingham Ala.	The home of A. G. Gaston, an influential Negro, was bombed.
Sept. 15	Birmingham Ala.	The bombing of the 16th Street Baptist Church resulted in the death of four Negro girls.
Sept. 18	St. Augustine Fla.	Four Negroes were beaten when they drove their car near a Klan rally. Four Klansmen were arrested on Sept. 19 and released on bond. On Oct. 16, one of the beaten Negroes was convicted of assaulting

two of the Klansmen. On Nov. 5, a jury found one of the Klansmen innocent, and charges against the other three were dismissed.

Sept. 25	Birmingham Ala.	Two bombs were exploded in a Negro neighborhood.
Sept. 30	Birmingham Ala.	State Police arrested two men in connection with racial bombings. The suspects, Robert E. Chambliss and Charles Cagle, had Klan records. A third man, John W. Hall, was subsequently arrested. On Oct. 9 the City Recorder found the men guilty of possessing dynamite and sentenced them to 180-day jail sentences and $100 fines. The three were released on bond. On June 16 and 18, 1964, they were found not guilty by a jury.
Nov. 16	Tuscaloosa Ala.	Two explosions, eighteen hours apart, shattered windows in a Negro neighborhood and jolted the University of Alabama campus.
Nov. 16	Rayville La.	Over 1,000 Klansmen assembled amid the glow of burning crosses.
Nov. 19	Tuscaloosa Ala.	A dynamite bomb exploded near the dormitory of a Negro co-ed at the University of Alabama.
Dec. 8	Dawson Ga.	Gunfire and an explosion damaged the home of a Negro voter-registration worker.

1964

January	McComb Miss.	A cross was burned in front of a Negro minister's home.

Jan. 18	Louisiana	More than 150 crosses were burned near Negro homes, churches and schools in five parishes.
Jan. 25	Atlanta Ga.	During civil rights demonstrations, Klansmen clashed with Negro students.
Jan. 31	Vicksburg Miss.	Crosses were burned in seven different places.
Feb. 15	Black Lake La.	Klan burned a cross at a meeting.
Feb. 16	Jacksonville Fla.	A bomb caused extensive damage to the home of a six-year-old Negro boy who attended a previously all-white school. On March 3, William Sterling Rosecrans, a "close associate" of North Florida KKK leaders, was arrested and charged with the bombing. On March 12, the FBI arrested five Klansmen, Barton H. Griffin, Jacky Don Harden, Willie Eugene Wilson, Donald Eugene Spegal and Robert Pittman Gentry, in connection with the bombing. On March 13, Rosecrans, who is from Indiana, pleaded guilty and a month later (April 17) was sentenced to seven years in federal prison. On June 30, the five Klansmen went on trial and a week later Jacky Don Harden and Robert Pittman Gentry were acquitted. A mistrial was declared in the cases of the other three Klansmen. Retrial began on November 16 and nine days later a jury acquitted the Klansmen of charges they conspired to violate the civil rights of the six-year-old Negro boy.

April 18	Notasulga Ala.	The Macon County High School was destroyed by a fire. The school had recently been ordered to desegregate, and white students were boycotting it.
April 18	Bogalusa La.	Three men in black hoods abducted a millworker, accused him of failing to support his child, beat him with a pistol and whipped him.
April 18	Jackson La.	Bob Wagner, a newsman, was seized by Klansmen near one of their meetings, and was beaten.
May 2	Jackson Miss.	Two young Negroes disappeared suddenly and their bodies were accidentally found in the Mississippi River in July by a large group of men who were looking for three missing civil rights workers. On Nov. 6 two men, one an acknowledged member of the Klan, were arrested on charges of killing the Negroes. They were freed on bond pending a trial.
May 2	Mississippi	Crosses were burned in 64 counties on the same night.
May 29	St. Augustine Fla.	Night-riders shot up an unoccupied beach cottage and fired into an automobile, narrowly missing an aide to Dr. Martin Luther King.
June 16	Philadelphia Miss.	A group of armed white men surrounded the Mt. Zion Methodist Church, beat Negroes and burned the church to the ground.
June 17	Jackson Miss.	A Negro was abducted by a group of hooded men and was flogged.

June 20	Fayette Miss.	A Negro civil rights worker was chased from his car by a group of white men.
June 20	McComb Miss.	Explosions on one night occurred at the homes of two Negroes suspected of civil rights activities; at the barbershop owned by another; and at the homes of two white men who had made remarks opposing KKK violence.
June 21	Branson Miss.	The Sweet Rest Church of Christ Holiness was rocked by an explosion.
June 21	Maben Miss.	A crowd of whites, many of whom were armed, circled a car containing six Negro civil rights workers. Passengers were spat upon, cursed and threatened.
June 21	Philadelphia Miss.	Three civil rights workers, two of them white, were murdered. On Dec. 4, the FBI arrested twenty-one men, charging them with conspiring to violate the constitutional rights of the three young men. Several of the defendants were members of the Klan. The men were released on bond. On Dec. 10, a U.S. Commissioner dismissed the charges against nineteen of them. On Jan. 11, 1965, the government presented to a federal grand jury the confessions of two of the men, one of whom is an acknowledged member of a Klan. The Grand Jury handed down indictments on Jan. 15 against most of the original defendants. On Feb. 25, a U.S. District Court judge dismissed felony indictments against

seventeen men, but ruled they must stand trial under a misdemeanor charge. An eighteenth defendant was to be tried separately in Atlanta.

| June 22 | McComb Miss. | The homes of two Negroes active in the civil rights movement were bombed. |

| June 25 | Ruleville Miss. | A Negro church was bombed. |

| June 25 | Longdale Miss. | Another Negro church was hit by a fire bomb. |

| June 27 | McComb Miss. | A Molotov cocktail mixture of oil and kerosene was hurled against the front door of the McComb *Enterprise Journal*. A note around the bottle was signed "K.K.K." |

| July 4 | Enfield N. C. | Cross-burning. |

| July 7 | McComb Miss. | Three explosions destroyed a section of the civil rights "Freedom House." |

| July 11 | Athens Ga. | Lemuel Penn, a Negro educator, along with a companion, had completed summer training at Fort Benning, Georgia. They were driving home when they were fired on and Penn was killed. On Aug. 6, four men identified as Klansmen, were arrested in connection with the killing. On August 31 two white men went on trial. A third man's confession, later repudiated, was read. On Sept. 4, a jury found the two Klansmen not guilty. On Oct. 16, the four Klansmen, along with two others, were indicted by a fed- |

eral grand jury, charged with acts of intimidation and violence against Negroes. On Dec. 29, the federal indictments against the six men were thrown out by a U.S. District Court judge. A state charge of murder is still faced by the Klansman who originally confessed a role in the slaying. Another man was charged with being an accessory after the fact.

July 12	Natchez Miss.	Two Negro churches were leveled by arsonists.
July 13	Elm City N. C.	An attempt to burn a Negro church that an integrated group planned to paint led to the arrest of two men. The KKK had warned that it would prevent efforts to conduct integrated projects at a church.
July 14	Wesson Miss.	The owner of a gas station was beaten by three masked and hooded men. He had refused to join the Klan, had hired Negro help and allowed them to use the cash register.
July 17	McComb Miss.	The Zion Hill Freewill Baptist Church was burned, and two men were roughed up by three white men.
July 18	Atlanta Ga.	Cross-burning at a Klan meeting.
July 19	Madison Co. Miss.	The Christian Union Baptist Church was destroyed by a fire.
July 19	St. Augustine Fla.	A 20-foot cross was burned at a Klan rally.

July 24	St. Augustine Fla.	A fire bomb was tossed into a recently-integrated restaurant. Later that day, warrants were sworn out against five Klansmen charging them with burning a cross on private property without permission.
July 30	Meridian Miss.	The Mount Moriah Baptist Church was destroyed by fire.
July 31	Brandon Miss.	The Pleasant Grove Baptist Church burned to its foundation.
August 1	Farmerville La.	A 50-foot cross was burned at a Klan meeting.
August 13	Raleigh N. C.	Cross burned on lawn of governor's mansion.
August 15	Natchez Miss.	Dynamite demolished a nightclub and bar, serving an all-Negro clientele, located across the street from a building housing the local Freedom School.
August 15	Greensburg La.	Several crosses were burned.
August 15	Greenwood Miss.	A Negro was shot while seated in his car. (He had been severely beaten the previous month.)
August 15	Jackson Miss.	A Negro was shot, a white civil rights worker was clubbed, and at least six crosses were burned.
August 15	Mississippi and Louisiana	Scores of crosses were burned, many of them fired at 10 p.m. by obvious pre-arrangement.
August 27	Jackson Miss.	A bomb shattered the windows and doors in the office of a small weekly

newspaper, whose anti-Klan editor had won a Pulitzer Prize for her crusading editorials.

August 29	Natchez Miss.	A cross was burned at a Klan rally.
Sept. 2	Enfield N. C.	Cross-burning.
Sept. 3	Enfield N. C.	Several crosses were burned.
Sept. 6	Canton Miss.	A dynamite blast ripped through a white-owned grocery in a Negro neighborhood.
Sept. 7	Summit Miss.	Three predawn bomb blasts damaged a home, a store and a shed, all owned by Negroes.
Sept. 9	McComb Miss.	Dynamite damaged the home of a Negro minister.
Sept. 17	Canton Miss.	Two Negro churches used for voter registration activity were burned.
Sept. 19	Philadelphia Miss.	Two small churches were hit by fire.
Sept. 20	McComb Miss.	The home of a Negro woman active in civil rights work was blasted. On Oct. 1, three white men, who had membership cards in the KKK, were arrested, and one of them was also charged in connection with the Sept. 9 bombing. On Oct. 12, the three men, along with another individual, were indicted in connection with the bombing. On Oct. 24, the four men, plus five others who had been seized in connection with

the bombing, entered pleas of guilty and *nolo contendere*. After designating various sentences for the nine men, the judge suspended the sentences.

Sept. 21	McComb Miss.	Dynamite bombs hurled from passing cars damaged a church and Negro home.
Sept. 21	Enfield N. C.	Cross-burning.
Sept. 23	McComb Miss.	A bomb was hurled at the home of a former Negro policeman.
Sept. 23	Columbia S. C.	A cross was burned in front of the governor's mansion.
Sept. 25	Natchez Miss.	An explosion ripped a hole in the lawn at the home of the mayor. Another blast occurred at the home of a Negro.
Sept. 26	Farmville N. C.	A minister was threatened, harassed and searched while attending a Klan rally.
Oct. 4	Vicksburg Miss.	A dynamite explosion heavily damaged a Negro church building that had been used as a voter registration headquarters.
Oct. 31	Ripley Miss.	Fire destroyed the Antioch Baptist Church, which had been used as a Freedom School.
Nov. 17	Laurel Miss.	A union official was kidnapped at gunpoint and whipped by masked men.
Nov. 29	Montgomery Ala.	A dynamite bomb wrecked the carport of the home of a Negro family.

Dec. 10	Ferriday La.	Several white men poured gasoline on a shoeshop and after setting fire to it, prevented a Negro from leaving. He subsequently died in a hospital.
Dec. 13	Montgomery Ala.	An explosion was set off outside a Negro church. Three men were accused of the crime and received six-month sentences, but were released on probation after ten days in jail. One of the men had been indicted in 1957 in connection with bombings of Negro churches and homes.

1965

January	Center Tex.	A number of crosses were burned, including six in one night.
Jan. 17	Jonesboro La.	Fires destroyed two rural Negro churches.
Jan. 23	New Bern N. C.	Three explosions wrecked a Negro funeral home and two cars during a civil rights meeting. Six days later, the FBI arrested three men, one of them an Exalted Cyclops of a Klan.
Feb. 16	Mobile Ala.	Two Negro youths were wounded by shotgun blasts.
Feb. 28	Lowndes Co. Ala.	Armed white men disrupted church services and warned a minister to leave the county by sundown or he would never be found.
March 5	Indianola Miss.	A Freedom School and library burned to the ground.

March 9	Selma Ala.	Rev. James Reeb from Boston was fatally clubbed. Two days later four men were arrested.
March 21	Vicksburg Miss.	A Molotov cocktail was thrown into a desegregated cafe.
March 21	Birmingham Ala.	Four time bombs were discovered in Negro neighborhoods.
March 22	Birmingham Ala.	Two more bombs were discovered in the Negro community.
March 25	Lowndesboro Ala.	Mrs. Viola Gregg Liuzzo, a white civil rights worker, was shot and killed while driving on the Selma-Montgomery highway. Four Klansmen were charged with violating the civil rights of Mrs. Liuzzo.
March 29	Meridian Miss.	Fire bombs were tossed at two Negro churches.
April 1	Birmingham Ala.	A dynamite bomb wrecked the home of a Negro accountant, and two other bombs were found at the home of the Mayor and a City Councilwoman.

2. Violence and the White Ghetto, a View From the Inside
by Peter Young
Consultant to the Commission

Background of Peter Young

Peter Young describes his qualifications as follows:

Born January 24, 1932, in Montclair, N.J. Educated in the private and public schools of Montclair and Pasadena, Cal. U.S. Air Force service from 1951–1955. Graduated (with honors) from Louisiana State University in

1957. Graduate student (history) at University of North Carolina, 1957–1960. Newsman in North Carolina—country editor at Raeford, TV "star" in Raleigh—1960–1965. Walked into a Klan cow pasture in 1964, and hasn't been the same since (neither has the Klan). Couldn't pay his bills as a newsman, so "sold out" for the public relations thing. Is presently Public Relations Director for the largest ad agency in New Jersey. Resides with Italian-American wife in Summit. Discovered "the white ghetto" in 1964, named it in 1965, and has lived to see the George Wallace campaign convince *all* the skeptics that it really exists.

Holder of Social Science Research Council Fellowship as an undergraduate at LSU for honors thesis ("The Negro Community of Huntsville, Ala., 1881–1894"). Holder of Woodrow Wilson and Southern Fund Fellowships. Recipient of four awards from the N. C. Press Association and a first place award (1961) from the National Editorial Association. One of five North Carolinians cited by that state's Fine Arts Commission (1962) for "distinguished contributions to the arts."

Agitator, trouble-maker, rabble-rouser, non-conformist, maverick, Presbyterian, etc. Has been active with Committee of Southern Churchmen in behalf of low-income Southern whites.

(For a description of the white ghetto, see text, Chapter 4.) With respect to specific kinds of violence in the white ghetto:

An environment which is impoverished on all levels—cultural as well as material—breeds violence on a massive scale, almost as a way of life. There is the violence of car wrecks, the violence of Saturday night drinking sprees and squabbles, the violence of hunting accidents, the violence of spouse against spouse, the violence of suicide via alcohol or the pistol and, indeed (and almost as an afterthought), the violence of race against race. This description of violence in the white ghetto is a mirror image of similar conditions in the black ghetto. And for most of the same reasons.

No act of racial violence occurs in the South for which "The Klan" is not blamed. I do not contend that the

Klans-people I have known are Sunday School types, just simple, misunderstood "agrarian reformers." But I will say that most of the Klan leaders I have known have behaved far more responsibly than this society had any right to expect.

In North Carolina, Dragon Jones preached the gospel of "ballots, not bullets," to people who had never been reached by any kind of organization.

Unfortunately, there was a built-in contradiction. Insofar as the leaders of the "white ghetto" were able to articulate a program, they envisioned a North Carolina that would keep Negro citizens in subjugation. The Tar Heel Kluxers were thus committed to an illegal end that would (hopefully) be achieved by legal means.

This is a contradiction bound to explode under pressure. [But our response should not focus on repressing "The Klan" as such; this is the very focus that has tended to block constructive action in the white ghetto.]

Furthermore, to paraphrase George Orwell, "All Klans are created equal; but some Klans are more equal than others." We *all* know that some Klan organizations such as the one in Mississippi have been responsible for numerous acts of criminal violence. But even with the Mississippi militants, it will be more productive to concentrate on the white ghetto environment from which this type of aberrant behavior springs.

As for the more narrow problem of assassination, I can not imagine the Klan officers I have known engaged in a meeting to plot the killing of a national leader. What I *can* imagine is the ease with which a paramilitary team of tough, professional killers can be recruited out of the white ghetto for almost any target with a high enough price on his head. [In such a case the most morally reprehensible and dangerous person or group is that which conceives and finances the assassination, but this likewise demonstrates the need for constructive work to reduce the population of the white ghetto from which such a person or group can recruit its killers.]

Beyond the assassinations, there is the related white ghetto phenomenon called "nigger-knocking." "Nigger-knocking" is the random murder of a black citizen, usually on the road, for the purpose of intimidating the local black community. A publicized example was the killing of Lemuel Penn on a Georgia highway in 1965. Unpublicized examples occur almost daily on Southern rural roads; the Sheriff finds only a black body, with no clues available to hunt down the slayer. As a general rule, law enforcement agencies are virtually helpless either to prevent or to solve this kind of crime.

As lynching became counter-productive—because of the pervasive influence of television, and also because of the ease with which law enforcement agencies can infiltrate mobs—the grand old Southern sport of "nigger-knocking" came on to take its place. Its utterly random quality makes it more effective than lynching as a control device. And the fact that it is executed by only one man, or at most a carload, minimizes the chances of detection.

The dull terror "nigger-knocking" generates tends to preserve local institutional arrangements, but it is also an important addition to the more basic economic factors (mechanization of Southern agriculture) in stimulating the continuing black migration out of the South and into the dry tinder cities of the North. One of the most popular 45-rpm records distributed by the United Klans of America is entitled, "Move Them Niggers North." At every level of activity, both legal (if reprehensible) and illegal, this remains as a principal and primitive goal of the white ghetto. Said one white supremacist:

"Why waste all this poverty money on some nigger kid trying to make him into a good little boy? A 10-cent bullet will make him a good little boy forever."

My own *very* rough estimate would be that several hundred black people die each year in the South as a result of "nigger-knocking." I note also that the technique is spreading to the North, with "nigger-knocking" incidents reported recently in both Cincinnati and Cleveland.

I have never known a Klan officer to advocate "nigger-knocking," either publicly or privately. The officers I have known are aware that "nigger-knocking" is a frequent occurrence. But they are as helpless as everybody else when it comes to describing the remedy, even when, on occasion, they can make a shrewd guess as to which one of "the boys" was out riding with his carbine the night before.

Curiously, the militant black leaders with whom I have discussed "nigger-knocking" are remarkably unconcerned. One mentions several hundred black bodies a year littering the Southern roads, and the black leaders reply: "Hell, we lose that many each year just in Newark because of narcotics or bad housing." This is a way of saying that the real victims of "nigger-knocking" are the "nigger-knockers." How sad, how true.

One final aspect of [white ghetto violence] remains to be considered. A local Klan leader in North Carolina told me in September 1968 that he had expelled 39 "drunks, radicals and troublemakers" so far this year from the one unit under his jurisdiction. He added, "And as soon as we got rid of that bunch of bad apples, we found we were getting a better class of members than ever before."

Naturally, I was very happy for him—but the difficult question remains: Where do the drunks, radicals and troublemakers go when they are expelled from Klan groups and cut loose to act on their own? I suspect that in all too many instances they are out on the highway with real guns loaded with real bullets.

It is not generally appreciated (*and it must be*) that the white ghetto has hundreds and thousands of *seriously* disturbed men, all armed, many of whom are alienated even from the local Klan organizations.

What to do, what to do? Perhaps there will be government officials who will ask about the white ghetto that very same question they have asked so many times about the black ghetto:

What in the world do those people want?

And the answer, of course, is that "those people" want pretty much what everybody else wants: a little piece of turf to call their own, some sense of control over their own lives, a decent minimum of economic security, an end to government harassment and insults. Ordinary folks (white or black) have absurdly simple demands but, paradoxically, these demands can not be translated into reality without massive changes in our socio-economic-political system.

Quick fixes? I can think of several.

1. *Stop the scapegoating.* The crisis we are in has NOT been caused by five angry Kluxers in North Caro-

lina, 13 bi-sexual Trotsky-ites in the East Village, or even 81 promiscuous teeny-boppers in Berkeley. The crisis is systemic; The System has failed to meet the basic needs of several different groups which now, admittedly, are aggravating the situation by throwing handfuls of sand into the delicate machinery.

2. *Lower by several levels police harassment.* All law enforcement agencies must use paid informers, but I believe this practice has gone out of control in America. We now have a police apparatus which rivals anything the Tsar of Russia or, for that matter, Mr. Stalin, ever had. Half the political activists in America are on some government payroll for the purpose of spying on the other half. And this practice will be about as effective here as it was for the Tsar, which is to say that it will not be very effective at all.

3. *Flood the white ghetto with resource people.* The existing network of social services in the white ghetto is grossly inferior to that provided in the urban black ghetto. There is a desperate need for health and legal services, for skilled family counselors, for dedicated social workers and youth workers, for tough young chaplains, etc. For example, if the emergency is as serious as both the Freeman Commission and I have found it, then the government might well begin by drafting young doctors for two years service at Rural Health Centers.

4. *Experiment with carefully supervised "cultural exchange" programs within the United States.* I think often of the Klan children in the white ghetto. They are doomed to a life of mediocre inferiority unless we quickly change their life style of extreme cultural deprivation. Most of these Klan children have never heard a "live" symphony orchestra, witnessed a professional play, toured a museum, read a poem. That is why I sometimes get just a little bit irritated, when I read in my newspaper that the State Department has sent Leonard Bernstein and the New York Philharmonic on a 20-day tour of Japan. Doubtless, there are sound foreign policy reasons for exhibiting the best of our culture abroad; how much more important it is to exhibit the best of our culture to our own people who are not even aware it exists. Would it be madness to offer the New York Philharmonic to

Dragon Jones for 20 days? "You make all the arrangements, Bob, and don't forget the colored children if you
want a deal like this again." No, that would not be
madness. It might be the beginning of an end to madness!

Or another possibility; what would 100 North Carolina
Klans-people make of the central [Negro ghetto] Ward
in Newark or an Indian reservation? If I know the
Klans-people, they might very well decide that the black
folks in Newark and the red folks of the reservation
needed some, er, ah, technical assistance in how to use
guns and bullets in order to get an intolerable situation
straightened out quickly. But that's just one of the
chances you'll have to take.

5. *Accept the limitations of the political process.* Some
of my colleagues in the Committee of Southern Churchmen have noted that many Christians have gone beyond
the old rule that we should "render unto Caesar the
things that are Caesar's." All too many of the brethren
have permitted Caesar to define the terms on which they
would participate in the secular life. That is a fatal error,
because it arouses expectations which can not be fulfilled.
The political process is one tool among many—and perhaps not the most important tool at that—for building
the beloved community.

3. Summary of Tapes Made by Peter Young

North Carolina
Ku Klux Klan

Ku Klux Klan Rally

September 1968, Four Oaks, N.C.
(in Eastern North Carolina, near Smithfield)

An editorial note: We urge you to attend the recent Klan
rally through the summary of the tapes that follows and talk
to some of the boys of the North Carolina Klan the same
way. You will find the members of the Klan shocking in the
race hate they manifest: For example, Robert Jones' remarks
about the assassination of Martin Luther King in his speech at

the Klan rally. But it should be remembered that these people are also earthy, vigorous, and alive. They are God's children, as Mr. Young points out, and our fellow citizens. A response to them which is simply repressive would probably be ineffective. More important, such a response would be immoral. It is high time that we who are capable of doing so, help break the chain of ignorance, isolation, and poverty to which these persons are responding.

Peter Young comment (0–47)

The Klan rally was taped with the consent of Klan leaders. The speeches were rough. The speakers did not hold back on racism. The rally opened and closed with a prayer, which was not taped. Before the rally started, there was country music, also not taped except for a small portion at the beginning of the tape.

A number of the references in the Klan speeches cannot be understood without knowing the following: There had been recent racial disturbances in neighboring Smithfield. The Klan had been blamed in part for the disturbances. Also, the town of Four Oaks had tried to prevent the Klan rally, by passing an ordinance requiring a permit to rally.

The dominant mood at the rally was one of rage, ignorance, and paranoia. This is an explosive mixture which cannot be dealt with exclusively by police measures. It represents a great challenge to our society, and the tragedy is that in the past that challenge has only been met with police measures. (End of Peter Young comment.)

Klan rally tape begins:

(Some recorded music, announcement about souvenir sales and soft drink concession. (47–77) First speaker introduced (77–83).

E. J. Melvin, local officer of the Klan (83–194):

Glad to be among white people. Klan is here to stay. Time to make your stand. The Smithfield *Herald* is a "nigger paper." The paper blamed the recent troubles on the Klan. Klan was not involved in the troubles. They (Negroes) have been financed and encouraged by high government officials. So they will riot and they will move into smaller towns and even out into the country. Klan does not burn buildings or destroy property. When Negroes burn a town, if they are arrested they are turned loose and given a $10 tip. Klan is not violent but is 100 percent for self-defense. The Communist plan to destroy our children by putting them in schools with Negroes is happening before our very eyes. Also breakdown of law and order and Christian religion pursuant to the Communist plan.

A government publication which was later suppressed demonstrated that Negroes have twenty percent less intelligence than whites. This is no shame; the Lord made them that way. But white children will be penalized for going to school with Negroes because they will be held back to the Negro pace. You would not eat with or go to church with a Negro, but your children are being put under Negro teachers.

You should use your vote to elect proper city officials. For example, the officials at Four Oaks tried to forbid the Klan rally but would have given Negroes full permission to march. Officials should enforce law and order. The poverty aid programs take your funds and give them all to the Negroes. This is a result of local officials who are getting paid off to channel funds to Negroes.

History books are being changed. George Washington is being depicted as a drunkard. They are talking about the role of Negroes in our civilization—they actually said that two regiments of Negroes beat the South during the Civil War. In fact, our nation was founded on the principles of Christianity and manhood; not the appeasement and cowardice we have now.

Our only hope is to vote for George Wallace, who is a man. Be sure to vote. Negroes are registering to vote whether they are literate or not; so get white people registered who may have previously been turned down for flunking their literacy tests. Our greatest weapon is the vote and the rallies where the truth, which will not be printed in "nigger newspapers," can be told (155–164).

Has never owned a slave: neither have you. We are slaves; we have to work for a living. Negroes do not. They riot and live off of federal money.

The Communists are behind the race mixing and agitation. This is confirmed by J. Edgar Hoover. It is not racial unrest, it is "nigger unrest." The trouble is going to move from the big cities to the small towns and into the countryside. When they try to march across the South, they will have to march over the blood of Klansmen.

Unite to protect your children. We want to work through the vote but if it comes to self-defense we will die in the Cause. (End of speech.)

Announcer (194–206):

Move in closer so you can hear better. This is the largest crowd you will ever be in and "not smell a nigger" (laughter). (Introduces Sybil Jones, wife of J. R. Jones, the Grand Dragon, as "the boss" of the Grand Dragon.)

Sybil Jones (206–335):

There are no miracles or Santa Claus. We created our own problem. We have known for 30 years that the Communists have been at the country. The Negro problem is the biggest problem today in one sense, but in another sense the problem is that we would not fight thirty years ago and now we have to fight to keep from going under. Klan has done a great deal of good since organized in 1961.

This is the most pathetic story she has heard: Twin brothers were drafted into the Army, and were sent to Vietnam. When one was returning home in an airplane, coffins were also being shipped back in the same airplane. He recognized the serial number of his twin brother on one of the coffins.

Contrary to what you might suppose, you are deeply affected by the destruction caused by the rioting Negroes. Property destroyed could have been yours.

Just recently a white girl was raped nine times by three Negroes and had to have 17 stitches taken in her breast. This could have been your wife or daughter. Will your wife or daughter be raped and your son killed in Vietnam and your house burned down before you realize that this is your problem? You make me sick if you say you can not fight City Hall. They tried to make her daughter sit with Negroes, so she took her out of school. If God could look into your brain, would He see a whipped dog with his tail between his legs or would he see a man? This is your country, you must fight for it. Is this still the home of the free and the land of the brave?

She does not advocate violence, but she approves of the following story: There was a Negro peeping Tom and burglar. A man said if he tries this on me he will never bother another person. The Negro did make the mistake of starting the climb through the man's bedroom window. The man waited until the Negro was halfway through and then blasted him nearly in half with a shotgun. When the coroner came to take him away, the man would not let the Negro be carried through the house. He said that is not the way he came in. Take the "black s.o.b." back out the window (laughter) (286–302). She would do the same whether the person was white or black because anyone who would try to get through a window would be a Negro whether he was white or black. This is not violence; the Constitution gives us a right to protect our homes.

Men in Russia live behind an iron curtain; but a lot of men here live behind an iron petticoat and that is "pathetic." Step out from behind the petticoat and be a man. ("Be a man; join the Klan" was the KKK recruiting slogan 1964–65—Ed.).

Women, it would make you feel good if your men did not have to ask you every time they made a 50-yard dash behind the house (i.e., visit the outhouse—Ed.).

Believes in Patrick Henry, "Give me liberty or give me death." Theologians say that God is dead and better red than dead. Her God is not dead and they will have to bury her before they take over. (End of Sybil Jones, 335.)

Announcer (335–353):
Can buy Klan records and souvenirs, refreshments. Donate a dollar and get a chance at a prize. Introduces J. Robert Jones, Grand Dragon.

J. R. Jones (354–619):
Read where the Klan was dead; this is the biggest funeral he has ever been to. Joke: after the Civil Rights Bill they integrated everything including the astronauts. They sent a monkey and a Negro into orbit with sealed orders. The monkey was to open his first. When the monkey opened his orders he began mashing buttons and the Negro thought "if the monkey has that much to do I wonder what I will have to do?" When he opened his orders they read, "Don't forget to feed the monkey."

Got a call from a person in Smithfield saying for God's sake get down here, the Negroes are tearing the town apart. When the Klan arrived the Negroes had torn up all they wanted and then gone to bed and the Klan patrolled the streets. The next day the Smithfield paper blamed the trouble on the Klan because the Klan had placed a billboard up on the highway two years previously (We have a picture of the billboard which says "welcome to Klan territory"—Ed.), and also because they buried a Negro in a Negro cemetery (reference unknown—Ed.).

He has nothing against the Negroes in Smithfield. He wants nothing to do with them. The first one to break the law will be the first one to die (400).

LBJ can burn "nigger town" (Washington, D.C.) if he wants to, but he can't burn North Carolina. North Carolina belongs to him (Jones) and the Klan.

The riots are 90 percent Negro and just a while ago Washington said that it was all the white people's fault. They tried to stop the riots with a truckload of welfare checks. They say riots in New Jersey were caused by racists. He is the biggest racist in North Carolina because he races around North Carolina in his car working for the white people. This is the only kind of racist he knows.

(There follows the story of how Jones learned of the assassination of Martin Luther King, Jr.—set out verbatim.)

> But let me tell you, and I'm not gonna take up much of your time—but let me tell you about some of the things that's happened in our State and some of the things that's happened in your county in the last 90 days. Start with the time that Martin Luther King stuck his head in one too many garbage cans and got his head blowed off. [laughter]

> Now I found out something that night. I try to learn something every day. But I bet you people didn't even know it. I got home—I was speaking at Pfeifer College down in Stanley County—and soon as I got home the boob tube was on and the first thing that I heard, "Martin Luther King had been assassinated," and I felt, "Lord God, I done learned something." [laughter] Really!

> You assassinate a King, a Queen, the President of the United States, maybe even a Governor, but who in the name of God ever heard of assassinating a nigger? I thought you killed them [laughter] (416–429).

Saw on TV Negroes looting, rioting, and burning in Washington, D.C., and police officers standing by and not doing anything (437). Never thought he would ever see it with his own eyes. Saw a post office by mistake flying the flag at half mast (in honor of Martin Luther King, Jr.—Ed.). Ran it up to the top of the pole. Heard that the Negroes were burning down North Carolina, so drove back from Florida. Found a flag at half mast. Ran it up to the top of the pole; told the postmaster that if he wanted to do well in Granite Quarry (home of Jones and headquarters of the North Carolina Klan —Ed.), he would not fly a flag at half mast for a Negro Communist, whether instructed to do so by the Postmaster General or LBJ, himself (470).

Found Klansmen in the National Guard facing the savage animals (Negroes) with fixed bayonets but with no ammunition for their rifles. Gave ammunition to all the Klansmen in the National Guard. Would not ask them to face the savages unarmed. Not asking to start trouble, but entitled to protect property in self-defense (470–490).

You will fight for your property but you will not stand up for your children. You would not associate with Negroes or white trash [sic], but you make your children go to school with them. Advocates sending children to private schools. A man asked him (Jones) what the man should do? The man's daughter had to go to school with Negroes. Negroes call up and asked her for dates. Jones replied, "When are you going to bury them?" (514–518) Ought to be willing to spend $20 a month to send children to private schools for a segregated education. "Don't that sound reasonable to you?" [Crowd gives no response]. (525).

Fourteen years ago the Supreme Court required desegregation because the Negro schools were not adequately teaching Negroes, so now they are requiring white people to go to the same inadequate schools.

Out of all the riots, only two people were booked for murder and those were two white policemen doing their duty —protecting the rights of the humans [sic], in Detroit (545) (the reference is to the Algiers Motel case—Ed.).

Washington is debating the nomination of Abe Fortas as Chief Justice. Abe Fortas helped draft the charter of the United Nations which supersedes the U.S. Constitution. In other words they are trying to put in a man to uphold the Constitution who had destroyed the Constitution.

Remember the Communists. "Fight for the right; die if you must. But always remember, in God we trust." (Jones's motto with which he regularly concludes his speeches.—Ed.)

Asks for donation to the Klan for the Klan radio program (579) and literature, etc. Not being members of the Pepsi-Cola Co. or the Ford Foundation, the Klan does not have the federal government behind them. Negroes march, they call it black power; let us march and call it white power. Black power is five Negroes pushing a Cadillac. (End of speech, 619).

(Comment by Pete Young and the announcer during the collection of funds for the Klan) (624–687).

Speech by Klan chaplin: (name unknown—Ed.) (688—2d side 103)

If Klan is dead we have just buried 7,000 people. There are approximately 1,000 cars in the parking lot. The Klan is being persecuted because of people like the Methodist minister on the town board whose wife teaches in "niggertown." Klan has not taken advantage of the Negro; the Communists have. Prior to Communism, whites and Negroes got along well together because Negroes stayed in their places. (Reads at length from the Bible (Isaiah) which describes rebellion against the word of God and various kinds of disruption—analogized to Negro troubles.) Things were all right while true Christian preachers and officials upheld segregation. A race of spotted people would be ridiculous. The Bible demonstrates that God segregated everything. Place a Negro beside a white person and you do not have to be told the difference: first, you smell him; he has kinky hair (end of side one of tape, 804).

Some preachers say it is God's will to integrate and intermarry but this is a lie; if it were not a lie, he would have only made only one race.

Genesis tells us about the first negro, Nimrod, who decided to build tower to heaven before God had paved the way to heaven through Christ's appearance on earth. Nimrod must have been a Negro because he acted just like one. God intervened (5–17).

The reason Martin Luther King can see LBJ anytime he wants to is because Martin Luther King's wife is the daughter of LBJ by a concubine marriage (17–23). (The references to Martin Luther King, Jr., are all in the present tense as if he were still alive, although he had been assassinated several months previously—Ed.) LBJ is a "nigger."

Has been throughout the crowd and has not smelled a single "blue gum." His father said, "Don't get bitten by a blue-gummed nigger. They're the deadliest of all." [laughter] (30).

Maintain segregation; do not allow intermarriage. The Bible says that the body is the temple of the Lord. It would be ridiculous if the Lord had to live in a polkadot temple (36).

(There follows a story, apparently about how badly Negroes smell. Tape partially not understandable—Ed.)

God said that man was to get his living by the sweat of his brow, not sitting home receiving a welfare check. But the government has said that as long as your skin is black and you smell bad you can draw a welfare check (48).

Story: Expert on odors was brought in to determine who smelled worse—a goat or a Negro. They put the man in a closed room and let in a goat and the man fainted. Then they let in a Negro and the goat fainted (52).

Do not knuckle down to the opinion of your fellows; pay attention only to God's will. He has only one boss, God Almighty. Working for Him through the Klan in these rally fields. God will never condemn you for doing His will and you can do His will better through the Klan than through a church that belongs to the United Council of Churches (which has taken a pro-civil rights, antisegregationist stand— Ed.) (62).

Every time he wanted to do something, he always came and asked his wife; she was the boss and still is, but when he decided to join the Klan and told her, she started to say something and he said shut up because he was standing up and being a man (69). It was three days before he saw her—then one of his eyes became unswollen enough so that he could dimly see her [laughter].

Teasing about his wife. His wife is a great help to him as he goes around preaching the will of God to keep whites segregated from Negroes who are filthy and carry venereal diseases. Had a German shepherd he was very fond of—it was the only one that ever bit his wife. It got eaten up by syphillis just like

Negroes and so he shot it and that is what we ought to do with Negroes that have syphillis (78). This is not violence; this is self-preservation.

Health, education and welfare is "nigger health, nigger education and nigger welfare." They have done nothing about yours.

In conclusion, if they come to riot and burn and rape, give them equal rights, like he is going to do. He is going to give the first bunch half the bullets and save half the bullets for the second bunch. [laughter—applause] (87)

Do not just live your religion on Sunday, live it all through the week and when you are called before God to make an accounting, be able to say you did the best you could. Look forward to the day that Jesus Christ comes and we will no longer have any trouble with LBJ, the Jews, the niggers, and the Communists. God bless you. (End of speech.) (103)

(Description of walking over to the cross, the cross-burning ceremony, itself, by Pete Young and Pat Gurne) (103–185).

Interview with Exalted Cyclops, Billy Flowers

This is right after the cross-burning ceremony at the rally site. (End of second side of tape.) (185):

This is the biggest Klan rally ever in the area. Interest raised by racial troubles in Smithfield. "The niggers have started a fire and we're gonna keep it burning." (198) Had approximately 500 new applications for the Klan since the trouble in Smithfield. The Smithfield merchants that had formerly thought the Klan was not needed and had been hostile to it were the ones who called on the Klan to protect their property during the racial disturbances. There was no bloodshed in Smithfield because the Klan was there in force.

Interview With Grand Dragon J. R. Jones (September 1968)
(Takes place the day after the Klan Rally summarized above.)

The previous week, the Klan had a rally in Statesville, N.C. and Dragon Jones came home and was about to go to bed at 12 midnight when the phone rang. A young man from Smithfield said "Bob, for God's sakes get down here; they're tearing our town up." Jones made two telephone calls (presumably to Klan organizations—Ed.) and then drove approximately two hours to Smithfield with 11 of his boys. When Jones arrived, there were approximately 500 armed Klansmen in Smithfield. (This figure is probably substantially inflated—Ed.) The Klansmen patrolled to protect Klansmen's property until daylight. There was no bloodshed—no shots were fired.

Jones drives himself hard, often going 48 hours without sleep. He smokes sometimes five packs a day and drinks gallons of coffee.

When he got home last night there were five armed Klan security men guarding his house. (His 13-year-old daughter had seen a carload of Negroes driving up and down the private road that leads past his house and had called Klan security guards—Ed.) They were protecting his property. This is done all over the state for Klansmen, and for law enforcement officers who may have to be "out on a ride protecting us."

Jones drives himself at this pace because he is afraid that the country will fall to the Communists. He believes that we have to return Constitutional government to the people with state's rights.

The FBI has had a bug on Jones' telephone for the last three years. Once a month, the FBI collects the names of the people that Jones has talked to. Jones has asked the FBI several times to pay the phone bill but they refuse. Jones started the Klan going again in North Carolina because of the Communist infiltration and takeover of the country, and the National Council of Churches. The whole mess started in 1913 when the United States monetary system was turned over to the Zionist Christ-hating Jew and taken out of the hands of Congress where it belonged. (The reference is to the Federal Reserve Bank—Ed.) Also, the Supreme Court or the Senate of the United States in 1945 voted that the charter of the United Nations supersedes the Constitution of the United States.

Jones had been in the Klan under Eldon Edwards, but the leadership was so bad in the State that Jones left the Klan completely, but thereafter the state of the nation got so "nasty" that he could not stand it. His daughter became of school age and Jones did not think she should have to go to school with Negroes. They were having turmoil with SNCC and CORE and a lot of civil rights activity, so nine men in the Salisbury area got together and petitioned Mr. Shelton, the Imperial Wizard, to start a North Carolina chapter of the United Klans of America and Jones was elected Grand Dragon. This was August 17, 1963.

The Klan recruits a new crop every year to replace those that die or move away or leave the organization. The membership is also reduced when Jones from time to time expels radicals, drunks, trouble-makers, and rabble rousers. He is trying to build an organization with good people. Sometimes these rabble rousers go into some way-out type of organization like the Minutemen.

Klansmen are unfairly prosecuted by the authorities. They get long sentences for minor infractions of the law, whereas a Negro can hardly break his way into jail. For example, a Klansman got 18 months for violating a 500-year-old law against terrorizing. All that was done was that one shot was fired into the house of a Negro and no one was hurt. Sometimes Klansmen have trouble getting lawyers to represent them.

Perhaps 3 percent of the Klansmen are college graduates. (Probably a gross overstatement. We know of only one college graduate in the North Carolina Klan—Ed.) In 1965 the average Klansman in North Carolina had 11½ years of education, was around 35 years old and made approximately $5500 a year.

No representative of the U.S. government has ever come to talk to Jones about what constructively might be done to help the poor white people. The only contact with the federal government is the FBI bug. Jones does not know whether the FBI has infiltrated the Klan, but the Klan has infiltrated the FBI. Some persons have been approached to tell the secrets of the Klan, but the secret of the Klan is that it has no secrets. The usual proposition for a Klan informer is dues and 10¢ a mile and from $200 to $900 a month. They identified an FBI informant in one of the klaverns. They wanted to expel him, but Jones said no. Now that they knew who he was they could tell him what they wanted the FBI to know.

If anything constructive is going to be done in North Carolina with the ordinary white folks it would have to be done through the Klan. Jones would talk to a representative of the U.S. government about constructive programs as long as the representative was not part of the FBI.

The poverty program hasn't worked because it was set up ridiculously. Approximately $50,000 was allocated to the county and $30,000 of it went to three people for salaries. They say they are looking for poor people to work and they pay some person $12,000 to $15,000 a year to see that the work is done. They just take people from one $15,000 job to another $15,000 a year job and have not helped a soul. There is a feeling among ordinary white folks in North Carolina that the war on poverty, like the Civil Rights Act, is for Negroes only.

It is the poor white people who can not afford a lawyer that get thrown in jail. If you have money to fight it you can stay out of prison. If you are black or have some dealings with the civil rights, the NAACP or the ACLU will send an attorney down for you, but Jones would rather go to jail than have an ACLU attorney. (An outstanding ACLU attorney offered to represent Klan officers at the 1965 HUAC hearings; he was turned down—Ed.)

When Jones was in the Navy, he refused to salute a Negro officer. He said if they hung the uniform on a tree he would salute it all day, but he would not salute a Negro; Jones had to leave the service. Jones is unhappy that there is a Negro on the North Carolina Highway Patrol, appointed by Dan Moore, the governor, and that there is a Negro treasurer.

The two races are on a collision course. If Jones knew the answer he would be smarter than most people. One answer is to organize white people. If we go to the ballots, everyone can win—black, white, red, yellow or brown. But if we go to bullets, everyone will lose. Shooting is not the answer, but Washington, D.C. has also proved beyond any doubt that integration is also not the answer.

The members of the (Eisenhower) Commission do not send their children to Washington, D.C. schools; they send them to Virginia schools that are segregated or to private schools that Jones cannot afford. There are no members of the House of Representatives pushing integration where their own children are concerned. The man running for lieutenant governor in North Carolina pushed integration in his county. When there was full and total integration in his county he put his children into private schools. Ordinary white people cannot afford private schools.

Time is running out. Jones has done everything in his power to keep down violence in North Carolina. If it hadn't been for the Klan all hell would have broken loose. But economically nothing has changed. Taxes keep going up: salaries remain the same. People that are poor will be poor next year and the people that are rich will be richer. But the Klanspeople have never asked the federal government for any aid. They just own a little bit of property and do not want any Federal stamp put on it, because it is theirs. The wisdom of this was demonstrated when the federal government came in with federal aid to schools and then took over the schools.

With respect to Vietnam, Jones is in favor of fighting Communism wherever he can. None of the Klansmen have ever desecrated the flag or burned a draft card. He thinks the average American citizen will keep sending his sons off to Vietnam as long as the country is in trouble.

Interviews With Klan Members, 1965

The following six statements of Jones, Mars, Hamby, Dorsett, Reagan, and Creel are from tape interviews taken and edited by Pete Young and Ted Crane in 1965 as part of their copyrighted unpublished manuscript "White Ghetto." The Task Force gratefully acknowledges the kind permission of Messrs. Young and Crane to use this material for the purposes of this report.

J. R. Jones:

This is some facts about J. R. Jones, born July twenty-sixth 1928, in Salisbury, North Carolina. Born in Rowan County, my father's name was Peyton M. Jones, he was a railroad man —Yard Conductor, 51 years on the Southern Railroad. My parents were in the Klan before I was born, and soon as I found out about it, I did join it.

I attended Rowan County High School and went in the Service as soon as I was old enough to go in Service. I was in the Navy, discharged in 1950, came back to Salisbury, met my wife Syble and we were married. Went to Washington, D.C., worked at the U.S. Supreme Court building there in the Electrical Department. After that I moved back here to Granite Quarry and was a bricklayer by trade until a bad accident. For a time I was also on the road as a salesman.

In June of 1963 myself and eight others got together one night in Salisbury and decided that something had to be done —that we'd sat down long enough. All of us were previous

members of the United States Klans which had as its Imperial
Wizard Eldon Edwards out of College Park, Georgia. At his
death his Klan started to die out, but a few of us finally
decided that we would try to keep on as a national organiza-
tion and not stay purely as a state group. We wrote a letter to
Mr. Robert M. Shelton, Imperial Wizard of the United Klans
of America out of Tuscaloosa, Alabama. He in turn sent
Robert Scoggin, Grand Dragon of South Carolina out of
Spartanburg, up to Salisbury in the middle or so of July 1963.
We got about 80 men together and were granted a Provisional
Charter into the United Klans of America, and I was appointed Grand Dragon at that time for a period of 90 days.
On August seventeenth I was elected as the Grand Dragon for
a three year term and I held my first state meeting on August
twenty-first.

One night of the very first that I get to stay home, about
seven-thirty the phone rang. I answered and the lady said,
Mister Jones? I said, yes ma'am. She said, I'd like you to come
down and whip my son-in-law. What's he done? Every night
for two years she says, before bedtime he beats my daughter.
She told me his name and who she was and the addresses and
I told her, I said, young lady, the first night he beat your
daughter I felt sorry for her—but if she don't have no more
sense than to stay and take a beating every night for two
years, I couldn't care less. I will not send anyone down there
to whip him, but I'll be happy to call him and tell him you
asked me to. She screamed her head off said, NO—don't get
my name mixed up in it—she hung up.

One Sunday afternoon we were supposed to have a rally up
in Lenoir, North Carolina. My Night Hawk went on ahead to
set the rally up, and was there before me. And when I got
there, the grass looked awful green and smooth and I got to
walking the property over and I thought, man, this is a fine
place to hold a rally. I walked on out to where the Cross was
set, and I come up over this little hill right next to Number 9
Green on the Golf Course. Best rally site I ever had. After
about ten minutes, the owner came down there waving a
seven Iron—he was mad, and Scared to Death. He says I
don't know what you're doing on this property, but GET
OFF. So I told him that it was MY property—I had a legal
Lease for twenty-four hours, and I was going to have me a
rally wasn't nothing he could do about it. But I did go to see

the men we got the Lease from, and it just so happened we'd made about a Fifty-Foot Mistake, on the wrong side of the road where he had no business. We did leave and had a good rally that afternoon across the street.

My average day will consist of 10 to 15 cups of coffee, about three packs of cigarettes and about 18 hours. I drive upwards of fifteen hundred miles a week, and in seven months to the day last year I ruined a 50,000 mile Warranty on a Dodge Dart. I get up around six a.m.—the phone starts ringing so I'm awake and up, around thirty calls a day come in on various matters of importance.

The reason for my joining the Klan in the first place, I was worried about the 1954 Supreme Court decision on school de-segregation—the Black Monday decision. I started checking and checking close, and found out that it's not the niggers themselves that's in charge of these various Civil Rights organizations—the niggers do not have the brains or the money to finance this Revolution on such a scale. These Executive Positions of CORE and the NAACP—their Boards of Directors and their Policy Makers are all white. And a good many of them are now, or have been associated with the Communist Party. The more these Communists gain control, the more violent these organizations get, and they're getting worse and worse every summer. This country's being torn apart by this Civil Rights Mess—this ain't no small thing that's going on—and these Communists are making all they can out of it. If Lyndon gets into office another four years, I think we'll even have some niggers on the Supreme Court and then you can look for the complete breakdown of all individual state government in the South. These niggers are getting their Rights and I think they should, but not at the expense of ALL Rights guaranteed to all states and people under the Constitution.

This investigation of the United Klans coming up in October is one example. They're fixing to outlaw the Klan from Interstate Travel and holding our rallies and from taking our message to the Public. They didn't think about investigating us until we came out in the open and now we've done it, it's got them Scared to Death. That's the last thing in this God's world they expected us to do. The Klan today is having its largest revival since about a hundred years. So far, we're the ONLY organization—except the Birch Society—that's fighting this Socialistic Federalism on a nation-wide scale. If this Situation ever comes to a head, I truly think that we could have another Civil War if the Law Courts ever try to enforce Integration of all public schools in the South come nineteen sixty-seven or eight. No matter what happens, there's going to be a whole lot of hurt before this thing's over.

* * *

Grady Mars:

Well first off, my name is Grady Mars, I am Chief of Security Guard for the United Klans in North Carolina. I was borned in Kempfer County Mississippi, on March 15, 1924 in the town of Philadelphia. I entered Military Service in October nineteen and forty-two, stayed in the Service a fraction over 20 years. I retired in February of '62 and set up residence in Warren County North Carolina. During my time in the Service, I was in the 82nd Airborne until I was injured in a Parachute Jump. During the last 18 years of my service I was in the Military Police and in the Air Police. I got married in 1951, my wife Jane and I have a daughter that is 12 years of age.

In March of 1964 I joined the United Klans of America. I brought into the Organization 18 years of police experience and techniques. I had listened to Mister Jones talk at three different rallies, and I was familiar with the Klan from many years ago in my home state of Mississippi. I will say this: the Klan of today is entirely different from what it used to be. The United Klans of America has drawn the best men and women out of these other organizations and is completely a modern corporation with our own full-time employees— which I am one—we are working on a Group Insurance Program and a Pension Program. We have a good solid depth of leadership, many bright young fellas who are ready and able to take over. Today we have generally adapted ourselves to modern needs and just like our government's Foreign Policy, we do not get out here and make trouble for aggressive purposes but we do maintain a quiet position of strength to protect ourselves. The way I see it, this Nigger Situation is just getting up into gear and we are preparing ourselves for the Ultimate Crisis that will come our way sooner or later.

As Vice-President of North Carolina, I am also the Chief

Security Guard and by this I have the sole responsibility for all the Security Guards within the state. I help to organize various Training Programs and such, so far as my officers are concerned. We provide security not only for the Klanspeople but for all of our visitors at any of our rallies. Most of our young fellas have had Military Training and know how to conduct themselves when faced with an Emergency. We have many Drill Instructors who rotate around the state from Unit to Unit each week drilling the boys in the art of self-discipline. I do have four men with a Belt in Karate and such as this, and we try to teach every man the basics of this type of things. Some of my Captains can put a hundred armed Klansmen at a given point with one hour's notice. My Security Guard never sleeps. At any time of the day or night, someone is patrolling the Nigger Areas, somebody will be standing by a Base Station Radio. All our cars are equipped with C B radios and with our Relay Stations I can talk to any Unit in the state or get a message out to them even while I'm driving along the road. Our oath binds us to the Realm and to the Imperial Wizard, and my men are just as tough on a fellow Klansman—tougher maybe—than they would be on a Trouble Maker from the crowd. They have no loyalty to any member of their Klavern that would prevent them from acting in a way to promote the welfare of the Organization as a whole. If a Klansman gets drunk on the lot during a rally or shows up drunk—the first time could be accident—if it happens twice that's no accident and he gets thrown off the lot and out of the Organization unless he wants to stand trial and defend his actions before his Klavern. It doesn't happen often, but so far it has happened twice this year. You're only allowed one mistake. If we ever do have trouble with these niggers bustin' into a rally, we don't want some half-drunk Ku Klux shootin' anybody. Of course we all hope that there is no Violence, but Integration has never worked in 200 years and it won't be accepted by the whiteman overnight. Johnson is forcing this Issue so's to get the Minority Votes or either for some other reason, and the Klan is prepared to fight if necessary. This is a War and we will do all in our power to win it and protect ourselves and our families.

* * *

Boyd Hamby:

My name is Boyd Lee Hamby, I was born in Caldwell County North Carolina, September the thirteenth, 1934. I moved to Lexington North Carolina and was married in nineteen and fifty-two, September the thirteenth on my seventeenth birthday. I went in the service September the twenty-third nineteen and fifty-four and spent three years, three months and fifteen days in the Service of which some two years and some few days were overseas in Germany as a Peacetime Soldier. I got out of the Army on January the eighth, 1958.

Living all my life in the South, I have heard of the Klan ever since I was a little boy. I'm not sure, but I think my grandfather was a member—that was a pretty closely guarded secret in those days. So three years ago, I guess it was, I was approached by a man from Lexington and he mentioned the United Klans of America and I was very much interested. So when the Dragon—Mister J. R. Jones came over, I was at the first meeting in my area.

My present position is Grand Night Hawk for the state, and I am also a Lieutenant Colonel in our newly organized Corps in charge of V I P Security. We take care of all visiting Dragons at the State Rallies and we are body guards for the Imperial Wizard and his staff. This is part of a new step-up in our security measures to prevent an Assassination or anything of that nature. I have a detail of 10 men that work with me around the platform to make sure nobody from the crowd can get to our speakers at the rallies. Some in uniform and some in their street clothes. The rest of our Security Guard is scattered out through the crowd, on the move all the time circling the back areas of the audience to guard against a long range bullet from a rifle. Other men see that the traffic is handled in an orderly manner and help the local Law direct the cars.

I am in charge of setting up and putting together the rallies in North Carolina. It involves quite a bit of traveling since I am on the scene for all the rallies and I have to drive anywhere from fifty to sixty thousand miles a year in my duties. I'm supposed to check and see that everything goes off without a hitch—the property leases, the Cross, the local Sheriffs

—I even get the blame for the weather. If anything goes wrong, the responsibility comes back up to me.

First of all we obtain the land preferably, say, a 20 acre field. We try to get a lot that's high and dry and if possible one that belongs to a Klansman or a friend to the Organization. This land is leased to us for one day—a 24 hour period from eight in the morning on the day of the rally until eight the next day. We have printed Lease Forms signed by everyone concerned and notarized and the rally site becomes our property for that 24 hours. Then we set the date of the rally on the same day as we have the Lease for. We usually have a back-up site picked out somewhere nearby so that we can go ahead and have our meeting if the original owner asks us to let him out of his obligations at the last minute.

Then we start moving in. It is usually my job to drive the truck out to the rally site. The local Unit furnishes the Cross —most of them run 60 to 70 feet. A lot of them use Telephone Poles, but mostly a green Pine tree or a Gum—something not too big, and straight. The Lewisburg Unit, I believe it is, got them a good one built a while back and they been using the same Cross at all their rallies for about three years now.

They usually go out the day of the rally in the morning about daylight. They get a committee together the night before and they go out to a farm or some property owned by a Klansman, and they will select the main pole for their Cross and cut it down. They trim it up good, get the branches off close and then it is taken to the rally field. Then it will be put together and a cross-arm put on. We try to make it up in proportion, and the distance from the cross-piece up to the top of the shank is equal to one half the length of the cross-piece. A lot of the boys go to work by nine in the morning but there's usually someone around to collect the Feed Sacks or the burlap bags and begin wrapping the Cross. I would say anywhere from four to five layers of burlap are put on, or something similar that will hold oil. The bags are put on with bailing wire or just nailed on with shingle tacks. Then the Cross is soaked with a solution of half gasoline and half kerosene. Most Crosses need soaking down three or four times, and I've known some to take up to 40 gallons of oil before they're completely saturated. Especially if you get wet weather like this afternoon, you want to soak the Cross up pretty good. Then right before dark, usually around six o'clock the Cross is erected. We hire a local wrecking service to come out and help us. We all take turns digging the hole which wants to be at least four feet deep and about two feet wide. Then we sling a long rope around the upper end of the shank near the cross-piece and the wrecker sets his boom hitch up on as high as he can reach. The Cross is then raised up until it slips down into the hole and the boys on the rope keep it straight and steady while we fill in around the base. I always set my Crosses at an angle so that the outline shape can be seen clearly from the side.

The Klan as a whole in years past has had a name for being violent and standing up. I do believe that by having this reputation that it has held down a lot of Racial Incidents that we would have had in the South, had it not been that the niggers knew the Klan was there and were afraid of what it would do. And today, as the Klan is having its biggest revival since the Civil War, these niggers are moving out of the rural areas of the South as fast as they can. I am not saying that the Klan of today is violent—they are not responsible for every Incident that crops up, although more often than not we do get the blame for any Violence. But everyone knows that the Klan is serious, they will fight if necessary—we could become militant anytime if this Revolution is pushed to extremes. I wish we could all live together—when I say together I don't mean Integration, I believe in Segregation. Before this interview is over, there is one little thing that I would like to say: I believe in what I'm fighting for—I believe in White Supremacy political and social. If I did not believe in this I would be home with my family—I have a wife and five children. So there's one little remark I'd like to make: I had rather be killed fighting for Something, than to live for Nothing.

* * *

George Dorsett:

This is George F. Dorsett. I was born in Saint Louis Missouri, June the eighth nineteen and seventeen. I came to Greensboro North Carolina and all my schooling was in Greensboro. I was ordained when I was 21, and I pastored in Greensboro for about four years—started the South Side Baptist Church in Greensboro. Pastored it for a while. Then I resigned there and went on an Evangelistic Tour of Texas and Mexico with my wife and two boys. After we returned from this—we were gone five years—we came back to Greensboro and I accepted a call to the Sydney Avenue Baptist Church in Burlington, and I pastored there approximately five years along with my Radio Ministry. I was on WBBB in Burlington and at the same time I was carrying a program over WGBG in Greensboro, a weekly program and a daily program every morning. I did my Evangelistic Work all along, up in the mountains and down through South Carolina—had an old brown tent that I conducted my Services in. After that I was with a local funeral home in Greensboro—we spent right much of our hours at work there—they were long hours, and I would ride the Ambulance and conduct many of the Funerals.

Then the Supreme Court passed the ruling on School De-Segregation, and many of the concerned white people began to join the White Citizen's Council in Greensboro. Various towns were using their Courthouse for these meetings, and several family groups had me to speak at their neighborhood meetings. The P T A associations were also becoming concerned, and I spoke at many of the High-schools in the area.

Then in the latter part of '56 I think it was, the Reverend James Cole was organizing through North Carolina—Cat-Fish Cole—and he was the Imperial Wizard of his own Klan group. He was an Evangelist also, and I met him several times on the Sawdust Trail on various trips and tours around the mountain country. There was another Evangelist working this area at that time and we met several times on the trail—his name was Billy Graham, I guess you've heard of him. We all went our separate ways. Many of the families who were in the White Citizens' Council joined in together with Cole's Klan at that time and I also joined. I spoke at many of the rallies around North and South Carolina which we conducted mostly in our large circus tents. I was appointed the North Carolina Chaplain by Reverend Cole, and worked closely with him in the activities of the Klan. Then he was arrested because of Maxton, North Carolina, and the skirmish we had there, and he was put into the Penitentiary for two years for inciting a riot, although he wasn't even present at the time. During his imprisonment his Klan died down, but many groups of us continued on with our family meetings and Sunday services.

After a while the United Klans Of America began to send their Organizers around the state, and we became interested. James Cole had operated mainly in North and South Carolina and we were attracted by the idea of joining a National Organization with a Planned Educational Program. They were legally chartered in seven states at that time, and employing men and women on a full-time basis. We all joined in with Mister Shelton's organization, because we realized that if we all stayed divided we would probably fall, but united we could stand firm together. At the 1964 National Convention I was elected Imperial Kludd of the Klan. I'm assured that the growth of the Klan in America will keep pace with this Civil Rights Situation and surpass even the old days. The Klan is always changing and responding to the needs of its people, when pressure is put on the white man the Klan will rise, this has always been true and will continue to be true.

It takes a lot of Ministers to make up our organization— many individual Units have one, and every Province must have an ordained Minister. I think it's one of the greatest opportunities, the families are already gathered, and it's almost like accepting a Congregation. Many families in various Klans of the same area get together on Sundays and have their own Community Services and picnic lunches, and I spend right much of my time going around to these meetings. I find the people very easy to get along with, they're reasonable ordinary men and women with the problems and jealousies that all of us have. It's true that where you have thousands of people in an organization you will get some men and women whose character is doubtful and who might bring shame to the Order under some circumstances. I find that's the same in the church—I've pastored churches where some of my members have gone off to do things that were not Christian. And I've known preachers who have left their family and run off with their Pianist or their Secretary and committed sins like that. But you cain't say that all preachers are criminals because of that, or that there's nothing to the church because one member's involved in a sin or a crime.

I think the white ministers of America have helped the negro spiritually but our hands are tied now, because we cain't help them like we did. Back in the early part of my ministry I preached at many of the negro churches for their Rally Day. When I was doing my radio broadcasts they would often invite me to come and speak, and the Offering would go towards their Building Fund. We did this many, many times, and my wife and I had a lot of good friends among the negroes in those days. We shared our Christian Beliefs together and kind of re-inforced each other in our religion. But now a Touchy Situation has been created, and white ministers don't get invited to speak in negro churches anymore. And it is true that he might cause more friction and ill-will than he might do good. Now a days a man cain't carry his maid home no more without thinking about it, and making sure she sits up front with him. These Socialist Organizations that are pushing Integration from this purely Physical Standpoint have succeeded in developing all the ingredients of a national Race War, and the pot's on the boil. I look for increased rioting all over in America, and I think the North is going to suffer the worst of all.

The Scripture tells us that God is not the author of Confusion. He himself through Divine Process made the white species separate from the black, and mankind is trying to force them together and confuse the various characteristics and skin color. In Acts 17:26, in Daniel chapter seven, and Revelation 11:15 and 21:24, all nations are to remain segregated in their own part of the earth. God forbade intermarriage between Israel and all other nations in Exodus 34:12 and Deuteronomy 7:3. The mixing of races caused Dis-Unity among God's people, as we learn from Number Eleven.

I don't think there's ever been a time in the history of the United States when we were at such a Critical Stage. There's never been so much confusion and chaos, and so many important laws passed so fast—they say they are broadening our Civil Rights, but seems like all they do is Broaden Federal Control of our Rights. We've had our assassination, and this Revolution that has started up is only the beginning. If this Integration Process was of God, it would go peacefully.

* * *

Tommy Reagan:

This is Tommy Reagan. I've been about seven years in Electronics and I was a Salesman selling to T.V. Repair Shops and Retail Stores. So one day I was sitting home between trips and this old boy who I used to know, asked me if I would come with him to a Klan meeting. I'd been dying to go to one, so naturally I jumped at the chance, you know. I had set back and watched for years what was going on, knowing full well what was happening. But I thought some other man on the street would step forward and fight this thing. Well, of course, nobody did. I've lived about half my life now—maybe more'n that and if I die tomorrow you can say that I tried and that I did what I could for what I believe in.

So we went out there, six of us in the one car and we finally turned into the yard of this old home on the outside of town. I was sitting up in the front next to this old boy who had invited me along, and as we were going down this driveway we were stopped by a man in a robe and he mumbled something to my friend who was driving and my friend said something back, and he let us on by. At that time I didn't know nothing about Passwords or nothing like that. I asked him what he said and he said, I don't know but it musta been the right thing. We drove around the backside of this old house, you know, and we all got out.

Pretty soon I found myself alone out there, and this big Klansman was leading me around the back into this back room, and he sets me down in this chair. I couldn't figure out what happened to the other boys, and they all went into the house another way. So I was setting there you know, and I kept on hearing shuffling of feet in the next room and I was wondering what was going on, but I wasn't about to ask this old boy you know, because he looked rough enough to me like he wasn't about to take the first word. So I kept my mouth shut and finally he brought me into this big room. I was confronted by a roomful of robed and masked Klansmen in white robes, with one all red robe in the center of the front row. When I saw all those robes together in that room, you couldn't a run me out of there—I been in it ever since.

When I was a kid, I shot marbles with the niggers and I got along with them. But a law is made for the Majority, or should be. That's the whole principle that our nation's Democracy is based on. But when you have to call out the United States Army into the streets of your own home town to force these niggers into White Society—where they don't belong and can never belong—it's not a good law, it's just not a good law. I was talking to my Insurance Agent over at the house the other evening, my wife had us some lemonade out on the front porch. He said he'd join the Klan himself, but he was afraid. I know he was scared because he told me so and I could tell from talking to him. Great big tall Texan, you know, could gather me up and half break me in two and he was scared. That's the trouble with the white man in America today concerning the nigger: they don't love him, they don't hate him—but they don't want to have to fight him.

* * *

Robert Creel:

My name is Robert M. Creel, I was born in a small south Alabama town on fifth October 1930. I lived there until I was approximately six months old, we moved away and we moved to Jefferson which I finished Elementary Schooling in Jefferson county. Then we moved to Hopewell Virginia where I attended Highschool. We moved back to Alabama because we only went up there, we had to have an operation on my father's hip which was at the Medical College of Virginia in Richmond. I went into the Army at the age of 17 and continued my studies and was in the Medical Corps for six years. I have a wife, her name is Billy, and we have three children.

In 1954 right after I got out of the Army I attended a public rally of the United Klans of America and I listened and I said, that's for me. I been in it ever since. I was the type of Klansman that I did more listening than any talking, then I gradually worked my way up to Grand Dragon. I got my father into the Klan, also I went through the Masonic Lodge and carried him through the Masonic Lodge. My wife is the E. C. [Exalted Cyclops] over Unit One of the Ladies Auxiliary here in the state. When I go into a town or one of my organizers we don't say who can come into the Organization and who can't. We ask for volunteers and we set up a Screening Committee, and the local citizens say whether a family is acceptable or not, because those men and women know each other and been knowing each other sometimes for generations. Half the D.A.R. in this state have relatives in the Klan.

I've never thought about going underground for the simple reason that this country's got a sickness of Socialism, and Socialism cannot be stamped out by secret underground organizations. The Federal Government never thought of investigating us until we got organized and came out in the open ready to fight them with finances and political backing on their own terms. These Communists are not impatient if they can elect a Liberal here and one there—and take away a Right this year and maybe one more next year, they're satisfied. One of their principal doctrines is that Communism must be built by non-Communist hands, and Liberals like Emanuel Celler and Jacob Javits and Abe Fortas of the Supreme Court—these men are playing right into their hands. See how many well-meaning people—college students and college faculty members—even some of the more Liberal Ministers of your churches have got out here in the streets and marched and demonstrated with these Socialist Civil Rights groups in the name of "Christian Tolerance." A lot of well-meaning people have contributed their money, sincere believers in the Principle of Integration—in the philosophical idea of it—but they have never seen the actual forced Race Mixing. Many of these people would hesitate if they realized the Constitutional Changes that this Civil Rights Revolution is bringing about. Many of these people out here marching would hesitate to have a nigger for a neighbor—they'd hesitate to send their young daughters into school with that bunch that pissed on the steps of our State Capitol. Half of these Protesters ain't never seen a real southern nigra, or had to sit down and eat together with one, or smell one.

I think the problem that's facing our nation is twofold. The nigra has lost his fight here in the South—these Civil Rights gangs are concentrating on your northern cities now, because they can put more direct pressure on the Legislatures. You haven't had any major riots here in the South and you're not going to have one. This Revolution has forced the white people together here in the South and is certainly responsible for this recent tremendous growth of the Klan. But on the other hand for the last three years the N double A CP's been sending these niggers North as fast as they could. Washington D.C. was their first Target City, and now they're concentrating on Philadelphia, Baltimore and New York City. In ten years these nigras could elect all the city officials in every big city of America, and that's just what these Civil Rights organizations want. They want to spread the trouble so that the whole nation becomes infected with riots and Federal Intervention. We've won our battle against these outside Civil Rights agitators here in the south—now our fight is with the local courts and the Federal Government. They intend to force this issue by September 1967, and you can look for the Big Trouble to start then. I hope we don't get gouged into a Shooting War, because certainly that's what these Communists want. We're hoping to hold the lid on the best we can, otherwise this whole country's lost for both of us, White and Black.

* * *

Klan-Sponsored Radio Program

We have a tape of the Klan-sponsored radio program. It is one-half hour of live country music supplied by Skeeter Bob and His Country Pals broadcast once a week over three radio stations. It is called Country Pals. The music is straight country style music with no racist lyrics. Listeners, however, are urged to donate to the Klan and write in for free tracts such as "The Ugly Truth about Martin Luther King." Listeners are also informed that 20 "segregationist" records are available, at $1 apiece and that they can send in for a list of the records and order them from the United Klans of America, P.O. Box 321, Granite Quarry, N.C.

Tapes of "Segregationist" Records

We have tapes of nine out of the approximately forty songs represented by the twenty "segregationist" records referred to in the Klan-sponsored radio program.

The Klan "segregationist" records started in approximately 1964 when the Klan brought out its first 45-rpm record entitled "Move Them Niggers North." They are semi-underground records, not generally available. They sell for $1 at Klan rallies and are available through the offices of the United Klans of America. They are also, we are told, in some rural juke boxes. They are not as yet played on the radio.

They strike all the themes of the white ghetto: (1) vigilantism, (2) racist violence, (3) resentment that the government directs welfare and government aid to Negroes but does not respond to the plight of the poor white. In quality and style, they are quite professional country music. This music be captures the raw hatred, fear, and resentment of the persons to whom the Klan appeals. Note the repeated references to Martin Luther King, Jr., in the summary of the music selections below. He apparently was the symbol of the Negro threat to these people. Note the line in selection seven: "Martin Luther's got to go/That's one thing that we all know."

Summary of Music Selections

1. "His Name was Levi Coon" (Cajun Ku Klux Klan) (86–128). (This is now the best seller of the Klan's "segregationist" records—Ed.)

A ballad that tells the story of a Negro who tries to get service in a restaurant because of the new civil rights bill. The waitress refuses to serve him, and when the Negro refuses to leave the waitress calls the Cajun KKK. The Cajun KKK arrives. The Negro is terrified and laments, "Why did I ever listen to that demonstrator King?" The KKK ties his hands and they both knew (the Klansmen and the Negro) that he would be tortured. The ballad draws the moral that Negroes should mind their own business and leave white folks be or else they will be terrorized by the Klan.

2. "I Don't Like Niggers" (Nigger-Hatin' Me). (128–171)

An expression of disgust and hate directed at all Negroes. The flavor of the song is expressed in the line "There are only two things that will make me puke/a hog eating slop and a big black spook." It also contains the line "Stick your black head out and I'll blow it (shoot it off)."

Other lines: "You have to be black to get a welfare check/ and I'm broke (the white singer of the song)/No joke/I ain't got a nickel for a coke/I ain't black you see/so Uncle Sam won't help poor nigger-hatin' me."

"Mirror, mirror on the wall/who's the blackest of them all/A man named King, there ain't no doubt/he's a-causin' lots of trouble with his baboon mouth."

3. "We Don't Want Niggers in Our School, We're Not for Integration" (171–208).

The theme of the song: Outside agitators are coming down South to take Southern schools away from the people and change Southern ways. Contains the lines: "We must prove to

Martin Luther that we stand for what is right/no court or left-wing liberals can ever make him white."

3. "Move Them Niggers North" (If they don't like our southern ways move them niggers north) (208–251).

The theme of the song: South has been invaded by trash that is going to take away its schools and its way of life from you and me; it is time to make a stand.

Contains the lines: "I like our Southland like it is, I'm sure that you do too/Old Martin Luther thinks it's his, I know he's wrong, don't you" (208–251).

5. "Make Your Stand" (Ku Klux Klan recruiting record). (251–303)

The theme of the song is contained in its opening lines: "All around this land there's too many people who are afraid to say where they stand/but I'm not one and I'm proud to be counted as a member of the Ku Klux Klan."

Also: "There ain't no way the government's gonna help you unless your skin is black."

6. "Segregation Wagon" (303–355).

Song links Southern ways with "states' rights" and conservatism. Blames problems on "sorry lookin' bunch of trash" from the North trying to take away Southern customs. Urges everyone to get aboard the segregation wagon.

7. "Nigger, Nigger, Tell Them Lies" (355–393).

Theme expressed in the following excerpts:

"They're marching for equality/they'll never be as good as me."

"Martin Luther's got to go/that's one thing that we all know." (Goes on to urge that Martin Luther King be tarred and feathered.)

"Puffy lips and kinky hair/living off the old welfare."

"They might as well give up the fight/no federal court can make them white/it's all up to you and me/let's beat the NAACP (move 'em North)."

8. "Wop, Wop, Bam, Bam, Who Likes a Nigger?" (393–451).

Chorus: "Wop, wop, bam, bam, who likes a nigger" (three times), next line: "and the hate in everybody is getting much bigger."

The first two verses are two racist jokes. First verse: LBJ sees some white people pulling a Negro on water skis in Louisiana and congratulates them on their progressive civil rights ideas. When he leaves, the two white people say that LBJ may be smart but he does not know anything about hunting alligators. Second verse: a rich man goes to a dentist and asks him to pull a bad tooth of his Negro chauffeur. The dentist says it will cost $200 because in Mississippi they don't allow Negroes to open their mouths and therefore he will have to go up through the Negro's bottom to get the tooth out. The last verse compares Negroes to various animals such as dogs, apes and mules. The Negro comes out worse. "The mule works for his living by the sweat of his neck/a nigger lives off the welfare check. Niggers might be smarter as a general rule/but in a spelling contest, I'll take the mule."

9. "They're Looking for a Handout."

Theme expressed in the chorus: "They're looking for something free/they're looking for a handout from you and me/and with the consent/of the President/they're gonna get their way."

The verse says that Negroes won't work. All they will do is demonstrate so that they can get handouts. But someday Negroes will have to go to work and stop holding out their hands for handouts. The Lord said that salvation is to be earned by the sweat of the brow. Urges Negroes to reform and become "good little niggers" once again (451–525).

The following is a recitation by Grand Dragon Jones, also available from the Klan on a 45-rpm record upon why the Klan burns crosses. It is recited with the hymn "The Old Rugged Cross" played in the background.

> Out of the wonderful of the sacred pages of this old book divine, comes the Sad Sweet Story of Calvary's rugged but Holy Cross. This old Cross is a symbol of Sacrifice and Service, and a sign of the Christian Religion sanctified and made holy nearly 19 centuries ago, by the suffering and blood of 50 million Martyrs who died in the Most Holy Faith. It stands in every Klavern in the United Klans of America as a constant reminder that Christ is our Criterion of Character, his teachings our rule of life, blood-bought and holy, sanctified and sublime. This Cross was once a sign of Ignominy and Disgrace, but being bathed in the blood of the Lowly Nazarene it has been transformed into the symbol of Faith, Hope and Love. It inspired the Crusaders in the Middle

Ages in their Perilous Efforts to rescue the Holy Land from the Most Heathen Turk, and is today being used to rally the forces of Christianity against the ever increasing hordes of Anti-Christs and the enemies of Pure Americanism. As light drives away darkness and gloom, so a knowledge of Truth dispels Ignorance and Superstition. As fire purified gold, silver and precious stones but destroys the dross, wood, hay and stubble, so by the fire of the Cross we mean to purify and cleanse our virtues by the fire of His Sword. Who can look upon this sublime symbol, or sit in its Most Holy Light without being inspired with a desire and a determination to be a better man. By this sign we shall conquer . . .

* * *

Interview with Will Campbell, September 1968

The Reverend Will Campbell is of Southern poor white background. He was born to a Mississippi tenant farmer. He was graduated from the University of Mississippi, did work at Wake Forest and Tulane, and received his doctorate at Yale University. He is a Baptist minister.

Reverend Campbell was student chaplain at the University of Mississippi until forced out of that position after being labeled a "crusading radical" because he preached and practiced integration. He is the author of the book, *Race and the Renewal of the Church*. He is executive director of the Committee of Southern Churchmen, a small group subsidized by national denominations and foundations as the "last fragile link" from mainstream America to the "white ghetto" from which the Klan draws its strength. He first began his concern in this direction in 1954. As task force consultant, Mr. Young puts it: "It is not enough to talk about the poor white; we must talk to the poor white." Reverend Campbell talks to the poor white.

(Interview). There were a number of incidents leading up to his dismissal as student chaplain of the University of Mississippi. One such incident: He was chided for playing ping pong with a Negro. He replied that he thought this was precisely the Southern way—each had a separate but equal paddle and they were separated by a net.

When the Supreme Court decision came down about school integration, he saw that if everyone in Mississippi would agree to follow the decision of the Supreme Court wholeheartedly, it would take at least ten years just to work out the logistics. But the attitude in Mississippi was "Never." And "never" is still prevailing. Now it is not just the white citizens councils and the Ku Klux Klan, but also Negro groups have taken up the cry.

Reverend Campbell blames this situation on the church and includes himself in the blame. At Little Rock, he and other churchmen walked with the Negro children to school. The church's plea was for law and order—that the governor should follow law and order and admit the Negro children in accordance with the law. But the church had something much more radical to say and should have said it—that the relationship should not be one of law and order, but one of love and equality. The irony is that now all three candidates for the presidency (Nixon, Humphrey, and Wallace—September 1968) are campaigning on the issue of law and order. Law and order works well for the middle class, both black and white, but not for poor people. Poor people equate law with order and order with the scheme of things that keeps them in their place. Reverend Campbell remembers his father agonizing on Christmas Eve when he thought his children were in bed asleep because his children were waiting for a Christmas that would not come for them. He can remember a tenant farmer crying when the rain did not come in time for his cotton crops because this meant that law and order would take his farm away from him.

Law and order, however, worked to keep poor people in their place until the last few years, when both blacks and whites have refused to accept the middle-class version of law and order. It is ironic that poor blacks and poor whites consider each other enemies, when the enemy is elsewhere.

There was a TV special on the Ku Klux Klan which accurately told the story of Klan atrocities, but deliberately ignored the conditions of the poor white people from which the Klan draws its strength. There is an invisible empire of selfish greed to acquire and control power. In fact, just a few people do control political power in this nation. That is why the Wallace campaign is so interesting and, in one sense, the healthiest thing in a long time because it is a challenge to the political power elite. Unfortunately, the challenge is in the wrong direction. Black people talk of participatory democracy; down South, Wallace is participatory democracy at work.

There is more participatory democracy to be found in the Klan for the poor white than in any other way reasonably open to him. He has no other route to participate in controlling his own affairs. He has been ignored. The "Gentry" position has prevailed against populist movements in which poor whites participated.

Huey Long nearly formed a coalition between blacks and poor whites and even more his brother, Earl Long. Earl Long was probably crazy, but so are a lot of politicians, and he had been crazy long before he was condemned on that ground. The Gentry got Earl Long when Earl Long objected to the Gentry's purging of black voters. The Gentry got him when there was a threat of poor whites and blacks getting together and voting against Standard Oil.

The establishment fears war between the races less than an alliance between them. A war between the races can be handled as a police problem or else a favored group can be allowed to get the upper hand. When Reverend Campbell was young in Mississippi, a poor white could kill a Negro with impunity. The Gentry coalition could always play one group against the other, but could not handle the two groups if they got together.

Reverend Campbell does not believe that there has been a calculated plot on the part of the Gentry to maintain power. This is just the common, human drive to power and the common, human failing of creating scapegoats for problems. The Gentry has projected on poor whites and perhaps all Negroes for years that somehow it is they that are causing the trouble. The Establishment projects its guilt on Negroes or on the Klan or the like, then ritually purges the guilt. This is what the House Un-American Activities Committee did in attacking the Klan. But the ritual purging of the Klan has done nothing to alter the basic condition of the poor white which remains and continues to breed the same problems.

There have been no really effective government programs tailored to the poor white. The Council of the Southern mountains out of Kentucky has done some work in the mountain Appalachian region, but this is not the same problem. There is no race question. The people there are all white and the area has been so exploited by strip-mining that they are almost all poor. The Establishment attitude towards the poor whites in Appalachia is also more sympathetic. The poor whites in the rural South carry guns and are thus too uppity for the establishment.

The rape of Appalachia was so complete that there is complete despair, but the man who carries a gun has not yet despaired. All the whites in Appalachia can do is moan their folksongs of despair. The other poor whites have not despaired; they carry guns in increasing number with increasing determination and perhaps with increasing effectiveness.

Perhaps this is leading to a concentration-camp society. If the only response to the poor white violence is more controls —a police response—then there will be created a spiral of more violence and more controls. As long as the government sees violence only as something to be controlled, all we really have is a fascist state; we have lost our freedom.

As a first response to violence, we must recognize that we are all potentially violent. Reverend Campbell spoke to a group of VISTA volunteers. They were from the North, East, and the West, but not the South. Reverend Campbell said that he came from Mississippi and approximately one-half the audience turned off. He said he was a Baptist minister and half the remaining audience turned off. In order to make some contact he said, "I am pro-Ku Klux Klan because I am pro-human being." The Ku Klux Klan for poor whites stands for peace, harmony, and freedom. Freedom means "I do what I want, when I want to and have some control over my own destiny." The Klan uses violence like the violence the United States uses in Vietnam. The United States is in Vietnam to ensure peace, harmony, and freedom, but the United States has to do it with violence and that is what the poor whites and blacks are doing. They are getting together to ensure their own peace, harmony, and freedom and they are doing it with violence. A member of the audience said to Reverend Campbell, "You call yourself a Christian minister, but Christ could not get into the Ku Klux Klan." Reverend Campbell asked how Christ would do on a VISTA exam and whether Christ could have been a delegate to the Democratic convention.

The members of the audience said that Reverend Campbell sympathized with uneducated people because he was uneducated—in other words that he was dirt. They assumed this because of their own prejudice about persons of poor white, Southern backgrounds.

The Reverend Campbell told them of his academic honors

and said, in conclusion, that he had seen more hostility and hate from this group of VISTA volunteers than he had ever seen at the Klan gatherings he had attended. At that point they were shouting at him "Hell, no" and the like. "I asked them whether they were shouting expressions of love."

If we accept the fact that we are all potentially violent and stop looking for scapegoats, such as Klansmen and Negroes, we can at least start working constructively at the roots of our problems.

White Backlash

Summary of Tony Imperiale Tape

Anthony Imperiale is head of the North Ward Citizens Council in Newark, N.J., a white ethnic quasi-vigilante group. Imperiale's organization is a prototype of an indigenous urban white-backlash group responding to real or perceived threats from the urban Negro. It should not be forgotten that Newark is corrupt. The mayor has refused to turn over his personal financial records to a grand jury, pleading the Fifth Amendment. Imperiale's platform in that regard is genuinely reformist. Imperiale at the time this tape was made was running for councilman-at-large in Newark. He won. Indeed, he led the ticket.

Imperiale Campaign Speech

I can restore law and order because I have no deals with any man. I have nothing to gain but to bring law and order back to Newark to see that my family and children and property are safe. We do not want a recurrence of the riots of 1967. FBI reports show that crime in Newark is skyrocketing. I do not promise to lower taxes or get anyone a job. I promise to serve you as I served the North Ward Citizens Committee as its president. We cannot stand more of what has been going on: radicalism on both sides, white and black.

I belong to the Model City Program in Newark and Tuesday night when I went to a meeting they tried to stop me from entering the building. I was threatened with physical violence. There were forty or more black radicals. I recognized some from LeRoi Jones and the Panthers. I could not call the police because the police would not respond for me, but my chauffeur saw that I was in danger and called the North Ward, and sixty of our men came down so that no one harmed me. The point is that this is a federal program and they tried to intimidate me.

The Mayor says he is going to try to get funds to start civilian patrols in the Central Ward (the Negro ward). He claims this should be done for the so-called ghetto area. I went to Washington to get federal funds to set up a civilian patrol program in the North Ward (Imperiale's white district) and the other areas of the city, black as well as the white, and I was pushed from pillar to post. It is all right for the Central Ward but not for the North Ward where I am called a paramilitary organization. Now, the Mayor wants additional taxes for civilian patrols after having condemned civilian patrols and having refused policemen and firemen a raise. You cannot have good law enforcement when you deny policemen and firemen a raise and slap them in the face by proposing civilian patrols.

A raise for policemen could be paid out of sales taxes which would take in $108,000,000 a year. But this money is being directed into anti-poverty programs which benefit only the Negroes and not our kids. I saw myself in the Central Ward ten portable pools placed there under the United Community Corporation smeared with manure, human waste, cut and destroyed. You do not read about this because it is kept quiet. Our kids were denied portable pools. Why is there no investigation? They will raise our taxes again. You can do something about this by voting for me. I do not say I can do much but at least you will have a voice. Right now, we have nothing. The press in Newark does not print the crime reports or the FBI statistics nor what is going on in the Central Ward where decent Negroes themselves have become the victim of black radicals.

After you elect me, I will need you to continue to support me. Nothing can be done without you people any more than the North Ward Citizens Committee would have become famous for its patrols and escorts without its members. I do not intend to sell my home and run.

There is $127,000,000 of federal money coming to Newark

under the Model Cities Program. They are going to put up skill centers not just for one ethnic group but for everyone. They are not going to take down the homes they originally had in mind, but instead they are going to place the center in a portion of the land that was to be a parking lot for the College. This is a county project and there would be no tax to the city, yet it would be an asset for the city if whites as well as blacks could attend it and be trained. Private enterprises controlled by clergymen should not be tax exempt. If we continue tax freeloading, Newark will become a ghost town. We cannot get any more taxes out of our people; there should be state aid and federal aid.

Do not let them take the stadium out of this area and relocate it. Let them use it for the children in our ward no matter what their color. The kids of this ward do not have blazer canteens like the other side of town. Our kids just hang around the corners. I went down to the Central Ward and saw the old furniture place beautifully refurnished with close to 700 kids in the building. There was not one white person. It was a blazer canteen for the kids. I am 100 percent for it and I do not care if they were all black, but our kids in the North Ward need this sort of thing too. They are running the city on a separate basis. The hypocrites, pacifists, and cheap candy-ass liberals and politicians are playing favors because that is where the vote is. They worry more about the vote than property and lives. I will do something to oppose this.

A man told me that he thought I was a nut when he first heard me talk. He remembered I said that when it comes to his doorstep he would awake. It came to his doorstep; his daughter was raped. I said now you want to kill, but killing is not the solution. This could have been prevented if the people supported the administration and the police. If there were strong law enforcement, the rape would not have happened in a school. If you elect me you will set a precedent. I will be the first what they call vigilante to be elected. Call me what you want, you cannot change what I will do and what is in my heart.

Responses to question from audience after speech

The mayor refused to turn over his financial records, pleading the Fifth Amendment. I found out that the mayor does not have the immunity of the Fifth Amendment and so I demanded his resignation. I sent this to the newspapers, but of course they would not print it. If the councilmen truly want to represent their people they will do their duty and act. If not, I will charge them with misfeasance.

If I win I will do it without money. My signs are hand-made. I am an underdog. If I lose, you lose, because I want to prevent the chicken-livered skunks from selling out. I have had offers for no-show jobs and $2,500 and $5,000 to keep quiet. I have also been intimidated in particular by the Governor. He is a candy-ass liberal who had the audacity to say that I was like Al Capone or the brown shirts in Germany. These are the things that are hurting us, but we are going to win and our broom will have some very sharp whiskers on it.

Interview with Imperiale

A few weeks ago three bombs were set off in front of my (Imperiale's) office. The bombs went off at intervals of ten to fifteen seconds. There was at least one stick of dynamite in each bomb. It appears to be a professional job. It was probably not an attack on my life but more-or-less a calling card to try to scare me off. At first, I thought it was the black radicals but now I do not know. It could have been narcotics racketeers.

The narcotic problem in Newark is serious. It is responsible for a great increase in crime, both in the Negro as well as the white area. There are payoffs to the police, but it can be stopped. I am going to do the best I can.

With respect to the bombing, we called the FBI to try to get them to investigate, but they would not investigate because they said that our civil rights were not involved. But my civil rights as an individual to operate as a North Ward Citizens Committee were being infringed. What makes me mad is that if the bombing had happened in the Central (Negro) Ward, there would have been all kinds of FBI agents and authorities. When we get bombed, neither the mayor, the governor nor anyone else said it was a bad thing to have happened. No statement whatsoever was made in the papers.

After the bombing, many people in the North Ward wanted to go down to the Central Ward and kill black people, but thanks to the boys of the North Ward Citizens' Committee, who circulated through the crowd calming people down, there was no violence. Instead we held an emergency rally and kept people cool. No FBI officer or any government officer has ever come near us about the bombing. I thought the least that could be done was that the mayor or the governor or someone might have come up here. If they had, I would not have had to stay on the streets for four days and four nights straight keeping people calm.

The priests would not even come. I had to call twice and finally had to tell the priests, "get the hell over here, your people have been bombed." Finally, they came over just in time to go back to serve Mass. They did not even ask whether I was alive or any of the people hurt. They just walked down, looked at the people and that was it.

The white churches in Newark are so busy working with the black community that they are not taking interest in the people of the white community. Certain parishes play favoritism and Monsignor Dooley at St. Francis Church caused trouble by calling me a bigot, a vigilante, and a loudmouth. He told the people not to listen to me. When I warned them that he was going to raise them $10 a year to bring their kids to school, he said I was a liar but then the $10 raise came through. He said I was a liar when I said he was going to start bussing cross-town kids (Negroes) here free of charge when our kids have to pay, but it happened.

One day twenty parents in this neighborhood witnessed over a hundred bussed-in kids beating up on one 13-year-old girl. We called an emergency parents' rally. That Sunday, Monsignor Dooley got up on the pulpit and the hypocrite said that the situation was not as big as we said. That was a lie. If we had not had a couple of my men in there, the girl would have been dead. I tried to give testimony on the United Community Corporation up in Washington (McClellan Committee) but they would not listen to me or let me testify.

The night of the riot in the Negro area after the death of Martin Luther King, the leader of the UCC told the mayor to get his people out and UCC people would take care of it. Two UCC men with armbands on were arrested for looting a drugstore. They were caught by two narcotics detectives and the inspector told the detectives to leave them alone. What is going on when you catch men with bombs in their hands and then tell detectives to leave them alone? Also, Henry Romeo arrested two UCC youths looting a drugstore—took pictures and everything.

Leaders in the black community get interviewed on NBC and the reporter asks them about "the racist extremist Anthony Imperiale" and they say that Imperiale is a psychopath with his guns and all. Then we learn that the government was giving $115,000 to people like LeRoi Jones to make hate plays and they say they have no regrets. We learned that in Newark, Negro children are asked in school, "Do you hear the noise of the airplane? It is the white people coming to bomb Negroes."

Let the mayor and the United Community Corporation say that they are responsible for a calm summer. That is a lie. What made the summer cooler is that people like me were aware of what was going on and were not going to tolerate any more disorder. We are not going to tolerate policemen being pushed and kicked and shot at.

(The governor asked Imperiale to call off his patrols.)

I did call them off but not because the Governor asked. I was advised by my attorney and close friend and campaign manager to discontinue the patrols because two-thirds of the city was functioning pretty well, so give it a try. However, the patrols in the Central Ward (by non-Imperiale people) were continuing, not for peace but to spy on our policemen. When I saw this going on and after the bombing, Governor Hughes can go to hell. The patrols are out and are going to stay.

The Anti-Vigilante Bill will do nothing because I am not a vigilante. I am 100 percent for a paramilitary law because that would outlaw people dressed in uniforms getting together and practicing sabotage and overthrow of the government. I am not out to overthrow our government. I love the government and am trying to save it.

After the death of Martin Luther King, the North Ward Citizens Committee had double patrols because we did not want people coming to the North Ward and burning us out. One night just as I had parked my car and was standing by the door of the office there was a siren. A car comes up and Porky Pig the mayor and two reporters jumped out. The mayor pushed the door open and pushed me and said "Where is the gun, I saw a man here with a gun." I said there was no one with a gun. The mayor began to search the building and opened up my refrigerator. I said, "Get the hell out of here, you have no search warrant." I did not exactly place the mayor under arrest but I started to escort him to the door. When the mayor realized that his big bodyguard was not with him because one of my men had blocked off the back door the mayor did not need much pushing to start running out the door.

Gabe Pressman interviewed the mayor that morning and the mayor said that the white militants were responsible for the burning in the Central Ward. I am considered the leader of the white militants. They called the mayor and told him that the interview had been accidentally destroyed and they wanted to reinterview him. In the second interview the mayor thought better of his original statement and changed it to soft-pedal white militancy. But Gabe Pressman salvaged that part of the interview and ran on TV that white militants were responsible for the burning of the Central Ward. That night my wife and four children were threatened with death. Someone threw Molotov cocktails at my home that did not explode. I had to move my wife and four children out of Newark. My car was riddled with bullets. The mayor put my family through hell by accusing me of this and that is why I was angry with him. He made an accusation without proof that put the lives of my family in jeopardy.

People call me an extremist, a hater, and an advocate of violence but this does not bother me. I live in an integrated neighborhood and do what I know in my heart is best. People make threatening phone calls to me saying they are going to kill me and my wife and kids and burn their bodies but I turn it into a joke and say let me get some more insurance and be sure to kill my mother-in-law too. By not taking them seriously I have reduced the number of calls.

None of the poverty programs from Washington are directed to any of the children in the North Ward. The funds of the United Community Corporation are not directed toward the North Ward. Anything done in the North Ward is done by funds from individual donations. Last summer the Negro kids on the other side of town had portable pools but the North Ward had to be contented with a sprinkler on Seventh Street. In order to be ensured of the safety of the children, I stole two barriers from the city and blocked off the street. There is no swimming pool within walking distance from the North

Ward. They opened up a hydrant with a sprinkler. My building is used for checker-playing and pizza parties and dancing for the kids—also used as a day-nursery for mothers.

Every day I get complaints from the white kids in the neighborhood who have finished high school and have asked for jobs, but they are told that the employer has to hire Negroes first. This was actually told to one of the kids who said, "Then what the hell is the sense of going to school if I'm not going to have an opportunity to work and get a job?" I walked into the Human Rights Office in connection with a complaint of a white boy who had waited three hours for a job interview and a Negro walked in and they hired three Negroes and made the boy go home, though he was there first. When he complained, the employer said, "We have to hire a Negro first." At the Civil Rights Division there was a Negro behind the counter who said that there was no ground for complaint.

Boys just home from Vietnam said there were race riots there that were not reported. This is because of "bums" like Adam Clayton Powell, LeRoi Jones, Stokely Carmichael, Rap Brown who operate on the anti-poverty program. The government is trying to buy them off with money.

At the first Council meeting in Newark, the radicals ran the chambers, burning papers, and threatening to kill the councilmen. We said 'it's high time we stepped in', so we started to go to the council meetings. The first night I went I brought three hundred people. Each week we came, the radical group lessened and lessened. I got the radicals out with the help of our group.

With respect to the bitter fight over whether police dogs should be added to the police department, ministers from Catholic and Protestant churches played a bad role. They made it a racial issue. They made the accusation that the dogs were to be used against the Negroes. The dog does not know the difference, whether a person is black or white: he is trained to act on command. The ministers won, in that the Newark Police Department does not have a canine corps, but this issue brought about the formation of the North Ward Citizens Committee. The same clergymen who are now yelling for better law enforcement went against the canine corps. They are hypocrites.

The clergymen sat amongst the black people at the council

meetings saying these are my brothers; but how come I support the church and I am not their brother? There should be separation of church and state and if clergymen come to the council they should do so in civilian clothes so as not to exercise an undue influence.

After the riots following the Martin Luther King rally, the North Ward Citizens Committee drove trucks of bread to help the victims and help to transport some of the clothes to the fire victims, too, but the UCC took all the credit. Clothes that were not given to the poor were sold for rags. I brought this to the attention of the city council but nothing was done.

At a school in the Montclair suburb of Newark, a young white teenage girl was attacked by a Negro and had some sort of object shoved in her womb. And a fireman's daughter was assaulted in the hallway. There are now 17 policemen patrolling the corridors at Montclair High School but this does no good because they have orders not to put their hands on any of the black students. If a fellow is rowdy, he deserves to get hit with a nightstick. Orders preventing this are what is causing the trouble.

I first started walking the streets day and night talking to small groups, taverns, clubs, anyone who would listen to me. At first they called me crazy, but now I have the respect of thousands and millions of people. I did it not because I am a super-patriot but because I saw a city that I love well going to hell. I kept people with me by saying if you quit and the city were destroyed tomorrow you would be sorry. They have learned from the black people that the squeaky wheel gets the grease, so they're going to squeak, too.

Two views from the "Opposite" Perspective

Interview with Dan Watts (September 1968)

Dan Watts is a veteran editor of the Black Nationalist movement. For the last eight to ten years he has been putting out a magazine called *The Liberator*. He was trained as an architect, but gave up that career in 1959 to start *Liberator* magazine.

(Interview, 333—second side, 173). Watts has recently returned from Europe. The quality of white European racism is different from that in America. The Europeans' perception of Watts is different from the Americans' perception, but Watts cannot yet determine what precisely the difference is or why. Young suggests that the difference in attitude is caused by Watts' statement that unless the Negroes got a piece of the action, they would burn America down. The Negroes have not threatened to burn Germany, France, etc., down. Watts said Negroes do not really have the capability of burning America down. All they can do is disrupt things. The irresponsible elements of the black community talk of burning. Negroes are at fault for not having formulated a coherent set of demands for the white power structure. It disturbs him that white persons apparently think that the radical blacks represent the entire black community and that the whites are arming themselves against the black community. It is time for the verbal war department in the black revolutionary community to shut up. Lenin went into exile fourteen times (i.e., shut up). The white backlash coalition is dangerous and it is a time for everyone to back away from verbal warfare between the races. The black revolutionaries like Stokely Carmichael and H. Rap Brown use the so-called Afro hairdo and the dashiki costume, but the actual rioter out doing most of the fighting is a soul brother with processed hair.

Watts recalls at Columbia, when he was an undergraduate, a history teacher remarked that for all their corruption and hustling, the robber barons really did build a railroad for America, but the civil rights movement for all its hustling has built nothing yet, nothing but protest. You do not make progress through protest or through civil rights laws. You make progress through getting money and votes. The classic example is the Irish politician. It would do a lot more good if Negroes in New York, instead of being concerned when a Negro in Mississippi is denied his vote and working to get a law passed (Civil Rights Act), would vote in a bloc instead and get political power. The only place in America that is truly integrated is the polling booth where black people will not vote in a bloc for black people.

The Negroes believed the white liberals, symbolized by the *New York Times* and the *Washington Post,* when they said that white people of good will were willing to help Negroes. The liberals said to the Negroes, "You tell it like it is." When the Negroes told it like it is, the white liberals said, "Later, Baby." Now the Negroes are disenchanted.

Roy Wilkins and Whitney Young are ten years out of date. They are still telling the white people that Negroes do not really hate them: Negroes simply want to have the opportunity to be like white people. They do not speak for the black ghetto, but neither does anyone else. This lack of leadership creates the great potential for violence.

New York has a billion dollar budget for welfare but welfare destroys the soul. New York should take this budget and make people get up at 8 a.m. in the morning and work for it. Watts is not afraid of sounding like Bill Buckley because he knows how welfare can destroy the soul. With respect to welfare, white liberals have become an albatross around the neck of the black community.

There is a crisis now in American race relations. Negroes have gotten this far before in the Reconstruction era and in the renaissance of the 1920's. But they appear to be able to get no further. They have to say "black is beautiful." But if it really were beautiful they would not have to say it. No one says white is beautiful.

It will be necessary to restructure institutions so that black people can be a responsible part of their own communities or else the concentration camp and the gas chamber become a real possibility.

Interview with Paul Krassner (September 1968)

Krassner, age 36, might be called the elder statesman of the student rebellion. He is the editor of one of the first, if not the first, underground newspaper, *The Realist*, and is the founder of the Youth International Party, the "Yippies," which contributed substantially to the confrontation at the Democratic convention in Chicago.

(Interview, 39—290). Krassner wanted to present an alternative life style to that symbolized by the Democratic Party convention. He is not a violent person but believes philosophically in violence for self-defense. We must redefine self-defense. Revolution is the ultimate form of self-defense. Krassner does not think he is ready to buy a gun yet. He would be embarrassed. Whoever sold him the gun would know just what he was going to use it for, just like when he was in college and went to the drug store to buy contraceptives.

There comes a time in the cycle of resistance and repression when it is natural to buy a gun. Chicago police, in creating violence, played into the Yippie's hands. The police and the National Guard were taunted. It was like theater; each person, including the police, unconsciously played his part to dramatize the situation.

Krassner was on a program with a Minuteman-type who said everyone had the right of self-defense and they (the Minutemen) would not obey the gun control laws. Krassner replied that he was delighted to see that the man, in effect, supported the right of Black Panthers to arm and recognized that you did not have to obey laws if those laws ran counter to a higher law.

Violence against persons tends to come from police, sometimes even in a vigilante context. For example, the attack in New York by off-duty police against Black Panthers. The violence from protest groups is almost always directed only toward property with symbolic value, such as burning down ROTC buildings. Violence appears to be the result of a feeling of impotence toward being able to alter any national policies.

Krassner is 36 years old. The slogan, "Don't trust anyone over 30," is not to be taken literally. "Over 30" is an attitude of authoritarianism and condescension, not chronological age.

APPENDIX E

NATIONAL SURVEY QUESTIONNAIRE

I'm from Louis Harris and Associates, a national public opinion research firm. We're conducting a survey and we've been asking your neighbors some questions about violence in America today and would now like to ask you some.

1. As you probably know, the Government in Washington has made many decisions and taken many actions during the past few years which have caused people to come out either in favor of the government's actions or against the government's actions. Could you tell me what action the government in Washington has taken during the past few years that you have *objected* to most? Any others?

2a. Sometimes people feel so strongly about something that they take some action because of it and other times they do not feel strongly enough to take any action. Did you take any action because of your feelings about what the government has done?

2b. Do you happen to remember what that was?

3a. (HAND RESPONDENT SHOW CARD "A") When you want to find out what is going on in your local community, which *one* of the major forms of mass communications on that list do you use *most frequently* to get the news?

3b. Which one do you mainly *use* to find out about events in the nation and in the world?

3c. More specifically, from which one have you gotten the clearest understanding of what's going on in Vietnam?

434

3d. Which one has been your main source of information concerning unrest in the cities and riots in the U.S.?

3e. Which one has contributed most to your understanding of the causes and meaning of student protest and uprisings in the U.S.?

3f. In your opinion, which one seems to emphasize news about crime and delinquency the most?

3g. Which one seems to you to dwell the most on accidents and national disasters?

3h. In your judgment, which *one* tends to emphasize the use of guns, knives, or other instruments of violence?

3i. From which one have you learned the most about the life and work of a policeman?

3j. Which one do you most frequently choose when you want to get away from daily tensions and just relax?

4. Now, I'd like to pose some more specific hypothetical or imaginary choices about the news media to see about your preferences. (HAND RESPONDENT CARD "B") If you had to choose between *one* in each of the pairings on that card, which one would it be—a or b? (INTERVIEWER: GET ONE CHOICE FOR EACH PAIR)

      a. Read the editorial page
         OR
      b. Read the front pages of your daily newspaper

      a. Read the comic strips
         OR
      b. Read the want-ad section

      a. Go to a movie starring Bing Crosby
         OR
      b. Go to a movie starring John Wayne

a. See a James Bond movie
> OR
b. See a Walt Disney movie

a. Watch the Ed Sullivan Show on TV
> OR
b. Watch Gunsmoke on TV

a. Read a detective story
> OR
b. Read a love story

5a. Imagine that for some reason you could only watch one television program a week. From all of last year's or this year's programs, what would be your choice?

5b. What's the main thing you like about that program?

5c. Imagine further that you had the power to eliminate one television program from the air of all last year's or this year's programs. Which *one* would you eliminate?

5d. What's the main thing you dislike about it?

5e. Of the three major television networks—ABC, NBC, CBS—do you detect any difference in the amount of violence they portray in their entertainment programs?

5f. How would you rank them from *most* to *least* violent? (RECORD ONLY ONE IN EACH CATEGORY)
> Most violent
> Medium violent

5g. How do you feel about the amount of violence portrayed in television programs today, not including news programs—do you think that there is too much, a reasonable amount, or very little violence?
> Too much
> A reasonable amount
> Very little
> Not sure

5h. Apart from the *amount* of violence, do you generally approve or disapprove of the kind of violence that is portrayed on TV?

>Approve
>Disapprove
>Not sure

6a. (HAND RESPONDENT CARD "C") Here is a list of ways to communicate with others in your community. Please tell me which *one* you think would be the most effective way

>(1) to bring an issue to the attention of your local community? (RECORD BELOW)
>(2) to influence people's attitudes about the issue? (RECORD BELOW)
>(3) to get people in your local community to take a stand and take action on the issue? (RECORD BELOW)

>>A. Telling friends, relatives and acquaintances
>>B. Speaking out at club and church meetings
>>C. Sending a letter to a newspaper or magazine
>>D. Writing to your political representatives
>>E. Buying advertising space in a newspaper or magazine
>>F. Buying advertising time on radio or TV
>>G. Going from door to door with a petition or joining a community action program
>>H. Creating or joining in a demonstration even if it violates the law

6b. What about you personally, which way do you think *you yourself* would be most likely

>(1) to bring an issue to the attention of your local community? (RECORD ABOVE)
>(2) to get other people in your local community to agree with your point of view? (RECORD ABOVE)
>(3) to get people in your local community to take a stand and take action on the issue? (RECORD ABOVE)

7a. Some people don't pay much attention to the political campaigns. How about you—would you say that you have been very much interested, somewhat interested, or not much interested in following the political campaigns so far this year?

    Very much interested
    Somewhat interested
    Not much interested
    Not sure

7b. How about the election this November—are you registered or eligible to vote?

    Registered
    Not registered
    Not sure

7c. So far as you know now, do you expect to vote in November or not?

    Expect to vote
    Don't expect to
    Not sure

7d. If you had to decide right now whom do you think you will vote for for President this November—Nixon, Humphrey or Wallace?

    Nixon
    Humphrey
    Wallace
    Other (specify)

7e. (IF DON'T EXPECT TO VOTE OR NOT SURE IN Q. 7c) If you were going to vote, how do you think you would vote for President in the November election?

    Nixon
    Humphrey
    Wallace
    Other (specify)
    Not sure

7f. Regardless of how you may vote do you usually consider yourself a Republican, a Democrat, an Independent, or what?

Republican
Democrat
Independent
Other (specify)
Not sure

7g. (IF REPUBLICAN OR DEMOCRAT IN Q. 7f)
Would you call yourself a strong (Republican) (Democrat)
or a not very strong (Republican) (Democrat)?
Strong Democrat
Not very strong Democrat
Not very strong Republican
Strong Republican

7h. (IF REPUBLICAN OR DEMOCRAT IN Q. 7f) Was
there ever a time when you thought of yourself as a (Republican) (Democrat) rather than a (Democrat) (Republican)?
Yes, a Democrat
Yes, a Republican
No, never
Not sure

8. (ASK EVERYONE) Now I'd like to read some of the
kinds of things people tell us when we interview them and ask
you whether you agree or disagree with them. I'll read them
one at a time and you just tell me whether you tend to agree
or disagree (READ LIST):

People like me don't have any say about what the government does.
Voting is the only way that people like me can have any
say about how the government runs things.
Sometimes politics and government seem so complicated
that a person like me can't really understand what is
going on.
I don't think public officials care much what people like me
think.

9a. As you well know, there are a number of serious problems facing this country both at home and abroad. The question is: What should be done about them; We would like to
have *your* opinion about a few of these problems that many

people have told us they have thought about recently. Our first question is on the war in Vietnam. Which one on the list (HAND RESPONDENT CARD "D") comes closest to your opinion about what we should do in Vietnam? Just give me the letter.

    A. Pull our troops out now

    B. Keep our soldiers there but stop all bombing of North Vietnam and try to end the fighting

    C. Continue our present policies which include limited bombing of the North and trying to end the fighting

    D. Take a stronger stand, even if it means invading North Vietnam

    E. Win absolute victory, even if it means using nuclear weapons against North Vietnam

    F. Not sure

9b. Our next problem concerns racial segregation and desegregation. As you know, some people feel segregation is good, others that it is bad. How about you—are you in favor of segregation, integration, or something in between?

    Segregation
    Integration
    Something in between
    Not sure

9c. Do you think that white students and Negro students should go to the same schools or to separate schools?

    Same
    Different
    Not sure

9d. During the past year or so, would you say most of the actions Negroes have taken to get the things they want have been violent, or have most of these actions been peaceful?

    Violent
    Peaceful
    Not sure

9e. In your own words, what is "open housing"—what do the words mean to you?

9f. If people who were of a different race than you are, came to live next door to you would you move?

>Would move
>Would not move
>Not sure

9g. If many people who were of a different race than you are came to live in your neighborhood, would you move?

>Would move
>Would not move
>Not sure

9h. Would you like to see Congress pass an open housing law or reject it?

>Pass
>Reject
>Not sure

9i. (ASK EVERYONE) Do you think that the federal government is trying to get integration too fast, or not fast enough?

>Too fast
>Not fast enough
>About right
>Not sure

10. As you know, demonstrations have been occurring against some of the government's policies in Vietnam and on civil rights. Would you say that you are generally in favor of these demonstrations, sometimes in favor and sometimes against, generally opposed to them, or very strongly opposed to these demonstrations?

>Generally in favor
>Sometimes in favor, sometimes against
>Generally opposed
>Very strongly opposed
>Not sure

11. I'm now going to read you a number of statements that some people agree with and others disagree with. After I've read you the statement, I'd like to have you tell me (HAND RESPONDENT CARD "E") whether or not you *strongly*

agree with the statement, *just agree* with the statement, *disagree* with the statement, or *strongly disagree* with the statement. (READ LIST)

- (a) Justice may have been a little rough-and-ready in the days of the Old West, but things worked better then than they do today with all the legal red tape.
- (b) When a boy is growing up, it is important for him to have a few fist fights.
- (c) Our government is too ready to use military force in dealing with other countries.
- (d) One of the best reasons for people to have guns is to make sure that the government doesn't get too much power.
- (e) The people running the government in Washington would do a good job if everybody left them alone instead of trying to influence them all the time.
- (f) The police frequently use more force than they need to when carrying out their duties.
- (g) Some politicians who have had their lives threatened probably deserve it.
- (h) Human nature being what it is, there must always be war and conflict.
- (i) Everything changes so quickly these days that I often have trouble deciding which are the right rules to follow.
- (j) If people go into politics, they more or less have to accept the fact that they might get killed.
- (k) Groups have the right to train their members in marksmanship and underground warfare tactics in order to help put down any conspiracies that might occur in the country.
- (l) In dealing with other countries in the world, we are frequently justified in using military force.
- (m) People were better off in the old days when everyone knew just how he was expected to act.
- (n) What is lacking in the world today is the old kind of friendship that lasted for a lifetime.
- (o) What young people need most of all is strong discipline by their parents.
- (p) A few strong leaders could make this country better than all the laws and talk.
- (q) It is unfortunate that many civilians are killed by bombing in a war, but this cannot be avoided.

(r) Politicians who try to change things too fast have to expect that their lives may be threatened.

(s) Sex criminals deserve more than prison, they should be publicly whipped or worse.

(t) Any man who insults a policeman has no complaint if he gets roughed-up in return.

(u) A lot more people in government and politics will probably be assassinated in the next few years.

(v) The government in Washington is the enemy, not the friend, of people like me.

(w) Some people don't understand anything but force.

(x) The police are wrong to beat up unarmed protesters, even when these people are rude and call them names.

(y) Sometimes I have felt that the best thing for our country might be the death of some of our political leaders.

12a. As you probably know, a number of politically active persons have been assassinated in the past few years. Some people have responded to these assassinations in one way, while others have responded in another way. We are interested in the feelings you remember having when you first heard of the death of the following people, if you did happen to hear of their deaths. Did you happen to hear of the death of George Lincoln Rockwell, the head of the American Nazi party?

> Heard
> Not heard

12b. How did you happen to first hear about that?
> Television
> Radio
> Newspapers
> Magazines
> Member of my family told me
> A friend told me
> A stranger told me
> Not sure

12c. (HAND RESPONDENT CARD "F") Please tell me, for each of the lines on that card, how you felt when you first heard of the assassination of George Lincoln Rockwell. As you can see each line has one word at each end of it, and there are five numbers in between the two words. If you felt hopeful you would tell me number "1"; if you felt hopeless you would tell me number "5"; if you felt in between, neither hopeful nor hopeless you would tell me number "3"; and if you were leaning toward one or the other word you would tell me either number "2" or number "4". Now please look at the card and tell me the number that best represents how you felt when you first heard of the assassination of George Lincoln Rockwell.

Hopeful
Not surprised
Unafraid
Sad
At a loss
Hopeless
Shocked
Afraid
Angry
Relieved
Not affected

13a. Did you hear of the death of Senator Robert F. Kennedy?

Heard
Not heard

13b. How did you happen to first hear about that?
Television
Radio
Newspapers
Magazines
Member of my family told me
A friend told me
A stranger told me
Not sure

13c. Now could you look at that card again and tell me the number which best represents how you felt when you heard of the assassination of Robert F. Kennedy?

14a. Did you happen to hear of the death of Medgar Evers, a Southern civil rights leader?
Heard
Not heard

14b. How did you happen to first hear about that?
        Television
        Radio
        Newspapers
        Magazines
        Member of my family told me
        A friend told me
        A stranger told me
        Not sure

14c. Now look at CARD "F" again and tell me the number which best represents how you felt when you heard of the assassination of Medgar Evers?

15a. Did you hear of the death of Malcolm X, a leader of the Black Muslims?
        Heard
        Not heard

15b. How did you happen to first hear about that?
        Television
        Radio
        Newspapers
        Magazines
        Member of my family told me
        A friend told me
        A stranger told me
        Not sure

15c. Again tell me the number which best represents how you felt when you heard of the assassination of Malcolm X?

16a. Did you hear of the death of President John F. Kennedy?
        Heard
        Not heard

16b. How did you happen to first hear about that?
        Television
        Radio
        Newspapers
        Magazines
        Member of my family told me

A friend told me
A stranger told me
Not sure

16c. Now could you please tell me, for each of the lines, how you felt when you first heard of the assassination of John F. Kennedy?

17a. Did you happen to hear of the death of Dr. Martin Luther King, a national civil rights leader?
Heard
Not heard

17b. How did you happen to first hear about that?
Television
Radio
Newspapers
Magazines
Member of my family told me
A friend told me
A stranger told me
Not sure

17c. For the last time, tell me the number which best represents how you felt when you heard of the assassination of Dr. Martin Luther King.

18a. Imagine that Congress has passed a law that makes you pay just as many dollars in taxes as people who make a lot more money than you do—would you strongly approve, just approve, disapprove, or strongly disapprove of this law?
Strongly approve
Just approve
Disapprove
Strongly disapprove
Not sure

18b. Here is a list of actions which someone might take as a result of the situation I just described to you. Please tell me the letter of each action that you feel it would be all right to take.

18c. How about you personally, are you likely or unlikely to do this as a reaction to that tax law we talked about?
  A. Express an opinion to friends on what is happening
  B. Sign a petition about what is happening
  C. Organize a group who are interested in what is happening
  D. If nothing else worked, participate in an illegal sit-in to express one's feelings about what is happening
  E. If nothing else worked, participate in a physical assault or armed action because of feelings about what is happening

19a. Now here is another situation: Imagine that Congress has just passed a law prohibiting anyone from saying anything against the government—would you strongly approve, just approve, disapprove, or strongly disapprove of this law?
          Strongly approve
          Just approve
          Disapprove
          Strongly disapprove
          Not sure

19b. Looking at CARD "G" again, would you tell me the letter of each action you feel it would be all right to take if Congress did in fact pass a law prohibiting anyone from saying anything against the government? (RECORD BELOW) (MULTIPLE RECORD IF NECESSARY)

19c. (FOR EACH ACTION CHECKED ALL RIGHT IN Q. 19b) How about you personally, are you likely or unlikely to do this as a reaction to that situation?
  A. Express an opinion to friends on what is happening
  B. Sign a petition about what is happening
  C. Organize a group who are interested in what is happening
  D. If nothing else worked, participate in an illegal sit-in to express one's feelings about what is happening
  E. If nothing else worked, participate in a physical assault or armed action because of feelings about what is happening

20a. Now consider this example: Imagine that the government has just arrested and imprisoned many of the Negroes in your community even though there had been no trouble—would you strongly approve, just approve, disapprove, or strongly disapprove of what was happening?

> Strongly approve
> Just approve
> Disapprove
> Strongly disapprove
> Not sure

20b. Again tell me the letter of each action you feel it would be all right to take if the government has just arrested and imprisoned many of the Negroes in your community even though there had been no trouble. (RECORD BELOW) (MULTIPLE RECORD IF NECESSARY)

20c. (FOR EACH ACTION CHECKED ALL RIGHT IN Q. 20b) How about you personally, are you likely or unlikely to do this as a reaction to this situation?

> A. Express an opinion to friends on what is happening
> B. Sign a petition about what is happening
> C. Organize a group who are interested in what is happening
> D. If nothing else worked, participate in an illegal sit-in to express one's feelings about what is happening
> E. If nothing else worked, participate in a physical assault or armed action because of feelings about what is happening

21a. Here is another case: Imagine that in order to keep control of the country, the government starts arresting and shooting large numbers of innocent people including members of your family—would you strongly approve, just approve, disapprove, or strongly disapprove of this action?

> Strongly approve
> Just approve
> Disapprove
> Strongly disapprove
> Not sure

21b. Look at CARD "G" again and tell me the letter of each action you feel it would be all right to take if the government started to arrest and shoot large numbers of innocent people including members of your family. (RECORD BELOW) (MULTIPLE RECORD IF NECESSARY)

21c. (FOR EACH ACTION CHECKED ALL RIGHT IN Q. 21b) How about you personally, are you likely or unlikely to do this as a reaction to this particular situation?
- A. Express an opinion to friends on what is happening
- B. Sign a petition about what is happening
- C. Organize a group who are interested in what is happening
- D. If nothing else worked, participate in an illegal sit-in to express one's feelings about what is happening
- E. If nothing else worked, participate in a physical assault or armed action because of feelings about what is happening

22a. Here is another possible situation: Suppose you see a group of people who are deliberately blocking rush hour traffic to protest the war in Vietnam—would you strongly approve, just approve, disapprove, or strongly disapprove of what was happening?
> Strongly approve
> Just approve
> Disapprove
> Strongly disapprove
> Not sure

22b. Again looking at CARD "G", tell me the letter of each action you feel it would be all right to take if you saw a group of people deliberately blocking rush hour traffic to protest the war in Vietnam. (RECORD BELOW) (MULTIPLE RECORD IF NECESSARY)

22c. (FOR EACH ACTION CHECKED ALL RIGHT IN Q. 22b) How about you personally, are you likely or unlikely to do this as a reaction to this situation?
- A. Express an opinion to friends on what is happening
- B. Sign a petition about what is happening

C. Organize a group who are interested in what is happening

D. If nothing else worked, participate in an illegal sit-in to express one's feelings about what is happening

E. If nothing else worked, participate in a physical assault or armed action because of feelings about what is happening

23a. Now consider this last example: Your Senator has blocked legislation which you believe is essential to protect the rights of every citizen. The Senator has come to your town and is making a speech in a public auditorium to gain support for his point of view. (HAND RESPONDENT CARD "H") Keeping this in mind look at this list and tell me the letter of each action that you feel it would be all right to take. (RECORD BELOW) (MULTIPLE RECORD IF NECESSARY)

23b. (FOR EACH ACTION CHECKED ALL RIGHT IN Q. 23a) How about you personally, are you likely or unlikely to do this as a reaction to this situation?

A. Carry signs expressing disapproval of the position of the Senator

B. Boo during pauses in the Senator's speech where the Senator was expecting applause

C. Participate with others in systematically booing and stamping feet so that the Senator was unable to continue his speech and be heard

D. Throw rotten tomatoes or other objects which could not harm the Senator but which would demonstrate disapproval

E. Throw empty bottles or other objects which could not do serious or permanent harm to the Senator but which would demonstrate the extent of disapproval

F. Use a gun or other weapon to inflict serious enough harm to the Senator so that he would have to turn over his position to another person

23c. Now looking at CARD "H", please tell me the letter of each action that you think some of your *friends* would feel it is all right to take?

23d. (FOR EACH ACTION CHECKED ALL RIGHT IN Q. 23c) Do you think that some of your friends are likely to do this or not?

24. People take many kinds of action to express their views about political or social issues. Please tell me which of these actions you have ever taken to express your opinion on a social or political issue?

ACTIONS

Discuss with friends

Write a letter to a newspaper or to an elected official

Contribute money to an organization concerned about the issue

Sign a petition

Express your opinion in person to a government official

Organize a group

Participate in a legally permitted demonstration

Participate in an illegal but non-violent demonstration

Participate in a riot

25a. Now let's turn a moment to some other kinds of experiences. First, tell me if any of these somewhat dramatic things have ever happened to you: As a child, were you spanked—frequently, sometimes, or never?

Frequently

Sometimes

Never

Not sure

25b. By whom were you spanked?

Mother

Father

Relative

Acquaintances

Other

Not sure

26. (INTERVIEWER: ASK THE FOLLOWING SERIES OF QUESTIONS ABOUT EACH OF THE FIVE SITUA- TIONS LISTED BELOW ALWAYS FOLLOWING THE INSTRUCTIONS AND RECORD ANSWERS BELOW.

ASK THE WHOLE SERIES OF QUESTIONS [26 a-g] FOR EACH SITUATION BEFORE MOVING ON TO THE NEXT SITUATION.

SITUATION 1. EVER BEEN SLAPPED OR KICKED ‚ BY ANOTHER PERSON

SITUATION 2. EVER BEEN PUNCHED OR BEATEN BY ANOTHER PERSON

SITUATION 3. EVER BEEN CHOKED BY ANOTHER PERSON

SITUATION 4. EVER BEEN THREATENED OR ACTUALLY CUT WITH A KNIFE

SITUATION 5. EVER BEEN THREATENED WITH A GUN OR SHOT AT

26a. Have you (READ SITUATION)?
    Yes
    No
    Not sure

26b. How many times would you estimate that this has happened to you?
    Once
    Two or three times
    Four or more times
    Not sure

26c. Did this happen to you as a child or as an adult?
    Child
    Adult
    Both
    Not sure

26d. Now let's just consider the most recent time that this happened. In what kind of situation did it happen?
    Fun or play
    Sports
    Anger or conflict
    Military combat
    Other
    Not sure

SITUATION 1. EVER BEEN SLAPPED OR KICKED BY ANOTHER PERSON

SITUATION 2. EVER BEEN PUNCHED OR BEATEN BY ANOTHER PERSON

SITUATION 3. EVER BEEN CHOKED BY ANOTHER PERSON

SITUATION 4. EVER BEEN THREATENED OR ACTUALLY CUT WITH A KNIFE

SITUATION 5. EVER BEEN THREATENED WITH A GUN OR SHOT AT

26e. What was your relationship to the person (READ SITUATION)?

> Family member
> Friend
> Acquaintance
> Stranger
> Other (specify)
> Not sure

26f. Did anyone intervene to stop the action?

> Yes
> No
> Not sure

26g. Who intervened?

Family member of one or both persons involved
Friend of one or both persons involved
Acquaintance of one or both persons involved
Stranger to both persons involved
Other (specify)
Not sure

27. (INTERVIEWER: ASK THE FOLLOWING SERIES OF QUESTIONS ABOUT EACH OF THE FIVE SITUATIONS LISTED BELOW, ALWAYS FOLLOWING THE SKIP INSTRUCTIONS AND RECORD ANSWERS BELOW. *ASK THE WHOLE SERIES OF QUESTIONS [27 a-g] FOR EACH SITUATION BEFORE MOVING ON TO THE NEXT SITUATION.* THIS SERIES OF QUESTIONS DOES NOT RELATE TO YOU PERSONALLY BUT WHETHER OR NOT YOU HAVE SEEN THE FOLLOWING SITUATIONS.)

SITUATION 1. EVER SEEN ANOTHER PERSON SLAPPED OR KICKED
SITUATION 2. EVER SEEN ANOTHER PERSON PUNCHED OR BEATEN
SITUATION 3. EVER SEEN ANOTHER PERSON CHOKED
SITUATION 4. EVER SEEN ANOTHER PERSON THREATENED OR ACTUALLY CUT WITH A KNIFE
SITUATION 5. EVER SEEN ANOTHER PERSON THREATENED WITH A GUN OR SHOT AT

27a. Have you (READ SITUATION)?
> Yes
> No
> Not sure

27b. How many times would you estimate that you have (READ SITUATION)?
> Once
> Two or three times
> Four or more times
> Not sure

27c. Did you see this happen as a child or as an adult?
> Child
> Adult
> Both
> Not sure

27d. Now let's just consider the most recent time that you saw this happen. In what kind of situation did it happen?
> Fun or play
> Sports
> Anger or conflict
> Military combat
> Other (specify)
> Not sure

SITUATION 1. EVER SEEN ANOTHER PERSON SLAPPED OR KICKED
SITUATION 2. EVER SEEN ANOTHER PERSON PUNCHED OR BEATEN

SITUATION 3. EVER SEEN ANOTHER PERSON CHOKED

SITUATION 4. EVER SEEN ANOTHER PERSON THREATENED OR ACTUALLY CUT WITH A KNIFE

SITUATION 5. EVER SEEN ANOTHER PERSON THREATENED WITH A GUN OR SHOT AT

27e. What was your relationship to the person?
> Family member
> Friend
> Acquaintance
> Stranger
> Other (specify)
> Not sure

27f. Did anyone intervene to stop the action?
> Yes
> No
> Not sure

27g. Who intervened?
> Family member of one or both persons involved
> Friend of one or both persons involved
> Acquaintance of one or both persons involved
> Stranger to both persons involved
> Other (specify)
> Not sure

28a. Have you ever spanked a child?
> Yes
> No
> Not sure

28b. What was your relationship to the child?
> Parent
> Other relative
> Teacher
> Babysitter
> Acquaintance
> Stranger
> Other (specify)
> Not sure

29a. Have you ever slapped or kicked another person?
>Yes
>No
>Not sure

29b. How many times would you estimate that you have done this?
>Once
>Two or three times
>Four or more times
>Not sure

29c. Did you do this as a child or as an adult?
>Child
>Adult
>Both
>Not sure

29d. Now let's consider just the most recent time that you slapped or kicked another person. In what kind of situation did it happen?
>Fun or play
>Sports
>Anger or conflict
>Military combat
>Other (specify)
>Not sure

29e. What was your relationship to the other person?
>Family member
>Friend
>Acquaintance
>Stranger
>Other (specify)
>Not sure

29f. Did anyone intervene to stop the action?
>Yes
>No
>Not sure

29g. Who intervened?
>Family member of one or both persons

Friend of one or both persons involved
Acquaintance of one or both persons involved
Stranger to both persons involved
Other (specify)
Not sure

30a. (ASK EVERYONE) Have you ever punched or beaten another person?
Yes
No
Not sure

30b. How many times would you estimate that you have done this?
Once
Two or three times
Four or more times
Not sure

30c. Did you do this as a child or as an adult?
Child
Adult
Both
Not sure

30d. Now let's consider just the most recent time that you punched or beat another person. In what kind of a situation did it happen?
Fun or play
Sports
Anger or conflict
Military combat
Other (specify)
Not sure

30e. What was your relationship to the other person?
Family member
Friend
Acquaintance
Stranger
Other (specify)
Not sure

30f. Did anyone intervene to stop the action?
> Yes
> No
> Not sure

30g. Who intervened?
> Family member of one or both persons involved
> Friend of one or both persons involved
> Acquaintance of one or both persons involved
> Stranger to both persons involved
> Other (specify)
> Not sure

31. Have you ever been in a situation where you had to defend yourself with a knife or a gun?
> Yes
> No
> Not sure

32. Now I would like to get your judgment on some questions concerning the possible effects of television violence. (REPEAT BEFORE EACH STATEMENT BELOW: "HOW LIKELY IS IT THAT TV. VIOLENCE (READ STATEMENT). IS IT LIKELY, POSSIBLE, OR UNLIKELY?")
> Plays a part in making America a violent society
> Allows viewer to blow off steam by watching violence, thus decreasing the likelihood of their being violent
> Makes people insensitive to real acts of violence that they hear about or see
> Provides entertainment and relaxation without harmful or bad effects
> Triggers violent acts from people who are maladjusted or mentally unstable
> Supports and strengthens traditional American values

In this section, we would like to know if you would approve or disapprove of people taking certain actions in a variety of imaginary situations.

33a. Are there any situations that you can imagine in which you would approve of a parent spanking his or her child assuming the child is healthy and over a year old?

Yes
No
Not sure

33b. Would you approve if the child
Was noisy and getting on the parent's nerves
Had been disobedient all day
Had been expelled from school
Had broken a law

34a. Are there any situations that you can imagine in which
you would approve of a parent beating his or her child?
Yes
No
Not sure

34b. Would you approve if the child
Was noisy and getting on the parent's nerves
Had been disobedient all day
Had been expelled from school
Had broken a law

35a. Are there any situations that you can imagine in which
you would approve of a husband slapping his wife's face?
Yes
No
Not sure

35b. Would you approve if
The husband and wife were having an argument
The wife had insulted her husband in public
The wife had been flirting with other men
The wife had been unfaithful

36a. Are there any situations that you can imagine in which
you would approve of a husband shooting his wife?
Yes
No
Not sure

36b. Would you approve if
The husband and wife were having an argument

The wife had insulted her husband in public
The wife had been flirting
The wife had been unfaithful

37a. Are there any situations that you can imagine in which you would approve of a wife slapping her husband's face?
       Yes
       No
       Not sure

37b. Would you approve if (READ EACH STATEMENT):
       The wife and husband were having an argument
       The husband had insulted his wife in public
       The husband had been flirting
       The husband had been unfaithful

38a. Are there any situations that you can imagine in which you would approve of a wife shooting her husband?
       Yes
       No
       Not sure

38b. Would you approve if
       The wife and husband were having an argument
       The husband had insulted his wife in public
       The husband had been flirting
       The husband had been unfaithful

39a. Are there any situations that you can imagine in which you would approve of a public school teacher hitting a student?
       Yes
       No
       Not sure

39b. Would you approve if the student had
       Been noisy in class
       Been repeatedly disobedient and uncooperative
       Destroyed school property
       Hit

40a. Are there any situations that you can imagine in which you would approve of a public school teacher punching or beating a student?

> Yes
> No
> Not sure

40b. Would you approve if the student had
> Been noisy in class
> Been repeatedly disobedient and uncooperative
> Destroyed school property
> Hit

41a. Are there any situations you can imagine in which you would approve of a policeman striking an adult male citizen?

> Yes
> No
> Not sure

41b. Would you approve if the citizen
> Had said vulgar and obscene things to the policeman
> Was demonstrating against the war in Vietnam and carrying a Viet Cong flag
> Was being questioned as a suspect in a murder case
> Was attempting to escape from custody
> Was attacking the policeman with his fists

42a. Are there any situations you can imagine in which you would approve of a policeman shooting an adult male citizen?

> Yes
> No
> Not sure

42b. Would you approve if the citizen
> Had said vulgar and obscene things to the policeman
> Was demonstrating against the war in Vietnam and carrying a Viet Cong flag
> Was being questioned as a suspect in a murder case
> Was attempting to escape from custody
> Was attacking the policeman with his fists
> Was threatening the policeman with a gun

43a. Are there any situations you can imagine in which you would approve of a teenage boy punching another teenage boy?

> Yes
> No
> Not sure

43b. Would you approve if the teenage boy
> Didn't like the other boy
> Had been ridiculed and picked on by the other boy
> Had been challenged by the other boy to a fist fight
> Had been hit by the other boy

44a. Are there any situations you can imagine in which you would approve of a teenage boy knifing another teenage boy?

> Yes
> No
> Not sure

44b. Would you approve if the teenage boy (READ EACH STATEMENT):
> Didn't like the other boy
> Had been ridiculed and picked on by the other boy
> Had been challenged by the other boy to a fist fight
> Had been hit by the other boy

45a. Are there any situations that you can imagine in which you would approve of a man punching an adult male stranger?

> Yes
> No
> Not sure

45b. Would you approve if the stranger
> Was in a protest march showing opposition to the other man's views
> Was drunk and bumped into the man and his wife on the street
> Had hit the man's child after the child accidentally damaged the stranger's car
> Was beating up a woman and the man saw it
> Had broken into the man's house

46a. Are there any situations that you can imagine in which you would approve of a man choking a stranger?

> Yes
> No
> Not sure

46b. Would you approve if the stranger
> Was in a protest march showing opposition to the other man's views
> Was drunk and bumped into the man and his wife on the street
> Had hit the man's child after the child accidentally damaged the stranger's car
> Was beating up a woman and the man saw it
> Had broken into the man's house
> Had knocked the man down and was trying to rob him

47a. Are there any situations that you can imagine in which you would approve of a judge sentencing a person to one or more years of hard labor?

> Yes
> No
> Not sure

47b. Would you approve if (READ EACH STATE-MENT):
> The person is an atheist or believes that there is no God
> The person is demonstrating after having been denied a demonstration permit
> A man refused to serve in the Armed Forces of the United States
> The person is an agitator who has incited people to riot
> The person has threatened to kill the President of the United States

48a. Are there any situations that you can imagine in which you would approve of a judge sentencing a person to death?

> Yes
> No
> Not sure

48b. Would you approve if:

The person is an atheist or believes that there is no God

The person is demonstrating after having been denied a demonstration permit

A man refused to serve in the Armed Forces of the United States

The person is an agitator who has incited people to riot

The person has threatened to kill the President of the United States

The person had been found guilty of first degree murder

The person was proven to be a traitor

49a. Do you own firearms?

Yes
No
Not sure

49b. How many (READ LIST) do you own?

Rifles
Pistols (handguns)
Shotguns
Muzzle loaders
Other (specify)

49c. How many (READ LIST) did you acquire used?

Rifles
Pistols (handguns)
Shotguns
Muzzle loaders
Other (specify)

49d. From whom do you usually acquire used firearms?

Sporting goods store
Hardware store
Another kind of store
A friend
Member of a gun or target club
Another private party
Not sure

49e. (ASK EVERYONE) Have you ever sold or traded a pistol, a rifle, or a shotgun?

> Pistol
> Rifle
> Shotgun

49f. (IF YES IN Q. 49e—OTHERS SKIP TO FACTUAL)

> Sporting goods store
> Hardware store
> Another kind of store
> A friend
> A member of a gun or target club
> Another private party

FACTUAL:

F1. What is your age?

F2a. Are you married now and living with your wife (husband)—or are you widowed, divorced, separated, or single?

> Married
> Widowed
> Separated
> Divorced
> Single

F2b. (IF MARRIED) How long have you been married?

> 5 years or under
> 6 to 10 years
> 11 to 15 years
> 16 to 20 years
> 21 to 25 years
> 26 to 30 years
> 31 to 40 years
> 41 to 50 years
> 50 or more

F3a. (ASK EVERYONE) Do you have any children under 18 years of age?

> Yes
> No

F3b. (IF CHILDREN) How many children under 6 years of age do you have? How many children ages 6 to 13 do you have? And how many children ages 14 to 18 do you have?

        Under 6

        6 to 13

        14 to 18

F4. Record Position of Respondent in Household:

        Male head

        Female head (no male head)

        Wife

        Son

        Other male (specify)

        Daughter

        Other female (specify)

F5. What is the last grade of school you attended?

        4th grade or less

        5th grade to 8th grade

        Some high school

        High school graduate

        Some college

        College graduate

        Post-graduate

F6. Have you had any other schooling?

        Yes

        No

F7. What other schooling have you had?

F8. (ASK EVERYONE) Is the head of the household an hourly wage worker, salaried, or self-employed?

        Hourly wage worker

        Salaried

        Self-employed

        None of the above:

        Retired

        Student

        Military service

        Housewife

        Unemployed

        Other (specify)

F9. What type of work does the head of the household do?
(PROBE FULLY—FIND OUT WHAT JOB IS CALLED,
DUTIES INVOLVED, ETC.)

F10. (IF NOT HEAD OF HOUSEHOLD) Do you also
work full or part-time?
> Full time
> Part time
> No

F11. There's quite a bit of talk these days about different
social classes. Most people say they belong either to the middle class or to the working class. Do you ever think of
yourself as being in one of these classes?
> Yes
> No
> Not sure

F12. Well, if you had to make a choice, would you call
yourself middle class or working class?
> Middle
> Working
> Not sure

F13. What would you say your family was when you were
growing up—middle class or working class?
> Middle
> Working
> Not sure

F14. What is your religion?
> Protestant
> Catholic
> Jewish
> Other
> Not sure

F15. What church is that?
> Baptist
> Methodist
> Lutheran
> Episcopalian
> Other (specify)
> Not sure

F16. (ASK EVERYONE) Would you say you go to church regularly, often, seldom or never?

> Regularly
> Often
> Seldom
> Never
> Not sure

F17. Where were you born?

> State:
> Foreign Country:

F18a. Were you brought up mostly on a farm, in a town, in a small city, or in a large city?

> Farm
> Town
> Small city
> Large city
> Not sure

F18b. Which city was that? In what state?

> (city)   (state)

F19a. How long have you lived in your present house (apartment)?

> Less than one year
> One to four years
> Five to nine years
> Ten to nineteen years
> 20 years or more
> All my life

F19b. How would you compare this neighborhood with the one you left? Is it less expensive, more expensive or about the same?

> Less expensive
> More
> About the same
> Not sure

F19c. What about the location of your present house (apartment)—is it closer to the center of the city, further out from the center of the city, or is it about the same as your old neighborhood?

> Closer to center of city
> Further out from center of city
> About the same
> Not sure

F20. For statistical purposes only, we need to know your total family income for 1967. Will you please look at this card (HAND RESPONDENT CARD "I") and tell me which letter best represents all the money the members of this household either earned or received from salary or wages or other sources, such as pensions, stocks and bonds, real estate, or other investments, in 1967 before taxes?

> A. Under $3,000
> B. $3,000 to 4,999
> C. $5,000 to 6,999
> D. $7,000 to 9,999
> E. $10,000 to 14,999
> F. $15,000 to 19,999
> G. $20,000 to 24,999
> H. $25,000 and over
> I. Not sure/refused

F21. Using the same scale tell me which letter represents the income of the head of the household only?

> A
> B
> C
> D
> E
> F
> G
> H
> Not sure

F22. Do you own your own home here, or rent or what?

> Own
> Rent
> Other (specify)

F23. What kind of work did your father do for a living while you were growing up?

F24. So far as you and your family are concerned, would you say that you are pretty well satisfied with your present financial situation, more or less satisfied, or not satisfied at all?

> Pretty well satisfied
> More or less satisfied
> Not satisfied at all

F25. During the last few years, has your financial situation been getting better, getting worse, or has it stayed the same?

> Getting better
> Getting worse
> Stayed the same
> Not sure

F26. Now looking ahead and thinking about the next few years, do you expect your financial situation will stay about the way it is now, get better, or get worse?

> Stay the way it is
> Get better
> Get worse
> Not sure

ASK Q. F27a. OF MALES ONLY—SKIP FEMALES TO F28.

F27a. What is your present military status:

> Veteran
> Active
> Reserve
> Never been in service

F27b. What branch of the service were you or are you in?

> Navy
> Air Force
> Army
> Marine Corps
> Coast Guard

F27c. (IF NAVY) What unit were you in—the Naval Air, on a Destroyer, on a Carrier or what?

> Naval Air
> Destroyer
> Carrier
> Other (specify)

F27d. (IF AIR FORCE) Were you in the Strategic Air Command or in the Tactical Air Command or what?

> Strategic Air Command
> Tactical Air Command
> Other (specify)

F27e. (IF ARMY) Were you in a Combat Arms unit or what?

> Yes, combat arms unit
> No
> Other (specify)

RECORD THE FOLLOWING—DO NOT ASK:

F28. *Ethnic Group or Racial Background:*
> White
> Negro
> Oriental
> Puerto Rican
> Other (specify)
> Not sure

F29. *Economic Level:*
> A
> B
> C
> D

Respondent's Name (PLEASE PRINT):

Address:
City/town:
State:
Telephone No.
Telephone Area Code

THIS IS A BONA FIDE INTERVIEW AND HAS BEEN OBTAINED ACCORDING TO MY AGREEMENT WITH LOUIS HARRIS AND ASSOCIATES, INC.

Interviewer's Name:

Interview No. Date
Time of Interview (o'clock)
Length of Interview (hours)
Sample Point No.
Validated by
Date validated

SPECIAL RESEARCH REPORT

Sheldon G. Levy

ATTITUDES TOWARD POLITICAL VIOLENCE

1. Method

This section seeks to identify the characteristics of persons within the United States who support political violence, based upon an analysis of the national sample. The survey instrument was administered by Louis Harris and Associates during October 1-8, 1968.[1] The final sample included 1,176 adults (aged eighteen or over). Comparisons of the survey data with census data indicate that the sample conforms closely with the expected distributions on basic demographic characteristics. The major exception was a slight overrepresentation in the sample of Negro respondents. The paper that follows uses weighted data to compensate for this overrepresentation. A copy of the entire interview schedule may be found in the Appendix Volume of this Report.

The research effort is to determine how Americans feel political problems should be approached. In order to examine this problem carefully it is important to consider the feeling that citizens of the country have about a wide range of problems.

Caution should be used against the ever-present tendency to leap from attitudes to behavior. The results are based on a sample who were interviewed in their own homes. In addition to the possible biases that may exist in the interview situation, there is the problem of determining, on the basis of publicly expressed attitudes, the behavior in which individuals are likely to engage. The relationship is difficult to determine.

Nevertheless, attitudes that are expressed in private to interviewers have been found to relate to the behavior of the individual, and the material is, therefore, important for developing tentative hypotheses about the basis of political violence in the general population.

The material is a link between the social conditions that the person sees and the behavior in which he engages. It is an attempt to study how the people of this nation feel about political violence and the implications that it has for the current political activity which is occurring and the possible political violence that may emerge.

People differ in several ways on the problems of political violence. Two major attitudinal differences are between expectation and endorsement. Some people may expect violence while they do not endorse it. Others may both expect as well as endorse the use of violence to obtain political goals.

People also differ in the conditions under which they would feel that a resort to political violence is justified. Some people may feel that current problems are sufficiently severe, and that the democratic processes are not moving fast enough, and therefore might believe that political violence is justified. Others might feel that the provocation offered by the social environment would need to be far more severe before they would endorse political violence as a means to remove social obstacles.

Thus, in addition to the difference in the expectations and endorsement of violence, there is a difference in the conditions under which these attitudes are expressed. An examination of both the attitudes and the social conditions will form the basis of this section.

It is, of course, not possible in a survey interview to observe what people actually do. It is, however, quite possible to ask them to indicate the behavior in which they have previously engaged. Therefore, there will be an attempt to determine what political and social actions individuals have taken in the past. Another section will relate attitudes toward political violence to political behavior as reported by the respondent.

Respondents in the national sample were given a list of twenty-five items with which they could either agree or disagree. These items are reproduced in Table 1, and range over a wide domain of attitudes. Some deal with family discipline, others with governmental violence, others with assassination, and so forth.

One way of examining the results is to consider each item separately and to investigate the attitudes of the respondents to them. Another way is to group items on the basis of those that seem to go together. For example, items that appear to deal with assassination could be analyzed, then those dealing with family discipline or police force, etc. Still another way, and the one that is used here, is to determine empirically the items that group themselves. One method available for grouping is called factor analysis. This method is based on the concept of correlation where the correlation, in turn, is based on the concept of a linear relationship between two variables. The particular correlation considered is Pearson's Product Moment Correlation.

Suppose that two variables are given to a group of individuals and they are asked to respond to both. To be concrete, consider items 2 and 3 in Table 1. The first of these items says that it is important for a growing boy to have fist fights. The second says that our government is too ready to use force in dealing with other countries. On a subjective basis the two items do not appear to be related but this is not necessarily the case. It could well be that most of the people who disagree with item 2 would agree with item 3, and those who agree with item 2 might disagree with item 3. If this were the case, then the items would be said to be empirically related to each other.

Table 1—Items Used to Obtain Psychological
Orientation of the Population

1. Justice may have been a little rough-and-ready in the days of the Old West, but things worked better then than they do today with all the legal red tape.

2. When a boy is growing up, it is important for him to have a few fist fights.

3. Our government is too ready to use military force in dealing with other countries.

4. One of the best reasons for people to have guns is to make sure that the government doesn't get too much power.

5. The people running the government in Washington would do a good job if everybody left them alone instead of trying to influence them all the time.

6. The police frequently use more force than they need to when carrying out their duties.

7. Some politicians who have had their lives threatened probably deserve it.

8. Human nature being what it is, there must always be war and conflict.

9. Everything changes so quickly these days that I often have trouble deciding which are the right rules to follow.

10. If people go into politics they more or less have to accept the fact that they might get killed.

11. Groups have the right to train their members in marksmanship and underground warfare tactics in order to help put down any conspiracies that might occur in the country.

12. In dealing with other countries in the world, we are frequently justified in using military force.

13. People were better off in the old days when everyone knew just how he was expected to act.

14. What is lacking in the world today is the old kind of friendship that lasted for a lifetime.

15. What young people need most of all is strong discipline by their parents.

16. A few strong leaders could make this country better than all the laws and talk.

17. It is unfortunate that many civilians are killed by bombing in a war, but this cannot be avoided.

18. Politicians who try to change things too fast have to expect that their lives may be threatened.

19. Sex criminals deserve more than prison, they should be publicly whipped or worse.

20. Any man who insults a policeman has no complaint if he gets roughed-up in return.

21. A lot more people in government and politics will probably be assassinated in the next few years.

22. The government in Washington is the enemy, not the friend, of people like me.

23. Some people don't understand anything but force.

24. The police are wrong to beat up unarmed protesters, even when these people are rude and call them names.

25. Sometimes I have felt that the best thing for our country might be the death of some of our political leaders.

The actual relationship would be considered a negative one because the "agrees" generally coincided with the "disagrees" and vice-versa. Nevertheless, there would be a great deal of predictability from one variable to the next. That is, given the score of a person on the first item one would know, for most people, how he would respond to the second.

Similarly, the correspondence could be the one in which those who agree on the first also agree on the second and the "disagrees" in the first case were also generally the "disagrees" in the second. In this instance there would also be a relationship. It would, however, be a positive one. The predictability would still be high but it would be "agree" to "agree" and "disagree" to "disagree."

It is also possible that items 2 and 3 are statistically independent. That is, those who agreed with item 2 would be divided approximately equally so that some agreed with number 3 but some disagreed. Similarly, this situation might occur for those who disagreed with number 2. In this case there would be no correlation between the two variables. One could not predict, knowing the response on one item, what the response of an individual would be on the second.

It seems quite reasonable to suppose that in many cases, items are found to be correlated because a single underlying psychological train is at the basis of the response. One need not insist that the items that do correlate with each other do so because a psychological trait or dimension is operating, but it seems reasonable that this is really the case. Thus, one major reason for trying to determine which attitudinal statements group together empirically results from the search for a reduced number of psychological dimensions which will explain why people respond the way they do.

One of the most commonly used techniques for determining which items are empirically grouped is Factor Analysis. The basis of factor analysis is the interrelationships that exist between pairs of variables. Suppose, for example, that all twenty-five items described above were intercorrelated with each other. That is, suppose #1 was correlated with #2, #3, #4, etc., that #2 was correlated with #3, #4, etc., and so forth.

It is possible to consider a correlation between two variables to be comparable to a distance between those variables. Then all of the distances (as measured by the correlations) could be placed into a geometric space. Factor analysis is a technique that allows a determination of the number of dimensions that are necessary to describe the distances between the variables. Because the dimensions may be interpreted to be basic psychological traits or characteristics that lead people to respond similarly to a set of items, the factor analytic technique is a useful one for determining both the number of the dimensions in the space and the psychological basis of the dimensions. In addition, the technique allows a method for determining which dimensions are the most important. Our discussion follows the order of importance of the dimensions.[2]

2. Dimensions of Psychological Orientation

Authoritarian Traditionalism (I) The first dimension that emerged appears to be based on a concept that involved both an appeal to authority and a longing for tradition. This factor is the largest that emerged from the analyses and consists of the following six items.

Item 16. A few strong leaders could make this country better than all the laws and talk.

Item 13. People were better off in the old days when everyone knew just how he was expected to act.

Item 1. Justice may have been a little rough and ready in the days of the Old West, but things worked better than they do today with all the legal red tape.

Item 14. What is lacking in the world today is the old kind of friendship that lasted for a lifetime.

Item 9. Everything changes so quickly these days that I often have trouble deciding which are the right rules to follow.

Item 15. What young people need most of all is strong discipline by their parents.

Items 15 and 16 are appeals to authority rule and the other

items all indicate that life was better in the past than it is today. In general, a person endorsing these items would be expected to have relatively little tolerance for social ambiguity.

Expectations of Assassination (II) The second most important psychological trait that appeared from the analysis deals with those items for which endorsement indicated an expectation that politicians, or certain subsets of politicians, either had to accept the fact that they might get threatened or assassinated or that there actually will be a large number of assassinations in the next few years. The items that represent this attribute are:

Item 10. If people go into politics they more or less have to accept the fact that they might get killed.

Item 18. Politicians who try to change things too fast have to expect that their lives may be threatened.

Item 21. A lot more people in government and politics will probably be assassinated in the next few years.

Use of Police Force or Endorsement of Authority (III) Endorsement of the items that formed the third psychological trait indicate general support of the police. Respondents who scored high on this trait tended to disagree with the first two items and agree with the last two. The last item is interesting because it indicates a general orientation to severe punishment of sex offenders but makes no explicit reference to the role of the police. This trait consists of the following items:

Item 24. The police are wrong to beat up unarmed protestors, even when these people are rude and call them names.

Item 6. The police frequently use more force than they need to when carrying out their duties.

Item 20. Any man who insults a policeman has no complaint if he gets roughed up in return.

Item 19. Sex criminals deserve more than prison, they should be publicly whipped or worse.

The Government as an Enemy (IV) This trait appeared to be about equal in importance to the previous one that concerned the use of police force, and consists of the following three items:

Item 25. Sometimes I have felt that the best thing for our country might be the death of some of our political leaders.

Item 7. Some politicians who have had their lives threatened probably deserve it.

Item 22. The government is the enemy, not the friend, of people like me.

Items 25 and 7 are an endorsement of either threat to or the death of political leaders. Item 22 represents a perception that the government is the enemy of the respondent. It is not very surprising that an endorsement of Item 22 also leads to an endorsement of Items 25 and 7, which represent the removal or implied removal of political leaders, either by death or through direct threats. The three items come close to representing the concept of alienation from the political system, although true alienation might consider that what happens to the government is irrelevant rather than directly involving a judgment that the government and its leaders are dangerous. Nevertheless, alienation is a reasonable concept to apply to the endorsement of these items.

International Use of Force (V) The last attribute that emerges from the analysis is comparable to the third attribute. The third attribute dealt primarily with police force, whereas the fifth deals with the use of force in international relations. High scores were obtained by agreement with the first and third items and disagreement with the second. The dimension consists of the following items:

Item 12. In dealing with other countries in the world we are frequently justified in using military force.

Item 3. Our government is too ready to use military force in dealing with other countries.

Item 17. It is unfortunate that many civilians are killed by bombing in a war but this cannot be avoided.

3. Discussion of Factor Analytic Traits

Tables 2 and 3 present the results for both the unrotated and the rotated solution. The unrotated solution resulted in two major dimensions. The size of the dimension can be evaluated by examining the proportion of the variance accounted for by the factors. Table 2 indicates that the first factor, which accounted for 19 percent of the variance, was

Table 2—Unrotated Factor Solutions of Psychological Orientation to the Population

VAR	I	II	III	IV	V
001	.5390	-.1003	-.3043	.0672	.0558
002	.3280	-.0536	.0723	.0675	.2231
003	.0941	.5203	-.3225	.2434	-.3206
004	.3570	.2377	-.1232	-.3811	.2921
005	.4390	.0406	-.1187	.2278	.4098
006	-.0547	.6330	.1399	.3580	.1560
007	.3857	.4098	-.0252	-.2289	-.0220
008	.3923	-.0205	.3083	.1152	.2038
009	.5537	.1542	-.1194	.0732	.0703
010	.5216	.2573	.4134	.0101	-.2204
011	.5190	.2358	.0480	-.0552	.2512
012	.4233	-.3001	.3191	-.0201	.3495
013	.6082	-.0926	-.3496	.1038	-.0507
014	.5870	-.1596	-.2158	.3020	-.1564
015	.4633	-.3657	-.0799	.3405	-.0866
016	.4992	.0344	-.1053	.2311	.0820
017	.2999	-.3922	.4230	-.1274	.1695
018	.5311	.2511	.4012	-.0090	-.2379
019	.5492	-.1339	-.2395	.0082	-.1266
020	.5170	-.3528	-.1131	-.2190	-.1753
021	.4526	.1038	.3619	-.0797	-.3793
022	.3208	.4285	-.2047	-.3180	.1276
023	.3562	-.1236	.2820	.0720	-.2533
024	-.2430	.4697	.2214	.4606	.1331
025	.2614	.4174	-.0464	-.4570	-.0448
LATENT ROOT	4.7413	2.2745	1.5352	1.3374	1.1315
PROPORTION OF VARIANCE	.1897	.0910	.0614	.0535	.0453
CUMULATIVE PROPORTION OF VARIANCE	.1897	.2806	.3420	.3955	.4408

about twice as large as the second factor, which accounted for 9 percent of the variance. These two factors are the only two that are sufficiently large to warrant discussion. (The loading of a variable represents how close it came to the dimension. The size of the loading is restricted to a range between −1.00 and +1.00.) Although the principal axes solution accounts for the relationships to a greater extent than do the rotated solutions, rotation frequently results in a greater ability to recognize the psychological basis for the responses.[3]

Table 3 indicates again that the first two factors were the largest. However, they as well as the remaining factors are much closer together than they were in the principal axis solution. The Authoritarian-Traditionalist dimension ac-

Table 3—Rotated Factor Solutions of Psychological Oriented to the Population

VAR	I	II	III	IV	V
016	.6910	.1101	-.1721	.2007	.1847
013	.6593	.1028	.2160	.0679	-.0509
001	.6507	.0468	.1568	.0918	.0390
014	.5902	.1334	.1583	-.0596	-.1010
009	.5160	.2939	-.0348	.0685	.0206
015	.4674	.0279	.1698	-.0687	.1331
025	.0167	.1631	.0018	.7370	.0402
022	.1243	-.0313	-.0325	.6837	-.0966
007	.0811	.2453	.0354	.6054	-.1354
010	.1102	.7988	-.0255	.0530	.0321
018	.1096	.7346	-.0071	.1239	.0038
021	.1187	.6576	.0733	.0998	.0410
024	-.0642	-.0145	-.7867	-.0531	-.1103
006	-.1249	.1579	-.6190	.1273	-.2353
020	.2581	.2385	.6127	-.0286	.0595
019	.3082	.1234	.3558	.2482	.0175
012	.2018	.1654	.0074	.0271	.7051
003	.1682	.1356	.1715	.1513	-.6857
017	.0049	.1993	.1996	-.0503	.5591
002	.1141	.0353	.0336	.0179	.0876
005	.2274	.0317	.0143	.0139	.0658
011	.2393	.2882	-.1032	.2481	.2143
008	.1364	.1943	-.0280	.0558	.1420
023	.1016	.1783	-.0104	.0817	.1280
004	.1601	.0602	.1333	.2916	-.0105

SUM OF THE SQUARED
FACTOR LOADINGS

| | 2.6560 | 2.1689 | 1.7682 | 1.7360 | 1.5445 |

PROPORTION OF VARIANCE

| | .1062 | .0868 | .0707 | .0694 | .0618 |

CUMULATIVE PROPORTION
OF VARIANCE

| | .1062 | .1930 | .2637 | .3331 | .3949 |

counted for 11 percent of the variance and the Expectations of Assassination Factor accounted for 9 percent of the variance. (The maximum amount of variance which can ever be accounted for by all of the factors is 100 percent.)

Two important points to keep in mind in the interpretation of the factors are:

1. The factors that are obtained from a factor analysis depend heavily on the subjects that were used, and even more so on the items that were included. The dimensions or psychological traits that were derived from this analy-

sis do not represent the basic psychological components of the citizenry of this country. They do represent important dimensions, *when the particular set of items that were used in this analysis are included.* It must be remembered that the items were selected because they represented ideas or attitudes that were considered relevant to the problem of political violence. It is obvious, of course, that they only represent a small portion of those items.

2. The factors indicate the dimensions that are important for a group of subjects, not the placement of those subjects on a dimension. For example, consider items #16 and #13 from the first factor. These two items both appeared on the first factor because they were reasonably highly correlated with each other. But one does not automatically know how any given Respondent answered these two items. *If* he said he agreed with item #16, the chances are that he also said that he agreed with #13. But he may have disagreed with #16. Thus, although given the response on one variable, it is possible to predict fairly well the response on the second variable; one is not able just from a knowledge of the factors that emerged, to determine how each subject responded.

At least as important as the determination of the factors themselves is a determination of where respondents located themselves on the factors. Who, for example, were the high authoritarians, and who were the low authoritarians? Who were the respondents high in expectations of assassination and who were low?

The following section will examine, therefore, both the level of response as well as the characteristics that appeared to lead to high or low placement on the factors. Although a mathematically economical way to do this is to examine the factor scores of the respondents, the substance of a factor was contained in the individual items. Consequently, the description that follows examines the separate items after they have been grouped in the manner that emerged from the factor analysis.

The Authoritarian-Traditionalist Trait—Although six items formed this dimension, the level of agreement differed, depending on the item. The amount of agreement for each of the items is given in Table 4. The items are arranged in the order of their loadings in this factor.

Table 4—Proportion of Agreement for Each of Six Items of the Authoritarian Traditionalist Trait

Item	Percentage who Agreed or strongly Disagreed
16	56
13	47
1	51
14	72
9	50
15	86

The two items that received substantially more support than the others consisted of items 14 and 15. Item 15 stated that, "What young people need most of all is strong discipline by their parents." Fully 86 percent of the population supported this idea. Even among those who were 30 years or less in age, agreement reached 80 percent. Apparently, for the nation, parental discipline is considered essential.

In the whole sample, 72 percent endorsed item 14 which stated that, "What is lacking in the world today is the old kind of friendship that lasted for a lifetime." Even among those 30 or younger, almost 2/3 (63 percent) agreed with this item.

In general, the population of the country appears to feel that modern life has elements that are confusing and which make living less personal than many desire. Although the youngest age group is less likely to endorse a return to conditions of the past when these are tied to regulation of one's life, the indication is that parental discipline and friendship are highly regarded values.

Table 5 presents the results for different groups in the population. For the items that formed this dimension, educational level was the basis for greatest discrimination among respondents. The next most consistent discriminating variable was the amount of political activity in which the individual had previously engaged. Finally, income was an important variable for discriminating among individuals in the population. The higher the education, or the higher the previous political activity or the greater the income, the less likely was the respondent to endorse the items. The results indicate that those individuals who had not gone beyond the eighth grade were twice as likely to endorse some of the items on this dimension than were those who had at least some college.

Table 5.—Endorsement percentages of respondents on the authoritarian-traditionalist items by education, political activity and income

Item Number	Education				Political Activity			Income		
	≤ 8th Grade	Some H.S.	H.S. Grad	College	Low	Medium	High	≤ $5,000	5,000-9,999	≥ $10,000
#16	67	62	53	47	63	54	44	63	57	47
		RANGE = 20				RANGE = 19			RANGE = 16	
#13	66	55	45	31	57	45	30	62	45	36
		RANGE = 35				RANGE = 27			RANGE = 26	
#1	63	62	50	34	61	47	32	56	52	44
		RANGE = 29				RANGE = 29			RANGE = 12	
#14	84	83	73	52	80	71	53	82	75	60
		RANGE = 32				RANGE = 27			RANGE = 22	
#9	69	63	47	31	62	47	36	62	51	38
		RANGE = 38				RANGE = 26			RANGE = 24	
#15	90	92	89	77	90	88	73	87	89	82
		RANGE = 15				RANGE = 17			RANGE = 7	

Greater endorsement occurred with increasing age. The largest differences occurred between those respondents who were 65 or under compared to those who were over 65.

It is apparent that endorsement of the items which formed the authoritarian-traditionalist dimension come from those individuals who have benefitted least or who have the least to look forward to, while the less authoritarian in the population are those who have been politically active in the past, or who have gained the most.

Expectations of Assassination—The agreement that respondents gave for the items that formed this attribute are presented in Table 6.

Table 6.—Percentages of agreement for the items of the expectations of assassination trait

Item	Percentage who Agree or Strongly Agree
10	51
18	51
21	55

There is very little variability among these items. More than half of the population agrees with each. Overall, the population at large appears pessimistic about the chances of survival of its political leadership.

However, subgroups do differ substantially in the degree to which they endorse the above items. Education and previous political activity were again important discriminating variables; region of the country in which the individual resides was also an important variable. In fact, the range between the lowest and highest groups is comparable to the variability found among the educational groups. The results are presented in Table 7.

Table 7 indicates a great deal of consistency among the characteristics of the high and low groups. The low groups are consistent with those that were low on the Authoritarian-Traditionalist trait. It is interesting to note that these groups are the ones that generally identified with the national leaders that were assassinated (the two Kennedys and King), although they are unwilling to accept political assassination as inevitable.

The high expectation groups are again those who have gained the least. The picture for them now is pessimism coupled with a greater value on authority and days past. The new

Table 7. –Endorsement percentages of respondents on the expectations of assassination items by education, region, and political activity

Item Number	Education				Region				Political Acitivity		
	≤8th Grade	Some H.S.	H.S. Grad	College	East	Midwest	South	West	Low	Medium	High
#10	65	60	48	36	39	51	66	48	62	47	39
		RANGE = 29				RANGE = 27				RANGE = 23	
#18	66	59	53	46	48	52	67	63	63	51	52
		RANGE = 20				RANGE = 19				RANGE = 12	
#21	62	53	52	44	44	56	61	55	62	62	44
		RANGE = 18				RANGE = 17				RANGE = 18	

characteristic that emerges in these groups is that of region (the South or West). This finally must lead to a reevaluation of the reasons that these regions appeared less identified with the national leaders who were assassinated. Although it is still possible that the explanation lies in the reduced amounts of support that individuals in these regions gave to the political leaders, it is also possible that it is simply a consequence of a greater expectation of assassination. Greater expectations might lead to smaller surprise when an event does happen. Of course, the two explanations could be coupled with each other: it is possible that pessimism has been generated by a general alienation, especially toward national leaders, and that this alienation may have then led to lack of support.

Use of Police Force or Endorsement of Authority—The third most important trait to emerge deals primarily with police force and the endorsement of authority. The percentage agreement or disagreement with each of the four items that formed this attribute are given in Table 8.

Table 8.—Percentage agreement or disagreement with items of the police force attribute

Item	Percentage
24	45*
6	65*
20	56
19	40

*Percentage disagreement.

There is fairly wide variability across these items. The greatest disagreement is with the item that states that the police frequently use more force than is necessary. Two-thirds of the population disagree with this, but there is a great deal of discrepancy between Negroes and whites, as will be indicated later. Least support is given to the severe punishment of sex offenders. Although there are wide racial differences on the items dealing specifically with police force, there is virtually no difference between the races on the treatment of sex criminals. On the other hand, wide variability on this item was obtained based on past Political Activity; 51 percent of those who were low but only 23 percent of those who were high endorsed the item.

The most important discriminating variables are race, education and age (Table 9).

Table 9.—Endorsement percentages of respondents on the use of
police force items by race, education, and age

Item Number	Race		Education				Age			
	Negro	White	≤8th Grade	Some H.S.	H.S. Grad	College	≤30	31-50	51-65	65+
24*	19	49	52	40	48	40	39	42	51	54
	RANGE = 30		RANGE = 12				RANGE = 15			
6*	23	72	59	60	73	64	34	27	25	27
	RANGE = 49		RANGE = 14				RANGE = 9			
20	41	59	71	65	56	45	41	53	67	81
	RANGE = 18		RANGE = 26				RANGE = 40			
19	39	40	56	49	41	22	35	37	42	53
	RANGE = 1		RANGE = 34				RANGE = 18			

*Percentage Disagreement.

The differences between the high and low groups are more difficult to interpret in the case of the Police Force trait. The strikingly new characteristic to emerge is the very low disagreement of Negroes with items 24 and 6. In fact, Negroes stand alone in their opinions about the police. In general, older citizens are more supportive of the police. Rural residents are more supportive and metropolitan city residents are less supportive. In general, the attributes of the high versus the low groups are predictable from the results of the Authoritarian-Traditionalist attribute, with the notable exception of the attitudes of Negroes.

The Government as an Enemy Trait—The Alienation Dimension shows small agreement in the population for any of the items.

Table 10.—*Percentage Agreement with the Items in the Alienation Dimension*

Item	Percentage
25	9
22	9
7	19

Although support is generally low, one out of five Americans believes that some politicians who have had their lives threatened probably deserved it. The variability on item 25 is too small to make interpretations. The other two items generally indicate the "have-nots" are higher in alienation than the "haves." These results are consistent with those previously presented on the Authoritarian-Traditionalist and the Expectations of Assassination dimensions. However, the salient result on this dimension must remain the small amount of agreement in the population for any of the items.

International Use of Force—The percentage agreement or disagreement in the population is given for the items on this dimension in Table 11.

Table 11.—*Percentage Agreement or Disagreement for the Items on the International Use of Force Dimension*

Item	Percentage
12	62
3	53*
17	73

*Disagree.

There is considerable support in the population for the inevitability of death in war time (item 17) and for justification of the use of force by the U.S. government in dealing with other countries (item 12). Although over half of the population disagrees with the idea that we are too ready to use military force in dealing with other countries, there is still substantial feeling in the population that this is the case. Almost four respondents in ten (39 percent) agreed with the statement that, "Our government is too ready to use military force in dealing with other countries."

The discriminating variables on this dimension did not differentiate to as great a degree as they did on the first three factors. Although the most important variables were region, income and education, only region was a consistent discriminator. The results indicate that residents of the East are the least supportive of the government's use of force in international relations while residents of the South are more supportive. Similarly, analysis of the income variable indicates that the low income group ($\leq$$5000) is more opposed to the government's use of force in international relations than is the high income group ($\geq$$10,000). Although education is a fairly important discriminator on the first two items, the results are not consistent. Thus, the highest educational category is the least likely to agree that the United States was frequently justified in using force when dealing with other countries (55 percent agree or strongly agree) but they are also most likely to disagree with the statement that our government is too ready to use force in its dealings with other nations (61 percent disagree or strongly disagree). The reverse was true for those who had less than a completed high school education: whereas 68 percent agree with the first statement, only 43 percent disagree with the second.

The results on item 3 are especially interesting. This item read: "Our government is too ready to use military force in dealing with other countries." Among the highest groups are the male veterans (66 percent disagreement) and those who earn $10,000 or more (63 percent disagreement). The male veterans have a substantial investment of their lives in the international activity of this country, while those who earn at least $10,000 may well believe that the international activities of the United States are being conducted in their interests. On the other hand, the low groups on this item are those who contribute the most to the draft (the less educated and the low income). They are also those groups who have gained the least from the domestic and international activities of the country.

Analysis of Other Items

The items that did not appear in any of the dimensions and the percentage who agree with them are given in Table 12.

Table 12.—Percentage Agreement with Items not Falling on One of the Major Dimensions

Item	Percentage
23. Some people don't understand anything but force.	78
2. When a boy is growing up, it is important to have a few fist fights.	70
8. Human nature being what it is, there must always be war and conflict.	58
5. The people running the government in Washington would do a good job if everybody left them alone instead of trying to influence them all of the time.	26
4. One of the best reasons for people to have guns is to make sure that the government doesn't get too much power.	10
11. Groups have the right to train their members in marksmanship and underground warfare tactics in order to help put down any conspiracies that might occur in the country.	26

The responses for the overall population indicate that alienation in the population from the government is small. Only 10 percent of the population agrees with item 4. Much greater endorsement is given to item 11, namely, that underground training is legitimate to help put down conspiracies that might occur. One in four Americans endorses this position. In general, those who are in the most insecure position feel the greatest danger.

Although a substantial majority of the population do not agree, still one out of four Americans believes in not trying to influence the government. As on the previous two items, the greatest endorsement comes from those in the worst position in the society, the Negroes (46 percent), those with only a grammar school education (42 percent), and those whose income is under $5000 (40 percent). On the other hand, those who have the most influence and have gained the most, infrequently agree. These are those who earn $10,000 or more (13 percent), the college educated (14 percent) and the high politically active (19 percent).

Although a substantial number of Americans believe war is inevitable, 37 percent disagree. Given the historical conflicts between groups, this may be taken as evidence of a fair amount of optimism in the population. Or perhaps it is a consequence of the nuclear age which does not allow for both the inevitability of war and the survival of the human race.

On the other hand, a larger percentage of individuals (78 percent) feel that force may be necessary in dealing with some individuals (Item 23). A substantial percentage (70 percent) also feel that some experience with violence is a necessary part of growing up (Item 2).

4. Response To Governmental Injustice

In this section, we seek to provide a more complete picture of public attitudes by examining specific situations in which respondents might conceivably find themselves. The emphasis is on hypothetical conditions of governmental injustice. Many studies emphasize attitudes toward violence that are considered an inappropriate response to social conditions, but few focus on attitudes connected with social conditions that may justify more extreme measures. Violent action is probably a product of the social condition, the perception of the social condition, the attitudes and motives of the respondent, as well as the response style or political habit. The usual attitudinal studies, of which the previous material is a good example, frequently make the judgment that the social condition is an inappropriate environment in which to express the attitudes toward violence that some do.

Through the use of a set of hypothetical situations, this section presents a number of social conditions which are perceived by almost all of the respondents as constituting social injustices. The major problem is to examine their attitudes toward political violence when this is the case.

Just as a democracy cannot survive if it has important segments of its population who use violence to achieve political goals, neither can it expect to maintain itself over a long period of time if its citizenry are unresponsive to extreme provocation. The first problem has been investigated. This material will present the results that are relevant to the second.

This section examines the political responsiveness of the population under conditions which, for the most part, do not exist. The aim is to try to estimate how people might respond under conditions of governmental injustice and to relate these responses to political behavior taken in the past because of feelings about political and social issues.

The Governmental Injustice Items

Most surveys of attitudes ask individuals their opinion about contemporary issues. The intention of this study was to go beyond this in two major ways. The first was by developing hypothetical situations which varied in the degree to which the respondent considered them unjust. The range covered was from mild injustice to extreme injustice on the part of the government. In addition, two other situations were described. One was a protest against the government that would ordinarily be considered illegal. The other was an appearance by an unpopular senator to give a speech.

In addition to the situations, the responses were designed to go from a purely attitudinal one (strong approval to strong disapproval of the situation), to a mild response (discussion with one's friends), to a severe response (physical assault or armed action). Thus, legal responses as well as those that would ordinarily be considered illegal were included. The responses were designed to examine both the extent to which the population felt a response would be all right in a situation as well as their estimate of their own likelihood of actually engaging in it under the conditions noted.

The hypothetical situations and the responses are given below. The senator question is presented separately because the responses that were offered here differed from those used in the first five cases.

1. Imagine that Congress has passed a law that makes you pay just as many dollars in taxes as people who make a lot more money than you do.
2. Imagine that Congress has just passed a law prohibiting anyone from saying anything against the government.
3. Imagine that the government has just arrested and imprisoned many of the Negroes in your community even though there has been no trouble.

4. Imagine that, in order to keep control of the country, the government starts arresting and shooting large numbers of innocent people including members of your family.

5. Suppose you see a group of people who are deliberately blocking rush hour traffic to protest the war in Vietnam.

After the degree of approval or disapproval was ascertained, the respondent was asked to indicate each action that he felt it would be all right to take.

These were:

A. Express an opinion to friends on what is happening.
B. Sign a petition about what is happening.
C. Organize a group who are interested in what is happening.
D. If nothing else worked, participate in an illegal sit-in to express one's feelings about what is happening.
E. If nothing else worked, participate in a physical assault or armed action because of feelings about what is happening.

The responses were designed so that the person could not say no to one of the illegal responses because he felt a legal response would do the job. Thus, those actions that would ordinarily be considered illegal (D and E responses) were introduced with the phrase, "If nothing else worked, . . ."

After the "all rights" were recorded, the respondent was asked, "How about you personally, are you likely or unlikely to do this as a reaction to (the particular situation) we talked about?"

Schematically, the design of these items can be represented in three dimensions: (1) the degree of provocation offered by the situations, (2) the degree of reaction offered by the response alternatives, and (3) the personal endorsement alternatives. Figure 1 presents this conceptualization for the first four hypothetical situations.

After the five situations were presented, a final one was given which read as follows:

> "Your senator has blocked legislation which you believe is essential to protect the rights of every citizen. The senator has come to your town and is making a speech in a public audience to gain support for his point of view."

As before, a set of responses were offered that allowed the respondent to indicate those which he felt were all right as well as those in which he felt he was likely to engage. In

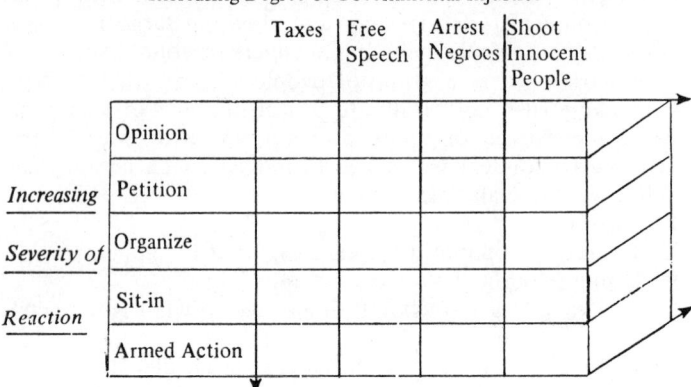

Figure 1. Conceptualization of Governmental Injustice Items

addition, however, a projective technique was used. After responding for himself, the respondent was asked to indicate which actions he thought some of his friends would think it would be all right to take, and, then, for those that were indicated, whether he thought some of his friends would actually be likely to do them. Thus, this item allowed the respondent to remove himself one step further from an indication of personal actions by asking for an estimation of some of his friends' endorsement and behavior.

The responses offered were:

A. Carry signs expressing disapproval of the senator.

B. Boo during pauses in the senator's speech where the senator was expecting applause.

C. Participate with others in systematically booing and stamping feet so that the senator was unable to continue his speech and be heard.

D. Throw rotten tomatoes or other objects which could not harm the senator but which would demonstrate disapproval.

E. Throw empty bottles or other objects which could not do serious or permanent harm to the senator but which would demonstrate the extent of disapproval.

F. Use a gun or other weapon to inflict serious enough harm to the senator so that he would have to turn his position over to someone else.

Findings

Respondents were first asked if they strongly approved, approved, disapproved, or strongly disapproved of the situation that was described. The results are presented in Table 13.

Table 13—Degree of Approval–Disapproval for Each of the Five Hypothetical Situations

			Issue		
Action	Taxes	Free Speech	Negro Arrest	Shooting Innocent People	Vietnam Protest
Strongly Approve	2	2	1	1	3
Approve	1	2	0	0	4
Disapprove	21	27	31	10	39
Strongly Disapprove	74	68	65	87	51
Not Sure	2	3	4	1	5

The results indicate that the greatest amount of approval is given on the Vietnam Protest item, but this response is only given by one out of 14 adults. The next least amount of disapproval is given to the Negro arrest situation. Further, the tax law is disapproved to a greater extent than is either the infringement of free speech or the Negro arrest situation. The shooting and arresting of innocent people clearly is the most strongly disapproved item in the list.

Actions That Individuals Would Take

For each of the situations, individuals were asked to indicate which responses they felt it would be all right to take because of their feelings about the situation. In addition, they were also asked for each item to which they responded yes, if they would be likely or unlikely to engage in the behavior indicated in their responses. Table 14 presents the results for the "all right" responses for each situation.

Table 14—Percentages Endorsing Each Response by Issue

		Issue			
Action	Taxes	Free Speech	Negro Arrest	Shooting Innocent People	Vietnam Protest
Express Opinion	74	73	76	67	75
Sign Petition	73	73	69	65	58
Organize a Group	61	64	61	67	50
Illegal Sit-In	11	17	18	37	8
Physical Assault	3	9	9	48	10

Table 15 presents the percentage of respondents who said a particular action was all right, who then said they were likely to engage in it themselves. The table further gives the product of the "all right" percentage and the "likely" percentage; that is, the percentage who said yes to both the "all right" alternative and the personal likelihood alternative.

Table 15—Percentage of (a) Personally Likely and Percentage of (b) Both "All Right" And "Likely"

		Issue			
Action	Taxes a/b	Free Speech a/b	Negro Arrest a/b	Shooting Innocent People a/b	Vietnam Protest a/b
Express Opinion	93/69	94/69	94/71	97/65	62/69
Sign Petition	88/64	89/65	88/61	94/61	83/48
Organize a Group	54/33	65/42	64/39	83/56	56/28
Illegal Sit-In	53/6	66/11	69/12	83/31	55/4
Physical Assault	43/1	71/6	59/5	86/41	68/7

Examination of Tables 14 and 15 indicates the degree of opposition in the population to wholesale arrest and killing by the government to keep control. Almost one out of two respondents indicates that physical assault or armed action would be all right to take (and fully 86 percent of these indicate that they would be likely to engage in this response). Similarly, the other possible responses in this situation have higher proportions of individuals who are likely to engage in the response than in other situations. The relatively low percentages of legal responses to this situation are probably due to the consideration that, for such extensive provocation, these actions would be ineffectual. Substantiation for this point of view comes from the fact that a smaller proportion of individuals endorse the illegal sit-in response than endorse the armed action response.

Other results are consistent with those presented for the approval-disapproval response. Although the proportion of those who indicate that an illegal response in the Negro Arrest situation is slightly smaller than in the Free Speech Infringement case, the overall percentage who indicate they would be likely to respond this way is the same. The tax situation, in terms of illegal responses, is the least provocative one. Again, this may be a consequence of the feeling that this situation could be remedied through legal means. It should be noted, however, that the respondent was asked if the illegal response would be all right, "if nothing else worked . . ."

The responses can generally be ordered, based on the proportion in the sample that say each action would be all right. Even this ordering has some reversals depending on the situation. In the Free Speech and Negro Arrest situations, the last three responses—organizing a group, illegal sit-in, and physical assault—are approximately equal in the proportion of those who say it is all right and who then indicate they would be likely to engage in the action.

The Hypothetical Senator

For the overall responses, individuals indicated that it would be all right to carry signs, but it would not be all right to engage in more severe forms of activity. The range was from 92 percent endorsement for carrying a sign to one percent endorsement for using a gun. Only for the carry-a-sign response was there more than a majority endorsement. However, the interpretations of what one's friends would think would be all right to do are quite interesting. Only in the case of the first response is there a greater percentage of endorsement for the individual himself than for his friends, when the whole sample is considered. For the second most serious response—booing—friends are considered much more likely to think that this action would be all right than the individual himself. This relationship continues through all of the remaining responses. (It also holds for the likely responses. In fact, for all of the responses, individuals more frequently indicated that their friends would be likely to engage in the behavior than was indicated for the respondents themselves.)

As can be seen from Table 16, seriousness of the response is in the order listed. More people would be willing to carry signs than to boo; to boo than to participate in booing and stamping of feet; and so forth. This ranking holds for the analysis of friends as well as for the white and nonwhite subgroups separately.

Table 16—Percentages of All Right and Likely Responses For Self and For Friends

Response	Self		Friends	
	All Right	Likely	All Right	Likely
Carry a sign	92	59	90	70
Boo	36	66	49	81
Participate in booing and stamping of feet	17	60	30	78
Throw tomatoes	5	55	13	63
Throw empty bottles	2	20	7	48
Use a gun	1	14	3	52

Differences between the two subgroups are presented in Table 17, but only for the answers that individuals gave about those responses which they thought their friends would think appropriate to take. White and nonwhite subgroups are comparable in proportions believing their friends would think it was all right to carry signs. However, for all of the more serious responses a much greater proportion of nonwhites indicate that their friends would think that a response was all right. Thus, in the case of booing, 59 percent of the nonwhites

*Table 17—Endorsement of All Right Response to Express
Disapproval of the Senator who was Blocking Essential Legislation*

Response	% Overall rates		% Subgroup Rates (Friends)	
	Personal	Friends	White	Nonwhite
Carry a sign	92	90	90 (n=657)	91 (n=158)
Boo	36	49	46 (n=332)	59 (n=102)
Participate in booing and stamping of feet	17	30	26 (n=187)	47 (n=81)
Throw tomatoes	5	13	9 (n=69)	28 (n=49)
Throw empty bottles	2	7	4 (n=31)	20 (n=34)
Use a gun	1	3	2 (n=11)	7 (n=12)

compared to 46 percent of whites indicated that their friends
would think this action was all right. In the next case, the
percentages are 46 percent to 26 percent, and so on. In fact,
fully one out of five nonwhites indicates that he thinks his
friends would think it would be all right to throw bottles that
could do some physical damage to the senator, whereas only
one out of 25 whites give this response for their friends. The
interpretation of the results is somewhat difficult because the
situation was clearly described as one in which the individual
senator was blocking legislation which the individual thought
was essential to protect the right of every citizen. However,
his status as a senator does make him legally elected, although
nonwhites might question the legality of the election if they
assumed he were from a state in which nonwhites were deprived of their voting rights.

Tax Issue

For the tax issue, political activity, educational level, and
age discriminated most among respondents. These results are
presented in Table 18. For most of the responses the various
subgroups did not differ greatly from each other. The exception to this was in the endorsement of the response to organize a group. In this instance there were sharp differences, with
low political activity or low education or older age associated
with smaller rates of response. The greatest differences oc-

Table 18.—Proportions of response on tax issue by political activity, education, and age

Response	Political Activity			Education				Age			
	Low	Medium	High	≤8th Grade	Some H.S.	H.S. Grad	Some College	≤30	31-50	51-65	65+
Strong Disapproval	71	77	72	71	79	76	71	74	76	76	69
		RANGE = 6			RANGE = 8				RANGE = 7		
Express Opinion	76	73	74	80	75	71	74	71	71	78	82
		RANGE = 3			RANGE = 9				RANGE = 11		
Sign Petition	66	76	78	69	74	72	75	77	74	68	70
		RANGE = 12			RANGE = 6				RANGE = 9		
Organize A Group	51	62	81	51	54	62	70	70	63	56	48
		RANGE = 30			RANGE = 19				RANGE = 22		
Participate In Illegal Sit-In	9	9	22	11	13	6	14	14	12	8	7
		RANGE = 13			RANGE = 8				RANGE = 7		
Participate In Physical Assault	3	2	6	4	3	3	2	3	3	2	4
		RANGE = 4			RANGE = 2				RANGE = 2		

Table 19.–Proportions of response on free speech infringement by political activity, education, and age

Response	Political Activity			Education				Age			
	Low	Medium	High	≤8th Grade	Some H.S.	H.S. Grad	College	≤30	31-50	51-65	65+
Strong Disapproval	56	72	79	52	62	67	82	76	69	67	51
		RANGE = 23			RANGE = 30				RANGE = 25		
Express Opinion	74	72	73	81	70	70	72	70	71	74	83
		RANGE = 2			RANGE = 11				RANGE = 13		
Sign a Petition	67	76	75	67	76	71	78	76	75	70	69
		RANGE = 9			RANGE = 11				RANGE = 7		
Organize a Group	54	66	82	47	60	66	74	71	68	59	47
		RANGE = 28			RANGE = 27				RANGE = 24		
Participate In Illegal Sit-In	11	16	34	12	17	12	25	23	19	13	8
		RANGE = 23			RANGE = 13				RANGE = 15		
Participate In Physical Assault	4	8	21	5	6	7	15	14	9	5	3
		RANGE = 17			RANGE = 10				RANGE = 11		

Table 20.–Proportions of response on arrest and imprisonment
of Negroes by political activity, race and age

Response	Political Activity			Race		Age			
	Low	Medium	High	Negro	White	≤30	31-50	51-65	65+
Strong Disapproval	59	68	74	86	61	70	67	66	53
		RANGE = 15		RANGE = 25				RANGE = 17	
Express Opinion	77	76	74	83	75	75	74	74	83
		RANGE = 3		RANGE = 8				RANGE = 9	
Sign A Petition	63	72	76	78	68	72	68	70	64
		RANGE = 13		RANGE = 10				RANGE = 8	
Organize A Group	52	64	77	76	59	69	64	59	46
		RANGE = 25		RANGE = 17				RANGE = 23	
Participate In Illegal Sit-In	11	18	37	43	14	23	19	14	13
		RANGE = 26		RANGE = 29				RANGE = 10	
Participate In Physical Assault	6	9	21	24	13	13	11	5	7
		RANGE = 15		RANGE = 11				RANGE = 8	

Table 21. –Proportions of response on shooting of innocent people by political activity, education, and age

Response	Political Activity			Education				Age			
	Low	Medium	High	≤8th Grade	Some H.S.	H.S. Grad	College	≤30	31-50	51-65	65+
Strong Disapproval	83	90	91	79	86	88	94	93	87	87	79
		RANGE = 8			RANGE = 15				RANGE = 14		
Express Opinion	67	67	68	73	66	64	66	65	65	66	74
		RANGE = 1			RANGE = 9				RANGE = 9		
Sign A Petition	62	65	69	65	66	62	66	66	63	64	67
		RANGE = 7			RANGE = 4				RANGE = 4		
Organize a Group	61	68	77	61	63	67	74	71	66	69	59
		RANGE = 16			RANGE = 13				RANGE = 12		
Illegal Sit-In	29	37	56	31	36	34	43	45	39	30	23
		RANGE = 27			RANGE = 12				RANGE = 22		
Physical Assault	36	50	71	30	43	51	59	60	52	37	30
		RANGE = 35			RANGE = 29				RANGE = 30		

curred on the item about previous political activity. While only 51% of those classified as low on this item, and 62% of those classified as medium, said the response would be all right, 81% of the highly politically active responded this way. Systematic influence of previous political activity may also be noted on both the "sign a petition" as well as the "illegal sit-in" response, although the differences between the extremes are not nearly as great.

Free Speech

The same three variables appeared to be of primary influence in discriminating among respondents in the Free Speech Infringement case (See Table 19). However, large variability was obtained on several of the responses. Even the amount of strong disapproval varied greatly among subgroups. Thus only 52% of those with not more than an eighth grade education, whereas 28% of those with a college education, strongly disapproved of the government's action.

For almost all of the responses, there was a tendency toward greater endorsement of a response with increasing political activity, with increasing education and with decreasing age. The exception occurs on the "express an opinion" response, which is highly endorsed by everyone including the groups that are noticeably lower in the endorsement of other responses. The response to organize a group and illegal sit-in again has the greatest variability among subgroups. However, there are also substantial differences in the level of endorsement on the physical assault response. Thus, while only 4% of the low, and 8% of the medium politically active groups said this response would be all right "if nothing else worked . . .", over one in five (21%) of the high politically active took this position.

Negro Arrest

The analysis of the Negro Arrest situation resulted in political activity and age being important discriminating variables. Race was a very important variable. (See Table 20.) In fact, for every response, including strong disapproval, Negroes gave the highest response rate. In addition to strong disapproval, there was great discriminability among subgroups on the "organize a group" and "illegal sit-in" responses. As expected, higher levels of previous political activity and lower age led to increasing percentages of endorsement.

Table 21 presents the results for the item concerning the shooting of innocent people. Political activity, education, and age are again the most important discriminating variables. It is important to observe that even for a situation so severe as this one, there is a fair amount of variability in the proportions that strongly disapprove of the government's actions. Only 79% of those who did not go beyond eighth grade, and 79% of those over age 65, expressed strong disapproval. On the other hand, 94% of those with some college education, and 93% of those between 18 and 30 years of age expressed strong disapproval.

Although substantial variability exists among subgroups on both the "organize a group" and the "illegal sit-in" responses, by far the greatest difference of opinion exists in the endorsement of the "physical assault" response. Only 36% of those low in political activity endorsed this most extreme response, but the percentage rose to 71 among those high in political activity. Comparable differences based on education and age may also be noted.

Vietnam Protest

Finally, the results of the Vietnam Protest case are presented in Table 22. Although political activity and education still are important discriminating variables, residence now also appears to be important. It will be recalled that this situation involved a protest against the war in which rush hour traffic was being blocked. It may be noteworthy that suburbanites expressed the greatest amount of strong disapproval.

Generally, there was relatively little variability among subgroups for the various responses. Greatest differences of opinion again occurred on the "organize a group" response. Consistent with the previous analyses, lower levels of political activity or of education were associated with lower rates of agreement that the response was all right. However, although residence discriminated importantly across the responses, there was no consistent pattern. Although suburbanites expressed the greatest amount of strong disapproval, rural residents were highest in their endorsement of the "express an opinion" response. This finding is consistent with the general finding in

Table 22.–Proportions of response to Vietnam protest by political activity, residence and education

Response	Political Activity			Residence				Education			
	Low	Medium	High	Metro City	Suburban	Urban Town	Rural	≤8th Grade	Some H.S.	H.S. Grad	College
Strong Disapproval	46	53	55	46	61	43	52	43	53	51	56
		RANGE = 9			RANGE = 15				RANGE = 13		
Express Opinion	76	24	74	72	73	73	82	80	70	71	80
		RANGE = 2			RANGE = 10				RANGE = 10		
Sign a Petition	53	58	66	58	63	54	55	54	61	55	61
		RANGE = 13			RANGE = 9				RANGE = 7		
Organize a Group	43	52	60	47	58	48	48	42	49	52	54
		RANGE = 17			RANGE = 11				RANGE = 12		
Illegal Sit-In	6	7	18	13	9	3	6	8	6	6	11
		RANGE = 12			RANGE = 10				RANGE = 5		
Physical Assault	9	8	17	13	8	8	9	8	12	9	10
		RANGE = 8			RANGE = 5				RANGE = 4		

these analyses that highest endorsement rates for the "express an opinion" response were frequently found among those groups who were lowest in both amount of disapproval and in the endorsement of the other responses. The other two responses that would ordinarily be considered legal (sign a petition and organize a group) had highest endorsement among suburbanites, but the ordinarily illegal responses (illegal sit-in and physical assault) had highest rates among the residents of metropolitan cities. These findings may have occurred because of the different racial composition of these two residential areas.

What information has this examination of the response rates to the hypothetical situation provided?

First, a particular social situation is perceived as differentially unjust by subgroups in the population. If strong disapproval is taken as a measure of the degree to which a political event is seen as unjust, then it is apparent that Negroes are more antagonized by the arrest and imprisonment of Negroes than are whites, and suburbanites are most antagonized by the Vietnam Protestors who blocked rush-hour traffic than are those who live in other residential areas.

Far more important, however, is the finding that those subgroups in the population who were most violent in their attitudes and expectations, as measured by the psychological dimensions, are least disapproving and responsive to actual instances of governmental injustice and even illegal protest (as presented in the Vietnam situation). Thus, although they have strong generalized attitudes towards violence, they also are the most passive in their political responsiveness to actual government injustice.

Strong evidence exists to support the inference that it is among those who have the least to look forward to (e.g., the elderly), among those who have benefitted the least from the resources of the country (e.g., the low income, the poorly educated and the Negro) and among those who have been least active in their utilization of the channels of political influence (e.g., the low politically active), that the greatest danger exists. Their generalized attitudes toward violence as well as their passivity in the face of governmental injustice provide a ready basis for manipulation by demogogic leadership, both through the creation of scapegoat enemies and through the manipulation of generalized hostility. It seems reasonable that a democratic society can secure its domestic tranquility by no better means than to provide a stake and a reward to those who are deprived.

Political Complaints and Political Action

Confirmation of the judgments provided above can be obtained in the brief analyses that follow. These will demonstrate that, not only are those groups with the greatest endorsement of political violence and expectations of violence the least responsive to possible instances of governmental injustice; they are the least provoked by governmental action and are also least likely to use the channels of political influence.

Respondents were asked the following question, "Could you tell me what action the government in Washington has taken during the past few years that you objected to the most?"

It should be apparent that the chosen topic differed greatly among respondents. The multiple responses will not be examined here. The major point is the examination of those who did not respond, that is, who either said none, or who didn't know.

The results presented in Table 23 indicate clearly that it is the least advantaged who did not list any response.

Table 23—Don't Know Responses to Past Governmental Actions
(in percent)

Income

$5,000	$5,000–9,999	$10,000
36	24	17

Education

8th Grade	Some High School	High School Grad	College
36	35	22	15

Race

Negro	White
45	23

Age

30	31–50	51–65	65+
24	20	30	34

Political Activity

Low	Medium	High
38	22	8

There are many other explanations for these results other than the argument that the respondents were unprovoked. The high percentage of "Don't Know" responses may be due to lack of information or to poor memories. The striking racial difference and the substantial difference between the medium politically active and the high politically active make this judgment more difficult.

Another explanation is that these are the groups that are most intimidated by the government and consequently least willing to express a complaint. The evidence is consistent with this hypothesis. But the hypothesis is not inconsistent with the conclusion reached previously that it was among these groups that the greatest passivity to governmental injustice resided. Intimidation may be one cause of passivity.

The amount of passivity in the population is further reinforced by an examination of the past political behavior of the respondents. Respondents were presented with the following item:

Please tell me which of these actions you have ever taken to express your opinion on a social or political issue:

1) Discuss with friends

2) Write a letter to a newspaper or to an elected official.

3) Contribute money to an organization concerned about the issue.

4) Sign a petition

5) Express your opinion in person to a public official

6) Organize a group

7) Participate in a legally permitted demonstration

8) Participate in an illegal but non-violent demonstration

9) Participate in a riot

Because previous political activity was based on this question, it is not surprising that this variable provided the greatest discrimination among respondents. (Those classified low answered 0 or 1 item, those classified as medium answered 2, 3, or 4, and those who were high answered 5 or more.)

Almost all of the respondents (97%) indicated that they had discussed things in the past with their friends. Further, there was practically no variability among subgroups. So few respondents indicated that they had participated in a riot that there was no variability on this response among subgroups. The other responses did, however, yield sufficient variability among subgroups to warrant analysis. The results are presented in Table 24 for educational level, race, and region, as well as for the past political activity.

Those who have benefitted the least are the least active. One exception to this pattern occurs among Negroes. Although their response rate is smaller than is that for whites on the less severe forms of activity (letterwriting, petitioning, and expressing an opinion in person) they are more active, proportionately, on the more severe forms of activity (organizing a group, legal demonstrations and illegal demonstrations). However, the response rates are far lower, overall, on those activities which Negroes dominate compared to those which whites do.

5. Summary

The results indicate that although there is a relatively small amount of alienation from the government in Washington substantial numbers of citizens long for the old days, expect the assassination of their political leaders, and endorse the use of force on the part of both the police and on the part of the nation in its dealings with other countries.

When the characteristics of the groups are examined, it appears that those who have benefitted least in the society are the most authoritarian and traditional and are most likely to believe that assassination of their political leaders will occur.

Relative to the use of police force, the more educated the individual is, or the younger he is, the less will be the endorsement. However, the major difference occurs between Negroes and whites with the former far more opposed to the use of police force than the latter.

The pattern reverses somewhat on items related to the international use of force, with those who have most benefitted in the nation tending to be less critical than those who have least benefitted.

Further, it appears that the least advantaged in the society are more likely to endorse the right of groups to train in underground tactics.

The impression that the data give is fairly clear: The less a person has gained in society and the less he has to look

Table 24. – Past political activity by education, race, region and rating on political activity

Response	Education				Race		Region				Political Activity		
	8th Grade	Some H.S.	H.S. Grad	College	Negro	White	East	Midwest	South	West	Low	Medium	High
Letters	15	22	31	52	18	34	31	33	22	47	2	36	87
		RANGE = 37			RANGE = 16		RANGE = 25				RANGE = 85		
Money	17	26	25	53	36	31	27	33	27	46	2	34	76
		RANGE = 36			RANGE = 5		RANGE = 19				RANGE = 94		
Petition	31	40	58	72	41	54	52	57	39	70	3	74	96
		RANGE = 41			RANGE = 14		RANGE = 31				RANGE = 93		
Opinion in Person	15	19	24	45	14	29	28	23	24	37	1	30	80
		RANGE = 30			RANGE = 15		RANGE = 14				RANGE = 79		
Organize a Group	4	7	6	15	13	7	11	6	5	11	0	3	44
		RANGE = 11			RANGE = 6		RANGE = 6				RANGE = 44		
Legal Demonstration	1	6	7	16	15	7	16	5	2	13	0	4	44
		RANGE = 15			RANGE = 8		RANGE = 14				RANGE = 44		
Illegal Demonstration	0	2	3	6	10	2	6	1	1	4	0	1	16
		RANGE = 6			RANGE = 8		RANGE = 5				RANGE = 16		

forward to, the more likely he is to believe that violence is inevitable and even justified. The pattern is far more complex than this, for different groups are frustrated in different ways. Nevertheless, the warning is unmistakable. When individuals or groups are disadvantaged either in the concrete rewards that they obtain, or the status that they achieve, or the access that they have to channels of political influence, or in a combination of these, violent expectations and opinions endorsing violent behavior are likely to occur.

The evidence presented indicates that there are conditions under which most people would feel the government was acting unjustly. Rather clear distinctions are made among various situations as determined by the endorsement of responses that vary in strength. Generally, the population is unlikely to endorse any but legal responses to remove different provocations, but given a sufficiently antagonistic political situation (such as the shooting of innocent people by the government in order to maintain control of the country) substantial numbers agree that even armed action may be an appropriate response.

Although the responsiveness of citizens is affected by the severity of the provocation, adults appear, except in the most extreme instance, reluctant to endorse illegal action even when these responses are introduced with the phrase, "if nothing else worked . . ." The evidence, therefore, indicates substantial passivity in the population to possible unjust acts of the government. The evidence, in fact, would seem to indicate that under most conditions of governmental injustice (except for the most extreme one), responsiveness in the population is not substantially higher than is their response to an illegal protest against the Vietnam war.

The data from the senator question further indicate that respondents are more likely to believe some of their friends would engage in illegal responses than they are to attribute such responsiveness to themselves. Moreover, nonwhite responsiveness to the unpopular leader was higher than white responsiveness.

References

1. Some of the items were selected for the survey from standard tests by James McEvoy, who, along with Bill Gramson, de-

signed other items specificially for the study, and who also
suggested the factor analysis.

2. The dimensions were obtained by rotation to the veremax
   criterion.

3. Although 25 factors were extracted in the principal axes solution, only the first five are presented here. The first ten factors
   were used in the rotation, and again only five are presented.

SUPPLEMENTS

INTRODUCTION

In this supplement we have assembled papers on assassination in nine specific countries or regions of the world by nine different authors who have made a special study of political violence and its relation to the particular region or country. The papers range in scale from brief statements with respect to two Scandinavian countries to highly detailed treatises. This is an outstanding collection of writings. It provides insights into the difficult problem of assassination at many different levels. We have drawn directly upon these writings in our introductory survey of assassination and its relation to political systems and in our discussion of the preconditions for and effects of assassination.

The knowledge to be gained from these papers is not limited to what is broadly structural or theoretical. For example, we may cite the following specific conclusions which are by no means a complete catalog but rather a general gleaning from those which can be drawn from the individual studies.

In the Middle East as well as in Latin America, political violence has been typically the only channel open to effect changes of the political structure. While both the Middle East and Latin America have a high incidence of assassination and political violence, in the latter region violence has not typically been directed against the Chief Executive. The Middle East, however, presents the opposite picture. This may be evidence of the influence of cultural traditions on assassination. The Middle East has a history of assassination of Chiefs of State from the time of the first caliphs, the successors to Mohammed. Latin America, in contrast, has a tradition which legitimized the head of state as part of an hierarchical order established by God. China also reflects the influence of cultural tradition. Institutionalized respect of parents, ancestors, and authority has apparently kept at a minimum the incidence of assassinations even in that overcrowded country. There are instances of assassination, however, and they usually occur during the changes of dynasties wherever the general level of political violence is high. Although there has been a high level of political violence in the United States from its inception, assassination appears to be considered in the United States as "European" or "foreign." This tradition may be a significant influence in channeling violence away from deadly assault against officeholders, even though other factors conducive to assassination may be present.

Eastern Europe demonstrates the effectiveness of assassination when systematically used in conjunction with other acts of terror as an instrument of ideologically-based social change. Such assassination and terror in Russia and Poland were effective in overthrowing autocracies in the former country or expelling foreign rulers in the latter. The experience of the British in the Middle East—Palestine, Cyprus, South Yemen —also verifies the effectiveness of systematic assassination and terrorism as a weapon of an indigenous people against foreign rulers. Germany and Japan demonstrate that such systematic assassination and terrorism are not necessarily the weapons of reformers against autocracy or foreign rule. In both countries, the governments—a moderate democracy in the case of Germany and a moderate semi-democratic government in Japan —were intimidated and ultimately brought down by systematic acts of assassination and terrorism. No one in the United States should underestimate the effectiveness of systematic terrorism, even when employed by a relatively small group, in destroying an established government.

France affords another illustration to democracies: that political violence does not necessarily stem from organized, ideologically-based movements that deliberately adopt a tactic of terrorism. Violence may be brought on by the unresponsiveness of the government to the reasonable demands of groups within the society, in effect requiring violence as the only available avenue for reform.

The experience of Canada has particular interest to the United States in demonstrating that political violence can be generated where a minority group perceives itself as culturally threatened and insufficiently represented in the central government, even when the central government is not in any way physically repressive and where formal civil rights are guaranteed to and in fact honored with respect to the members of the minority group.

The short survey of assassination in England tends to verify an hypothesis of this report: that even when an assassination is the immediate product of a deranged mind, high levels of political strife tend to focus such a mind upon political figures and thus trigger the assassination event.

The experience of Australia should warn us against too simplistic an analysis of the causes of political violence in the United States. Australia has a population of which a high percentage have guns, a frontier tradition, an immigrant population, and yet a low rate of assassination and political violence.

Finally, the Scandinavian countries suggest that countries need not devise clever strategies to avoid assassination and political violence if their populations are racially and religiously homogeneous, if they are small yet have a sufficiently sound economy to sustain a welfare system that more or less eliminates poverty, and if they do not have the burden of maintaining international order. A curious feature related to violence in such countries is the high rate of suicide.

A glance at the table of contents will suggest the breadth of the material in this volume.

SUPPLEMENT A

POLITICAL VIOLENCE AND TERROR IN 19TH AND 20TH CENTURY RUSSIA AND EASTERN EUROPE

by Feliks Gross*

1. Introduction

A long historical experience of political violence suggests that a clear distinction should be made between isolated political assassinations perpetrated by individuals and tactically motivated assassinations, the object of which is to promote general upheaval or terror.

Since the creation of states, men of politics have been assassinated by aspirants to power. Tyrants were killed by those seeking freedom, vengeance, or desiring to establish a tyranny of their own. Statesmen were killed by political fanatics and the mentally disturbed. These are, however, cases of isolated, temporary conspiracies by individuals. Elimination of a single person or of a few was the goal of such attempts.

The Russian and East European past, however, suggests a long history of tactical terrorism. Individual assassination in this case was a political method, a tactic guided by a strategy that led to systematic violent activities against individuals. Unlike the first type of assassination, which was a rather unique occurrence, tactical terrorism had in certain cases a duration extending over a long period of time. In the United States, perhaps the violent activities of the Ku Klux Klan best represent this type of tactic.

*Brooklyn College

519

Terror was used as an instrument for accomplishing different objectives. It was waged against brutal foreign conquerors and tyrannies, as a means toward reorganizing the society in terms of a government based on political rights and representative institutions. Individual assassination, however, was also waged as a means to destroy democratic institutions and cow conquered peoples into submission.

Since only a systematic tactical terror was of long duration, the question must be asked: What were the conditions of the durability of this tactic?

The existence or formation of a party was the first, and essential, condition. As a rule, this party was a secret, highly-disciplined and centralistic organization, with clear and definite goals. Frequently, such parties had the support of committees abroad, sometimes even the support of foreign governments.

Second, an increase of political assassinations has usually been precipitated by certain social and political situations. Extended periods of terror appeared in political cultures that already had traditions of violence. A change of conditions frequently, but not always, resulted in cessation of terror. Professionalization of terror, e.g., in Bulgaria, however, carried the previously established patterns into different political situations when a relatively moderate peasant government was in power.

Finally, terror attracted certain personality types. Here again, under conditions of very oppressive rule, a person otherwise nonaggressive and humane might turn to violence.

We find ourselves, rather suddenly, in an historical period of intellectual confusion and physical violence. The issue of violence and its past history became of practical significance in a time of appeal to physical violence in domestic politics, as a way of interfering with the business of education and government.

There are, of course, times in history, as noted in this paper, when violence is one of the few roads left open for those who fight for the rights of man against the oppression of others. Man was and is forced sometimes to use violence in his struggle for emancipation and freedom.

The experience of the past hundred years, discussed in this paper, teaches that a clear distinction must be made between (1) struggle and violence against domestic autocracy, (2) violence against foreign conquerors who exterminate nations or enslave peoples, and (3) violence waged against democratic institutions, as was done by the fascists, Nazis, and their satellites.

Violence has generated violence; blood has called, in the past, for more blood. Terror, even in the name of the highest ideals, has created, in the end, political habits that have moved into the patterns of political life, and have continued even after conditions were changed.

Violence—we must always ask: For what? Why? Against whom? These are also questions that must be asked today. The attempt of an Armenian militant, a Dashnak, against a Turkish commander who ordered the massacre of his kinfolk, is morally a different type of act from the assassination of a humane President, or of a senator of a republic who advocated help to the underprivileged. Again, there is a profound moral difference between an attempt by a group of militants in a self-governing and democratic community to shoot from a rooftop firemen and policemen called to an emergency, and an assault by Serbian Yugoslavs against a Ustashi militia which moved into their village to kill their families.

Violence in Eastern Europe and Russia was a result of an historical tragedy and led to new tragedies. At times, in Russia, as a consequence of the tactics of terror, the moral structure of man and society was undermined and the sense of direction lost.

The advocates of extreme violence may not realize that this means, ultimately, killing. And killing as a political method will sooner or later produce a class of professionals.

Democratic institutions and the continuity of our civilization are a result of a slow and difficult development within a very subtle political framework. Once this framework is broken, it may take generations to restore.

2. Types and Function of Terror

Legitimacy and Violence

The humanizing effects of democracy and our civilization have an influence on our thinking and selective perception of the past. It seems to have become almost forgotten that the use of violence and assassination to achieve political power, remove an adversary, or change a dynasty was a general historical phenomenon for centuries in societies organized into the complex political form of the state. Next to assassination as a means to gain wealth and property, assassination to gain political power seems to be tragically frequent in past history.

Western civilization, during a slow historical process, has humanized political institutions. Humanization means here above all limitation, reduction, or abolition of the use of violence, cruelty, and killing in the business of internal government. It seems that the reduction of political murder and assassination as a means of transferring power or changing dynasties is a slow development, influenced by the Church and philosophy.

The major concept which reduced political assassination was the concept of legitimacy rooted in the duality of Church and state. It was the ecclesiastic hierarchy which validated the hereditary legitimacy of the dynasties and maintained in that way a control over the orderly transfer of power. Of course, political murder was still abundant in medieval times. The Church itself indulged in terror toward dissidents. Nonetheless, a foundation was laid toward the concept of power based on legal and philosophical (or theological) premises as the only legitimate power. The paramount legitimacy of elective power, established already in antiquity, both in Greece and Rome, continued in medieval cities and guilds. The complex legal and philosophical concept of legitimacy of power became fundamental in Occidental politics. Few ideas in our civilization could be found which contributed more to the political and cultural continuity of Europe and America than this one. Only in a few modern states, where well-established concepts of democratic legitimacy, based on general will or majority rule, were associated with political freedom and relative equality, or absence of excessive exploitation, did a nonviolent power transfer and nonviolent political struggle become fully accepted and institutionalized. It became a shared value, a political custom or way of life.

"Sultanism" and the Transfer of Power by Assassination

In imperial Rome political assassination was frequent. At the time of the Emperor Constantine, it became a method later called "sultanism," a continuous murder of all possible pretenders to power, or competitors, until no one but the ultimate ruler survived. In the fourth century A.D., Licinius, a competitor for power with the future Emperor Constantine, did away with the "families of Galerius Severus and Maximus Daia, including their innocent children." Even the widow and daughter of the Emperor Diocletian were assassinated, while Constantine later arranged for the assassination of Licinius. After the death of Constantine, his brothers, first Constantius, and then Dalmatius, were murdered.[1] This was the same Constantine who established the Christian Church as the religion of the Roman Empire. It was, however, a period of transition, with the disintegration of old values, including the idea of legitimate succession. At such times power is based on winning the allegiance of the military.

While the idea of legitimacy slowly regained acceptance in Western Europe, it was by no means free from political murder. In highly civilized Muslim Spain in the eighth century political assassination was frequently practiced. "Of a total of 20 (governors, appointed from Damascus or North Africa) only three survived as long as 5 years: those who did not fall in battle were murdered by their rivals."[2] In the Ottoman Empire political assassination as a process of consolidation and transfer of power was part of the general use of violence in politics and absolute rule and, as we shall see, may have contributed to a "political style" or political cultural pattern in which assassination and terror became one of the few avenues of struggle against autocratic rule. When Sultan Murad III (1574–1595) left 20 sons out of 47 surviving children, one of them, his successor Mohammed III (1595–1603), ordered the murder of his 19 brothers, to eliminate competitors.[3]

This pattern of eliminating competing dynasties by assassination continued in the Balkans (in a far milder form, however, in terms of means and number of victims), especially in Serbia, even after liberation from the Ottoman yoke, from 1817 until 1903. Once a political pattern is well established and internalized in the political behavior of individuals, or institutionalized in groups, it has a tendency to continue, so that it is difficult to break the pattern. Turkey is no exception, but rather a representative of the pattern. In Persia, where sultanism was a major political device, the succession of the two major dynasties was "seldom undisputed and decided without bloodshed."[4]

Most recently, sultanism reappeared in modern totalitarian

states. Hitler's elimination of Roehm, Schleicher, and so many others in the infamous bloodbath of 1934, and Stalin's purges, were assassinations of possible competitors.

Renaissance: Tyranny and its
Political Style

Political assassination makes a new appearance in Europe in the early Renaissance, with the struggles between the papacy and emperors (Hohenstauffen). The old medieval legitimacy based either upon hereditary rights with succession validated and legitimized by ecclesiastical authority or upon elective power, was slowly weakened in parts of Italy. Italy now had a "multitude of political units—republics and despots—whose existence was founded simply on their power to maintain it."[5] From Sicily, from the South, came the centralizing style in politics, which broke the medieval freedoms and old legitimacies, and also introduced the Saracen mode of securing power. These new trends were manifest in Emperor Frederick II—the *stupor mundi*, but the ruthless and cruel style of government is associated also with the name of his son-in-law and vicar, Ezzelino da Romano.

> The conquests and usurpations which had hitherto taken place in the Middle Ages rested on real or pretended inheritance and other such claims, or else were effected against unbelievers and excommunicated persons. Here for the first time the attempt was openly made to found a throne by wholesale murder and endless barbarities, by the adoption, in short, of any means with a view of nothing but the end pursued * * *. The example once set was not forgotten and his fall led to no return of justice among nations, and served as no warning to future transgressors.[6]

It is difficult, if possible at all, to prove this one single causal sequence which the Swiss historian suggests as the major or even the only determinant. Nonetheless, the trend appears and carries with it the traditions that prevailed in other, neighboring parts of the Mediterranean or Middle East, as established by the Sarcens, Arabs, Persians, or earlier, the Byzantines.

The sultanic patterns moved into Europe with the beginnings of this great period of cultural renaissance. They destroyed the old and subtle fabric of representative-municipal or dualistic hereditary-dynastic legitimacy, and brought in political assassination more as a political style based on fear rather than on shared values and consensus.

Macchiavelli, in his *Prince*, described its working, and advised the Prince to apply cruelty in order to keep his subjects united and faithful. The Prince, taught the Florentine scholar, must abstain from taking the property of others, but not necessarily from taking their lives, "for men forget more easily the death of their father than the loss of their patrimony."[7] Political assassination is now moving in time, and step-by-step a political style, a way of doing the business of politics, and in a broader sense a political culture, is becoming well established.

Legitimacy supplied elements of continuity and personal security because of the public institutions based on law and acceptance of shared values. It is true that these institutions collapse if they cannot change during times of upheaval. But the new style destroyed the very subtle and yet very shallow foundations of limitation of power, the very foundation of individual security.

Political assassination as a style of maintaining, transmitting, and consolidating power resulted in tactical political assassination as a means to oppose autocratic power. This time political assassination as a tactic against autocracy had not a legal, but a philosophical legitimacy based upon the principles of individual and political freedom. Autocracy without recognized legitimacy permitted violence from two fronts: from other competitors for autocratic power, and from opponents and citizens struggling for restoration of freedom. This meant frequent struggles by citizens for their own lives, and for the survival of their families and neighbors.

Thus the idea of systematic political assassination appears in Europe as a tactic of struggle not only between competitors for power, but also as a means in the struggle for principles of freedom and legitimacy, i.e., as a tactic in the ideological struggle.

Macchiavelli, in his *Discourses*, describes the legal means of defending and maintaining liberty in a Republic. He discusses the reasons of change from liberty to servitude, and asserts that a state born in blood and violence will change through blood and violence, because it germinated through the injury of many, thus inculcating a spirit of vindictiveness. Such an environment generates the idea of assassination as a political method. When a state created through consensus is changed, there is no danger comparable to that of a state brought into existence through violence, wherein blood calls for vengeance.[8] When violence is accepted, political assassination becomes a method, generating its own logic of perpetuation.

Political assassination of this historical period has concrete and definite functions: capture of power, removal of adversaries and competitors, and consolidation and maintenance of power by terror. In rare instances, the victim has been a tyrant and the issue was liberty, with perhaps the idea of establishing a Republic. In most cases, however, assassination was an act of vengeance, sometimes an act of retribution for injustices and injuries done by the powerful.

Political Assassination: Systematic and Tactical

Political assassination as a rational act for a definite goal has been a frequent occurrence in past history; in fact, it was in some cultures an accepted method to win and maintain power. Assassination because of political oppression or from psychological or emotional motives can probably be traced also to the historical past. However, political assassination as a systematic activity, as a major part of political tactics, advanced by an organized political group for achievement of an ideological goal, seems to be a 19th-century phenomenon, a consequence of the struggle against autocracy and foreign rule.

The reaction against the French Revolution in Central and Western Europe retarded the development of democratic institutions. Monarchies and autocracies lacked the will to resolve the social problems of the new industrial society. At this point, the traditions of the French Revolution suggested the established and effective type of revolutionary tactics. In Russia, however, which lacked this tradition of a popular revolution, where the peasantry was either passive, or loyal to the Tsar, or rebellious at times, but without broad political goals, where the government was more similar to an Oriental autocracy than to contemporary European monarchies, assassination became a political tactic. It spread to the Balkans, again as a tactic in response to foreign oppression.

Terror

During the second half of the 19th century, a theory of terror was developed by revolutionary Russians in their struggle against autocracy. Unlike political assassination as an isolated act, terror—in terms of 19th-century revolutionaries and later in terms of some resistance groups during World War II—became a systematic, tactical course of action with political objectives. Terror was directed primarily at key decision-makers or administrators, or used vindictively against persons responsible for cruelties and oppression; for one of the functions of terror was retribution and deterrence. The leaders of these organizations expected that assassination of an oppressive administrator would restrain his successors from perpetrating the same despotic acts. This was the objective in the assassinations of high-ranking German officers in Poland during World War II. The major function of terror in Russia was, however, to weaken the government and the autocratic institutions of the Tsarist Empire. In words of the Populist theoretician Stepniak, in 1892:

> A victory, immediate, splendid, and decisive, such as that obtained by an insurrection, is utterly impossible by means of terrorism. But another victory is more probable, that of the weak against the strong, that of the "beggars" of Holland against the Spaniards. In a struggle against an invisible, impalpable, omnipresent enemy, the strong is vanquished not by arms of his own, but by the continuous extension of his own strength, which ultimately exhausts him, more than he would be exhausted by defeat.

> Such is precisely the position of the belligerent parties of Russia.

> The Terrorists cannot overthrow the government, cannot drive it from St. Petersburg and Russia; but having com-

pelled it, for so many years running, to neglect everything and do nothing but struggle with them, by forcing
it to do so still for years and years, they will render its
position untenable. Already the prestige of the Imperial
Government has received a wound which it will be very
difficult to heal. An Emperor who shuts himself up in
prison from fear of the Terrorism is certainly not a figure
to inspire admiration.[9]

Terrorism was clearly directed solely against a tyrannical
government (we shall return to this issue later).

The Russian Populist theoretician of terror and author of
an essay on terroristic struggle, Nicholas Morozov, formulated
in 1880 the tactical objectives of terror:

The Terrorist Party * * * must press without mercy a
system of continuous terror, to punish the government
for its every attack on freedom; it must achieve its demoralization, disorganization, and weakening. The Party
must incapacitate the government and render it powerless
to take any kind of measures to suppress ideas and activities directed toward the people's welfare.

With these two courses the Party will make its mode of
struggle traditional and will annihilate every despotism in
the future.[10]

The objectives here were clearly formulated: terror is directed against autocracy; its objective is a slow process of
weakening the government. After over a quarter of a century
of terror, from 1880 until before the outbreak of World War
I, this objective was to a certain extent achieved. At times the
government was weakened and confused.

Nevertheless, terror as a system of action was only one of
the means in the arsenal of revolutionary strategy. Usually,
terror was combined with other actions, such as propaganda,
or even, as in Macedonia, with guerrilla tactics. The preference of Russian revolutionaries was also based on moral considerations. The "Central Terror" which they practiced was
directed solely against carefully selected major representatives
of the Russian autocracy, such as the Tsar himself, governors,
and high-ranking police officers. It did not hurt innocent people; it was discriminating. In a sense—in their view—it was
both tactics and punishment.

Terror was to a large extent an instrument of those who were "outs" and who wanted to destroy the autocratic institutions. After World War I, systematic individual assassination or terror was used by the extreme right against democracy. Political techniques are similar to tools. Some—not all, of course—are "neutral" *per se;* they can be used for a variety of contradictory objectives. The objectives are decisive in a political, and above all in a moral sense, because ideology and objectives control the choice of means.

Mass Terror

In contrast to ordinary terror, mass terror is a political tactic of the "ins". It is an effort to consolidate power, and usually to eliminate groups of innocent people defined as class, race, or a nation. Thus, the objectives of mass terror are broader than those based solely on a rule by fear.[11]

J. N. Steinberg, the first Russian Commissar of Justice, member of the S.R. (Social Revolutionary Party), opposed Lenin precisely on the issue of mass terror. He describes the latter as a *system* of violence, dispensed from above. Mass terror is a detailed, well-thought-out plan of threat and punishment by which the regime bends a population to its absolute will.[12] The rule of mass terror was usually in the past, and still is, a government of a minority that maintains its power primarily by manipulation of fear, not by consensus.

Kautsky suggests as one of the causes of mass terror during the French Revolution, the weakness of the new republican state, which could not properly exercise its power and secure food from the rural areas for the few urban centers. This may explain the coercive actions and counteractions of the revolutionary government in the Vendee and Brittany, but it does not explain the entire Terroristic period.[13]

It is the fear of the survivors which is seminal. The fear of suffering, humiliation, loss of life and liberty influences their behavior. Thus, the terrorized submit to the decisions of the terrorists, and obey their orders. Society slowly splits into three groups: (1) those who command and control the elements of violence or identify themselves with the latter; (2) the passive mass of obedient, predictable "subjects" or "citizens" manipulated frequently into manifestations of emotional and symbolic expressions of loyalty and love for their tormentors; and (3) a rapidly declining, divided group of those who are either indifferent (but not manipulatable) or opposed. The latter again are divided into various orientations, and are usually called "enemies of the people."

The ruled are continuously warned about the imminent dangers from the "enemies of the people," who in various historical periods carry various names. Some of them in the past really represented the *ancien regime* and the status quo. Others, however, opposed the government for a variety of reasons, and these were usually the "outs" who challenged the power of the rulers and fought for freedom, toleration, and human dignity. Identification of opponents as enemies of the people supplied the rulers an excuse for their annihilation.

Contradictions of Terror and
Mass Terror

The distinction between terror and mass terror was essential in theory and practice to the revolutionary movement in Russia. The populist revolutionaries, members of the "People's Will," later of the Social Revolutionary party, opposed mass terror as a means of consolidation of power. They opposed it above all for ethical reasons, because it was directed against an innocent mass of people and defeated the very principle of freedom and ethics. They favored, however, terror or systematic assassination as necessary and relatively humane tactics. The terror spared innocent victims who so often suffer in any spontaneous revolution. The targets of terror were confined solely to those regarded as really responsible for the tyranny.

The famous case of Ivan Kalayev inspired Camus to write a play, *The Just,* in which he attempts to explore the mind and personality of a Social Revolutionary terrorist.[14] Kalayev threw a bomb and killed Grand Duke Sergei in February 1905. The assassination was at first planned for on February 2, but on this day, the Prince's wife and two children were in the carriage. Kalayev refused to destroy innocent persons. He repeated his attempt on February 4. According to the reports, he did not try to escape, because he believed that the assassination was necessary. Nevertheless, he believed that it was a sin for which a man should suffer the penalty of his own life.[15]

The Bolsheviks, on the other hand, rejected terror as "adventurism," approving, however, mass terror as a necessary instrument of consolidation of power. J. J. Steinberg, the first Commissar of Justice who opposed Lenin on this issue, writes that "from the very days of October, Lenin strove to impress his colleagues with the absolute necessity for violence, execution, terror." He did not believe that the victory of the Revolution could be achieved without mass terror.[16] Trotsky, in his discussion with the Austrian Social Democrat, Karl Kautsky, a strong opponent of violence and mass terror, argued that:

> Terror is helpless—and then only in the long run—if it is employed by reaction against a historically rising class which does not want to leave the scene of operations. *Intimidation* is a powerful weapon of policy, both internationally and internally. War, like revolution, is founded upon intimidation. A victorious war, generally speaking, destroys only an insignificant part of the conquered army, intimidating the remainder and breaking their will. The revolution works in the same way: it kills individuals and intimidates thousands. . . .

Trotsky answers also the question of those he calls sarcastically "high priests" of liberalism and the "holy men" who asked what is then the difference between Tsarism and Red terror: the first was directed against the proletariat, the latter against the bourgeoisie.[17]

Today, in terms of history and experience, perhaps mankind has learned that logic and abstract concepts and theories of violence detached from ethical valuation destroy nations. But first such logic destroys our own individual humanity.

Historical Pattern of Mass Terror

A historical pattern, once established, has a tendency to continue. The Bolshevik theoreticians had before them, as one of the historical models of their revolution, the French Revolution and the French terror. The latter had a great and most tragic historical antecedent—the Inquisition. These three great mass terroristic experiences had several things in common, but one element was paramount: the belief that a minority has the right to kill and destroy entire sections of a population to pursue what it believes is a paramount ideological or religious principle. All three of these terroristic movements have shown the hidden dangers in misinterpreting fundamental idea systems by abstract logic and confused theories. In the name of salvation, liberty, and social equality man was destroying those who had to be saved and liberated. Thus freedom was equated with annihilation. The abstract and misinterpreted ideas justified the moral issue, thereby legitimizing cruelty. The three experiences in mass terroristic enterprise were a prelude to the most monstrous one—the Nazi extermination camps. Ideas have their own fate, and travel in ways different from those intended by their originators.

A mass terroristic enterprise, once well-established and rooted in a strong ideology or religion, becomes a powerful institution and may last for centuries.

Random Terror

Random terror, in its strategic and tactical objectives, is more related to the individual than is mass terror. Random or indiscriminate terror has as its goal the weakening of government, erosion of institutions (this is especially true in the case of a terroristic struggle against a democracy), and intimidation of the decision-makers. The technique is simple: explosives are placed in places where men congregate—post offices, cafes, railroad or bus stations, banks, etc. Indiscriminate terror was applied by the Algerian revolutionaries against the French government in metropolitan France, when bombs were placed in public places, such as cafes. The tactics of random terror were already used half a century before, by the Bulgarian revolutionary groups in their struggle against the Turkish government, for example in the Salonica Coup of April 29, 1903. In this carefully prepared action, bombs were planted in public places, and thrown in the vicinity of sidewalk cafes, music halls, and post offices.[18] Random terrorists seem to be free of those moral considerations that restrained the Russian terrorists. Death, mutilation, suffering are directed indiscriminately, victimizing entirely innocent people, accidental bypassers, children, women, workers, office clerks—whoever happens to be at the scene.

Focused Random Terror

During World War II, random terror appeared in what may be called "focused" terroristic attempts, when explosives were placed in cafes where German officers met. (This was, for example, the case in the resistance action in Cracow, Poland, in the Cafe "Cyganeria," organized and accomplished by the Polish-Jewish underground. The cafe was a meeting place for German officers and civilians.) Here, the action was clearly directed against foreign invaders. Its objectives were: (1) punishment, (2) intimidation, and (3) an important *acte de presence*, a warning that "We are here, and the city does not and will not belong to you. You are criminals and you, and your successors, shall be punished."

Dynastic Assassination

Several distinctions must be made at this point. First of all, we have separated systematic, tactical destruction from isolated, unconnected cases of political assassination. We have also distinguished individual terror from mass terror and random terror. We shall limit ourselves in this paper primarily to the type of terror that involves tactical, systematic human destruction.

It is, however, necessary to add still another type of assassination which is not necessarily systematic: assassination as a means of changing dynasties and political orientations associated with a ruling dynasty, a type of assassination related to "sultanism." This was the case in the century-long Serbian feud between the Obrenovich and Karageorge families, which ended in 1903 with the assassination of the last Obrenovich king and his wife by partisans of the Karageorge dynasty. We may call this dynastic assassination. Its objective is the elimination of a ruler or of a family, as well as a change of ruling elites, and usually, a change of political orientations.

Tactical and Strategic Objectives of Terror

A further distinction should be made between the tactical and the strategic or ideological objectives of terror. Tactically, the objective of terror has been the punishment, intimidation, weakening, or slow disintegration of government. Strategic-ideological goals have been broader, and form the basis of what we may call the moral and ideological legitimation of terror by the actors of an historical tragedy.

Thus, tactical terror in the past was directed against the representatives of a foreign rule that was oppressive and cruel. Usually, no avenues of change or redress were open, and this was the only way to liberation. It required courage, skill, and determination. Terror was in most cases combined with at least beginning or full-scale guerrilla warfare. It was justified in the eyes of revolutionaries as a national war, even more significant than "regular" warfare, because, as a rule it was the last resort of those who were oppressed and sometimes abandoned by the civilized world. This was the case in Macedonian, Armenian, and Bulgarian terroristic action against the Turkish rule of Abdul Hamid at the end of the 19th century and prior to World War I. Similar in nature was the Polish terroristic action, closely related to the Revolution of 1905, the latter of which had its roots in the tradition of century-long insurrections against Russian autocratic rule. The goal in some cases was autonomy, and in others the restoration of national independence.

During World War II, the choice under German occupation in Eastern Europe was between slavery, slow death by starvation, and extermination, or freedom, dignity, and struggle by all means open to a free man, including tactical terror. Under such conditions the legitimacy of terror was clear to the militants and was rooted in their basic values. There was, in their perception, no other choice for those for whom freedom and dignity was a higher value than life itself.

The terroristic action of the Russians was strategically directed against autocracy, but the goals of individual terrorists were not necessarily identical. The major groups, however (not all, of course), advocated some kind of a democratic and socialist state. At times, they were willing to cease terroristic action for the price of constitutional political rights. This was, at least, stated in a letter of the revolutionary committee of the Populist party, written to the successor of Tsar Alexander II after the latter's assassination in 1881.[19] It should be stressed again, that the goals were not identical. And what some extreme groups who advocated terror envisaged was, in fact, a dictatorship—a new tyranny, of course—but only as a means of establishing a perfect rule of liberty.

The third group of strategic objectives was the destruction of democracy. The terrorists of the difficult era that followed World War I directed their action against representatives of democracy, and directly or indirectly against democratic and republican institutions. Tactical terror of the pre-Nazi German organizations was, combined with other legal and illegal actions, directed, in fact, against the Republic and democracy.

The fascist groups in Eastern Europe which at times practiced individual assassination, directed their actions against the young, democratic, republican institutions or governments of political moderation. Other brutal and ruthless forms of struggle were used by these groups, rather than systematic, individual terror. The Croat fascists, the *Ustashis*, however, used both individual assassination against the Yugoslav King and later, during the war, mass terror against the defenseless Serbian, Greek-Orthodox, and Jewish population.

Terror and Isolated Assassination

In addition to these five major strategic types of terror—tactical, random, random-focused, mass terror, and dynastic assassination—Europe had its share of isolated, unconnected political assassinations. The latter are isolated acts of elimination, originating in the rational or emotional motives of individuals, sometimes prepared or supported by organized groups. But they are not the systematic, tactical actions of well-organized, ideological, frequently paramilitary groups, usually combined with more extensive revolutionary activities, such as guerrilla warfare, mass manifestations, strikes, and mass unrest.

It seems that the United States, England (not Ireland, however), Switzerland and the Scandinavian countries have not had in their past a history of systematic and tactical terror operated by well-organized, ideological groups, although the United States has had some isolated political assassinations. The Ku Klux Klan in the United States has practiced tactical terror. Tactical, systematic terror, in contrast to the isolated assassination, is part of a broad revolutionary strategic plan. Its continuity is rooted in a centralistic party organization, as well as in an ideology or goals which have at times a broad appeal.

3. Terror in Russia

The theory of tactical terror developed, and perhaps originated, in Russia. Terror as a major revolutionary tactic, or as a part of the entire tactical-strategic design of a mass revolution or insurrection was practiced in Eastern Europe and Russia at the end of the 19th and the beginning of the 20th centuries. Nineteenth-century Western Europe and America witnessed sporadic, isolated attempts to assassinate political personalities as well as the formation of some rather minor political groups (e.g., the "microparties" of the anarchists) which leaned toward tactical terror. The Ku Klux Klan, for example, practiced a special kind of violence, assassination, and terror. The advent of various types of fascism changed the pattern, however, and Europe again had its share of individual and mass violence. Previous to this, terror had never assumed the political role it played in Russia, in Russian-occupied Poland, and in the Balkans. In a sense, tactical terror was a Russian and Balkan revolutionary tactic, associated with well-organized and dedicated groups. A different form of terror appeared after World War I as a part of the general policy of intimidation and destruction of democracy. At this time it became an instrument of the extreme right and Nazism.

Terror as a Political Style

In Russia, the Balkans (particularly Bulgaria), and later in Poland, the causes of terror were various. Terroristic struggle flourished under different conditions and was an outcome of different traditions or ideologies. Nevertheless, in Russia the continuous terror for more than 30 years after 1874 impressed Thomas G. Masaryk as a new phenomenon of a terroristic revolution. Terror was conducted by a minority that followed a dramatic, tragic way of life which impressed the rest of the nation. The terroristic action—from the shores of the Baltic to the Aegean and Adriatic, from the Gulf of Finland to the Bosphorus—developed within a quarter of a century into a political style of violence.

In the Balkans, particularly in Bulgaria, terror continued after World War I, or appeared later, as in Croatia. This time, as in other Western European countries, terror was directed against weak, nascent democracies, or against the more stable institutions of relatively moderate autocratic governments. In the end, the way was open to brutal dictatorship and war, a logical consequence of the politics of violence.

Russian terror was not a cause of this development, but it was one of the elements contributing to the establishment of a revolutionary-terroristic style in the politics of Eastern Europe at the beginning of the 20th century.

Polish revolutionary activity had its own style and insurrectionist traditions. Bulgarian (IMRO) and Armenian (Dashnaks) revolutionary organizations were, however, to a certain extent influenced by the Russian revolutionaries. A leader of the Macedonian revolutionary organization, Kostia Todorov, was at one time a member of the Russian Social Revolutionary party. Both parties were united by a common bond of struggle against autocracy and tyranny, Russian or Turkish, and by a vision of a new and better society. What the parties planned, or what they were trying to achieve, and what they did achieve are another matter. Some of the most tragic consequences were not anticipated at the beginning. At the turn of the century, however, Russian revolutionary thinkers, some of them active terrorists, suddenly discovered the brutalizing effects and the self-destructive logic of individual terror.

From Political Assassination to Tactical Terror

The history of a revolutionary movement involves far more than a study of its vicissitudes and ideas. A revolution does not appear suddenly; it is a result of a long and continuous process, of an accumulation of social and political contradictions. It may take decades and a sudden crisis or castastrophe, such as war, to accelerate the process and generate a revolution.

After the failure of the Decembrists in 1825, and after sporadic attempts to create revolutionary organizations, a political movement of a radical democratic orientation appeared between 1861 and 1863. The movement evolved slowly and reappeared in 1872 as an agrarian-socialist and radical movement, with some sections leaning toward anarchism. The largest and most influential group of the Populists decided to appeal primarily to the masses of peasantry, and to workers in the countryside. This movement was known as the "migration to the people." The migration of the young students and intellectuals to the countryside with the apostolic mission of social and political liberation, started at the beginning of 1874, and failed. Many activists were arrested and sentenced, while the peasants were, at best, indifferent, and mostly hostile to the "white hands" from the cities. No significant political reforms followed. After this experience and failure, and after a revolutionary lull during 1876 and 1877, at a conference of the Populists in 1879, a centralistic, disciplined, underground organization was formed, tightened by strict secrecy. Terror was chosen as its major tactic. But even the terroristic section of this party, now called the "People's Will," had its antecedents. Writings which recommended tactical terror had appeared earlier, about 1876.

The terroristic group was only one section of a political organization. The movement split. The splinter group, the "Black Partition," emphasized the significance of economic transformation and social revolution, as opposed to terror. Other groups, prescribing terror, appeared at this time. One group was composed of workers called "the Northern Russian Workers Association."

At the same time, liberal movements began to be more active; "constitutionalists" advanced the ideas of a constitutional rule. The ideology of the "People's Will" was not monolithic. The dominant trend was radical-democratic and agrarian-socialist. The program stressed the demands for political liberties and representative government. A political alliance with the liberals was viewed as a necessary future policy. The extreme wing of the party was anarchist, and this faction contained within it the germs of totalitarianism.[20]

Some of the revolutionaries opposed the terroristic tactics at the party conference of 1879, and terror was by no means the only tactic or the only activity.

Early Political Assassinations

Isolated political assassinations and attempts at assassinations had already occurred prior to 1879 in Russia. There was an unsuccessful attempt by Karakosov to assassinate Tsar Alexander II in 1866.[21] In 1878, Vera Zazulich shot and wounded the police prefect of St. Petersburg, General Trepof, after he had mistreated political prisoners. She was acquitted. She impressed the jury and public opinion by her defense and by her description of the oppressive conditions in Russia and the brutality of the police and government. In the same year there was shooting in Odessa by a group of revolutionaries resisting arrest. One of them, Kovalsky, was sentenced to death and executed in spite of the warnings of the revolutionaries. In retaliation, the chief of the secret police, General Mezentieff, was stabbed to death by Stepniak in Petersburg. Again, early in 1879, Prince Kropotkin, governor of Kharkov, whom the revolutionaries made responsible for the brutal treatment of political prisoners, was assassinated. In April 1879, an unsuccessful attempt was made to assassinate the Tsar.[22]

In November, when the Tsar was leaving for Livadia, a dynamite charge was exploded along the way. A few months later, a bomb in the Tsar's winter palace exploded, injuring 53 persons and killing 10 of the Tsar's guards.[23] This was not the end of attempts at assassination. There were still sporadic acts (although the attempt at the winter palace was organized by the Northern Workers Group), and at the same time a continuous intensification of a trend.

Beginnings of a Systematic Terroristic Struggle

In August 1879, the "People's Will" sentenced Emperor Alexander II to death. In March 1881, the Tsar was killed when a bomb was thrown at his sledges.

In 1880, the period of systematic terroristic struggle began. Discussing the earlier patterns of political assassination, Morozov wrote in his *Terroristic Struggle:* "All these actions of that time were accomplished continuously and in succession when the terroristic struggle did not become yet a part of a system." Now a "system" was here. The terroristic struggle continued, with varying intensity and temporary declines, for 30 years.

Opposition to Terror

Meanwhile the "Black Partition" evolved into the Social-Democratic movement, influenced by Marxist theories. The Social-Democrats were opposed to terror. Political change, they argued, is a result of historical, socio-economic changes, and not of a single act. Assassination of officials cannot effect such a change of the entire system. The revolution should be an act of the people of the working class. Soon (1903), the Social-Democrats split into two factions: the Mensheviks and the Bolsheviks. The split was a result of a long discussion and inner dissensions. The Mensheviks represented a rather Western, democratic orientation, while the Bolsheviks drifted toward the theory and practice of a small centralistic party (a vanguardist party) and future party dictatorship. Neither of these parties favored individual terror.

Nechayev and Burtsev

Theoreticians of the "People's Will" also believed that political change must be accomplished with the wide participation of the people. However, in their ranks a variety of tendencies were present, including the pressure exerted by the intransigents and extremists.

Although the extremists had a very small following and minor influence, the views of their theoretician, Nechayev, reflect the intensity of feelings. The extremist views of Nechayev go beyond the theories of Morozov or Tkachev. Sergei Nechayev wrote of the groups opposing revolution in Russia:

Karakozov's deed must be viewed as a prologue . . . . The most important of these opposing groups are:

1. All persons who occupy higher government posts and have authority over the armed forces and who carry out their command work with a special zeal.

2. People who possess large economic power and use it exclusively for themselves or to help the state.

3. People who argue and write for hire, i.e., journalists bribed by the government and writers who try to obtain government money by flattery and denunciations.

The first group must be exterminated without any argument.

The second group must be deprived of its economic power and means, which should be used for the work of national liberation; if they cannot be so used, this power and means must be destroyed.

The third group should be made silent by any kind of means (if only by depriving them of their tongues).[24]

Nechayev's social and political views were similar to the anarchists, and were linked for a time with the views of the anarchist Bakunin.

This was not, however, the position of the committee of the "People's Will." The Russian historian and Populist Nicholas Burtsev stated the official position of the movement in *Narodnovolets* (No. 2, 1897):

. . . We will be the first to manifest a complete cessation of the terrorist struggle, when the government honestly shows a desire to give up its present scurrilous policies. We are in favor of terror, however, not because we like it, but only because in our judgment there is no other possible method of struggle with the government at this moment, which, without the aid of terror, could force the government to grant concessions. Whenever there arises the possibility of an honest government, one that believes in its own policies—independent of the Pobedonostsevs —even one that arises under the pressures of liberals affiliated with Loris-Melikov, and that openly professes with sufficient guarantees the coming of a new era for Russia—we, too, as Stepniak, will "applaud the adoption of peaceful means" and will then be opposed to terrorism, as we are now opposed to it in free nations.

We count as indispensable conditions in a successful political struggle: freedom of the press, of assembly, and of the individual. With these conditions as bargaining points we will then go so far as we can toward our sacred ideals, but without the use of terror . . .[25]

It was this position, and a theory of ethical, democratic socialism, which prevailed when the Social Revolutionary party was formed in the early years of this century, at a time when the tensions and social conflicts were about to culminate in the Revolution of 1905.

Motivation and Some of the Determinants

The inclination toward terroristic tactics in Russia grew slowly before it was accepted as a major political technique by a small revolutionary group called the "People's Will" (Narodnaya Volya). Terror was conceived as a means of weakening the government. At first, this was the tactical orientation of a small, idealistic group, composed largely of students and members of the educated classes, i. e., the *intelligentsia*. Masaryk's remark was penetrating when he wrote that the Russian revolutionary movement of the 1870's and 1880's was above all political, that "it was an aristocratic struggle for freedom waged against tsarist absolutism."[26]

The ideology of the young revolutionaries was, in spite of its collectivist appeal, individualistic, even personalistic. The large participation of women was striking. Women were early admitted to Russian universities; already, in 1886, about a thousand women studied in Russian academic schools. Among women sentenced for political crimes, the percentage of educated women was very high.[27] Thus the "People's Will" was a movement of an educated, and to a large extent an isolated, few. They identified themselves with the peasantry and the working class, but their appeal to both met with little response at this time. The peasants mistrusted the educated. In terms of the peasants' perception of social classes, of their culture and behavior, these young students, future officials, and doctors were closer to the "upper classes" than to the peasantry. The movement, accordingly, was socially isolated, but highly motivated and youthful.

Political conditions in Russia had always been oppressive. Political freedom and representative government in a Western sense were absent. The Tsar was virtually an autocrat. The situation of the peasantry even after the Emancipation in 1861 was very difficult. The socio-economic conditions reflected profound class differences and inequalities.

These conditions alone may not have produced a terroristic, organized action, however. The emotional, psychological, and ethical appeal of this movement of the young and educated, although difficult to explain and evaluate in precise terms, had very much to do with their strong motivation. Contradictory sentiments and ideas rooted in a strange, dogmatic reasoning supported by iron logic were at that time one of the characteristics of Russian political and philosophical thinking, which was influenced so strongly by German philosophy. The revolutionaries displayed a type of religious and apostolic zeal. In their argumentations theology was displaced by philosophy, social science, and logic, but their reasoning was still guided by a maximalist, absolute ethics.

Most of the revolutionaries were atheists. But they had transformed their childhood religious emotions, concepts, and strong ethical principles into a political ideology and revolutionary cause. There were differences in personality types, of course. Moreover, different revolutionary tactics appealed to different personality types, and membership changed with the changing conditions and times.[28] Some penetrating insights into the psychology and personality of these men were given by Dostoyevski (who tended to be rather negative), but perhaps more important by Stepniak (himself a terrorist), Lavrov, Berdyaev, Masaryk, Savinkov (V. Ropsin), and recently by Camus.[29] None of the terrorist movements of Europe produced literature of such philosophical depth and tragic contradictions. None has raised so courageously the moral dilemma. Those arguments and dilemmas tormented the revolutionaries and pointed to terrorism as a self-destructive process. In the end, some of the idealists discovered that they were henchmen in the service of a great cause and moral principle, but still henchmen. The question asked at the end was an elementary and fundamental one: Who has the right to kill; does anybody have this moral authority?

It is difficult to explain this complex and tormenting metaphysics and behavior without dwelling on problems of value structure, personality, modes of thinking, the history of Russia —in short, on culture. It may be remembered that Russia since its rebirth in the 16th century was an autocracy, and that violence was frequently applied simply as a matter of exercise of power. The Tsar himself, Ivan the Terrible, killed his own son.

Political institutions with their roots in Oriental autocracy did not supply any sufficient means of political and socio-economic change. The centralistic and absolute government discouraged tendencies toward local government, although efforts to liberalize the entire system through legal means were made continuously. The autocratic institutions, maintaining their power by coercion, even violence, supported by religious orthodoxy, generated a strong hostile response and promoted the organization of centralistic parties that endorsed the tactics of violence as an effective method of change.

Ideology and Objectives of the Terrorists

Yet it was among these terroristic revolutionary groups in autocratic Russia where democratic ideas flourished. There were several factions, some of them minor, whose objective was—as was stated before—establishment of dictatorship, as a transitional stage toward a truly free society, a society free of any coercion. Here rationalism worked in harmony with perfect ideals and logical contradictions, so impressive and convincing to novices. Theories were also advanced (by Morozov and Tkachev) that terror should continue under constitutional rule, because even under such rule, a tyranny might appear, e.g., of a type found in Bismarck or Napoleon.[30] Through intimidation and elimination of future tyrants, terror would keep the future, perfect world free from autocracy. These late regicides were, however, in a minority and formed an insignificant faction or separate party. The main party, the core of the "People's Will," had democratic traditions and clear democratic objectives. In 1878, the "People's Will" stated clearly and sharply in an "Urgent Note" its differences with the group which "indulges in Jacobinistic tendencies and methods of a centralistic organization."[31] In a letter which the committee sent after the assassination of Tsar Alexander II in 1881, the revolutionary committee asked the Tsar to introduce a representative form of government, free press, and freedom of speech and assembly as conditions of a pacific development and cessation of revolutionary tactics.[32] After the assassination of President Garfield, in the official organ of the revolutionary terrorists, *Narodnaya Volya* (No. 6, October 23, 1881), a declaration appeared which deserves attention in the United States today:

The Executive Committee, expressing its profoundest sympathy with the American people on account of the death of James Abram Garfield, feels it to be its duty to protest in the name of Russian revolutionaries against all such deeds of violence as that which has just taken place in America. In a land where the citizens are free to express their ideas, and where the will of the people does not merely make the law but appoints the person who is to carry the law into effect, in such a country political assassination is the manifestation of a despotic tendency identical with that to whose destruction in Russia we have devoted ourselves. Despotism, whatever may be the parties or whoever may be the individuals that exercise it, is always blameworthy, and force can be justified only when employed to resist force.[33]

The choice of the revolutionary tactic is a human decision within the compelling conditions created by the society into which the political actors were born. This is also the case with terroristic tactics. The choice of such tactics was not a consequence of historical necessity. Conditions indicated that such tactics would be efficient, but the choice was made by the revolutionaries. Terrorism was a stage in a long process, and was developed into a political style. The social revolutionary Stepniak wrote in the 1890's: "The revolution, especially the Russian revolution, is a strangely fantastic monster, and there are no means of divining where it will stop, or the leaps it may still take, if the whim seizes it."

The Government's Reaction to Terror

Terroristic tactics were continued by the social revolutionaries. The terroristic struggle and political insecurity had contributed to the extension of the powers of the police state. An extensive, secret, political police network was built, the Okhrana, an augury and antecedent of future organizations of this type: the Soviet GPU under Stalin and Hitler's Gestapo. Okhrana, with its ruthless methods, became a hated organization and a target of the terrorist revolution. It penetrated deeply into the revolutionary party. Some of the secret agents ("provocators") became leaders of the terrorists.

The story of Azev, a leader of terrorist squads, shocked the public opinion of the world. Alexander Gerasimov, the head of the dreaded political police Okhrana, called it later, in his memoirs, "conspiracy under my orders." Azev was a secret agent of Okhrana: before accepting the leadership of the terroristic squads, he consulted the head of the secret police, Gerasimov. Gerasimov in turn discussed the matter with the Minister of Interior, Plehve. It was Azev, an agent of Plehve's own department, the secret police, who planned and directed the assassination of Plehve.[34]

Terroristic tactics eventually became self-defeating. The government, however, felt the continuous threat of violence. The tactical prediction of terrorist theoreticians had been fulfilled: the government was occupied with problems of its own safety, and it was indeed weakened. Of course, terrorist action was not the only cause.

Terror, however, continued after 1905, even after the experimental representative institution, the duma, was proclaimed in August 1905. It even continued into the time of the third duma after 1907.

Prime Minister Stolypin responded to the political assassinations by court-martialing those accused of political crimes, and sentencing those who were found guilty to death. But the number of executions began to decline; in 1911, 73 sentences were passed.[35]

In September 1911, Premier Stolypin was assassinated. This was perhaps the last major act of the terroristic revolution, which began in an unsystematic way in 1876, became tactical about 1879, and began to disappear about 1911.

The Size of the Terroristic Party

The terroristic party undoubtedly had a powerful impact on Russia. Systematic political assassination and the heroic deeds of revolutionaries had an influence on public opinion in a country that was under an autocratic rule and where representative institutions as late as at the beginning of the 20th century were only in rudimentary form. How large was the party that planned and executed this revolutionary tactic of terror, so unique in Western history? Ludwik Kulczycki, historian of the Russian revolutionary movement, wrote half a century ago that the party had at the time of its highest development about 500 members.[36]

Outside the party, however, was a large group of sympathizers who were not members, but shared at least part of the party's general political attitudes, although they might have disagreed on sections of the program. Kulczycki estimates that the sympathizers of the "People's Will" who supported this party's struggle against absolutism and in favor of free institutions, probably amounted to between thirteen and nineteen thousand persons, largely students and workers.[37] As the party grew in influence, its appeal to the workers and later even to the peasantry increased.

Whatever the differences in the estimates, the numbers of the party membership were small indeed. The terroristic action was performed by small, secret squads. In the three attempts to assassinate Tsar Alexander II about 50 populists participated.[38] Thus, the small groups, applying the tactics of individual systematic terror, exercised an unusual disproportionate influence over the entire country.

Terror and Representative Institutions

Why was terroristic action of such long duration in Russia?

The terroristic struggle coincides with the time of a very slow advance of limited representative institutions—the establishment of the Zemstvo. Since 1870 the liberal representatives of the Zemstvos had met occasionally, and to their conference in Kieff in 1878 they even invited several prominent revolutionaries, urging cessation of terrorism. Some revolutionaries even joined the "League of Oppositional Elements." The liberals had stressed the need for freedom of speech and press.[39] After the Revolution of 1905, the first national representation, the duma, was elected by 1906. While the socialists boycotted the election, the Constitutional Democrats (KD) were the strongest party.[40] Thus, during the period of terrorism weak representative bodies did exist, and even a national representation, weak and incomplete as it was, made its appearance. There were also liberal parties, tendencies, and groups.

Because of the latent discontent and opposition to absolutism in the few cities of Russia, the revolutionary pressure, despite the small numbers of the spearheading party, was far stronger than the government's response and institutional changes. It is true that for a long time, in the countryside, revolutionaries had little appeal. But in a centralistic state like Russia, cities, even the few urban centers Russia had at this time, play a paramount role in political ecology. In the towns opposition to the Tsarist regime grew among the *intelligentsia*, students, and the working class. They were a minority, but nevertheless a dynamic minority. The institutional changes, the slow and hesitant advance toward some kind of representative form, which in fact did not affect the deep and acute class divisions, were too inadequate to meet the demands and pressures of the moderates in the revolutionary groups. The terror and assassinations continued in spite of court-martials, the Okhrana, and executions.

A government that desires a peaceful transformation and continuation of its rule must sense the needs of the time and the nature of revolutionary pressures and demands, not solely in terms of the number of voters, but also in terms of real social needs and the potential mass-appeal of the pressure groups. The government and its responsible leaders must perceive the need for changing socio-economic inequalities at a proper time and in a proper way. Without such wisdom, the revolutionary process will follow its logical course.

4. Violence and Terror against Foreign Rule in Eastern Europe

Origin of the Polish Revolutionary Movement

The terroristic action of the Polish revolutionaries from the Polish Socialist Party (P.P.S.) is of quite a different origin, and a consequence of a different political situation, from that of the terror of the "People's Will" or of the Social Revolutionary party.

The Russians fought their own government, the Poles fought a foreign one. Rationalization or legitimation of violent physical struggle against a foreign invader and a foreign oppressive government was supported by national attitudes and values. The legitimacy of a struggle against a foreign invader is generally accepted in Western civilization.

Thus, in terms of the ideology or philosophy of the movement, and in terms of ethics, the Polish revolutionaries, it seems, were not tormented by the moral and philosophical problems as were the Russians. Perhaps their modes of thinking and their values were also quite different from those of their Russian comrades. For all their philosophical and historical traditions, the Polish revolutionaries did not leave behind them voluminous philosophical discussions about the moral and philosphical nature of political assassination that the Russians did.

It may be safely argued that the terroristic struggle of the Poles was far shorter in time and far less significant a tactic. It was only ancillary. But the revolutionists from the Polish Socialist Party left an important mark on the political culture of their country and on its literature. Some of the most gifted writers of that country, Zeromski, Brzozowski, Strug, to mention the most prominent, were inspired by the revolutionary pathos of the struggle and the tragic life of its heroes.

The goals of the Polish Socialist Party—both social and political—originated in the Polish revolutionary movement which had its roots in Poland's own past. It was not an offshoot or a derivative of the Russian revolutionary movement.

Since 1794, almost every generation of Poles has taken up arms against foreign invaders. Insurrections occurred in 1794, 1831, and 1863. The revolutionary traditions, the struggle for independence, were a part of the Polish tradition, especially among the nobility and the educated classes.

In the early years of the Polish Socialist Party, the insurrectionist traditions were represented directly by some members (such as B. Limanowski) who still participated in the insurrection of 1863, or others (such as J. Pilsudski) whose families were actively engaged in or sympathized with the insurrection.

The Polish Socialist Party

Socialist organizations and ideas appeared early in Poland.[41] At the conference in Paris in 1892, a program was adopted which proclaimed as basic objectives the national independence of Poland and the establishment of democratic socialism. A future Polish state was envisaged as a republic. Self-government, representative institutions, freedom of speech, press, and assembly, as well as other political rights formed an essential part of the program, which also advocated extensive labor legislation and gradual nationalization of land, the instruments of production, and means of communication.[42]

The insurrectionist traditions, however, represented only one element in this party. Political and social democracy and labor legislation reflected the basic ideology of the working class which this party really represented.

While the "People's Will" was above all a party of the educated classes, the young Russian intelligentsia, students, and revolutionaries who identified themselves with the peasantry and the working class, the Polish Socialist Party at the turn of the century, and on the eve of the Revolution of 1905, had not only a powerful appeal to the working class; its relatively large membership was also composed of workers, students, and members of the intelligentsia. Many workers were active in the revolutionary and terroristic struggle.

This was indeed a workingman's party, representing his interest and his struggle, appealing to his values, sentiments, and economic needs.

Absence of Terror in the Austrian Part of Poland

Poland was partitioned in the 18th century by Russia, Germany, and Austria. In the Austrian part, the constitutional monarchy guaranteed political, and to an extent, national rights to a variety of ethnic groups. The monarchy had not only a representative government, with a house of parliament in Vienna, but also a large measure of self-government, even autonomy. The Polish part was administered by a governor (viceroy) appointed in Vienna, but it also had its own diet. Even the school system was administered with the assistance of national councils. The Russian part was the most oppressive, having autocratic rule and denying national rights, even the use of the Polish language in schools and offices.

The revolutionary action of the Polish Socialist Party was conducted only in the Russian part. Systematic violence, in the form of tactical terror, such as attempts to assassinate high administrative representatives, governors, and police directors, appeared as a part of revolutionary tactics only in the so-called "Congress Poland." After 1846 in the Austrian part no attempt at an armed insurrection was made, no systematic political assassination was organized by the Poles.

In Galicia, in the Austrian part, Polish Socialists (P.P.S.D. —Polish Social-Democratic Party) followed the tactics of European socialists, supporting vigorously representative institutions, organizing trade unions and social insurance for workers, and fighting for progressive labor legislation. The party was well represented in the Parliament in Vienna, in the provincial diet, and municipal governments. The representatives in the Parliament soon won recognition and fame as gifted and responsible democratic leaders and legislators.

The case of Poland in the first decade of our century is instructive. A measure of political rights and self-government was a sufficient policy to secure a peaceful, and in a way, after the general franchise of 1907, a parliamentary method of social and political change. It may be suggested that a similar measure of political freedom and self-government would have prevented the development of violent struggle and individual terror in Russian Poland. This experience and the very tentative assumption cannot, however, be mechanically generalized and applied to other nations and cultures; the experience here is limited by time, culture, and social conditions.

The Nature of Terror in Poland

The political assassination in the Russian part as practiced by the revolutionaries of the Polish Socialist Party was tactical, but it neither had the systematic, continuous character of the terror of the Russian revolutionaries, nor was this action as paramount a tactic as in the former case. In fact, the individual assassination of the high representatives of the Russian government, identified by the revolutionaries as responsible for the oppression or brutality, begins with the revolution of 1904 and appears only as one of several methods in the revolutionary tactical pattern.

The Revolution of 1904–05 was in Poland a powerful social movement, advanced by strikes, propaganda, mass manifestations, and military actions more related to partisan warfare.

An armed conflict between the Russian soldiers and the Poles, led by the militants of the Polish Socialist Party, took place in Warsaw in 1904. It was the first armed conflict since the Polish insurrection of 1863. Manifestations and armed conflicts took place in other parts of Russian Poland. In 1905, an attempt against the hated chief of police of Warsaw was made by Okrzeya a militant of the P.P.S. Okrzeya paid with his life.

In 1905, numerous attempts against governors, police chiefs, and many others followed. One of the best known and most spectacular was the attempt against the governor-general Skallon in Warsaw in 1906. On Wednesday, August 15, 1906 (known in history as Bloody Wednesday), tactics of terror were directed against individual policemen on duty in Warsaw. They were attacked and shot by the militants of the P.P.S. An attack on the train at Rogov in 1906 was an organized partisan action, involving a number of revolutionists acting according to a detailed plan, under a disciplined command.[43]

Opposition to Terror and Direct Action

The Polish Socialist Party was not the sole representative of socialist ideology, although it was undoubtedly the dominant party of the working class in Poland. S.D.K.P.L., the Social Democracy of the Kingdom of Poland and Lithuania, rejected terror and did not advocate an independent Poland. It envisaged Poland as an autonomous province or state within the future Russian Socialist Republic. The Polish Communist Party evolved later, after 1917, from the S.D.K.P.L. But terror and direct action was also opposed within the Polish Socialist Party. The party split in 1905. The revolutionary faction (PPSFR) continued its direct action, a kind of guerrilla warfare combined with individual terror and the tactics of political assassination.

Internal Political Terror

The terroristic struggle, however, attacked a wider circle than the hated representatives of an oppressive government.

The operation involved larger numbers of people than the militants alone. Some were corrupt, others betrayed their trust. The organization was sooner or later penetrated by secret agents. Under the conditions of an underground struggle, the party became highly secret and disciplined. The safety of party members and the maintenance of secrecy did not leave many choices. Punishment by death was the price a former member paid for treason or even weakness. Neither did the party tolerate those who wanted to leave it, after some experience. Police agents, once discovered, paid with their lives. Internal terror became in that way a means of maintaining discipline and secrecy.

The Russian revolutionaries (or Macedonian revolutionaries as we shall see later) met similar problems of secrecy and police action. They solved them in a similar manner—by death. In consequence of this tactic, the circle of victims of the terror grew larger, and terroristic, uncompromising struggle influenced the lives, destinies, and sometimes personalities of the militants.

The military activities of the revolutionary faction of the Polish Socialist Party, with the political assassination of individual representatives of the Russian government as one of its tactics, did not last as long as the Russian terroristic struggle. About 1908, the terroristic action began rapidly to decline. Thus, the intensive stage of terroristic action did not last longer than 4 or 5 years in Poland.

The Termination of Systematic Terror

How was terror terminated in Poland?

The terroristic and guerrilla tactics were displaced by military preparations for a war against Russia, and eventually by the professionalization of the militants. In 1908, the leader of the fighting squads, Joseph Pilsudski, began to organize a nonpartisan nucleus of the future Polish Army—the Union of Direct Struggle. Later, an organization of "Riflemen" (Stsheltsy) was formed, and from this the Polish Legion evolved in Galicia, headed by Pilsudski. This was the first regular Polish military unit since the insurrection of 1863, and was once again the nucleus of the Polish Army. The commander of the Legion, a former leader of the fighting squads,

became the first chief of state of the Republic. The story of
the Irish resistance and struggle for independence, for all its
differences, bears certain similarities to the Polish struggle.

The Polish revolutionary movement and its terrorists were
thus broadening the legitimacy of the movement. At first, the
legitimacy of the terroristic movement was ideological, in
terms of a party. Now the movement claimed national and
historical legitimacy, which called for national loyalty. The
name of the military formation as well as its symbols were
those of the Polish military formation in the times of the
French Revolution and Napoleon. The attempts to define Polish history reinforced the legitimacy of the revolutionists.
Thus a secret, underground, and militant movement was channeled into a formal military structure, and assumed national
symbols and legitimacy. However, only a part of the revolutionaries were absorbed by the military structure. The revolutionary struggle, with terror as a part of it, was now channeled
into preparation for war.

Terror by the Armenian Dashnaks as a Defense and Struggle Against Turkish Massacres

The massacres of Armenians inspired by the Turkish government assumed the proportions of mass extermination or
genocide. An Armenian revolutionary organization known as
the Dashnaks (Hai Heghapokhakan Dashnaksowtiwn) answered the Turkish massacres with a broad gamut of tactics.
One of the tactical actions was terror, directed against Turkish
and Tsarist government officials and Kurdish beks, who were
regarded by the Armenians as responsible for the massacres.
The strategic objectives of terror by the Dashnaks were
vengeance, punishment, intimidation, or defense.

The Armenian Massacres

The Dashnaks faced a situation different from that of the
Poles. The Turkish government was even more autocratic than
the Russian tyranny. Arbitrary violence of both minor
and higher native officials, especially in the countryside, was a
frequent occurrence. Violence in the transfer and changes of

power, and individual and mass violence exercised against the subject Christian population was a recurrent phenomenon, a matter of administrative routine. The position of the Armenians in Turkey was also different from the Serbian, Greek, Bulgarian, or Albanian minorities. The first three could always look for protection and support from Serbia, Bulgaria, or Greece. Albanians were fighting men of the mountains who could defend themselves. Large sections of the minority population were Moslem and identified themselves with the Ottoman Empire. Many served in the Turkish Army. The Armenians were defenseless and without allies. Deprived of their national independence, they were divided between Turkey, Russia, and Persia, and abused and mistreated by the Kurds, a nomadic people. The Turkish government used the nomadic and primitive Kurds against the Armenians. Armenians appealed to the Congress of Berlin in 1878 for support in their attempt to gain administrative reforms. They had a certain limited representation of their religious and civil affairs through their "National General Assembly." In 1889, persecution of the Armenians began, as both the Turkish and Russian governments saw the problem in terms of the "Armenian danger." In 1894, massacres of Armenians were resumed in the province of Bitlis; Kurds, aided by Turkish troops, destroyed 25 villages, killing indiscriminately any Armenians they found. The Pasha commanding this pogrom was decorated.

After an Armenian protest in Constantinople in 1895, massacres followed in the capital, and again there were mass killings on a genocidal scale in Asia Minor, organized by Turkish officials. According to British reports, about 30,000 Armenians perished in this massacre. In August 1896, after an Armenian protest action, in Constantinople, there was another Armenian massacre, with the assistance of Turkish soldiers and police officers. About 6,000 persons were killed. A British diplomat reported that it seemed "that the intention of Turkish authorities [is] to exterminate the Armenians."[44]

Massacres continued, while Western powers protested with no real effect. Again, after a brief, hopeful period, the Young Turkish Revolution in 1908 was followed by the massacre of Armenians at Adana.[45] Finally, in 1915, another massacre of Armenians shocked world opinion. The American ambassador called the massacres "the murder of a nation"; the British government published a document on *The Treatment of Armenians in the Ottoman Empire, 1915–16* (London, 1916). Mass deportations ordered by the government were followed by new massacres of the helpless and innocent population.[46]

Such were the social and political conditions which resulted in the revolutionary tactics of terror and direct action by the Armenian Dashnaks against the Turks.

The Dashnak Party

The intolerable condition of Armenians living under the Turkish yoke and the revolutionary fervor among university students in Russia, brought together a cross section of Armenian students in the summer of 1890. Through the main efforts of Christopher Mikaelian, Simon Zavarian, and Stephan Zorian, the Dashnak Party was founded in October 1890. It was comprised of people with diverse social backgrounds; the prime concern of all these people was the liberation of Turkish Armenia.[47]

Mikaelian and his wife, the founders of the party, were formerly members of "Narodnaya Volya" (People's Will). The Dashnak Party advocated the independence of Armenia and advanced a socialist and democratic program. Direct action was only a part of its political strategy and tactics. The tactics of terror may have come through Mikaelian and his experience in the Russian revolutionary organization "People's Will."

Mikaelian favored terror against those responsible for the Armenian massacres. The Dashnaks, together with the Macedonian revolutionary organization IMRO, planned to assassinate Sultan Abdul Hamid. Mikaelian, however, was killed in Bulgaria while experimenting with explosives in 1904. The unsuccessful attempt of the Armenian revolutionaries against the life of the Sultan took place in 1905.

The Dashnaks, as was mentioned earlier, also conducted guerrilla activities as early as 1897 against the Kurdish persecuting bands. Their direct, revolutionary activities had two major objectives: punishment of those guilty of anti-Armenian crimes, and defense against the Kurds and Turks who harassed Armenians. Furthermore, the party hoped to impress the European powers and the Turkish government with the needs for reforms, civil rights and protection for the Armenians.[48]

As late as the early 1920's, the Dashnak terrorists assassinated those whom they regarded as responsible for the Armenian genocide. Terror, in the Armenian case, developed under the specific conditions of a disintegrating Turkish Empire and national persecutions. The acts had wide moral support among the Armenians. The Dashnaks later played an important role in the government of the short-lived Armenian Republic, after 1918. The Republic was later seized by and incorporated into the Soviet Union.

Polish and Armenian Terroristic Tactics Compared

The Polish and the Armenian terroristic actions developed under entirely different historical conditions and within a different socio-political environment. Certain characteristics, however, were common to both movements: both were national struggles against a foreign and oppressive government; and terror was only one element in the general strategy and tactics of both movements. But the Dashnak terroristic and guerrilla activities were of longer duration than the Polish, lasting over a quarter of a century.

5. Political Assassination in Balkan Politics

The Nature of Political Assassination

Political assassination in Serbia and Bulgaria must be considered in its sociological and historical context.

Serbia won its limited freedom during the struggle of its people in the early years of the 19th century; Bulgaria achieved this status almost 70 years later. Both nations had been under Ottoman rule for centuries. Individual assassination in the transfer of power, and especially in the succession of power, was a frequent occurrence in Turkey—almost a matter of court routine. Violence was equally applied and abused in an arbitrary manner in the business of ruling her subject peoples. The Turkish occupation of the Balkan peninsula in the 14th and 15th centuries froze the medieval societies there and arrested cultural progress. After emancipation from Turkish rule, the Balkan societies emerged with a primitive, almost medieval (although colorful) peasant folk-culture and economics.

The political habits of the early Balkan leaders were shaped by the heavy and dangerous pressures of Turkish rule. Serbian men of politics were hardened to armed struggles, cunning in negotiations, and ruthless in politics, both with the Turks and in competition and fights with their own people. Thus, armed struggle and violence in Serbia, which in the early years of the 19th century was a "folk-society" of free peasantry, was directed chiefly against the Turks, and, when the struggle was local, also against competing families. These peasant families slowly grew into dynasties that represented not only definite interests but also political orientations. Political assassination was a simple means in the power struggle of eliminating a competitor and changing a political course of action. Assassination was usually perpetrated by organized groups of partisans of a family or dynasty.

At the turn of the century, dynastic factions formed secret, highly-disciplined organizations, with the support and membership of army officers. Assassination was the ultimate tactical means toward desired political change. Unlike Russian terror, assassinations in Serbia during this period were mostly single, isolated acts attempted by conspirators for a definite purpose of eliminating a ruler or statesman. The ultimate end was power, associated with a change of the elite. But power for what? Both the elite and the ends were nationalistic. The conspirators desired a union of the entire Serbian or South Slavic population into one Serbian Kingdom.

This type of assassination became common early in Serbia's history. It must be remembered, however, that Serbian politics was influenced by Turkish example, and that the Turks practiced government by violence not only against the Serbs but also in their own politics.

Dynastic Feuds and Assassinations

Kara George, the liberator of the Serbs and the founder of the Karageorgevich dynasty, while escaping from the Turks, killed his own father in 1787. The old man had refused to cross a river, since his courage was failing, and Kara George preferred to see him dead rather than have him fall into Turkish hands. The hero of the Serbian uprising returned to his country, after many vicissitudes, in 1817, in an attempt to regain influence and extend the borders of his country.

Milosh, the founder of the Obrenovich dynasty, was ruling Serbia at that time. Kara George urged him to join forces against the Turks. Milosh, however, informed the Turkish pasha of Kara George's presence in Serbia. On the demand of the pasha, Kara George was murdered and his head sent to Constantinople. The liberator of Serbia had been assassinated with the complicity of the ruler of the newly liberated nation. "The tragedy," writes Temperley, "was of the dreadful Aeschylean type, for Kara George is said to have murdered the half brother of Milosh."[49]

Thus at the outset the pattern was established for future dynastic succession and violent change. Eight sovereigns span the period from 1817 to 1945, three of whom were murdered. If Kara George, in his role of liberator, is also considered a national leader, then the ratio is four out of nine. Two rulers were deposed, and one abdicated.[50] In 1903, King Alexander, the last Obrenovich, and his wife were shot by a group of conspirators, led by Colonel Apis, who was later the founder and leader of the Black Hand, a secret organization. Later, some members of Alexander's government met the same fate. With this assassination the feud between the Karageorgeviches and Obrenoviches was finally terminated.

This was not, however, solely a ruthless struggle for political power. The reign of the last Obrenovich had been unconstitutional. He suspended a liberal constitution and appointed a military cabinet. His political orientation was pro-Austrian, at a time when millions of South Slavs, Serbs, and Croats were under Austro-Hungarian rule. The political orientation of the Karageorgeviches, conversely, was pro-Russian. It is true that Alexander's successor, King Peter Karageorgevich, was the best king Serbia had ever had. He was a man of personal integrity, simplicity, and courage, a truly democratic king, strongly identified with the peasantry. Nevertheless, the dynastic change was effected by a brutal assassination.[51]

The Black Hand and the Assassination of Archduke Ferdinand

The young Serbian kingdom had democratic tendencies and institutions. The international situation, with its tensions, nationality problems, and ardent patriotism led young students and officers to the formation of a number of nationalistic societies. Large areas of South Slavic territory were under Austro-Hugarian rule. In addition, after the Congress of Berlin, Austria-Hungary annexed Bosnia and Herzegovina, which had previously been occupied by Turkey. The population of this area was predominantly Serbian. A pan-Serbian program of the union of all Serbs, and later South Slavs, into the Serbian state had at this time a great appeal.

A secret nationalistic organization was founded in Belgrade in 1911, the Union of Death, better known as the Black Hand. Its goal was a national state of all Serbs, including those under Austro-Hungarian rule. This secret organization included a number of high officers in key positions in the army, among them "Apis" Dimitryevich, Colonel of the General Staff and chief of Serbian intelligence. Its membership was not large, but it was influential, and had branch committees in various parts of the kingdom as well as in some towns in Turkey and Austria-Hungary which were inhabited by Serbian minorities.[52]

The organization was dedicated to its national goals through the revolutionary struggle, including terroristic action. The Black Hand reached the height of its power during the Balkan wars. Members of the organization were among those who intitiated, organized, and executed the assassination of Archduke Francis Ferdinand in Sarajevo on June 28, 1914, which precipitated World War I, itself a consequence of far more complex circumstances.[53]

The Black Hand, by means of secrecy and individual violence, and with its members placed in key positions in the army, exercised powerful control over the government and the dynasty. In 1917, members of the organization were arrested and accused of planning the assassination of Prince Alexander. A silent struggle went on for a time between the government and the Black Hand. One of the latter's most outstanding and dedicated members, Colonel Apis (D. Dimitryevich), a man recognized by many Serbs as an outstanding patriot, was sentenced and executed.

Professionalization and Institutionalization of Terror

Terroristic activity as a political tactic has shown in the past two tendencies: professionalization and institutionalization.

After a time, a professional class of terrorists gains influence in and control of the terrorist organization. Meanwhile, sporadic and transient conspiracies, once the act of terror has been repeated, change slowly into permanent and highly disciplined institutionalized associations. Such institutionalized groups of strong ideological and group loyalties gradually become independent and exercise a powerful influence on the political life of the nation. Their disciplined organization and use of terror make them aggressive. The manipulation of fear by terror, the use of terror against those who are unskilled in violence or unwilling to use it, give such groups an influence and strength that extends far beyond their numbers. This was the case in the transformation of the Macedonian revolutionary organization IMRO, which at first directed its struggle and individual terror against the Turks, and later practiced assassination and violence in Bulgarian domestic politics.

The Komitadji of Macedonia and Terroristic Action

The struggle against Turkish rule in Macedonia was led in the last quarter of the 19th century by insurgents called *haiduci* in Slavic, or *kleftis* in Greek. They were called *komitadji* by the Turks, since the fighting bands were under the command of committees.

In 1894, the first central committee of the Macedonian revolutionary organizations was formed. It was called the Internal Macedonian Revolutionary Organization (IMRO) (the Bulgarian name was Vatreshna Makedonska Revolutionarna Organisaciya (VMRO). Modeled on the Italian Carbonari in some of their rituals, this secret, highly disciplined organization was directed by a central committee, and controlled a number of detachments of a secret political army.[54]

The Turkish rule was oppressive, especially for the peasantry. Taxes were burdensome and the peasant was defenseless against the abuses of tax collectors, passing troops, or the police. In certain areas and at various times, Turkish rule, incompetent and corrupt though it was, was still tolerable. But repeated persecutions, abuses of the local population, and massacres, called for self-defense and for emancipation of the subject peoples from the oppression. Macedonian peasants were too often subjected in their daily life to humiliations and extortions.[55]

In 1895, new bands of *komitadjis* infiltrated Macedonia from Bulgaria. Now the Macedonian Internal Organization began its revolution with a wide uncompromising struggle, combining the tactics of guerrilla warfare with terror against Turkish officials and their allies. The revolt reached its peak in 1904, but also continued during the Balkan wars.

Terroristic activities were not limited to attacks against oppressive Turkish officers and administrators. The death penalty was used to maintain discipline and secrecy and to punish any embezzlement of party monies by minor collectors of dues. Sudden raids and executions were used to terrify neutrals and opponents.[56]

During the Balkan wars, the *komitadji* rapidly began to lose their democratic and liberal orientation. An auxiliary army of certain Bulgarian *komitadji,* writes Todoroff, "committed regrettable acts of violence and brutality against the Turkish population."

IMRO had begun as a democratic and revolutionary organization to fight the Turks. One faction advocated a Balkan Federation with an autonomous Bulgaria, the other favored incorporating a liberated Macedonia into Bulgaria. The pro-Bulgarian and anti-Serb faction gradually predominated. During World War I, the *komitadji,* supported by the Central Powers, fought against the Serbs.

During and after World War I, professionalization and institutionalization of the one-time revolutionary guerrilla organization occurred. After so many years, terroristic action had become a profession. "Little by little," wrote Kostia Todoroff, "the idealists perished in the fighting, but the professionals survived. . . ."[57]

One of the factions of IMRO now became an independent organization, a state within a state, terrorizing those Bulgarian governments which favored cooperation with Yugoslavia and opposed war and continuous, irredentist action in Macedonia. Terror and political assassination were one of the tactics of a major fraction of IMRO: their goal was annexation of all Macedonia, including the Yugoslav parts of Macedonia. A minor faction continued to advocate the old program of a Balkan federational democracy with an autonomous Macedonia.

Sanguinary internal struggles and assassination between factions and their leaders became similar to Turkish "sultanic" practices. When the peasant leader and Prime Minister Stambuliiski ordered arrest of the *komitadjis,* in his effort to protect the Yugoslav border from terroristic raids, the terrorists answered with the assassination of the Minister of War, Dimitroff (October 1921), and a district prefect, Kozlovski. Eventually the *komitadji* leader Alexandroff gave his support to the military opponents of Prime Minister Stambuliiski. The latter was finally murdered by the Macedonian terrorists with the complicity of an army officer.[58]

As a consequence of the struggle between factions, there arose the phenomenon of internal terror. Alexandroff was killed in September 1923, in the presence of his former friends, at a party conference. In the words of Todoroff, "these conflicts turned out to be really massacres, for the Organization was openly aided by the Bulgarian police and military. Three hundred persons were killed."[59]

The terror spread throughout Bulgaria and abroad. A number of prominent democratic and moderate statesmen were killed, while internecine warfare between leaders followed in Bulgarian towns, in the city of Milan, and in a theater in Vienna. Plotting and conspiracy continued in foreign embassies in Vienna and in suburban villas. Killer squads from Sofia tracked their victims in the streets and squares of the Austrian capital. "It is impossible," says Roucek, "to detail all the terrorist acts perpetrated in Yugoslavia and Greece."[60]

The goals had changed, the idealists had disappeared, the professionals were now dominating the organization and directing the deadly tactics. The organization had become professionalized, institutionalized, and directed against different targets. Assassination as a method of achieving an objective was now being used in entirely different socio-political conditions.

6. From the Terror of the Totalitarians to the Underground Struggle Against Conquerors, 1918–1945

The Political Situation, 1918–1945

A catastrophe, such as war, has frequently had a decisive impact on political strategy and tactics. What we call "crisis" is, in fact, a basic change of situation, and this change affects the decisions and actions of political leaders and their parties.

World War I brought an increase of political controls. Extensive control of individual travel and ration cards and rationing of food and goods increased the power of the state and of the bureaucracy far beyond the prewar legal limits. The War also effected psychological and emotional changes, or displacement and redirection, at least in its initial stages. The revolutionaries of Russia had to choose between either the struggle against the Tsar or the struggle against the German armies. This situation did not prevent the formation of underground movements. Terror, however, was a political tactic, which under the conditions of the War began, for many reasons, to decline.

Individual political assassinations did not disappear; but they were rather exceptional. In this category are the assassination of the Austrian prime minister Sturgkh by a young socialist, pacifist, and physics instructor, Friedrich Adler, in Austria, and the assassination of Rasputin, the influential, self-appointed religious preacher of peasant origin who was killed by Russian aristocrats. Each assassination took place at a critical moment at the end of the war, in two countries that were in a mood of defeat. In Austria, it was a protest against prolongation of the war; in Russia, it was an attempt to eliminate a person whose influence was regarded as responsible for the nation's military reverses.

The 19th century came to an end in 1914. The new historical period began in 1918 with the emergence of independent East European states and the disintegration of the old empires. Former leaders and members of the revolutionary and terrorist groups were now not only legitimized; they also played a prominent role in the building of nations.

Former Terrorist Parties and Revolution in Russia

In Russia, Victor Chernov, one-time leading member of the Social Revolutionary Party and active during the democratic stage of the 1917 Revolution, was elected president of the short-lived Constituent Assembly of 1917. He and other members of his formerly terroristic party—it was a direct descendant of the "People's Will"—defended with vigor democratic institutions and the ideology of the new Republic. They opposed the death penalty and any attempts to introduce dictatorship into Russia. The famous terrorist Borys Savinkov was minister of interior in the Kerenski government. Having been terrorists in times of autocracy, these former advocates of tyrannicide opposed, in their new role of democratic leadership, any form of terror, especially mass terror. The programs and declarations of the "People's Will" and of the Social Revolutionary Party of the underground past became the guidelines of the S.R. members of the government.

After Trotsky and Lenin seized power and dictatorship had been gradually introduced, the Social Revolutionaries once again took up opposition. Terror and assassination attempts were made by some of the members of the Social Revolutionary Party. V. Volodarsky, the Petrograd commissar of propaganda, and M. S. Uritzky, chairman of the Petrograd Cheka, were assassinated. Assassination attempts were made against Lenin, and the German Ambassador, Mirbach, was murdered. These were acts of factions of the S.R. rather than of the party itself. Social Revolutionaries would, perhaps, have hesitated to apply with equal effort the same violent tactics of terror against a government born in a revolution as they applied to the autocratic Tsarist regime. But even if they had decided in favor of terror tactics, they would never have had the chance to carry them out. Arrests, imprisonment, and mass terror by the government was again their tragic destiny. The attempt against Lenin by Dora Kaplan and the killing of the German ambassador were exceptional. Now the fury of mass terror and exile removed this party from the arena of the Revolution.

Former Fighters and Democracy in Poland

In Poland, the members of the once revolutionary faction (so-called FRAK) of the Polish Socialist Party returned from Siberian prisons, liberated by the Revolution. Others were released from the armed services. Some of them now took responsible positions as members of the parliament (Sejm), trade unions, and municipal government. Thomas Arciszewski, a former hero of the anti-tsarist struggles later to be Polish prime minister, was elected to the parliament. His special interest was a children's aid society. Jan Kwapinski, at one time a leader of direct action involving terroristic anti-tsarist tactics, was now a member of the trade union. He later became mayor of Lodz, the textile center and second largest

Polish city, and was also a minister in the Polish government. Joseph Pilsudski, the leader of the FR revolutionary faction, who directed the action at Bezdany against soldiers in a Russian train and commanded the Polish Legion during the war, was the first chief of state.

It is evident that once the political and historical situation that had been conducive to direct, terroristic action was changed, most of those then engaged in revolutionary activities, involving tactics of individual violence and guerrilla warfare, have afterwards shown political statesmanship and moderation, and have defended democratic processes.

Former Komitadji in a New Bulgaria

This experience described above has not been limited to Russian and Polish revolutionaries. Kostia Todorov, once a leader of the *komitadji* in Macedonia, who once participated in an attempt to assassinate Sultan Abdul Hamid, later became Bulgarian minister to Belgrade, and afterwards was undersecretary for foreign affairs in the government of Stambuliiski. Under the latter's guidance, Todorov actively supported a peaceful policy with Bulgaria's neighbors, especially in the vital area of the Yugoslav–Bulgarian borderland, Macedonia. Stambuliiski and Todorov now cooperated with the Yugoslav government in defending the local population against the raids and assassinations of the Bulgarian *komitadji*, who of all terrorists perhaps continued their activities for the longest time.

Effect of Former Patterns of Violence
on the Political Behavior of Leaders

Those revolutionaries who were dedicated to democratic principles or to socialist or peasant ideologies generally rejected violence as a means of political power, and tended to promote progressive and humane changes. This was not true, however, of all terrorist groups. A faction of IMRO, the Macedonian–Bulgarian organization, continued its terroristic activities. Former members of the fighting squads of the Polish Socialist Party could now be found in municipal government, as burgomasters of towns, administrators of social security.

members of parliament, and in many other civic or state functions. During the period of their underground life, they discussed, both in their circles of self-education and in underground
publications, the problems of establishing and maintaining
representative institutions. Now this activity was proving to
have been fruitful. One of the achievements of the democratic
Polish socialists, among whom were the prominent old fighters
who had used the tactics of terror, was to promote a social
legislation which was not a "paper" legislation, but a well-ad-
ministered social security and social health insurance program.

The old struggles, however, left certain characteristics, as
manifested in their analytical skills and political behavior, and
even in their daily habits. Many of them understood violence.
They could see the dangers approaching when Hitler came to
power, while many statesmen and democratic parliamentarians
of other countries either viewed Nazism through rigid theories
and concepts or were victims of a wishful thinking that was a
reflection of their own fear. The old revolutionaries also knew
how and when to use a variety of tactical means, including
violence itself. They were courageous and skillful, yet nonviolent, when fighting for restoration of democratic rule in their
own country during dictatorship. They used whatever remained of representative institutions to maintain and extend
democratic ways, and organized demonstrations and political
strikes. When the Germans overran their country, the same
men who led the Revolution of 1905, Thomas Arciszewski
and Casimir Puzak, organized the extensive network of the
Polish underground, and resumed the guerrilla and terroristic
struggle, including the use of individual, tactical terror against
the invaders.

Significance of the Political Situation

The foregoing discussion has shown the primary significance of socio-political conditions as a causative factor in the
use of tactical terror. It must be stressed, however, that the
experience described above is also determined by cultural
conditions, and that it is limited in time. It has proven valid
only in a limited number of specific cases, wherein men of an
unusual type of personality have effected a democratic resist-

ance against autocracy in certain countries. Representative government and independence were the primary goals of the terroristic struggles. In those cases where these goals were achieved, the former fighters moved into positions either of political leadership of government or of opposition to it.

New and Old Patterns of Political Assassination

Were the patterns of political assassination, when they reappeared between 1918 and 1939, new, or were the tactics the same but the goals different?

The assassinations were now directed against democratic institutions and their representatives. The tactical and strategic objective of violence was political power for the extreme right and elimination of internal dissenters within the party and of external political opponents without. Democratic institutions had become weak, and many governments were frequently unable to cope with urgent socio-political problems. Parliaments, having become coalitions of shaky majorities composed of numerous minority parties, or of parties divided into hostile camps, were frequently unable to pass laws and form governments. In such a climate of weakness and sometimes of disintegration, assassination reappeared in a new pattern of violence against democratic leaders. However, until the German conquest, assassinations were surprisingly infrequent in the northern part of Eastern Europe, and also in Yugoslavia and Greece. Wherever assassination and tactical terrorism reappeared, it was closely related to an increase of interethnic and interideological tensions.

In the Baltic countries (after the period of unrest and the subsequent formation of republics) assassinations were practically absent; in fact, there were no major assassinations until the German takeover. In Poland, which had had a tradition of insurrections and terror against foreign rule, political assassinations were rare, and the practice of tactical terror was limited to the nationalistic Ukrainian secret organizations that were responsible for the assassinations of the minister of interior, Pieracki, and of a leading proponent of Polish-Ukrainian rapprochement and reconciliation, Holowko.

In Bulgaria, however, IMRO had split into factions, with its dominant anti-Yugoslav section leaning toward extreme nationalism and continuing its irredentist activities. Internal terror decimated its ranks, even while it continued its tactical terrorism against moderate and progressive Bulgarian statesmen.

During the late 1920's, radical nationalistic movements with fascist leanings appeared in Yugoslavia, Rumania, Hungary, and, later, in Poland. These pro-fascist parties exercised intimidation and violence against democratic representatives and national minorities. A nationalistic and Catholic right-wing, pro-German, and separatist party became increasingly significant in Slovakia. The Rumanian Iron Guard and the Croat Ustasha widely practiced all kinds of violence, including terror, in a ruthless form.

Isolated Political Assassination and Tactical Terror in Poland

Systematic tactical violence may be defined as terror. In Eastern Europe and Russia, far more than in the United States, political assassinations have been ideological, i.e., organized and executed by well-organized groups. Yet there is no evidence—as far as this writer knows—of such organization in the assassination of Gabriel Narutowicz, the first elected Polish President of the Republic, in 1922. Narutowicz was elected by a coalition vote of the parties of the left and center, and also by ethnic minorities. A campaign of defamation, led by the newspapers of the nationalistic right, increased the tension and enhanced the buildup of hostility and hatred. This psychological pre-assassination stage, in the form of a campaign of defamation, seems to be a seminal force in isolated political assassination. It breaks the weak, rational restraints and the control of emotions, exculpates the assassin before his act, and seems to promise him a hero's place in the pages of history. There was such an emotional and psychological climate created by the parties of the extreme right in the case of Narutowicz's murder, but—so it seems today—there was no connection whatever between the parties of the right and the perpetration of the act itself.

The assassination of Narutowicz, who was a friend and choice of Pilsudski, left an impress on Polish interwar history. Pilsudski, the leader of socialist resistance against tsarist rule, commander of the Polish Legion during World War I, organizer of the Polish armed forces, and the first chief of state of his country, never recovered from this tragedy. His attitude toward the right-wing parties that opposed his rather liberal reforms from the beginning, was now changed into a far deeper distrust of the Polish nation and doubts about the political maturity of sections of his country. The assassination also made him doubt whether representative institutions would be feasible in such a divided nation. The country had been divided previously, and now old hostilities were resurfacing. The old fighters against tsarist rule, who once used the tactics of violence, were now defending democratic institutions and warning against hatred and violence.

After the political coup of Marshall Pilsudski in 1926, the former chief of the Air Force General Wlodzimierz Zagorski was imprisoned in 1927 and disappeared under mysterious circumstances.[61] It is generally believed that he was assassinated by some of Pilsudski's adherents. The case was never fully clarified, and was a stain on the record of this political group, which was regarded as responsible for the death of one of their opponents.

These are the only major Polish cases of assassination within the 20 years of Poland's independence. It should also be remembered that some members of a secret Ukrainian nationalistic organization assassinated two representatives of the Polish government; in 1931, Tadeusz Holowko, a man of progressive traditions and leanings, with a long pro-Ukrainian record, and, in 1934, Bronislaw Pieracki, a harsh minister of the interior.

Yugoslavia and the Ustasha; Assassinations of King Alexander and Stephen Radic

Interethnic tensions and hostilities, intensified and manipulated by pro-fascist or nationalistic parties, resulted in the reappearance of individual violence in Yugoslavia, in a far more intense form than in Poland.

After the *coup d'etat* of King Alexander, Ante Pavelich founded a fascist and terroristic Croatian organization, *Hrvatski Ustasha* (Croatian Upriser). The party was organized along totalitarian lines. Its goal was the creation of a separate Croatian state, carved out of Yugoslavia—a totalitarian Croatia. The Ustashi had camps in Hungary and Italy, and were supported by both governments. From there, they tried to organize raids into Yugoslavia. The Croatian fascists also engaged in terror. In October 1934, they succeeded in assassinating King Alexander of Yugoslavia and French Foreign Minister Louis Barthou.

After the invasion of Yugoslavia by the Axis armies, a kingdom of Croatia was established under an Italian protectorate. The Ustashi, headed by Ante Pavelich, formed a government, and extended their terroristic tactics to include mass terror. Their cruelty towards the innocent Serbian, Greek-Orthodox population can only be compared with the German massacre of the Jews in Poland and Russia, or with the Turkish massacres of the Armenians. The Ustashi were responsible for the genocidal extermination of over 500,000 Serbs (according to estimates). They also operated the notorious concentration camp at Jasenovac in Slovenia.[62] The Ustashi, like the Nazis, the Rumanian Iron Guard, and other fascist groups, used terror tactics for the attainment of power, and mass terror for consolidation.

The new Croatian organization of the extreme right, formed by some of the former members of the Ustasha, have continued to the present time (autumn, 1968) their tactics of terror. An intensification of violent activities in Yugoslavia was noticeable in the summer of 1968. The new Croatian nationalistic groups violently oppose the liberal and federalistic policy of Tito's government, and would prefer a program for a totalitarian Croatian state. They operate, according to West German sources, from Germany (Bavaria) and Spain.[63]

Although the Ustashi reflected an extreme fascist trend, ethnic tensions and hatred have always been intense in Yugoslavia, which is, after all, a union of several South Slavic nations. The democratic Croatian peasant party was itself under continuous pressure from Serbian nationalists. Stephen Radic, one of the most promising democratically oriented Yugoslav statesmen, was shot in the Yugoslav Parliament with two of his followers, by a Montenegrin member, in front of the entire assembly.[64] This political murder was an isolated act, not a result of organized and systematic tactics. The intensification of ethnic hostilities and manipulation of hatred are both powerful instruments in politics which easily accomplish the desired end—the generation of violence.

The Rumanian Iron Guard and Terror—
Assassinations of Iorga, Duca, and Others

Extreme nationalism and antisemitism produced in Rumania a native form of fascism, the Iron Guard. The Iron Guard derived its tactical strength, as did most of the fascist parties, from ethnic, religious, and racial tensions. It utilized these tensions for direct action in the form of mass and individual violence. The Iron Guard was founded in 1924 as the "Legion of the Archangel Michael" by Cornelia Zelea Codreanu, who was of Ukrainian-German origin. Nationalistic and rabidly antisemitic, the Iron Guardists had a substantial following in the Rumanian universities. In their ruthless activities they practiced a variety of violent tactics, inciting the population to pogroms and outrages against Jews, democrats, and moderates who opposed them. Fascist students and Iron Guardists, in open disregard of the law and of the elementary rights of others, shot down public officials, and even fellow students. Codreanu shot down the prefect Manciu in court (1924), participated in the assassination of Prime Minister Ion Duca (1933), and finally, in 1938, was killed with 13 other guardists "while trying to escape."[65] Again, in 1937, terrorists attempted to assassinate a courageous rector of the University of Yassi because of his opposition to antisemitic terrorism.

In 1936, a student, Mikhail Stelescu, who had resigned from the organization, was killed in a hospital in Bucharest by 10 Iron Guardists. The assassins were students from 19 to 23 years of age.[66] The University of Bucharest could conduct classes only with difficulty in 1936. Student strikes and antisemitic incidents were continuous. When General Antonescu took over the government of Rumania in 1940, the Iron Guardists murdered more than 60 political prisoners and kidnapped and cruelly murdered the leading Rumanian historian, Professor Nicola Iorga, who was a former Rumanian prime minister and himself a nationalist. A leading peasant party economist, Virgil Madgearu, met the same fate. Outrages against Jews followed afterwards.

This is only a random sample of the numerous killings and outrages perpetrated by the Iron Guard. The fascists found support among the students. Their goals were expansionistic, nationalistic, and antisemitic, and their animosity was directed against moderate and liberal statesmen, who, in spite of the terror in 1938, gave at least legally equal rights to minorities through a nationality statute.[67]

Foreign Support

The new terroristic fascist groups were recruited mainly from the nationalistic educated classes, university students, the *declasses* who had never finished their academic education, and former army officers. Together they formed a certain cohesive class of marginals, uprooted, inspired by fascism and its successes. They were outside the ruling elite. In times of growing unemployment among the educated and lack of job opportunities for young graduates, the new fascist movement had its promise and attraction. Universities, with their traditional curriculum and petrified structure, offered, at graduation, few choices of practical employment. In addition to the socio-economic situation, extreme nationalism, manipulated by powerful political parties and at various times by some of the East European governments, contributed to a climate of ethnic tension of high psychological intensity. Hostilities and aggressive urges at such moments were easily released and channeled toward targets pointed out by the fascist party. The party's tactic was terror. Thus, violence and terror were natural conductors for aggressive impulses—they supplied the avenues of release and satisfaction. Such action was promising in terms of glory and success, powerful fascist states supplied the evidence to support this belief.

Terroristic movements on a large scale usually had a strong outside support in the form of money, weapons, and printed material from abroad. This type of tactic is rather expensive political business, involving as it does a small army of professionals. Money was frequently collected abroad or was supplied by foreign governments. Italy, Germany, and Hungary were such bases for the fascist terroristic movements in the Balkans.

The Soviet Union

Political assassination in the Soviet Union was institutionalized in the form of mass terror, and legitimized by ideology. It is beyond the scope of this essay to discuss the political assassinations performed on Stalin's order in various countries. Stalin's massive scale calls for volumes, not chapters. The assassination of Sergei Kirov in 1934, friend of Stalin and member of the Politburo,[68] was the beginning of the great purges in which thousands of innocent people were executed. The assassination of Kirov still remains a mysterious affair. The purge trials and executions were, in fact, judicial assassinations.

Until this time, however, the mass terror initiated soon after the Soviet seizure of power continued with varying intensity. During the Civil War, White troops, fighting the young Soviet Republic, practiced their own "White terror," and massacred whomever they captured and suspected.

The internecine carnage during the period of the Revolution calls for a special study of the human potentialities for violence and brutality. Individual assassinations in such a climate become, because of sheer numbers, quantitative statistics. In human destiny, an individual act is the measure of the man, and a window to an understanding of his mind. Quantity or vast numbers alone cannot reveal this.

The assassinations of 1918—an attempt by the revolutionary Dora Kaplan on the life of Lenin, and in July the assassination of Count von Mirbach, the German ambassador by social revolutionaries[69]—were rather isolated acts. The motive for the assassination of Mirbach can be understood only within the context of the strange theoretical and tactical thinking of Russian intellectuals. According to Steinberg, the objective of this assassination was to "reestablish the former equilibrium of the Revolution" and remove the German influence from the Russian Revolution. The fury of the Bolshevik terror was later directed against the opposing Russian socialist parties. The mass terror destroyed any compassion for the individual. Numbers were registered, but few were impressed by the massive statistics of human suffering.

World War II: Tactical Terror and Resistance

With the outbreak of World War II and its foreign conquests, the pattern of violence changed. Violence became the primary method of the Germans in dealing with their conquered territories. While the German conquest advanced, a ruthless terroristic regime was imposed by the Ustashi, Iron Guard, and other Axis satellites. Italians in the Balkans were far more moderate, relatively restrained as compared with the Germans, and this was especially true in their dealings with their Croat, Rumanian, and Hungarian allies. Mass murder, massacres, and concentration camps cover the pages of history of this tragic period. Terror as a political means of maintenance and consolidation of power was widely used.

It was impossible during those days to separate terror from mass terror; both were closely related and were only a variation of general tactics. Generally, the fascist conquerors extended individual terror to large proportions (executions of hostages, prominent leaders, etc.). The borderline between terror and mass terror was thus broken.

The conquered nations did respond politically to conquest. Satellite governments appeared in all countries, with the single exception of Poland. At the same time, active resistance appeared in almost all conquered territories.

Resistance to foreign occupation in times of war is tantamount to a second war. Such a type of warfare is complex. The tactical-strategic pattern of resistance had a broad choice of methods. Terror was only one, and a rather ancillary, tactical device of the struggle; it was a part of general warfare, and not a simple assassination. The militants of the resistance sometimes displayed unusual daring, as, for example, the assassination of Reinhard Heydrich, deputy chief of the Gestapo and chief of security police and "genius of the final solution," in May 1942, by members of the Free Czechoslovak Army, who had been parachuted from England.[70]

Terror, especially in countries which had a long revolutionary tradition, now had definite objectives. It was not solely a separate act of vengeance, although the motive of retribution cannot be denied.

First, terror was a powerful weapon of intimidation. The Germans responded to terror with the mass execution of hostages. Yet a Nazi administrator or a Gestapo officer was haunted by the fear that he might not escape the fatal bullet or knife from the avengers of the resistance.

Second, terror, applied as internal terror directed against those regarded as or accused of being traitors, informers, or blackmailers, was a coercive sanction. It was one of the methods of maintaining national solidarity in the resistance, by eliminating the corrupt elements and intimidating those who were weaker.

Third, terror was an important act of retribution, an act of justice against those who were guilty of oppressive and cruel acts.

Fourth—and this was one of its most important functions —terror through hearsay spread general fear, an intense fear, perhaps even more so than mass terror. Grapevine rumor spread the news rapidly, attention was usually focused on some frightful detail, which was especially effective in terms of the psychological vulnerability of the subject. Thus, terror became a powerful device for intimidating the conqueror through sourceless reports.

Finally, terror was a means of eliminating decision-makers and leaders. The most dramatic case of such an attempt was the conspiracy of some German officers in their attempt to assassinate Hitler.

The Patterns of Resistance

Tactical terror at that time had one element in common in all East European and Russian resistance movements. It was primarily (although not solely) directed against a foreign conqueror, and thus it had local native support, which gave it a strong legitimacy in terms of national shared values as well as the sympathy of substantial sections of the population.

The patterns of resistance, however, varied from country to country. This was due to differences in historical traditions, skills, personality, and the specific local conditions of the struggle.

Russia had an impressive and effective tradition of partisan warfare, extending back long before the time of Napoleon's invasion. The Cossacks, although they were Ukrainians, had throughout history a reputation for unorthodox tactics. The major pattern of Soviet resistance was primarily straight partisan warfare.[71] The partisan units were sometimes built around a kind of specialized skeleton structure of regular soldiers (this was especially the case in the other occupied countries). The units were usually led by army officers. The network was organized and controlled by the Soviet authorities, so that not only was this a spontaneous movement, it also represented an organized and centrally directed type of warfare. The main tactics were guerrilla, not terror, tactics.

In the Balkans, the Yugoslav underground was organized in guerrilla units. The old traditions of fighting the Turks in small bands supplied a general pattern of action. Again, terror was not a major tactical device.

In Yugoslavia, fratricidal struggles between the Chetniks, led by General Draja Mikhailovich, and partisan groups, led by Tito, as well as the massacres of the Ustashi, resulted in a human catastrophe of historical magnitude. Internal terror and the elimination of prominent partisans of the Chetniks or Ustashi in towns or villages also took place. This holocaust was precipitated in the midst of war and invasions by the Germans and Italians. Old hostilities between the Albanians and Serbs in Kossovo revived. The Serbs were killed by Hungarians in Novi Sad and by the Ustashi in a Serbian land overrun by fascists. It was a genocidal slaughter of the Serbs; mass assassination had subsumed individual assassination.[72]

The Polish Underground and Legitimation of Terror

The Polish underground had traditions extending back more than a hundred years when the war started. These traditions were revived almost immediately after the country had been invaded and occupied.

The first meetings which led to the formation of a Polish underground began as early as October 1939.[73] The Poles organized an underground state, with courts of justice, schools, political authorities of their own, and an underground Home Army (AK). The basic pattern of an underground state headed by an underground national government was established for the first time in Poland during the insurrection of 1863. During World War II, the major political parties formed the Council of National Unity—a kind of underground parliament—which in turn elected the "Home Council of Ministers," composed of a vice-prime minister and three ministers.[74] The home authorities had their counterpart in London, where the Polish government in exile resided, headed by a president and prime minister, together with the Polish Army in exile. The legal continuity of the Polish state was thus maintained. The decision of the Polish underground authorities and the sentences of the underground courts had their legitimacy in terms of their acceptance by the members of the Resistance. The sentences of the underground courts were announced with the traditional "In the name of the Polish Republic." The underground state had its department of justice, headed by the former dean (president) of the Warsaw Bar, attorney Leon Nowodworski. The judges were carefully selected Polish professional judges. Sentences had to be confirmed by the competent District Plenipotentiary of the underground and then sent to the District Director of Civil Resistance. The District Director finally transmitted the decision to fighting teams, for execution.[75]

Many of these sentences were carried out. Before this was done, the commanding officer made an attempt to read the sentence to the condemned.

On June 15, 1943 the Gestapo killed all persons gathered for a wedding celebration at Zbydniow, except the young bridal couple, who had gone to the town photographer to have their pictures taken, and two young boys hidden in the attic. The death sentence was passed against Gestapo official, Fuldner, who was in charge of this outrage, by an underground court. A few days later, while he was conferring with two visiting Nazis from Cracow, a group of underground fighters surrounded the house, and the commander of the group read him the sentence. He was then shot in the presence of the Nazi officials, who were asked to report this to the governor. The chief of civil resistance, Korbonski, radioed the story to London. The news about the execution of the sentence was later broadcast from London.[76] There were many cases similar to this. Sentences were also carried out against those regarded as traitors.

This type of individual violence was indeed a kind of self-defense. In terms of the resistance groups, headed by the Council of National Unity, this was a legitimate way of enforcing justice. The act had legitimacy in the eyes of large sections of the population, which stood behind the Council of National Unity. However, there were many assassinations in this ruthless struggle which did not have legitimacy of quasi-judicial proceedings. There were also fratricidal incidents.

The communist resistance groups organized in a "People's Army" (Armia Ludowa, AL) were relatively small and weak, as compared with the AK. Their tactics were primarily directed toward partisan warfare.

A small but aggressive fascist and antisemitic Polish underground organization killed several prominent democratic leaders and Jews. Various bands also assumed the role of "independent" underground groups. Waclaw Zagorski, a captain in the Polish underground home army, wrote later:

> We all tried a taste of the underground, and in this jungle we all believed at one time that the day would come when no one would be persecuted, followed, and trapped like an animal, no one would kill anybody, no one would need a disguise or a false passport, or need to look for a shelter in a strange home.
> Our underground paths have crossed and led to various places. Some in this struggle have forgotten their real goal; for them it was only important who kills whom, not who instigates the oppression of man against man; their goal was only their own freedom. From the underground they went into the depth of the jungle . . . .[77]

Zagorski again touched the great dilemma of political and ideological assassination; of moral ends and destructive means, of intentions, visions of a better world, and unanticipated consequences. Dilemmas of similar nature tormented Savinkov, the Russian revolutionary of a generation before.

The rule of the Nazis in the countries they occupied was characterized by violence, massacres, genocide, and mass extermination. Individual assassination, with the sanction of the German state and its cruel laws, was a part of this policy of racial extermination. Mass and individual terror became routine. Were these acts of individual, ideological assassination judicial murders? A dogmatic mind may argue that they were the legal acts of public authorities, supported by the laws of the conquerors.

The massacre of about 10,000 Polish officers in Katyn was probably executed by Soviet authorities under an order (perhaps misunderstood) from Stalin. The Soviets directed the large-scale deportations and mass imprisonment of Polish citizens. Stalin had treated his own countrymen in a similar way. This was the Soviet method of maintaining and consolidating power. Isolated cases of assassination also occurred. Marian

Bogatko, husband of the authoress Wanda Wasilewska, was shot to death in Lwow in 1940. Polish underground circles suspected that this was done by the Soviet political police. Bogatko had publicly expressed strong criticism of the Soviet occupation. Yet one cannot exclude the possibility that this was an act of some political groups, although terror was not practiced in this area and at this time by the Poles. Two prominent Jewish socialist leaders, Alter and Ehrlich, were executed by Soviet authorities—after a trial. These cases of political violence against individuals were different in their sociological nature, in the motivation of the actors, in scope, and in terms of juridical norms. Their quasi-legal basis does not alter the fact that they were political acts, perpetrated by political decision makers, for political objectives. The purpose was to remove any kind of opposition and any potential critics or competitors.

We have described in this short discussion a difficult and dangerous borderline, wherein a legal act is immoral and a moral act is illegal in terms of those who control power and the means of violence. Only a limpid moral judgment and humaneness can suggest in such cases the true ethical distinction.

7. Overview: Russian, Balkan, and Polish Terrorism

Causation of Terror

Whether an assassination is vindicated by public opinion and ultimately legitimated depends upon the historical context. This is also important for determining whether the sociological situation is conducive to political-ideological assassination or to systematic terror.

We shall limit ourselves here primarily to the factual material already presented in this study. The cases which were discussed occurred at certain times and in certain political cultures. The causative factors might be different in other political cultures and in other periods of time. Furthermore, a moral distinction must be made between terror applied against a domestic autocracy or against a foreign occupying power and terror directed against representatives of democratic institutions.

Causes of Terror Against
Autocracy and Foreign Rule

In the Polish and Russian cases, two major socio-political conditions could be identified from past experience which resulted in terroristic response: (a) oppressive foreign rule and conquest, or (b) oppressive domestic rule without any expectation of institutionalized, legalized avenues of change. We may call this a dead-end situation.

What is meant by "oppressive"? It means acts of physical brutality, including murder, limitations of freedom, humiliation of persons, economic exploitation, denial of elementary economic opportunities, and confiscation of property. Definitions cannot illustrate the humiliation and deprivation the Armenians and Bulgarians suffered under Turkish rule, or the Serbs under Croatian Ustasha government, or the Jews in Germany, or the areas of Eastern Europe occupied by the Germans or Soviets. The moral, political, and economic subordination of ethnic groups or of a nation by extreme coercive measures, to the point at which an oppressed people views such conditions as no longer tolerable, results—under certain circumstances—in situations in which revolutionary committees may favor the choice of violence as the only adequate response.

The chances of such a response are enhanced under foreign occupation. We shall call this factor "sociological," because essentially it arises out of ethnic or class subordination or stratification as well as from foreign control of political and social behavior through extreme coercive measures.

The case of Poland prior to 1918 is quite illustrative. In Galicia, the Austrian-occupied part of Poland, tactical terror was absent, while in the Russian part terror was directed against important government representatives. Russian rule was oppressive and autocratic relative to the rule in Galicia, because the latter enjoyed a large measure of autonomy and individual political rights. Later, terror was revived by the Polish underground fighters during the brutal German occupation.

In the Balkan area, the systematic terror at first employed against Turkish officials in Macedonia was later institutionalized by the terroristic organizations of IMRO. Their terroristic activities continued, but without their former sociological justification. The Armenian terrorism of the Dashnaks was primarily a response to Turkish massacres and persecutions. During World War II, terrorism in the Balkans was reactivated in a similar way.

The condition generating terroristic action was usually that of a certain high-intensity threshold level of oppression, which theoretically at least could be measured by the enormity of oppressive acts, such as destruction of households, massacre of the subjugated people, the number of persons of the subjugated ethnic group who were political prisoners, and the limitations imposed on freedom of movement and freedom of expression. Arbitrary values can be assigned to each type of oppression and a composite index formed of all those types of occurrences. Yet a quantitative index cannot express the qualitative nature of human suffering and humiliation. Difficult as it is to evaluate the nature of oppression, however, the fact that there are various intensity levels seems to be obvious. Fascist Italian rule, for example, oppressive as it was, was less oppressive for the Jewish people than that of the Nazis.

Factor Analysis and Model A

The sociological factor is a relevant but not a *sufficient* causal factor; it may even be asked whether it is at *all* times a *necessary* cause. Oppression must be perceived *qua* political oppression by a group of people. Consequently, one of the contributing causal factors of a systematic terror thus far has been the formation or existence of an organized group, guided by an ideology. Ideology determines the strategy and tactics. The terroristic tactic was obviously a consequence of the choice of such a tactic by a party that had definite ideological objectives. This tactic was anchored to those objectives.

The members of the terrorist committee, however, had a choice of alternatives, of which there are always at least two: perish or fight. History might supply cases where man has chosen self-destruction or total submission in the form of slavery rather than direct, armed resistance or action. In some cases, e.g., in the case of the Russian terrorists, there were certain opportunities for effecting change by means of weak representative bodies; or there were other revolutionary alternatives, at least in terms of theory, such as a revolution made by the people, i.e., as a spontaneous act of the masses rather than an act of a few terrorist groups.

We now arrive at the third factor: personality type. The choice of tactics, even under such oppressive conditions as tsarist rule or Nazi occupation, was mostly a voluntaristic act, a consequence of choice. Leaders and militants of strong principles and beliefs, and of a certain personality structure, were those who joined the revolutionary party of the "People's Will" in Russia or the underground Polish movement during World War II.

Where systematic terror was part of the tactics of the struggle against autocracy, these three factors were present: (a) an oppressive sociological situation; (b) existence of a revolutionary party; and (c) existence of "activist" personality types, i.e., persons who took a definite stand in relation to the situation and had, or developed, the will to act.

The revolutionary party operates in a certain socio-political situation, and it both responds to it and tries to affect it. In this sense, there is an interdependence between the situation and the activities of the party. But interdependence does not suggest as yet the causation of terroristic tactics. Causation, in terms of systematic tactical terror, required in our cases the three major causal factors antecedents mentioned above.

We shall now illustrate the causation of systematic terror in Model A.

MODEL A

Causation of Tactical Terroristic Acts Against Foreign Rule or Autocracy

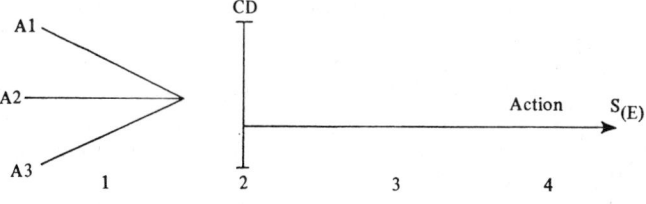

Systematic terroristic acts were the sequence-effect (SE) of the following antecedents.

1. The presence of three antecedents was seminal:
    A1 — Antecedent 1. The perception of socio-political conditions of oppression.
    A2 — Antecedent 2. The existence of a political party with an ideology and the tactics of direct action.
    A3 — Antecedent 3. The presence of activist personality types who are willing to make a political choice and respond with direct action and violence to conditions of oppression.
2.   CD — The choice and decision were made within the conditions which were a result of an interplay of the three factors, A1, A2, and A3, and the terroristic action chosen.
3. Action — Terroristic action followed.
4.   SE — Sequence-effect. The terroristic act was accomplished.

Briefly, the interplay of the three causal factors A1, A2, A3 were necessary, in the cases discussed here, to result in an effect: tactical terror.

Causation of Terror Against Democracy:
the Preassassination Stage

Where the political rights of citizens are respected, as in a democracy, the element of direct, physical oppression, such as in the case of foreign conquest or domestic autocracy, is absent. Even under the rule of the peasant party of Stamboliiski, who was later assassinated by a conspiracy, the government, in spite of all its shortcomings and harsh measures, was far milder than the dictatorship which followed in Bulgaria.

The socio-political antecedents, our sociological determinants in all these cases, are not the same as those necessary in the case of the antiautocratic terror of the tyrannicides. It is quite possible that terroristic action can be started by an extremist party against a strong and vigorous democracy, although this has not happened thus far in Switzerland or England. However, such action usually begins when representative institutions are weak or in decline, or when democratic values have lost their appeal and have ceased to motivate and inspire individuals. Such a situation was called by the French sociologist, Emile Durkheim, *anomie*. In the German Weimar Republic the representative institutions were weak, because, after the castastrophe of the war, the government was unable to cope efficiently with the socio-economic problems of the nation. During this period, two courses of action by parties of the extreme right could be noticed: attacks against and vilification of representative institutions, and a campaign of insults and defamation against the leading persons of democratic persuasion. Whatever the overt or covert objectives of such tactics were, there followed as a consequence an adverse reaction of public opinion toward the Republic. This tactic of moral attack and destruction was intensified: we may call this stage the preassassination stage. At a certain point of this stage, there were attempts to assassinate representatives of democracy. These attempts could sometimes be displaced on other persons, and thus the person singled out in the defamation campaign was not necessarily the object of physical violence. This preassassination technique is quite frequent—Stalin usually destroyed his opponents morally prior to their physical destruction.

Is such a campaign conscious or not? Is it directed or spontaneously formed? It is not easy to give a general answer. Every case requires a careful study. The process of defamation has appeared frequently in the past, during the preassassination stage, in a variety of forms: articles in newspapers, animadversions in public speeches and private gossip, posters, and inscriptions on walls, subways, and railroad stations.

Before the assassination of President Gabriel Narutowicz in 1922 in Poland, in a preassassination stage, a vituperous defamation campaign was launched against him by the parties of the right. The assassination was an isolated, political act of killing, and not a result of a terroristic tactic. The assassin, Eligius Niewiadomski, believed that he had performed a heroic act and a patriotic duty. There was neither a conspiracy nor an organized terroristic party. But in the climate of vilification, once the political actor was "morally" branded, the psychological restraints of a potential assassin were weakened or even removed. The assassination was now justified; in his view—and in the view of some Polish nationalists—the act had legitimacy. The assassin represented a psychological personality type with certain tendencies, perhaps with subconscious aggressive or even deviant urges. Many such persons walk the streets of large cities. Once a "moral" sanction was given to individual violence by what potential assassins could regard as public opinion or political authority, aggression was released, and sometimes was probably displaced on other persons rather than on the "target-persons" of the defamation propaganda.

Violence and disorders resulted in the past in a situation of relative insecurity and disintegration or weakening of democratic institutions. In such a climate assassination appeared. In Germany a process of defamation of Rathenau preceded the murder of this prominent German statesman.

Where can we draw a borderline between bold, legitimate criticism and defamation? It is difficult to define defamation precisely, nor can the practice of it be effectively prohibited. To prohibit it would destroy the will and courage to criticize legitimately. Perhaps eventually it would even destroy freedom of speech. The practice of defamation is rather a symptom than a cause.

The weakening or breakdown of democratic institutions was not a sole or an isolated antecedent of violence: The difficulties in the functioning of democratic institutions were used by antidemocratic parties in the tactics of eroding them.

A terroristic tactic is also a matter of decision and choice, made by the leaders of a party. Such a tactic is a consequence of a set of values or of an ideology. Again, a certain type of personality must be present, for not every member of a rightist party would be willing to make such a decision.

We may now illustrate the analysis of the causation of tactical terror and political assassination in a democracy in Model B.

MODEL B

Causation of Individual Violence as a Tactic
Against Democratic Institutions

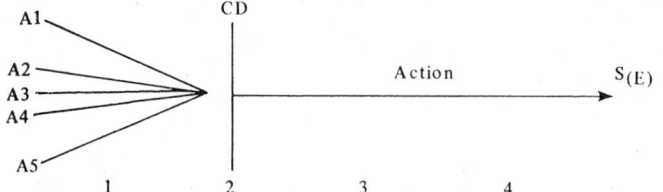

1. Political assassination of democratic representatives is a sequence-effect (SE) of the following antecedents:

    A1 — Socio-political determinant. Weakening of shared democratic values and/or crisis of democratic institutions.

    A2 — Existence of a party or a temporary conspiracy with the ideology and tactics of direct violence.

    A3 — Preassassination process of defamation and actions of the party directed against democratic institutions.

    A4 — Presence of certain personality types, with propensities toward overt aggression once the foregoing antecedents are present.

2.   CD — The choice and decision are made by the terrorist group or terrorist party.

3. Action — Organization and release of violence against target-person.

4.   SE — Assassination follows as the sequence and effect of the antecedents and decisions.

Antecedents are the necessary but not sufficient set of causal variables. The will, which reflects the personality of the decision-makers and affects the choice and decision of tactics, is a trigger and a necessary causal variable.

The terroristic action may be planned by the party. In the past, however, the parties were frequently inspired, supported, or even directed by an outside government.

A General Hypothesis

The experience of a century in violent political behavior (terror and political assassination) in Russia and Eastern Europe, including the Balkans, suggests some rather striking but tentative findings, or hypotheses:

1. Assassinations and individual terror have appeared or increased in the past in Eastern Europe (including the Balkans) in periods of intensification of ethnic tensions (Yugoslavia, Rumania, Bulgaria, Poland). Socio-economic tensions before or during the terror did not result in tactics of individual violence.

2. Ideological-political inequalities and tensions rather than social and economic conditions contributed to revolutionary

situations in which terror was waged by underground parties in Russia (in the 19th and early 20th centuries). In Russian revolutionary theory, terror and violence were primarily legitimated as tactics toward achievement of political objectives (representative government, democracy, or dictatorship) and not of socio-economic goals.

Duration

How long does terror last as a systematic tactic? In the past, the duration has varied. The longest duration of tactics of individual terror in Russia and Eastern Europe was about 40 years (IMRO), and of mass terror in Europe 600 years (Inquisition).

Once terror begins it is very difficult to arrest it. Assassination calls for vengeance or retaliation, as terror releases counterterror. A tragic chain of reciprocity, once initiated, cannot be easily stopped, since it is motivated by strong emotions. A short, tentative table of the durations of terroristic actions illustrates this. The data on duration are not precise, but are gross approximations.

Duration of Tactics of Individual Terror Against Autocracy and Foreign Rule (Approximations)

Polish Socialist Party under Russian occupation	4–5 years
Armenian Dashnaks	25–30 years
Russian Populists and Social Revolutionaries	30 years
IMRO (Internal Macedonian Revolutionary Organization) (periods of struggle against foreign rule and domestic moderate governments before and after two Balkan wars and World War I)	40 years (and more)

Duration of Terroristic Tactics Against Democracy and Moderate Governments (Approximations)

Croatian Ustasha	35 years
Macedonian IMRO (2nd period)	20 years
Rumanian Iron Guard	15 years

Institutionalization

Both terror and mass terror have had periods of long duration. Once the terroristic group is institutionalized, terror activity becomes a part of "institutional" behavior; it creates values of its own, and has its own discipline and routines. Institutions, especially bureaucracies of mass terror, have a tendency to perpetuate and extend the life of their organization. They resist termination. After institutionalization, professionalization of terroristic parties appears. Terroristic activity for those who are actively engaged in it becomes a full-time occupation; their livelihood depends on the party. This tactic requires careful preparation, planning, and deadly skills. It necessitates secrecy, which again conflicts with regular, daily, 8-hour employment.

In most of the cases discussed in this essay, the core of the terroristic organization became professional. As the years passed—some of those organizations lasted for two or even three revolutionary generations—this type of revolutionary activity became a way of life.

Once the socio-political situation changed, at least in the cases of the Russian Social Revolutionaries and the Poles, the revolutionaries knew how to terminate their terroristic activities. They became members of representative institutions and channeled their energies into building a short-lived democratic society. But some could hardly adjust to new conditions. In other cases, however, as in the case of certain sections of the Macedonian IMRO, the objectives were changed and terroristic activities did not cease. The professionals continued to apply terror in internal and external struggles.

The extension of the duration of terroristic tactics was also dependent on the response in the social base, i.e., the response of the social class the party claimed to represent, or in other cases, the response of social or ethnic groups. Some of the terroristic parties had stronger support than others. At certain times, the terroristic activities of the underground movement in Poland had, in the cities at least, broad national support. IMRO at the turn of the century, in its terroristic activities against the Turks, had the support of the Bulgarian peasantry. The Black Hand of Serbia had strong influence in the army and among the younger educated classes. This class or ethnic support contributed to the strength of the terroristic parties and to their duration.

But the major factors of duration were: (1) the sociological situation within which the party operated; (2) the nature of the party organization and its ideological appeal; and (3) the

personalities of the party's leadership and militants, as well as
its recruits of new members.

Diffusion of the Terroristic Pattern

Once terror was initiated in one country, the news was
disseminated abroad, so that violence was emulated elsewhere.
In Eastern Europe, the Russian "People's Will" and the Social
Revolutionary Party were influential outside of the country
Since the 1890's their tactics had been assimilated by revolutionary parties in Eastern Europe, the Balkans, and Russian
Armenia. A kind of political style developed, which to a
certain extent was a result of terroristic tactics. This type of
tactics imposed—as a condition of individual and group survival—a certain style of political behavior, even a style of
personal life. After the situation had changed and the way of
life of the militants had been modified, something yet remained of the past.

Those who fought against autocracy by way of assassination
were frequently men and women of high principles and education. For some, this was a tragic and traumatic experience that
left lasting impressions. The terroristic fascist and authoritarian parties moved from terror to massacres, mass terror, and
genocide, which have changed the history and destiny of nations and contributed to the formation of hostile attitudes and
painful memories which are difficult to eradicate or alter. Yet
after World War II, mankind did recover rather miraculously
from this ghastly past, even if on a superficial level only.

Some Reflections

The use of terror, violence, and political assassination on a
systematic scale, directed against democratic and free societies, debilitates slowly the entire political fabric and erodes
representative institutions. It forces, sooner or later, a resolute
action in defense of democracy, which may also result in
limitation of freedom and establishment of repressive measures that are contradictory to democracy; or, an intimidated
populace may yield to a vocal and aggressive minority.

Democracy, by definition, is a political system in which respect for a dissenting minority and government by consent, not by violence, are fundamental premises. Democracies, conceived as governments of free peoples, never have developed adequate ways of combatting continuous systematic violence, and particularly individual tactical terror and assassination. Free societies view individual political assassination as an exceptional, isolated occurrence. We believe that a country in which a citizen enjoys freedom and relative welfare should be free of violence. Current experience seems not to confirm fully such an assumption. Political violence has appeared, even in societies in which personal freedom was a supreme value.

It is of paramount significance to understand better the conditions that are conducive to political assassination, because the control of such conditions suggests that a humane policy of prevention is far more preferable and workable than a policy of repression. Political situations can be manipulated, however, and small terroristic groups may operate for a time in a democratic society by using their political rights as a shield.

The lessons of the past are a message of warning: once the politics of violence and terror is established, it is difficult to reestablish representative institutions that will function as well as they did previously. Violence creates conditions in which an arrogant and brutal minority can seize power and rule over an intimidated and passive population for many years.

Only a few great civilizations, and even these for rather short periods in history, were able to maintain governments based on democratic legitimacy, free elections, government by consent, and the protection of dissident minorities. Democracies decline by the slow erosion of faith in the efficacy of their institutions and by means of violence. An understanding of the conditions in which individual violence grows, the ways by which it can be controlled by democratic means, the setting of limits for violent political behavior, and defining the conditions under which force must be used to protect representative institutions, are areas requiring calm judgment, investigation, serious thinking, and the advocacy of wise and humane proposals.

References

1. Jacob Burkhardt, *The Age of Constantine* (New York: Doubleday, 1956), pp. 266, 271, 277.
2. Harold Livermore, *A History of Spain* (New York: Grove Press, 1960), p. 67.
3. L. S. Stavrionos, *The Balkans Since 1453* (New York: Rhinehart, 1958), p. 159.
4. William S. Haas, *Iran* (New York: Columbia University Press, 1946), pp. 95ff. See the dynasties of Safarid and Rayars, which span almost 350 years.
5. Jacob Burkhardt, *The Civilization of the Renaissance in Italy* (English ed.; New York: Harper & Brothers, 1958), I, p. 22.
6. *Ibid.,* pp. 24–25.
7. Niccolo Machiavelli, *The Prince* (New York: Modern Library, 1940), p. 62.
8. Niccolo Machiavelli, "Discorsi Sopra la Prima Deca di Tito Livio," in *Tutte Le Opere* (Florence: Barbera, 1928), p. 212.
9. Stepniak, *Underground Russia* (New York: Charles Scribner's Sons, 1892), pp. 32, 257.
10. Nicolas Morozov, *Terroricheskaya Borba* [Terroristic Struggle], published in London in 1880, reprinted in *Da Zdrastuyet Narodnaya Volya* (Paris, 1907), pp. 48ff. This essay on terror was regarded 50 years ago as a bibliographical rarity.
11. Feliks Gross, *Seizure of Political Power* (New York: Philosophical Library, 1957), pp. 98–139.
12. I.N. Steinberg, *In the Workshops of the Revolution* (New York and Toronto: Rhinehart & Company, 1953), pp. 134ff.
13. K. Kautsky, *Terrorismo E Communismo* (Milan: Bocca, 1946), pp. 34–35. Originally written in 1919; also an English edition. This writer used the edition which was available at this time.
14. Albert Camus, "The Just," in *Collected Plays,* translated by Stuart Gilbert, (London: Hamish Hamilton, 1965).
15. Steinberg, *op. cit.,* footnote 12, pp. 128–131.
16. *Ibid.,* pp. 144–145.
17. Leon Trotsky, *Terrorism and Communism* (University of Michigan Press [1920], 1961), pp. 58–59.
18. Fredrick Moore, "The Macedonian Committees and the Insurrection," in Luigi Villari's *The Balkan Question* (New York: Dutton & Company, 1905), pp. 204ff.
19. Gross, *op. cit.,* footnote 11, pp. 101ff.
20. For a history of the Russian revolutionary movement at this time, see Ludwig Kulczycki, *Revolucja Rosyjska* (Lwow: Poloniecki, 1911), Vol. II, Chapters IV–VI, pp. 102–325; Alphons Thun, *Geschichte der Revolutionaren Bewegung in*

Russland (Leipzig: Dunker-Humbolt, 1883), p. 186 (conference at Lipeck and Voronesh); and Gross, *op. cit.,* Chapters V and VI, pp. 81–132.

21. Kulczycki, *op. cit.,* I, p. 457; Thun, *op. cit.,* footnote 20, p. 37.
22. Gross, *op. cit.,* pp. 99–100.
23. Morozov, *op. cit.*
24. Excerpts from an article by Sergei Nechayev in "Narodnaya Rosprava," in V. Burtsev, *Za Sto Lyet* (1800–1896) (London: Russian Free Press Foundation, 1897), pp. 93–94.
25. Gross, *op. cit.,* pp. 109–110.
26. Thomas G. Masaryk, *The Spirit of Russia* (London: Allen and Unwin, 1919), II, p. 107.
27. C. Lombroso and R. Laschi, *Il Delitto Politico e Rivoluzioni* (Turin: Bocca, 1890), p. 229; and especially Appendix III, "The Nobles and Russian Women in Political Movements," which contains a digest of a study by N. W. Tarnovsky on "Modification of Delinquency Patterns According to Social Class," which appeared in *Uridicheskii Viestnik* (Moscow, May 1889). According to it, 25 percent of the women sentenced for political violations were "educated women." (The digest does not specify the level of education.) The fact is, however, that among women sentenced between 1874 and 1883 for common crimes, none had higher education, only 29 had gymnasium (high school), 35 had elementary education and 21,348 were illiterate.
28. Gross, *op. cit.,* "Personality," pp. 14ff.
29. Masaryk, *op. cit.,* footnote 26, Albert Camus, *l'Homme Révolte* (Paris: Gallimard, 1951); Stepniak, *op. cit.,* footnote 9, (also his novels); V. Ropsin (Boris Savinkov), *The Pale Horse* (London: Allen and Unwin, 1918); Nicolas Berdyaev, *The Origin of Russian Communism* (London: Bles, 1955).
30. Morozov, *op. cit.*
31. "The Urgent Note," *Obshchina,* No. 8–9, October 1878, signed by Vera Zazulich, Stepniak (Kravchinski), and others; reprinted also in Burtsev, *Za Sto Lyet.*
32. For full text, see Gross, *op. cit.,* pp. 102ff.
33. The text is quoted here from Masaryk, *op cit.,* II, p. 545 (translation by Eden and Cedar Paul); for early comments and the protest of *Narodnaya Volya* against the assassination of President Garfield, Alphons Thun, *op. cit.,* p. 201; also Gross, *op. cit.,* p. 109.
34. Gross, *op. cit.,* p. 125ff. For details, see Boris Nikolayevski, *Istoria Odnovo Predatiela Terroristy i Politicheskaya Politsia* (Berlin: Petropolis, 1932); Alexander Gerasimov, *Der Kampf Gegen die Erste Russische Revolution* (Berlin, 1934).

35. George Vernadsky, *A History of Russia* (first published by Yale University Press) (New York: New Home Library, 1944), p. 194.

36. The British historian, Sir Bernard Pares, estimated the membership of the "People's Will" in 1881 at about 500, organized in 12 local branches, with special subcommittees. L. Boguczarski, who used sources similar to Kulczycki, suggests that the party by 1881 was far weaker. It had a Central Committee of 28, and did not have more than "several tens" (between 50 and 90) membership. See *Cambridge Modern History* (Macmillan and Cambridge University Press, 1934), XII, p. 310; Boguczarski, "Is Istorii Politicheskoy Borby 80 Godov," *Russkaya Mysl* (April–May 1910), quoted by Kulczycki, *op. cit.*, Vol. II, p. 394.

37. Kulczycki, *op. cit.*, Vol. II, p. 390.

38. *Ibid.*, Vol. II, p. 395.

39. Pares, *op. cit.*, pp. 306ff.

40. Vernadsky, *op. cit.*, pp. 190ff.

41. Adam Ciolkosz, *Zarys Dziejow Socjalizmu Polskiego* (London: Gryf, 1966); Feliks Gross, *The Polish Worker* (New York: Roy, 1945), pp. 107–144.

42. Gross, *The Polish Worker, op. cit.*, footnote 41, pp. 151ff.

43. Tadeusz Jablonski, Zarys Historii P.P.S. (Warsaw, 1946), pp. 44–50; Jan Kwapinski, *Organizacja Bojowa* (London: Foreign Committee of P.P.S., 1943), pp. 15–21; H. Wereszczycki, *Historia Polski, 1864–1918* (Warsaw: Wiedza, 1948), pp. 253ff.; Leon Wasilewski, *Zarys Dziejow Polskiej Partji Socialistyczne* (Warsaw, 1925).

44. William Miller, *The Ottoman Empire and Its Successors* (Cambridge University Press, 1936), pp. 426–430.

45. *Ibid.*, pp. 480–481.

46. *Ibid.*, p. 538; Henry Morgenthau, *The Tragedy of Armenia* (London: Spottswoode, Ballantine and Co. Ltd., 1918); Arnold J. Toynbee, *Armenian Atrocities, The Murder of a Nation* (New York: Hodder and Stoughton, 1915), also *The Treatment of the Armenians in the Ottoman Empire* (London, 1916); Joseph Guttman, *The Beginnings of Genocide, Armenian Massacres in World War I* (Armenian Historical Research Association, 1965), (no place of publication given), contains a collection of documents and the memoirs of Naim Bey.

The Armenian Academy of Science made estimates of the number of victims of the Turkish massacres. It is difficult to check the accuracy of this data. The data may, however, be of interest. Mr. Ara Caprielian, who assisted with dedication and ability my researches in this area, supplied the sources and translations.

A statistical record of Turkish massacres of non-Turks in the Ottoman Empire is as follows:

1822	Greeks massacred on Kios	50,000
1823	Greeks massacred in Misolinki	8,000
1826	Turkified foreign soldiers in Istanbul	25,000
1850	Assyrians in Mosoul	10,000
1860	Armenians and other Christians in Lebanon	12,000
1876	Armenians and Bulgarians in Bulgaria	14,000
1877	Armenians in Bayazid	1,400
1879	Armenians in Alashgerd	1,250
1881	Armenians and other Christians in Alexandria	2,000
1892	Turkified Armenians and foreign soldiers	3,500
1894	Armenians in Sassoun	12,000
1895	Armenians in the provinces of West Armenia	300,000
1896	Armenians in Istanbul	9,570
1896	Armenians in Van	8,000
1903	Armenians, Greeks, Bulgars in Macedonia	14,667
1904	Armenians in Sassoun	5,640
1909	Armenians in Cilicia (Adana)	30,000
1915	Armenians in West Armenia and Turkey	1,500,000
1918–20	Armenians in Kars and Ardahan	50,000
1918	Armenians in and around Baku	30,000
1919	Armenians in Kunvijlar	10,000
1919	Armenians in Cilicia (Adana)	50,000
1921	Armenians in Hajun	20,000
1922	10,000 Armenians and 20,000 other Christians in Izmir	210,000

Aramayis Mnatsaganian, *Hai Jzoghovurdi Voghbergowtiune* [The Tragedy of the Armenian People] (Yerevan, 1965), p. 65. See also Viscount Bryce, "The Future of Armenia," *The Contemporary Review,* CXIV (1918), p. 605.

47. Ara Caprielian, "The Formative Period of Armenian State-hood," unpublished Master's dissertation, Graduate Division of the City College of the City University of New York, December 1, 1966; and "Origins of the Armenian Revolution-ary Federation," term paper presented at this writer's seminar on Russian and East European Social Movements, Graduate School, New York University, December 1967; Louise

Nalbandian, *The Armenian Revolutionary Movement* (Berkeley, 1963).

48. Caprielian, "Origins of the Armenian Revolutionary Federation," *op. cit.,* p. 41.
49. Harold W.V. Temperley, *History of Serbia* (London: Bell & Sons, 1917), pp. 180–195; William Miller, *op. cit.,* p. 57. For the general pattern of violence in Balkan politics, see Joseph S. Roucek, *Balkan Politics* (Stanford University Press, 1947).
50. Data from Ferdinand Schevill, *The History of the Balkan Peninsula* (New York: Harcourt Brace, 1922), p. 543.
51. Miller, *op. cit.,* pp. 454ff.
52. Ernest C. Helmreich, "The Black Hand," in *Slavonic Encyclopedia* (New York: Philosophical Library, 1943), pp. 100ff.
53. Zdenek J. Slouka, "Black Hand and European Politics," a research paper for a graduate seminar at New York University on Social and Political Movements in Russia and Eastern Europe.

    Louis Adamic, in his *My Native Land* (New York: Harper, 1943) indicates that many secret organizations were active at that time. However, according to Adamic, the young conspirators against the Archduke were provided by the head of the terroristic department of the Black Hand with guns, and he helped them through the borders. Colonel Apis (Dimitriyevich), the chief of intelligence of the Serbian Army and prominent in the Black Hand, according to Adamic was not directly involved (p. 293). Helmreich, *op. cit.,* footnote 52, states that "Members of the Black Hand were responsible for the assassination." C.E. Black and E.C. Helmreich in *Twentieth Century Europe* (New York: Knopf, 1950), write: "The plot actually had been planned and put into execution by members of the Serbian Black Hand Society." (p. 51).

    Victor Serge, after the First World War, met some of the survivors of the conspiracy. According to their declaration, Colonel Dragutin Dimitriyevich (pseudonym Apis), chief of the Black Hand, was among the initiators of the attempt and received assurances of support from the Imperial Russian military attache in Belgrade. Victor Serge, *Memoirs of a Revolutionary* (Oxford University Press, 1963), p. 181.

54. Roucek, *op. cit.,* Chapter VI; Roucek, "IMRO," in *Slavonic Encyclopedia,* pp. 531–532; Kostia Todoroff, "The Macedonian Organization Yesterday and Today," *Foreign Affairs,* VI (1928), pp. 473–482. Todoroff gives 1894 as the year of the founding of IMRO, Roucek, 1893. On taxation and

Turkish administration, see Edwin Pears, "A Description of Turkish Government," in Luigi Villari's *The Balkan Question,* pp. 14–43.

55. On Turkish rule in Macedonia, see Dr. Bogirade Tatarcheff, "Turkish Misrule in Macedonia," in Villari, *op. cit.,* pp. 167ff.

56. For a description of internal terror, see Christo Silianoff, "Briefe und Beichten 1928), pp. 171ff. A good description of IMRO is in Roucek, *op. cit.,* footnote 48, and Frederick Moore "The Macedonian Committees and the Insurrection," in Villari, footnote 54, *op. cit.*

57. Todoroff, *op. cit.,* footnote 54, p. 475.

58. *Ibid.,* pp. 479–480.

59. *Ibid.,* p. 480.

60. Roucek, *op. cit.,* p. 156.

61. Joseph Rothschild, *Pilsudski's Coup d'Etat* (New York: Columbia University Press, 1966), p. 184.

62. See the article "Ustasha" in the *Grande Dizionario Enciclopedico* (1962), and Dinko Tomasic, "The Ustasha Movement," in the *Slavonic Encyclopedia* (New York, 1949), pp. 1337–1341.

63. "Yugoslavien, Attentate," *Der Spiegel,* October 21, 1968.

64. Hugh Seton-Watson, *Eastern Europe Between the Wars* (Cambridge University Press, 1945), p. 224; Serge, *op. cit.,* p. 182.

65. Seton-Watson, *op. cit.,* pp. 206–209.

66. Roucek, *op. cit.,* pp. 221ff.

67. Seton-Watson, *op. cit.,* footnote 49, pp. 206–215; Roucek, *op. cit.,* pp. 220–224. Robert Lee Wolff, *The Balkans of Our Time* (Harvard University Press, 1956), pp. 194–195; Black and Helmreich, *op. cit.,* pp. 548–549.

68. Serge, *op. cit.,* p. 278.

69. Steinberg, *op. cit.,* p. 244.

70. William L. Shirer, *The Rise and Fall of the Third Reich* (New York: Fawcett, 1959, 1960), p. 1289.

71. A major work in this area, with large and excellent documentation, is John A. Armstrong, ed., *Soviet Partisans in World War II* (University of Wisconsin Press, 1964). On the patterns of the underground struggle, see Gross, *Seizure of Political Power, op. cit.,* pp. 330ff.

72. For an account of Chetnik guerrilla warfare and fratricidal struggles, see David Martin, *Ally Betrayed* (New York: University Press, 1966), pp. 111–113.

73. Stefan Korbonski, *W Imieniu Rzeczypospolities* (Paris: Instytut Polski, 1954), pp. 11ff.; English translation *Fighting Warsaw* (Minerva Press [no place given] 1956), ed. 1968,

Chapter 1, p. 9; Zygmunt Zaremba, *Wojna i Konspiracją* (London, 1957), pp. 85–115.

74. Zaremba, *op. cit.,* p. 202.
75. Korbonski, *op. cit.,* 73 (English text), pp. 120–127.
76. *Ibid.,* pp. 210ff.
77. Gross, *Seizure of Political Power, op. cit.,* pp. 345ff.

SUPPLEMENT B

ASSASSINATION AND POLITICAL VIOLENCE IN 20TH CENTURY FRANCE AND GERMANY

By Harold Deutsch*

1. Introduction

Political turbulence has profoundly affected the history of France and Germany during the 20th century. France, since 1789, has witnessed two periods of Napoleonic rule, a Bourbon restoration, the rule of a cadet branch of the house of Bourbon, and three republics. More than one of these regimes generated dramatic constitutional changes of its own. Civil strife has been endemic at times, and occasionally has flared into civil wars that have increased the strains already imposed by external conflict. Extremists of both the Right and Left alternated or contended with one another in producing public disorder and violence. As a result of this, repressive measures were enforced which were propitious in the germination of regimes of a marked dictatorial character.

Nineteenth century Germany presented, on the surface at least, an appearance of order and stability, when compared with the upheavals in France. A number of revolutionary flurries—only the widespread and in some respects profound government of 1848 can be dignified by more serious terminology—failed to achieve any considerable change in the political situation. Both national unification and the abrogation of absolutistic institutions were accomplished in gradual stages in which there was little internal violence. Political and economic developments together with three victorious foreign

*University of Minnesota.

wars (in 1864, 1866, and 1870–71) effected unification. The successes in the wars made rather easy a task that might otherwise have offered almost insurmountable difficulties.

In most German states there were no significant constitutional changes after the 1850's, and the constitution of the German Empire endured without alteration from its establishment until the debacle of 1918. Thus the Germans had a considerable authoritarian tradition which promoted the habits of obedience and submission. The veneration of legal formalities and of orderly procedure was often accepted even by the sharper critics of the prevailing system. There was much truth in the biting comment, ascribed to Lenin, that if German revolutionaries should storm a railway station, they would hesitate to venture out upon the platform before purchasing the appropriate tickets.

Both France and Germany in the 19th century witnessed political assassination attempts upon prominent public figures. In the majority of cases these attempts centered on the sovereign as the symbol of authority and of the prevailing order. The persons involved in such plots were often deranged or were exhibitionists who hoped to emerge from obscurity to snatch a moment of glory for themselves. Only the assassination of August von Kotzebue (1819) by Karl Ludwig Sand and the plot of Count Felice Orsini against Napoleon III (1858) deserve to be qualified as having wider political significance.

2. The Early 20th Century

At the turn of the century France was in a state of unrest that reflected the bitter heritage of generations of internal and external conflict. Since the final establishment of the Republic in the second half of the 1870's, the clash between French Catholicism and persons of anticlerical persuasion had alternated, in successive stages, between exacerbation and mitigation. Often the moderates on both sides encountered as much enmity from within their own ranks as from their opponents. The diplomatic efforts of Pope Leo XIII and of Cardinal Lavigerie to effect a greater political neutrality among French Catholics by a less firm identification with reaction was only partly successful. The encyclical *Au Milieu des Solitudes*

(1892), which recommended rallying to the Republic, encountered the opposition of most of the hierarchy and the larger part of the Catholic press. Both did not hesitate to fulminate against "Papal Republicanism."

All of the passions, memories of former injuries, and sequelae of the social and political conflicts of the late 19th century were reflected in the Dreyfus affair. As the only Jewish officer attached to the general staff, Captain Dreyfus was regarded as an interloper and was the natural target for the suspicions and resentments of the military caste. The fact that he also came from a wealthy family only increased his vulnerability. By dealing severely with him, the Republic (and not only the army as its most steadfastly Catholic and conservative agency) had a chance to show that it could not be influenced by "Jewish gold." This explains why so many who at first glance would seem logically to have appeared as his natural defenders against persecution, not only failed to rally to his support but joined in opposing a review of his case. The case also offered an opportunity for the Republicans to show that they could be as zealous in guarding the national prestige and honor of the army as their royalist and Bonapartist critics.

Only gradually did the frantic efforts to uphold the conviction of Dreyfus reveal the forces and motives which lay behind them. Thus the case of the thoroughly unheroic and uninspiring Dreyfus, which Clemenceau later trenchantly described as "abysses beneath the Dreyfus affair,"[1] became the focus for all the contending passions and forces in the Third Republic. On one side were the ultranationalists, militarists, clericals, and what remained of unreconstructed monarchists. They posed as defenders of morality, honor, and national security against the supposed plots of a Jewish world syndicate abetted by atheists, Freemasons, pacifists, and cosmopolitans —everything in other words that they labelled unFrench.

The opposing coalition which eventually comprised the Dreyfusards was slow to form and close ranks. The intellectuals who gave it inspiration and leadership were themselves in many cases not free of anti-Semitism. The socialists also had shared widely in the denunciation of Jewish influence in banking and the busi ss world. Only after the extremists of the Right had fully evealed their hand did such socialist leaders as Jules Guesde rally to the Dreyfusard cause.

The fury of the passions engendered by the case repeatedly

inspired public disorders of varying dimensions. In the month after the publication of Zola's famous open letter to President Faure, *J'accuse*, for example, violence flared out in Algiers and in the major towns of the Republic. Mobs paraded the Paris boulevards with standards and chants that demanded death to Zola and the Jews. In a dozen cities large crowds plundered Jewish shops and set fire to them and to the synagogues. Jewish-owned factories were invaded and their machinery wrecked. In the provincial towns, particularly, the riots turned into pogroms. The police in many cases fraternized with the demonstrators and echoed their slogans. Many towns organized boycotts against Jewish shops, and petitions flooded the government to deprive Jews of the vote, expel them from France, exclude their children from schools, and to dismiss those who were public employees. Other mobs threatened and occasionally manhandled leading Dreyfusards. Huge protest meetings were held and sometimes ended in bloody clashes. Zola's own house was stoned by students, and for weeks such men as he and the Clemenceau brothers went in peril of their lives. If Zola had been acquitted it is likely that the waiting mob would have invaded the Palace of Justice and murdered him and his defenders. Their lives were probably saved when they received the maximum sentence, which helped to turn the bloodthirstiness of the mob into an orgy of triumph. "I shall not try to describe the riotous, fraternal joy of this evening," wrote an observer in *Le Figaro*.[2]

The outcome of the affair, though from the Dreyfusard standpoint a happy one, was not the restoration of political harmony. Harmony, in fact, had never existed in the Third Republic, or for that matter in 19th-century France. The orgy of hate which had characterized the national hysteria had been too extreme to permit feeling to be maintained at such a level. In fact, emotional exhaustion was so great that when Dreyfus was finally rehabilitated it caused no great outpouring of feeling. But rancor was too deep in the victors to encourage an attitude of magnanimity. The other side had appealed too often to force and to the exercise of indiscriminate authority to allow a spirit of forgiveness.

The response of the radical Republicans who emerged victorious from the affair was political vengeance on a large scale. The army was purged of its least trustworthy officers, with about 5000, or roughly one-fourth, of the officer corps being retired. But the army was indispensable and the counter-attack against it required some limits. A more devastating assault was made upon the Church with the Law of Associations (1901) and the separation of Church and State (1905). In many localities feeling again arose, and there was considerable resistance to government measures. The Grand Chartreuse distillery had to be occupied by force. Government inventory-takers were sent to inspect Church treasures to prevent impoverished clergymen from disposing of them to dealers and collectors. Riots developed from the action of parishioners who stood armed guard over the altars or set animal traps to snare unwary officials. Bands of young Church supporters sometimes invaded the churches to "defend" them despite the pleas of the clergy for order.

The situation gradually became tranquil as more moderate counsels prevailed in the government. As members of the Sarrien cabinet (1906), the more flexible Aristide Briand as Minister of Religion and the basically sensible Clemenceau as Minister of the Interior made extensive concessions in the actual application of the harsh legislation. The riot-breeding inventories were dropped and the clergy left free to use the churches without the formation of the lay associations which the law demanded and which violated all precedent. During the 8 years before 1914 there was an armed truce between the old contestants in which each seemed content with freedom from the other's attack.

In the period 1906–1914 public violence in France in many cases originated in labor troubles and in disorders which derived from the rise of syndicalist socialism. Clemenceau now demonstrated his ruthlessness by crushing strikes with the liberal use of troops for the protection of strikebreakers. His own first ministry, which lasted an astonishing 3 years, showed his basic lack of understanding of the social question. Now in his fourth decade in French politics, the age had passed him by at the very moment when the radical Republic had acquired enough political room to deal vigorously with such problems. Instead troops were regularly employed against strikes, union organizers were arrested and otherwise harassed, and *agents provocateurs* and police spies were active. The military was also called in to suppress the mass demonstrations of desperate winegrowers who were threatened with disaster by phylloxera. The high-handed arrest of their leaders led to rioting and mutiny by peasant soldiers. Meanwhile Clemenceau did nothing to support an income tax measure already passed by the Chamber through the Senate. He was apparently motivated in part by political jealousy of its promoter, Joseph Caillaux.

This rigid resistance to social reform alienated many young leaders who had expected the Republic to use its victory for more than defense vested interests. Another consequence was the estrangement between the Republic and socialism. The latter, influenced also by the decisions of the Amsterdam Congress of the Second International of 1904, now abandoned the policy of coalescing with radical bourgeois parties. In 1905, Jean Jaures, the greatest figure in the history of French socialism, joined the Marxist leader, Guesde, in forming the Unified Socialist Party (formerly, *Section Francaise de l'Internationale Ouvriere*—SFIO). The parliamentary representation under Jaures largely hewed to the reformist line, which just then was also emerging in Germany and elsewhere, but among the French workers themselves there was growing disillusionment with the parliamentary process. In 1902, the CGT and the *Federations des Bourses du Travail* had merged under the former designation and became increasingly attracted to syndicalist practices. French unionism had a strong localist and federalist tradition; the syndicalist emphasis on an economy based on workers' syndicates had a correspondingly strong appeal. The watchword was direct action and the supreme ideal of such action was the general strike for the overturn of bourgeois society. To increase militancy and class consciousness in the intermediate stages, local strikes, widespread sabotage, and, wherever anarchism lingered, stark terrorism, were approved means. The brutal police repression which these tactics were likely to arouse was not unwelcome to the more radical elements, for it would contribute to increase class consciousness.

The last decade before 1914 thus witnessed renewed violent expression in the political life of France. Among the worst offenders was *Action Francaise*, which had become increasingly respectable through the support of wealthy conservatives and the approval of Pius X and much of the French hierarchy. Upper-middle-class youth was widely enrolled in its *Camelots du Roi* (Newsvendors of the King), which frequently was in the limelight by its physical attacks on teachers, its destruction of bookshops that sold liberal or radical literature, and its public meetings. The violence and disorder thus created were dealt with too gently. The increasing international tension and the return to chauvinism made nationalist extravagances among young people more acceptable to the authorities. Fear of the rising tide of socialism increased conservative sympathies. The excesses of the *Action Francaise* attacks upon Jean Jaures, such as accusing him of being a paid revolutionary agent of Germany, contributed to his death. He was killed on the eve of the war by a nationalist fanatic who had been aroused by such defamation.

The early 20th century witnessed the same contrast between conditions in France and the relative order and stability in German affairs that was characteristic during the 19th century. Undoubtedly this can be partly ascribed to a continuance of the more uniform character of German political life. The most serious clashes between contending religious, social, and political forces already seemed to be of the past. During the 1870's Bismarck had gradually overcome the ultraconservative charge that he was treasonous to Prussia when he incorporated her into the new Reich. That period had also seen both the rise and decline of the bitter struggle between the Bismarckian state and the Catholic Church (the *Kulturkampf*). In the eighties, this had been followed by Bismarck's prolonged attack on Marxian socialism. All of these conflicts had left scars, but by 1900 many of them had healed over.

German socialism in the decade and a half before 1914 was the most imposing form of socialism, in terms of following, discipline, and organization. Except for one severe attack on it in 1907, it had steadily and at times sensationally gained in parliamentary representation. By 1912 it had polled an amazing 35 percent of the popular vote. Meanwhile, neither socialist agitation nor industrial strikes had produced anything similar to the public violence that was afflicting France and many other countries. The acute miseries of the workers in some of these countries had been largely overcome in Wilhelmian Germany. After 1890, and especially after 1900, employment had risen faster than the population, and there was a corresponding increase in wages. In dealing with the discontents of the workers, Bismarck had judiciously followed a policy of firmness combined with leniency. His social insurance laws, which were further extended in the nineties after his departure, had nearly eliminated the type of abject poverty that resulted from undeserved misfortune. German legislation also provided for regulation of wages, time off from work, grievance procedures, and safety measures. Bismarck, in effect, had insured against exactly those major discontents which originate in miserable conditions. These policies probably rank among the supreme examples of a statesman's recognition of not only immediately critical pressures, but also of future dangers. They were a vital factor in securing a state of political peace in Germany until 1914.

3. Political Violence in the Early Weimar Republic

In times of prolonged war, modern states have usually found it necessary to impose drastic restrictive measures on their political activity. Great emphasis is placed on public order, and every imaginable appeal is made to assure national unity. Those venturing to resist are usually accepting the risk of severe punishment. Advocates of a "premature" peace, in particular, risk denunciation as sympathizers or even agents of the enemy.

This was the situation in France and Germany in World War I. In France, the principal party leaders proclaimed an *Union Sacrée* and formed a coalition cabinet that included such unlikely members as the Marxist Jules Guesde, who had heretofore uncompromisingly denounced the participation of socialists in bourgeois cabinets. In Germany, William II announced that he "no longer knew any parties, but only Germans." Harking back to a type of political truce that had prevailed in besieged medieval cities, the parties agreed to adjourn their quarrels and rivalries in a *Burofrieden*. For a time, even the most radical and recalcitrant Social Democrats were whipped into line by the severe party discipline, as in the case of voting the war credits. Coincidentally, appeals were made, as in France, for industrial peace. This united posture was maintained with considerable success until the last year of the war. Then the metal workers' strike of January 1918 and a coincident unrest in French heavy industry were struck down with such harsh methods as the mobilization of strikers. On both sides political unity continued to weaken. In the summer of 1917, the war-weariness of the armed forces had been demonstrated by a mutiny in the German navy and a far more serious mutiny in the sadly mismanaged French army.

In France, the victory restored national morale for a time and led to the most conservative surge that had thus far been registered in 20th century politics. Germany after the defeat endured for half a decade violent domestic strife, widespread demoralization, and economic chaos. At times the very continuance of the nation seemed to be in doubt.

To understand the political, economic, and social climate in which the new German Republic had to seek to establish itself, the situation must again be seen in historical perspective. On the eve of the war there had been every evidence of a rising liberal movement in Germany. The Reichstag election of 1912 for the first time in the history of the Empire had a majority of its members from parties which, in one measure or another, demanded drastic alteration of the prevailing political order. Two votes of no confidence, though without legal implications under the existing constitution, served notice that a program of steps leading to a system in which the executive was responsible to the parliament was envisioned. If this trend had continued and the elections of 1917 had confirmed or strengthened the verdict of 1912, the government of William II would have been in a difficult situation. No chancellor had yet been able to govern without the assurance of a parliamentary majority, and the skillful use of the power of the purse could curb any government that observed constitutional forms. That would, in fact, have become the issue: William II in time would have had to either yield or choose the risky alternative of using force to subvert the constitution along reactionary lines.

The war and then the collapse of the German Empire in 1918 destroyed any hope of progress toward a more liberal Germany. Among the more fateful features of the government was the utter lack of preparedness of those who were suddenly placed in positions of high responsibility. Only a few weeks before the portents had seemed to favor victory. Awareness of defeat came not as a gradually maturing realization but with the virtual effect of a thunderclap. Among the Social Democrats who stepped into leading positions many, including their chief, the later President Friedrich Ebert, felt that the change was too precipitate and would have preferred the continuance of the monarchy in modified form. They were professionally

parliamentarians with little or no experience in public administration. The situation they encountered would have over-
whelmed the most experienced statesmen—too much was
being demanded of them in every respect.

Another important factor in the situation was that the German 1918 revolution took place in the shadow of the Russian
revolution of almost a year earlier. That convulsion had represented the triumph of extremism over the forces of moderation. Now, in the Germany of November 1918, political and
economic chaos was already advancing rapidly and the
chances of the revolution getting completely out of hand were
obvious. At the moment the majority (moderate) Socialists
who had assumed responsibility for leadership could not possibly conceive of things not going fast or far enough. It is small
wonder that they viewed with dread the appearance of such
symbols of political turnover as soldiers' and workers' councils
and mutinous formations of sailors and soldiers. Yet they
clung to such signs of continuity and stability as the existence
of the monarchy and sought, or at least accepted, the backing
of such traditional pillars of the old society as the army
leadership and the bureaucracy. The ingrained German love
of order also played a role. Not only Ebert but many of his
associates "hated revolution like the plague." This made it
easy for them, for example, to support so traditional a symbol
of bourgeois liberalism as the calling of a national assembly.

Part of the price of this procedure was the split among the
workers that endured until the end of the Republic. They had
gained little thus far in Germany from following the parliamentary road. Ebert's policies now alienated many of the
Independent Socialists, who had broken away to oppose the
war in its later stages, and especially the radical Spartacist
party of Karl Liebknecht and Rosa Luxemburg. What now
came to be called the Weimar Republic was never to experience the working class solidarity that had existed under the
Empire.

The reactionaries, on the other hand, had succeeded in
remaining in the army and the bureaucracy. They had at first
backed the Republic—up to a point. As long as men like
Ebert were there to restrain the more radical workers, they
had grudgingly cooperated with the government. Once the
Left was under some control, those who wished to turn the
clock back were again prepared to strike out on their own.
They hated the compromise with the moderate Left which

circumstances had forced on them. They were also averse to the moderate socialism which the Republic seemed to favor, and denounced what seemed to them the excessive spirit of accommodation which the Republic leaders were showing toward the demands and pressures of the victorious Western powers. In considerable measure these enemies of the Republic on the Right were frankly revanchist in spirit and intention.

The Republic and its leaders of the Weimar Coalition (Social Democrats, Centrists, and Democrats) now became the victims of some of the most outrageous political slanders of which history has record. The lost war and the hated peace were in effect dumped on its makers. After all, had they not come to power at the moment of national disaster? Were they not its beneficiaries? Was it not they who had signed the nefarious treaty against which the Right had protested? Could they not be described as the political blood brothers of the leaders of the Western nations who had ruined and then humiliated Germany? The ultranationalist gospel as preached by General Ludendorff, eager to unload the responsibility that was so largely his for the defeat of 1918, was received with enthusiasm by reactionaries and Nazis. According to Ludendorff, the Republic's founders had not only gained by the nation's misery but were directly instrumental in bringing it about. The traditional bogeys of European ultranationalists from the days that antedated the Dreyfus case—the Jews, socialists, and Freemasons—were again trotted out as scapegoats. Ardent Protestants found satisfaction in adding another international force—Catholicism—for good measure. This strange assortment of bedfellows was alleged to have hatched up a plot against Germany that commenced with the launching of the war against her, involved the assembling *ad infinitum* of allies for the hostile coalition, and climaxed in treasonable machinations to cheat Germany of the victory which was claimed to have been imminent in 1918. Thus the legend of the stab-in-the-back was built up to become a central feature of that real stab-in-the-back, the victim of which was the German Republic.[3]

Reckless and irresponsible charges of this type were soothing to wounded national pride and provided welcome relief for the antagonisms and frustrations of millions of desperate, maddened men in the terrible years that immediately followed the war. They were embroidered or interwoven with all the usual accusations about supposed Jewish rapacity and cultural demolition activities, the intrigues of Freemasons, and the social incendiarism of the Marxists. In a period of breakdown of authority and of weakening or unreliable state instruments of control such as the army and police force, this was an effective incitement to violence. The years 1918 to 1923 stand almost alone in German history in the abandonment during this period of the usual restraints on the ruthless and vengeful paying off of political scores. In this period there were about 400 political murders, countless clashes between contending groups consisting of from a few men to entire mobs, and fights ranging from tavern brawls to street battles.

By far the larger number of these outrages were perpetrated by members of the Right. They displayed all the traditional intolerance of elements that might threaten long-established vested interests. The snobbery of a "superior" caste that looked upon itself as born to be among the rulers of men reacted sharply to the threat posed to it by the egalitarian Republic. Instruments were readily at hand in the irregular military formations on which the Republic at first had to rely. It had proved impossible to hold together any of the units returning from the front. The war-weariness of most of the men, the tempting proximity of their homes, and the desire to become reestablished as quickly as possible in civil life re-sulted in almost automatic military dissolution the instant they had arrived at their domestic bases. At the same time a sprinkling of elements in every unit really had nowhere else to go. Among these were the very young volunteers or draftees who had never had a civil occupation, having often gone di-rectly from school into the army. In the older groups there were also to be found rootless men who had no families or none to which they felt particularly drawn. Many marriages had been broken under the strains of wartime conditions. Civil life had nothing to offer to such groups that was more attrac-tive than the camaraderie of the barracks or, under existing conditions, the security of being clothed, fed, and housed at government expense. There were also among them many rowdy types who found much that was attractive in a rough-and-ready sort of existence. Among the officers, there were the old regulars who had known only a military existence and who shrank from the uncertainties of civil life.

In its desperate need to maintain itself against the pressures of the Spartacists in the first months after the war, the government tolerated and even welcomed the formation of these Free Corps. They somewhat resembled the regiments privately raised by military entrepreneurs in the days of mercenary armies. In a number of cases they even bore the name of the general who recruited and commanded them. Aside from helping "to restore order" in the troubled months after the Armistice, they served in such embattled border regions as Upper Silesia and, with Allied tolerance, in the Baltic area to preserve it from Bolshevik takeover. Meanwhile they were becoming an embarrassment to the Republic and, to a lesser extent, to the regular forces which were now being formed under the designation of Reichswehr. The latter had welcomed for a time the presence of irregular formations which circumvented Allied restrictions. For their future purposes, however, they distrusted them and some of their officers, who were inclined to serve their own interests.

An organization more specifically designed to evade the restrictions of the Versailles Treaty was the so-called "Black Reichswehr." Its formation was a result of the acute tensions on the Eastern frontier. In the years 1920–1921 there arose the possibility of a clash between Germany and Poland. The Poles engaged in a military adventure in Upper Silesia, and it was considered possible that they would invade East Prussia. The commander of the Reichswehr, Colonel General Hans von Seeckt, felt it imperative to organize forces to supplement his 100,000-man token army. Thinly disguised as *Arbeits-Kommandos* (labor battalions), about 20,000 men were raised and trained in East Germany. Inevitably, this created a certain amount of talk, especially on the part of Leftists who had reason to believe that such formations might be used against them. Complaints were made to the Reich Disarmament Authority or to the Allied Control Commission. When the persons who made the complaints could be identified, they were likely to be brutally murdered by ultranationalists who conceived of themselves as operating in the style of the late medieval *Femegerichte*. The degree to which such murders were sanctioned by the military authorities who presided over the activities of the Black Reichswehr remains undetermined. It was certainly among the less savory of the German efforts to circumvent the restrictions of the Treaty of Versailles.[4]

When the Free Corps were disbanded over a period of months in 1920, their unruly elements tended to drift to Bavaria where the fiat of the Reich government was weak.

The area had become a hotbed of discontented reactionary activities of every description. There had been much armed conflict during the revolutionary phase in Bavaria, and the contending parties had acted with a barbarity that left animosities which remained until the end of the Republic. An Independent Socialist premier, Kurt Eisner, had been assassinated, hostages put to death, and the more radical revolutionaries shot in droves after their attempt to establish a regime of the extreme Left had been defeated. A period of Rightist agitations followed, with strangely divergent groups such as Bavarian separatists, Nazi centralists, and Prussian reactionaries collaborating with or betraying each other. Many plots and *Putsch* (takeover) attempts also characterized this era. The most significant of these were as described in the following paragraphs.

The Kapp Putsch, March 12–17, 1920

The Kapp or Kapp-Luttwitz Putsch might have succeeded if it had been better prepared and executed. The reaction against the Versailles Treaty and the Republic that had accepted it had been bitter, and the army leaders, horrified at the idea of wartime comrades firing on each other, generally adopted a neutral position. But the coup was so completely mismanaged that the government, which withdrew from Berlin and called for a general strike, nearly won by default. The coup had a positive result in that the more perceptive military leaders realized, little as they liked the Republic, that they had no choice but to work through it to restore German power. In particular, Seeckt gave notice that he would in the future not tolerate any Putsch attempt, whether it orginated from Right or Left, and that he expected from the military loyal adherence to the Republican Constitution. Except when the troops of the Putschists in their frustration fired on a jeering crowd as they withdrew from Berlin, the incident had caused almost no bloodshed.

The Ruhr Revolt, March–April 1920

The Ruhr workers, persuaded by the extreme Left, refused after the Putsch had collapsed to abandon the general strike or the arms they had seized. It became necessary to use force, and for this purpose the government used Free Corps troops who were not involved in the Kapp affair. There was heavy fighting and ruthless suppression, and both the wounded and captured were put to death. In the following months, Seeckt banned any singing of the Free Corps anthem.

Mutiny of the Black Reichswehr, September 30–October 2, 1923

This was an effort by Prussian reactionaries to force Seeckt's hand during the national crisis after the abandonment of passive resistance against French occupation of the Ruhr. Major Buchrucker, the organizer of the Black Reichswehr, formed the plot under the impression that Seeckt would approve or would not object to a *fait accompli*. When Buchrucker discovered he was mistaken, he lost his head and ordered the 4500 men he had collected to occupy a number of East German fortresses. Seeckt calmly ordered the Reichswehr to move against the mutineers and succeeded in suppressing them in short order. The Black Reichswehr was thereupon dissolved and Buchrucker himself was sentenced to 10 years imprisonment.

Leftist Outbreak in Saxony, October 1923

This was another of the sequelae of the Ruhr occupation and the end of passive resistance. The government of Saxony was led by Social Democrats, but had compromised with the Communists to the point of accepting two Communist cabinet members and organizing a Red Militia. Saxony became a prey to riots and acts of sabotage. The Social Democratic premier announced the new Reich government of Stresemann and proclaimed a Dictatorship of the Proletariat. Seeckt ordered the local Reichswehr commander to suppress the movement, and governing authority was vested for a time in a Reich commissioner.

The Munich "Beer Cellar Putsch," November 8–9, 1923

This incident was important not only for its immediate serious implications, but also because it was the first great thrust for power by the Nazis. It was previously mentioned that Bavaria's relative independence of the still weak Reich authority had made that part of Germany a meeting point of anti-Republican plotters. Now the Prussian reactionary Ludendorff endorsed National Socialism. The Nazi party derived its membership from men of every imaginable discontent, frustration, and political illusion. Perhaps no other German political group could match them in the use of ruthless opportunism as a principle of action.

Thus Hitler, an advocate of the extreme Reich centralism, did not hesitate when it suited him to attempt a coalition with the Bavarian separatists, who were no less cynical in trying to make use of him and his followers. In the general breakdown of authority after the Ruhr episode of 1923, the Nazis saw their chance to take over, first in Bavaria and then in Berlin. They had organized a large body of party militia brown shirts or storm troopers, and also counted on winning over the army and police. The Reichswehr district commander, General von Lossow, had objectives that were much closer to those of the Bavarian legitimists (supporters of the restoration of the house of Wittelsbach) than to those of the Nazis. By November 1923, all parties were on a collision course. Hitler tried to frighten his uncertain allies into an action that he believed would put him in power. Instead he frightened them into looking to their own safety. On the critical day of November 9 he was left alone with his Nazis and General Ludendorff to face the police. The famous march through Munich had ended in a fiasco that also shattered the dream of a greater march to Berlin. With their leaders killed, wounded, imprisoned, or in exile, political existence of the Nazis seemed over.

The Episode of Rhineland Separatism

Many Germans had never been satisfied with the Bismarckian Reich. The Catholic Rhineland, West-oriented and contemptuous of much in the Prussian tradition, was in 1919 amenable to proposals to set up a state of its own within the German commonwealth. Had French policy been content with the severance of the left-Rhinish territories from the Prussian state alone rather than from the Reich itself, it might have been successful in the attempt.

At the Versailles conference the French had made an effort to annex the Rhineland. They had to content themselves in the treaty with the separation of the Saar territory under League jurisdiction and a long-term Allied military occupation of the Rhineland itself. They now (1923) determined to exploit this occupation by erecting at least a buffer territory. In this way, together with their occupation of the Ruhr, they soon drove the Rhinelanders to abandon any thought of loosening their ties with their fellow Germans.

In spite of the nationalistic feeling in Germany, the French continued to implement their policy through military and civilian agents whose assignment was to divide the German people. A common procedure was to disarm the regular authorities and leave them at the mercy of gangs of hoodlums and criminal elements attracted from all parts of Germany and many other parts of Europe to pose as "separatists."[5] Episodes involving the beating and pistolling of officials were common whenever local government agencies were seized. Murders thus perpetrated went unpunished and the police were forbidden even to investigate them. Conditions were especially frightful in the Bavarian Palatinate. Soon the terror backed by the French was answered by a German counterterror against the separatists. The French were finally compelled to abandon their policy as a result of the publication in the British press of critical accounts by the correspondent G. E. D. Gedye and the report of British Consul General Clive. The Belgians, who, with some embarrassment, had supported the French, now retreated. The French, finding themselves isolated, gradually abandoned their efforts.

The main significance of these incidents probably was their influence on developments in other parts of Germany. During French occupation of the Ruhr, "passive resistance" often became active sabotage, such as the demolition of trains and signal points. The French responded not only by shooting the saboteurs, but by arresting union leaders and industrialists who would not cooperate with them. Reactionaries and Nazis were thus furnished with sufficient martyrs to enliven their propaganda for two decades. Gedye may have overstated matters somewhat when he wrote: "The driving force behind all German extremist appeals was always the situation on the Rhine."[6] There can be no doubt, however, that it aroused national feeling everywhere in Germany and contributed to the outrages which occurred at that period in many parts of the Reich.

This survey should make it obvious that in a period of so many political convulsions and economic misery there could only be constant ferment and a disposition to resort to violence. Most of the Putsch attempts were preceded and followed by rising and receding waves of public disorder. Deep hatred and a conviction about the unmitigated evil character of opponents and opposing causes confused the minds of many. In few periods of history has the idea that the end justified *any* means been received with such widespread acceptance.

Given the normal complement in any society of persons who are mentally disturbed or who have criminal tendencies, the situation in Germany could hardly fail to produce political murders on a scale scarcely known since the civil conflicts of the late Roman Republic or the religious struggles of the Counter-Reformation. These murders included openly declared enemies of the old order like Karl Liebknecht and Rosa Luxemburg, "traitors" like the Centrist Matthias Erzberger (identified with the making of the Armistice), Foreign Minister Walter Rathenau (considered to be too yielding to Allied demands), and those more clearly treasonous such as the Rhineland separatists. Stresemann for a time was marked for death because he gave up the passive resistance in the Ruhr, and Seeckt because he would not join in making a Rightist coup. The number of lesser known persons who were murdered was in the hundreds.

Because of the conservative sympathies of many of the judges, those assassins or would-be assassins who were caught were often acquitted or received ridiculously light sentences.[7] Many of those implicated in murder or Putsch attempts "had their day in court." Some of the more prominent, like Adolf Hitler, used their trials as a platform for propagating their political beliefs or to vilify the Republic. Such laxness on the part of the judicial authorities encouraged others to disregard personal restraints. In estimating the factor of deterrence, it is worth noting that, despite the hatred felt for the Allied Western powers, no attempts were made on their representatives, since it was known that in such cases it would not be easy to escape punishment.

The statistics on political murders in Germany for the years 1918 to 1922 may be found in E. J. Gumpel.[8] It should be noted that the inclusion of 1923 would have given an even more impressive picture. That was the year of the murders and lynchings in the Rhineland separatist imbroglio and of 11 or 12 of the *Feme* murders.

After 1923 the political turbulence in Germany receded. With the Dawes Plan and the Treaty of Locarno foreign tensions were greatly reduced. The stabilization of the mark and steady economic progress also contributed to improve the socio-political situation. The government was controlled by moderate conservatives who had become, like Stresemann for example, cautious from painful experience. The election of Hindenburg increased the feeling on the Right that the "Red Republic," however contemptible, no longer was capable of effecting revolutionary social change. It was only when the economic situation once more became perilous that the German political scene again became unsettled.

4. The German Political Crisis, 1929–33

After 5 years of comparative tranquillity, the elections of 1928 seemed to indicate that the Republic's days of tribulation were over and that it had withstood all shocks successfully. Nationalists, Nazis, and Communists suffered various degrees of setbacks, and the Weimar Coalition of the early postwar days had finally returned to govern at the Reich level. The press of the Western world hailed the 10th anniversary of the Republic with sincere congratulations. It proved, however, to be only a temporary renewal.

The reaction of the country to the catastrophe of the depression showed again the many weaknesses of the Republic. Many of these had seemed well on the way to being overcome, but actually had only been papered over. The artificial growth of the economy had not really given anyone a sense of security, especially not to those classes that had suffered most during the inflation. The middle class in particular had not been able to restore the financial reserves that had given it so much of its character. The few years of relative prosperity had not been sufficient. The Republic also had failed to engage fully middle-class loyalties, while the supporters of the old order regarded that class with only grudging tolerance. The divisions in the working class had become more seriously accentuated with the establishment of the Communist Party.

The rapidly growing strength of the Nazis with the advent

of the depression failed to generate any sense of alarm; on the contrary, it appeared to fit in with the Marxian thesis that the final phase of dying capitalism would be a short period of something like a fascist dictatorship. Consequently, the Communists were prepared to cooperate with the Nazis in whatever seemed to promise the destruction of the prevailing order. Eloquent appeals by such Social Democratic leaders as Prussian Premier Otto Braun to set limits to the obsessed attacks on the Republic received sneering rebuffs. According to the report of the British ambassador, Sir Horace Rumbold, the Communists did not even shrink from supplying funds to the Nazis when the latter were hard-pressed.

No attempt will be made here to analyze intensively the character and meaning of Nazi ideology and political practice. Reference is made only to those aspects that contributed more directly to heightening the atmosphere of turmoil and multiplying the appeals to violence and that became so commonplace after the great Nazi electoral advance in September 1930. Hitler's agitation was calculated to increase hatred, flatter every prejudice, and exploit every grievance whether real or imaginary. The Nazis exalted the "will to power" that was determined to destroy everything in its path. They scorned Christian ideals such as humility, mercy, forbearance, and adherence to a sharply-defined code of ethics. All rules governing conduct were measured in terms of their effectiveness in achieving Nazi aims.

The use of force was lauded as the natural and proper expression of the "fighting spirit" (*Kampfgeist*) appropriate to man, and as a vital form of that perpetual struggle which was the major impetus in the advancement of mankind.

It was thus inevitable that the Nazi revival at the beginning of the thirties should take numerous forms of violent expression. Because marching and parades achieved such purposes as promotion, organization, and auto-intoxication, demonstrations were especially popular with the Nazis. Besides parades, public ceremonies (mourning, paying honor, dedication of plaques and buildings, etc.), meetings, conventions, and the like were employed to gather crowds, attract attention, or challenge to combat. Such occasions were in fact often calculated to goad opposition groups into interfering and making physical attacks. Or a demonstration once underway would sometimes result (whether intended or not) in a riot. A particularly preferred form of action was to interfere with the demonstrations of other parties. For both Nazi defense and attack Hitler established the first and most effective of the German party militias of that era, the Brownshirts, or Storm Trooper (*Sturmabteilung*). These were intended to both protect Nazi public affairs and interfere with those of their political enemies. Though most of the street battles of that period were between Nazis and Communists, the *Saalachiacht* (meeting hall encounter) often found the two parties together in interrupting a meeting of the Social Democrats. A Nazi mob might invade such a hall through one entrance while the Communists were coming in from another. Then, having disposed of a common enemy, they might engage each other for good measure.

The growing arrogance and bellicosity of the Storm Troopers was a potent stimulus to the development of parallel formations of rival parties. Thus the Communists organized their *Rotfront* (Red Front) and the Republicans their *Reichanbanner*. The *Stalhelm* (Steel Helmets) were in a somewhat different category, being essentially a veterans organization that predated these others. In their close association with the Nationalists, however, they resembled a party militia.

Even before the Nazi electoral surge of September 30, 1930, public order had deteriorated to a point where the Federal Minister of the Interior, Karl Severing, could state in the Reichstag on March 13 that 300 policemen had been wounded and 14 killed during the previous year.[9] By that time no Sunday passed without blood being shed in the German streets. Intermittently, the governments of the various states which controlled the police force took such remedial measures as forbidding outdoor meetings and parades, dissolving the *Rotfront*, and prohibiting the wearing of Nazi uniforms and emblems. In the end the Bruening government adopted the drastic step of suppressing the SA and the SS (the latter were the black-uniformed elite guard within the party militia).

If such actions as those described above had been applied consistently against the Nazis, they might have been effective in checking them. Hitler and his followers respected nothing but force; no concessions or compromise, no internal appeasement could ever restrain them. But a consistent policy of this kind was exactly what the harried government of Bruening (March 1930–May 1932) and its reactionary successor, headed by Papen and Schleicher, were unable to achieve. A psychological and very real political consideration was that the Communists had developed along with the Nazis (though not to the same degree). They too had taken to the streets with similar viciousness and enthusiasm, and had given the country a Red scare that in many areas became nearly hysterical. Accordingly, many Germans were reluctant to place severe restrictions on the Nazis, who were the only group that could effectively take to the streets and compete for the support of the worst victims of the depression. As elsewhere in the world, when it seemed that some choice had to be made, the bourgeois sections of society never hesitated in preferring Fascism over Communism. Beyond this, the mere electoral advance of the Nazis and Communists had destroyed the old balance of forces in the Reichstag. The latter could have exercised a steadying influence throughout the period of crisis.

Rendered more arrogant than ever by their voter support, the Nazis after the September 1930 election demonstrated new excesses of violence. Clad in SA uniforms and marching in military formation, they entered the Reichstag and conducted themselves in so rowdy a fashion that the proceedings had to be repeatedly suspended. At the same time, Nazi mobs for the first time on a large scale broke the windows and made shambles of Jewish shops. From then on it became merely a question of how much they could get away with in flouting every traditional standard of public conduct. Though it involved only the brutal murder of a single man, what was at stake was most tellingly demonstrated when a gang of Nazis invaded the home of a Communist in the upper Silesian village of Potempa and beat him to death before the eyes of his family. Though the country was loud with expressions of horror and disgust, Hitler did not hesitate to come to the support of convicted assassins and denounce the "monstrous" sentence that had been passed upon them. It was a presage of the horrors that were to characterize the 12 years of his rule which lay ahead.

5. The Nazis in Power

Although short of actual civil war, public and private violence of many kinds had marked the rise to power of the

Nazis. It was also a major element in turning Hitler's rule into a complete dictatorship. It was to characterize many aspects of national life while he was the absolute master of Germany.

The compass of this study does not include a description of the many ways in which brute force was practiced in the actual governance of the Reich. Thus we shall pass over the arbitrary imprisonments, the systematic harassment of citizens by the regular or special police forces, the incarceration of a million Germans in concentration camps, and much else that either belongs in the category of traditional operations of government to maintain order or formed part of the terror apparatus of the totalitarian state. Beside this, however, Hitler's 12 years witnessed many types of violent action which were not publicly acknowledged and can only be described as lawless. Accordingly, a brief summary of the main characteristics of the Third Reich must suffice.

The Sanctioning of Internal Violence

Restraints on Nazi groups were at a minimum in the first year and a half of the regime. In many parts of Germany the SA in effect was allowed to run wild. It invaded the homes of Jews or political opponents with whom it had a score to settle in order to beat them up or it dragged them off to its cellars for a more thorough going over. In the process there was likely to be a good deal of plundering and vandalism. Often enough political pretexts were made to cover the vengeance for private grudges. The police were unhappy about the state of affairs, but were themselves much intimidated and thus hesitated to interfere. Persons with influential connections fared best if there was a chance to summon help and if it arrived in time. This type of outrage was less frequent after the crushing of the SA leadership in June 1934.

The Use of Violence in Establishing the Dictatorship

In this category would be included the setting afire of the Reichstag and the political exploitation of it which followed. Though it remains to be finally proven that the fire was set at the orders of Goebbels and/or Goering, it is at any rate certain that the Communists did not do it. By the cynical exploitation they made of the arson, the Nazi leaders can at the very least be called accessories after the fact. Far more sinister was their involvement in the ghastly Blood Purge of June 30-July 2, 1934. This blow at the SA, which might have had some excuse if it had been meant to put an end to the organization's lawlessness, really derived from the ambitions of Ernst Roehm's rivals and Hitler's suspicions concerning his loyalty. Though it is possible that Roehm was thinking of a coup to take over the regime, there was no proof of this and Hitler simply decided to take no chances and to strike first. Instead of using the regularly constituted agencies charged with maintaining order and authority—the army, the police, and the courts—he employed the SS in an action that could have no pretense to legality. Up to 300 SA figures and other personages were seized and shot. An undetermined number of individuals were included solely because Hitler or such Nazi leaders as Goering and Himmler, who directed the purge, found it convenient to settle at the time with various old enemies. The Reich cabinet tamely submitted to Hitler's demand for a retroactive legalization of what had been done.

Continued Anti-Semitic Excesses

After Hitler's seizure of power, there was no further assurance of security in person or property for the Jews in Germany. Aside from the danger of incarceration in concentration camps or of arrests on flimsy pretexts, there was always the prospect of being plundered or assaulted. The crowning mass action against the Jews, previous to the deportations during the war, was the infamous pogrom of November 1938 launched under the direction of Goebbels and involving the wholesale plundering of shops and burning of synagogues.

Murders Ordered by Hitler

Both before and during the war there were mysterious deaths of prominent individuals known to have incurred the enmity of Hitler or other Nazi officials. Some were reported to have been killed while resisting arrest or trying to escape. Others were said to have perished in accidents. In most cases the proof as to what really happened will never be found. Before passing too sweeping a judgment, it is also necessary to remind ourselves that because a person may be held capable of anything does not make him necessarily guilty of *every-thing*. Yet there can be no doubt about the murder of the former French Minister of the Interior, George Mandel, who was claimed to have died in an auto accident, or of the governor of Tripolitania, Italo Balbo, who undoubtedly was killed in an airplane crash, but in one that resulted from German antiaircraft fire. There is also no question but that Hitler gave instructions for the assassination of French Generals Giraud and Weygand, although the transmission of the order was fortunately sabotaged by the Chief of Intelligence, Admiral Wilhelm Canaris. There is a considerable likelihood that the plane crash which took the life of the builder of the Autobahnen, Fritz Todt, was arranged in the highest quarters. There are also the more casual orders to liquidate certain people which, although not published to the world, Hitler did not even try to hide. An example of this is the shooting at his command of the professional blackmailer Schmidt, who knew too much of the facts in the 1938 frameup by Himmler's agents of Colonel General von Fritsch on homosexual charges. There are finally the scores of political prisoners whom Hitler had put to death without pretext of a trial in the closing days of the war.

Incitement to Mob Action Against Allied Aviators

As the Allied bomber offensive mounted against Germany, Hitler tried to conceive some means of retaliation and deterrence. At one time he seems seriously to have contemplated the execution of all captured aviators. Dissuaded from this, he allowed Goebbels to make a number of denunciations of Allied air attacks which were a plain incitement to mob action against aviators who were taken prisoner. A number of such lynchings did occur.

6. Anti-Hitler Plots and Assassination Attempts

In a totalitarian society there is no room for legitimate dissent or opposition. The only alternative to abject submission or to resignation is to operate in a clandestine way. Yet the means available to a tyrant for suppression are so numerous that the chances of a successful coup, even when engineered by men with some control over such instruments of power as the military and the police, are minimal. It is important, at the least, to have access to the dictator's person, but success in this still leaves uncertainties. In the case of Hitlerite Germany, where the military took an oath of unquestioned obedience, the only way to bring about a change was to assassinate the head of state.

The men who conceived the first major plots against the regime in 1938 and 1939–1940 found it hard to adjust themselves to acceptance of this fact. Most of them were motivated by moral considerations that often had a strong religious basis. It was difficult enough for them to accept the notion of having to use violence to accomplish their ends. To carry violence to the point of murder was more than some of them could assent to, even as late as 1944. In 1938 and 1939 their plans called for seizing the person of the dictator by the use of commando-type groups of officers, students, and workmen. It was expected that Hitler would be held for a show trial that would reveal fully the criminality both of himself and of his regime. Actually, the young realists who composed the troop conspired among themselves and with some of their more hardheaded backers, believing that Hitler would be found to resist capture, in the sense in which the Nazis often employed the term, and that they would have no choice but assassinate him.

The 1939–1940 plot was premised on the idea of making a prisoner of the dictator. But Army Chief of Staff Franz Halder failed to carry out the coup he had promised for November 5. Thereupon a small inner group fell back upon the assassination attempt they had scheduled for the evening of November 11, the night before Hitler's intended offensive in the West. Inability to obtain the necessary explosive forced the cancellation of this plan also, and a few months later Hitler's stupefying triumph in the West left his opponents for a time without hope.[10]

By the time plans for the overturn of the regime were resumed in 1942, a grimmer, more realistic spirit dominated coup preparations, which thereafter centered frankly on Hitler's assassination. Half a dozen specific plans for his elimination were formulated, leading finally to the actual bomb attempt of July 20, 1944.

7. Germany Since 1945

When the Allied armies entered Germany in 1945, they anticipated major problems in establishing and maintaining control over a population which had seemed to fight the war with such fanatic determination. There had been much talk about the formation of Nazi guerrilla bands who would snipe from hidden positions. It was also expected that there would again be *Feme*-type murders of persons accused of collaboration with the occupying forces.

Nothing of this sort developed. Instead the victors found an utterly cowed and docile population too physically and emotionally exhausted to think of further resistance. It often seemed to the occupiers as if the overriding concern of everyone they met was to deny his Nazi past. The only place where there was difficulty worthy of mention was in West Berlin, where some murders and many kidnappings of Germans who were considered too friendly to the West were engineered at the orders of its own Soviet ally.

This generally tranquil state of affairs continued throughout the fifties. The Germans worked hard, kept their political quarrels at a moderate level, and almost universally welcomed reconciliation with their former Western enemies. It was not until the years 1966–1968 that there again arose any problem about public order. And then it came as the result of a worldwide social, cultural, and political malaise which found expression particularly in the discontents and dissents of the younger generation. In trying to maintain public order, German authorities encountered the same difficulties as did those in other countries in trying to maintain a proper balance between concession and police action. In this respect the German experience probably has been no more instructive than that of other countries.

8. The Later Third Republic

With the exception of the year 1934, public disorders in France during the twenties and thirties never reached the level of intensity of the Dreyfus affair. These last decades of the Third Republic, however, were not without their share of turmoil. Both victory in the war and the mere passage of time allowed many wounds to heal and gave the Republic a degree of security that it had not previously known. In the minds, if not always in the hearts, of many Frenchmen it had for the first time become identified with France. Between moderate groups of the Left and Right, between the Army and the Republic, and between the Church and its antagonists, the mood was distinctly conciliatory.

As early as 1920, however, danger signs became visible. The split in the socialist ranks, evident throughout Europe, between gradualists and Communists became endemic in the French labor movement. Reactionary businessmen reneged on wartime promises to accept collective bargaining and the right to strike. A moderate prosperity, however, continued during the 1920's, and the nation's complacency increased when the world depression did not affect France.

When the Depression finally did come, the psychological unrest was marked. There were charges of widespread corruption in the government. Cynicism among the people was fostered by the casual and irresponsible way in which governments rose to power and were overthrown or reconstituted. Not conflict over issues but the whim or convenience of the participants seemed to determine governments.

The Stavisky scandal which broke sensationally with the suicide of this shady operator in January 1934 precipitated a crisis of confidence such as the Republic had not experienced since the days of the Dreyfus affair. Not only political leaders but parliamentary institutions as such appeared to be implicated. For 7 years this financial adventurer had managed to stay out of court despite a variety of charges against him. Meanwhile he blithely continued his questionable dealings while high-level government officials attempted to protect him. The general loss of confidence was accentuated by the feeling that in playing politics the governing political groups had dissipated the primacy in Europe which France was believed to have enjoyed at the beginning of the thirties. The democratic Europe that followed the 1918 victory had vanished. Dictatorships had multiplied until Italy, Poland, Austria, Portugal, Yugoslavia, Turkey, and, most ominously, Germany were tyrannically ruled. Other Baltic and Balkan states were in danger. The disputes about the effects of France's German policy were particularly acrimonious. The Left accused the Right of having prevented timely concessions to the faltering Weimar Republic; the Right replied with charges that the Left had been guilty of weakness in dealing with the traditional enemy.

France was thus plunged into a state of frustration in which the old hatreds and dissensions were revived. What gave the situation a most serious character was that extremist groups of the Left and Right now had the choice of alternatives not available early in the century. The Communists, under the direction of Moscow, pursued the aim of world revolution and were, as in Germany, prepared to go to any length to bring down the bourgeois Republic that was the first obstacle in their path. They were especially vicious in their efforts to ruin the "social Fascists" (Socialists) who dared to compete with them in the proletarian market place. As for the ultras on the Right, insofar as they no longer pursued the phantom of monarchism, they were increasingly attracted to Fascism.

Fascist leagues and paramilitary organizations were growing rapidly in France in the early thirties. *Action Francaise* and Maurras' *Camelot du Roi* were gaining influence. Disapproval of Pius XI, who did not hesitate to place *Action Francaise* on the Index Expurgatorius, had little effect on those who were concerned with action and whose ostentatious support of the Church had often been a cover for promoting reactionary and nationalist causes. The disapproval of the Church only made it easier to draw inspiration from Fascist sources, especially as Mussolini was soon providing financial support for French reactionary activity. As with the Nazis in Germany, the more ultrareactionary fringe of the business community was prepared to subsidize any group that raised the banner of anti-Communism or was eager to use the Communist brush to tar any cause which promoted social welfare. Thus the champagne king, Pierre Taittinger, became the patron of the *Jeunesse Patriotes*. Perfume magnate Francois Coty, who was treated by those who had hereditary wealth as an interloper and was kept waiting at the door of its most exclusive club, that of the regents of the Bank of France, took out his frustrations by financing the *Solidarité Francaise*. Both of these organizations took their inspiration from Italy's Black Shirts.

This was far less clearly the case with the *Croix de Feu* of Colonel de la Rocque, which started as a veterans' organization and grew into a mass movement. Fortunately de la Rocque lacked the ruthlessness, dynamism, and driving ambition of a Mussolini or a Hitler. With his appeals for "moral pressure" and showing himself as an example of selfless dedication to the national welfare, he seemed something of a mystic. But the spirit of the movement was strongly authoritarian and its trappings quite obviously aped Fascist and Nazi models. There were uniformed and armed formations, "maneuvers" held on country estates, and "lightning mobilizations" via automobiles and airplanes. Most followers of de la Rocque, however, were conservative bourgeois who, although they had lost faith in the processes of parliamentary government, did not wish to adopt Fascism. The more genuinely Fascist elements which for a time associated themselves with the *Croix de Feu* dropped out when they realized that de la Rocque had no program for taking over power. By 1937 whatever threat of Fascism there was in the movement was fading away when it turned itself into a *Parti Social Francais*. What was left of real Fascists then departed to join the sinister *Cagoulards* (hooded men), who got much of their financial backing from Mussolini and can be considered as a conspirational group. By this time also, Jacques Doriot, once the leader of French Communist youth, had left that part of his life behind him and formed the increasingly Fascist *Parti Populaire Francais*, competing with the *Cagoulards* for the allegiance of ruffian elements.

Prime Minister Edouard Daladier's frivolous approach to the Stavisky affair had outraged the nation. On the day he was to present his new government to the Chamber, February 6, 1934, a vast mob, drawn largely from the Rightist organizations but including also a Communist contingent, converged from the Place de la Concorde toward the bridge which alone separated the mob from the Palais Bourbon where Daladier was addressing the Chamber. In the end the exhausted police lines managed to hold, but only after 14 persons had been killed and 650 injured.

Thus ended the most violent day Paris had seen since the Commune. The Left loudly insisted that there had been a plot to overthrow the Republic. Such a claim, however, rested almost entirely on circumstantial evidence, and in fact most of the evidence indicates otherwise. There is no doubt that the Rightist leagues were out to make trouble, but nothing shows that an organized coup was contemplated. Obviously the more Fascist-minded components of the mob would have been happy to send the parliament packing if they had been able to force the bridge and invade the Chamber. The Republic in that sense may have had as narrow an escape as in the Boulanger affair of the 1880's.

The remaining history of France in the thirties records the agonies of a Republic which had lost much of its faith in itself and failed to find any unity and strength to attack any of its major problems with vigor and purpose. For a time it seemed as if a process of polarization was taking place in the ranks of both Left and Right. The mounting Nazi threat had at last prevailed upon Moscow to shed for a time its policy of universal subversion of bourgeois institutions. One aspect of its new line was the promotion of "popular fronts," i.e., alliances with other sectors of the Left, with a common defense against Fascism as the principal rallying cry. This had an astonishing effect on traditional nationalist positions. For two generations French reactionaries had prided themselves on being the most uncompromising defenders of the national cause. The formation of a Popular Front and its combination of far-reaching social demands with a stand against the international manifestations of Fascism now led to an amazing *volte face*. By no means the entire Right was prepared to accept the ultras' slogan, "Better Hitler than Blum!" But much of conservative France was henceforth a drag on any policy of severe restraint of the German dictator.[11]

As so often before, although now with somewhat reversed roles, Frenchmen denounced each other as agents or dupes of foreign powers. There was the usual combining of this with arguments about armament and who should pay for it. There was also now added the question of who was to manufacture the arms, with the Popular Front favoring nationalization of the arms industry.

Thus the middle and late thirties saw much continued social and political conflict. Even the religious issue was revived because of its role in the nearby civil war in Spain. Accordingly, demonstrations on one side or the other of foreign causes combined with marches, rallies, and clashes over domestic issues to bring new violence to the streets. There were numerous strikes, including a number of sit-in affairs which at first had considerable success. Then the collapse of the Popular Front and a more conservative shift again brought the government over to the side of the employers. In November 1938, the workers who had occupied the huge Renault plant were cleared out by force at the orders of the Daladier government. A general strike which followed on November 30 was broken when Daladier called up the railway and public-service workers. The failure of the Popular Front to live up to the high hopes that had been placed in it did much to destroy faith in the Republic among those who had been its strongest backers. The French body politic was afflicted with a profound malaise that explains much about the failure of the nation in the test it had to face in 1940.

Despite the many conflicts and disorders of the thirties, political assassination was insignificant. Only two prominent Frenchmen were victims of assassins, and in neither case did the incident relate in any way to the contemporary French scene. The deadly assault on President Doumer (May 1932) was the act of a madman. The twin murders of Foreign Minister Barthou and King Alexander of Yugoslavia had more political connotations, but these were of an international rather than a domestic order. In this latter case there is the possibility that the sole target was Barthou's fellow victim, the King, thus making Barthou's death incidental or even accidental. Another possibility is that both were to be removed and that the real instigator was the chief beneficiary of the act— Adolf Hitler.[12] Actually, the more likely culprit is Mussolini, who had no more scruples than Hitler in such matters and who had long been and continued to be the patron of the Croatian extremists who were directly involved.

9. France After World War II

The France of the Fourth Republic that emerged from World War II was a sorely tried land whose faith in herself was perhaps at the lowest point in several centuries. The fall of the Third Republic in 1940 had clearly reflected the defects not only in the military establishment but in the very moral fiber of the nation. There had been too little resistance to the Nazis, and that little came too late to prove a truly redeeming experience. However brave a show the French tried to put on, it was hard to ignore that the liberation had come as the gift of outsiders. Frenchmen also carried with them bitter memories of the era of appeasement and of a large measure of collaboration with the invaders.

Undoubtedly the Fourth Republic also continued to suffer from many of the debilities that had wrecked its predecessor. It could no more master so vast a problem as the decolonization that beset the old empire-builders of Europe than the Third Republic had been able to deal with the threat of Nazi Germany. It stumbled badly during the Algerian situation, which indeed in the late fifties seemed almost beyond any solution.

The Fifth Republic, the child of Charles de Gaulle, seemed for several years to be little better. For much of its first decade it suffered from the fact that it seemed to have no future. Its institutions were too much tailored to De Gaulle, who, after all, was mortal. For over two further years France was caught up in a fever of violence and disorder that threatened to consume her. Riots of every dimension, a general strike, an armed insurrection in Algiers, terror and counterterror, an army that for months was within an inch of open revolt—Europe for generations had seen little to compare with it. Hundreds—usually the more moderate elements on both sides—were murdered. The Secret Army Organization (OAS) seemed prepared to stop at nothing to prevent a settlement it abhorred. For years de Gaulle's life was in constant danger from plots.

Despite the extent of these convulsions, peace and order were in the end established almost miraculously. In the mid-sixties France seemed to enjoy a stability that was rare in her recent history. The year 1968, however, proved that old tensions continued beneath the surface and that the society of the Fifth Republic would have to face the same dissatisfactions and resentments in the younger generation that trouble its neighbors. The riots of May that seemed at times to approximate a revolutionary situation clearly demonstrated how an authoritarian regime faces the same difficulties in maintaining a balance between concession, reform, and police measures that confront other more flexible democracies.

10. Summary and Conclusion

The history of 20th-century France and Germany can provide much insight into the situations that lead to or arise from public violence and political assassination. The experience of the two countries reflects both situations peculiar to them and phases of their national life that are European or worldwide in their implications. Each illustrates the extensive interplay of political, economic, social, and cultural factors.

The German experience is in some respects unique in that the country had to face the consequences of two defeats in a single generation. Yet, the sequelae of World War I differed very much from those of World War II. The first produced a sudden, unexpected, and therefore never entirely comprehensible situation that threw the nation into a turmoil which can perhaps only be compared in this century to that which prevailed in France during the Algerian crisis of the late fifties. The Germans also found that those upon whom responsibility for leadership was thrust were dazed and unprepared.

The history of the German revolution of 1918 also argues that at certain points in time one may pay too heavy a price for law and order. However high a value may be assigned to law and order, it is questionable whether it represents a final criterion to which all else is relative and subordinate. One can make too many and too serious compromises and break too insufficiently with an outlived past to allow construction of an adequate design for the future. It seems particularly dangerous to leave in positions of power the supporters of an old order that has clearly been sentenced to oblivion.

The effective use of human foresight may be the quintessence of statesmanship. Bismarck's social legislation probably did much to forestall in Germany an unrest that was familiar at the time in many neighboring countries, including France. The French Third Republic paid heavily for the rigidity of Clemenceau in failing to respond to the needs of the age. The history of the 20th-century, including that of the United States in such matters as its dealings with its Negro citizens, affords plenty of examples of the crises of nations that "waited too long."

Repression, especially if it is applied without limit, can do much to repress the violent expression of discontent. Yet it clearly contributes nothing in dealing with the continuing ills of society. The experience of France in the thirties offers important lessons in this regard. In particular, repression seems to be self-defeating in countries where a critical situation has been left to develop to a point at which alleviation without violence is no longer possible. Perhaps the most striking example of this is to be found in France's fumblings with the problem of Algeria, which bred some of the worst horrors of our century, in a situation where reasonable concessions 10 years earlier might have led to a solution.

The situation is palpably different in cases where dissident groups indulge in the practice of violence as a principle of action. Here any concept of appeasement loses all meaning and compromise is only seized upon to smooth the way for more outrageous demands. Groups like the Nazis, the practitioners of force *par excellence*, respect only force in return and can never be turned aside on either domestic or international issues, except by the unquestioned readiness of their opponents to use force when necessary.

The phenomenon of ultra-authoritarian or totalitarian states has confronted those who must deal with them with moral problems that are unfamiliar in countries where democratic processes are available to register protest and dissent. It has been noted but may well be stressed again, that when the opportunity to protest and dissent is denied, the only justifiable recourse for dealing with tyranny is political assassination.

In countries where an accumulation of wealth sufficient to affect the national budget is possible for individuals—a problem unsolved and not even attacked in France and Germany —there arises the grave menace of political fringe elements in the business world who have the capacity to subsidize what are in effect political armies—at times really paramilitary organizations. French and German experience should at least make us aware to what such financing of extremists (and this is not unknown in the United States) can ultimately lead. The experience of both these countries also provides significant examples of the dangers of national hysteria, notably among groups that feel threatened in their social and economic position, especially where the threat is conceived to be of an international character. In the case of both the Weimar Republic of Germany and the French Third and Fourth Republics it was shown that one of the most serious situations a nation can face is a crisis of confidence in which doubts occur not only about specific political leaders but about parliamentary institutions and the basic structure of society.

In conclusion, in situations of serious public violence neither total suppression nor total concession are adequate responses. A judicious balance of firmness and conciliation, as perhaps was best illustrated in de Gaulle's handling of the Algerian problem, is required.

References

1. Jean Martet, *Clemenceau* (New York, 1930), p. 292. Leon Blum put it even better when he said that Dreyfus, had he not been Dreyfus, could never have been a Dreyfusard.
2. Nicholas Halasz, *Captain Dreyfus; the Story of a Mass Hysteria* (New York, 1955), p. 156.
3. Ebert unwittingly contributed some of the inspiration for the legend by making a speech to returning soldiers in which he credited them with not having been defeated on the field of battle. One of the more eloquent analyses of the inception and propagation of the legend is that of Galo Mann, *The History of Germany Since 1789* (New York and Washington, 1968), p. 346.
4. One of the better discussions in English of the Black Reichswehr is that of John Wheeler-Bennett, *The Nemesis of Power: the German Army in Politics, 1918–1945* (2nd ed., New York, 1946), pp. 92–95, 111–112.
5. G.E.D. Gedye in *The Revolver Republic: France's Bid for the Rhine* (London, 1930), p. 236, stated that in the Bavarian Palatinate 75 percent of all separatists came from outside the region.
6. *Ibid.*, p. 38.
7. For a discussion of this situation, see Franz Neumann, *Behemoth: the Structure and Power of National Socialism* (New York, 1942), pp. 20–23.
8. E.J. Gumpel, *Vier Jahre Politiscker Mord* (Berlin, 1922), pp. 73–82:

	Left Groups	Right Groups	Total
Committed by	22	354	376
Not expiated	4	326	330
Partly expiated	1	27	28
Expiated	17	1	18

9. W. William Halperin, *Germany Tried Democracy. A Political Survey of the Reich from 1918 to 1933* (New York: Norton Library, 1965), p. 425.
10. For the story of the 1939–1940 plot, see Harold C. Deutsch, *The Conspiracy Against Hitler in the Twilight War* (Minneapolis, 1968).
11. See Charles A. Mioaud, *The French Right and Nazi Germany, 1933–1939* (Durham, N.C., 1943).
12. This is emphatically the view of William Herzog, *Barthou* (Zurich, 1938), pp. 255–303.

SUPPLEMENT C

C. POLITICAL ASSASSINATIONS IN CHINA, 1600–1968

By Daniel Tretiak*

1. Introduction

This study examines political assassinations as well as other forms of death, violent and nonviolent, of elites in China during the past 350 years, from the end of the Ming dynasty (1368–1644) until the present.

For each major time period, the level of political violence within the general political environment will be discussed, followed by quantitative and comparative data on the incidence of violent deaths, particularly assassinations, of officials. The relationship between the aspects of politics and assassinations in Imperial China and the relationship between the breakdown of the traditional system and the commensurate increase in assassinations, as well as other forms of violent death will also be discussed. The paper concludes with a discussion of the legitimization of political assassinations in China, and an assessment of the usefulness of assassination from the points of view of both the Chinese political system and the assassination-planners.

Major findings of the study include:

1. Elites die violently during periods of dynastic decline and decay, but quite rarely during periods of relative peace.

2. Political assassination—one of the several forms of violent death—occurs concurrently with general violence in the society. Yet, with certain exceptions, there are on the whole

*Advanced Studies Group, Westinghouse Electric Corporation

fewer instances of assassination than of the other forms of violent death (execution, suicide, or death in warfare), even in periods when the violent death rate is quite high.

3. Like nearly all of the violent deaths in China, political assassinations, in the main, have occurred as part of the process of conflict between elites. In contrast with what appears to be the case in the United States, for example, assassinations in China have generally not been the result of random acts committed by individuals acting alone. Rather, because assassinations are part of the process of elite conflict, they usually occur as the result of collective planning, even if the act is invariably committed by one person acting alone. (In recent times, there have also been a few cases of assassinations of political figures for mainly personal reasons.)

4. The overwhelming majority of the Chinese elite died naturally, during the period under study, and this can be related to the strong influence of the political socialization process, with its emphasis on respect for authority figures, a process through which Chinese of many stations have passed. Additionally, however, high-level officials particularly were protected from attacks on their lives by good security provisions. Moreover, since guns were not widely available in China until the latter part of the 19th century, officials were threatened by less effective weapons during the 1600–1850 period.

5. Generally speaking, the Chinese did not approve of political assassinations; yet, under certain conditions, assassination obtained the tacit if not explicit approval of many Chinese.

6. Occasionally, the Chinese desired the goals of assassins if not the means they used to attain them; and in certain periods, assassination was a quite effective means for attaining certain goals. On other occasions, those who planned political assassinations suffered a sharp decline in their political fortunes as a result of public disapproval of their activity.

We turn first to a quantitative examination of the incidence of violent and nonviolent deaths* of Chinese officials, all of

---

*By nonviolent death is meant the death of an individual through illness or old-age. Violent death here has several forms:

execution (mainly of an official by the Imperial Government);
suicide (as a preferred alternative to execution by either the Government, or anti-Government rebels);

whom must be considered to have been of high rank,[1] first in the late Ming period, then in the Ch'ing (Manchu; 1644–1912) period, and finally in the Republican (1912–49) and Communist (1949–present) periods.

2. Political Assassinations in China, 1600–1968

a. Political Assassinations at the End of the Ming Dynasty, 1600–1644[2]

The Ming dynasty's final years were characterized by intense conflict between eunuchs surrounding the various emperors and bureaucrats dissatisfied with this state of affairs. Furthermore, local rebellions were developing in China proper, as well as in Manchuria in the northeast. In the latter area, the struggle was first among the Manchus; then, after one of their number had succeeded in establishing himself as leader, the decaying Ming dynasty was successfully challenged militarily. The last Ming emperor committed suicide in 1644, and the Ch'ing (Manchu) dynasty was proclaimed.

Given this environment of high violence involving political elites, we would expect to find that, in the period 1600–1644, the rate of death due to violence was higher than in periods of

---

death in warfare (mainly between the Chinese Empire and its opponents, either internal or external);
and assassination.

All four violent forms are considered politically-related in varying degrees.

For the purposes of this paper, political assassination is a form of death that occurs suddenly to an individual who is involved in politics as the result of *covert* planning by one or more other individuals. Generally speaking, the target can be involved at any level of politics in a political system. Here focus is on high-ranking individuals, mainly but not exclusively in Government service.

The above definition of assassination allows one to differentiate sharply between assassination, on the one hand; and execution and suicide on the other. But all three types of violent death of political officials are, of course, related. They are all *violent* forms of death, as opposed to nonviolent ones (natural causes and disease being the two main forms).

relative peace in the Ch'ing dynasty after 1681.† This expectation is confirmed by comparing the results in table 1 and table 3 (below).

Table 1
Cause of Death of Eminent Chinese, et. al., 1600–1644

(N=38)

	Percentage
Natural Causes	61
Suicide	13
Execution	11
Assassination	3
Warfare	13
Total	101*

*Excess due to rounding

Because both Chinese and Manchus were involved in conflict among themselves and against each other, the rates of all forms of violent and nonviolent death for each group are quite similar, although there are differences in the rate of occurrence of the various forms of violent death—as table 2 shows.

Table 2
Cause of Death for Chinese and Manchus, 1600–1644

(N=37)

	Han Chinese	Manchus
	(in percentages)	
Natural Causes	59	60
Suicide	18	7
Execution	9	13
Assassination	5	—
Warfare	9	20
Total	100	100

As was noted, the Manchus were involved in much local warfare among themselves, both in the late 16th century as well as in the period 1600–1644; thus, a larger percentage

---

†We do not have data for the *entire* Ming dynasty; nevertheless, there can be little doubt that the rate of violent death of elites during most of the dynasty was much lower than in its last 44 years.

(20 percent) of Manchus were killed in warfare than were Chinese (9 percent).

The one assassination recorded was extremely important: in 1620, the Ming Emperor, T'ai-ch'ang, was in all likelihood the victim of a successful Court plot to poison him. This event was, of course, symbolic of the decline in political authority in the latter years of the Ming dynasty. Even the Emperor was no longer inviolate. (As is noted below, a similar case occurred at the end of the Ch'ing dynasty.)

In sum, the rate of violent death of officials increased concurrently with the generalized violence which was occurring in Chinese society at the end of the Ming period. The rates changed markedly when the Manchus began to restore order after 1644.

b. Political Assassinations During the Ch'ing Dynasty, 1644–1912

Introduction.—The overthrow of the Ming and the establishment of the Ch'ing dynasty in 1644 were not followed by immediate peace. Separate groups loyal to various Ming princes continued unsuccessfully to try to establish autonomous local bases throughout China. It was not until 1681 that the last major internal challenge to the Manchus was crushed.

Afterwards, although local rebellions developed from time to time in various areas of the Empire, the period from 1680–1840 was one of general peace. But from 1840 until the end of the dynasty, internal and external threats seriously undermined the position of the Ch'ing rulers: for example, from 1850–65, the T'ai-p'ing rebellion raged through much of southern and central China. Beginning in 1840, foreign nations began to challenge the Manchus' supremacy over their realm. Although there were respites from these challenges, in the end the dynasty fell. Especially in the last years of the dynasty, the Manchus, in contrast with the Chinese, were victims of violent deaths, including assassination. This method was particularly used in the final decade by the Chinese against the Manchus. Indeed, the Manchus who did not want to relinquish control were intimidated into doing so by a successful assassination attempt against one of their number. The data in tables 3 and 4 illuminate these points.

Table 3
Cause of Death of Eminent Chinese, et. al., 1645-1912*
(N=365)

Cause of Death	Time Period														Average for total period 1645-1912	Total N
	1645-1660	1661-1680	1681-1700	1701-1720	1721-1740	1741-1760	1761-1780	1781-1800	1801-1820	1821-1840	1841-1860	1861-1880	1881-1900	1901-1912		
Natural Causes	59.5	75	97.4	90	89.3	82.3	91.3	88.9	96.2	100	75	75	87.5	73.3	84.1	307
Suicide	10.8	8.4	2.6	3.3	/	11.8	/	7.4	/	/	12.5	/	12.5	/	5.2	19
Execution	18.9	14	/	3.3	7.2	5.9	8.7	3.7	/	/	/	10	/	6.7	6	22
Assassination	2.7	2.8	/	3.3	3.6	/	/	/	/	/	/	/	/	6.7	1.4	5
Warfare	5.4	/	/	/	/	/	/	/	/	/	8.3	15	/	13.3	2.5	9
Uncertain	2.7	/	/	/	/	/	/	/	3.8	/	4.2	/	/	/	.8	3
Total**	100	100.2	100	99.9	100	100	100	100	100	100	100	100	100	100	100.0	/
N for each time-period	37	36	39	30	28	17	23	27	26	19	24	20	24	15	/	365

*It was arbitrarily decided to determine cause of death for 20-year periods, with two exceptions; 1645-1660 and 1901-1912. The latter exception is self-explanatory; the dynasty fell in 1912; the former one coincides with the end of the reign of the first Ch'ing emperor, and with the beginning of the consolidating, long reign of the K'ang-hsi Emperor, 1661-1722.

**If not 100%, result due to rounding.

Table 4
Comparison of Causes of Death for Chinese and Manchus, 1645-1912
(in percentages)

Death Form

	Period	Natural	Suicide	Execu-tion	Assassi-nation	Killed in Warfare	Un-certain	Total
Han Chinese (N=288)	1645-1660	51.8	10.4	24.1	3.5	6.9	3.5	100.2
	1661-1680	72.7	9.1	15.2	3	/	/	100
	1681-1700	100	/	/	/	/	/	100
	1701-1720	95.2	/	4.8	/	/	/	100
	1721-1740	91.3	/	8.7	/	/	/	100
	1741-1760	90	/	10	/	/	/	100
	1761-1780	94.4	/	5.6	/	/	/	100
	1781-1800	90	5	5	/	/	/	100
	1801-1820	95.5	/	/	/	/	4.5	100
	1821-1840	100	/	/	/	/	/	100
	1841-1860	79	10.6	/	/	5.3	5.3	100.2
	1861-1880	75	/	6.25	/	18.75	/	100
	1881-1900	90.5	9.5	/	/	/	/	100
	1901-1912	90.9	/	9.1	/	/	/	100
	Average for entire dynasty	85.4	3.8	6.9	.7	2.1	1.0	99.9
Manchus (N=63)	1645-1660	87.5	12.5	/	/	/	/	100
	1661-1680	100	/	/	/	/	/	100
	1681-1700	100	/	/	/	/	/	100
	1701-1720	87.5	12.5	/	/	/	/	100
	1721-1740	100	/	/	/	/	/	100
	1741-1760	75	25	/	/	/	/	100
	1761-1780	80	/	20	/	/	/	100
	1781-1800	83.3	16.7	/	/	/	/	100
	1801-1820	100	/	/	/	/	/	100
	1821-1840	100	/	/	/	/	/	100
	1841-1860	60	20	/	/	20	/	100
	1861-1880	75	/	25	/	/	/	100
	1881-1900	100	/	/	/	/	/	100
	1901-1912	25	/	/	25	50	/	100
	Average for entire dynasty	82.5	7.9	3.2	1.6	4.8	/	100

Thus, table 3 shows that during the periods of high internal conflict (1645–80 and 1840–1912), the percentage of natural deaths was considerably lower than in the long period of general peace (1681–1840). The differences in the form of death in the periods 1821–40 and 1841–60 are striking: in the former period 100 percent of all deaths recorded were due to natural causes; in 1841–60, only 75 percent—one of the lowest rates for any of the Ch'ing time periods—were from natural causes. In the 1841–60 period, the death rate due to warfare was 8.3 percent and that due to suicide was 12.5 percent. (An individual frequently preferred to die the latter way rather than face torture and execution at the hands of an enemy.)

With one important exception, most Ch'ing political assassinations recorded in *Eminent Chinese of the Ch'ing Period (ECCP)* took place during the early years of the Ch'ing dynasty. (Two which occurred during the period 1701–20 and 1721–40 both involved Tibetans killing one another, but are nevertheless included in the sample.) As was noted earlier, one of the last Ming emperors was probably a regicide; similarly, in 1908, the Kuang-hsu Emperor (b. 1871) was probably killed on orders from the aging Dowager Empress Tz'u-hsi (b. 1835) just before her own death a day afterwards. Both the late Ming and late Ch'ing regicides were signs that the dynasties were doomed and that respect for their authority among even their own supporters was declining rapidly.

Although assassinations, as expected, occurred at the beginning and the end of the dynasty, the high assassination rate (6.7 percent) for the 1901–12 period is based on only one case, the regicide of the Kuang-hsu Emperor. After the causes of death of Manchus and Chinese are compared, a more careful examination will be made of other late-Ch'ing assassinations and assassination attempts not mentioned in ECCP. (See Political Assassination in Traditional China, below.)

Chinese and Manchu causes of death: a comparison.— While the rule of the Manchus was strongly resisted by many Chinese in its early stages, from the K'ang-hsi period (1661–1722) until the final years of the dynasty, anti-Manchu sentiment was not high. In large measure this situation existed because even before the Manchus assumed power, they had accepted many aspects of Chinese culture. Furthermore, the new Ch'ing dynasty officials recognized that, if they were to rule China successfully, it would be necessary to attract the support of Chinese scholar-officials. Efforts were made to this end even before 1644, as well as thereafter; consequently, although the Manchus provided the ruling house as well as many military leaders, the overwhelming majority of officials were Chinese. However, as the dynasty began to crumble in the late 19th century, young Chinese revolutionaries began to attack the dynasty on the grounds that it was foreign (Manchu), not Chinese.

Because the Chinese generally were less prevalent in the military leadership than the Manchus and because the support of the Chinese was essential to the life of the dynasty, we would expect a higher percentage of Chinese than of Manchus to die from nonviolent causes throughout the dynasty. Accordingly, over a period of time, a greater percentage of Manchu military elites than Chinese would die in war. Also, a greater percentage of Manchus than of Chinese would naturally be the victims (or intended victims) of assassination attempts, at both the beginning and end of the dynasty.

These results are basically confirmed by the data in table 4. To be sure, the rate of death due to natural causes for both Chinese and Manchus for the entire period, 1645–1912, was virtually the same: 85 percent for the Chinese, and 82.5 percent for the Manchus. However, these long-term similarities should not obscure two substantial short-term differences:

1. From 1645–60 and 1661–80, a greater percentage of Chinese died violently than did Manchus—the latter were the victors, the former the victims in the mopping-up operations of the periods.

2. This imbalance was corrected in favor of the Chinese during the long period of relative peace, 1681–1840. During that 160-year span, the death rate due to natural causes was 95 percent for Chinese and 89.2 percent for Manchus. The difference is accounted for not by assassinations or war, but rather by executions and suicides; Manchu wrongdoers were usually permitted the honorable way out, the Chinese were often less leniently treated.

Table 4 shows that no Chinese and no Manchus were assassinated during the 1681–1840 period. As noted in the discussion after table 3, the assassinations that did occur in this period involved Tibetans. Thus, the period of dynastic strength coincided with a low degree of death by violent means for both Chinese and Manchus, with the ruled (Chinese) actually having a lower rate of death by violence than did the rulers (Manchus).

A further examination of late Ch'ing assassinations.—Political assassinations at the end of the Ch'ing dynasty were more numerous than was revealed by data from ECCP; furthermore, these assassinations were the result of strong anti-Manchu sentiments held by Chinese revolutionaries.[3] Important cases are listed and described briefly in table 5.

Table 5

*List of Important Assassinations in the Final Years
of the Ch'ing Period**

1. In 1905, an assassination attempt (by bombing) was made by one Wu Yueh against five ministers (three of whom were Manchus) enroute to observe foreign systems of government. Wu was an anti-Manchu revolutionary with strictly political motives. None of the 5 intended victims were killed, although Wu was killed in the blast.

2. Two years later, in 1907, the Governor of Chekiang, En-ling (a Manchu) was assassinated by Hsu Hsi-lin, a revolutionary leader of the anti-Manchu T'ung-meng Hui (a predecessor organization of Sun Yat-sen's Kuomintang). Hsu's efforts were part of an attempt to begin an insurrection in Chekiang province. Although Hsu succeeded in killing the provincial governor, Hsu himself was captured and executed; moreover, the insurrection attempt failed.

3. After the Kuang-hsu Emperor's death in 1908, a Prince-Regent, Tsai-feng, was appointed to handle affairs for the child-emperor, P'u-i. By this time, Chinese political activities against the Manchu dynasty were rife; one strong current of these was anarchism. One of those influenced by anarchist thoughts was Wanç Ching-wei, nominally a member of Sun Yat-sen's T'ung-meng Hui. In 1910, Wang attempted, but failed, to assassinate the Manchu Prince Regent—a purely political act designed to draw attention to the revolutionary cause. The anarchist movement specifically espoused the carrying out of political assassination, but the anarchists were more successful in the plotting than in the doing.

4. Following the unsuccessful attempt against Tsai-feng, two Manchu provincial officials, Fu-ch'i and Feng-shan posted in Kuangtung Province, a hotbed of Kuomintang revolutionary sentiments, were assassinated by Chinese in separate acts in 1911.

5. In 1912, anti-Manchu forces, including Sun Yat-sen, demanded that the boy-Emperor abdicate; but the Manchu Court—a leader of which was Liang-pi—did not want to acquiesce in Sun Yat-sen's order. On January 26, 1912, Liang-pi was assassinated by one P'eng Chia-chen for political motives, and the ultimatum of the revolutionaries was quickly met.

---

*An-sha shih mainly describes assassinations in the late Ch'ing period, implicit confirmation of our main thesis that assassinations are more likely to occur in China in periods of general violence than in periods of relative peace. An assassination before the last decade of the Ch'ing dis-

c. Political Assassinations in the Republican
Period, 1912–49

The fall of the Manchu dynasty was followed by nearly 40 years of constant, wide-scale conflict, as Chinese of various political persuasions struggled to reestablish the authority of the Central Government.

Yet the levels and forms of violence varied: immediately after the Manchu dynasty fell, a republic was formed with Yuan Shih-k'ai at the helm. Yuan's use of political violence against his opponents was notorious and in fact, contributed to his fall. During the period following Yuan's death (1916) military conflict was high, as numerous warlords sought to establish local, regional, and, when possible, national bases of power. In addition to conflict between warlords, there was the more ideologically based clash between the Chinese Communists and the Kuomintang (Nationalist Party); from 1927 until 1936, the two groups were in a constant state of armed struggle, with the Communists suffering numerous defeats at the hands of the Nationalists who, however, were unable to vanquish the Communists entirely.

The increasing threat of the Japanese after 1937 made it incumbent on Chinese to sublimate their internal differences to protect the nation; Communist-Nationalist hostilities thereafter declined somewhat. However, some Chinese, led by Wang Ching-wei, participated in forming a pro-Japanese puppet government in Nanking. Hostility was high between this regime and that of Chiang Kai-shek in Chungking; political assassination was a constant device used by each group against the other, especially during the period 1938–40. During World War II, however, political assassinations subsided as a result of a truce between the Chungking and Nanking governments.

With the end of World War II, violence between Communists and Nationalists broke out again, resulting in the defeat of the Kuomintang and the establishment in 1949 of the Communist-led People's Republic of China on the Mainland and of Chiang Kai-shek's Republic of China on Taiwan. During most of the period, 1949–68, a higher degree of political

cussed in *An-sha shih* took place in August 1870. Then, an important official, Ma Hsin-i, was knifed while walking in the street by one Chang Wen-hsiang. Although investigations showed that the assassin's motives were personal, some thought the death was politically motivated.

stability prevailed on both the Mainland and Taiwan than had existed during the 1912–49 period on the Mainland.

The preceding survey of the Republican period suggests that the highest percentages of violent deaths to officials would occur in the 1920's and 1930's, but that during the entire period (1912–49), the rates would be higher than during the post-1950 period—or during the 1681–1840 period of prolonged relative peace in the Ch'ing dynasty, for that matter. Moreover, as we expected, we find that the assassination rate is quite high during the entire period, with other forms of violent death also quite prevalent.

Table 6 reveals the major findings.[4] Quite clearly, compared with more peaceful periods, the rate of *natural* death is considerably lower during each decade (or fraction thereof) from 1912–50, and the rate for violent death is higher. During the entire Republican period, the number of assassinations was highest in the 1931–40 decade (four), although the percentage of assassinations (relative to all forms of death) was highest in the 1912–20 period (11 percent). The assassination rate during each decade of the entire Republican period was higher than the average for the entire Ch'ing period (1.4 percent), but the rates for the Republican period are quite similar to those of the late Ming and of the early and late Ch'ing years. This result is to be expected, because all four periods were ones in which intra-elite conflict and general violence were high. It should also be noted that the percentage of those killed in battle (table 6) was lower than expected (3.3 percent), but that the high rate for executions (9.5 percent) was correlative with the conflict level of the period.

Assassinations in six of eight recorded cases were directly a part of the process of conflict among disputing elites, as the following brief descriptions (in table 7) of the cases show.* Two other assassinations against political figures were mainly committed for personal reasons, although there were political overtones as well.

---

*This list is by no means complete: nearly half the individuals whose biographies will appear in the *Biographic Dictionary* cannot yet be tabulated. Consequently, two key assassinations—those of Sung Chiao-jen, an early leader of the Kuomintang (by Yuan Shih-k'ai, in 1913); and Wen I-to (an important poet and leader of the Democratic League; probably by Kuomintang agents, in 1946) are omitted. Furthermore, even if the entire *Dictionary* were published and all entries considered, certain individuals might not appear in the *Dictionary* and would therefore not be considered in the analysis. Therefore, a listing follows of several other

Table 6

Causes of Death in the Republican and Post-Republican Periods, 1912-1968

(N=211) (in percentages)

Cause	1912-1920	1921-1930	1931-1940	1941-1950	1951-1960	1961-1970	Average of all cases
			Year				
Natural	78	52	68.5	63	92.3	100	75.4
Assassination	11	7.4	7.4	2.2	/	/	3.8
Suicide	/	/	5.5	2.2	5.1	/	2.8
Execution	/	26	9.3	17.4	/	/	9.5
Killed in Battle	11	7	5.5	2.2	/	/	3.3
Unknown or Uncertain	/	3.5	3.7	8.7	2.6	/	3.8
Accidental	/	3.5	/	4.4	/	/	1.4
Decennial Total	100	99.4	99.9	100.1	100	100	100

Table 7

Brief Description of Political Assassinations, 1912–1950
(arranged chronologically, by type)

I. Assassinations of political figures for strictly political reasons.

    1. Ch'en Ch'i-mei. Anti-Manchu revolutionary assassinated by Yuan Shih-k'ai in 1916. May have been revenge for Ch'en's having planned the assassination of Chang Ju-ch'eng, the garrison-commander of Shanghai loyal to Yuan Shih-k'ai.

    2. Liao Chung-k'ai. Leading member of left-wing Kuomintang. Assassinated in 1925 by individuals linked to Hu Han-min, leading member of right-wing Kuomintang.

    3. Lu Po-hung, Shanghai civic leader and industrialist. Assassinated in 1937, probably by Kuomintang agents, for continuing to contribute to hospitals while city under Japanese occupation.

    4. Liu Chan-en (Herman Liu). Shanghai civic leader. Assassinated in Shanghai in 1938 by Chinese who were Japanese agents.

    5. Ch'en Lu. Foreign Minister in the pro-Japanese puppet government headed by Wang Ching-wei; assassinated by pro-Kuomintang elements in 1939.

    6. Li Chao-liu. Communist guerrilla leader, assassinated in Harbin in 1946. Assailants unknown.

II. Assassinations of political figures mainly for personal reasons.

    1. Hsu Shu-cheng. Warlord assassinated in 1925 by one Lu Ch'eng-wu to avenge father's death.

    2. Chang Tsung-ch'ang. Shantung warlord assassinated in 1932 by nephew of man Chang executed in 1927.

---

assassinations which took place from 1912–1950; the significance of individuals varies.

Name[5]	Position	Year of Assassination
1. T'ang Yu-lu	aide to T.V. Soong	1931
2. T'ang Shao-i	politician: Puppet Gov.	1938
3. Chou Feng-chi	politician: Puppet Gov.	1938 (?)
4. Chi Yun-ch'ing	Green gang leader	1938
5. Ho Tien-fang	militant in puppet gov.	1938
6. Fu Hsiao-an	pro-Jap. Shanghai mayor	1938
7. Lu Lien-k'uei	Detective in Shanghai	1938
8. Chang Hsiao-lin	Green gang leader	1938
9. Yang Chien	Sec. of Academia Sinica	1943 (?)
10. Wang Ching-wei	Pres., Puppet Gov.	1935 (unsuccessful attempt)
11. Li Kung-p'o	leader of Dem. League	1946

12. It might also be noted that Japanese occupation officials were also frequently targets for Chinese patriots during World War II. (In fact, Japanese were targets from the late 1920's.)

Some students of Chinese history have considered the Republican period as postdynastic, somewhat comparable to the Ch'in (255–209 B.C.), the Sui (581–618), or the late Ming–early Ch'ing periods. Although there is no representative sample of data for the Ch'in and Sui periods, late Ming–early Ch'ing data may be usefully considered in comparison with the data for the Republican period. Thus, one would expect to find some comparability between the patterns of cause of death in both periods, as well as between late Ch'ing and Republican patterns.

Table 8 compares (in percentage terms) the forms of death during the late Ming–early Ch'ing, late Ch'ing, and Republican periods. In only one period, 1881–1900, does the rate of natural death exceed the Ch'ing dynasty average of 84.1 percent. Otherwise, the rate of death due to natural causes is quite similar in the late Ming (61 percent), early Ch'ing (59.5 percent and 75 percent for the first two time periods), and the Republican period (58 percent and 66 percent for the two time periods). The rate of death from natural causes is considerably higher in each of the late Ch'ing time spans, with the exception of the bloody 1841–60 period. From 1861–1900, various Chinese and Manchu officials tried to restore the dynasty's strength. Their partial success is reflected in the data for the 1861–1911 period, which show relatively high natural death rates.

Compared with the two other periods of high violence (late Ming–early Ch'ing and late Ch'ing), assassination levels are highest in the Republican period, although they are also high in the last decade of the Ch'ing dynasty. Assassination rates in Republican and late Ch'ing time spans exceed those for the late Ming–early Ch'ing period.

If lower natural-death rates are representative of the periods of high conflict, whether these be late Ming, early or late Ch'ing, or Republican, we would conversely expect that higher natural-death rates would exist in periods when the positions of high-level elites were relatively legitimized, whether during the long Ch'ing period (1681–1840) or the shorter post-Republican period (1951–1968, with the years 1966–68 being noteworthy exceptions).

Table 9 shows the comparison of these periods. If the data reflect reality with any degree of accuracy, the last 18 years have been years in which the overwhelming majority of high officials on Taiwan and the Mainland died naturally and not

Table 8
Cause of Death: (1) Late Ming-early Ch'ing;
(2) Late Ch'ing; (3) Republican
(in percentages)

Cause of Death	Late Ming-early Ch'ing			Time Period 1841-1860	Late Ch'ing			Republican Period	
	1600-1644	1645-1660	1661-1680	1841-1860	1861-1880	1881-1900	1901-1911	1912-1930	1931-1950
Natural Causes	61	59.5	75	75	75	87.5	73.3	58	66
Suicide	13	10.8	8.4	12.5	/	12.5	/	/	4
Execution	11	18.9	14	/	10	/	6.7	19	13
Assassination	3	2.7	2.8	/	/	/	6.7	8	5
Killed in warfare	13	5.4	/	8.3	15	/	13.3	8	4
Unknown or Uncertain	/	2.7	/	4.2	/	/	/	3	6
Accidental	/	/	/	/	/	/	/	3	2
TOTAL	100	100	100.2*	100	100	100	100	99	100

(Note: If percentages are not 100, result due to rounding.)

Table 9

Cause of Death: (1) Ch'ing Dynasty, 1681–1840;
(2) Post-Republican Period, 1951–1968
(in percentages)
Time
Period

Cause of Death	1681–1840 (N=209)	1951–1968 (N=75)
Natural Causes	92.3	96
Suicide	3.1	2.7
Execution	3.4	–
Assassination	1.0	–
Killed in Warfare	–	–
Unknown/Uncertain	1.0	1.3
Accidental	—	–
TOTAL	100.8*	100.0

*Excess due to rounding.

by violence; indeed table 9 suggests that the percentage of violent deaths was lower than even in the relatively peaceful 1681–1840 period. (The violence of the Cultural Revolution [see the following section] may alter upward the 1951–68 percentages, however.)

d. The Communist Period, 1949–68

With the establishment of the Chinese People's Republic (CPR) in 1949, overt forms of political opposition ceased. During the CPR's early years many local-level political opponents, especially rural landlords and the urban bourgeoisie, were stripped of their property and either executed or imprisoned. Especially after the Hundred Flowers Period (1957), many intellectuals were subjected to psychological and physical torture. Yet, if only because the regime held an overwhelming balance of force against its opponents, there seem to have been no cases of political assassination of high officials since 1949 on the Mainland. Purge victims have either committed suicide (e.g., Kao Kang, in 1954) or simply disappeared from public life (e.g., P'eng Teh-huai disappeared in

1959). These conclusions about the absence of political assassinations have not been invalidated by the events of the Great Proletarian Cultural Revolution (1966–68), as far as is known.

The Cultural Revolution was launched in China, in the summer of 1966. One of its major manifestations was the removal, for various reasons, of many Party-Government leaders on all levels: national, provincial, and local. Many targets of purges fought back, supported by other bureaucrats as well as by some sectors of the society at large. Although Chairman Mao Tse-tung, the initiator of the Cultural Revolution, lacked sufficient support to effect a sweeping replacement of all political leaders, many did lose their posts. On various levels of the Party and State structures, conflict was extensive between many entrenched bureaucrats and their supporters on the one hand, and Mao and his supporters on the other.

Consequently, since August 1966, violence unparalleled in the history of the People's Republic erupted on the Chinese Mainland. Most of this violence was political in nature, although economic goals also figured in the dispute. If the Feierabends' categories are used to list the types of domestic conflict which erupted in China in the 1966–68 period, the following types occurred:[6]

1. Micro-strikes

2. Micro-demonstrations

3. Micro-riots

4. Arrests of significant and insignificant persons

5. Imprisonment of significant and insignificant persons

6. Terrorism and sabotage

Although political assassinations and executions have not been common occurrences during the period thus far,[7] numerous former political elites have been either removed from previous positions[8] and/or subjected to cruel psychological and physical punishment. As a result, some ex-officials have attempted, sometimes successfully, to evade further difficulties by committing suicide.[9] In late 1966, P'eng Chen (former mayor of Peking), Lu Ting-yi (former Minister of Propaganda), and Lo Jui-ch'ing (former Chief of Staff of the People's Liberation Army) were reported to have unsuccessfully attempted to commit suicide. (Another story, by a Japanese correspondent in Peking, claimed that Red Guard posters called for execution of the three by firing squad.) The Yugoslav news agency, Tanyug, reported that Yang Hsiu-feng (then President of the Supreme Court) had, like P'eng, Lo, and Lu, also unsuccessfully attempted to commit suicide. An actual suicide was that of the former Yunnan Provincial Communist Party First Secretary, Yen Hung-yen, in the summer of 1967.[10]

As a result of prolonged and harsh physical and psychological attacks, old leaders have died because their physical constitutions could not stand the strain. Victims of this sort have undoubtedly included Yeh Chi-chuang (died 27 June 1967, age 74; Minister of Foreign Trade, 1952–67), Chiang Kuang-nai (died 8 June 1967, age 79; Minister of Textile Industry, 1952–67), and Li Ta (died 24 August 1966, age 77; President of Wuhan University since 1952, as well as one of several founders—Chairman Mao was another—of the Chinese Communist Party).[11]

The lack of evidence of political assassinations of high-level Communist officials is replicated by an examination of incidents of violence at the local level. Despite the numerous acts of anomic violence in Canton, for example, the political assassination of only one low-level, local-Party person was reported in *SCMP:* one individual was said to have been killed by a hand grenade while working in his factory office.[12] Two other instances were reported in which local political figures were killed, but apparently not for political reasons: a local official was killed by "class enemies" and a railway leader by "thugs."[13] Whether these were politically inspired is uncertain.

Gun availability during the Cultural Revolution.—Political violence among groups competing for local power (e.g., workers, students of various levels and degrees of education, certain members of the Army, and low-level bureaucrats) was a constant feature of the Cultural Revolution almost from its inception. Because the number of people killed and wounded has been exaggerated and played down both inside and outside China, it may never be possible to know just how many people were victims of the violence of the Cultural Revolution. Yet one fact seems quite certain—the increased availability of guns resulted in much bloodshed, involving countless individuals, particularly in Chinese cities. Of 46 references in *SCMP* to local-level violence, fully half referred to the use of guns by one or both parties to the conflict. In Wuhan, a major urban center in Hupeh Province, 50,000 guns were reportedly available on one occasion. While no accurate public data exist for gun availability in Kwangtung province or its capital (Canton), many reports of violence in that province describe gun use. Chinese newspapers report guns being obtained by warring factions from at least two sources: (1) seizure from P.L.A. arsenals; and (2) seizure from arms shipments (presumably being made via rail or truck) enroute to Vietnam. Again, while no public data exist as to the number of guns seized from either of these two sources, the amounts were probably substantial.

Guns were reportedly used in 50 percent of the 46 cases of violence which appeared in *SCMP* and one would expect the number of fatalities to be quite high, as in fact it is. Fatalities occurred in 16 of the 23 cases (about 70 percent) where guns were reportedly used. Even in the 23 reported clashes where the use of guns was not specifically referred to, fatalities were reported in nine (nearly 40 percent) of the cases.

Given the random nature of the data, it is difficult to determine the number of casualties resulting from these clashes, except to say that in numerous cases individuals have been killed and wounded. Indeed, for the purposes of this report, there is no need to indulge in body counts; many people, probably a large part of them youths, have been killed or wounded as a result of the conflicts which ensued during the period of the Cultural Revolution.

Concluding remarks about violent deaths of elites in Communist China.—Since the establishment of the Chinese People's Republic, political violence against high-level officials was quite limited until the Cultural Revolution began in mid-1966. For many years, Chinese Communist high-level officials had been noted for their cohesion and limited conflicts. Within the society at large, the Communist Party if not necessarily widely esteemed, controlled almost all of the weapons in Chinese society, so that it was difficult for opponents to use violence against high officials. Low-level officials were also generally free from violent attacks, although they were subject to some threats, particularly during the aftermath of the Great Leap Forward (1959–61).

It was not until the Cultural Revolution that high-level officials were among the main targets of criticism and attack. As far as it is known, high-level officials have not been assassination victims; but, as it has been shown, suicides and attempted suicides have been reported, as have the deaths of elderly persons caused by the strain of the Cultural Revolution. Formal executions have not been reported as yet.

Nevertheless, certain aspects of the Cultural Revolution have been so violent that it would not be surprising if, in the future, verifiable reports appeared which would show that occasional executions and assassinations of important officials took place during the 1966–68 period. Such expectations cannot be avoided in view of the frequent correlation, in Chinese history since the late Ming period, of all forms of violent death, including political assassinations, with general political violence in China. This expectation is, if anything, strengthened by the increased availability of guns in Chinese society during the past several years.

3. Politics and Political Assassination in Traditional China

Despite the rather high rate of political assassinations in China from 1900–1950, the long-term data given in the previous section shows that there has generally been a low incidence of political assassination of elites. In order to understand why this is so, it is necessary to examine the relationship between authority figures at the national level (e.g., the Emperor) and subordinates (e.g., the bureaucracy). A similar relationship existed on the local level between the Emperor's surrogates, the bureaucracy, and the local inhabitants.

During most of Chinese history, Confucian ideology was influential in molding the behavior of the Chinese political elite. Among other things, Confucian literature stressed the importance of respect for superiors, whether they be near or distant, one's father or the Emperor. From their earliest years, young Chinese were educated in the Confucian classics; it was necessary that these and other literary classics be memorized by future bureaucrats. Thus, the educational process was carried out not only for learning's sake but also for its didactic function. It was necessary not only to learn what one studied, but to use moral precepts of the Confucian literature to guide one's behavior in adult life, whether in the bureaucracy or outside it. And a main precept emphasized was respect for superiors.

The inculcation of respect supported the hierarchical nature of traditional Chinese Government, in which the Emperor—embodying religious, symbolic, and political roles—was supreme lord over all. The political power of the Chinese Emperor in periods of dynastic strength was great; furthermore, the awe and respect which he commanded added to his prestige within Chinese society. He was literally and figuratively conceived of as the Son of Heaven; thus, harm to his personage, or even to that of his subordinates, was considered a crime of consummate magnitude.

The main political functions of the Emperor included the carrying of a heavy daily administrative burden as well as supervising civilian and military personnel.[14] Relations between the powerful Emperor and the bureaucracy over which he presided were often in a state of tension; yet the system generally functioned quite well. Individual bureaucrats infrequently perceived their positions threatened by the Emperor or his family. (As tables 3 and 4 showed, most high-level elites died naturally during the Ch'ing period, particularly from 1681–1840. See also table 9.)

Positions in the Chinese civil service were generally attained by achievement, not solely by ascriptive criteria; i.e., although a high socioeconomic position helped one's chances for entry into the civil service, it was still necessary to pass standardized examinations. Although some individuals might be accepted into the service because they were from the imperial family, most applicants had to pass the examinations. Those successful were assured positions and probable advancement, free from the excessive competition from individuals lacking the overall qualifications for a particular bureaucratic position.

Although the influence of Confucian learning and morality contributed to politically socializing the bureaucrats into accepting and even strengthening the power of the Emperor, relations between the ruler and his bureaucracy were complicated by problems which were created by the basic nature of their roles in the political system. As Professor Levenson has pointed out:

The ambivalence of bureaucracy toward monarchy and of monarchy toward bureaucracy was comprehended in the ambivalence of each toward feudalism: bureaucracy had some, at least, of the dynamics of feudalism without the statics, monarchy had the reverse.

But the conflict between the Emperor and the bureaucracy, whether it was in their relationships toward feudalism or central authority, was "far from extreme, for after all, the social roles of bureaucracy and monarchy were only clashing, not incompatible, and were complementary even as they clashed."[15]

Although the bureaucracy acknowledged that the Emperor was the central authority of the traditional Chinese political system, there was sufficient hostility in the Emperor-bureaucracy relationship to warrant instituting provisions to assure the Emperor's safety at all times. For the bureaucracy's loyalty to the Emperor was, in the end, loyalty to the Emperor as the leader of the system, not to the Emperor personally. If the Emperor was perceived in a highly negative way, loyalty to him might be withdrawn, even if not necessarily given to another.

a. Security Measures

The Chinese Emperor was protected by elaborate security measures in order to defend him from attacks by overly hostile bureaucrats or other Chinese dissatisfied with his rule. The Imperial Palace in Peking was surrounded by high walls and well guarded by troops especially selected for this purpose. Entrance into the Palace was strictly regulated and granted only to high and trusted officials. Although Ming Emperors did not tour the realm, both the K'ang-hsi (1661–1722) and the Ch'ien-lung (1736–96) Emperors did tour on several occasions. Yet, generally speaking, the Emperor did not appear frequently in public; and when he did, commoners were not permitted to draw near enough to attack him nor even to gaze on him.

Individuals charged with performing security duties varied with the dynasty:

1. If the dynasty was a non-Chinese one (i.e., Mongol or Manchu), non-Chinese often held key positions in the Imperial Court, even if the bureaucracy was still staffed mainly by Chinese. The non-Chinese recognized that they had a common interest with the Emperor in protecting him from plots or hostile policies emanating from the bureaucracy. The gains derived from protecting the Emperor far outweighed those which might be gained from removing him.[16]

2. If the dynasty was Chinese (ie., T'ang or Ming) eunuchs were employed by the Emperor to mediate between himself and the bureaucracy. According to Karl Wittfogel, eunuchs "not infrequently . . . were responsible for their sovereign's personal safety (as heads of his bodyguard)."[17] Eunuchs were not perceived as threats by the Emperor, since it was he who had given them posts (which were often very powerful) and they had much to gain by the Emperor's continuing to hold his position. Because eunuchs were very often successful in influencing imperial decision making, they—more than the Emperor—were often strongly attacked by the civil service bureaucracy.[18]

Although Chinese Emperors may have perceived potential threats from the bureaucracy, it was nevertheless necessary for them to obtain and preserve the respect of the bureaucrats if the Chinese political system was to continue functioning. Disciplinary measures could be enacted; yet a reign of terror instigated by the Emperor against the bureaucracy would only have destroyed all semblance of order in the country. Thus, despite tendencies toward conflict within the system, conflict boundaries were generally preserved. And one of these was to avoid widespread removal by assassination (or execution, for that matter) of the Emperor or his bureaucrats. It is more than mere coincidence that the two probable regicides (see Assassinations, 1600–1968, above) in the past 500 years in China were committed by persons within the Court, from the Emperor's own entourage and not by members of the bureaucracy or the common people. Political interests militated against mutual conflict between the Emperor and his bureaucrats; furthermore, Confucianism, the political ideology of the dynastic nation-state, exerted a powerful influence on both ruler and subject, reducing strife between the two. The interrelationship may be depicted as follows:

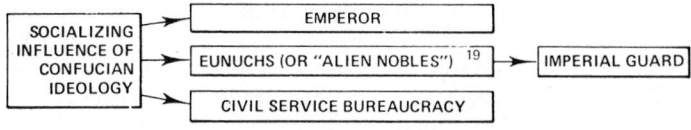

When such a system worked effectively, there were very few violent deaths of any kind among high officials. Good Emperors and good officials knew the importance of behaving properly, a behavioral pattern reinforced by mutual self-interest which required that intra-elite conflict be minimized if the imperial system was to persist. During most of the Ch'ing dynasty this system functioned reasonably well. Then, beginning with the T'ai-p'ing rebellion (1850–65), the authority of the Ch'ing government was increasingly called into question as a result of failure to deal successfully with domestic and foreign threats. By the end of the 19th century, Court conflict among the Manchus and ultimate disillusionment with the Manchus by Chinese officials brought the dynasty to its collapse. Table 5 suggests the degree to which assassination played an increasingly important role in causing the fall of the Ch'ing dynasty.

b. Assassinations in the Warlord Period

Although elite-level politics in traditional China were characterized by an order that existed because of the tension between the Emperor and the bureaucracy, there was violence rather than tension, and disorder rather than order in the Republican period as extensive conflict took place among provincially and regionally based warlords. After unsuccessful efforts had been made to reconstitute a strong central government in 1912, warlords established political control over local areas as a result of their military power. Most warlords were not content to be mere local leaders; using military force, they clashed with one another in an attempt to expand the areas which they governed. For 20 years (1915–35), warlordism was a significant aspect of the Chinese political scene, even as attempts, particularly by Chiang Kai-shek, were beginning to succeed in establishing a strong central government.

Viewed in terms of how order was traditionally maintained in China, the central problem of the warlord period was the failure of any single figure (or group) to become established as the new authority of the Chinese state. Moreover, the old bureaucracy had disappeared and a new one had yet to be established. The breakdown of the traditional system had come suddenly and rapidly and while competing warlords desired to monopolize national power (or at least hold a major share of it) their opponents were competent enough and had sufficient resources to thwart the reinstituting of a strong central government.

It is well known that a main feature of the post-Ch'ing period was the clash of warlord armies; additionally, two forms of political assassination were features of the times:

1. Warlords tried, rarely successfully, to have a rival assassinated; or
2. Warlords attempted, with some success, to have the subordinates of a rival assassinated.

Thus, for example, after the Manchurian warlord Chang Tso-lin was assassinated by the Japanese in 1928, Chang Hsueh-liang (Chang Tso-lin's son) had two former aides of his father assassinated because he suspected that the two had aided the Japanese in his father's murder. He also saw in them rivals to his own authority in Manchuria.

The assassination of equals was a less common occurrence than that of subordinates. For example, the latter were often removed when a warlord would invite a rival and his aides to a banquet. Although the rival might be spared from the attacks which took place in the dining hall, frequently the subordinates were less fortunate. This situation may have resulted, in part, from the subordinates giving their lives to protect their leader from death.

Some of the limits of conflict which the Emperor and bureaucracy observed in the traditional system seem also to have been instituted by the warlords. Although these regional leaders' authority was not nearly as legitimated as that of their dynastic predecessors, they commanded some respect from both their equals (other warlords) and subordinates. Thus, there seems to have developed in the post-World-War-I period a sort of code of honor between the warlords themselves, which required that the leaders mutually respect an opponent's life, even if his inferiors could be killed. This code may have developed as a result of the nature of warlord conflict. During most of the period, no single warlord had enough power to establish central control alone; invariably, it was necessary to share even local or regional power with an ally, whose reliability could never be taken fully for granted. In an era of unstable alliances, today's enemy could be tomorrow's friend; hence, enemies could be vanquished or forced to retire, but not executed.

Furthermore, traditional respect for superiors from inferiors may have extended into the transitional, warlord period. Many warlords were surrounded by individuals whose criteria for status were both ascriptive and achievement, and in some cases, being competent military personnel, they were also from the warlord's family, locale, or province. The persistence in the transitional period of some, if not all, traditional Confucian values governing interpersonal behavior meant that close personal ties were helpful in reducing conflict within warlord groupings; subordinates in a warlord's camp held enough of the traditional values of respect for leaders so that they were not a constant source of violent threats to their chiefs.

It might be noted that if a private individual wished to assassinate a warlord, his chances of successfully doing so would be slight: security measures, given the semimilitary nature of the warlords' existence, were very good. As table 7 showed, most of the assassination victims were not warlords; and those that were were relatively minor figures killed not by their opponents or subordinates, but by individuals for mainly personal reasons. Both warlords cited in table 7 were killed in public places (railway stations), not in the comparative security of their homes or camps.

Thus, the respect which warlords commanded from subordinates (who knew from childhood to give respect to superiors, an authority pattern reemphasized in the military environment) as well as the security enforced to protect warlords, made warlordism not very risky for the chieftains, although this was not the case for his aides and foot soldiers.

c. Gun Availability in Pre-Republican China

A major concern of Americans is the relationship between the availability of guns and the general level of anomic violence in the society as well as the relationship to political assassinations. In China before the final decades of the Ch'ing dynasty, the level of sophistication of firearms was low enough so that Chinese officials did not have to fear assassination from guns.

The Chinese learned how to use gunpowder in relatively large but primitive cannons long before the start of the Ming dynasty (1368); however, there was very little improvement made, in size or scale, in these early weapons over the next several centuries.[20] Then, as a result of increased contact with the West beginning in the mid-19th century, modern weaponry became more available, both through imports and domestic production. Over a period of time, hand weapons proliferated through the society and were used extensively at various times during the Republican period. Political elites, as was noted earlier, were regular targets of assassins using these weapons.

Gun Availability since 1950.—However, following the Communist takeover in 1949, the Mainland regime attempted to monopolize access to weapons by collecting as many privately held weapons as possible. This effort was basically successful, although some Chinese did hide a limited number of weapons from the police. As was noted in the discussion of the Cultural Revolution, the level of violence undoubtedly increased and remained high due to the rather easy availability of guns since late 1966. Conversely, the success of various provincial authorities, via the Chinese Army, in reducing the availability of guns in the country facilitated the maintenance of uneasy calm as 1968 ended.

4. On the Legitimacy of Assassination of Chinese Officials

In any political system which, generally speaking, highly respected its political leaders, one must expect that violent acts committed against high officials would not be legitimized but rather abhorred. Thus it was in traditional China. It may have been somewhat dangerous for one to be an official during interdynastic periods, and it took some time for new authority figures to emerge once a dynasty was overthrown. But after a new dynasty was established and its authority legitimized by the Chinese, violent deaths, by any means, of elites were quite rare. Most high-ranking officials died naturally.

Thus assassinations were not in any way legitimized by the spirit of Chinese politics during the traditional period. Any assassination attempts against the Emperor or his officials would have been subject to the strictest censure and punishment, for such acts would have been viewed by many other Chinese as disturbing the natural order of society.

However, when that order was disrupted due to the emergence of rebellious groups which challenged the ruling dynasty, the use of assassination became less subject to censure, particularly if it was carried out against non-Chinese (as in the late Ch'ing period). As Manchu rule neared its end, there was so much hostility by some Chinese revolutionaries to the ruling elite that assassination came to be used as a weapon, particularly against Manchu officials of the Ch'ing monarchy. Such a tactic seems to have been considered acceptable by some Chinese, although senior Chinese officials undoubtedly did not approve these actions.

Following the fall of the Ch'ing dynasty, assassinations became fairly regular occurrences during the warlord period as well as in the late 1930's. Their frequency was not a sign of widespread approval, however. While warlords may have considered the use of assassination as an acceptable tactic against an opponent (or more likely, the latter's subordinates) such behavior did not mean that all Chinese involved in the political process believed that assassination of political opponents was a proper way to deal with conflict. Indeed, when assassination was used by Kuomintang officials against one another, the assassin's faction was condemned by other factions, not (as in Japan, for example) praised for the righteous motives which prompted the act. Thus, after the assassination of Liao Chung-k'ai by Hu Han-min's aides in 1925, Hu's political fortunes in the Kuomintang steadily declined. Similarly, many Chinese believed that the Kuomintang was responsible for the 1946 assassinations of Li Kung-p'u (a leader in the left-of-center Democratic League) and Wen I-to (a Chinese poet and Democratic League member); being implicated in these assassinations only added to the difficulties of the Nationalists in establishing their authority after World War II ended.

After 1949, the Communist government succeeded in re-establishing reasonably strong central control over China; even though its officials were feared, if not universally respected, the regime monopolized the use of terror in society. Thus it was difficult, if not impossible, for individuals or groups opposed to the Communist government to assault high officials of that government. Only with the Cultural Revolution (1966–68) were physical attacks by Red Guards against Party and State officials legitimized by some, but not all, sponsors of the Cultural Revolution. Consequently, much strife ensued between new and old groups contending for power throughout the country, sanctioned for reasons of his own by Chairman Mao Tse-tung.

Mao and his cohorts did not specifically state that the Red Guards, for example, could use violent means to oust "party powerholders taking the capitalist road"; indeed, on several occasions, they warned against such use. Nevertheless, by officially sanctioning the removal of the Party elite, it became a matter for local discretion as to how the goals of the Cultural Revolution could best be attained. Additionally, although violence was discouraged, Mao and his aides made no apologies for bloodshed, claiming that "revolution is not a dinner party."

Hence, from the very beginning of the Cultural Revolution generalized political violence was semilegitimized by some, if not all, Chinese political elites; those opposed to Mao and his policies had no choice but to retaliate against their attackers —which they did, often with great effectiveness.

As the Cultural Revolution continued, some of Mao's supporters, including his wife, Chiang Ch'ing, encouraged Red Guards to use guns against their opponents. But, as the Chinese military made its weight felt, those same elites who had first encouraged rebels to use weapons reversed their original position.

During the past 500 years of Chinese history, the use of political assassination by one group of elites against another or by private citizens against senior officials has not been considered legitimate behavior in the Chinese political system, except under certain conditions. During long periods of relative internal peace (e.g., 1681–1840) the authority of the regime was established throughout most of China and its officials respected. Even in relatively violent periods during Ming and Ch'ing times, assassination was not widely used against senior officials.

However, with the decline of Ch'ing power in the late 19th century, Manchu officials were no longer immune from personal assault. Assassinations took place with relative frequency in the final decade of Ch'ing rule; furthermore, the late Ch'ing patterns carried over into the Republican period, although assassination was less legitimized when used by Chinese against one another than when used by Chinese against the Manchus.

5. The Impact and Effectiveness of Assassination in China

Although assassinations as a way of settling political disputes in China have at best been made partially legitimate by some elites, there have been periods when assassination has been used effectively and with some impact. Thus, even the unsuccessful assassination attempt in 1910 by Wang Ching-wei against Tsai-feng, the Prince Regent (see table 5) dramatized the cause of anti-Manchu Chinese radicals. Additionally, the successful assassination attempt against Liang-pi two years later so intimidated the Ch'ing Court that the dynasty turned power over to the Republican forces.

But because assassination as a tool in political conflict was not totally acceptable to many Chinese during the Republican period, it often harmed the interest of the assassins' faction, even if a given assassination attempt succeeded. Furthermore, as in the 1938–40 period, those who plotted assassinations could in turn become the victims of counter-plots. Hence, outer limits to violence developed and leaders of both the Kuomintang and the Puppet regime (in Nanking) entered into a tacit truce, agreeing not to assassinate opponents or members of the latter's camp.

6. A Postscript:
Some Relevant Comparisons on Political Assassinations in China and the U.S.

1. In China, an increase in assassinations is very clearly related to a general period of domestic violence, somewhat like the situation that took place in the U.S. after the Civil War. The occurrence of assassinations is more likely during periods of civil violence, when the authority positions of elite and officials are called into question, than in times of civil

peace. However, in the Chinese case, it seems far more difficult for the authority's legitimacy to be reconstituted once it is called into question, than in the American case (compare the rather long period of violence and violent death from 1850–1950 in China and the recovery in the South after the Reconstruction era ended; or, for that matter, the immediate power transfer after President Kennedy's death).

It might be added that when the Chinese wear themselves out through extensive civil conflict, the political assassination rates (as well as the rates for all violent deaths) drop to a very low level (none of the Chinese or Manchus studied were assassinated from 1681–1840 and 1950–68). But there are greater extremes of violence in China, with assassinations and high violence lasting for much longer periods of time, and then stopping.

2. Generally speaking, lower level officials in China, as in the United States, were less prone to face violent death than higher level ones when violence was rife through the land. But, only two Emperors since 1368 have been killed by assassination in contrast with four U.S. Presidents since 1789; in China, the victims tend to be the Emperor's subordinates.

3. For purposes of comparison, Manchus in the late Ch'ing period in China can be considered as functional equivalents of carpetbaggers and others in the U.S. South after the Civil War —both were outgroups. However, the performance of each outgroup as a ruling elite differed considerably: the Manchus were politically socialized into accepting many Chinese values before taking over as a new dynasty; they were not simple conquerors. In contrast, the Reconstructionists came as pure conquerors and were not empathetic with Southern values. Rather, in contrast with the Manchus, the Reconstructionists tried to ram new values down the throats of the Southerners. Because the Manchus were basically Sinicized by 1650, their rule was basically accepted by 1660, and fully so by 1680.

4. With reference to the study of political assassinations, political socialization brought quick legitimacy to the Manchu rule and, consequently, a low incidence of assassination of Manchus by Chinese until the end of the dynasty. Then, as anti-Manchu feeling became ethnically expressed, particularly from 1907–12, the assassination level in China increased (25 percent of 1901–1912 sample). Although the papers on political assassination in China and the U.S. are based on different

samples, it remains clear from the data in both papers that when the legitimacy of the outgroup is questioned, assassinations rise.

5. This brings us to the matter of efficacy of assassinations. In China, as in the U.S., the result is mixed.

A. When assassination is used against the outgroup (Manchu or Reconstructionist), it is a rather effective weapon: in the end, the assassins get rid of the outgroup—the desired goal. The assassins will face little, if any, political disapproval.

B. However, when assassination is used by Chinese against other Chinese, the result is less clear. For example:

1. There was general disapproval of assassination by many Chinese during the warlord period as well as afterwards.

2. Consequently, groups backing assassinations often suffered a political demise (as in the case of Hu Han-min and Liao Chung-k'ai—1925; and the KMT implication in the death of Wen I-to).

3. At one particular time, 1938–40, Chinese assassinations against other Chinese were rife (on a relatively high rank of elites); some Chinese had become collaborators of the Japanese, and thus became targets of Kuomintang, and Kuomintang leaders were targets of the collaborators.

6. Random U.S. cases of assassination—that is, those not in the Reconstruction period—seem, in the main, not to be the result of planned acts by politically motivated groups, while in China assassinations have been planned actions by groups for political purposes in nearly all cases. Even when personal revenge is an issue, political overtones are also present. (See table 7, for example.)

7. *Brief Concluding Remarks.* The Chinese case is relevant for comparison with the American one if only because it reveals intensities in assassination rates rarely seen in the United States, as well as periods of civil violence of longer time-spans and greater depth than we have seen in the United States. The Chinese case is instructive because it demonstrates some of the relationships which one can expect to find when social and political order breaks down and elites conflict to such an extent that restoration of order is long in coming.

Hence, we come back to the beginning. The occurrence of political assassinations is very strongly related to how a political system copes with the authority problem. Put differently, is the focal point of central authority—Emperor, President, or Chairman—made legitimate and accepted both by other elites and populace? The Chinese case suggests that when the answer is yes, all forms of violent deaths, including assassinations, will occur infrequently; when the answer is no, we can expect an increase in violent deaths of officials.

References

1. The basic source for information on late Ming and all Ch'ing officials is the biographic dictionary, *Eminent Chinese of the Ch'ing Period* (see reference 2); due to the focus of that work, this paper concentrates on high-ranking individuals. However, there is little reason to suspect that officials at lower levels were more likely targets for assassination than higher ones. Entry into the civil service was highly desired by Chinese families; the risks to life for entrants into the service do not seem to have been in any way extraordinary, but the benefits may have been. (See Ho Ping-ti, *The Ladder of Success in Imperial China* [New York: Columbia University Press, 1962].) While Professor Ho does not specifically examine the form of death of Ming and Ch'ing officials, in none of his 27 case histories (appendix, pp. 267–318) is there a reference to the violent death of an official, let alone to assassination.
   Security provisions for protecting local-level officials from attacks was undoubtedly minimal; no guards specifically for protection purposes seem to have existed. See Ch'ü T'ung-tsu, *Local Government in China Under the Ch'ing* (Cambridge: Harvard University Press, 1962), Chapter V.

2. The source for data for the final 44 years of the Ming dynasty (1368–1644) as well as for the entire Ch'ing (Manchu; 1644–1912) dynasty is Arthur W. Hummel, ed., *Eminent Chinese of the Ch'ing Period* (Washington, D.C., 1944), 2 vols. (hereafter, *ECCP*). Time limitations permitted the writer to tabulate data from only one-half the total pages in each volume. This yielded 403 officials, slightly more than half the total names given separate entries in *ECCP*. (Individuals who did not have separate entries were not considered.) *ECCP* contains approximately 800 separate biographies of Han Chinese, Manchus, Mongols, Tibetans, etc. in all walks of life. While the emphasis is on political and military figures, scholars, artists, etc. are also included. The focus in *ECCP* is, by definition, on *eminent* Chinese (and individuals of non-Chinese groups) who lived in the Ch'ing

period; thus, the concern here must be with high-level officials, not local-level functionaries who did advance along "the ladder of success". Because any study of political assassinations in any political system must, in the end, be limited as to time and level of analysis, we find the limitations imposed by *ECCP* entirely acceptable, and in no manner restrictive to the study.

3. That fewer cases of political assassination are tabulated than we know occurred is a deficiency in *ECCP* which must be pointed out and remedied. Although no collection of data exists in which to place this sample contextually, we must list and discuss the cases. Because the editor of *ECCP* had to determine arbitrarily which individuals would receive separate entries and which would not, some assassination cases are considered in *ECCP* in connection with separate entries of individuals not assassinated. References to other cases were found in *An-sha shih* (A History of Assassinations), which is Vol. 16 of *Man-ch'ing Pai-shih* (Stories of the Ch'ing Dynasty), (Shanghai: New China Book Company, no date).

4. The data for this table are derived from entries in Howard Boorman, ed., *A Biographic Dictionary of Republican China* (New York: Columbia University Press, 1967), Vols. I and II. The remaining volumes have not yet been published. Volumes available list all entries through the surname Ma— a total of 360. There were 149 names dropped from the cause-of-death sample: in the case of one because the individual was a European; in the case of another because he was assassinated by the Japanese; the remaining 147 because, at the time of the *Dictionary's* publication, they were still alive. (Deaths subsequent to publication were not considered.) These 360 entries constitute more than one-half the *Dictionary's* projected total of 600. Thus, for both *ECCP* and the *Dictionary* slightly more than half of all separate entries were examined.

5. Items 2 to 8 from Y.C. Wang, "Tu Yueh-sheng (1885–1951): a Tentative Political Biography," *Journal of Asian Studies,* Vol. XXV, No. 3 (May 1967) pp. 433–455.

6. The Feierabends' 30 categories may be found in their article "Aggressive Behaviors within Polities, 1948–62; A Cross-National Study," *Journal of Conflict Resolution,* Vol. X, No. 3 (September 1966), p. 255.

7. No single source for obtaining data on these events could be considered wholly satisfactory. Ideally, we need records of all levels of government in China to do the job. Such data are not available to the writer—if to anyone; thus one source, *Survey*

of the China Mainland Press (SCMP) was arbitrarily chosen. *SCMP* is a publication of the U.S. Consulate General, Hong Kong. During the Cultural Revolution, *SCMP* released regularly numerous translations of materials published by the Red Guard and other organizations in China. These publications normally were smuggled out of China and sold to the highest bidder, primarily in Hong Kong. Red Guard papers, unlike the official press in China, often reported current developments in China in an unvarnished manner. As such, they were extremely useful to foreign observers of the Mainland. *SCMP* was examined for the period June 1967–August 1968; all entries dealing with violence at all levels in China were studied. Yet, the data cannot necessarily be considered representative of all political violence which occurred throughout China. It is far easier to obtain in Hong Kong Red Guard materials from nearby provinces (e.g., Kwangtung) than from more distant areas (e.g., Hopei, Manchuria); consequently, there is a built-in regional bias to the data. If all Red Guard newspapers available in libraries in the U.S. and Japan were examined this bias could not be corrected, unless these libraries did not have the same bias. Thus, the data, while interesting, have limitations which must be understood. Kwangtung province undoubtedly had violence of a very high level for the entire period for which we have data. Analysis of the limited data extant for other provinces in no way contradicts the main conclusion about the slight relationship between general political violence and political assassinations in Kwangtung. Thus, the relevance for other regions of the Kwangtung data may be strengthened.

8.   An excellent list appears in *Far Eastern Economic Review Yearbook 1967* (Hong Kong), p. 148. See also Parris H. Chang, "The Father Idols," *Far Eastern Economic Review* (August 22, 1968), pp. 351–353; Mr. Chang describes the purge in the Chinese Communist Party at the Central Committee level as well as the provincial one. For a useful summary of the extent of the purge in the State Council and various Ministries, see Donald Klein, "The State Council and the Cultural Revolution," *China Quarterly*, No. 35 (July–September 1968), pp. 77–95.

9.   For a mid-1968 account of suicides involving purged individuals, see "Comrade Chang Ch'un-ch'iao Holds Forum at the Office of the Shanghai Municipal Revolutionary Committee," *Huo-chu T'ung-hsun* (Torch Bulletin, Canton), No. 1 (July 1968); in *Survey of China Mainland Magazines,* No. 622, pp. 11–12.

10.   Kweichow Provincial Radio, July 13, 1967.

11.   For the official obituaries of Yeh and Chiang, see *SCMP,* No.

3873, p. 2. No official source has admitted that the two Ministers died as a result of persecution, but that they did is a widely-held view of observers of the Cultural Revolution. For an unofficial but undoubtedly true account of the persecution suffered by Li Ta and his ensuing death, see "Truth of the Persecution of Comrade Li Ta by T'ao Chu and Wang Jen-chung," *Na-han Chan-pao* (Outcry Combat Bulletin, Canton, January 1968); in *SCMP,* No. 4144, pp. 1–8.

12. *SCMP,* No. 4108, p. 6.

13. See *SCMP,* No. 4224, p. 3, and No. 4227, p. 11, respectively, for the two citations.

14. Teng Ssu-yü and John K. Fairbank, *China's Response to the West* (Cambridge: Harvard University Press, 1954), p. 17.

15. Joseph R. Levenson, *Confucian China and Its Modern Fate,* Vol. 2 (London: Routledge and Kegan Paul, 1964), p. 27.

16. Karl A. Wittfogel, *Oriental Despotism* (New Haven: Yale University Press, 1957), pp. 593–60.

17. *Ibid.,* p. 355.

18. *Ibid.,* pp. 354–358.

19. The term is Wittfogel's, *op. cit.,* pp. 359–360.

20. Wang Ling, "On the Invention and Use of Gunpowder and Firearms in China," *Isis,* Vol. 37 (1947), pp. 160–178. See also L.C. Goodrich and C.S. Feng, "The Early Development of Firearms in China," *Isis,* Vol. 36, (1945–1946) pp. 114–123.

SUPPLEMENT D

ASSASSINATION IN JAPAN

By James R. Soukup*

1. Introduction

For the purpose of considering the subject of assassination, the history of modern Japan can be divided roughly into two uneven periods. The first era comprises the years from the Meiji Restoration of 1868 to the Second World War; the second from the war to the present. In the first era, Japan's top national leaders faced an almost constant threat of death by assassination. In the postwar years they have been largely free of such attempts.

The first three-quarters of a century of modern Japan witnessed the assassination of two prominent Meiji oligarchs, three Prime Ministers, one former Prime Minister, three Cabinet members, two high ranking Foreign Ministry officials, and two leading socialists. Three eminent businessmen and two generals also were murdered for political reasons, and other leading political figures were the targets of unsuccessful attempts.

Recorded incidents of lower level assassination attempts are noticeably lacking. A few incidents occurred in conjunction with local riots or revolts protesting economic hardship and/ or repressive measures by government officials, particularly during the 1870's and early 1880's. Undoubtedly, additional cases can be uncovered, but certainly their number or repercussions would not have been significant. Those persons involved in assassination attempts were evidently convinced—

*University of Texas.

with ample reason—that their "causes" could best be "drama-tized" by selecting nationally prominent figures as their targets. Moreover, they were usually ultranationalists obsessed by a feeling that the nation was in danger.

The assassinations tended to cluster in the seventeen years between 1920 and 1936. In the decade from 1920–30, during the so-called "era of party government," six of the 18 cases cited above took place; these included two Prime Ministers, a Zaibatsu financier, and two socialist leaders. The most dangerous years for government officials, however, were those from 1932 to 1936. Eight of the above 18 victims, including a Prime Minister, a former Prime Minister, and two Finance Ministers, were killed in this brief 5-year span. Furthermore, their deaths were the products of organized plots rather than isolated acts by individual assassins, as was the case in most of the prior incidents.

In contrast, the postwar years have been largely unmarred by acts of assassination. Three unsuccessful attempts were made on the lives of two communists from 1947–49. The most numerous, and potentially most dangerous, postwar incidents occurred during and immediately after the Security Treaty negotiations of 1960. Moderate socialist, Jotaro Kawakami, and Prime Minister Nobusuke Kishi suffered stab wounds in June and July of 1960. Then in October of 1960, Inejiro Asanuma, Secretary-General of the Socialist Party, met his death gruesomely at the end of a sword wielded by a 17-year-old, anti-leftist fanatic. Finally, in December of 1961 police authorities uncovered and promptly aborted a plot to strike down the Ikeda Cabinet. Among the conspirators were persons who had played prominent roles in prewar assassination efforts of ultranationalist groups. Since this conspiracy was thwarted there have been no further incidents, with the exception of the 1964 attack on Ambassador Reischauer by an insane would-be assassin.

In reviewing the assassins, one is immediately struck by the fact that they have almost always been rightists. Supporters of the left have not employed political assassination as a means of influencing the course of Japanese politics. During the prewar years, any leftist remotely suspected of such tendencies was imprisoned. On one occasion, the high treason trial of 1910–11, 12 anarcho-syndicalists were put to death for an alleged plot to take the Emperor's life. (Subsequent evidence indicated that the charges were probably false and that the defendants were framed by the Katsura government.) The most likely explanation for the lack of left-wing assassination attempts is not, however, that they were prevented from doing so. The more salient point is that they were probably aware of the fact that the Japanese public would react sharply against both them and their cause if they resorted to such tactics. Many prewar Japanese were willing to condone assassination if it was motivated by a higher ideal such as patriotism or loyalty to the Emperor, but they were not favorable to such acts committed in the name of socialism, particularly since they regarded socialism as largely a foreign import.

Left-wing elements in Japan today must be wary of any action that has even a remote possibility of rekindling such sentiments. Tactically, they are on much safer ground when they accuse the government of not taking proper steps to guard against a revival of right-wing groups noted for their history of assassinations. Furthermore, the leaders of left-wing parties and labor unions do not suffer the same frustrations as in the prewar years. Although they have not succeeded in gaining governmental power, they hold positions from which they can derive substantial benefits and prestige. They have organized mass demonstrations, but have sought to avoid bloodshed. There is considerable evidence that most left-wing party and union leaders, like their conservative counterparts, dislike the more violent actions which have accompanied some recent student outbursts.

Students from the so-called Sampa factions, which are critical of both established socialist and communist organizations and the government, may present a problem in the future. It is not inconceivable that the potent mixture of youthful idealism and disdain for "the establishment" could produce a new breed of assassins on the left. As yet, however, this has not transpired.

2. Causes of Assassination

Militarization and the idealization of the warrior code are often cited as major factors responsible for the resort to assassination in prewar Japan. The 1878 murder of Meiji bureaucrat, Toshimichi Okubo, by samurai disgruntled by his opposition to military ventures in Korea and loyal to their military hero, Takamori Saigo, certainly lends support to this contention. Furthermore, high ranking military men sympathized with and, in some instances, actively encouraged young army and navy officers and cadets when they participated in the 1932 assassination of Premier Inukai, a man who opposed expansionist efforts in China. Nor can it be denied that many Japanese tended to glorify the medieval 47 *ronin* who murdered the slayer of their feudal lord and later committed collective suicide. Certainly, many assassins were inspired by the story of the 47 *ronin* and others who, in warrior-like fashion, were willing to commit political murder as an act of loyalty to lord, Emperor, or nation.

It is inaccurate to explain assassinations solely in terms of militarism especially since this concept did not deeply pervade Japanese society. Moreover, internal violence and disorder did not (and do not) normally characterize the Japanese people. Rather self-control and social harmony, closely related values, are highly esteemed tenets of Japanese social thought and action. More importantly, emphasis on militarism obscures more fundamental aspects of prewar political problems in Japan.

Almost all of the assassins, particularly those of the 1930's, were ultranationalists motivated by a combined sense of national peril and national destiny. They viewed their victims as men who were too willing to make concessions to foreign powers (e.g. the arms limitations agreed upon at the Washington Naval Conference), too reluctant to embark upon a course of military expansion, and too involved in political corruption and money-making activities that sapped national strength. As for the Japanese public, it was too prone to excuse assassination if it could be justified on grounds of patriotism and loyalty to the Emperor. What mattered was not the means used, but the purity of the assassins' goals and motives, and the purest of goals and motives were those related to patriotism. The trials of those responsible for the 1932 murders of Inukai, Finance Minister Inoue, and Mitsui President, Baron Takuma Dan, were graphic examples of such characteristics. The defendants were permitted to embark upon long diatribes alleging that their victims had weakened the nation while they were seeking to renew national vigor and strength. Their testimonies evoked considerable public sympathy in and out of court, so much so that they received light sentences. Thus, a distorted form of nationalism, not just militarism *per se*, created a climate conducive to assassination.

A further probe into the backgrounds, values, and attitudes of the ultranationalists reveals that many of them were basically traditionalists disturbed by some of the innovations and characteristics of a country in the throes of change. First of all, some of the civilian participants in assassination attempts were disappointed and frustrated men who, in a modernizing society, could not meet the necessary prerequisites and qualifications for their chosen professional and/or business careers. Secondly, their military cohorts among the young officers and cadets of the "Imperial Way" faction in the armed forces, although deeply concerned about their careers in the light of the disarmament policy of the Party Cabinets, were also disturbed by the economic distress in the rural areas. After all, many of them either came directly from rural areas or were exposed to the bitter complaints of rank-and-file soldiers disgruntled by the economic hardships confronting their rural households. Verbally, both the civilian and military ultranationalists attacked Zaibatsu financiers for their emphasis on money making—a characteristic that was frowned upon in old Japan—and the politicians for entering corrupt relationships with businessmen. At the same time, they extolled the virtues of "men of the soil." In other words, some of the assassins were men who found it difficult to adjust to the changes accompanying Japan's modernization and/or feared that traditional values were being destroyed. The most obvious example of this phenomenon can be seen in the attitudes of the samurai rebels and assassins of the 1870's, but traces of it can also be found in the ultranationalist cries for a *Showa Restoration* (italics are mine) during the 1930's.

Some historians dealing with the late 1920's and early 1930's merely cite the existence of economic hardships, particularly in rural areas producing silk and other cash crops hard hit by world depression; the ultranationalists' feeling that this economic crisis could only be overcome by expansion abroad; and, hence, their determination to remove any persons who stood in the way of an expansionist escape. I am convinced, however, that the social-psychological dimension is more relevant to assassination than the economic one.

Certain features of the party system also apparently affected the rate of assassination. In their struggle for power, party

factions sometimes subsidized civilian rightists, not to eliminate rivals physically but to disrupt their operations (for example, by ransacking their headquarters). Ironically, the
money often found its way into the hands of individuals who
eventually turned on the politicians. Furthermore, not only the
rightists but a sizable number of average Japanese were also
repelled by the politicians' involvement in scandals and questionable ties with business interests. While such conditions did
not directly breed assassination they made it much easier for
the public to accept such actions when perpetrated by fanatics.

Many of the conditions conducive to prewar assassination
do not prevail in postwar Japan. Militarism is largely discred-
ited and exerts little physical or moral influence in politics.
Significantly, members of the Self-Defense Force refused to
become involved in the 1961 conspiracy. Although there has
been an obvious resurgence of nationalist sentiment, the postwar brand of nationalism differs significantly from its prewar
antecedent. Today's nationalism is a much more realistic and
self-confident variety, one that is less receptive to movements
that cry out in terms of "divine mission" and "national peril."
The respect for party politicians remains low but the satisfaction with the overall political-economic system, particularly in
the light of recent economic progress, seems substantial. There
are traces of discontent among tradition-minded farmers and
owners of small enterprises and, more significantly, among
unorganized workers and lower middle class elements in the
cities. However, the ruling Liberal-Democrats have attempted
to meet some of the demands by farmers and small entrepreneurs. Moreover, despite other potential dangers of the movement, the new Buddhist party (Komeito) has provided an
outlet for the pent-up frustrations of substantial numbers of
the urban discontented. Probably the most significant fact about
the discontented is that they are beginning to express themselves in the more pragmatic terms of economic self-interest
rather than in the emotion laden symbolisms of the past that,
in this author's opinion, lend themselves more to bloody outbursts.

All of this is not to say that there cannot be a sudden
resurgence of political murder in Japan. If outside powers
were to force Japanese political leaders to make what were
perceived of as humiliating concessions or if there were a
sharp downturn in the economy, there could be a revival of
plots against governmental leaders. For the moment, however,

anything other than the occasional depraved act of an individual assassin is unlikely.

3. Impact of Assassination

The deaths of key Japanese politicos contributed to the weakening and eventual demise of the short-lived party governments in prewar Japan. Prime Ministers Hara (assassinated 1921) and Hamaguchi (assassinated 1930), strong men with the ability to pull together diverse elements, possessed qualities sorely needed in the faction ridden parties of Japan. Their successors lacked their abilities and, accordingly, the parties could not develop sufficient capacity to cope with Japan's problems in the 1920's and 1930's.

Not only the deaths of such leaders but the manner of dealing with assassins also adversely affected the politics. Specifically, the fact that the assassins of the early 1930's were treated with leniency—indeed, in some cases, as heroes rather than villains—led many politicians to fear for their own lives. As a result, following the death of Prime Minister Inukai, the parties made deals with military leaders which compromised themselves out of any meaningful role in Japanese politics.

The assassinations of 1930–36 simultaneously accelerated the development of an aggressive foreign policy. Specifically, the deaths of Prime Ministers Hamaguchi and Inukai and Finance Ministers Inoue and Takahashi, all of whom advocated retrenchment of the military budget, removed obstacles in the path of those who supported an expansionist course of action.

Care should be taken, however, not to attribute too much impact to the assassinations. The prewar roots of democratic party politics were fragile while those of ultranationalism were strong and widespread. The assassinations merely hastened rather than determined subsequent developments.

4. Effectiveness of Assassination

The most effective assassins were undoubtedly the ultranationalists of the 1930's, but even these men would have to be regarded as only partial successes. They were intent upon

promoting overseas' expansion and replacing party government with some form of military rule. As indicated in the
preceding section, their actions removed obstacles in the path
of an imperialist policy and hastened the demise of the parties
and the ascendancy of the military. However, most of them
also wished to put in control of the government men of or
sympathetic to the Army's Imperial Way faction and to relieve
economic distress in the countryside with sweeping reforms.
Their efforts to achieve these latter aims failed.

The last important and most bloody effort on behalf of the
Imperial Way faction, the coup attempt of February, 1936,
was put down and the ringleaders were executed. From that
time on power was firmly in the hands of the so-called Control Faction of the Army. Although members of this latter
faction were repelled by the unrealism of the assassins' total
views on foreign policy, they were in general sympathy with
the expansionist aims of the ultranationalists, particularly as
they applied to China. In fact, they found that the assassinations of the early 1930's were quite useful for their own
purposes. However, they were not as receptive to plans for
agrarian reforms and other plans to alleviate the suffering of
the lower classes. As a matter of fact, it is doubtful that even
the generals of the Imperial Way faction would have supported far-reaching reforms.

In the final analysis, the civilian ultranationalists and their
young officer cohorts who engaged in assassination were
largely tools in the hands of the manipulators from above.

SUPPLEMENT E

ASSASSINATION IN LATIN AMERICA

By Karl M. Schmitt*

1. Introduction

Force, violence, and threats of violence have occurred so frequently in political contests in Latin America that one can well argue that violence is a normal feature of its political life. Furthermore, there seems to be a fairly high correlation between revolutionary activity and the assassination of lower- and middle-level political figures. On the other hand the assassination of chief executives seems to occur rather infrequently as compared with most other areas of the world.

In the 162 years since the assassination of Jean Jacques Dessalines of Haiti, over 30 rulers and former rulers of Latin American states have been murdered. These killings, however, are not distributed evenly among the 20 countries of the area. Bolivia heads the list with about 10, and Mexico, the Dominican Republic, and Haiti follow with three each. Conversely, Argentina, Brazil, Chile, and Cuba have not experienced the assassination of any of their chief executives, although several attempted assassinations have occurred, and an Argentine former president was murdered 10 years after relinquishing his office. The same countries that have these relatively high levels of assassination of chief executives also have high levels of assassination among less important political leaders. Political murders of provincial and local officials and opposition leaders occurred frequently in the troubled times from 1910 to the early 1930's in Mexico. Assassination of political opponents

*University of Texas.

was a common activity of the Trujillo dictatorship in the Dominican Republic (1930–1961) and among the would-be heirs of the dictator, who was himself assassinated; assassination of opposing political leaders has also occurred frequently in Haiti under the dictatorship of Francois Duvalier (1957–present).

Several other countries, however, such as Guatemala and Colombia, have been plagued with political murders by opposing political factions, although they have experienced low levels of assassination among their chief executives. Estimates run as high as 3,000 deaths in Guatemala in the past 2 or 3 years, while in Colombia the violence between the late 1940's and the early 1960's accounted for at least 250,000 deaths. Obviously not all of these latter can be classified as assassinations, but certainly several thousand can be.

Although assassinations of national leaders seem to occur in clusters in Latin America, the time element seems to be irrelevant. Several such assassinations were carried out around the turn of the century, several more in the late 1920's and early 1930's, and four between 1955 and 1961, which are the last major assassinations so far. There seems to be little relationship among these clusters at any time, and it would be difficult to demonstrate that high-level assassination is on the rise or decline on the whole for Latin America.

2. Causes of Assassination

In the Iberian tradition of which all of Latin America (except Haiti) is heir, the republican descendants of the kings, whether prime ministers, presidents, or caudillos, have inherited an aura of "sacredness" to a much higher degree than their counterparts in the United States and most of Western Europe. Franco in his long years of Spanish rule has never been shot at, nor was Salazar after his consolidation of power in Portugal. By law, customs, and tradition, chief executives in Latin America are regarded with awe and respect by the masses. The wealthy or elite are inclined to treat the peccadillos and foibles of presidents with some leniency and permit them to retire in safety even when they are deposed by force. This live-and-let-live attitude, highlighted by the general respect accorded to the right of asylum, is rooted not only in humanitarianism and reverence for the symbols of authority, but also in the practical recognition that today's revolutionary may be tomorrow's president. The elder Somoza of Nicaragua was never particularly disturbed that opponents might try to unseat him or kill him in a fight, but he was horrified at the thought of assassination. His attitude seems widely shared.

Although dictators account for most of the victims of assassinations, dictatorship of itself does not explain assassination in Latin America. For one thing, too many chief executives of the area have been strong men if not outright dictators, so that an accurate comparison cannot be made with more limited chief executives. Neither do religious-ideological issues account for assassination. It is true that García Moreno of Ecuador was killed by an opponent of his theocratic state in 1875 and that Alvaro Obregon was assassinated in 1929 by a religious fanatic opposed to the Mexican government's policy toward the Catholic Church, but these are isolated cases. In the three great social revolutions of Latin America (Mexico 1910, Bolivia 1952, and Cuba 1959), no top officials of the old regime were murdered by the victors. Diaz of Mexico was permitted to go into exile and so were the defeated leaders in Bolivia.

Assassinations of high-level officials seem to occur with some frequency in times of strife and revolution, but not always. In addition to Obregon, Mexico's two assassinated presidents held office during the fighting phase of the Revolution between 1910 and 1920. In neither case were economic or ideological issues paramount, but the drive to political power by their opponents was. Bolivia's rash of assassinations in the 19th century reflected simply the drive to power by contending caudillos, and three of the four latest assassinations in the Caribbean (1955–1961) seemingly were motivated by attempts to seize power by political opposition groups, generally under conditions of political turmoil or recent drastic changes in political alignments. Only the assassination of Somoza of Nicaragua in 1956 does not fit the pattern. The Nicaraguan dictator was murdered by a neurotic young man who was encouraged by disgruntled opponents of Somoza, but he had no broad support. As compared with assassinations of U.S. chief executives, those in Latin America were perpetrated less by fanatics or unstable persons, and more by daring political adventurers bent on seizing power for themselves or for their superiors.

When we turn our attention from top national officials to lower political leaders as victims of assassination, the conditions under which political murder occurs are more predictable. Where the authority of the national government is respected and enforced, where local and provincial government is firmly established, low-level assassination is rare. Where the authority of the national government has collapsed and where factionalism and rivalries harass the nation, the incidence of this kind of assassination increases. Whether the rivalries are based on economic, political, or ideological issues does not seem relevant; the important factor appears to be the presence or absence of recognized authority. A weak government is tempted to remove its opponents by murder rather than by due process of law, and where authority has collapsed or is denied respect, the opponents of the government have less qualms about attacking officials who attempt to enforce regulations that are unpopular. Cuba in the pre-Castro years experienced a series of weak governments that could command little obedience from important sectors of the population and could not impose a rule of law and order. Street battles occurred between rival political bands, and political leaders were machinegunned from speeding cars in broad daylight. Mexico from 1910 to the early 1930's witnessed frequent gunfights and murders by rival political factions. Zapata, the peasant leader, was murdered by the weak government of Carranza in 1919, and Villa was murdered in 1923 by those who feared a revival of his popularity and influence. Assassination is rare now in Mexico, but has become common in neighboring Guatemala where rival political factions are engaging in gang warfare, murders, kidnappings, and arson. The government, torn by these rival forces, lacking broad-based popular support, and fearful that the military might decide to give its allegiance to one of the factions, has not been able to contain the violence. Conversely, Argentina, Brazil, Uruguay, and Chile, with strong though not necessarily popular national governments, have a very low incidence of assassination of either high- or low-level officials. Guerrilla bands in Venezuela, Peru, Ecuador, and Bolivia have killed some local and provincial officials in recent years, but they have not been able to win sufficient support to sustain their activities or to escalate conflict to the point where violence and assassination threaten the government or reach levels comparable to those of Guatemala and Colombia in recent years.

3. The Impact of Assassination on Political Systems

The effects of assassination on a political system can be measured crudely by studying the post-assassination period in terms of changes in personnel, changes in policies, and changes in the nature and character of the political system. We can term these low, medium, and high impacts respectively. The lowest kind of impact would be that in which another person was appointed to fill the position occupied by the victim. Usually, however, a series of shifts occurs wherein a sort of musical chairs is played in filling vacated positions. The greatest impact, however, occurs when not only the old political system itself is destroyed and a new one substituted, but when drastic changes occur in the socioeconomic structure of a nation. Most assassinations produce a situation somewhat between these extremes.

Latin America has experienced low, medium, and high impacts from assassination. Two of the more recent assassinations of dictators in Latin America are excellent examples of low- and high-level impacts. The murder of President Anastasio Somoza of Nicaragua in 1956 brought few changes in that country. His two sons smoothly took over their father's chief functions, the elder as president, and the younger as commander of the armed forces. Very few personnel changes occurred in important political positions, and, except for a certain easing of restrictions on the political opposition, there were not many policy changes. At the present time, 13 years after the assassination, the younger son is president and governs in the tradition of his father. In contrast, the murder of Generalissimo Rafael Trujillo of the Dominican Republic set in motion a chain of events that not only overthrew dictatorial government and substituted a more limited and open system, but it rid the country of the Trujillo family. Although the socioeconomic structure has not been radically altered, the political system has been profoundly changed in terms of personnel, policies, and structure. Ironically, the man who is president today (but elected in his own right) served as Trujillo's puppet president at the time of the assassination.

An example of an intermediate type of impact from assassination is furnished by Brazil, a country not known for assassination. This is a case in which the attempt did not come off as planned. In 1954, during the administration of Getulio Vargas, assassins attacked Carlos Lacerda, a sharp-tongued newspaper critic of the regime. Lacerda was only wounded but his companion, a major in the air force, was killed. The armed forces demanded a military investigation and the government consented. The trail soon led to the official household of the president himself, the primary instigator being the commander of the palace guard. A vociferous opposition demanded the resignation of the president, and when the military added their pressure, Vargas committed suicide. We need not detail the confused chain of events that followed the suicide that resulted from the assassination except to note that there was a substantial change in personnel, a greater intervention of the military in politics, and a shift in policies toward rapid and substantial economic development. The assassination and attempted assassination did not "cause" these changes directly; but they served as a catalyst to point up the stagnation of political life and the socioeconomic unrest that festered beneath the surface of Brazilian life.

We must now ask what accounts for the different political responses to assassinations. Although it is obvious that impact of assassination varies according to the country and the time, it appears that national characteristics, the size of a country, and secular trends have little bearing on the question. It would also seem that the political importance of the victim would be critical, but the murder of the Brazilian air force major had far greater repercussions than the murder of the President of Nicaragua. What is important then?

Basically, the critical factor in determining the impact of assassination is the nature of the political system in a given country at a given time; i.e., the characteristics of the administration or ruling regime, the political opposition, and the conspiracy. In Nicaragua, the Somoza regime, despite its dictatorial features, had certain popular characteristics. Somoza played the role of a "man of the people" and kept his ties to numerous groups and interests. In fact, he was killed at a labor union dance. The opposition was weak and fragmented, with virtually no organized mass support; the conspirators, principally exiles, had at best weak ties with the opposition within the country. When these conditions are included with the fact that Somoza's two sons had been groomed to succeed their father, the outcome is not surprising.

In the Dominican Republic on the other hand, Trujillo had

alienated important sectors of the populace, including members of the elite and middle class. Opposition was growing steadily in the late 1950's as the repressions of the dictator became more cruel and senseless. The conspirators had contacts with persons in high places, and many individuals and groups were prepared to act once the assassination occurred. Although the immediate result of the murder was the execution of most of the assassins, opposition to the regime steadily mounted. Moreover, Trujillo's sons and brothers were not prepared to assume the responsibility of power, and within 6 months the system was overturned.

In Brazil, Vargas enjoyed considerable popularity; but by 1954 his administration was coming under increasing criticism for its corruption and stagnation. The clamor over the death of the air force major, particularly because the conspirators were linked with the administration, supplied the occasion for the voicing of dissatisfaction and for pressuring the president to resign. Vargas' followers were dismayed and demoralized, at least temporarily, while the opposition moved from a position of strength.

Finally, it must be noted that international conditions can have at times some effect on the political aftermath of assassination. In late 1961, intervention by the United States prevented an attempted return of members of the Trujillo family to the Dominican Republic. The intervention met with virtually no criticism from within the Dominican Republic or from other Latin American states. Trujillo supporters were shaken by the profound upheaval in the country, and the family was thoroughly disliked elsewhere in the hemisphere. In fact, the year before the assassination all other Latin American states had broken relations with the Dominican Republic because of Trujillo's attempt to assassinate President Betancourt of Venezuela in 1960. Generally, in Latin America, however, other states have not intervened after an assassination in one of the countries, and therefore have not influenced its impact.

4. Effectiveness of Assassination as a Political Technique

If we wish to determine the political effectiveness of the assassination of officeholders according to the degree of correlation between the motives of the assassin or assassins and the net result of the deed, we must conclude that in Latin America assassination has not been a very useful technique to attain one's political ends. Furthermore, if we examine the more recent examples of assassination, we find that the technique has been very dangerous personally, not only to the immediate perpetrators but also to those who conceived and planned the action. One may argue, however, that the assassination of opposition leaders by officeholders has at times been efficacious in improving the position of weak or unstable governments.

Apart from a few strongmen who have bludgeoned their way to power over the corpses of their opponents (and this occurred mostly in the 19th century), few assassins have gained political power or forced basic changes in political policies. It is true that Victoriano Huerta in Mexico gained control of the central government after assassinating President Madero in 1913, but he could not pacify the country afterwards and was eventually driven into exile. Moreover, the young religious fanatic who murdered President-elect Alvaro Obregon in 1929 because of the Mexican church-state conflict achieved nothing in terms of his own and his supporters' ends. The conflict between the government and the Catholic Church eventually ended, but not as a result of the death of Obregon, while the assassin and his accused accomplice were sentenced to long prison terms.

One might argue that the murderer of President Somoza of Nicaragua had little motive other than removing the dictator, and that in these terms he attained his ends. It may be argued further that since he had demonstrated earlier something of a martyr complex, even his death at the hands of Somoza's aides was not an unqualified disaster. His accomplices, however, entertained some vague hopes of a collapse of the Somozas' power and to profit from it. In this they were greatly disappointed. Most were seized and imprisoned; a few were killed under peculiar circumstances. Except for the removal of the elder Somoza, little had changed, and the assassination in general must be regarded as a failure from the point of view of the assassins.

The assassination of Trujillo in the Dominican Republic is more difficult to judge as to its political effectiveness, in that while the hated dictator was removed and his regime destroyed, political affairs progressed beyond the control of the assassins and in ways not to their liking. Some of them, of course, were motivated largely by revenge for abuses committed against themselves and their families. Yet all but two of the some 10 or 12 members who were actively connected with the plot were eventually killed, some after excruciating tortures, by the family and agents of the slain dictator. The two who escaped remained in hiding after their plans for immediate seizure of the government had fallen through. In the turmoil of the next few months they remained largely undercover, fearing assassination from friends of Trujillo. They eventually emerged, and today both have some importance as political figures in the country. In the main, however, events have passed them by.

On the other hand, Mexican governments in the 1920's and 1930's certainly strengthened their hold by ruthlessly exterminating revolutionary and would-be revolutionary leaders. The present Bolivian government also fortified its position by killing Che Guevara after capturing him in late 1967. Che alive could have been a rallying point for other potential revolutionaries; Che dead meant a substantial weakening of armed opposition.

In conclusion it must be said that in Latin America, except in a few cases, assassins of officeholders have not achieved the political ends they were seeking. Their major achievement was that they removed the victim from political affairs. Most of the assassins were rewarded for their efforts with execution or imprisonment. Few are remembered as heroes or martyrs, and fewer still achieved political power as a result of their deeds. A number of assassinations have brought substantial political changes in their wake, but generally in ways not desired or foreseen by the assassins. The most satisfied assassins are those who simply want to "get" the victims, and are not much concerned about the consequences either for themselves or for society. Government-inspired assassinations of opposition leaders have had mixed results; in some cases they have strengthened regimes and in others they have produced an effect that was the reverse of what was intended in that they resulted in the destruction of the administration.

SUPPLEMENT F

ASSASSINATION IN THE MIDDLE EAST

By Carl Leiden*

1. Some Introductory Comments

It is seldom easy to gather data on assassination, but the problems of doing so in the Middle East are unusually formidable. There is no single source of data for the area: files of Middle Eastern newspapers are in some cases impossible to locate (in certain areas newspapers have only existed in recent years) and, in any case, are likely to omit or misrepresent information about such things as assassinations.

Moreover, Middle Eastern rulers are not unwilling to embroider plots or attempts against their own lives, for they often feel that their positions are enhanced by successful escapes (sometimes from imaginary threats). Arabs will sometimes refer to *baraka,* a sort of spiritual blessing which we may call good luck. All citizens feel that if their rulers have such luck, so will they. It is tempting for a Nasser or a Kassem (Iraq, 1958–1963) to enlarge upon the dangers in which he lives (nonetheless real) in order to emphasize the importance of his survival. Kassem took great pride in the numerous "attempts" made on his life; some of his simpleminded followers concluded that he was invincible. He was killed in a coup, however, in 1963.

All of this suggests that we are not ever likely to get full and reliable data on assassinations in the Middle East. We must be cautious in using the data we possess.

---

*University of Texas.

2. Overview

The Middle East is largely Arab and Muslim, although not exclusively so. The history of the Arabs and of those they converted to Islam is filled with violence and bloodshed, including assassination in all its forms. Three of the first four caliphs (successors to the prophet Muhammed before the establishment of the first hereditary dynasties) were assassinated; if one examines the many centuries of subsequent history, one finds an inordinate number of assassinations and incidents of political violence. Much of this, it must be said, sprang from the nature of the system at the top, rather than from spontaneous violence from below. It is also essential to remember that death was a common fate (along with castration, blinding, etc.) contemplated for defeated ministers, unsuccessful generals, and others, who, in more modern times, might be expected to retire to innocuous pursuits in private life. To some degree the Middle East is not unlike this today. When the young officers overthrew King Farouk in Egypt in 1952, there were long disputes over whether he should be executed or permitted to go into exile. In another age, few would have hesitated to apply the more draconian measure.

The very word "assassin" is derived from an Arabic word (for those who use hashish) used to describe an Ismaili Shia sect of Muslims in the 12th and 13th centuries whose leaders used assassination as a deliberate policy to further their political ends. Their first victim was Nizam al-Mulk in 1902. (This sect is described very fully by Bernard Lewis in his *The Assassins: A Radical Sect in Islam* [New York: Basic Books, 1968].)

The Middle East is generally thought to be part of the developing world. Its development, however, has been uneven. Many of the conditions and the characteristics of its earlier history remained until the beginning of this century and in some isolated pockets still continue. As late as the end of the 19th century, a reformer, Jemal al-Din al-Afghani, urged direct action against those rulers who were unsympathetic to his views. Nasiruddin Shah, the ruler of Iran, was the most prominent victim of this movement; he was assassinated in 1896.

Since the turn of the century, the Middle East has endured extreme turbulence and instability. This period witnessed the firm establishment, and ultimately the disengagement, of foreign control. Two world wars were partly fought within the area. Great movements of populations occurred: Bulgarian, Turkish, Greek, Armenian, Jewish, and other. The infection of nationalism was nurtured to white heat during the twenties and thirties. The Zionist crusade for the establishment of a national home for the Jews was finally successful. Israel was established in 1948 and subsequently fought three wars with the Arabs. After the end of the Second World War, the machinations of the big powers continued to engulf the Middle East as an area of intervention.

All of these and more contributed to those conditions which, at the very least, did not still the historic attachment to assassination. However, the danger of assassination has varied from country to country in its intensity and, more importantly, has varied with the atmosphere of deep political frustration. Egypt produced a number of significant assassinations in the last half-century. Butros Ghali Pasha (the first Christian Prime Minister) was killed in 1910 because Egyptian nationalists thought that he was selling out the Suez Canal interests to foreigners; in 1945 the Premier Ahmed Maher Pasha was announcing in Parliament Egypt's entry into the war against Germany when he was killed by another nationalist. In 1924 Sir Lee Stack, the British Commander-in-Chief of the Egyptian army, was shot down in the streets of Cairo. (The British government sought a fantastic measure of political revenge for this deed and one can argue that its political repercussions have been almost without measure.)

The frustrations within Egypt also produced some religious fanaticism that came to be centered largely in the so-called Muslim Brotherhood. Coming to maturity during the Second World War, the Brotherhood became engulfed with war-centered issues and with the overriding issue of Jewish penetration into Palestine. It began to use all the instruments of violence, including assassination, to further its aims. A number of lower level opponents of the Brotherhood were liquidated, and in December 1948 it assassinated the Premier Nukrashy Pasha. Fearing the Brotherhood, yet finding itself unable to proceed openly against the Brotherhood, the government retaliated by having the Supreme Guide of the Brethren, Hasan al-Banna, shot down in Cairo (1949). In 1954 the Muslim Brotherhood attempted to shoot Nasser, and as late as 1966 some of its (outlawed) members were punished for continuing plots against Nasser's life. However, the number of assassinations (and attempts) have been fewer in Egypt after the Revolution (1952), and it is difficult to escape the conclusion that most Egyptian assassinations were products of nationalist unrest.

There is hardly any doubt that the Zionist presence in Palestine catalyzed the "need" for assassination within the area. There was a great deal of low-level violence, including assassination, in the thirties and immediately after the war, reminiscent of Ireland after the First World War (and Cyprus in later years). Jews and Arabs killed large numbers of one another and both Jews and Arabs harassed the British (who controlled Palestine until 1948). In 1944 two Jewish youths, members of the extremist Stern gang, shot Lord Moyne (British Minister of State for the Middle East) in Cairo; in September 1948 Count Folke Bernadotte, UN mediator, was machine-gunned in the new city of Jerusalem, allegedly by members of the same gang. It becomes almost impossible to chronicle the enormous chain of killings and retaliations, singly and in mass, that have occurred and continue to occur in and around the Arab borders with Israel.

Syria and Jordan, neighboring states to Israel, have endured a spate of assassinations since the late 1940's. In March 1949 Col. Husni Zaim became the strongman of Syria but was murdered in a coup in August. In July, Zaim had surrendered Antun Saada (leader of the Syrian National Party [the *Parti Populaire Syrien* (PPS)], who was attempting a coup in Lebanon) to Lebanese authorities who were supposed to kill him on the spot. His murder, or execution, was delayed a few hours, but out of it a number of assassinations were spawned. Political revenge was finally meted out to Riad al-Sulh, the Lebanese Premier, when he was murdered in Amman in 1951 by a follower of Saada. Zaim himself, by playing false to Saada, had lost enough support to make his vast collection of enemies move against him. The coup was led by Col. Sami Hinnawi, but the young officer who shot Zaim out of hand was Fadlallah Abu Mansur, a member of the PPS (Parti Populaire Syrien). Hinnawi was, in turn, deposed by Col. Adib Shishakli in December 1949 and some months later was permitted to leave for Lebanon. In Beirut, he was assassinated by Ahmed al-Barazi in private revenge for the murder of his cousin Muhsin al-Barazi who had been killed with Zaim. Shishakli ruled for several years but was, in turn, forced into retirement in 1954. Shishakli ultimately went to Brazil where he was assassinated by a Druze in revenge for his alleged activities against the Druze in Syria. The strongman who emerged from the army was Lt. Col. Adnan al-Malki, but he was shot by a military police sergeant (a member of the PPS) in April 1955. Since then, in Syria, assassination on a high level has somewhat abated but has continued to exist on lower political levels.

We have mentioned the assassination of Riad al-Sulh in Jordan in 1951. The same year saw the assassination of King Abdullah (the great moderate voice on Israel) in Jerusalem. The years that followed produced much political violence in Jordan (which, after 1949, was a weirdly patched political system) including attempted coups, assassinations (for example, the death of Prince Majali in 1960), riots, and war. Complicating it throughout the last decade has been the intermittent call from other Arab leaders (Nasser, for example) to the Jordanians to rise up and kill King Hussein. (Hussein's position in the fall of 1968 was a highly dangerous one, confronted as he was with the violent pressures from the Palestine liberation groups. It was a situation highly conducive to assassination.)

Iraq has had its modicum of violence over the years. The first King of Iraq, Faisal I, held the country together until his death in 1933. His son Ghazi (d. 1939) was less able; it was during this period that the campaigns against the Assyrians were carried to maturity and the army began to insist on its independence. The first coup occurred in 1936 (the Minister of Defense Jafar al-Askari was assassinated in its course). The strongman of this coup was Bakr Sidqi, who was himself assassinated in 1937. More coups, a war, and the turbulent politics of the forties and fifties followed. In July 1958, the King, Faisal II; his uncle, the former regent, Abdul Ilah; and General Nuri al-Said were all murdered in the coup by General Kassem. Kassem lasted until 1963 and survived a number of assassination attempts but was finally killed in still another coup. Turbulence has continued to characterize Iraq.

There has been relatively little assassination (or its attempts) in Saudi Arabia (or perhaps, more accurately, we should say that there has been little evidence that such assassinations have taken place), but in the peripheral areas—

Yemen, Aden, and South Arabia (South Yemen), and the Persian Gulf principalities—the incidence of assassination has been very high. In Yemen, attempts have been fairly common against the *imams* (the rulers) and two have died in this manner (Yahya in 1948 and Ahmad from wounds in 1962). Yemen has been in revolution since 1962. The British Colony of Aden reverberated with low-level political violence in the sixties and the short-lived South Arabia Federation (of British manufacture) was brought to its knees by assassination attempts and threats against those who purported to govern it.

The stability and democratic aspirations given Turkey by Mustafa Kemal Pasha have contributed to a lack of assassination. In the 1950's there was a period of low-level violence as the Democratic Party (of Bayar and Menderes) sought to maintain its supremacy, but this was brought to an end by the 1960 revolution. Iran, on the other hand, has witnessed a number of assassinations. Several attempts have been made against the Shah himself (in 1949 and 1965). General Ali Razmara (the Prime Minister) was assassinated in March 1951, when Iran entered the turbulent nationalist period of Mossadegh. Assassinations and attempts have continued since that time (the Prime Minister Ali Mansur was assassinated in 1965).

In Afghanistan, the isolated assassination or its attempt still occurs. In 1919 Habibullah Khan (the King) was assassinated; a decade later his son Amanullah was driven from the throne. The strongman who emerged, Nadir Shah, was assassinated in 1933 (his brother, the ambassador to Germany, was assassinated shortly before in Berlin by an Afghan student). Several attempts have been made against the present king or his ministers in recent years, but the rate is generally low. The same can be said of Pakistan. The most significant high-level case in that country was the assassination, in 1951, of Liaqat Ali Khan, the Prime Minister. His death was not without its consequences, as he was the strongest and ablest personality on the Pakistani political scene at the time.

In summary: The Middle East has had a fairly large number of high-level assassinations in the last half century and a large but indeterminate number of low-level ones. Furthermore, the Middle East is an area where assassination as a deliberate political policy of one government against another (for example, King Saud of Saudi Arabia was accused of spending several million dollars in an abortive attempt to kill Nasser) continues to be employed. The area also continues to display a great amount of other kinds of political violence and turbulence.

3. Causes of Assassination

It is difficult if not impossible to be precise in a question of this kind. A sufficient requirement for assassination is the existence of one man appropriately motivated. Any society spawns a portion of such individuals; chance, circumstance, opportunity, and so on will account for the presence or lack of isolated assassinations of this kind.

More general statements of environmental causation can, however, be hazarded. Although there is little philosophical justification of assassination among Islamic commentators, there is undoubtedly a tradition of assassination. Political authority in the Middle East was (and continues to be) largely centered in individuals whose support was heavily personal. Such conditions can make assassination a tempting weapon in that more than the victim is likely to be destroyed by the deed.

The Middle East is an area where dictatorship (of mild to severe forms) prevails, and there is probably no constitutional, legal way of altering a government. Few Middle Eastern rulers subject themselves to periodic examination by their electorates. This breeds extreme methods of opposition. It is well to add that the notion of responsible opposition, so common to the West, has not taken deep root in the Middle East. Opposition of any form is equated with obstructionism; few Middle Eastern rulers hesitate to root out even the mildest forms of opposition. Where there are no legitimate forms of opposition, it should hardly be surprising that violence is contemplated by whatever political forces that possess ambition.

The central basic causes—conditions that give rise to or increase the probabilities—of assassination are (1) the unresolved problems of political development (political systems not yet stabilized), (2) the extreme fragmentation along religious, ideological, and cultural lines (Syria, Iraq, and Iran, for example), and (3) the pressure of nationalism.

An assassin must feel more than a casual distrust or distaste for his victim. The factors that give rise to such intense feeling of hate or fear are usually ideological or religious, as in the case of the Middle East. Ideological commitments in a period of rapid political change is a potent mixture. Nationalism is an ideology which unifies the people against the "enemy." The Middle East has been buffeted about by strong outside forces in the last half century. It has been invaded, despoiled, and exploited by much of the world. In the struggle to find dignity, independence, and freedom, Middle Easterners have felt compelled to use all weapons that come to hand. Killing an individual who impedes, in some real or fancied way, the "progress" dear to the assassin's heart does not seem to be such an awful thing. No group of people in the Middle East has been immune to the temptations of assassinations. Religious convictions have merely rationalized the deed rather than lessened the likelihood of its occurrence.

This discussion of causes is perforce incomplete. The psychology of assassination is not wholly determinative. But an examination of Middle Eastern high-level assassinations compared with those in other parts of the world suggest the above conditions as being conducive to assassination. As the fervor of nationalism abates and as political stability and ideological tolerance come to characterize the area, almost certainly the rate of high-level assassination will begin to fall off.

4. The Impact of Assassination

We must distinguish here between the survival of the political system and the embarrassments and difficulties generated for the ruling elite of that system by an act of assassination. The basic systems themselves in the Middle East do not appear to have been imperiled by assassination. Multiple forms of violence, including assassination, may bring about systemic changes. In the Middle East, the best examples are the events in Cyprus (in the fifties), Palestine (in the thirties and forties), and Aden and South Arabia (in the sixties). It is not accidental that Great Britain was involved in all of these; the systemic changes brought about were the exclusion of the British and a rejection of the political patterns projected by the British for the period after their departure.

On the other hand, assassination has had some very major

consequences in specific cases. This, of course, is a function of the role of the person assassinated and of the nature of the crises faced in the post-assassination period. When Nadir Shah of Afghanistan was assassinated in 1933, his country lost the man who had given it stability and direction. He had been a man of great energy, ability, and resourcefulness, yet his death had relatively little impact. Afghanistan was a backwater in the world of 1933; little in the nature of social change would have occurred in any case. The King's son, Zahir Shah, and Zahir's uncles combined to assure tranquility for the system. It would be difficult to discern impact here except in terms of "what might have been." In the same year (1933), King Faisal of Iraq died—of a heart attack, not assassination—and the impact was much more severe. His son Ghazi was irresponsible, and the death of a strong King unloosed political forces that were difficult to control (and in the event were not controlled). The difference between Iraq and Afghanistan in the impacts of the deaths of their rulers does not lie in the fact that one was assassinated and one was not, but rather, it lies in the nature of the political problems facing the countries. The death of Abdullah in Jordan in 1951 was surely significant in the fact this was a crucial year for his country and for the Arab world. His death brought to the throne Talal (who was mentally disturbed) and upon his abdication, Hussein, who was virtually a boy. On the other hand, the multiple assassinations in Syria seem of little significance. The death of one army leader simply meant that another took his place. The successor might be more or less able than the man he replaced, but this was about all that could be said.

Similarly the assassination of Nukrashy Pasha in Egypt in 1948 was of relatively little significance. But the death, in retaliation, of Hasan al-Banna, head of the Moslem Brotherhood, was of considerable significance because of his position in his religious movement—there was simply no way of replacing him. Moreover, the Brotherhood entered its most crucial period at that time; the absence of al-Banna was of cardinal importance.

An assassination can have a high impact when (1) the system is highly centralized, (2) the political support of the victim is highly personal, (3) the "replaceability" of the victim is low, (4) the system is in crisis and/or in a period of rapid political and social change, and (5) if the death of the victim involves the system in confrontation with other powers.

5. The Effectiveness of Assassination

This hinges on motive. If the assassin merely seeks revenge against the victim, then his death accomplishes the purposes intended. On the other hand, if the assassin hopes to achieve other ends, the whole question reverts to impacts.

Let us phrase a hypothetical case. We know that a number of attempts have been made against the life of Muhammad Reza Shah Pahlavi, the ruler of Iran. In general, attempts to kill him could come from two distinct groups: those who believe that he is too revolutionary and those who believe that he is not revolutionary enough. His death would certainly plunge Iran into crisis. His son is but a child and the strongman who ultimately would replace him would (in the opinion of most students of modern Iran) be someone much to the *left* of the present King. Thus a successful assassination, if engineered by the first group, would be in fact a tragic error; for the second group it would likely lead to goals aimed at, although accomplished by considerable risk.

Professor Bernard Lewis has argued of the original Assassins that their policy of assassination did not lead to any long-run control or domination of the target systems. It seems safe to say that assassination in the Middle East as a *deliberate* instrument of policy is a highly uncertain, risky, adventure with little probability that systemic or other far-reaching changes will be brought about. Of course, assassins do not always reason this way.

6. Conclusion

There have been a great deal of assassinations along with other forms of violence in the Middle East. The area is in the throes of finding itself and sorting out its political and ideological future. There are few channels of opposition or of criticism open; much change takes place because of violence or its threat. (Parenthetically it should be said that a number of Middle Eastern countries have regulations on the acquisition and possession of firearms, but these are easily circumvented.) It is not likely that the incidence of assassination will fall off until some sort of stability (not just political) comes to the area. This alone will not assure the end of assassination but will, in effect, limit assassinations to the unpredictable lunatic fringe that exists everywhere.

The alleged assassin of Senator Robert Kennedy is of Middle Eastern origin. It is natural to ask whether this origin contributed in any way to the assassination. It is difficult to buttress logically any assertions of this kind. About all that can be said is that the Jerusalem and Palestine—Sirhan is apparently west-bank Palestinian rather than east-bank Jordanian—of his youth was the scene of incredible violence (including the high-level assassinations of Count Folke Bernadotte and King Abdullah). No part of these experiences or their environmental conditions would have lessened whatever tendencies he possessed to assassinate those with whom he disagreed.

SUPPLEMENT G

ASSASSINATION AND POLITICAL
VIOLENCE IN CANADA

By Denis Szabo*

1. Introduction

Violence has been a matter of concern for governmental and nongovernmental bodies in recent years. The amount of literature devoted to this topic has recently greatly increased as a direct consequence of increased interest in the study of criminological aspects of violent behavior and also increased concern with general disruptive manifestations of violence in several strata of the population. Many etiological theories of violence have been proffered by existing criminological literature, and recently the interest of social scientists has been directed towards violent aspects of social unrest, violence in developing nations, and links between violence and the process of social change and development. This interest represents a new development away from the pure criminological and penological concern with detection, conviction, and treatment of violent offenders, a move towards the political science aspects of violence in the process of national development.

Canada has experienced at least its share of political violence. To understand such violence, this paper will discuss the sociocultural and historical context in which Canadian political violence has occurred.

*This is an abbreviated version of a paper written for the Commission by the Department of Criminology, University of Montreal, under the supervision of Denis Szabo. The paper was originally written in French but was submitted to the Commission in English translation.

700

2. Problem of Canadian Identity

Canadian national identity is in large part a reaction against a long-term supposed threat from the United States to its independence and traditions. Loyalty to the British Crown has been one effective means of providing sentiment against United States intervention and control. The social consequence of Canadian allegiance to a British monarch has been the acceptance of a national purpose based on the principle of "indivisibility of the Commonwealth."

Nationalism in English-speaking Canada has undergone some curious changes. At one time it represented a left-wing, often pro-United States protest against the Imperial connection and the closed economic-political-ecclesiastical system sustained by this connection. As Vincent Masset has put it: "There are some people in Canada with strong nationalist feelings who think that their end could only be achieved through a republican form of government." Today it is often the leftwinger who is most anti-American and pro-British.

The most "traditional" form of Canadian nationalism would seem to continue in the French Canadian protest movements with their anti-English and anti-Establishment overtones directed at those within Canadian borders who represent English cultural, political and economic domination. As English-speaking Canadians seek to isolate Canada from the United States, French Canadians look for means to assure their own safety, surrounded as they are by over 200 million English-speaking North Americans. In a sense, both English-speaking and French-speaking Canadians want to protect their respective minority cultures from being absorbed.

3. Historical Context of Political Violence in Modern Canada

From the Battle of the Plains of Abraham to Louis Riel

French Canadians strongly adhere to the motto "*Je me souviens*" and they remember the heroic period of New France. French Canadians like to point out that they are the original *canadiens* "for tradition is a stronger force there (Quebec) today than anywhere else in North America."[1]

The French had one great rival in North America, the English, who were more concerned with trade than glory. New France was an economic threat and harassment to New England, which then included New Brunswick and Nova Scotia. In 1759 the conflict reached its climax when Wolfe defeated Montcalm in the historic battle on the Plains of Abraham at Quebec City. This defeat condemned the French colonists to permanent subordination to the British.

The possibility of a secessionist movement in New England caused the British decision to strengthen their hold on New France. The Quebec Act of 1774, called the Magna Carta of French Canada, granted religious and political rights to the French Canadians. It gave them a legal basis for resisting assimilation. The Quebec Act was evidently a contributing factor to the landlords and clergy remaining loyal to the Crown during the American Revolution. *Les habitants* were indifferent to the struggle for independence and resisted helping either side. Despite the Quebec Act, the movement for American independence did not help the French-Canadian cause. Thousands of English loyalists moved into Canadian territory until the French were outnumbered.

The British were confronted with the problem of establishing representative government in a colony split into two hostile ethnic groups. They sought to solve the problem by dividing the colony into two fairly homogeneous provinces. The Canada Act of 1791 established a predominantly French Province, Lower Canada (Quebec), and upper Canada, each with an elective assembly.

The ethnic conflict, however, persisted in Lower Canada. The English wanted state-controlled schools, whereas the French considered education a religious matter. The rural French were aligned against the urban English on the control of finances and taxation. In 1837 a rebellion erupted in Lower Canada but was quickly suppressed. It resulted in the abolishment of the separately elected assembly for Lower Canada.

Lord Durham, an advocate of colonial reform, was dispatched to Canada to investigate conditions and difficulties and to make recommendations for reform. In his report, Lord Durham, an idealist, recommended that the French group be obliterated by progressive assimilation into the English culture. The Union Act of 1840, the result of the Durham Report, brought the two former colonies into a union of Canada East

(Upper Canada) and Canada West (Lower Canada). The Province of Canada, as the union was called, was placed under a single legislature in which the two sections were equally represented. The new governmental arrangement was plagued by political instability that intensified the fear of American annexation.[2]

In the face of external threat and internal deadlock, representatives of Upper and Lower Canada met with representatives of Newfoundland, New Brunswick, Nova Scotia, and Prince Edward Island to discuss the possibility of a confederation of all colonies in British North America. The first conference was held in Charlottetown, Prince Edward Island, in 1864; later that year there was a constitutional convention held in Quebec City. Unlike the Philadelphia convention in 1787, the Quebec meeting had to consider certain delicate ethnic and religious issues, which are still prevalent in Canada today. The ethnic-religious "reconciliation" enabled the delegates to tentatively formulate a scheme of consolidation or federation between the Province of Canada and the Maritime provinces to be known as the Dominion of Canada. After approval by the provincial legislatures, the confederation proposal was sent to the British parliament for ratification. The British North America Act of 1867 and subsequent enactments by the British parliament are, in effect, the Canadian Constitution.

The ethnic conflict was supposedly resolved during the confederation debates in the Province of Canada in 1865. The confederation arrangement, then, was based on a compact between the English-speaking majority and the French-speaking minority. The compact, from a political standpoint, created a centralized form of federalism with a certain amount of provincial autonomy.

The compact, from a social standpoint, preserved the bicultural and bilingual character of the country. The Quebec Act of 1774 was the cornerstone in the preservation of the French cultural heritage and provincial identity. The Durham Report, on the contrary, envisioned the assimilation of the French-speaking minority by the English-speaking majority; but the compact resolved these differences by granting provincial autonomy in the fields of language, religious, social, municipal, and educational institutions.

The compact, from an economic standpoint, gave to the

Dominion Government the power to regulate commerce. This resolved the conflict between the commercially-minded English and the agrarian-minded French.

The compact was simply a union of the various provinces to the English-speaking majority; however, to the French-speaking minority, "it is a pact or treaty between the French and English which guarantees to each group an equal right to its own faith, language, laws, and customs."[3] The British North America Act was the legal description of this compact or agreement. This enactment by the British Parliament followed the Quebec resolutions, but there were important alterations to the compact. These changes were never referred back to the colonial legislatures for consideration. In other words, the Canadian Constitution has never been formally approved in its entirety by the Canadians.

In conclusion, to the English-speaking Canadian, the confederation agreement or compact meant majority rule; to the French-speaking Canadian, it meant minority rights. The English were mainly concerned about federal control and the commercial aspects of confederation. The French were concerned about provincial autonomy and the cultural aspects of confederation. The compact, in the final analysis, resolved to some extent the conflict between the English and French cultures.

From Louis Riel to Modern Separatism

Since confederation, the Riel insurrection, the separate-school question, and the conscription issue are the more serious crises that have threatened national unity and intensified the ethnic-religious conflict; each are discussed in the following paragraphs.

The expansion of Canada to the western territories created certain difficulties. Hudson's Bay company reluctantly relinquished its control to Dominion authority. However, the *metis* (halfbreed French-speaking nomads) were alarmed at the prospect of land exploitation and Canadian domination. Louis Riel, a young *metis* rebel, established a provisional government, *la nation metisse*, in the Red River area above Minnesota. Riel, irresponsible and unstable, enraged by continued English-Canadian opposition to the protest movement, executed Thomas Scott, a provocative English-Canadian, for insubordination. Despite unfavorable repercussions in Ontario to the Scott incident, the Dominion Parliament passed the Manitoba Act of 1870 creating the Province of Manitoba. Predominantly French-speaking, Manitoba had provisions for ethnic equality in terms of denominational schools and official bilingualism. There is no question that the Riel uprising secured provincial status with ethnic equality and protection of *metis* land titles.

The binational character of Manitoba was short-lived in the face of rapid legislature which abolished separate denominational schools and the official status of the French language. The developments in Manitoba and the defeat of remedial legislation in the Dominion Parliament provoked considerable bitterness. In 1884, in Saskatchewan, the government system of land survey disregarded *metis* land titles, and Riel, leader of *metis* discontent, returned from exile in Montana to lead another struggle against the Dominion Government. The agitation became a rebellion which included the formation of a provisional government and an armed attack against the police at Duck Lake. The Cree Indians, who had similar grievances, massacred the inhabitants of three settlements. Canadian militia soon captured the rebel stronghold at Batoche and crushed the remaining resistance. Riel was arrested and condemned to death. The harshness of the sentence created additional controversy.

Ontario, heavily Protestant and remembering the death of Scott, considered Riel a rebel and a murderer.[4] Quebec considered Riel "the champion of an oppressed minority whose death was nothing short of martyrdom."[5] Riel's execution led to public demonstrations in Quebec and to the election of Honore Mercier, a political opportunist with an emotional, anti-Dominion following, as Premier of Quebec. Edgar McInnis, a Canadian historian, states that "Riel became a symbol of all the deep-rooted antagonisms that continued to divide Canada along racial lines and that contributed in a major degree to the revival of sectionalism which marked the final decades of the century."[6]

Canadian participation in the military defense of Great Britain through the years has generated much bitterness and hostility between English and French Canada. According to the French-Canadian viewpoint, Canada was not obligated to defend British imperial interests. The French felt that the Canadian armed forces were discriminatory because they were English oriented, and ultranationalists were afraid of the loss of French identity through the assimilation policies of the armed services.

Revival of the controversial separate-school question exacerbated and embittered the 1917 conscription controversy. In 1916 Manitoba abolished bilingual schools, and shortly thereafter Ontario restricted the establishment of French-language schools and confined the teaching of French to the early grades. Quebec considered such actions a flagrant repression of minority rights.

During World War I, when Prime Minister Robert Borden decided that compulsory military service was necessary, he wanted to secure the support of his parliamentary opposition to avoid a disastrous ethnic-religious cleavage. He aimed at political coalition and military conscription. Wilfred Laurier, a French-Canadian moderate, declined an invitation to help Borden form a coalition or "Union" government. He realized that conscription would divide the country and that as a matter of practical politics, to be associated with it would mean his relinquishing control of Quebec to the adherents of nationalism and isolationism. Disregarding Laurier, the leader of the Liberal party, Borden was able to bring about the formation of a Union government of English-speaking Liberals and Conservatives. The 1917 national election results, excepting Quebec, overwhelmingly supported the Union government. Quebec was virtually isolated from the mainstream of Canadian politics.

The enactment and eventual enforcement of conscription provoked serious rioting in Quebec. The provincial legislative assembly finally tabled a motion stating that "Quebec would be dispelled to accept breaking of the Confederation pact of 1867 if in the other provinces it is believed that she is an obstacle to the union, progress and development of Canada."[7]

Because of its involvement in World War II, Canada was again confronted with the conscription problem. During the 1940 election campaign, Prime Minister Mackenzie King pledged not to impose conscription for overseas service. In 1942, in order for Canada to maintain its military commitments, a national plebescite was held to release the Government from its pledge. The referendum resulted in a 72 percent "no" vote in Quebec, the remaining provinces voting 80 percent in favor. Because the vote intensified ethnic friction and sharpened Quebec's opposition, King refused to adopt conscription immediately. Only late in 1944 was compulsory military service adopted, but it was limited rather than total conscription. Although his approach satisfied neither extreme, King was able to maintain the delicate ethnic balance.

Canadian dualism (or the existence of what some Canadians call the "two solitudes") and the inherent conflict involved in this concept are problems of some magnitude today. One of the main reasons for the continuation of tension and hostility is the lack of communication and socialization between the two groups.

Each group has a stereotyped, derogatory view of the other. The English Canadian thinks that many French Canadians are church-dominated; the French Canadian thinks *les anglais* are badly in need of the Church. To many English Canadians, a French Canadian is a backward peasant, "a medieval fossil clinging rigidly to an outmoded way of life."[8] On the other hand, French Canadians think of *les anglais* as having a dual allegiance to Great Britain and Canada. This was evident during the heated parliamentary debate 2 years ago over the adoption of a national Canadian flag. The traditional English wanted to retain the Red Ensign with the Union Jack in the upper masthead corner. To the French Canadian this was an example of the loyalist mentality clutching the colonial symbol.

For almost 200 years since British conquest, Quebec has slumbered peacefully, content to be isolated from the rest of Canada. The winds of change, industrialization and urbanization, have intensified the conflict between the solitudes, English and French. Quebec is in a state of gradual transformation from a backward agrarian society to a modern industrial society. The French Canadian is concerned about the economic domination of the English Canadians and Americans in his province. The French Canadians have nothing like a proportional share of economic power although they comprise almost a third of the country's population. This economic discrimination is based on the fact that positions in industry are geared for the English. It should be pointed out, however, that the church-controlled education of Quebec has not been oriented particularly toward participation and advancement in the modern world. Jean Lesage, former Premier, and the late Daniel Johnson, implemented programs of "economic liberation" that involved more provincial control and government participation in the development of natural resources and industry. The conflict between the English-speaking and the French-speaking Canadians now involves the economic, as well as the cultural and social, spheres.

The ethnic-religious conflict may also be explained because of different ideologies. Ramsay Cook in *Canada and the French-Canadian Question*, says that French Canadian philosophy might be termed Rousseauian because it is mainly concerned with *la survivance* or group survival.[9] In contrast, the philosophy of the English Canadian is Lockean because it is basically concerned with individual rights.[10] It could be said that at the present Quebec ideology is less on the defensive and more on the offensive.

4. Fertile Ground for Political Violence: Quebec

Outline of the Sociopolitical and Ideological Situation in Quebec

Having given the historical background, we now present an outline of the sociopolitical and ideological situation in Quebec.

This concerns the problem of the preservation of the cultural heritage and the coexistence of two cultures. During the course of evolution and struggle, two main trends emerged with French Canada: on the one side were the avowed Federalists and on the other, the Separatists.

The former visualize greater autonomy within the French-English community in Canada. The latter nurture ideas of revolution, and their goal is to separate from the rest of Canada and to achieve independence by every possible means. Our present study focuses upon the option for violence.

French-Canadian national, or patriotic, movements failed in the past because they did not find solid enough support from the public. There had to be an ideological superstructure and widespread national education before such a movement could be successful.

The grievances of the French-Canadians arise in part from

the increase in legislative centralization by Ottawa. In addition, it has been suggested (Richer 1938) that the autonomist feeling in Quebec rests on the fact that Confederation had a bad effect on French-Canadian life because it imposed a "materialistic outlook, similar to that of the Anglo-American."

The other grievance lies in the organization of the political parties. The Anglo-Canadian bloc runs the show, and this is still true today: the English-speaking people dominate the political parties and these in turn dominate French Canada.

French-Canadians, as we have already stated, are divided into two groups: Federalists and Separatists. The former are represented by the two traditional parties: the Union Nationale and the Liberals. The separatists are divided according to the means to be chosen to achieve independence: the vote or *violence*. The advocates of violence believe that the revolutionary tradition of French Canada has been nothing but a long and constant struggle to maintain ground and that the revolution must completely sever itself from its past pattern of misunderstanding and compromise. This is the theory espoused by the Front de liberation Quebecois (FLQ). They adopt the tactic of guerrilla warfare, which they call "the strategy of the exploited." They believe that "propaganda through action" is an effective means of attaining their objectives. With these tactics, the FLQ promotes or uses force, violence, and even terrorism.

To illustrate the degree of violence, the following paragraphs describe the events that took place in a first and second wave of violence.

The First Wave

The 8th of March, 1963, marked the beginning of the attacks; three military establishments were the targets of Molotov cocktails. The 29th of March marked the destruction of one of the symbols of colonialism: the monument to General Wolfe on the Plains of Abraham in Quebec City. The movement continued its activities by dynamiting some railroad tracks near Lemieux moments before Prime Minister Diefenbaker passed through during his election campaign.

Several days after the discovery of a strong charge of explosives near the TV tower on Mount Royal, the general headquarters of the Royal Canadian Mounted Police in West-mount was dynamited, and the next day, April 20, the antiter-rorist squad of the City of Montreal defused explosives that had been placed in the corridors of Central Station. This day marked the death of the first victim of the terrorist move-ments; a guard named O'Neil at the Army Recruitment Centre in Montreal was killed when a bomb exploded. The FLQ, in its fight against national symbols, tried to destroy the Dominion Monument in Montreal. During the following weeks, Selbec Copper Mines, a large mining concern, was attacked and Federal mailboxes were bombed in the predomi-nantly English and independent City of Westmount. The ex-plosion of a bomb claimed a second victim, Police Sergeant M. Leja, of the bomb-detonation squad.

The arrest of several members of the FLQ temporarily broke up the organization, but like the Arab commandos in Algeria, it soon resumed activities as the Armee de liberation Quebecois (ALQ). In 1964, it executed spectacular raids against military installations in Montreal and the industrial complex at Shawinigan Falls. On August 28 of that year the ALQ held up an armament factory in Montreal, resulting in the deaths of two factory employees and the arrest of five activists.

The dissolution of the ALQ marked the initiation of an-other new movement, the Front de Liberation National (FLN) which announced its title at the beginning of 1965. It did not hesitate to use violence in its fight against Anglo-Canadian imperialism in Quebec and was the group held responsible for the burning of the car of Leon Balcer of Trois Riviere; Balcer was leader of the Progressive Conservative Party of Quebec and an ardent advocate of the visit of Queen Elizabeth II to Quebec.

The objectives of the first terrorist movement were the destruction of colonial symbols and the military, police, and postal systems. If such acts claimed a number of victims, these murders were but accidental, because assassination was not the aim of the movement. However, because of these "assassi-nations," the organization lost the confidence of the Quebec separatists, as illustrated by the articles in the Quebec French press which supported the movement until the casualties oc-curred and thereafter became antiterrorist. The FLQ had the support of the French population as long as its activities were concerned only with demoralizing the English-speaking people and making them take cognizance of the reality of French presence in Quebec.

The Second Wave

An intermediary wave of terrorism was unleashed on Quebec from August 6 to August 27, 1966. An alleged FLQ group attacked industrial enterprises, supporting the unions against them, and committed several holdups and armed robberies to obtain money, arms, munitions, and explosives.

The second attack of violence brought about the death of two people. On May 6, a bomb at the La Grenade factory took the life of Mlle. Therese Morin, and on July 14 Jean Corbo, FLQ activist, was killed by the bomb he was transporting to the Dominion Textile factory.

From April 2 to April 4, the group stole dynamite and munitions from the Waterloo Marble Works and then robbed the Elysee Theatre of $2,415 on May 1. One June 9, the home of M. Gaston Deserres was robbed of $500; on April 15, rifles and ammunition were stolen from the Mont-St-Louis College; and on August 27, a conspiracy to hold up the Jean-Talon Theatre was uncovered.

The attack against national symbols was launched by the explosion of a bomb near the monument of Dollard des Ormeaux at Park Lafontaine and June 3 during an election rally in which former Quebec Premier Jean Lesage was taking part, a bomb exploded in a lavatory of the Paul Sauve Arena.

This second wave of violence might be regarded as a period during which the FLQ terrorist group was setting itself up financially and acquiring arms; they attacked only important Anglo-Saxon industry that was at odds with labor and national and political symbols, such as the Dollard des Ormeaux monument and the election meeting of Jean Lesage.

This second wave caused the death of two persons and the arrest of 11 members of the FLQ terrorist network, whose leaders were presumed to be Pierre Vallieres and Charles Gagnon. Vallieres was condemned to life imprisonment for the death of Mlle. Therese Morin; Charles Gagnon, acquitted at the beginning of April 1969 of the charge of manslaughter in the case of Jean Corbo, was nonetheless condemned to 2 years in prison for conspiracy in armed robbery at the Jean-Talon Theatre.

The Third Wave

The point of departure of the third movement could be considered the cry of "Vive le Quebec libre," uttered by General de Gaulle on his visit to the 1967 International Exposition in Montreal. These words revived the national feeling of French Canada and made possible the creation of the separatist Mouvement Souverainete Association in October 1967 by M. Rene Levesque, which joined the Rassemblement Nationale (RN), in the fall of 1968 to become the Parti Quebecois.

The objectives of the third wave of terrorism, from 1968 to 1969, were not only to destroy symbols of colonialism and federalism in French Canada, but also to become frequently associated with the labor and union disputes and conflicts. On May 11, 1968, a bomb was placed in the Seven Up Co., where personnel had been on strike for some time. Liquor Commission stores, on strike since the month of June, became the targets for bombs on September 8 and 26. On September 20, the barracks of the Black Watch Regiment—the first federal objective of the second wave—was bombed, then the Offices of the Ministry of Labour, and on October 14, the Club Renaissance and the Reform Club, two political clubs. Labor conflicts were supported by the terrorists on November 13 and December 14, when the company and management of Domtar were the objects of attack. On December 14, Chanbly Transport and its director, Charles Senecal, were subjected to bombings and on November 20, another store of the Liquor Commission.

The large industrial and commercial companies, representing Anglo-Saxon power in Montreal, were the objects of several criminal attempts: On November 15, Lord & Co.; on November 18, Structural Steel; and on November 22, Eaton's Department Store, where the police found two charges of dynamite; and on December 12, the private home of the President of Structural Steel was bombed.

From December 31, 1968, to February 25, 1969, the objectives of the terrorists were, for the most part, government buildings and the executive offices of large Anglo-Saxon companies: the Federal Tax building, the Government Offices on McGill St., the store of the Queen's Printer, the barracks of the Regiment de Maisonneuve, the RCAI building, the Bank of Nova Scotia, the RCAF building, and on February 14, the Montreal Stock Exchange, where the explosion demolished a part of the premises and was responsible for wounding a good many of the personnel working in Place Victoria.

The end of 1968 was marked by several radical movements; worker and union strife was at the bottom of some of the violence against companies and their directors, but with the beginning of 1969, the political objectives of French separatism resumed predominance.

5. Conclusion

Violence and terrorism are perfect weapons for revolution that seeks to abolish a regime or institutions that are promoting the interest of only a number of its citizens. It is an ardent force designed to break resistance through terror.

It is through action that minorities manage to awaken the spirit of independence and the spark of audacity without which no revolution would ever take place. Such action spreads more propaganda in a matter of days than thousands of pamphlets. In Canada, the revolutionists generally proceeded by depositing explosives or bombs on certain property that had been chosen for previously selected objectives. The violence was directed against symbols of English-speaking domination, against Federal or Anglo-American property, and not specifically against those individuals who were "incidentally" wounded or killed. This is a specific kind of political violence which contains a predominant element of propaganda. The form, consisting of acts designed to alert and awaken, was aimed at informing the public, making them aware, and gaining their support in finding a solution to the social, cultural, economic, and political problems of Quebec; support which they could not obtain, they explained, through legal means.

A distressing and sobering aspect of political violence in Canada is that one cannot begin to compare the domination of the French Canadians by the English-speaking Canadians with the cruelty or violence that took place in Tsarist Russia or Hitler Germany and the extent of suppression that may have "justified" violence under those regimes. It is important to realize that the perceived political, socioeconomic, and psychological oppression of the French part of the population by the English-speaking portion, as described above, was sufficient to produce serious political violence without physical oppression or curtailment of physical freedom by the perceived dominant majority.

References

1. Mason Wade, *The French-Canadian Outlook,* Carleton Library No. 14 (Toronto: McClelland and Stewart Ltd., 1964), p. 1.
2. In February 1863, the *New York Herald* called for annexation "peaceably if possible, forcibly if necessary." Mason Wade, *The French Canadians, 1760–1945,* p. 319.
3. *Ibid.,* p. 42.
4. Edgar McInnis, *Canada: A Political and Social History* (New York: Holt, Rinehart and Winston, 1960), pp. 333, 364.
5. *Ibid.,* p. 364.
6. *Ibid.,* p. 338.
7. Ramsay Cook, *Canada: A Modern Study* (Toronto: Clarke, Irwin & Co., Ltd., 1963), p. 175. The British North American Act makes no provision for secession.
8. Charles Wagley and Marvin Harris, *Minorities in the New World* (New York: Columbia University Press, 1964), p. 185.
9. Ramsay Cook, *Canada and the French-Canadian Question* (Toronto: Macmillan of Canada, 1966), p. 146.
10. *Ibid.*

SUPPLEMENT H

ASSASSINATION IN GREAT BRITAIN

By the Task Force Staff

1. Introduction

It is often said today that the United States and Great Britain are in a "special relationship." We are bound by the ties of a common language, cultural tradition, history, legal system, and similar democratic political institutions and philosophy. We were allies in the two great wars of this century.

The United States and Great Britain differ markedly, however, in the number of civil strife and assassination events that they have experienced during the period 1918 to 1967. Great Britain, relative to the other nations discussed in these reports, has had a low incidence of political strife and a low incidence of assassination events. The United States, on the other hand, during these same periods has experienced high levels of political strife and a high incidence of assassination events.

When a larger time perspective is employed, however, a comparison of the history of assassination of top governmental leaders of Great Britain with that of the United States is not as favorable to Great Britain. Assassination data for Prime Ministers of Great Britain since 1800 and monarchs of Great Britain since the reign of Queen Victoria in 1837 are listed below.

2. Assassination Attempts

Monarchs

No successful attempts have been made on the life of the Monarch of the United Kingdom in recent times, but the following attempts are recorded:

H. M. Queen Victoria 1837–1901—

1. June 10, 1840, Constitution Hill, Westminster.

Edward Oxford, a potboy, discharged two pistols at Her Majesty's carriage. He was charged with shooting at Her Majesty but acquitted on grounds of insanity and confined in Bedlam [a mental institution].

2. May 30, 1842, Constitution Hill, Westminster.

John Francis, a cabinet maker, fired a pistol at Her Majesty's carriage. He was convicted of High Treason and sentenced to death, but the sentence was later commuted to transportation for life.

3. July 3, 1842, St. James's Park.

John William Bean, age 18, pointed a loaded pistol at Her Majesty's carriage. He was tried for the offense and committed to Newgate Gaol for the assault.

4. May 19, 1849, Constitution Hill, Westminster.

William Hamilton, an Irishman from county Limerick, fired a blank charge at Her Majesty's carriage. He was found guilty of presenting a pistol toward Her Majesty and sentenced to be transported for 7 years.

5. May 27, 1850, Cambridge House, Piccadilly.

Robert Pate, a former Army officer, struck Her Majesty on the forehead with a stick. He was charged with assaulting Her Majesty, a plea of insanity was rejected, and he was sentenced to be transported for 7 years.

6. March 2, 1882, Windsor Railway Station.

Roderick McLean fired a revolver at Her Majesty's carriage. He was tried for the offense, acquitted on grounds of insanity, and detained during Her Majesty's pleasure in a mental institution.

On July 16, 1936, in Constitution Hill, Jerome Pannigan k/a George Andrew Campbell McMahon, born 1902, threw a loaded revolver at the person of H. M. King Edward VIII. McMahon apparently intended only to draw public attention to himself and this cannot be classified as an attempt upon the life of the King. At the Central Criminal Court on September 14, 1936, he was sentenced to 12 months' hard labor for "Wilfully producing a revolver near the person of the King with intent to alarm His Majesty."

Prime Ministers

One Prime Minister only has been assassinated in the United Kingdom since 1800. On May 11, 1812, in the lobby of the House of Commons, Spencer Perceval was shot through the heart by one Bellingham, a commercial agent, who had a grievance against the Government. He was tried at the Old Bailey on May 15, 1812, sentenced to death despite a plea of insanity, and hanged 3 days later.

Metropolitan Police records contain details of three other incidents which may be classified as attempts.

1. On January 20, 1843, at Charing Cross, Daniel McNachten shot Edward Drummond, Private Secretary to Sir Robert Peel, the Prime Minister. Drummond died of his wound the following day and McNachten was tried for his murder. A plea of insanity was accepted, and he was detained in a mental institution. It was believed, at the time, that McNachten had mistaken Drummond for the Prime Minister.

2. At the Central Criminal Court on March 10, 1917, three persons were convicted of conspiring to murder the Prime Minister, David Lloyd George. Alice Wheeldon was sentenced to 10 years' penal servitude, Alfred Mason to 7 years and Winnie Mason to 5 years. The group, who were all conscientious objectors, believed that the Prime Minister was responsible for the loss of life in the First World War and had conceived amateurish plans to assassinate him by stabbing him with a needle dipped in curare.

3. On March 22, 1954, a parcel, addressed to Sir Winston Churchill, was delivered to 10 Downing Street, S.W.1. Upon examination, it was found to contain a substance which, if ignited, would have burnt vigorously. A note attached to it suggested that it had been sent as a warning.

The facts produced in this memorandum have been obtained by research which cannot be described as exhaustive, and it may well be that during the 19th century further attempts were made on the lives of the reigning sovereign or Prime Minister which have not come to light.

However, if case no. 3 listed above is to be discounted as lacking serious intent, it might be considered significant that out of a total of nine assassination attempts seven involved firearms and all occurred before the possession of firearms became strictly controlled by the Firearms Act of 1937.

The foregoing shows seven assaults on the sovereign of Great Britain during the period 1840 to 1936, none of which were successful, and four assaults on a Prime Minister of Great Britain from 1812 to 1954, of which only one, the assassination of Prime Minister Spencer Perceval in 1812, was successful.

Several of these attempts do not appear to merit consideration as assassination attempts. The package sent to Winston Churchill, the revolver thrown at King Edward VIII, and the firing of a blank at Queen Victoria were probably more gestures of protest than serious assault attempts. Similarly, the assault on Queen Victoria with a stick may not have had the purpose of seriously injuring her. Nonetheless, the four remaining attempts upon a sovereign and the three remaining attempts upon a Prime Minister, comprising a total of seven attempts during the period of 1812 through the present, are quite comparable in number to the total of nine attempts on Presidents of the United States or presidential candidates from 1835 to the present (see Chapter 2 of the Task Force Report).

The assassination data of Great Britain differ markedly from those of the United States in one respect, however. Although assassination attempts on Presidents or presidential candidates occur at relatively regular intervals in our history since 1835, most assassination attempts in Great Britain occurred in the 19th century. Indeed, there is a striking collection of assassination events in the decade beginning June 10, 1840, and ending May 27, 1850. During this period, no less than 4 of the 7 serious attempts occurred and 7 of the 11 total events reported occurred. Except for the present decade in the United States in which assassination attempts against a President and a presidential candidate occurred, no decade of our history experienced more than one such incident.

The collection of assassination attempts in the 1840's in Great Britain may simply be a function of imprecise collection of data. If accurate, however, this phenomenon is important because it seems to bear out the theory developed in Chapter 3 of the Task Force Report that assassination incidents are related to the general level of political strife, whether or not the incidents themselves are a result of a coherent political goal, such as seizure of power or alteration of policy. In the three decades preceding the 1840's Great Britain experienced much political turmoil as a result of Britain's shift from a mercantile and agricultural nation to an industrial nation. Violent protests by workers against the introduction of machines, the lowering of wages, and the unemployment of skilled labor resulting from industrialization racked Great Britain during the first half of the 19th century. One wave of protest took the form of destroying the machines themselves. Groups of men, known as Luddites, would periodically storm factories and destroy machines; such groups were active from 1810 through the 1820's.

In 1815, Parliament was unresponsive to the demands of the working class and passed the Corn Laws for the purpose of protecting agricultural producers. These laws guaranteed producers a certain price for grains, and the effect was to raise the price of bread, the staple diet of most workers. For decades thereafter, working men and the poor rioted from time to time against the hardships introduced by the simultaneous effects of the Corn Laws and the lower wages caused by the introduction of machines.

The passage of the Corn Laws brought home to both workers and the industrial middle class that Parliament—whose members were elected according to population patterns set in the 16th and 17th centuries—was controlled by the agricultural interests and the landed gentry. There followed great demands for reform of Parliament to reflect the shift of population to the cities. The infamous "Peterloo" massacre of August 16, 1819, occurred when soldiers were ordered by a local magistrate to disperse a huge crowd that had come to hear orators speak in favor of reform in Parliament. Parliament was reformed in 1832, but working-class protests continued because property qualifications were put upon suffrage, thus, denying most workers the vote. The 1830's marked the rise of a new radical workingmen's organization, the Chartist movement. The Chartists demanded immediate vote for the working class, reasoning that if the working class were given the vote, the harsh economic conditions of industrialization would be ameliorated. Riots instigated by Chartists advocating "physical force" occurred in the early 1840's.

The Anti-Corn Law League was also active during the 1840's. Torchlight parades, mass meetings, and some riots occurred early in the 1840's, and in 1846 the Corn Laws were repealed. Working-class supporters of the Anti-Corn Law League then turned their full attention to political reform and support–for the Chartists grew. The high waves of Chartism were in the years 1838, 1842, and 1848 and closely linked with immediately preceding periods of trade depression. In 1848, a year of revolution on the Continent, Chartism reached its peak, and several armed clashes with authorities occurred in Liverpool, London, and elsewhere. In 1850, prosperity and the rise of working-class unions with limited economic goals combined to remove the basis of popular Chartist support, and radical working-class protest subsided.*

There are many imponderables. We do not, for example, know why so many assassination attempts against Prime Ministers and monarchs accompanied the turmoil of the 1840's; whereas the first three decades of the 19th century in Great Britain, which also experienced much civil strife, witnessed only one such event, the successful assassination of Prime Minister Spencer Perceval in 1812. The conjunction of great political turmoil and assassination events in the 1840's, however, remains a striking phenomenon.

Apart from the gesture toward Winston Churchill in 1954, the last two decades of British history have shown no direct assassination events. This, of course, is in dramatic contrast to the history of the United States during those two decades. During this period, Great Britain experienced relatively little civil strife or turmoil.

As to the applicability of the foregoing to the United States: the history of Great Britain during the 1840's indicates that assassination events will continue until the causes for underlying civil turmoil cease to exist or are ameliorated. It suggests, as do much of the other data at the command of this Task Force, that the surest way of eliminating the evil of assassination from our national life is to meet and to solve the pressing social problems of our era as Great Britain had to meet and to solve the problems presented by industrialization.

---

*The turmoil in Great Britain during this period is examined in greater detail in "On the Origin and Resolution of English Working Class Protest," by Ben C. Roberts, in the Report of the History Task Force of this Commission.

SUPPLEMENT I

ASSASSINATION IN AUSTRALIA

By Murray C. Havens*

Australia, with a society which is, perhaps, more similar to that of the United States than any other country, provides a sharp contrast with the United States and most other parts of the world with regard to total number of assassinations. In fact, there seems to have been only one successful political assassination in the history of the country and only two unsuccessful attempts at a prominent level. From our examination of Australian sources, however, we have been unable to discover examples of unsuccessful attempts against less important figures. What accounts for the infrequency of assassinations in Australia? And what meaning, if any, does the absence of assassinations in Australia have on the causes and consequences of such actions elsewhere?

The first assassination attempt in Australia occurred on March 12, 1868, well before the federation and independence of Australia in 1901. A visiting member of the royal family, Alfred, Duke of Edinburgh, was shot in the back at close range in the Sydney suburb of Clontarf. The wound did not prove dangerous. His assailant, an Irishman named O'Farrell, was subsequently executed.

A successful assassination took place in 1921 in South Australia. A relatively minor State legislative candidate was killed in a rural railway station by his apparently insane opponent. To the extent that an insane person can have a motive, this is the only politically motivated killing of a political figure since the federation and independence of Australia

---

*University of Texas.

and, probably, the only one in the entire history of the country.

Another major assassination attempt did not come until June 19, 1966, when the leader of the Labor Party, Mr. Arthur Calwell, was shot after addressing a political rally at the townhall of Mosman, another Sydney suburb. The would-be assassin, a young man named Peter R. Kocan, thrust his sawed-off .22 rifle against the window of Calwell's car and fired. Calwell's facial wounds, resulting largely from flying glass, were painful but not fatal. Kocan was sentenced to life imprisonment.

Australia has been remarkably free of attempts on the lives of its political leaders at all levels. There has never been an attempt against a chief of state or head of government, and only the two nonfatal shootings noted above mar the perfect security of political figures at both high and low office levels in Australia.

Accounting for Australia's freedom from assassination is not easy or simple. The scholar can only suggest possible explanations, which would be necessarily tentative. At the very least, however, the evidence presented by Australian history may serve to cast doubt on some of the explanations offered for the frequency of political murders elsewhere.

For example, the Australian experience seems to contradict the belief that assassinations in America are somehow related to the fact or the myth of the frontier. Australia's frontier experience was just as real as that of the United States and a great deal more recent. Indeed, most of the country is still very sparsely populated. Australia has a land area approximately equal to that of the 48 contiguous states, but its population is only 6 percent of that of the United States and is primarily concentrated in five large cities. Although frontier mythology has taken a somewhat different form in Australia, it certainly has been present. The real frontier had its share of violence. There were plenty of "bushrangers," or outlaws; the most famous of these, Ned Kelly, may reasonably be regarded still as the great Australian hero. As in North America, the aboriginal population were removed by violence from areas deemed attractive for white settlement; they were exterminated in Tasmania and driven from the lush coastal regions of the mainland into the bleak interior.

The character of Australian settlement cannot readily account for the absence of political deaths. Beginning as a convict settlement, often poorly administered and always poorly supported from the homeland in its early days, there was nothing in the background of the population to account for the absence of this particular form of violence.

Until after the Second World War, the overwhelming majority of Australian settlers were from the British Isles; however, many of these were Irish, and events of the period just before Irish independence suggest that there is nothing inherently incompatible between Irishmen and assassinations. Although Australia has a somewhat more homogeneous population than the United States, it is by no means perfectly so. Major religious differences have always existed because of the Irish presence. Also, some immigration from the European Continent and America was present from an early period. Australia lacks the ethnic variety of America only in the absence of a large and conspicuously different ethnic group, like the American Negro, Mexican, or Puerto Rican. (The aborigine is very small in numbers and concentrated in the "outback." There has never been much prospect of black African immigration, and influx of Orientals and Melanesians was cut off fairly early by restrictive immigration legislation.)

Security measures taken for the protection of Australian politicians have scarcely been responsible for their safety. The Prime Minister had only minimal protection until recently, and only after the wounding of Calwell was this protection extended to a few other prominent political figures. Like the United States, Australia has prided itself on the ready accessibility of its officeholders. The politician who cannot be seen casually and on short notice runs the risk of being considered snobbish, undemocratic, and unresponsive to popular wishes. Were he suspected of being motivated by concern for his personal safety, he might even be charged with cowardice. When Prime Minister Holt announced, after the Calwell shooting, that additional bodyguards would be made available for important personnel of all political parties, several men for whom the protection was intended strongly denounced this step.

The argument that the availability of firearms is closely related to the incidence of assassination is also contradicted by Australian evidence. Guns in Australia can be secured almost as readily as in the United States, and in rural areas they are owned by a high proportion of the population. Guns are probably less common in Australian cities than among American urban dwellers, but this is a matter of individual choice rather than prohibitory restrictions.

Many of the aspects of Australian life that have been discussed would lead us to expect a high level of violence, and such violence has been present in certain forms. Rough language is common, and Australians have often prided themselves on their readiness to brawl and their effectiveness in doing so. Moreover, such violence is not confined to nonpolitical arenas. Even on the floor of Parliament, the standard of decorum is surprisingly lax from the perspective of an American political observer. Verbal violence is the rule, and members freely insult each other. In the early decades of the century, parliamentary sessions sometimes became so disorderly as to prevent the conduct of business. Literary and conversational references to the need to wipe out certain, most, or all politicians are commonly encountered. (Note the frequency of such demands in the well-known mystery novels of Arthur Upfield, for instance.)

Yet this violent side of Australian life stops sharply at a point short of assassination. Indeed political deaths of any kind have been rare. There are many demonstrations and disorders, often on the scale and of an intensity that would lead an outsider to call them riots, but the rioters almost always emerge alive. However, both racial violence and labor disputes have led to a small number of deaths over the years. For example, more than 20 persons died in the celebrated battle at Eureka Stockade, which ended a rebellion in the Victorian gold fields in 1854. Otherwise political disputes have been settled without the effusion of fatal quantities of blood.

At least one possible explanation for the absence of assassinations and other extreme forms of political violence in Australia lies in the relative unimportance of politics to the society throughout most of its history. The tendency to speak disparagingly of individual politicians is usually extended to politicians as a whole and politics itself. The principal demand made of the political order may be that it should leave the citizen alone, and it has done precisely that far more than in most societies. The society has been rapidly expanding throughout its history, leaving plenty of scope for individual activity beyond the bounds of any particularly systematic social control. Even where public policies were deemed necessary and important, they were often supported by virtually the whole population (as with Asiatic exclusion) or were problems chiefly of means rather than ultimate goals (as with transportation policy and resource development).

Certain questions that have led to violence elsewhere were irrelevant to Australian politics for part or all of its history. Foreign affairs could be largely ignored until 1941 as not much of a problem and as a British responsibility, anyway. (The bitter and eventually successful opposition to conscription in the First World War must be noted as an exception, however, to this generalization.) From the time that independence began to seem feasible, there was little dispute over the basic character that the Australian Government was to assume. Democracy itself would have been rejected by some settlers in the earlier convict days, but well before 1901, the Australian commitment to democracy was beyond serious dispute. Independence itself, with the maintenance of initially strong ties to Great Britain, encountered few objections. The real problems in the establishment of the Federation were chiefly questions of economic policy and the need to balance the economic interests of the six states. In addition, there was less basis for the ethnic and religious disputes that have engendered violence in many political systems. Friction between Irish Catholics and the remainder of the population has always been a feature of Australian history; but this friction, though varying in intensity, has been kept within tolerable limits.

Australian politics has focused chiefly on economic questions. Even such issues as immigration have been viewed widely and by many people chiefly as economic problems. Furthermore, by the late 19th century, a majority of the Australian population had achieved, on a reasonably dependable economic basis, at least a minimal standard of living. Hence, the economic disputes were not usually over matters of life and death but over various means to achieve widely agreed-upon economic goals or over the distribution of economic rewards beyond the bare necessities of life. These are matters that are by their nature "compromisable." The histories of many other countries suggest that men are much more likely to kill each other over differences of religion, language, ethnic background, or abstract political principle than they are over economic interests (unless the interest involves a struggle for survival). But these matters of high emotional commitment have usually been kept out of Australian politics, perhaps largely through luck and partly through farsighted leadership, both in formal government and in other social institutions.

In the last few years, like much of the rest of the Western world, Australia has encountered a substantial increase, especially among young people, in intense commitment to various political values. This development may lead to a higher level of political violence, possibly including assassination attempts, but this is, as yet, far from certain. The attempt on Calwell in 1966 was related only in limited degree to the intensity of political conviction. There have been large-scale and occasionally somewhat violent demonstrations; but most of these have been closely tied to the question of Australian participation in the Vietnam conflict or related issues, such as conscription, nuclear testing, and so forth. Whether the termination of the war would end this new aspect of Australian politics or whether the emotional commitment engendered by the war can be carried over to other issues is not presently clear. If the latter is the case, Australian politics will surely be more violent in the near future than it has been through most of its past. The decline of such commitment would presumably lead to a relaxation of potentially violent political tensions in Australia, unless the situation were complicated by a drastic reduction in the presently rather high standard of living (not very likely) or by a recurrence of critical problems in foreign affairs (very likely, indeed). Ethnic or religious friction could theoretically lead to violence also, but religious differences, as in the United States and Western Europe, appear to have become less, rather than more, relevant to the political arena; the largescale immigration in recent years from Eastern and Southern Europe, chiefly Italy and Greece, has produced no critical political disturbances. The position of the aboriginal population has attracted considerable attention; there are signs of developing political organization and leadership among aborigines, but this group remains too small to occasion major political strife on a national basis. In the localities where they are concentrated, especially in the Northern Territory, an increase in tensions involving this group perhaps can be expected.

What have been the consequences of assassination and assassination attempts in Australia? The most important may have been sheer shock. Perhaps because of the rarity of such events, Australians have tended to react with considerable dismay to these occurrences. Overt symptoms of such shock were clear in the aftermath of the Calwell shooting in 1966; press accounts of the two earlier episodes suggest a similar pattern of response. In societies in which political killings are more "normal," such reactions are more difficult to discover.

The successful 1921 assassination appears to have produced no significant political consequences of a tangible character, but the attempts of 1868 and 1966 led to concrete developments. The attempt on the Duke of Edinburgh, having been undertaken by an Irishman, was widely attributed to a Fenian plot and produced a noteworthy increase in tension between the Irish and other Australians for some time thereafter. This was manifested in religious friction as well, particularly because the issue of public educational facilities was just becoming important. The shooting of Calwell, motivated in part by opposition to the Australian Labor Party, its leader, and its Vietnam policy, but even more by a desire for personal notoriety, led to a tightening up of security precautions for Australian political leaders in general. This step was bitterly resisted by some of those leaders, especially in the opposition Labor Party, because of fear that it would interfere with the traditional Australian relationship between the politician and his supporters. For this reason, among others, the Calwell episode may be considered a major blow at Australian political innocence—perhaps the final blow at an innocence which was first severely shaken half a century earlier at Gallipoli. "The lucky country" was not free of the world's evils, after all. If these considerations are relevant, it cannot be said that Australian assassination attempts have been without impact.

On the other hand, if one attributes to the would-be assassins O'Farrell and Kocan motivations based on attempts to calculate rationally the likely political consequences of their actions, they were probably disappointed and would have been equally disappointed had their victims died. The Duke of Edinburgh was not in a position to modify significantly British policy in Ireland or in Australia, and his death could only have led to more harshly repressive measures, if it led to anything at all. Calwell did leave the Labor Party leadership less than a year after he was shot, but this development was due to internal party disputes that had reached a high level of intensity several months before the assassination attempt and to the loss by the party of the general election several months afterward. This outcome was in no way related to his wound. If O'Farrell wanted to make merely a symbolic gesture against Britain and British government and if Kocan wanted merely personal recognition, both were presumably satisfied with their efforts and would have been more satisfied still had their victims died. But if either wanted something more than this, then the practical political consequences achieved by his action were surely not those he anticipated and desired.

SUPPLEMENT J

ASSASSINATION IN FINLAND

By Inkert Auttila*

Only three political assassinations seem to have been recorded in the history of Finland since the country was constituted as a separate political entity in 1809.

In 1904, the Russian General-Governor of Finland, N. I. Bobrikov, was assassinated by a civil servant who committed suicide immediately afterwards. The next year, the Procurator (i.e., the Attorney General) E. Soisalon-Soininen, was assassinated by a member of one of the so-called activist groups, working for Finnish liberation from Russian rule.

The next assassination took place in 1922, when the Minister of the Interior, Heikki Ritavuori, was shot by a mentally disturbed right-wing extremist, who opposed the Minister's leniency in dealing with the Red prisoners after the Liberation War—Civil War of 1918.

During the disturbances in the 1930's, some semi-Fascist organizations temporarily threatened the democratic order and several incidents took place where political personages were kidnapped and, as a symbolic act of scorn and demonstration, were transported to the Russian border. In a few cases, Communists and persons involved in Socialist movements were manhandled, and a couple of unsolved homicides are recorded. However, because these homicides were directed against unknown and insignificant persons, they cannot reasonably be classified with the above-mentioned political assassinations.

The background of the assassinations of Bobrikov and Sois-

---

*Institute of Criminology, Helsinki.

alon-Soininen is obvious. At this time, Russia strengthened its grip on Finland, the Constitution was set aside by imperial decrees that were generally considered unlawful, and a considerable proportion of the Finnish people perceived the situation as a freedom fight against Russian oppression. In history books, the perpetrators of the two acts are treated neutrally or with approval; in particular, the slayer of Bobrikov is, with some reservations, spoken about as a patriot.

The general glorifying of the Bobrikov assassination may have provided the psychological background and model for the murder of Ritavuori in 1922. Ritavuori's policy of leniency against the prisoners of war placed him in the "enemy camp"; criticism against him in right-wing newspapers was furious, and the assassin probably sought to emulate the "hero" role of the slayer of Bobrikov. Psychiatrists found the perpetrator, an architect and member of the nobility, to be mentally disturbed.

The hypothesis that political assassinations are strongly influenced by "precedents" is strongly substantiated by the Finnish experience. In the beginning of the century, the anarchist assassinations in Russia were a general subject of comment and concern in Finland, as in Europe at this time. Knowledge of precedents combined with a situation of political frustration may be a general background for political assassinations. During the last decades, there has not been any feeling of political frustration in Finland that could be reasonably applied to a scapegoat within the country.

Considering the above-average level of crimes of violence in Finland, the number of Finnish political assassinations may seem small. On the other hand, because Finland is a small country, political power may be more accessible through legitimate channels than in a larger country. The size of the country may explain the differences in the number of political assassinations when the democracy factor is held constant.

SUPPLEMENT K

ASSASSINATION IN SWEDEN

By Klas Lithner

Since just before the end of the 18th century, there have been only two assassinations in Sweden.

The first assassination occurred in March of 1792, when King Gustavus III was shot at a masquerade at the Royal Opera at Stockholm. There was a political plot among several members of the higher nobility who were displeased because the King had made himself practically lone ruler several years before and severely curtailed the power of the Parliament. Some were inspired by the French Revolution. A captain by the name of Anckarstrom, a member of the lower nobility, became the tool of the plotters, who saw the masquerade as a very good opportunity. There had been rumors about a plan to assassinate the King, but the King did not heed the warnings. The shot was not mortal, but he died several weeks later of complications from the wound. Anckarstrom, the murderer, seemed to be a man with a general grudge against the world.

The second assassination took place at night, between June 26 and 27, 1909, when Czar Nicholas of Russia and his Czarina were on a state visit to Stockholm. A young anarchist by the name of Hjalmar Wang, 22 years old, waited in a park between the castle and a big hotel where there had been a state dinner for the many participating officers. When three high-ranking officers passed, Wang suddenly rushed them and shot and killed a major general in the Swedish Marines. Immediately afterwards he committed suicide; consequently, it was impossible to investigate his motives in detail, but Wang had

731

been an active anarchist for several years. At the time, he was a deserter from his military service, which he should have started some months earlier. He had very lively contacts with anarchists from Russia and the Baltic provinces, who lived in Stockholm as political refugees from Russia. From this small group emanated strong activistic, political propaganda directed against the Royalty, the Church, and the Army. As a safety measure but without direct legal authority, the Stockholm police took several of the leading foreign anarchists into preventive arrest during the visit. From conversations with Wang's associates reported after his death, it was believed that Wang had intended to assassinate the Czar, possibly in cooperation with his political associates; however, when, for some reason, he became unable to do so, he chose instead to kill a uniformed officer, a symbol of "the Establishment."

During the period 1933 to 1945, when there were several small but active Nazi parties or party factions in Sweden, there were rumors that they considered the use of political violence, but there were no incidents.

The probable reasons explaining why there have been practically no political assassinations in Sweden in modern times are the following:

1. There has been a gradual democratization process where the old political rulers have relinquished their former power without a direct fight.
2. The kings have been content to become more and more symbols and less and less rulers.
3. Sweden is a homogeneous country with a long tradition of political cooperation between the parties.
4. There is no tradition of political violence.
5. At least during the latter decades, there has been a close control over the ownership of firearms.
6. A law concerning mentally ill persons has made it possible to certify persons who threaten violence.

ANNOTATED BIBLIOGRAPHY

Assassination, Terror, and Political Violence

Books

Alexander, Charles C. *The Ku Klux Klan in the Southwest.* Lexington: The University of Kentucky Press, 1965. x+288 pp. A useful study of the second Ku Klux Klan in the Southwest from 1915 to 1944, with particular emphasis on the 1920's.

Baker, Dean C. *The Assassination of President Kennedy: A Study of the Press Coverage.* Ann Arbor: The University of Michigan, Department of Journalism, 1966. 55 pp. + appendix of 45 pp. An analysis of the extent and quality of coverage by American newspapers of the assassination of President Kennedy.

Bell, Daniel, ed. *The New American Right.* New York: Criterion Books, 1955. xii+239 pp. A collection of essays on modern American right wing politics. Among the contributors to this volume are Richard Hofstadter, Seymour Martin Lipset and Talcott Parsons.

Bell, Daniel. *The Radical Right.* Garden City: Doubleday & Co., Inc., 1963. xiii+394 pp. An expanded, enlarged and updated version of the *New American Right.*

Bishop, Jim. *The Day Lincoln was Shot.* New York: Harper & Bros., 1955. viii+308 pp. A popular account of the events of Lincoln's last day, preceding his assassination.

Bornstein, Joseph. *The Politics of Murder*. New York: William Sloan Associates, 1950.
An account of several important twentieth-century assassinations in the Western world and their impact on national and international affairs.

Bowen, Don R., and Masotti, Louis H. *Civil Violence: A Theoretical Overview*. Cleveland: Case Western Reserve University, Civil Violence Research Center, 1968. 24 pp.
A theoretical overview of empirical investigations of urban rioting in the United States in the 1960's.

Brooks, Stewart M. *Our Murdered Presidents: The Medical Story*. New York: Frederick Fell, Inc., 1966. 234 pp.
This book relates the medical case histories of the assassinations of Lincoln, Garfield, McKinley and Kennedy.

Briley, Richard, III. *Death of the Kingfish!* Dallas: Triangle Publishing Co., 1960.
A popular account of the life and death of Huey Long, Senator from Louisiana.

Bromberg, Walter. *The Mold of Murder: A Psychiatric Study of Homicide*. New York and London: Grune & Stratton, 1961. viii+23 pp.
This book explores psychological factors leading to murder.

Byas, Hugh. *Government by Assassination*. New York: Alfred A. Knopf, 1942. x+369 pp.
This book explores the rise of militarists in Japan through the use of assassination. Written during World War II, the work is flawed by its anti-Japanese bias.

Chalmers, David M. *Hooded Americanism*. Chicago: Quadrangle Books, 1968. x+431 pp.
An excellent account of the first, second and third Ku Klux Klans in the United States. Particular emphasis is placed on the history of the second Klan.

Chisholm, Maj., Henry J. (USAF). *The Function of Terror and Violence in Revolution*. Unpublished dissertation, Georgetown University, 1948. 202 pp.

An analysis of the technique and function of terror as a political tactic in the 20th century.

Christowe, Stoyan. *Heroes and Assassins*. New York: Robert M. McBride & Co., 1935. 290 pp.
An historical account of Macedonian terrorists in the Balkans in the first third of the 20th century.

Connery, Robert H., ed. *Urban Riots: Violence and Social Change*. Proceedings of the Academy of Political Science, Vol. XXIX, No. 1. New York: The Academy of Political Science, Columbia University, 1968. vii+190 pp.
A collection of essays by political scientists, sociologists, economists and historians concerning the role of violence and social change, and the demographic, social, and economic preconditions of recent urban violence in American society. It also contains a selective bibliography of violence and social change.

Dedijer, Vladimir. *The Road to Sarajevo*. New York: Simon & Schuster, Inc., 1966. 550 pp.
An historical account of events and circumstances leading to the assassination of Archduke Franz Ferdinand in 1914.

Delzell, Charles F. *Mussolini's Enemies*. Princeton: Princeton University Press, 1961. xix+620 pp.
An account of the antifascist resistance in Mussolini's Italy.

Deutsch, Hermann B. *The Huey Long Murder Case*. Garden City: Doubleday & Co., Inc., 1963. x+180 pp.
This work relates the assassination of Senator Huey Long of Louisiana, and suggests possible motives of his assassin.

Donovan, Robert J. *The Assassins*. New York: Harper & Bros., 1952. x+300 pp.
The author recounts the story of each assassination or attempted assassination of a President of the United States, from the attempt of Richard Lawrence to assassinate President Jackson to the attempt on President Truman by Oscar Collazo and Griselio Torresola. The volume places special emphasis upon the life and character of each of the assassins.

The chapters on the attempted assassinations of Theodore Roosevelt and Franklin D. Roosevelt are the most extensive materials available on these subjects.

DuCloux, Louis. *From Blackmail to Treason*. London: Andre Deutsch, Ltd., 1958. 240 pp.
An account of political crime and corruption in France, 1920–1940.

Durham, M. Edith. *The Serajevo Crime*. London: George Allen & Unwin, Ltd., 1925. 208 pp.
This work contains useful background material on the assassins and the assassination of Archduke Ferdinand.

Edwards, George. *The Police on the Urban Frontier*. New York: Institute of Human Relations Press, 1968. x+89 pp.
The author, Police Commissioner of Detroit in 1962–63, provides an interesting analysis of the problems of police forces in 20th-century America, with a comprehensive set of recommendations for resolving these problems.

Eisenmenger, Victor. *Archduke Francis Ferdinand*. London: Selwyn & Blount, Ltd., 1928. 285 pp.
The life story of Archduke Franz Ferdinand of Austria.

Epstein, Benjamin R., and Forster, Arnold. *The Radical Right*. New York: Alfred A. Knopf, Inc., 1967. xi+239 pp.
A current report on the radical right—its activities, spokesmen and schemes.

Ferracuti, Franco, and Wolfgang, Marvin E. *The Subculture of Violenc*e. London: Social Science Paperbacks, Associated Book Publishers, Ltd., 1967. xxii+387 pp.
The authors present the thesis that subcultures that encourage their members to resort to violence in resolving personal problems may exist within societies whose general norms prohibit such violence.

Fortas, Abe. *Concerning Dissent and Civil Disobedience*. New York: Signet Books, 1968. 64 pp.

A legal analysis of the boundaries between dissent and civil disobedience, by a Justice of the United States Supreme Court.

Governor's Commission on the Los Angeles Riots. *Violence in City—An end or a beginning?* 1965. iii+101 pp.
A report on the Watts riot in Los Angeles by a commission appointed by the governor of California.

Graham, Stephen. *Alexander of Jugoslavia.* London: Cassell & Co., Ltd., 1938. 302 pp.
An account of the life and assassination of Alexander, King of Yugoslavia.

Gray, Lee Learner. *How We Chose a President.* New York: St. Martin's Press, 1964.
A brief account of the system used in the United States for the election of presidents.

Greenberg, Bradley S., and Parker, Edwin D., eds. *The Kennedy Assassination and the American Public.* Stanford: Stanford University Press, 1965. xi+392 pp.
A collection of studies and surveys on the reaction of the American public to the assassination of President John F. Kennedy.

Gross, Feliks. *The Seizure of Political Power.* New York: Philosophical Library, 1958. xxvii+398 pp.
An analysis of the use of force and violence in the seizure and consolidation of political power during the 19th and 20th centuries in Russia and Eastern Europe.

Groth, Alexander. *Revolution and Elite Access: Some Hypotheses on Aspects of Political Change.* Davis: University of California at Davis, Institute of Governmental Affairs, 1966. 72 pp.
An analysis of the revolutionary process.

Gurr, Ted Robert. *The Genesis of Violence: A Multi-Varient Theory of the Pre-Conditions for Civil Strife.* Unpublished dissertation, New York University, 1965. 646 pp.
A theoretical study of the preconditions for political violence, containing an excellent bibliography.

Guttmacher, Manfred S. *The Mind of the Murderer*. New York: Farrar, Straus & Cudahy, 1960. xii+244 pp.
A psychiatric study of different types of murderers.

Hall, Wilfred George Carlton. *Political Crime*. London: George Allen & Unwin, Ltd., 1923. 96 pp.
An account of various types of political crime, including regicide.

Hammer, Joseph Vaughn. *The History of the Assassins*. London: Smith and Elder, Cornhill, 1835. 240 pp.
An interesting account of the Islamic sect that practiced assassination as a political tactic in the 12th and 13th centuries.

Hartogs, Dr. Renatus, and Freeman, Lucy. *The Two Assassins*. New York: Thomas Y. Crowell Co., 1965.
An analysis of the lives of Lee Harvey Oswald and Jack Ruby.

Heaps, Willard A. *Riots, U.S.A. 1765–1965*. New York: The Seabury Press, 1966. 186 pp.
This volume illustrates in detail that urban mass violence is not a new phenomenon in the United States.

Horowitz, Irving L., ed. *The Anarchists*. New York: Dell Publishing Co., Inc., 1964. 640 pp.
A selection of essays by the major anarchists of the 19th and 20th centuries.

Janos, Andrew C. *The Seizure of Power*. Princeton: Center of International Studies, Princeton University, Research Monograph No. 16, 1964. v+99 pp.
An analysis of the various ways in which violence may be employed to seize political power.

Jászi, Oscar, and Lewis, John D. *Against the Tyrant: The tradition and theory of tyrannicide*. Glencoe, Ill.: The Free Press, 1957. ix+288 pp.
A useful study of the idea of tyrannicide in Western political theory, from the ancient Greeks to contemporary political theorists.

Johnson, Francis. *Famous Assassinations of History*. Chicago: A. C. McClurg & Co., 1903. xii+420 pp.
An account of 31 assassinations, from that of Philip of Macedon (336 B.C.) to the assassination of King Alexander and Queen Draga of Serbia (1903).

Joll, James. *The Anarchists*. Boston: Little, Brown & Co., 1964. 303 pp.
An intellectual history of anarchism. Chapter V concerns terrorism and propaganda by deed.

Kliman, Gilbert, and Wolfenstein, Martha, eds., *Children and the Death of a President*. New York: Doubleday & Co., Inc., 1965. xxix+256 pp.
A collection of studies on the reaction of children to the assassination of President Kennedy.

Kornbluh, Joyce L., ed. *Rebel Voices: An I.W.W. Anthology*. Ann Arbor: The University of Michigan Press, 1964. vii+419 pp.
An excellent and interesting history of the American labor movement through study of its songs. A useful selected bibliography is included.

Krinerman, Leonard I., and Perry, Lewis, eds. *Patterns of Anarchy*. Garden City: Doubleday & Co., Inc., 1966. 570 pp.
A collection of writings on the anarchist tradition.

Laney, Richard. *Political Assassination: The History of an Idea*. Unpublished dissertation, University of Utah, 1966. 285 pp.
A study of assassination and its theoretical justification, from the Greek city-states to modern times.

Lasswell, Harold D., and Lerner, Daniel, eds. *World Revolutionary Elites*. Cambridge: The M.I.T. Press, 1965. vii+478 pp.
A study in ideological movements, such as Communism and Fascism, and their leaders.

Leiden, Carl, and Schmitt, Karl M., eds. *The Politics of Violence*. Englewood Cliffs, N.J.: Prentice-Hall, Inc., 1968. x+244 pp.

A useful volume on violence, terror and the revolutionary process. This work contains interesting case studies on revolutions in Mexico, Turkey, Egypt and Cuba.

Levy, Sheldon G. *The Detroit Riot of July 1967: Communications, Processes and Reactions.* Paper prepared for delivery at the meetings of the American Psychological Association, December 2, 1968. 25 pp.
The author studies communications during the Detroit riot, the riot processes, and reactions to the riots. The riot is viewed as a system that includes the whole community; the dynamics and impact of the event are analyzed.

Menninger, Karl A. *Man Against Himself.* New York: Harcourt Brace & World, Inc., 1938. x+485 pp.
An interesting analysis of man's aggressive and destructive tendencies by one of America's leading psychiatrists.

Mijatovich, Chedomille. *A Royal Tragedy.* London: Eveliegh Nash, 1906. x+230 pp.
A contemporary account of the assassination of King Alexander and Queen Draga of Serbia.

Nall, James O. *The Tobacco Night Riders of Kentucky and Tennessee: 1905–1909.* Louisville: The Standard Press, 1939. 221 pp.
An excellent history of an organization of tobacco growers that used mask, match, gun, lash and hoe to fight the tobacco monopoly in the early 20th century.

National Advisory Commission on Civil Disorders. *Report.* Washington, D. C.: U.S. Government Printing Office, 1968. xv+425 pp.
A comprehensive report on the conditions underlying urban riots in the United States in the 1960's.

Nomad, Max. *Aspects of Revolt.* New York: Bookman Assoc., 1959. 311 pp.
A sympathetic account of 19th- and 20th-century radicalism.

Overstreet, Harry and Bonaro. *The Strange Tactics of Extremism.* New York: W. W. Norton & Co., Inc., 1964. 315 pp.

An examination of right wing extremism in contemporary America.

Pitmen, Benn. *The Assassination of President Lincoln and the Trial of the Conspirators*. New York: Moore, Wilstach & Co., 1865. 421 pp.
This volume contains much of the testimony taken for the military commission that tried the alleged conspirators in the assassination of President Lincoln.

Porterfield, Austin L. *Cultures of Violence*. Fort Worth: Manney Co., 1965. ix+237 pp.
The author outlines some philosophical, psychological and sociological stresses that play a part in violent acts.

President's Commission on the Assassination of President John F. Kennedy. *Report*. Washington, D. C.: U.S. Government Printing Office, 1964. xxiv+887 pp.
An exhaustive report on the assassination and assassin of President John F. Kennedy by a Commission chaired by Chief Justice Earl Warren of the United States Supreme Court. Also available to the public are 26 volumes of evidence and testimony before the Commission which support the conclusions of the Commission in its Report.

President's National Advisory Commission on Rural Poverty. *The People Left Behind*. Washington, D. C.: U.S. Government Printing Office, 1967. xiii+160 pp.
An excellent study of rural poverty in modern America. The report analyzes the conditions under which the rural poor live and suggests programs which should and may be employed to alter their plight.

Reilly, Michael F. *I Was Roosevelt's Shadow*. London: W. Foulsham & Co., Ltd., 1947. 128 pp.
A popular account of the job of protecting an American President by a former member of the United States Secret Service.

Rice, Arnold S. *The Ku Klux Klan in American Politics*. Washington, D. C.: Public Affairs Press, 1962. vi+150 pp.
This book documents the pervasive influence that the second Ku Klux Klan had in American politics in the 1920's.

Rosenberg, Charles E. *The Trial of the Assassin Guiteau.* Chicago: University of Chicago Press, 1968.
An excellent and extensive account of the life and character of the assassin Guiteau, including his trial. Special emphasis is placed upon psychiatric testimony presented at the trial by the defense and the prosecution.

Sanger, Richard H. *Insurgent Era.* Washington, D. C.: Potomac Books, Inc., 1967. 231 pp.
An analysis of the techniques of revolution in the 20th century. This work includes a useful appendix on political violence from 1945 to 1966.

Seton-Watson, R. W. *Sarajevo.* London: Hutchinson & Co., Ltd., 1925. 303 pp.
An admirable historical account of the social and political forces which led to the assassination of Archduke Ferdinand at Sarajevo.

Shearing, Joseph. *The Angel of the Assassination.* London: William Heinemann, Ltd., 1935.
An interesting account of the assassination of Jean Paul Marat by Charlotte Corday.

Stampp, Kenneth M. *The Peculiar Institution.* New York: Alfred A. Knopf, 1956. xi+436 pp.
An excellent account of the institution of slavery in the antebellum South and its impact on both whites and blacks. Chapter III relates the attempts, often violent, of slaves to obtain their freedom.

Storr, Anthony. *Human Aggression.* New York: Atheneum, 1968.
An investigation of the violence and aggressive impulses in man. The author rejects the traditional notion that equates aggression with hostile or bad behavior and also the idea that aggression is learned rather than innate behavior.

United States Senate, 88th Cong., 2d Sess., Rep. No. 1179. *Protecting Heads of Foreign States and Other Designated Officials.* 1964. 9 pp.
A collection and short discussion of some of the federal laws relating to protection of foreign officials in the United States.

Vizetelly, Ernest Alfred. *The Anarchist.* New York: John Lane Co., 1912. xiv+308 pp.
A study of anarchism and the tactics of anarchists. This work contains accounts of many of the assassinations perpetrated by anarchists in the late 19th and early 20th centuries.

Wolfgang, Marvin E., ed. *Studies in Homicide.* New York: Harper & Row, 1967. viii+323 pp.
A collection of essays on sociological, psychological and psychiatric aspects of homicide.

——. *Patterns of Violence.* Annals of the American Academy of Political and Social Science, Vol. 364, March 1966. vii+247 pp.
A useful collection of essays on violent behavior in man by contributors from different disciplines. Several of the essays concern violence in America in particular.

Wolfenstein, Victor E. *Violence or Nonviolence: A Psychoanalytic Exploration of the Choice of Political Means in Social Change.* Research Monograph No. 20. Princeton: Center of International Studies, Woodrow Wilson School of Public and International Affairs, 1965. 45 pp.
A study of the psychological disposition of political leaders to seek or avoid the use of violent means. The author provides case studies of Gandhi, Nasser and Lenin.

Articles

Abrahamsen, David. "A Study of Lee Harvey Oswald: Psychological Capability of Murder," *Bulletin of the New York Academy of Medicine,* 2d Ser., Vol. 43, No. 10, Oct. 1967, pp. 861–888.
A psychological study of Lee Harvey Oswald, based upon his writings and the known facts of his life.

Andronov I. "How Gandhi Was Murdered," *New Times,* Jan.–March 1965, pp. 9–13.
A brief account of the circumstances surrounding the assassination of Mahatma Gandhi.

Ashford, Douglas E. "Politics and Violence in Morocco," *Middle East Journal*, Vol. 13, 1959, pp. 11–25.
An analysis of political violence in Morocco since that nation became independent in 1956.

Banta, Thomas J. "The Kennedy Assassination: Early Thoughts and Emotions," *Public Opinion Quarterly*, Vol. 28, 1964, pp. 216–24.
This study seeks to ascertain the thoughts, emotions and speculations of the American public about the assassin of President Kennedy, within the first few hours after his murder.

Bwy, Douglas. "Dimensions of Social Conflict in Latin America," *The American Behavioral Scientist*, Vol. XI, No. 4, Mar.–Apr. 1968, pp. 39–50.
This study takes a close empirical look at political aggression and instability in Latin America.

Chaplin, J. P. "Commentary on Three Oswald Interpretations," *Journal of Individual Psychiatry*, Vol. 23, May–Nov. 1966, pp. 48–52.
An analysis of interpretations of Lee Harvey Oswald by psychiatrists of three classic schools of depth psychology: psychoanalytic, Adlerian and Jungian.

Corfe, T. H. "The Phoenix Park Murders," *History Today*, Vol. 11, 1961, pp. 828–35.
An account of the assassination of the Chief Secretary for Ireland and the Under-Secretary for Ireland in 1882.

Cornwell, Elmer E., Jr. "Presidential News: The Expanding Public Image," *Journalism Quarterly*, Vol. 36, Summer 1959, pp. 275–83.
This analysis of front-page news in a large daily and in a medium-sized daily over the last 70 years indicates that presidential news has increased more rapidly than either national governmental news as a whole, or Congressional news.

De Grazia, Sebastian. "A Note on the Psychological Position of the Chief Executive," *Psychiatry*, Vol. 8, 1955, pp. 267–72.

A study of the reactions of 30 analysands to the death of President Roosevelt on April 12, 1945.

Deware, Hugo. "Murder Revisited: The Case of Sergi Mirnovich Kirov," *Problems of Communism*, Vol. 14, 1965, pp. 75–80.
An inquiry into the assassination, in 1934, of Kirov, a leading Bolshevik and a member of the Politbureau.

Dietze, Gottfried. "Will the Presidency Incite Assassination?" *Ethics*, Vol. 76–77, Oct.–July 1965, pp. 14–27.
The author presents the thesis that the growth and power of the office of the presidency has increased the attraction to that office of assassins.

Feierabend, Ivo and Rosalind. "Conflict, Crisis and Collision: A Study of International Stability," *Psychology Today*, May 1968, pp. 26–70.
An excellent cross-national statistical survey of political aggression in 84 countries of the world, from 1955–61.

——. "Aggressive Behaviors within Politics, 1948–1962: A Cross-National Study," *The Journal of Conflict Resolution*, Vol. X, No. 3, Sept. 1966, pp. 249–71.
A systematic, empirical analysis of conflict behaviors within and among nations.

Fine, Sidney. "Anarchism and the assassination of McKinley," *American Historical Review*, Vol. LX, No. 4, July 1955, pp. 77–99.
An excellent and comprehensive account of the assassination of William McKinley and its effect upon anarchism in America.

Forkosch, Morris D. "Presidential Murder—The Constitutionality of a Statute Making It a Federal Crime," *Southwestern Law Journal*, Vol. 19, 1965, pp. 229–238.
An examination of the crime of murder of a President within the American federal legal system.

Frenkel, Dr. Richard E. "Protecting the life of the President," *Satellite Communications Research News*, 1968.
Analysis of the increase of threats against the life of the President since the assassination of President Kennedy.

Friedrich, Carl J. "Political Pathology," *Political Quarterly*, 8 January 1966, pp. 70–85.
An examination of the political meaning of corruption, secrecy, betrayal, treason, violence and propaganda.

Grantham, Dewey W., Jr. "Goebel, Gonzales, Carmack: Three Violent Scenes in Southern Politics," *Mississippi Quarterly*, Vol. 11–12, Winter–Fall 1958–9, pp. 30–37.
An interesting account of the assassinations of William Goebel, Governor of Kentucky, in 1900, Narcisco Gonzales in South Carolina in 1902, and Edward Carmack in Tennessee in 1908. Gonzales and Carmack were both newspaper editors.

Hastings, Dr. Donald W. "The Psychiatry of Presidential Assassination," *Journal-Lancet,* March 1965.
This article contains an analysis of each of eight actual and would-be assassins of American Presidents. The author concludes that all the assassins except Collazo and Torresola were psychotic.

Hennessy, Bernard. "Politicals and Apoliticals: Some Measurements of Personality Traits," *Midwest Journal of Political Science*, Vol. 3, 1959, pp. 336–355.
A study of the influence of personality factors on participation and nonparticipation in politics.

Jászi, Oscar. "The Stream of Political Murder," *American Journal of Economics and Sociology*, Vol. 3, 1943–44, pp. 335–55.
The author makes an interesting differentiation of tyrannicide from political murder, which he defines as the elimination of persons and groups by a ruler.

Katz, Joseph. "On the Death of the President: President Kennedy's Assassination," *Psychoanalytic Review,* Vol. 5, Winter 1964–5, pp. 661–4.

An analysis of the motivation of Lee Harvey Oswald and of the public reaction to the assassination of President Kennedy.

Kirschner, David. "The Death of a President: Reactions of Psychoanalytic Patients," *Behavioral Scientist*, Vol. 10, Jan. 1965, pp. 1–6.
A study of the reactions of eight female psychoanalytic patients following the death of President Kennedy. The author hypothesizes that President Kennedy stood for an idealized parent symbol for these patients.

Levinson, Daniel J. "The Relevance of Personality for Political Participation," *Public Opinion Quarterly*, Vol. 22, 1958–59.
The author analyzes the impact of intra-psychic influences upon political behavior.

Lipset, Seymour Martin. "On the Politics of Conscience and Extreme Commitment," *Encounter*, Aug. 1958, pp. 66–71.
A brief but excellent comparison between extremist political activity in the United States and that in Canada.

Marshall, John. "The 20th-Century Vehme," *Blackwood's Magazine*, Vol. 257, Jan.–June, 1945.
This article is a study of a terrorist, right wing organization that practiced assassination in Germany in the 1920's.

Massotti, Lewis H., ed. "Urban Violence and Disorder," *American Behavioral Scientist*, Vol. II, No. 4, Mar.–Apr. 1968, 56 pp.
A collection of essays and studies of urban disorder in the United States during the 1960's.

Nieburg, H. L. "The Threat of Violence and Social Change," *American Political Science Review*, Vol. LVI, No. 4, Dec. 1962, pp. 865–73.
An interesting theoretical analysis of the relationship between violence and social change in a political system.

Ogg, Frederick A. "Assassination of Rumania's Premier," *Current History*, February 1934.

This article describes the assassination on December 29, 1933, of Ion Duca, Premier of Rumania, and places the assassination in its political context.

Olsen, Marvin E. "Alienation and Political Opinions," *Public Opinion Quarterly*, Vol. 29, 1965, pp. 200–12.
This article considers the relationship of alienation to political attitudes toward such issues as governmental action programs, racial integration, freedom of speech and international organizations.

Padover, Saul K. "Patterns of Assassination in Occupied Territory," *The Public Opinion Quarterly*, Vol. 7, 1943, pp. 680–93.
A discussion of assassination as a pattern in several differing political cultures, past and present.

Parenti, Michael. "The Black Muslims: From Revolution to Institution," *Social Research*, Vol. 31, 1964, pp. 175–194.
A useful study of the Black Muslim movement in the American Negro community.

Progoff, Ira. "The Psychology of Lee Harvey Oswald: A Jungian Approach," *Journal of Individual Psychiatry*, Vol. 23, May 1967, pp. 37–47.
The author analyzes Lee Harvey Oswald in terms of the absence of a father figure, the nature of his mother, his feelings of inferiority and misfortune, his attraction to Marxism, his marriage and his tendency toward violence.

Rothstein, David A. "Presidential Assassination Syndrome," *Archives of General Psychiatry*, Vol. 11, Sept. 1964, pp. 245–54.
An excellent study by a practicing psychiatrist of patients committed to the Medical Center for Federal Prisoners in Springfield, Missouri, for the crime of threatening the life of the President of the United States.

——. "Presidential Assassination Syndrome: Application to Lee Harvey Oswald," *Archives of General Psychiatry*, Vol. 15, Sept. 1966, pp. 260–66.

The author analyzes the life and character of Lee Harvey Oswald in light of the results of his previous study of persons who threatened the President.

Roucek, J. S. "Sociological Elements of a Theory of Terror and Violence," *American Journal of Economics and Sociology,* Vol. 21, Apr. 1962, pp. 165–72.
A sociological analysis of the use of terror and violence as political and social weapons in the 20th century. The author differentiates among types of terrorism.

Rummel, Rudolph J. "Dimensions of conflict behavior within and between nations," *General Systems Yearbook,* Vol. VIII, 1963, pp. 1–49.
This study determines the dimensions of variations among nations with respect to their domestic and foreign conflict behavior during a period of contemporary history, determines the approximate position of each nation along these dimensions, and ascertains the relationship between the dimensions of foreign conflict behavior on the one hand and domestic conflict behavior on the other.

———. "Dimensions of Conflict Behavior within nations, 1959–1964," *Journal of Conflict Resolution,* Vol. X, No. 1, Mar. 1966, pp. 65–73.
A quantitative analysis. The author attempts to determine which conflict events occur most often in conjunction with other conflict events.

Schwartz, David C. "On the Ecology of Political Violence: The Long Hot Summer as a Hypothesis," *American Behavioral Scientist,* July–Aug. 1968, pp. 24–28.
A provocative inquiry into the theory that environmental factors of climate are connected with certain dimensions of violent behavior.

Stone, Lawrence. "Theories of Revolution," *World Politics,* Vol. 18, No. 2, Jan. 1966, pp. 159–176.
A summary review and critical examination of recent work

in the social sciences on the typology, causes and evolutionary patterns of revolution.

Tanter, Raymond. "Dimensions of Conflict Behavior Within and Between Nations, 1958–60," *Journal of Conflict Resolution,* Vol. X, No. 1, Mar. 1966, pp. 41–64.
This study presents evidence relative to the relationship between domestic and foreign conflict behavior. The author presents data for 83 nations for 1958 to 1960.

Tischendorf, Alfred. "The Assassination of Chief Executives in Latin America," *South Atlantic Quarterly,* Vol. 60, 1961, pp. 80–88.
An excellent analysis, covering the years 1806 to 1960.

Walter, E. V. "Power and Violence," *American Political Science Review,* Vol. 58, Mar.–June 1964, pp. 350–60.
A study of the relationship between power and violence in political theory.

Wharton, Don. "How the Secret Service Protects the President," *Reader's Digest,* Vol. 69, July–Dec. 1959, pp. 139–43.
A brief survey of how the Secret Service does its job.

Williams, John. "Assassinations," *Medico-Legal Journal,* 1965, pp. 93–100.
The author asserts that between 1865 and 1914 there was a marked increase in the number of assassinations of political figures among the nations of the world. He suggests that most could have been avoided had it not been for the factors of foolhardiness of the victim and the inadequacy of police protection.

Willner, Ann Ruther and Dorothy. "The Rise and Role of Charismatic Leaders," *Annals of the American Academy of Political and Social Science,* Mar. 1965, pp. 77–88.
An intensive analysis of the charismatic leader as distinguished from other leaders. The authors conclude that the possession of charisma depends upon the leader's ability to draw upon and manipulate the body of myth in a given culture as well as the actions and values associated with these myths.

American Political and Social Culture

Agger, Robert E., Goldrich, Daniel, and Swanson, Bert E. *The Rulers and the Ruled*. New York: John Wiley & Sons, Inc., 1964. xx+789 pp.
A study of politics and political power on the local level in American communities.

Cash W. J. *The Mind of the South*. New York: Alfred A. Knopf, 1941. xi+429 pp.
This volume contains an analysis of the social, intellectual and historical forces that created the American South. The chapters on the impact of Reconstruction in the South are particularly revealing.

Edelman, Murray. *The Symbolic Uses of Politics*. Urbana: University of Illinois Press, 1964. 201 pp.
An excellent analysis of the place and uses of symbols in politics.

Havens, Murray Clark. *The Challenges to Democracy: Consensus and Extremism in American Politics*. Austin: University of Texas Press, 1965. 119 pp.
A brief analysis of the American political system. Chapter III concerns the historical failures of American consensus, such as the American nativist movement and the Ku Klux Klan.

Jennings, Kent M., and Zeigler, Harmon L., eds. *The Electoral Process.* Englewood Cliffs, N.J.: Prentice-Hall, Inc., 1966. xv+304 pp.
A collection of essays by various contributors on the American electoral system.

Lasswell, Harold D. *Psychopathology and Politics*. Chicago: The University of Chicago Press, 1930. vii+285 pp.
An attempt to understand political life through psychological analysis of political leaders and activists.

MacIver, R. M. *The Web of Government*. New York: The Free Press, 1965. 373 pp.
An analysis of the origins and basis of government in human society.

Marcuse, Herbert. *Eros and Civilization*. Boston: Beacon Press, 1966. xxviii+274 pp.
A philosophical work by the man commonly said to be the intellectual father of the American New Left.

Meyer, E. Swing. *The Winning Candidate: How to Defeat Your Political Opponent*. New York: James H. Heineman, Inc., 1966. ix+244 pp.
A study of modern American political tactics and techniques.

Pomper, Gerald. *Nominating the President*. New York: W. W. Norton & Co., Inc., 1966. 304 pp.
An analysis of the nomination and election process of American Presidents.

Roche, John P. *Shadow and Substance*. New York: The Macmillan Co., 1964. viii+468 pp.
Essays on the theory and structure of politics.

Roche, John P., and Levy, Leonard W. *Parties and Pressure Groups*. New York: Harcourt Brace & World, Inc., 1964. 239 pp.
A collection of documents in American government, with excellent chapters on electing a President and campaign costs.

Weisbord, Marvin R. *Campaigning for President*. Washington, D. C.: Public Affairs Press, 1964. 208 pp.
A study of how presidential campaigning has changed in the United States from George Washington to Lyndon Johnson.